Men and Women in Revolution and War, 1600-1815

Men and Women in Revolution and War, 1600-1815

Thomas R. Rumsey

Casady School,
Oklahoma City, Oklahoma

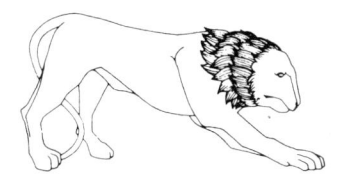

The Independent School Press
Wellesley Hills, Massachusetts

© 1985 by Independent School Press, Inc.

All rights reserved. No part of this publication may be reproduced or transmitted in any form or by any means, electronic or mechanical, including photocopy, recording, or any information storage or retrieval system, without permission in writing from the publisher.

PRINTED IN THE UNITED STATES OF AMERICA

0-88334-178-6

85868788
12345678

For my father

PREFACE

This book, like other history textbooks, owes very much to many historians, both living and dead, and a bibliography appears at the end in the hope that students will read some of their works. The debts that this author owes to others more able are countless, and he has labored to make that fact clear. The same is true, of course, with reference to the illustrations in this book. It is hoped, for those who believe that history can be painted, drawn, and engraved as well as written, that the many period art illustrations throughout the text will heighten pleasure and increase understanding. For the rights and reproductions of these works, the author is grateful to scores of curators and galleries, both in this country and abroad. If the number and quality of such illustrations exceed what is usual for texts of this kind, it is because a generous faculty grant made additional expenditure possible. For this very timely award, the author would like to thank Richard McCubbin, Headmaster of Casady School.

This book is a venture in collective biography, and it is hard not to be aware of criticisms leveled at the elitism of historical biographies as a *genre*. Biography is history with the masses left out; biography can fall into the trap of assuming that history's leaders were often in fact led. Yet biography can be entertaining, breathing life into the past for the individuals reading about it. In any case, the form has been used with a certain caution, and it has been supplemented with a lot of social history. If there are portraits of the "great" here, they would not necessarily be pleasing to Mr. Carlyle. If some of the men and women written about made things happen, some others stumbled, fumbled, and fell out of step with their times, bemused and unknowingly led by movements and other events beyond their understanding. Some were heroes; some were victims; some at the same or different times, were both.

In thanking the editor, the author has saved the most important contributor for the last. Throughout the editing of this book and its predecessor, Gordon Boice has offered application, enthusiasm, encouragement, and no little creativity. For all of these, he is much appreciated.

Oklahoma City, Oklahoma   Thomas R. Rumsey
Fall, 1984

CONTENTS

Chapter I: Sir Robert Carey's Ride — 1
    Introduction — 3
    Changing Patterns of Power — 3
    A General Crisis? — 7
    Imperfect Means of Social Control — 10
    The Challenge to Authority — 15
    Standards of Behavior — 21
    Domestic Relations and Demography — 24
    Agents of Instability and Mortality — 30
    The Inadequacy of the Medical Professions — 38
    Harbingers of Improvement and Change — 44
    Conclusion — 50

Portfolio: The Life of the Society, 1600-1815 — 53

Chapter II: The Troubled Journey Through the English Revolution, 1603-1714 — 61
    The English Civil War — 63
    James VI and I — 69
    The Struggle of Crown and Parliament — 76
    The Onset of the Civil War — 83
    Oliver Cromwell and the Rule of the Generals — 100
    Charles II and the Restoration — 113
    The Glorious Revolution and its Legacy — 120
    The Meaning of a Century of Rebellion — 125

Portfolio: Women, 1600-1815—Family, Mortality, Sexuality, Individuality—And the Changing Images of Children — 129

Chapter III: Great Wars and Great Powers in Central and Northern Europe, 1618-1721 — 145
    The Struggle for European Hegemony — 147
    Gustavus Adolphus — 151
    Cardinal Richelieu — 160
    Queen Christina and Her Successors — 169
    Russia in Europe — 177
    Conclusion — 190

Portfolio: Louis XIV—Art, Propaganda, and the Pursuit of Absolutism — 193

*Chapter IV: The Play of the Balance of Power in
    Western Europe, 1648-1715*   *197*
    Introduction   199
    Louis XIV and the French Monarchy   199
    The Dutch Republic and the House of Orange   207
    King Carlos II and the Spanish Dilemma   212
    The Duke and Duchess of Marlborough   217
    European Realignment   225

*Portfolio: The Health Professions—Physicians, Surgeons,
    Midwives, Anatomists, and Quacks*   *229*

Chapter V: The Enlightenment, 1600-1800   *239*
    A Scientific Revolution?   241
    René Descartes   243
    Galileo Galilei and Sir Isaac Newton   248
    William Harvey and the Human Universe   253
    The Scientific Revolution   259
    Voltaire   262
    Mary Wollstonecraft   271
    The New Science and the New Reason   277

*Portfolio: Science, Cities, Commerce, Transport,
    and Industrial Revolution, 1600-1815*   *281*

*Chapter VI: Stability, Commerce, and Industry in
    Eighteenth Century Britain*   *289*
    The Process of the Industrial Revolution   291
    The First Two Georges and Whig Politics   295
    Sir Robert Walpole and Caroline of Anspach   298
    Enterprise and the Politics of Commerce   304
    Josiah Wedgwood   306
    James Watt and the Chain of Innovation   309
    Adam Smith   313
    Men, Women, and the Industrial Revolution   317

Portfolio: Food, Drink, and Drunkenness, 1600-1815   *319*

Chapter VII: Rulers and Warriors in Eighteenth Century Europe   *327*
    Introduction   329
    Maria Theresa   330
    The Making of a Great Power   340
    Catherine the Great   349
    Britain, France, and Colonial Dominance   357
    Conclusion

Portfolio: Women Artists, 1600-1815   *365*

Chapter VIII: Revolution and War in France and Europe, 1789-1815	*371*
The Era of the French Revolution, 1789-1815	373
A Nobleman Out of Step	378
Robespierre and the Terror	385
Napoleon Bonaparte and the French Empire	391
The Duke of Wellington	401
The Congress of Vienna	410
The Consequences of the French Revolution	420
Portfolio: Francisco de Goya y Lucientes and the Tragedy of Total War	*425*
Epilogue: The European World in 1815	*429*
Appendix: Genealogical Tables	*433*
Bibliography	*443*
Index	*475*

LIST OF ILLUSTRATIONS

The Peasant's Misery. David Vinckboons	2
The Peasant's Pleasure. David Vinckboons	2
Southwark Fair. William Hogarth	11
The Cock Pit. William Hogarth	12
The Bitter Medicine. Adriaen Brouwer	31
The Quack. Adriaen Brouwer	41
Family Group. Adriaen van Ostade	52
A Dutch Courtyard. Pieter de Hooch	53
Skittles Players in a Garden. Pieter de Hooch	54
The Wigmaker, I and II. *A Diderot pictorial encyclopedia*	55
The Smokers. Adriaen Brouwer	56
The Suitor's Visit. Gerard Ter Borch	57
The Surprise. David Teniers	58
Tavern Scene. After Adriaen Brouwer	58
Credulity, Superstition and Fanaticism. William Hogarth	59
The Rat Killer. Rembrandt van Rijn	60
The Miseries of War—The Estrapade. Jacques Callot	60
Portrait of James I. Daniel Mytens	70
Portrait of Charles I. Unknown Artist	87
Queen Henrietta Maria and her Dwarf. Sir Anthony Van Dyck	88
Portrait of Oliver Cromwell. Unknown Artist	112
Portrait of Charles II. Studio of James M. Wright	119
The Proposition. Judith Leyster	129
A Girl and Her Duenna. Bartolomé Esteban Murillo	130
Mistress and Servant. Attr. Willem van Mieris	130
The Wedding of Kloris and Roosje. Cornelius Troost	131
The First Lesson of Fraternal Friendship. Etienne Aubry	131
Sir Thomas Astor at the Deathbed of his Wife. John Souch	132
The Saltonstall Family. David des Granges	132
Portrait of Saskia van Uilenburgh. Rembrandt van Rijn	133
Portrait of Elizabeth van der Meeren. Fans Hals	134
The Lady Governors of the Old Men's Home at Haarlem Frans Hals	134
Miss Catherine Tatton, and *The Honorable Mrs. Graham.* Thomas Gainsborough	135
Portrait of Miss Hoare. Sir Joshua Reynolds	135
Mrs. Renny Strachan. Sir Henry Raeburn	135
An Old Woman at Prayer. Nicolaes Maes	136
The Twins Clara and Albert de Bray. Salomon de Bray	137
Portrait of Clelia Cattaneo, Daughter of Marchesa Elena Grimaldi. Sir Anthony van Dyck	138
Girl with a Broom. Rembrandt van Rijn	138
Young Girl Plucking a Duck. Barent Fabritius	138

Child with Cherries. Salomon de Bray	138
The Sick Child. Gabriel Metsu	139
The Dancing Couple. Jan Steen	140
Illustration from J. Cats, *Silenus Alcibiadia Sive Proteus* . . .	140
The Bedroom. Pieter de Hooch	141
The Lacemaker. Nicholaes Maes	142
The Young Governess. Jean-Baptiste-Simeon Chardin	142
Las Meninas, or the Family of Philip IV. Diego Velázquez y Silva	143
The Hoppner Children. John Hoppner	144
Oval Medallion depicting Peter the Great and his Family	146
Portrait of Gustavus Adolphus of Sweden. M. Merian	154
Portait of Queen Christina of Sweden. David Beck	170
Peter the Great as the Founder of the Russian Navy. L. Caravak	188
Bust of Louis XIV. After Bernini	193
Louis XIV in Costume. Joseph Werner	194
Mademoiselle de la Vallière in Costume. Joseph Werner	195
The Family of Louis XIV. Attr. to Nicholas de Largillière	196
The Estates General, 1614. Jean Ziarnko	198
Portrait of Jean Baptiste Colbert. Philippe de Champagne	202
Portait of a Young Man in an Armchair. Rembrandt van Rijn	209
Portrait of Carlos II. Claudio Coello	212
Portaits of King Philip IV and Queen Mariana of Spain. Diego Velázquez	214
Portrait of John Churchill. Attr. Sir Godfrey Kneller	220
Title page from *The Grete Herball* . . .	229
Title page from Andreas Vesalius, *Humani corporis* . . .	230
The Kopster. Cornelius Dusart	231
The Anatomy Lesson of Dr. Tulp. Rembrandt van Rijn	232
The Dissection. Thomas Rowlandson	232
The Barber-Surgeons. Flemish woodcut	233
Illustration of a child in the womb. Sir William Hunter	234
The Lying-in Room. Adriaen or Carol Dusart	234
Pass-Room Bridwell. A. C. Rugin and Thomas Rowlandson	235
La Pharmacie Rustique. Gottfried Locher and Barthelemi Hubner	236
Self Portrait with Dr. Arrieta. Francisco José de Goya y Lucientes	237
Madhouse at Saragossa. Francisco José de Goya y Lucientes	238
Mural Quadrant from Tyco Brahe's Astronomiae instauratae mechanica	240
Portrait of Sir Isaac Newton. Unknown Artist	248
Portrait of William Harvey. Unknown Artist	253
Voltaire. Joseph Rosset	263
Portrait of Marry Wollstonecraft. J. Opie	273

The Astronomer. Jusepe de Ribera	281
Experiment with the Air Pump. Joseph Wright of Derby	282
Metamorphosis of a Frog. Maria Sibylla Merian	283
Robert Hooke's microscope and his drawing of a fly in his *Micrographica*	284
Nicolaus Copernicus in the Observatory in Frombork. Jan Matejko	285
Engraving of a canal and aqueduct	286
The Quay of the Piazetta. Canaletto, Venice	287
View of Dresden from the Right Bank of the Elbe. Bernardo Bellotto	287
View of Amsterdam. A. J. Visscher	288
Broad Quay, Bristol. Unknown Artist	290
Portrait of Robert Walpole. Studio of J. B. Van Loo	302
The Pancake Baker. Jan Steen	319
An Old Woman Cooking Eggs. Diego Velázquez y Silva	320
A Peasant Interior. Louis Le Nain	320
Peasants Drinking. Isaac van Ostade	321
Merrymakers at Shrovetide. Frans Hals	322
Tavern Scene. David Teniers the Younger	323
The Rake's Progress. Plate III. William Hogarth	324
Wine is a Mocker. Jan Steen	325
The Drunken Cobbler. Jean Baptiste Greuze	325
The Ugly Club [Serving the Punch]. Thomas Rowlandson	326
Portrait of Augustus the Strong. Nicolas de Largillìere	328
Portrait of Grand Duke Peter, Catherine, and Paul	352
Portrait of William Pitt. After R. Brompton	359
Mademoiselle Vigée-Lebrun and her Pupil Mademoiselle Lemoine. Marie-Victoire Lemoine	365
The Mystical Marriage of St. Catherine. Luisa Roldán	366
Danseen Branle, Pastoral #6. Claudine Stella	366
Self-Portrait. Judith Leyster	367
The Annunciation. Suzanne de Court	368
The First Step. Marguerite Gerard	369
The Marquise de Peze and the Marquise de Rouget with her Two Children. Elisabeth Vigée-Lebrun	369
Portrait of the Artist with Two Pupils. Adelaide Labille-Guiard	370
Napoleon in His Study. Jacques-Louis David	372
Trumpeters of Napoleon's Imperial Guard. Theodore Gericault	399
Los Desastres de La Guerra: Number 5.	425
The Third of May 1808 in Madrid. Francisco de Goya y Lucientes	426
The Colossus. Francisco de Goya y Lucientes	427
Saturn Devouring One of His Sons. Francisco de Goya y Lucientes	428

LIST OF MAPS

The Great Rebellion in England, 1642-1649	104
Cromwell's Scotland and Ireland	109
Hapsburg Dominance: The Holy Roman Empire in 1600	150
The Azov Campaign: Peter's Struggle to Reach the Black Sea	185
Key Battles Fought by the Duke of Marlborough in the War of the Spanish Succession	223
The Hapsburg Dominions at the Close of the Reign of Maria Theresa	339
Brandenburg—Prussia After the Peace of Westphalia, 1648, and Under Frederick the Great, 1742-1772	349
The Destruction of Poland: The Partitions, 1772-1795	356
Europe in 1810: The Height of Napoleonic Power—Wellington's Peninsular Campaign, 1809-1812 / Waterloo, Geography and Military Strategy / Napoleon's March on Moscow, 1812	406, 407
After the Congress of Vienna, Europe in 1815	418, 419

Chapter I

Sir Robert Carey's Ride: European Society in the Seventeenth Century

Soon London will be all England.
—King James I

The kernel of the Torah is, Thou shalt love thy neighbour as thyself. But in our days we seldom find it so, and few are they who love their fellow men with all their heart—on the contrary, if man can contrive to ruin his neighbour, nothing pleases him more.
—Glückel of Hameln

I pray God send my Lady a good delivery and a brave boy.
—Sir Charles Lyttleton to Viscount Hatton, 1682

Mary foh, honest? burnt at fourteene, seven times whipt, sixe times carted, nine times duck'd, search'd by some hundred and fifty Constables, and yet you are honest? Honest Mistress *Horsleach,* is this World a World to keepe Bawds and Whores honest?
—Thomas Dekker, *The Honest Whore*

The Scituation of this Monarchial Government Lies in the will of Kings, *alias* Conquerors, setting up Lords of Manors, exacting Landlords, Tything Priests and covetous Lawyers, with all those pricking bryars attending thereupon, to be Taskmasters to oppress the people, lest they should rise up in riches and power to disthrone them.
—Gerrard Winstanley, *The Law of Freedom In A Platform*

It is one of the disadvantages belonging to your sex that young women are seldom permitted to make their own choice.
—Lord Halifax, *Advice To A Daughter*

What will you do, sir, with four physicians? Is not one enough to kill any one body?
—Molière, *L'Amour Médicin*

The Peasant's Misery, **Top,** and *The Peasant's Pleasure.*
David Vinckboons
In early modern Europe, soldiers were often quartered in private households. In the first panel, a peasant family is irritated, impoverished, and threatened by the presence of mercenary soldiers, their mistresses, and their families, while in the second, the peasants, fed up with the soldier's depredations, take their vengeance. *Courtesy of the Rijksmuseum, Amsterdam.*

A. Introduction

It was March 24, 1603, a Thursday. On that day Elizabeth I, queen regnant, sovereign of England for longer than most of her subjects could remember, turned her face to the wall and died. Soon many began mourning, others still rejoiced, but for these things Sir Robert Carey had no time. By nine in the morning he had evaded the guard, taken horse, and clattered out of the courtyard of Richmond Palace to ride for Doncaster, Edinburgh, and James VI of Scotland. On March 27, exhausted, covered with the mud of the road, "be-blooded with great falls and bruises," Sir Robert Carey ended his difficult journey at the Palace of Holyrood. There, on that Saturday evening, he informed James Stuart that Gloriana, England's Virgin Queen, was dead without issue and that he, James VI, would be the first of his line and name to sit upon the English throne. Sir Robert Carey's journey, bringing with it news of sudden death, broken by a violent fall, was symbolic of the seventeenth century, a metaphor for the age.

B. Changing Patterns of Power; Transport, Trade, Communications

That Sir Robert Carey rode northward also carries with it a certain significance, for this is the century when the monarchies and states of northern and western Europe begin their historical moments, slowly superseding the city-states of Italy and the Mediterranean and the oceanic empire of Hapsburg Spain as centers of economic and political power. The speed of this change can be overstressed—at least some of the bankers of James I were Italian, exiled Spanish Jews founded financial empires in Amsterdam—but it is nonetheless true that in the seventeenth century the vital center of the European economy had begun its journey out of the Mediterranean and into the Atlantic, establishing trading links with the Baltic, the colonial empires of the Atlantic and the Pacific, the barracoons and slaving stations of the African coast, the forests of Brazil, the mines and *encomiendas* of Spanish America, and even with the Levant and North Africa. The masters of Dutch *fluits* of large capacity, requiring few hands, traded and re-exported bulk commodities from Brazil to the Baltic, making Amsterdam the Venice of the north. Where the Dutch went, the English followed, creating out of this occasionally violent apprenticeship a commercial and colonial empire, amassing a pool of wealth from which it financed an industrial revolution a century-and-a-half later.

Announced by Robert Carey's ride, a new dynasty, that of the Stuarts, came to rule in England for the rest of the century. Elsewhere too, new dynasties had, or soon would, come to power and influence. From Sweden the house of Vasa intruded into Europe during the Thirty Years' War and, in a series of conflicts given too little attention by historians of western Europe, waged war with the newly founded Russian dynasty of Romanov for control of the north. In France the house of Bourbon, freshly enthroned by the good fortune and realism of Henry of Navarre, came to maturity and dominance in the reign of Louis XIV.

It is also of note that Sir Robert Carey's ride was so violent and dangerous, for his was a century in which communications and travel were risky, life uncertain, terrifying, and, for most, fundamentally unjust. On the road to Holyrood, Carey "got a great fall by the way" and his horse, according to his own account, "with one of its heels gave me a great blow on the head that made me shed blood." Those who traveled and traded in seventeenth-century Europe would have understood Carey's misfortune all too well. The poor, of course, walked. Those who could afford to do so rode horses or took the new, badly sprung, and very dangerous coaches. In 1664 an acquaintance of Samuel Pepys, the great diarist of London life, was drowned while trying to cross the Thames on horseback. On another occasion Pepys noted that "a neighbour of ours Mr. Hallworthy . . . is also dead, by a fall in the country from his horse, his foot hanging in the stirrup and his brains beat out." In 1625 Asher ben Eliezar, on his way home to Reichshofen in Alsace, saved himself by clinging to willows when his horse fell backward into the water on the way up a river bank. In 1680 Sir Charles Lyttleton boarded the horseferry at Richmond, only to have his horse leap into the river. Lyttleton, who was weighted down by "greate French bootes and many cloathes," was fortunate enough to be pulled to shore. The seventeenth century was one of broken limbs, of bad backs, of ruptures, concussions, and piles.

Travel on horseback was not only dangerous, but slow. Only the fastest of post-horses, under the most ideal conditions, could make as much as seven miles in an hour. The average rider was lucky to make the more typical twenty to forty miles in a day. Coaches, even slower, brought their own set of problems. William Byrd of Westover, a Virginian who sampled the delights of London life in the early eighteenth century, was overturned in the Reading coach in 1718. Pepys wrote of a coachman of an acquaintance dead and buried because a coach-horse kicked in his head. Compounding the problem were the roads—rivers of mud in wet seasons, often badly cared for by local authorities, so badly rutted in England that carriages could not be pulled in double harness. During the English Revolution, teams of five oxen were sometimes insufficient to pull heavy loads of timber and weaponry, and more draft animals had to be reserved for the purpose. The conditions of the roads, and the insufficiency of the vehicles that ran over them, made it very difficult for merchants to move bulk goods like grain, coal, and timber overland. This, in turn, forced an overreliance on water transport, hindered the economic integration so necessary to industrialization, and delayed the economic development of interior areas without rivers. Canals, which required great outlays of capital to build, were only occasionally a solution in the seventeenth century.

Probably Sir Robert Carey did not rest in an inn on his way to Edinburgh, but he would not necessarily have been fortunate had he done so. Celia Fiennes, traveling in provincial England in the later seventeenth century, found "frogs and slow-worms and snails" in her room. On the way to Prague in the 1590s, Fynes Moryson was obliged to sleep in an establishment where ". . . women, Virgins, Men and Maids, Servants, all of us lay in one roome." Moryson was happy to sleep on the edge of such a company, "delighting more in sweet aire, then the smoke of a dunghill." German inns were little better in Moryson's estimation, offering "grosse meat, sower wine, stinking drinke, and filthy beds."

Within towns and cities the means of transport were more various but also prone to hazard. Streets, not always paved, were stopped with traffic, garbage, and street vendors. In London, drivers of hackney coaches put out eyes with their whips, overturned their vehicles in the deep gutters, and were regularly, though unsuccessfully, prosecuted for manslaughter. Traffic was noisy enough in the seventeenth century to keep Londoners like Pepys awake at night. Walking in the city was no alternative. Pedestrians were assaulted by coachmen or by thieves, had their pockets picked, their clothes bespattered with filth or their shoes sucked off by the mud. In 1676 John Evelyn, walking through unlit and obstructed London streets, injured himself severely enough on a timber to have to be carried home. In seventeenth-century Paris, the municipal government issued orders banning various obstructions from the streets, including manure heaps and piles of lumber, while servants in certain Spanish cities were threatened with public whippings in a vain effort to keep them from heaving pots of human ordure onto the pavements. Little wonder that the rich preferred the covered sedan chairs and horse litters that Fynes Moryson found in use in Genoa and Naples.

By design, as in Venice, or by circumstance, as when the Thames in London overflowed its embankments and flooded Westminster, many in the seventeenth century found it easiest to travel by water. The London watermen who regularly carried Pepys home constituted a genuine subculture; in 1676 there were some two thousand of them. The Thames thus became the chief artery of transportation for many Londoners, but the pilings around the bridges conspired to make even river travel dangerous. Watermen ran the bridges as if they were running rapids. Under the arches of London Bridge the water level could drop off as much as six feet as the current created swirling whirlpools strong enough to overturn boats. Similarly, on the river near Ulm, Germany, Fynes Moryson encountered "Barkes" drawn by horses, plying a trade subject to the hazards of violent current, drunken boatmen, and "the multitude of bridges."

Deep-water transport and trade brought with it the possibility of moving large and bulky cargoes, and greater profit, but added the dangers of navigation, epidemic disease, and piracy. Ships foundered in storms and broke up on reefs; crews and passengers sickened from plague or scurvy; cargoes were spoiled by either salt water or pirates. In 1617 Barbary pirates from North Africa struck Madeira, carrying away twelve hundred prisoners. Eight years later, the Barbary corsairs seized forty vessels from Le Havre alone off the Newfoundland banks. The Dunkirkers threatened European seaborne trade over a wide area, and at least one historian has claimed that piracy, particularly at the hands of the Dutch and the English, contributed to the decline of Venice. Monarchs also contributed to the difficulties of seaborne trade, seizing merchant vessels for military purposes, forcing merchants to import grain or military commodities at marginal profit, extorting money from merchant communities, or charging tolls. The Sound Dues, required by the Danish king of every vessel passing into the Baltic, were perhaps the most prominent example of the latter practice.

The Europe through which Sir Robert Carey rode was a region in the process of changing its economic and political orientation, and one in which states best suited and best situated for overseas trade were becoming more powerful. It was a Europe dominated by maritime or agricultural, not industrial, powers, in which full economic integration had not been achieved. Serious problems—internal and external tariffs, lack of standard weights and measures, currency difficulties, poor surface transport, slow communications, and an agriculture unable to feed adequately the mass of the population—remained.

C. A General Crisis?—Rich, Poor, and Economic Change

The land and people through which Sir Robert Carey and the seventeenth century moved were bound up in a struggle between continuity and change, between old and new, which would throw Europe into rebellion and revolution. H. R. Trevor-Roper and certain other historians, noting the disorders, dislocations, and revolutions of the times, have referred to a "general crisis" in the first half of the seventeenth century. The symptoms of this general crisis are numerous: the Thirty Years' War in Germany, the last phases of the revolt of the Netherlands against Spanish domination, the revolt of the Catalans in Spain, the crisis of 1650 in Sweden, the English revolutions of 1640-1660 and even of 1688, the aristocratic insurrection in France known as the Fronde, many and scattered peasant insurrections, a seeming increase in social tensions expressed in severe witchcraft prosecutions extending from England to Russia.

The causes of these events are more obscure. Marxist historians like E. J. Hobsbawm have pointed to the gradual change from a feudal economy based on land, to a capitalist economy based on investment and trade; to a rapid rise in prices; to a slowing in European expansion between 1600 and 1650; to a lessening of population growth—citing them all as causes of crisis. Other scholars see the general crisis as being caused by a struggle for power—between centralized monarchies and the old nobility, between great nobles and lesser landholders, or between monarchs and parliaments. Others cite a breakdown of authority occurring when governments and rulers, operating on fixed incomes derived from the land, were unable to meet the costs of governing when those costs were driven upward by inflation. Still others see the general crisis rising out of religious conflicts created at the time of the Reformation of the sixteenth century, aggravated by a disgust at the corruption and greed of royal courts and noble households.

Whatever the causes, contemporaries saw the world full of trouble, the times out of joint. "A general corruption hath overgrowne the vertues of these latter times," said the Englishman Barnabe Rich in 1614, "and the world is become a Brothell house of sinne." "These are days of shaking . . . ," said the preacher Jeremiah Whittaker, "and this shaking is universal: the Palatinate, Bohemia, Germania, Catalonia, Portugal, Ireland, England." John Evelyn, the seventeenth-century diarist, thought of the reign of Charles II as "wonderfull" and "miraculous" because it had survived "conjurations against him, Parliaments, Warrs, Plagues, Fires, Comets, revolutions abroad happning in his time with a thousand other particulars. . . ."

A particular sign of impending trouble to seventeenth century men and women was the masses of poor who increasingly crowded country lanes and cities, loud, lewd, obstreperous, unamenable to authority. The Englishman Richard Younge wrote in 1654, "Of Poor there are two sorts: Gods poor and the Devils: impotent poor and impudent poor." The impotent poor, as Younge called them, outstripped the generosity of private charity, while their impudent brothers and sisters strained the patience of magistrates and frightened more prosperous people everywhere. "The great Multitude of *poor* Wretches in all parts of the city is such," wrote Joseph Lister of the Paris poor, "that a Man in a Coach, a-foot, in the Shop, is notable to do any business for the numbers and importunities of the Beggars." In Rome, wrote an observer in 1601, "one sees only beggars, and they are so numerous that it is impossible to walk the streets without having them around." In Venice the municipal government took measures against the boatmen who brought beggars from the mainland, while in Paris the authorities tried to control the inflow of indigent by requiring badges to beg. The magistrates of Seville, who had to suppress a serious rebellion of the poor in 1652, likewise required the licensing of beggars. In England the poor were whipped through the streets, put to work, incarcerated, or sent back to the parishes of their origin. Many European cities built hospitals or prisons to house the indigent and criminals. Saltpetrière and Bicêtre were built in Paris; the London public could pay to see the mad in cages in the hospital known as "Bedlam," or to view imprisoned prostitutes beating hemp in the prison known as Bridewell.

There were so many kinds, varieties, and definitions of poverty in the seventeenth century that it is hard to calculate its extent accurately. As Carlo Cipolla has written, "The unemployed were confused with the poor, the poor were identified with the beggar, and the confusion of the terms reflected the grim reality of the times." In the late seventeenth century, Gregory King's statistics show an English population of some five and a half million. Perhaps one-quarter of these could be considered poor—among them groups as various as "cottagers," "paupers," "thieves," and "beggars," to use King's own terms. More recently, an economic historian calculated that between twenty and fifty percent of England's population before 1750 were impoverished by modern standards. Moreover, in an agricultural economy, where so much work was seasonal, underemployment was as serious as unemployment.

Adding to the potential for instability was the fact that in a population that was very youthful to begin with—perhaps forty percent of the population in England was under the age of fifteen, as opposed to about twenty-two percent in 1951—many of the wandering poor were also young, and to their elders the more dangerous for it. In the cities, the concentration of youth tended to be very pronounced. In Venice in 1642, some forty-six percent of the population was eighteen or under, while in Padua in 1634 thirty percent of the population was fifteen or under. Lest orphaned children grow into masterless men and women, society took severe measures against the parents of illegitimate children, and orphans were bound out as apprentices or servants by local authorities or charities. In Seville, where unwanted infants could be placed in a revolving window in a house next to the cathedral, the Brotherhood of Santo Niño Perdido was founded to aid abandoned children.

Blending into the masses of the poor, and paradoxically drawing strength from their misery, was a shifting and ill-defined underworld. Speaking its own jargon, often highly specialized in terms of criminal activity, this subculture imperfectly revealed itself in ballads, rhymes, folk poetry, and at markets and fairs. Indistinguishable from this criminal mass, at least in the contemporary mind, were the hoards of beggars and vagabonds turned loose upon country and town by the forces of enclosure, inflation, and economic change. Shifting between this underworld and the ranks of the more honorable poor were groups of traveling actors, minstrels, puppeteers, tooth-drawers, medical quacks, rupture-cutters, diviners, prostitutes, palm readers, boatmen, unlicensed preachers, poachers, squatters, midwives, cunning men, sorcerers, alleged witches, and street vendors. These, the masterless men and women of seventeenth-century Europe, preyed upon the powerful, reviled their laws, picked their pockets in theaters and cockpits, assaulted them on the streets, robbed them on the highway, killed their game in their own preserves, infected them with plagues and venereal diseases, and, in need and through fraud, obtained small portions of their wealth.

"The angry buzz of a multitude," wrote Lord Halifax, "is one of the bloodiest noises in the world." All over Europe, ruling groups, of whatever variety or kind, were faced with the problem of how to control large numbers of unwanted, youthful, and potentially violent poor. Those who possessed power and property were justifiably worried, for they had a great deal to lose. In most cities a small merchant oligarchy, often armed with a charter of privilege granted by a monarch, monopolized wealth and political power. In his classic study of the English provincial town of Exeter, Wallace MacCaffrey has estimated that three percent of the population owned fifty percent of the assessed property in the period 1540-1640. These merchant oligarchies, conservative and tradition-minded, often intermarried with the landed classes, shared their values, and sometimes bought their property.

On the land, economic inequalities could be as strongly pronounced. In seventeenth-century France the peasantry, four-fifths of a total population of twenty million, owned less than half the land. In Muscovite Russia, by fits and starts, an organized system of serfdom was developing under the control of the *boyars,* the great landholders. Contemporary commentators were agreed as to the suffering of the agrarian poor, though they allowed for regional differences. "As for the poor *paisant,*" said Fynes Moryson of the French peasantry, "he fareth very hardly and feedeth most upon bread and fruits, but yet he may comforte himselfe with this, that though his fare be nothing as good as the ploughman and poor artificers in England, yet it is much better than that of the *villano* in Italy."

D. *Imperfect Means of Social Control*

Traditionally the rulers of European society—whether nobles, church leaders or monarchs—had provided places, though meager ones, for the masses of poor. A hierarchical society of three estates—clergy, nobility, and a much larger group supporting the previous two—had been the way that Europe was organized since medieval times; but by the seventeenth century an increase in population, combined with rapidly rising prices, compromised traditional relationships. Lords of the manor, their fixed incomes unable to keep up with inflation, cast marginal peasants off their manors and enclosed their land to raise saleable sheep and other livestock. The guild structure, which had employed so many of the young, began to break down in the face of competitive capitalism. The Church, the major source of what charity and poor relief there was in the medieval centuries, found itself under increasing attack, prey to the same inflationary forces that affected government and nobility, weakened by political controversies with powerful sovereigns, challenged by the consequences of Reformation.

In fairness to the more fortunate, there were serious efforts on their part to assist the destitute and to mitigate suffering. W. K. Jordan, in a series of studies, has revealed a remarkable level of private charitable and philanthropic activity in Tudor-Stuart England. Thousands of parish clergy continued to cure souls, feed the hungry, and visit the sick; the gifts of the faithful and the activities of nuns staffed many hospitals, orphanages, and poorhouses. In studying seventeenth-century European society it is sometimes very difficult to distinguish philanthropy from religious duty, and religion from social control. In any case, these efforts seem to have fallen far short, eaten up by the same inflation that devoured so much else, defeated by an economy that could neither absorb nor feed all those dependent upon it.

It is also true that European society had within it certain rituals and customs to defuse discontent, to channel the violence of the youthful and poor. For centuries European peasant youth had, at carnivals and holidays, elected "Lords of Misrule," being allowed by society to mock and temporarily replace its leaders. As Natalie Zemon Davis has argued, such festive play gave youth the means to organize themselves, to discover how the society worked, and to be sure of their places within it.

Southwark Fair. William Hogarth
This engraving, and the one on the next page, illustrate the vivid public life of fairs, spectacles, and blood sports that drew the upper classes and the poor together and provided a natural environment for the quacks, petty criminals, beggars, prostitutes, and entertainers that formed the underside of European society. *Courtesy of The Brooklyn Museum.*

The Cock Pit. William Hogarth
Courtesy of The Brooklyn Museum.

Feast days, church ales, saint's days, name days, May Day, religious pilgrimages, and fairs reinforced the origins, both pagan and Christian, of European society. Carnivals, celebrated throughout Europe at the time of Lent, became ritualized metaphors for gluttony, sex, and violence. The rates of illegitimacy and homicide often went up during carnival time, as society purged itself of the tendencies that could destroy it. By the seventeenth century these festivals were perceived, rightly or wrongly, as threats to good order. The founders and leaders of the Reformation sometimes condemned such pleasures and pilgrimages, feast days and holy days, as empty and idle rituals, unnecessary for salvation, even harmful to it. William Stubbes wrote disapprovingly in his *Anatomie of Abuses* in 1587, "some spende the Sabbaoth day . . . in maintaning lords of misrule . . . , in Maie games, church ales, feastes, and wakesses; in pyping, dauncyng, dicying, carding, bowlyng. . . ." Richard Baxter, a seventeenth-century Puritan, wrote in his *Autobiography* of youthful sabbath days spent dancing under the maypole until dark, though only after time spent reading the *Book of Common Prayer*. The wisest of society's leaders might well have perceived such celebrations as a two-edged sword, as rituals that might channel discontent into play, or lead to social anarchy or disorder. Thus James I in his Declaration of Sports, issued in 1618, encouraged the continuation of such sabbath entertainments as archery, May-games, Whitsun ales, and Morris dances, but attempted to prohibit the more violent rituals of bull- and bear-baiting.

For many, the family filled the vacuum of authority left by the weakening of older socioeconomic relationships. Sixteenth- and seventeenth-century catechisms, designed to prepare youth for full membership in church and society, emphasized the fifth commandment. Parents, and particularly the male head of the household, were to be honored, respected, and obeyed, and this pattern of authority was extended, through them, to magistrates, monarchs, and all who ruled. "Now by parents wee understand not onely the natural parents," ran a late sixteenth-century English catechism, "but such as by the law of nature and of God, supply their places: as grandfathers, uncles, great uncles and aunts, brethren, sisters, kinsmen, and kins-women, Magistrates. . . ." One of the most usual condemnations leveled at the wandering poor by their social betters was their failure to observe the conventional rules of marriage and family life. Disobedience to parents was harshly dealt with in law and custom. In the *Ulozhenie* of 1649, a law code of Muscovite Russia, children who killed their parents were to be executed, while the killing of a son or daughter resulted in a year in jail. The Englishwoman Anne Lady Halkett was only expressing an aspect of the habit of obedience to parents when she wrote, ". . . I ever looked upon marrying without consent of parents as the highest act of ingratitude and disobedience that children could committ. . . ."

Others saw instruction in manners and courtesy, the elaboration of other social rituals, as a means to reinforce authority over the young and rebellious. In seventeenth-century France, manners and courtesy were used to emphasize the superiority of royalty over nobility, and the nobility over all others. A humiliating code of courtesy was imposed by Cardinal Richelieu and Louis XIII on all their subjects. At the Spanish court, a royal meal required the services of a large number of servants and inferiors. Every time the Spanish king dined, he was served in various ways by a steward, a clergyman, a major-domo, a butler, a carver, a cellarer, and a physician. Two mace-bearers and a footman were also in attendance. At most courts, and in many great houses, social rank was emphasized by social privilege. The distribution of articles productive of physical comfort, even the amount and kind of food received, was formalized and made dependent on power and rank. In the palace of Cardinal

Mazarin, a whole pig would be placed before the Cardinal himself, another was shared by sixteen of his pages, but his *valets de chambre* had to be content with two pig's ears. At the court of Charles I of England, a similar system approached the level of expensive absurdity. Powerful courtiers were entitled to receive more food than they or their servants could possibly eat, as well as the privilege of *bouge of court* whereby, again on the basis of rank, they received allotments of bread, ale, firewood, and candles. Many converted such privileges into money payments, or had their servants sell their allotments outside the court at a profit. Court etiquette often became so frozen that even extraordinary events could not disrupt the lines of authority. Philip III of Spain was inconvenienced, and perhaps even made mortally ill, by the fumes from a brazier in his court which nobody dared remove, fearing that by doing so they would offend the absent courtier charged with the responsibility.

Habits of courtesy were instilled in the literate from youth, and forced in a humiliating way on their inferiors. Books of etiquette were acquired by the powerful, and peasants acquired habits like touching cap or forlock when confronted with their social betters. "It is . . . necessarye for Fathers and Maysters to cause their Chyldren and servantes to use fayre and gentle speeche," ran a late-sixteenth century book on courtesy, "with reverence and curtesye to their Elders and Betters. . . ." As a contemporary English poet wrote:

> First I command thee God to serve,
> Then to they parents duty yeeld.
> Unto all men be courteous
> and mannerly in town and field.

The idea of obedience was also reinforced by economic policy, the formalized extravagance of courts, the granting of monopolies, and taxation. Mercantilism, the economic philosophy that prevailed with most monarchs and states, carried within it an insistence on obedience to authority. According to its tenets, gold and other precious metals were to be kept in the kingdom and hoarded for its benefit; the poor, whenever possible, were to be restricted in their wanderings and put to work, the better to make them productive and to limit dissent; manufacturing and industry were to be encouraged, the better to keep a favorable balance of trade and a stable kingdom. Privileged merchants were granted monopolies, giving them exclusive trading rights in a given commodity or in a given geographic area. In a similar way, the landed classes were given privileged positions at court, the right to marry wealthy wards or relatives of the monarch, honors, and pensions.

In return, sovereigns expected loyalty, obedience, and loans and gifts of money in times of financial need. Lest nobles become too powerful, they were expected to attend the sovereign's court, and to participate in its expensive round of masques, balls, hunts, rituals, and ceremonies. Great merchants as well as the landed classes were expected to feast and house the royal court when it progressed the country, and to ingratiate the monarch with expensive gifts.

Sir Robert Carey rode to the court of James Stuart at Holyrood for precisely these reasons: to demonstrate his obedience to a new English sovereign and to be granted his reward. There was, however, a flaw. Such a system of reward and privilege could only be sustained if monarchs and others in power possessed sufficient wealth to fund their official generosity, and sufficient authority and police power to overawe both their overmighty and desperately poor subjects. At precisely the same time that servants and philosophers at the courts of powerful kings were developing doctrines of royal sovereignty and absolutism, economic crisis and inflation were robbing monarchs of the wealth needed to reward those who helped maintain their authority. Simultaneously, those left outside the system came increasingly to resent it—merchants excluded from trading monopolies, nobility denied the favor of the court, guildsmen who had lost their living to merchant-capitalists, the agricultural laborer thrown off the land because of enclosure.

E. The Challenge to Authority and its Response: Crime, Violence, and the Law

Contrary to the beliefs of some, contemporary society is not the first to challenge and test authority. Authority in the seventeenth century, by the very fact that there were so few to enforce it, was obliged to fall back on severe measures, which in turn brought it contempt and diminished respect for government. As C. V. Wedgwood has remarked of the seventeenth century, "The outlook even of the educated was harsh. Underneath a veneer of courtesy, manners were primitive; drunkenness and cruelty were common to all classes, judges were more severe than just, civil authority more brutal than effective, and charity came limping far behind the needs of the people."

Too often, the mask of manners and obedience was ripped off, only to be badly and imperfectly reapplied by a legal system fundamentally unjust and lacking the means to enforce its edicts consistently. It is hard to escape the belief that seventeenth-century society was one in which law was at once overcodified and underpoliced. Seventeenth-century London had no formal police at all, and its citizens used the services of bellmen who would, for a fee, bring light and pike to bear on dangerous streets. Even in Paris, where the police chief La Reynie made strides in law enforcement, there were only eight hundred foot-patrolmen to cover hundreds of winding streets and meet the needs of a population of a half-million.

It is undeniable that when criminals were caught, the law dealt harshly with them. In seventeenth-century Muscovy, by the *Ulozhenie* of 1649, torture, generally in the form of beatings with the knout, was an accepted part of criminal investigation. Even confessed criminals were tortured, in an effort to oblige them to admit other crimes or to implicate accomplices. For a first theft criminals were beaten, mutilated by the loss of one of their ears, committed to prison, and then forced to hard labor and exile. Execution was mandated for murder, arson, stealing from a church, treason, a second robbery, or a third theft. Wives who murdered their husbands were suffocated to death by being buried alive. The Military Code of Peter the Great simply built on this existing body of law, and added to its savagery. Under Peter's Code there were some sixty-one capital offenses, to be carried out variously by shooting, hanging, breaking on the wheel, quartering, burning, and beheading. Most lesser crimes required mutilation or corporal punishment. In Russia, as with most of Europe, execution, exile, or beatings were seen as preferable to confinement in prison. Such prisons as there were tended to be seen as burdens on state revenue; therefore they were run as profit-ventures by contract jailers, where survival depended on the ability to pay keepers for necessities and privileges. A long sentence in prison was tantamount to a death sentence.

The seventeenth-century French also administered extreme punishments. The assassin of Henry IV was dealt with in a typically harsh way. Because he had stabbed his sovereign to death, the miscreant was first tied to a cross, a knife chained to his hand, and his whole arm committed to the flames. Thereafter hot oil, pitch, molten lead, and brimstone were poured on his living flesh, already rent by the application of red-hot pincers. Finally what remained of the carcass was pulled apart by four horses and destroyed by the mob. Hot pincers were often used on capital criminals. They were used in the execution of *La Pilosa,* the escaped convict and murderer who led a revolt in Palermo, Sicily in 1647, and Fynes Moryson noticed their use on murderers in Germany. For lesser criminals in France there were the galleys where men, with shaven head, eyebrows, and beards, and dressed in loincloths, were made to pull in groups of three a fifteen-foot oar.

In Germany, Fynes Moryson found a similar maze of violent custom governing criminal punishment. On two occasions, Moryson claimed that he saw men hanged in chains, with dogs suspended on either side of them to devour their flesh. "Great criminals" were nailed by the ears in public before execution; sons could lose their hands and their head for striking their father; alleged witches could be burned through the rectum by a burning iron, those who counterfeited coin could be immersed in caldrons of boiling lead; rapists and their accomplices could be beheaded. Between Dresden and Prague another English traveler found "above seven score gallowses and wheels, where thieves were hanged, some fresh and some half-rotten, and the carcases of murderers broken limb after limb on the wheels."

Even in England, famous for jurists, equity, and the Common Law, injustice was not unusual and punishment severe. The horror and humiliation of the traitor's death, which combined stripping, hanging, castration, disembowelment and quartering, was still practiced, and recorded in the diaries of Pepys and Evelyn. Capital crimes were likewise very many, though not always carried out, as with the woman who was condemned in 1637 for stealing one of the king's dishes. Most execution was by hanging, but it was a slow death as the neck was not usually broken. Relatives of the condemned often came to the place of public execution to pull on the legs, or beat on the chest, of the still living body to hasten death. As in other societies of the time, beating and mutilation were also occasionally ordered. In the case of William Prynne, who was condemned for seditious writing, the punishment was loss of both ears and the application of hot irons to both cheeks.

All over Europe, the law extracted horrible and symbolic penalties, and punishment was designed to reflect the heinousness of the crime. Thus, in the Netherlands, manslayers were executed and then buried in the same coffins with those they had slain; in England, suicides, guilty of self-murder, could be buried in obscurity at crossroads with stakes through their hearts. Out on a lark in 1661 with some ladies, Samuel Pepys was obliged to ride under the hanging corpse of a highwayman on Shooter's Hill, a site on the Dover Road outside London where travelers were often robbed. Highwaymen, their bodies soaked in tar as a preservative, were commonly so displayed; "a filthy sight it was," Pepys later recorded, "to see how his flesh is shrunk to his bones." For similar reasons, pirates were hanged on Wapping Dock, in full view of ship's crews as they worked their vessels from London down the Thames to the sea.

Authority redoubled its harshness toward sexual crimes, particularly with those believed to be deviant or illicit. In many European states, homosexual practices were punishable by burning. In

Palermo, Sicily a special piazza was designated specifically for execution of homosexuals. There in 1608, in an ironic turn of fate, the public hangman was burned for the crime for which he had executed so many others. In England the "Devilish and Unnatural Sin of Buggery" was also a capital crime, and it remained so into the nineteenth century. Social rank was not always a guarantee of safety. Mervyn Touchet, Second Earl of Castlehaven, was tried in 1631 for a litany of deviant acts, including the abetment of rapes on his second wife and stepdaughter as well as homosexual acts with his servants. Despite his noble status, Touchet was sentenced to death by hanging. Similarly, alleged witches, thought to be especially bestial because of sex acts with the devil, were sometimes burned. Incest could also be a capital crime. In 1632, in London, one Robert Robinson was hanged at Smithfield for raping the daughters of his second wife.

Where it did not do violence, the law humiliated and shamed. In Padua, those convicted of certain financial crimes were required to sit bare-buttocked in public; those guilty of adultery in England did public penance in a white robe or had to stand in the stocks in ignominy before passers-by. Many punishments required the victim to be publicly stripped, partially or fully, before whipping, branding, mutilation, or execution. For serious crimes, and even for some lesser ones, humiliation was extended to the family of those punished. When Ravaillac suffered the terrible penalties for assassinating Henry IV, his family suffered seizure of property and banishment. The ritual castration of traitors in England was a sign that the seed and family line of the criminal were thought to be corrupt.

The sense of justice was also diluted when, as it often was, it seemed compromised by wealth or power. Money was known to intersect with the law in various unfortunate ways. In Sicily, those guilty of certain consensual sexual offenses could commute their punishments according to a sliding scale of cash payments; in Seville, murderers could have their lives if widows of the victim accepted a sum of money in compensation; in many parts of Europe, legal officers were thought to be friendlier if gifts were given. Some sexual offenders in England suffered extreme penalties, but many thought the court of James I to be a center of homosexual activity, and that the Lord Chancellor, Sir Francis Bacon, indulged a passion for children.

By the seventeenth century, for all of these reasons, there had arisen a general mistrust of and disrespect for the law as well as all connected with it. Association with hangmen or executioners was surrounded by taboo. In Germany, Fynes Moryson asserted that executioners wore green caps so they would be recognizable to all who desired not to associate with them. In Poland, the hangman had such trouble in finding a wife that condemned female felons could be pardoned if they agreed to marriage. Throughout Europe, executioners were a caste apart, and the profession became hereditary in certain families.

Judges and lawyers were singled out for particular contempt. In the late seventeenth century, Sir William Smith, Justice of the Peace for Middlesex, proudly proclaimed that "The King and the laws have long fingers, and sometime or other they will reach the tallest malefactor." But all those who came before him did not agree, and he was obliged to fine a miscreant for publicly saying "I care not a turd for Sir William Smith." Benefiting from the growing complexities of the law, which necessitated increasingly specialized education, the legal classes in the seventeenth century grew fat on the fees of litigation. The powerful, who had once bludgeoned each other on the field of battle, now bludgeoned each other in the courts of law. In England, landed families sent their sons for a term or two to the Inns of Court to be instructed in the law, as they had once sent them to great households to be instructed in the sword.

Lawyers became the subject of satire, as in Racine's *Les Plaideurs,* while the English playwright Thomas Dekker wrote of ". . . The Lawyers ill-got monyes, That suck up Poor Bees Honyes." "Amongst the living Objects to bee seen in the streets of Paris," sneered Lister, "the Counsellors and chief Officers of the Courts of Justice make a great Figure: They and their Wives have their Trains carried up; so there are abundance to be seen walking about the streets in this manner." "He was so excellent a lawyer," wrote the biographer John Aubrey of Sir Walter Rumsey, "that he was called *The Pick-locke of the Lawe.*" Commented the English revolutionary Richard Overton, "I must be tryed by a Law (called the Common Law) that I know not, nor I thinke no man else. . . . The tedious, unknowne and impossible-to-be understood common law. . . ." In her study of seventeenth-century Seville, Mary Elizabeth Perry translates the words of a contemporary describing a legal system in which there was "no administration of justice, rare truth, little honor and fear of God, and less trust," and in which none were punished if they could "pay scribes, lawyers, and judges." Said Celia Fiennes of the English Court of Chancery, "This formerly was the best Court to relieve the subject but now is as corrupt as any and as dilatory," subject to delays that enriched lawyers and bankrupted plaintiffs and defendants.

In the seventeenth century the uncertain, unjust violence of the law left little reaction save contempt in a society also violent, and too used to pain and death. The short journal of young Thomas Isham of Lamport, kept as a Latin exercise, may serve as an illustration. In his diary Thomas Isham wrote of unknown people dying on the road and being buried unmourned in the churchyard, of children dying in the night, of an unidentified indigent girl found dead in a ditch, of a schoolmaster shut out of his own school and shot in the arm by his own pupils, of one man killed when the breech of his gun blew up and of another found unaccountably murdered and mutilated in a field, of too many women losing their lives in childbirth.

In city and town the violence of the law in fact became a form of public entertainment, in much the same way as the blood-sports of dueling, cockfighting, and bull- and bear-baiting. For many, there must have been little to choose between the sight of a wounded dog flung into the lap of a spectator by an enraged bull, an event that John Evelyn witnessed in 1670, and a traitor publicly killed and mutilated for assaulting his king, a happening witnessed by the same author more frequently than the first. "The apprentices have bine mutinous ab^t St. Giles and w^d have puld down a house," wrote Sir Charles Lyttleton disapprovingly in 1682; but he saw little reason to be critical of the behavior of his son, badly wounded in a duel in 1690. "*Drinking, Gaming and Whores,*" said a contemporary preacher with unusual candor of the passion for dueling, "these are the rotten bones that lie hid under the painted *Sepulchre* and title of *Honour.*"

Casual violence was practiced by all classes, even by the leaders of society and their servants, and the mob. In 1620, in the midst of a royal progress, two gentlemen set upon a retainer of the Earl of Southampton and spurred and beat him nearly to death. In 1663, a quarrel between two coachmen, one of them the king's, resulted in the laying on of whips and the loss of at least one eye—to the laughter and enjoyment of passers-by. In 1628, John Lambe, charlatan, astrologer, quack physician, and creature of the hated Duke of Buckingham, was set upon by the London mob as he left a theater and battered to death.

For all of its wrath and violence, the law was no match for the violence of the society it tried vainly to control, unable to cope very well with a wandering underclass created by demographic increase and economic instability. Legal institutions were simply not adequate for what they were called upon to perform. Thus in the late seventeenth century the unpaid justice of the peace for Middlesex, Sir William Smith, instructed his grand jury that they were obliged to investigate everything from heresies, treasons, suspicious priests, and robbers to questionable alehouses, cursers, libelers, disturbers of the peace, and those who fiddled with the price of grain.

In such a system, it was usually the poor or ignorant, who suffered the law's pains and humiliations. The pamphleteer author of *The Laws Discovery* wrote in 1653, "Many times murderers and notorious thieves are but warmed a little in the hand, because they can read; and another for a sheep or a trifle because he cannot read." "Whip me? out you toad:—whip me?" exclaims a character in one of Dekker's plays, "What justice is this, to whip me because Ime a begger? . . . I am starved, and have had no meat by this light, ever since the great floud, I am a poore man." "And is not this a slavery," asked the Englishman Gerrard Winstanley later in the century, ". . . That though there be Land enough . . . to maintain ten times as many people as are in it, yet some must beg . . . , or work in hard drudgery, . . . or starve, or steal, and so be hanged out of the way, as men not to live in the earth . . . ?"

In March of 1672 Thomas Isham of Lamport recorded in his diary a disquieting crime. A local shepherd had been found murdered in his cottage with all his family. The murderers, probably thieves, were long gone and were probably never caught. This incident, as much as any, revealed the powerlessness of the law in the face of a violent society. Yet no crime committed in the seventeenth century would astonish a modern urban-dweller. It is not the violence of seventeenth-century society that endangered it, but the violence and ineffectuality of its law. The contempt for law, and thus for the governments that made it, was what threatened to undermine the social order and made so many question the monarchies that ruled them. Had Sir Robert Carey been knocked senseless on his great fall from his horse he might well have been set upon by one of the wandering poor for whom monarchy, economy, and law had done nothing. If that had occurred he would have lost his horse and his clothes, and he would have been fortunate indeed to have been left alive in a ditch.

F. Standards of Behavior and the Coarseness of Life

The coarseness of the seventeenth century has impressed many social historians, and examples of cruelty, crudity, and indifference to suffering are not hard to find. Peter the Great, Tsar of all the Russias, impaled his rebellious palace guard on stakes, extracted the teeth of unwilling courtiers, forced servants to eat tortoises and drink vinegar, beat up his palace staff, and, on one occasion, tried unsuccessfully to oblige his wife to kiss a phallic symbol in public. James I once responded to a courtier's request that he meet the public by exclaiming, "God's wounds! I will pull down my breeches and they shall also see my arse!" On a fine day in 1663 Sir Charles Sedley, before a crowd of a thousand in Covent Garden, clambered onto a balcony, exposed himself, assumed various obscene postures, advertised a bogus powder claimed to have a remarkable effect on loose women, and finally, in a most unique way, drank a toast to Charles II.

It was a century just beginning to understand the idea of privacy and what in modern times would be thought of as the most elementary social decency. In April of 1662 Samuel Pepys was appalled when a corpse washed for four days in the Thames without being recovered, but his own wife squatted in a ditch when she felt the call of nature at a theatrical, and Pepys himself did not hesitate to beat his own servants with brooms or to box their ears. The Dauphin of France urinated on the wall of his own bedchamber. William Byrd of Westover lay with a prostitute on the grass of a London park. "He was much troubled with Flegme," wrote the biographer of the noted lawyer Sir Walter Rumsey, adding that the counselor often sat by the fire "spitting and spawling."

It was also a time of lying and libels, in which toleration was seldom thought of as a virtue but the reverse. "I would prefer not to reign at all rather than to reign over heretics," said the Spanish king Philip II, and his attitude of mind was expressed in the continued expulsion of Jews and Muslims; the doctrine of *limpieza de sangre,* or purity of blood; and the ritual of the *auto da fe,* after which heretics who admitted their errors were allowed the mercy of strangulation before being committed to the flames. In England, where missionary Catholics were still executed, Ephraim Pagitt published in 1647 his *Heresiography,* in which he condemned the many religious groupings not in agreement with his own Presbyterian views. After the revocation of the Edict of Nantes in 1685, French Catholics assaulted the Calvinists, or Huguenots, forced them to hold charcoal in their hands and poured boiling water down their throats. Blackness of skin was increasingly seen as a sign of blackness and inferiority within. In perhaps the most extreme act of intolerance, at least to modern minds, the studies of Philip Curtin show that some 1,325,000 slaves were imported from Africa to European colonies in the seventeenth century—as opposed to less than a fifth of that number in the preceding one.

The Englishman Sir Kenelm Digby was described by a contemporary, with some reason, as "the Pliny of our age for lying." In this distinction he had many competitors, as the men and women of the seventeenth century consistently cheated on weights and measures, watered milk and ale, and delighted in slander. "The use of talking is almost lost in the world by the habit of lying," observed Lord Halifax. In every village there seemed to be at least one "common swearer" or "bawling scold," and slander also reached the ears of the mighty. The author of the anonymous tract *Tom Tell Troath,* which appeared in 1621, began with a diatribe against all that was Catholic and foreign, and ended by slandering James I. In 1666 one

Harry Killigrew was banished from the court of Charles II for alleging that Lady Castlemaine, the king's mistress, had been when young "a little lecherous girl" known for certain acts of sexual precocity.

Crudity was often compounded by drunkenness. John Wilmot, Earl of Rochester, an admittedly extreme case, bragged that he had been drunk consistently for five years. "We heard that Chapman of Draughton," wrote young Thomas Isham in 1673, "being in drink in a house at Maidwell, said that Sir William Haslewood had no one in his house but sodomites and whores." Most contemporaries agreed that drunkenness was common, only quarreling over the area of Europe that was the most drunken. In his account of seventeenth-century Russia, Adam Olearius, a native of Holstein, wrote that intoxication affected "high and low, men and women, old and young," and that no one ever missed "an opportunity to drink and get drunk." In Saxony, Fynes Moryson found that drunks on their way out of cities "doe reele from one side of the streete to the other, as if it were too narrow for them," and that it was "no shame . . . to spewe at the Table in their next fellowes bosom, or to pisse under the Table, and afterwards in their beds." The author of an English account of Poland, written in 1598, described the Polish gentry as great "quaffers," though "not sleepy, nor heavy in their dronkennesse, as the Dutche . . . , and not surly, as the Germans."

Crowned heads and governments tried, though unsuccessfully, to discourage drinking. In 1607 the English Parliament passed an act against "the odious sin of drunkenness," but too often the good example was lacking. Later in the century Lord Halifax wrote, with more than a touch of irony, that "Great Drinkers are less fit to serve in Parliament than is apprehended." Few, however, seem to have heeded his warning that "Nothing is more frail than a man too far engaged in wet popularity." The Landgrave of Hesse founded a society to encourage temperance in drink, but its first president died of drink's consequences. Samuel Pepys was always resolving, heavy head pounding, to moderate his drinking, especially after he threw up at Westminster Hall. John George, Elector of Saxony, so fond of food and drink that he remained hours at table, dumped the last drops of steins of beer on servant's heads as a signal for more.

The coarseness of life, especially in a society in which there were such contrasts between wealth and poverty, such hostility between the few who ruled and the masses they ruled, such a gulf between the few who were literate and the many who were not, produced extremes in attitudes, in the way seventeenth-century people viewed their world. Some years ago the literary scholar Basil Willey called the seventeenth century "double-faced," writing of "an age half scientific and half magical, half skeptical and half credulous. . . ." Most intellectual historians date the modern scientific revolution from the seventeenth century, yet it was a century almost unbelievably ignorant and credulous by modern standards. In the early seventeenth century the Englishman Walter Yonge wrote seriously of a woman who ejected pins from her nose and mouth, of bloody rains, of prophecies found under the foundations of monasteries. At the other extreme, reacting against the credulity, baseness, and uncertainty of the times, were attitudes skeptical, satirical, even cynical. "It is the fools and the knaves that make the wheels of the World turn," Halifax wrote. "They *are* the World; those few who have sense or honesty sneak up and down single, but never go in herds."

For many in fact, faith and reason, magic and science, credulity and skepticism, were not opposed abstract concepts, but coexisted in uneasy tandem. At times, neither approach seemed sufficient to lessen the terror and coarseness of life, adequate to foster trust or reinforce social bonds. In Carlo Cipolla's essay on the effects of the plague in a seventeenth-century Italian village, we find one priest vainly trying to impose a proper quarantine to isolate the disease, while another insisted on leading a religious procession which might have encouraged its spread. Tuscan public health officials ordered the mass killing of dogs and cats, in the mistaken belief that they were responsible for the outbreak, while the rats, the true agents of the disease, were in consequence allowed to multiply more freely. Neither prayers nor pragmatism stopped the epidemic, as the people violated the quarantines that were curses to trade, the poor stole from the houses of plague victims, the gravediggers trafficked in the infected garments of the dead, the well-to-do opposed the extra taxes needed to isolate and care for the sick, and the physicians either fled the plague or were attacked by fearful people when they dared to report a new outbreak.

G. *Domestic Relations and Demography: Women, Children, and the Family*

In a society of such apparent coarseness, indifference, and brutality, the violence of the streets spilled over into domestic relationships and women and children could be terribly mistreated. In 1609 the English House of Lords heard the case of Sir John Kennedy who had, with the assistance of eighteen or twenty men, thrown his wife out of the house without any possessions or clothes. Many are the proverbs emphasizing the need to dominate women; not unusual are laws and customs that legalized or condoned the physical mistreatment of wives and children. When Sir John Brampston was sent away to school with his brother, an intemperate schoolmaster gave the latter "50 blowes with the great rod;" Endymion Porter perhaps represented contemporary attitudes more accurately when he limited the number of those who could discipline his child, and further instructed that he not be beaten "overmuch."

It is tempting to explain away much of the casual brutality toward women and children as a consequence of the general coarseness of the times and to religious attitudes emphasizing the inherent sinfulness of women and children. There is merit in these explanations. For many in the seventeenth century, as in preceding ones, all women were Eve reincarnated and therefore responsible for the sins of Adam and the death of Christ. A society in which the doctrine of original sin was deeply ingrained had more difficulty in assuming the innocence of children than our own.

More recently, social historians have come to believe that past domestic brutality and the violence of life which fed it were the results of still more powerful forces—the shortness of life, the frequency of disease, the filth and unpleasantness of ordinary human existence. Some have also argued that the goals of family life in the seventeenth century were different than they are in the modern world, that seventeenth-century families emphasized the objectives of the group and thus could be very indifferent to the goals of individual members. What is probably most true is that attitudes toward women, children, and the family intersected with the ultimate brutality of seventeenth-century life—early and frequent death.

"The building of a family," wrote Lord Halifax, "is a manufacture very little above the building of a house of cards." Marriage and family life were certainly no more stable in the seventeenth century than they are now, and perhaps less so. Among the upper classes marriage was an economic venture through which great families became greater by marrying into still more powerful ones. Women and heiresses were often judged less on personal qualities and more on the wealth they could bring into a family. Financial considerations often transcended private feeling. Thus in June of 1684, Dr. Edmund King wrote as follows to Viscount Hatton, one month after Lady Hatton died:

> ... your Lord^p I believe will doe well to have an eye to the support of yor familie, and look upon y^r glass how the sand runs, and give me leave to say I know a Lords grandaughter who is about 19, finely accomplisht, bredd by the Countess of K ____, her grandmother, 5 or 6000 ^{li}[£] certain or therabouts. Beautie inough, nay a large share, vertue, and hono^r unspotted.

Although many arranged marriages did grow into strong personal relationships, callousness and bad feeling sometimes grew when parents arranged matches for children who had little in common. As divorce or annulment were rarities, the result was violence, bad feeling, adultery, or separation. "Hence it is," wrote Richard Whately in his tract on marriage, "that divers houses are none other, but even very Fencing Schooles, wherein the two sexes seeme to have met together for nothing, but to trie masteries." Wrote the Frenchman Pasquier in similar vein, "Marriage . . . is a way of learning how to hate women."

At the other extreme of society, the poorer classes often delayed marriage for the same reasons that encouraged their betters to marry for wealth or power. Poorer men and women, because they could not afford to wed, or desired to limit the numbers of children for economic reasons, married at a later age than is customary today. In the village of Colyton, Devonshire, the average age for women at first marriage was thirty, while in Amsterdam it was nearly twenty-seven; in Geneva, it was twenty-four. In 1663 Samuel Pepys was told that the people of East Prussia habitually married late, the women seldom below thirty. In consequence, he added "They are not very populous there. . . ." Fynes Moryson, traveling through the Netherlands in the late sixteenth century, noted that many women remained single to a similar age. Late marriage in essence became a form of birth control in a society that possessed few other effective modes of contraception. Many, of course, never married at all. The spinster was a fixture of seventeenth-century society, as were younger sons of landed families who lacked the wealth to marry according to their station. The poor regularly formed genuine but unblessed unions simply because of the complexities and expense of church marriages. Therefore, for many people in the seventeenth century, marriage came later than it does today, if it came at all.

The instability and brevity of marriage was often made more so by the appallingly high death rate among spouses and children. Glückel of Hameln's family was not untypical. Her father married twice, and Glückel herself outlived two husbands. Of her children, a daughter died at the age of three, and two sons predeceased their mother. Elizabeth, the mother of William Taswell, died at age forty-three after giving birth to twelve children between 1649 and 1667. Of the twelve, seven died in infancy or childhood. In the small village of Foxton, Cambridgeshire, Philip Rayner married his wife Elizabeth in 1611. The couple had ten children in ten years, but six of them died before they came of age. The English clergyman and farmer Ralph Josselin was born of yeoman stock in Essex in 1617. His mother died when he was eight years old, and his father remarried when his son was in his early teens. In 1640 Ralph Josselin married

Jane Constable and fathered ten children. Of these, Ralph, the first of two sons named for their father, died at ten days old, while the second died at thirteen months. Yet another son, Thomas, died at twenty-nine, and two daughters, Mary and Anne, died respectively at eight and nineteen. John Wilmot, Earl of Rochester, died at thirty-three leaving a wife and four legitimate children, as well as an illegitimate daughter by Elizabeth Barry. The latter daughter died at thirteen, and Rochester's son and heir at age eleven. Adam Martindale (1632-1686) was a nonconformist minister from a yeoman family in Lancashire. While he was still an infant his mother died, and, at about the same time, his sister Jane defied the family, moved to London, married, and died of the smallpox. All but two of Adam Martindale's children died before their father. One child, Hannah, contracted a fever at the age of ten that left her crippled for life.

Death was so frequent that parents often could not know each other very well, or did not dare to do so. Children came to be associated with death or hardship. Richard Lane, a contemporary English clergyman, noted in his diary that his infant nephew was christened on the same day that Lane's sister, dead of the consequences of bearing the boy, was buried. Samuel Pepys no doubt spoke for some when he wrote, "and so home, where I find my wife not well—and she tells me that she thinks she is with child; but I neither believe nor desire it. But God's will be done." John Evelyn was sent to live with his grandfather when he was very young, and it was not until seven years later that his parents and all their offspring were reunited.

Children died so commonly that their names were forgotten, even by siblings or parents. Thus Sir John Brampston wrote of his father, "By his wife Bridget Moundeford John Brampston had manie children, some that died before his wife, Bridget, Mary, Thomas, and others. . . ." Micheline Boulant, in a study of French family life in a region near Paris, found that widowed spouses in the seventeenth and eighteenth centuries remarried rapidly, after several months or even weeks, that at least thirty percent of marriages were second marriages for at least one of the partners, and that when parents died children were scattered among relations. All of this created a family life that was "blurred," with houses full of step-mothers, step-fathers, step-brothers and sisters, and even illegitimate offspring. The youthful Louis XIII apparently experienced some confusion as to how to relate to the illegitimate children of his father by three different women. When Edmund Verney took Mary Blakeney as his third wife in 1588, he married a woman who already had children by both her previous marriages. This, the fact that Edmund Verney also had children, and the fact that his third marriage also produced a son, created jealousies among half-siblings over property that required a private act of Parliament to settle. One of these sons, Francis, quarrelled violently with his step-mother and step-brother, sold his share of the property to stave off creditors, and left England, never to return. In similar style, the young Ralph Josselin might have left home for Cambridge because of an inability to get along with his step-mother.

Bearing the most extreme sacrifices for their families were women. The absence of effective birth control techniques made more frequent the dangers of childbirth, already made mortal by imperfect obstetrics and hygiene. In 1606 Mary Pole died at thirty-eight after having given birth to her ninth child. John Evelyn watched the twenty-six-year-old Lady Godolphin waste away from puerperal sepsis. Jane Josselin was pregnant for nearly nine years of a twenty-year span during which she produced ten children. The mother of the Frenchwoman Angélique Arnaud suffered through a series of twenty pregnancies, the first fourteen of which were one year apart.

In their letters and prayers seventeenth-century women revealed their feelings about this central, and much-feared, event in their lives. "It pleases God that I continue ill with my coold," Lady Brilliana Harley wrote to her husband, "but it is, as they say a nwe disease; it trubelles me much more because of my being with childe; but I hope the Lord will have mercy with me; and, dear S^r, let me have your prayers for I have need of them." The same attitude of mind is also illustrated in the following prayer for women:

> O most gracious workman, let thy pitifulness amend the thing which our sinfullness hath marred, and either abate my pain, that I might not need of so great strength, tendance, and cunning, or else increase my strength, power and courage, that I may be able to overcome the pain of my travail.

The accounts of seventeenth-century childbirth that remain show that such prayers sometimes availed little. When Frances Drax was brought to bed of a child, she was in labor for a Saturday and a Sunday before a physician was called, a midwife finally determining that the child was positioned wrongly. There ensued a battle to save the child. Only when it was ascertained that the child was dead, on Monday night, did the focus of concern move to the mother. Despite all efforts, Frances Drax, praying, filled with medicinal cordials, lingered through Tuesday, and finally begged to be allowed to die. It was at least Wednesday before she could do so, with her child still within her.

Premature birth, as might be expected, brought equal danger. Alice Abdy, daughter of a London alderman and wife of Sir

John Brampston, was frightened, or jolted by a carriage, into premature labor in late December of 1648. Again in an effort to prevent early delivery and the loss of the child, Alice Abdy was attended by doctors and midwives, including a future president of the Royal College of Physicians, and by the skilled male midwife Hugh Chamberlen. Finally, it became obvious to the latter that the child would "have to be taken from her." "The question beinge," her husband wrote later, "...not soe much which way she should live as which way she should dye." Relatives were consulted, as was Alice Abdy herself. She desired the procedure to be performed, and so it was. The child, six weeks early, could not live even if not stillborn, and Alice Abdy followed her child to the grave in early February.

The death of Alice Abdy and her premature child is a painful reminder that the life expectancy of children continued to be very low in the seventeenth century. A study of the London parish of St. Botolph's at the turn of the century reveals that for every one hundred children born, seventy reached the age of one, while forty-eight attained their fifth birthday, and somewhere between twenty-seven and thirty saw fifteen. Pierre Goubert, in his studies of the Beauvais region of France, has concluded that out of every one hundred children born, one quarter died before they were one, another quarter before they were twenty, and yet another between the ages of twenty and forty-five. Only about ten reached the age of sixty. At certain times of year, especially in August and September demand allowed French priests and gravediggers to offer bargain funerals for children. In the Hôtel Dieu in Paris, it was said that there was a place known as the "Tower of Limbo" where the bodies of unbaptized and unwanted children were placed, and covered with quicklime.

High infant mortality was inadvertently encouraged by some of the customs of the time, and particularly that of putting children out of the home to nurse. John Evelyn was kept by a wet-nurse until he was two, with no apparent ill effects, but Samuel Johnson might have come by a life-long and disfiguring facial disease from his. Small children sometimes slept in the same bed as their nurses, and were occasionally "overlain" or suffocated. William Taswell's infant sister Maria died from this cause, and John Evelyn suspected that his young son Richard was accidently suffocated by his nurse. Sir John Brampston blamed the death of his namesake in 1640 on a nurse who allegedly "had let him catch the itch of her children," which she then compounded, and hid, with poultices. Doubtless nurses, and their sisters the midwives, were rightly blamed for some deaths, but they probably were not responsible for all that were attributed to them. Children simply died frequently during and after birth, and nurses or midwives, often poor women, often associated with the practice of witchcraft, were available targets for parental anxiety and rage.

Social custom flowed into the general uncleanliness of the time, with potentially harmful effects for young children. *Accouchment,* or confinement, in France was turned into a dangerous and infectious ceremonial by the upper classes, with the confined woman required to play host to families, children, friends, and hangers-on. In noble or royal families, all those in any way associated with the child could be present at birth. When Louis XIV was born, the princes of the blood saluted him before the umbilical cord was cut. In these and other ways, custom and demography undermined the stability of the family, and of the larger society.

G. Agents of Instability and Mortality: Disease, Nutrition, Hygiene

Childbirth and infancy, so difficult in the seventeenth century, were but the earliest contacts of human life with a world full of diseases that could ruin families or decimate populations. The reading of seventeenth-century diaries reveals a society in which sickness was chronic, badly understood, and often fatal. The London bills of mortality listed deaths from complaints as various, and unspecific, as "griping in the guts," "fright," "bleeding," "Broken legge," "headmould," "Stopping of the Stomach," "Winde," "Vomiting," and "Teeth." Terms often used, like "dropsy," "colic," "apoplexy," "fit," or "ague" could each refer to dozens of diseases, and merely described observable symptoms. Scrofula, or the "king's evil," for which the touch of monarchs was thought to be a cure, could refer to a number of diseases including afflictions of the throat, goiter, mumps, swelling of the salivary glands, facial disorders and discharges, running eyes, skin cancer, and even leprosy. "All our physicians can't tell what an ague is," so said a frustrated preacher in a sermon heard by Samuel Pepys in 1665.

People lived with ailments that they could neither understand nor have cured. Ralph Josselin, like many in the seventeenth century, suffered from eye trouble, but also was cursed with a nagging, running sore on his leg, liver pains, and sciatica. His children, not uncommonly for the time, suffered from ringworm, and his wife from ague and "fits." Samuel Pepys suffered from ailments of the same nastiness. While still a young man he was operated on for the stone, and for years suffered pain in his groin. One winter, his nose grew swollen and painful with the cold, and his mouth hurt with sores, while his face and neck were prone to boils. Pepys was always dosing

The Bitter Medicine. Adriaen Brouwer
This unhappy man, struggling to swallow a remedy that some practitioner has prescribed, symbolizes the unhappiness of an age where medicine was much less safe and helpful than it is today. *Courtesy of the Stadelsches Kunstinstitut, Frankfurt-am-Main.*

himself with "physic," in an effort to relieve blocked bowels. Frequent overindulgence in wine and spirits gave him hangovers heroic enough to keep him in bed, and a diet that overemphasized meat left him with all sorts of intestinal problems. In 1663, Pepys suffered from a cold severe enough to make him at least temporarily deaf, and some years later bad eyes made him give up his diary.

Some diseases, like smallpox, were terribly frightening. In the seventeenth century it killed perhaps one of four who contracted it, and many bore its disfiguring pockmarks. It was particularly destructive of the lives of young women because it had the potential for ruining physical beauty. "Mistress West, the Lord Delaware's daughter," wrote John Chamberlain in 1618, "one of our prime and principal beauties, is seized upon by the smallpox, which if they deal not mercifully with her she is quite undone, seeing her good face is the best part of her fortune." Smallpox ran through certain families, like the noble Russells, with a vengeance. In that family smallpox struck and killed Margaret, second Countess of Bedford, in 1565, while the third countess lost her beauty because of the disease; the fifth countess nearly died of it in 1641, as did the first duke of Bedford twenty years later. Not surprisingly, smallpox formed the substance of a horrible nightmare of William Byrd of Westover, who dreamed that his daughter had died of the disease. Consumption and whooping cough were also killers, contributing more deaths to the London bills of mortality in mid-century than any other diseases. Dysentery, the dreaded "bloody flux," also caused high mortality, as did fevers, the quartan, the tertian, others.

More frightening still was the Black Death, which struck the seventeenth century much as it had in medieval times, killing whole populations. During the plague epidemic that struck Italy in 1630-1631, Milan lost half of its population of 130,000, Venice more than a quarter of its population of 140,000. In eight years of epidemic between 1617 and 1664, Amsterdam lost 110,000 people. London lost 30,000 to plague in 1603, 60,000 in 1625, and 90,000 in weeks in 1665. "But Lord," wrote Pepys, "what a sad time it is, to see no boats upon the River—and grass grow up and down Whitehall-court—and nobody but poor wretches in the streets." In such epidemics whole families could be wiped out. In the village of Foxton, Cambridgeshire, the vicar had four little girls and a wife in 1625. By 1628 all were dead of the plague. In the village of Monte Lupo, in Tuscany, the plague first struck at the inn outside the village walls in the late summer of 1630. Between September 1 and October 6 the innkeeper Aurelio Mostardini lost a son, a daughter, a sister-in-law, and at least two other family members.

Venereal disease victimized many, disfiguring and even killing, making the "great pox" nearly as dreaded as the smallpox. In 1677 Dr. Edward Lake reported on the "great afflictions the Countess of Danby groaned under because of her two sons." Her eldest, Lord Latimer, and his wife were "sadly diseased with the pox, and did even begin to rott," while the younger son was sent to France in the hope of a cure. Such cures were unpleasant, imperfect, and painful, involving sweat-tubs, as well as doses of mercury and turpentine. Lord Rochester, whose health was possibly mortally compromised by the disease, tried to make light of such cures in an obscene poem. It reads in part:

> For all these Crying Sins of thine,
> The Suffering Part is always mine,
> 'Tis I am crammed with *Turpentine*.

The spread of venereal disease was furthered by widespread prostitution, which many observers noted but even the brutalities of the law could not control. In Madrid, prostitutes were so numerous in the Prado that gentlewomen dared not walk there; estimates of the number in Rome ran as high as 40,000. Thomas Coryate professed to be shocked at the thousands of prostitutes he saw in Venice, though he himself visited one. In Paris, even sending pimps to the galleys, and the shaving, whipping, and banishment of prostitutes did not end the problem. Louis XIV ordered the mutilation of prostitutes found with soldiers in the vicinity of Versailles, while in Toulouse convicted prostitutes were taken to a rock in the middle of the river, stripped, placed in a cage, dunked by the hangman to the point of drowning, and left on public view. Many municipalities favored more rational methods of dealing with prostitution and the spread of venereal disease, licensing prostitutes and isolating those who were sick.

Unfortunately for the health of the society, prostitution and venereal disease were not in the final analysis controllable. As poor women poured into the cities and failed to find work as maids, or even as casual laborers, they were obliged to join a growing army of temporary and more professional prostitutes. Many women, responding to economic change and the impermanence of employment, probably drifted in and out of prostitution as the need arose to feed themselves or their families. Lack of privacy, and the master-servant relationship, also assisted in making the distinction between prostitutes and working women unclear. Samuel Pepys did not hesitate to accost maids of friends and associates, as did William Byrd of Westover. The latter, possessed of an undeniably vigorous sexuality, incessantly prowled the streets of London for prostitutes. The prostitute became the object of humor and ridicule, but little understanding. Prostitution, and the venereal diseases it assisted in spreading, were but functions of the economic stresses of the times and of the wandering poor who found their way to the cities.

Disease must have inhibited the bonds of affection within families as individuals tried to cope with afflictions disfiguring, horrifying, or painful. Samuel Pepys, possibly because he had endured an operation for the stone, never fathered children, and his wife suffered from a painful gynecological complaint that at times made physical intimacy impossible. For many others, sexual relations were inhibited by frequent pregnancy, medical taboo, and even fatigue. In a society where the most ordinary acts of life were tiring, where travel was dangerous, and separation common, it should not be at all surprising that family ties were fragile, and often broke.

Disease and demography were also affected by the fact that seventeenth-century people, out of either choice or necessity, ate very badly. The rich were drawn to excessive eating, especially of meat, fish, sweets, and fruit. The family of the dukes of Bedford ate, according to their own kitchen accounts, beef, mutton, pork, calves' heads, veal, chicken, capons, salt fish, flounder, pike, lobster, crayfish, numerous varieties of fruit and sweets, and even some vegetables. For Samuel Pepys, a tailor's son and a crown servant anxious to emulate his betters, a good dinner consisted of oysters, hash of rabbit and lamb, beef, a dish of roasted fowl, a tart, fruit, and cheese. Prince Henry, the eldest son of James I, by the account of his physician "ate strangely to excess of fruit, and especially of melon and half-ripe grapes, and often eating his full of fish and of raw and cooked oysters beyond rule or measure at each meal, three or four days a week." "He had ruined his stomach with it . . . ," wrote the Venetian ambassador of the meat-eating propensities of Philip II of Spain, "and he would have died of it if nature had not given him a necessary relief: the disgusting infirmity of suppurating legs." Thus gout, quite wrongly, was seen as an aristocratic or royal disease, aggravated by dietary excess.

Fondness for meat and fish transcended spoilage or adulteration. Consequently it was often served spiced, stewed, pickled, salted, or marinated. Home at dinner with a guest, Pepys was once embarrassed to see little worms creeping out of the sturgeon that he served. He attributed the problem to bad preserving and pickle. All parts of the animal were enjoyed—head, tongue, cheek, ears, feet, and entrails. Meat-offal was often made up into pies or puddings. In Madrid the local meat pies, called *empanadillas,* were the subjects of jesting as to the precise origins of their fillings.

While the rich suffered from excess, the poor could literally die of hunger, and they were sometimes found dead in ditches, their mouths full of grass and earth. In the best of times the diet of peasants and poor townsmen was deficient. The peasants of Spanish Andalusia existed on a diet of rye bread, cheese, onions, and olives. French peasants of the Beauvais region lacked the means to support a pig or other livestock, and generally ate a low-nutrition diet of bread-and-dripping, soup, gruel, peas, and beans. In 1640 Gaston of Orléans, brother to the French king, wrote that a third of French subjects ate ordinary bread, another third oat bread, and the last third, lingering on the brink of starvation, ate acorns, grass, even the bran and blood which they picked out of streams near slaughterhouses.

All over Europe men and women anxiously watched the weather, fearing that it would turn against them and cause dearth. Diaries and letters are filled with the news of harvests and the prices of grain. In the early seventeenth century the Englishman Walter Yonge wrote of storms, poor harvests, high prices, and weather often too wet or too dry. Later in the same century Ralph Josselin recorded news of frosts, droughts, flooding, even a great wind in 1662 that pulled down houses and leveled crops. In 1647 heavy rains rotted the seeds in the fields of Sicily before they could germinate, causing widespread starvation. Pierre Goubert, writing of the famine in 1693-1694 in Beauvais, described it as a virtual massacre.

A diet poor enough to begin with was aggravated by high prices, shortages, and poor transport. Some sixty to eighty percent of the income of the mass of the population went for food, as opposed to about twenty-two percent in the United States in 1950. W. G. Hoskins has estimated that in seventeenth-century England one harvest in four was deficient enough to raise grain prices at least ten percent, an intolerable burden to those living on marginal incomes. Poor transport, particularly over land, made it impossible to move the bulk grain needed to alleviate localized and regional famine.

The result for all classes was nutrition- and famine-borne disease: rickets in young children who lacked the calcium found in milk; pellagra caused by diets heavy in corn and light in whole-grain cereals, legumes, meat, and fish; diseases of the eyes, possibly caused by the lack of vitamin A found in eggs, dairy products, and fish; scurvy caused by the lack of vitamin C found in fresh fruit. Shortages of minerals caused diseases like goiter to be common in certain regions of Europe. Traveling through southern France, Thomas Coryate saw men and women with "exceeding great bunches or swellings in their throats . . . some . . . as greate as an ordinary football with us in England." Nutritional deficiencies also caused various anemias. Chlorosis, often called the "green sickness" or the "virgin's disease," the latter because it affected so many women, was very common in seventeenth-century Europe. Dysentery, or certain forms of it, could also be fostered by famine, and attacks of dysentery sometimes signaled the last stages of starvation. Finally, nutritional diseases also affected the birth rate, as did famine itself. In seventeenth-century France, children seem to have been most often conceived in the more plentiful months. There is even some evidence of what one historian has called "famine amenorrhea," where food deficiency caused a temporary decline in the birth-rate. In many respects, the food profile of the mass of the population in seventeenth-century Europe resembles that of the Third World today.

Disease was also encouraged and transmitted by crowded conditions, which in turn discouraged the most elementary efforts in the area of hygiene and cleanliness. Strangers, masters, and servants, often in states of considerable uncleanness, shared chambers and even beds. Fynes Moryson, once proposing to share a bed with a stranger on his travels, was surprised when questioned on the cleanliness of his body and linen. "To my father's," wrote Pepys of a June day in 1660, "Where Sir Tho. Honywood and his family were come of a sudden, and so were forced to lie together in the little chamber. . . ." Pepys thought nothing of reading himself to sleep while his maid mended his breeches at his bedside, or of having his hair combed for lice; but in fairness to him he did get angry when his barber returned a periwig alive with nits, and was relieved when moving to new quarters allowed at least some of his servants to sleep in separate rooms. Cleanliness was not a measure of social rank, nor was it always practiced by the medical professions. Lady Anne Clifford remembered that at the court of James I "we were all lousy by sitting in the chamber of Sir Thomas Erskine." A brother in one of the hospitals of Paris, the Hotel Dieu, wrote in 1612 that it was an "urgent matter" to remove the mortally sick from the beds they shared with other patients "in order to avoid any apprehensions which they might have" and to avoid the odor of death.

The seventeenth century, like so many that preceded it, was a time of public filth and private dirt. Many were suspicious of bathing as possibly injurious to health, and at best an eccentricity. Adam Olearius treated the baths he found in Russia and Finland, ancestors of the modern saunas, as distinct oddities. Samuel Pepys, who barely mentioned bathing in all the pages of his diary, and who once attributed a bout of sickness to washing his feet, made fun of his wife's resolution to go regularly to a public bath-house: "she now pretends to a resolution of being hereafter very clean—how long it will hold I can guess."

Pepys' much-envied friend Thomas Povy had a bath in his house, as well as a well and a cistern, but the desire for private baths does not seem to have been strong. The third Peter Chamberlen, of the family of male midwives, sought a monopoly for making baths and bath-stoves, but it was never granted due to opposition or indifference. Lord Bacon, writing in 1638, recommended that one prepare for a bath as for an assault, coating the skin with oil and salve so that water might not penetrate the body.

Public baths grew up with the century at places like Baden, Epsom, Tunbridge Wells, and Bath. These were recommended by physicians and patronized by royalty, but contemporaries, who tended to visit them for medicinal or social purposes, wondered at the advisability of mixed bathing and saw baths of all kinds as centers of sexual activity and titillation. The busybody Thomas Coryate, on seeing garlanded women bathing at Baden in 1608, found it "a spectacle exceeding amorous" with "many passing Faire yong Ladies and gentlewoman naked in the bathes with their wooers," while in the early eighteenth century William Byrd of Westover saw the *bagnios* of London principally as a place to take whores. At times, however, the dangers ascribed to public bathing seem to have been well-founded. Contemporaries referred to people being pulled under by the current as they bathed in the Thames.

Pepys wrote nastily in 1665 that "the fine Mrs. Middleton is noted for carrying . . . a continued soure base smell that is very offensive, especially if she be a little hot." In this he was probably unfair, because uncleanness was a problem for all classes and most people.

The inconvenience and suspicion of bathing was heightened by a water supply that was uncertain and often polluted. Some cities, like London, possessed water wheels and systems of wooden pipes and conduits that pumped river water to fountains and even private homes, but such water was as likely as not to be filthy. According to Fynes Moryson, two river branches entered Padua, convenient to drive many mills, and contributing to trade, but also important because they "doe cleanse all filth of stables and privies." Rural villages were little better. Foxton, Cambridgeshire had its muck heaps, and it was also permissable to open cesspits and gutters into the village brook at night. In city, town, and village it was exceptional if travelers did not find streets caked with mud and manure, blocked with the offal of butcher's shambles, and piles of human ordure, much of which reached the water supply.

By the seventeenth century the chamberpot and the close stool, an often beribboned and decorated box that had to be emptied by servants, had replaced the medieval garderobe as a primary device for dealing with human waste. Servants responded to the increased responsibilities by dumping the contents of these devices on the streets of towns, adding to the gutter offal that corrupted wells and rivers. Palaces and public buildings, underequipped for purposes of sanitation, contributed to the problem of waste disposal. In the stairways, court, and passageways of the Louvre, in the words of a contemporary, "one sees a thousand ordures . . . caused by the natural necessities which are performed there every day." Anthony à Wood damned the courtiers of Charles II for leaving their excrements in chimneys, studies, coalhouses, and cellars while resident at Oxford. In such an environment Lister was probably not surprised to find in a city like Paris, where thousands of water-carriers were employed because the Seine had become a sewer, that one of his hosts had built a device to filter the river water through sand.

Even clothing could be an agent of filth and infection. While clothing was perhaps less a social divider than it had been in medieval times, the requirements of dress were real, often complex, and very expensive. Wigs, which came into fashion when Louis XIII suffered a disease that robbed him of his hair, grew ever larger and were nesting grounds for fleas and lice. Women needed many yards of materials for shifts, gowns, ruffs, coifs, petticoats, kerchiefs, headcloths, stockings, stays, and aprons; the men needed breeches, doublets, jerkins, shirts, hose, boots, and, by the end of the century, cravats. Hats were also an expense, worn even indoors until the custom was made impracticable by the wearing of wigs. Both sexes required cloaks, special clothing for walking or riding. Fashion and ceremony sometimes demanded elaborate stitchery, embroidery, cutlery, leather, and jewels. For the coronation of Charles II, the Duke of Bedford spent nearly £1,000 just for the liveries of his servants, including £16 to a wigmaker, £11 to a purveyor of feathers, £23 to a sword cutler and beltmaker, £293 to a laceman, and £103 to a tailor. Clothing, so expensive, and so necessary in a society where central heating was unknown, was often bequeathed in wills, taken to pieces to make new garments, or sold second-hand. The young Ralph Josselin sold off most of his clothes to pay debts, and Pepys had an article of clothing made from his wife's old petticoat.

Although lighter cotton prints and the so-called "new draperies" did begin to compete with the traditional heavier woolens, clothing must have been difficult to clean and therefore became a host for filth and vermin. In May of 1665 Pepys, though a tailor's son, mentioned that he felt hot and uncomfortable "in the same clothes I wore all winter." Authorities had to fight against a brisk trade in clothing during plague years. The typhus epidemic of 1623, from which John Donne sickened, could only have been caused by the lice which inhabited houses, clothing, and persons.

H. The Inadequacy of the Medical Professions

The burden of public health, of sickness and death, fell on groups of medical professions ill-prepared in terms of training and equipment, divided over modes of treatment, over criteria for licensing, and over questions of medical jurisdiction. While there was indeed substantial medical and surgical advance from the fifteenth through the seventeenth centuries—Ambroise Paré discovered that ligature was superior to cautery in the treatment of wounds; the Chamberlen family of male midwives developed a crude form of obstetric forceps; Thomas Sydenham carefully catalogued and described a variety of poorly-understood diseases; medical schools developed programs in clinical medicine, built botanical gardens and amphitheaters for anatomy; Vesalius, Harvey, and others made explorations in anatomy and physiology—it is arguable how many of these developments could be applied to a society poor and badly integrated, where the standards of medical training were many and various.

Physicians, sometimes indifferently or mysteriously trained, were licensed by many authorities including bishops, universities, guilds, and professional bodies like the Royal College of Physicians in London. By the seventeenth century, medicine was becoming a profession in terms of organization, but was not as yet so in terms of training and treatment. Though they quarreled philosophically over means of treatment, some devoted to the traditional four humors of ancient medicine and to the teachings of Galen, others to the chemical remedies advocated by the disciples of Paracelsus, physicians nonetheless considered themselves a medical elite. They visited patients and tested urine, often charging very high fees, but they frequently left actual treatment to those they considered their inferiors—to the barber-surgeons and the medicine-vending apothecaries. Some of the treatments that were prescribed—bleeding, blistering, purging, glystering, sweating—were often as frightening to the patient as disease itself. Prince Rupert, a military hero of the English Civil War, hid some of the symptoms of his last illness for fear of being bled. Still in part devoted to Galen's four humors, "the blood, the phlegm, the choler, the melancholy," physicians often felt that extreme measures were needed to keep the system in balance, and bleeding through one of forty-one veins designated for that purpose could accomplish remarkable things. According to one contemporary,

> [bleeding] quickeneth the spirit and purgeth the brains, helpeth the memory and maketh the senses more subtle, clarifieth and sharpeneth the sight, voice and wit, heateth the marrow, and wasteth such superfluous humours which make the marrow in the bones to be cold, it purifieth the whole senses, and removeth those fumes which ascend to the head and trouble the senses; it stayeth vomiting, and laxe.

Surgeons, because they often performed the scarification, cupping, and bleeding prescribed by physicians, were also much feared, and it was as yet an emerging profession infiltrated by rupture-cutters and other quacks. "Mr. Freeman called and set Blaxley's sister's leg; he did the same for a hound."—so runs an entry in the diary of Thomas Isham of Lamport. Nonetheless, surgeons did perform more complex procedures, and did so with some skill. Pepys, himself the beneficiary of a successful operation for the stone, mentioned that an aunt submitted to a mastectomy. Procedures were also known for caesarean section, though it was not frequently performed, and for plastic surgery. The Scots surgeon Thomas Lowe, whose treatise, *The Whole Art of Chirurgery,* was first published in 1597, mentioned surgical procedures involving the removal of tumors, the amputation of limbs, the repair of cleft palates and ruptures, the treatment of ulcers and fistulas, and the reproductive anatomy of women—in addition to the more usual bone-setting and bleeding. The particular curses of seventeenth-century surgery were the lack of good anesthetics and sterilization methods, compounded by the mistrust from the public. Simple fractures easily became gangrenous, and John Evelyn's brother died of the stone rather than submit to the same painful surgical procedure that eased Pepys.

The art of prescribing medicine had not yet become a science, and still seemed to be somewhat connected to magical technique. It was still believed that the living could be healed or helped by remnants of the dead. Ashes of bones were used to make aphrodisiacal powders, and a gout remedy prescribed for Charles II was made of calomel, sugar of lead, pulverized human bone, and the "raspings of a human skull unburied." Pepys carried a hare's foot as a remedy for colic. Desiccated skulls were said by some to be good for epilepsy, while the touch of a corpse would inhibit menstruation. The perspiration of cadavers was said to remedy hemorrhoids and tumors. In seventeenth-century France the gums of teething children were rubbed with a mixture of honey, butter, and the brains of hare and viper, while bed-wetting was remedied with porcupine meat. "Venice treacle"—consisting of vipers, white wine, opium, spices, licorice, red roses, germander, aloes juice, St. John's wort, and honey—was a common remedy in contemporary London.

Beverages like brandy, and even substances like tobacco were thought to have medicinal properties. "Mr. Chetwind," Pepys wrote of an acquaintance, "by chawing of tobacco, is become very fat and lusty, whereas he was consumptive." He also heard a doctor prescribe turpentine pills for the stone. In such a chaos of prescriptions, elixirs, glysters, vomitaries, powders, cordials, and treacles, quackery flourished. James II gave the Royal College of Physicians

The Quack. Adriaen Brouwer
Most of the common people were too poor to be able to afford the fees of physicians, who often would not perform surgery in any case. This left the field open to wandering quacks and unlicensed practitioners. *Courtesy of the Stadelsches Kunstinstitut, Frankfurt-am-Main.*

oversight of "all dealers in corrupt Medicines and druggs." It was an impossible task. Years earlier, reflecting the biases of his surgical profession, worried over the proliferation of harsh drugs, Thomas Lowe condemned those who promised "to heal all things by vomitaries and laxates," and caused their patients to end their days "by cruel vomiting" and "insatiable going to stool." The playwright Molière, in one of his satires of the medical profession, had a physician administer a concoction of animal droppings and powdered toads, but the point was lost on the army of mountebanks and quacks and apothecaries and physicians who prescribed remedies either useless or harmful.

The public, mystified by the many, frightening, and varied forms of possible treatment, went from doctor to doctor, quack to quack. Before her death in 1694, the daughter of Sir John Brampston consulted eleven physicians and four apothecaries. They disagreed as to the cause of the disease and the medicines required to effect a cure or ease her pain. "After all this expence," wrote Sir John, frustrated and worried over his dying daughter, "and the tryall of so manie medecines, doctors and apothecaries, there was not found any ... that ... gave ease"; "for at best they do but guess, and I am perswaded that most of them dissemble their opinions, and comply with the patient's desires and their owne profit." "With us, it is a profession that can maintain but a few. And divers of those more indebted to opinion than learning, and ... better qualified in discoursing their travails than in discerning their patient's maladies." So said the author of the tract *Tom Of All Trades* in 1631.

There were, of course, physicians moderate and cautious in treatments, familiar with the limitations of their profession and the benefits of rest and quiet. Among them were men like Thomas Sydenham, or advocates of natural childbirth and quiet healing like Percevall Willoughby. There were surgeons like Gaspare Tagliacozzi, who developed techniques for the replacement of lips and noses destroyed by mutilation or syphilus. But all of them together could not counter the cynicism of a public sickened by harsh remedies and unable to distinguish the able physicians from the "Mountebanks, Empiricks, Quacksalvers, Paracelsians ... , Wizards, Alcumists, Poor-vicars, cast Apothecaries, and Physitians men, Barbers, and Good-wives," who, in the words of one contemporary, confused people with their obscure degrees and deserved little but the title of "Doctorasse." The cynicism of many was summarized in the following verse:

> When any sick to me apply
> I physicks, bleeds and sweats 'em.
> If after that they chose to die
> Why verily I lettsom.

Other medical professions, like dentistry, were even less liberated from quackery. The dental profession was still largely in the hands of itinerant toothdrawers who practiced their profession at country fairs. Formidable individuals sometimes recognizable by their necklaces of extracted teeth, the toothdrawers practiced their profession with the aid of pliers and the more brutal grooved pelican, which gripped and removed teeth with a twisting motion. Teeth were also cleaned by scraping with metal instruments and application of *aqua fortis*, a solution of nitric acid. Contemporary diarists often refer to toothache and to sores in the mouth, to bad or rotten teeth, and the deaths of children were sometimes ascribed to problems connected with teething.

Nowhere are the problems, jealousies, and limitations of the healing professions better illustrated than in the controversy over the training of midwives. Though midwives had long been licensed by municipalities, bishops, and medical bodies, there seems little question that some midwives, as some physicians, were incompetent in assisting childbirth and caused the death of mothers and children. Unfortunately, in some areas of Europe, the largely female profession of midwifery did not receive the respect from the other medical professions that it might have merited, and not enough effort was made on the part of the medical establishment to make the training of midwives more professional. There were, however, notable individual efforts at improvement. Experienced male physicians and surgeons produced works designed to assist midwives, as did Louise Bourgeois, official midwife to the French court, and the Englishwoman Jane Sharp. More ambitious efforts at organization and training were often blocked by medical and licensing bodies anxious to protect and extend their areas of responsibility and jurisdiction. In England a proposal for a midwive's guild, instigated by the Chamberlen family of male midwives, was rejected on recommendation of the Royal College of Physicians, probably for reasons of professional jealousy and mistrust. In 1687 Elizabeth Cellier was equally unsuccessful with a plan for training midwives in London. In France, efforts to establish a school for midwives were successful, but in some areas of Europe the once-proud profession of female midwifery, often the only recourse for poor and pregnant women, was left in a medical backwater, associated in the public mind with witchcraft, incompetence, and death.

The fate of female midwifery is but a small illustration of the effect of the professionalization of medicine on what health care there was for the mass of the people. The medicine that the poor could afford—the cunning man, the white witch, the midwife—was increasingly attacked and despised by medical professionals whose remedies were beyond the means and understanding of the poor. Even the wealthier classes preferred at times to treat themselves, much as Lady Brilliana Harley prescribed remedies for her son by letter, and tracts on housewifery still underlined the responsibilities of women in tending to the health needs of their families. Into the breech stepped the quack and the rupture-cutter, the mountebank and empiric, at once causes and beneficiaries of the inadequacy of health care.

I. Harbingers of Improvement and Change

Though few in 1600 would have noticed it, European society carried within it the seeds of growth and improvement, as well as dissolution and revolution; some of them would eventually become agents of change, making life more civil, improving prospects for trade and prosperity.

The first of these harbingers was the phenomenal growth of the city, both in population and in economic importance. Cities have always been a force in the European past, so much so that historians like William C. McNeill have argued that European history would be more comprehensible if it were organized around cities rather than nation states. It is definitely true that between 1500 and 1700 cities grew markedly, especially in key areas of western Europe.

Patterns of urban growth reinforced the flow of economic power to the Atlantic. Older ports tended to decline. The population of the Spanish trading port of Seville dropped from 150,000 in 1600 to 125,000 in 1650. There was also noticeable population reduction in Italy. Venice lost 10,000 inhabitants between 1600 and 1700, dropping to 140,000 people, while Verona lost half of its population in half a century. Siena, Turin, and Vicenza also lost inhabitants. Amongst the cities of Germany, the record was more mixed. Frankfurt stood at 25,000 in 1600, dropped to 15,000 at the end of the Thirty Years' War, and stabilized, again at 25,000, by the end of the century. Nuremberg grew from 15,000 to 22,000 between 1600 and 1700. But it was Paris, London, and Amsterdam that experienced the clearest and most explosive growth: Paris was already a city of 300,000 in 1600, and stood at a half-million a century later—increasingly dominating the life of France and becoming a cultural and architectural model for Europe. Even so, London outstripped Paris, growing from 250,000 to 600,000 in the same period. Amsterdam nearly doubled in numbers, growing from 100,000 in 1600 to 180,000 by the end of the century. Even in areas that were still overwhelmingly rural, cities and towns were assuming a greater importance. Perhaps twenty percent of the inhabitants of England lived in towns and cities in the seventeenth century, while the urban population of France was something like seventeen percent.

Cities came to overawe and dominate regions and even states, forcing upon them increased economic organization and integration. They became centers of wealth, culture, philanthropy, services, and especially of the money capital so crucial to the development of foreign trade and domestic industry. The studies of F.J. Fisher and others have demonstrated that between 1540 and 1640 London became the driving force in the economic development of England. The area from which London was obliged to draw its food and supplies grew ever larger, even reaching into northern England. Agriculture was stimulated, particularly in the surrounding counties. Produce flowed into markets at Newgate, Cheapside, Leadenhall, and Gracechurch Street—so much so that several of these had to be enlarged, and new markets were created at Bishopsgate and Queenshithe. Grain and other commodities were brought in from both England and abroad, giving employment to merchants, factors, and middlemen. Shops and exchanges appeared as London and other cities became centers for luxury goods and commodity trading. London's growing need for coal created a profitable coastal shipping trade, causing in turn early growth of an English coal industry.

In the negative sense, cities like London, Paris, and Amsterdam were filthy and noisome places, with very high rates of mortality. John Graunt, one of the early urban demographers in European history, noted that in seventeenth-century London there were more burials than christenings. Nonetheless, the city grew, being able to do so because it absorbed so many from outside its walls. By so doing, London and other urban centers performed an important economic and social function: absorbing surplus population from surrounding rural areas, employing them as servants and apprentices, creating some jobs, and supporting the charities that fostered stability and eased want. At least four of Ralph Josselin's children were sent to London as servants or apprentices. By one estimate one Englishman in six had some experience of London during his or her lifetime; by another, it is calculated that some twenty percent of London's population consisted of servants.

Presiding over cities like London were groups of men described by Alan Everitt as "pseudo-gentry," akin to the landed classes even if they did not always invest in country property themselves. Conservative, competent, their wealth often increasing with rising prices, merchant oligarchies dominated their cities and gave them stable, if authoritarian, government. Even in times of crisis, as during the English Civil War, these urban oligarchies remained preoccupied with local issues and resisted disruption.

By the late seventeenth century many cities were substantially rebuilt of brick and stone, becoming in the process safer and cleaner. Under the care of a succession of sovereigns and ministers, Paris became an architectural marvel, the well-lighted and well-paved, though still dirty, city that Lister saw in 1698. Four-fifths of the old city of London was destroyed in the Great Fire of 1666, a catastrophe well-described by Pepys and others, but Londoners used the tragedy as an opportunity for reconstruction, giving full reign to the skills of architects like Sir Christopher Wren. "The citizens, instead of complaining, discoursed almost of nothing but of a survey for rebuilding the city with bricks and large streets." So wrote Henry Oldenburg of the spirit of the Londoners after the Great Fire.

In some parts of Europe, important developments in housing complemented the growth of cities. Though materials and standards varied widely, houses tended to be built or rebuilt with more internal subdivisions. Ceilings of plaster were built over first-floor halls and rooms, creating at first lofts and then bed-chambers. The creation of second floor rooms, in turn, required fireplaces and chimneys, enclosed staircases and eventually corridors and landings. By the end of the century more windows, and more glass, appeared. Wills reveal instead of mats the bequest of feather beds, the most cherished possession of the English yeoman, as well as carpets, table-cloths, cushions, pillows, linens, blankets, pans of brass and pewter, and even joined furniture. Wallpaper, tapestry, and paint replaced wainscoting in the homes of the more affluent. Ceiling heights were raised, and the sash window was introduced. Though many of the houses of the seventeenth century were small, cramped, and uncomfortable by modern standards, and though the very poor still lived in hovels with their animals and a few sticks of rude furniture, the first strides toward privacy had been made, and with it came new possibilities for human relationships.

Eating and drinking became more civil and pleasant exercises. Glasses made their appearance, replacing the common cup theretofore used; plates were substituted for trenchers and slabs of bread; the fork also made its appearance, partially replacing fingers; gentlemen stopped bringing their own knives to table. Pepys drank a "cupp of tea" for the first time in 1660, and by the early years of the eighteenth century William Byrd of Westover drank it in London with some regularity. Chocolate became a popular beverage in London and Paris. It was coffee, however, that became the drink of choice. In 1669 the ambassador of the Ottoman Porte served the bitter beverage to guests in Paris. Soon every European city had its coffee houses, which became centers of news, gossip and, in the minds of some monarchs, sedition. Wines, ordinary and fortified, as well as spirits, began to compete with the beer and ale that were already dietary staples. Foods like maize, or corn, and the potato began their march across Europe and into the diets of the poor. Tobacco, to the enjoyment of some and the horror of others, was used for purposes both pleasurable and medicinal.

For the literate classes, civility was also promoted by the many conduct books published. Tracts were printed on how to raise and educate children, how to make marriages successful, how to behave. A growing body of literature discussed, pro and con, the educability and powers of women. That there was an "educational revolution" in this period is a matter of dispute, both as to its effects and extent, but schooling was available, and some of the powerful did immerse themselves for a time in the universities or in institutions like the Inns of Court in London. Increasingly popular was the "grand tour," the lengthy pilgrimage through Europe undertaken by male aristocrats and their tutors.

For women, educational and other opportunities continued to be marginal. "I cannot but complain of . . . the great negligence of Parents," wrote Hannah Woolley, "in letting the fertile ground of their Daughters lie fallow, yet send the barren Noddles of their Sons to the University, where they stay for no other purpose than to fill their empty Sconces with idle notions to make a noise in the Country." The Englishwomen Anne Lady Halkett was taught to write, speak French, play the lute and virginals, and sew, but Russian women of the upper classes were kept secluded before and after marriage, and custom almost ritualized the separation of sexes in the Spanish monarchy. Many contemporaries noted a relationship between the duties of a wife and those of a servant. "It is ridiculous to see the wives of German foote-soldiers going to warre," commented Fynes Moryson, "laded with burthens like she-Asses, while the men carry not so much as their own clokes. . . . " Preaching before James I, Robert Wilkinson compared a good wife to a snail, "not only for her silence and continual keeping of her house, but also for a certain commendable timorousness of her nature."

Nonetheless, in both Protestant and Catholic states, women were able to use religion as a means to improve or maintain their status. In England, Puritanism, that complex religious brew that combined the ideas of the Reformation with native heresy, followed and expanded the more positive ideas of Luther and Calvin on the honored place of women in the family. Spiritual equality with men was admitted, and women served a valued function in the "little commonwealth" of the Puritan family. While women preachers and radicals played a part in the English Civil War, women preachers were suspect and most Reformers felt that women should be subject to their husbands. Interestingly, some Puritans attributed the spiritual strength of women to their sacrifices in childbirth. "Childe-bearing women," wrote Richard Sibbes, "bring others into this life with danger of their own; therefore they are forced a nearer communion with God because so many children as they bring forth they are in peril of their lives." Much the same was said of Mistress Jane Ratcliffe of Chester, blessed by a God impressed by her grief at the loss of an infant, "who made that an occasion to make her apparently his own child."

Both Protestant and Catholic women lived lives of real conviction, and some of them were exceedingly well-educated. Rachel Allen, daughter of a Lincolnshire clergyman, knew Latin, Greek, and Hebrew, and bore a son in 1608 who eventually became Bishop of Carlisle. Elizabeth Tanfield, the strong-willed daughter of the Chief Baron of the Exchequer, also knew four or five languages. Later she made a study of the Fathers of the Church, and converted to Roman Catholicism. This she kept a secret from her husband, Viscount Falkland, for twenty years.

Some social historians believe that women were harmed economically by the decline of guilds and the other consequences of approaching capitalism. In the case of guilds this was probably true, but in parts of Europe women continued to function economically much as they always had. On the fields of the manor of Sonning in Berkshire and Oxfordshire, women performed much as they had in previous centuries—working in field and manor house, giving birth, dying or surviving. In the seventeenth century, according to the researches of Doris M. Stenton, widows of copyhold tenants at Sonning were allowed to work "widow's estates," or tenancies, for the duration of their lives. Some women were even copyhold tenants in their own right, and some fewer still were freeholders. While women were victimized economically, some accumulated money through inheritance or economic activity. When the new widow of the London merchant Sir Nicholas Golds was remarried to a courtier, Thomas Neale, she was worth, according to Pepys, £3,000. The wags henceforth called her new spouse "Golden Neale." Glückel of Hameln, the widow of a Jewish merchant, became a successful businesswoman in her own right—and was able to provide dowries for all of her unmarried children save one. Women were often victimized when they came to the city to find work as maids, but some were able to exploit the opportunity to gain a degree of sophistication and education. According to *The Compleat servant maid, or the young maiden's tutor,* published in England in 1685, a female domestic servant should be knowledgeable enough to dress suitably, preserve perishables, write legibly, do sums, and carve. London maids went so far as to petition against their "surly madames" during the English Civil War.

One of the real obstacles to the improvement of women's status was the burden of their own sexuality, and the attitude of society toward it. A contemporary proverb held that women were "saints in the church, angels in the streets, devils in the kitchen, and apes in bed." The power of female sexuality was still feared. In the craze of witchcraft prosecution that struck Europe in the seventeenth century, alleged witches were sometimes accused of making men impotent. When Eleanor Radcliffe, Countess of Sussex, died of the consequences of venereal disease, contemporaries still saw an element of divine punishment in it: "a great and sad example of the power of Lust and the slavery of it," wrote John Aubrey, noting that she had formed a sexual relationship with one of her footmen after her husband's death. A young girl could begin work in one of the licensed brothels of Seville if she could prove that she was older than twelve, was not a virgin, was orphaned, and was not of noble status. The churching of women, a ritual that marked the reentry of women into society after the uncleanness of giving birth, was still practiced. The Reverend Rowland Davies wrote of churching no less than eight in a morning in 1689. Pepys, on seeing a group of "gallants" carrying off a woman, did nothing to help and seemed almost to envy them. The decline of witchcraft prosecution in the late seventeenth and eighteenth centuries, and the more humane discussion of family limitation by Catholic theologians, while important, seem modest gains in a society where attitudes toward women were often callous and disrespectful.

Despite such attitudes, the well-off of both sexes were able to enjoy the amenities of the new concept of the social "season," with time spent at country houses, in the major cities, at court, and at the spas. Pepys enjoyed the theater and his music; his contemporaries and successors were able to enjoy the masques, operas, paintings, architecture, and ballets commissioned by royal courts and their wealthy emulators. Fascination with plantings, parks, and gardens increasingly claimed the attentions of the upper classes. More genteel recreations like billiards and an antecedent of croquet became popular, and Charles II built new tennis courts at Whitehall. Card games of various kinds, lotteries, and tontines eased the passion of the upper classes for gambling, as did the horse race. "Angling is an art and an art worth learning," wrote Izaak Walton of another pursuit growing in popularity; "the question is whether you be capable of learning it." The third Stuart sovereign enjoyed a yacht given him by the Dutch government.

More profoundly, the Jewish community of Europe, though it still endured persecution, ghettoization, and clumsy and brutal attempts at Christianization, came to occupy an even more prominent place in seventeenth-century European society. In England, where Dr. Rodrigo Lopez was executed for allegedly trying to poison Queen Elizabeth in 1594, and where anti-Semitic plays like Marlowe's *Jew of Malta* and Shakespeare's *Merchant of Venice* were first performed, a petition was presented in 1649 for the readmission of Jews. The petition was rejected, but Cromwell allowed Sephardic Jews to return to London in the 1650s, and Charles II granted the English Jews a charter some years after his return to the throne. Though the population of Venice declined in the seventeenth century, the Jewish community within that city actually grew, participated very heavily in banking, and became an important link in supplying the foodstuffs that relieved Italian famines.

In Germany and the Holy Roman Empire the banking caste known as the "court Jews" became the valued and protected servants of the politically powerful, despite periodic expulsions, wars, and urban anti-Semitic outbreaks like the Fettmilch uprising in Frankfurt in 1612. In Poland the Jews became an important minority community, numbering a half-million in the 1640s, likewise serving the ruling classes in various capacities.

In 1648 the stability and welfare of Jews in central and eastern Europe was terribly compromised by the revolt of an unstable mass of Cossacks, Tatars, and peasants under the leadership of the renegade Bogdan Chmielnicki. Rising in revolt against Polish landlords, this huge and unbalanced army also fell upon Jews wherever they were found. When this horde entered the city of Nemirov they were joined by townsmen. Armed with swords, scythes, clubs, and lances, they attacked Jews tricked into leaving the town fortress. Butchering and raping, they pursued stragglers into the fortress moat, turning the water red. The toll from massacres like this one may have reached a quarter-million. Fleeing from Chmielnicki, Jews moved westward, burdening German communities with their numbers but creating a reservoir of talent important in the economic development of western Europe.

These refugees were joined by the continuing forced migration of *Marranos* and *conversos*, of Spanish Jews and so-called "new Christians," from the Iberian peninsula. Also moving westward, the *Marranos* and new Christians found homes in cities like Amsterdam, where they were joined by Jewish immigrants from Germany and eastern Europe. In Amsterdam, Jewish merchants diversified their interests beyond banking and moneylending, became involved in the foundation of the Dutch East and West India companies, and participated in a growing trading network extending from the Levant to the Baltic. Jews were prominent in the development of the Amsterdam stock exchange, and in 1657 the States General, acknowledging their importance, proclaimed Dutch Jews citizens of the Netherlands.

J. Conclusion

Sir Robert Carey's ride occurred in a troubled time, in a society on the edge of crisis. Seventeenth-century Europeans had a tendency toward violence, an inclination perhaps heightened, perhaps banked, by the continuing, terrible effects of the constants of their demography—food shortages, disease, lack of proper hygiene, frequent and early deaths. The people Sir William Carey knew had less stamina, labored under more chronic ailments and deformities, and were shorter than those in the western world today. Fewer were born healthy and fewer still lived to the Biblical three score and ten; fewer had enough to eat, and fewer ate wisely or well even if they had the means. Very few were literate; many more ignorant or credulous; an influential minority showed tendencies toward skepticism or even a cynical turn of mind. Manners only masked a coarse-grained life of brutality and blood sport, in which all classes still partook. The professions of law and medicine had not captured what we would call the public trust, and often merited only the fear or contempt of the common people. The more traditional institutions of state and Church, of monarchy and bureaucracy, found themselves threatened by the same inflationary pressures that obliged great landowners to enclose land, and the same economic instability that created large numbers of wandering poor. In consequence, underemployment and unemployment added to the sense of social distress, feeding crime and violence. Economic relationships were altered and misery increased. All over western Europe the rate of population growth slowed or stagnated, and in some of the Mediterranean lands it actually declined. The seventeenth was a century still reluctant to believe in the innocence of children, in the inviolability of women or of anybody else. At once superstitious and reasoned, credulous and skeptical, it emerges Janus-faced to confuse historians.

Into the balance can be thrown at best a few, and very tentative, signs of improvement: the growth and increasing economic importance of cities; improvements in housing; a stronger strain of civility in eating, manners, and games; signs of the survival and growing prosperity of the Jews, one of Europe's most vital minorities. Some social historians have argued as well that the family became more tolerant of individualism in the later seventeenth century, more respectful of the needs of the adults and children who gave it impetus. It does seem, though they were as yet willing to beat their children severely, that some families were concerned with the education of the young, with the welfare of their daughters in marriage and in life.

Whatever the merits of such conclusions, it is true that occasionally people rose above the terrors and coarseness of the time, the uncertainties of life, and the threat of death, to care deeply about one another. The letters of Lady Brilliana Harley, to her husband and especially to her son, reveal an affection that overcomes the instability of families and her own poor prose. "Beleeve me," she wrote to her husband in 1627, "I thinke I never mist you more then nowe I doo, or else I have forgoot what is past." To her son she wrote in 1638, "I may well say, you are my well-beloved child:

Family Group. Adriaen van Ostade
The affection between mother and child, and between siblings, seems to be a theme that emerges strongly in seventeenth- and eighteenth-century art. *Courtesy Pierpoint Morgan Library, New York.*

thearefore I cane not but tell you I mise you." Ralph Josselin worried over his many children, followed their lives with particular care after they left home and agonized when so many of them sickened and died. On the death of his daughter Mary in 1685, John Evelyn wrote, "Thus lived, died & was buried the joy of my life & ornament both of her sex & my poore family: God Almighty of his infinte mercy grant me the grace thankfully to resign my selfe...." The Countess of Manchester, hearing that a beloved niece had suffered a miscarriage, wrote to the woman's husband urging that she be restored to health before she was made pregnant again. "Wee have lost lately soe many relations out of this family," she concluded, "I cannot but be frighted wth the least rumore of illness in one so very neare unto mee, and for whom I have soe tender an affection...." For some in the seventeenth century, life still seemed the best answer to death. Never was this more striking than in the Jewish tradition. "I found in truth," wrote Glückel of Hameln after the death of her father, "no peace until, after the thirty days of mourning, I was blessed with a baby boy, through whom Loeb, my father's name, was born again."

Portfolio: The Life of the Society, 1600-1815

A Dutch Courtyard. Pieter de Hooch
This painting, and the one following, illustrate the emerging, comfortable bourgeois lifestyle of the seventeenth and eighteenth centuries. *Courtesy of the National Gallery of Art, Washington. Andrew Mellon Collection.*

Skittles Players in a Garden. Pieter de Hooch
Courtesy of the St. Louis Art Museum.

The Wigmaker, I and II, from Charles Coulston Gillispie. *A Diderot pictorial encyclopedia of trades and industries* (New York, 1959).

These two illustrations from Diderot's encyclopedia demonstrate the importance of wigs in the fashion of the period. *Courtesy of the History of Science Collections, University of Oklahoma Libraries.*

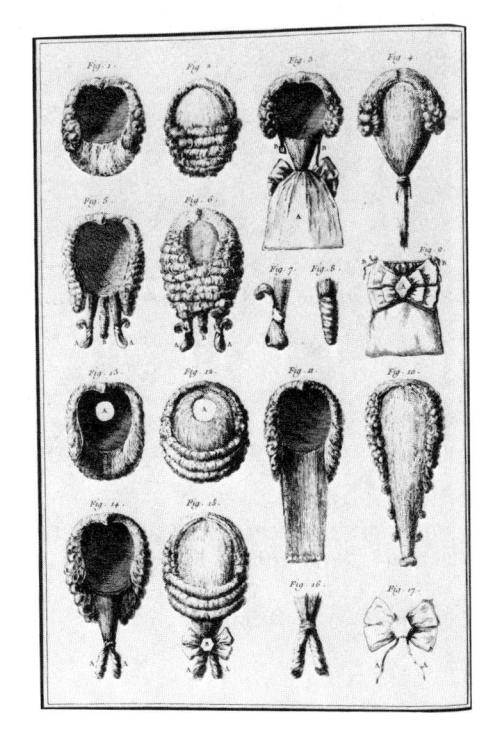

The Smokers. Adriaen Brouwer
Smoking first became a European habit in the seventeenth and eighteenth centuries, provoking this amusing painting by a member of the Dutch school. *Courtesy of The Metropolitan Museum of Art, New York. Bequest of Michael Friedsam.*

The Suitor's Visit. Gerard Ter Borch
In the seventeenth and eighteenth centuries, courtship was often a very public spectacle, undertaken as siblings and even parents looked on. *Courtesy National Gallery of Art, Washington. Andrew Mellon Collection.*

The Surprise. David Teniers
The need for servants could combine negatively with the power of men in the household to strain family relationships and victimize women. *Courtesy of the Philbrook Art Center, Tulsa, Oklahoma.*

Tavern Scene. After Adriaen Brouwer
For many women, the scarcity of work, underemployment, the instability of families, economic stagnation, and the limited nature of charity in the face of mass beggary and poverty offered little alternative but part-time or full-time prostitution. *Courtesy Graphische Sammlung Albertina, Vienna.*

Credulity, Superstition and Fanaticism. A Medley. William Hogarth
The great intellectual movements of the Scientific Revolution and Enlightenment, as Hogarth reminds us, may not have left as large a mark on the lives of contemporary Europeans as has sometimes been assumed. *Courtesy of the Yale Medical Library. Clements C. Fry Collection.*

The Rat Killer. Rembrandt van Rijn
This etching reminds that the dwellings of many who lived in this period of European history exhibited uncleanliness and vermin. *Courtesy of the Dallas Museum of Fine Arts. Gift of Calvin J. Holmes.*

The Miseries of War—The Estrapade. Jacques Callot
Punishment for even petty crimes could be savage in the seventeenth and eighteenth centuries. This illustration is a grim reminder that the governing powers of the period feared violence, crime, heresy, and revolt and fought them with cruelty. To underline the point, executions were public affairs, a combination of morality play and entertainment for the masses. *Courtesy of The Metropolitan Museum of Art. Rogers Fund.*

Chapter II

The Troubled Journey Through the English Revolution, 1603-1714: James I, Charles I, and Henrietta Maria, Oliver Cromwell, Charles II, James II, William and Mary, and Queen Anne

> It is strange to note how we have insensibly slid into this beginning of a civil war by one expected accident after another, as waves of the sea, which have brought us thus far; and we scarce know how, but from paper combats, by declarations, remonstrances, votes, messages, answers, and replies, we are now come to the question of raising forces, and naming a general and officers of an army. . . .
>
> —Bulstrode Whitelocke

> We are of all nations the people most loving and most reverently obedient to our prince, yet are we . . . too easy to be seduced to make rebellion upon very slight grounds. . . . Our clergy are become negligent and lazy, our gentry and nobility prodigal and sold to their private delights, our lawyers covetous, our common people prodigal and curious; and generally all sorts of people more careful for their private ends than for their mother the commonwealth. . . .
>
> —James I

> No man who knows ought, can be so stupid to deny that all men were naturally born free, being the image and resemblance of God himself.
>
> —John Milton

> A subject and a sovereign are clear different things.
>
> —Charles I

I tell you we will cut off his head with the crown on it.

—Oliver Cromwell

Truly, I think, if the King had had money, he might have had soldiers enough in England. For there were very few of the common people that cared very much for either of the causes, but would have taken any side for pay or plunder. But the king's treasury was very low. . . .

—Thomas Hobbes

But all rich men live at ease, feeding and clothing them by the labors of other men, not by their own; which is their shame, and not their Nobility; for it is a more blessed thing to give then to receive: But rich men receive all they have from the laborers hand, and what they give, they give away other men's labors, not their own; therefore they are not righteous Actors in the Earth.

—Gerrard Winstanley

Living in an age of extraordinary events, & revolutions he learn't . . . this truth which pursuant to his intention is here declared. That all is vanity W^{ch} is not honest, & that there's no solid wisdom but in real piety.

—John Evelyn, epitaph

The great Question which in all Ages has disturbed Mankind . . . has been . . . Not whether there be Power in the World, nor whence it came, but who should have it.

—John Locke

A. Religion, Rebellion, Revolution, and the English Civil War

Imagine the following untoward, absurd, even preposterous narrative of events: in the year 1603 a queen died, full of years, leaving her country seemingly secure and its monarchy popular. Less than forty years later an institution called the Parliament, while declaring itself the upholder of the law, rebelled against one of the successors of that most popular queen. Furthermore, this Parliament, though it professed itself to be very suspicious of armies, nonetheless created an army to fight against this royal successor. After nine years of struggle, in 1649, this army dominated and partially destroyed the Parliament that created it, and executed the sovereign, whom it had captured. A republic was then established, which proved not to work very well, and a general was made head of state. This general proceeded to run the country very much like a king, assuming powers beyond those of that unfortunate monarch who had recently been executed. After the death of the general, a period of intense confusion resulted: Parliament was called back into session, and in 1660 invited the son of the monarch who had been executed to come back from exile as king, to replace the son of the deceased general who had proved inept at ruling. This was accomplished, and the new king ruled for twenty-five years. When he died, however, he was succeeded by his brother, who was unfortunately quite stupid. Knowing very well what an army could do, and believing that this new king was going to use one against them, the members of Parliament revolted against this king as it had once revolted against his father. When this rebellion occurred in 1688 the king ran away, and Parliament at once invited his daughter and her husband to become the new sovereigns. After this, there were no revolutions in this country, and, indeed, its people came to pride themselves on the stability of their government. Though Parliament thereafter became increasingly the most powerful part of the government, kings and queens still ruled and the monarchy once again became popular.

Interestingly enough, the above narrative is not the work of novelist or storyteller, but of history itself; it relates, in admittedly simplistic terms, a sequence of events in seventeenth- and early-eighteenth-century England. Known variously as the Great Rebellion, the Puritan Revolution, the Struggle for the Constitution, and the English Civil War, this group of happenings has fascinated generations of historians as much as it appalled many of those who experienced it.

For Thomas Hobbes, whose *Behemoth* remains one of the best contemporary accounts of the conflict, the Civil War was a revelation of how "the actions of men" could lead to "hypocrisy and self-conceit, whereof the one is double iniquity and the other double folly." "After a Revolution," wrote Lord Halifax, applying his wit and cynicism to his experience of the Great Rebellion, "you see the same men in the Drawing Room, and within a week the same flatterers." Bulstrode Whitelocke felt the conflict to be the unfortunate result of "one expected accident after another, as waves of the sea," leading tragically from paper debates to the raising of armies. "Lord," a partisan of the king wrote at the outset of the struggle, "let no unseasonable stiffness of those that are in the right . . . no perverse obstinacy of those that are in the wrong, hinder the closing of our wounds. . . ."

This is not to say that all contemporaries saw the Great Rebellion as futile, its violence meaningless. Many detected in its battles and controversies the hand of God, and the tempering of constitutional and legal principles. Oliver Cromwell, who led his men into battle against the king to the singing of hymns, wrote on one occasion that "Religion was not the first thing contested for, but God brought it to that issue at last . . . and at last it proved that which was most dear to us." At another time, he remarked that "I profess I could never satisfy myself of the justness of this war, but from the authority of the Parliament to maintain itself in its rights." For Gerrard Winstanley, it was a righteous struggle of poor against rich. For the poet John Milton and many others, it was the struggle of free-born Englishmen against the centuries-old tyranny which had been imposed by William the Conqueror and his successors, the monstrous "Norman Yoke" that had destroyed the ancient liberties of a mythical "golden age." For political philosophers like John Locke it was a demonstration of what came to be known as the "social contract," a theory of government that held that rulers and ruled were bound by a solemn agreement the latter could break, even by force of arms, if rulers or governments failed to live up to the terms.

The conflicting attitudes of contemporaries and participants—a compound of indifference and idealism, cynicism and religious fervor, opportunism and principle—have reacted ever since on the biases and imaginations of historians, with equally varied results. As with many other historical episodes, the English Civil War has become an exercise in historiography, a great historical debate.

The often-tragic view of the seventeenth century writers and participants was counterpointed in the nineteenth century by a group of historians who saw the Great Rebellion as a landmark in the struggle for religious and constitutional liberty. These, the Whig historians, writing in the same century that produced the evolutionary theories attributed to the biologist Charles Darwin, and believing that they lived in a time when democratic government had reached its most perfect form, saw the English Revolution as an episode in a larger, even cosmic process. The Great Rebellion was nothing less than the seed-time of modern democracy and liberty, the germ from which English party government grew and evolved inexorably thereafter: ". . . in October 1641," wrote the Whig historian Lord Macaulay, ". . . two hostile parties emerged . . . which have ever since contended. . . . They were subsequently called Tories and Whigs . . . two rival confederacies of statesmen, a confederacy zealous for authority and antiquity, and a confederacy zealous for liberty and progress." Such views find their echoes in the magisterial works of S. R. Gardiner and Sir Charles Firth, as well as in the more modern efforts of G. M. Trevelyan and Maurice Ashley. While the contributions of the Whig historians have been real, Whig history has also carried within itself the sins of simple moralism and hindsight. In it the Civil War becomes a morality play in which evil, stupid, and reactionary Stuart kings contend with predictable lack of success against an enlightened, progressive Parliament.

Complementing the Whig view is an interpretation that sees the English Civil War as a religious struggle—a "Puritan Revolution." In the minds of some, Puritanism, the English contribution to the Protestant Reformation of the sixteenth century, fits in very well with the idea that the English Revolution was a struggle for liberty and representative government. It is true that some English Puritans seem to have been influenced by John Calvin's ideas on the right of resistance to ungodly authority. Many Englishmen seemed to react on religious and moral grounds to the real or imagined Catholicism of the early Stuart kings and their courts. "No Puritans in any narrow sense," wrote the historian William Haller of some of these men and women, "they and their successors were nevertheless fervid individualists in religion. . . . Consequently they gave their adherence to the preachers of that image of life and threw their weight against the baseborn clerics and upstart favorites whom they had, with increasing disgust, seen climb at the Stuart court into positions of wealth and authority."

The major problem with this Puritan interpretation lies in definition—*Puritanism* is a word increasingly hard to define. Coming into common use in the sixteenth century, the term had, by the seventeenth, become gawky with many meanings, and thus devoid of any meaning at all. In religious terms, Puritanism could denote the English disciples of Luther, Calvin, or Zwingli, or of all three; it could mean those who simply wished to purify the English church of empty rituals and ceremonies; it could signify those who advocated a presbyterian church structure, or a structure of independent congregations; it could even be identified, according to the historian A.G. Dickens, with the old English heresy of the Lollards, the name given to the disciples of the medieval English clergyman John Wyclif. Adding to the confusion was what Puritanism came to mean in purely *political* terms. By the seventeenth century, Puritanism had become the label for all who opposed any of the policies of the English monarchy. "In short," wrote one contemporary, "all that crossed the views of the needy courtiers, the proud encroaching priests, the thievish projectors, the lewd nobility and gentry . . . all these were puritans; and if puritans then enemies to the king and his government." Finally, there seems to be a problem with associating Puritanism with the Whig ideal of progress. The researches of Michael Walzer, among others, suggest that Puritanism looked back to the ideals of a cooperative medieval society, its followers uncomfortable with the economic changes of the seventeenth century, rather than forward to capitalism and democracy.

In the twentieth century, the idea of the English Civil War as a constitutional or religious struggle gave way to the concept of an English Revolution resulting from a class struggle. Drawing in a creative way from the philosophy of Karl Marx, another important nineteenth-century thinker, historians like R.H. Tawney, Christopher Hill, and Lawrence Stone have applied the Marxian theory of history to the English Revolution. When the Civil War began, argue these scholars, most of the aristocracy, feeling their social dominance threatened, took the side of the king, while most of the gentry, as the lesser landowners were called, rising economically, came to the defense of Parliament. The Great Rebellion thus becomes a true revolution, in which political changes were accompanied by changes in social structure. In the phrase of Christopher Hill, it was a "bourgeois revolution"—a struggle that revealed changing economic relationships and the declining economic power of the old landed classes.

This interpretation is interesting and attractive, but like its predecessors, it has its flaws: historians like H.R. Trevor-Roper have shown that some of the gentry suffered an economic decline even more severe than that of the aristocracy; other scholars have noted the instability of merchant families in the years before the Civil War; several studies of Parliamentary membership, as well as of English cities and regions, before and during the Civil War, show little relationship between socio-economic class and sides taken; religious affiliation is neglected as a cause of the English Revolution, or explained away as an intellectual expression of economic status. Puritanism becomes, in the tradition of Max Weber's *Religion and the Rise of Capitalism,* the ethic of the rising merchant classes and the gentry, while the reactionary royalists and aristocrats around the king adopt the more conservative beliefs of the Church of England or even Catholicism. In this way, consciously or unconsciously, those who follow this interpretation fall into the moralism of their Whig predecessors. Once again, those who side with Parliament are seen to be progressives, while the reactionary and bad sided with the king.

In more recent times, this so-called "gentry controversy" has perhaps generated more heat than light. Professor Lawrence Stone and his colleagues insisting that the fortunes of the gentry were rising; Professor Trevor-Roper writing with great force about a gentry in decline. Much ink and many pages in historical journals have been spent in what the historian J.H. Hexter has called the "Storm over the Gentry." But though partisans of both sides have battled themselves to a standstill, the gentry controversy still had a useful function to perform; it demonstrated that the English Civil War could no more be understood as a simple class struggle than it could be as a movement for political or religious liberty. Some new explanation had to be found.

A newer explanation, emerging in prototype from the wreckage of the gentry controversy, can be called the "court and country" hypothesis. As Professor Perez Zagorin, one of the leading exponents of this view, has observed, "the genesis of the English Revolution is not to be sought in a class struggle—for the leading sections of both sides in the Civil War included many who were drawn from the same economic class." According to this interpretation, what has been seen as a struggle for political ideas or economic interest becomes a struggle for power between one group benefitting from the favor of the Stuart kings, the "court," and another who did not enjoy such favor, the "country." Each group had a membership drawn from all social classes, and from a variety of religious persuasions, but religious, economic, and even ideological questions motivated the crucial question of power, and who should have it—the court which wanted to keep it, and the country which wanted to have more of it, or all of it.

Unfortunately for the Stuart kings and their court followers, economic and political difficulties made them unwittingly vulnerable to the assaults of the country party. Troubled by inflation and the rising costs of government, the court increasingly needed certain services supplied by the country group. From the ranks of the country party came many of the gentry and nobility who formed the unpaid backbone of royal government in the rural counties, the justices of the peace and lord lieutenants; from the country were elected many members of Parliament who voted the taxes needed to keep the government in operation; from the country party came many of the wealthy the court depended on for loans during times of crisis. As the financial position of the monarchy worsened, so the devotees of the court and country hypothesis argue, it did a very unwise thing.

Instead of following policies that would ingratiate it with the country party, the court party took actions that had the opposite effect. By 1640, the antagonism of the court and the country reached a crisis. Bankrupted and faced with an invading Scottish army, the court had to turn to a Parliament dominated by the country for funds. Using their power over the purse to advantage, the country party attacked the court party and tried to force the king to surrender much of his power to them. When the king refused, the result was civil war.

Thus the interpretations of the Civil War have come full circle. The "double iniquity" and "double folly" of the contemporary Thomas Hobbes became, in the nineteenth century, an idealistic struggle for political and religious freedom, and, in the twentieth, becomes once again a rather brazen struggle for power. "Truly, I think," wrote Hobbes in his *Behemoth,* "if the King had had money, he might have had soldiers enough in England." Such sentiments find their echoes in the musings of the court and country advocates three centuries later, as they return the English Revolution to the realm of political pragmatism and to the greed of men.

Of course this will not do. If the participants in the English Civil War were not the idealists that the Whigs believed, neither were they all the ruthless pursuers of power that some modern scholars believe them to have been. In truth, none of these interpretations, as creative and brilliant as they are, can accommodate all the complexities of the Great Rebellion or the ideas and passions of the men and women who were in some way involved. Among the participants there were political opportunists and power seekers to be sure, but there were also those who thought they heard the voice of God, or who believed that the king had violated the law, or who believed that Parliament had done so. There may have been those who fought out of frustration with their economic status, but there were also those who went to war out of conviction, putting aside perhaps forever a contented country existence, and who knew full well that they risked forfeiting their lands and fortunes to their enemies. Adding to the confusion is the fact that many who lived through these troubled times changed their minds as events unfolded, altering their loyalties or abstaining from the struggle altogether. Some in the country party who opposed the king in Parliament out of principle joined the king on the battlefield out of loyalty, or later conspired with the king against a parliamentary army of which they had grown afraid. The principled and unscrupulous peopled both sides, and for all sorts of reasons. In their idealism, their pragmatism, their hesitations, their unthinking decisions, and their sometimes imperfect understanding, the English who struggled through the period of the Civil War for a time turned their world upside down, and remade England for their heirs.

B. James VI and I: The Character of a King

It is safe to say that James VI and I is one of those sovereigns who has not been well-treated by historians. Lord Macaulay, who looked down with a moral disdain on the Stuart dynasty that James established in England, summed up the hapless James in one sentence: "He was indeed made up of two men—a witty, well-read scholar, who wrote, disputed, and harangued, and a nervous, drivelling idiot who acted." S.R. Gardiner, whose history of the Civil War remains one of the best secondary accounts of the conflict, felt that James "sowed the seeds of rebellion and disaster." The Tudor historian J.E. Neale reflected the biases of many of his colleagues when he wrote of James as "a weak sovereign who had neither the character nor the political skill to maintain the discipline of the past."

Such hostile opinions come, in part, from the analysis of contemporary, or primary, sources, and in part from the biases of the historians who have, and occasionally have not, read them. The judgments of the contemporaries of James are mixed and cannot by themselves account for the low esteem in which the first English Stuart has been held. To the Frenchman Sully, James was "the wisest fool in Christendom." On the other hand, contemporaries who observed James at close quarters tended to be more favorable. Another Frenchman in James' court called him "for his years the most remarkable Prince that ever lived. Three qualities of mind he possesses in perfection: he understands clearly, judges wisely, and has a retentive memory. His questions are keen and penetrating and his replies are sound." "He is patient in the work of government," wrote Sir Henry Wotton in 1601, and "makes no decision without obtaining good counsel." Said Bishop Godfrey Goodman at the close of James' reign: "He was the occasion of much peace in the Christian world. . . . While all the Christian world was in wars, he alone governed his people in peace. He was a most just and good king."

When James was judged harshly by some contemporaries, it was as much for his personal idiosyncracies and predilections as for his decisions of state. James was in truth an unregal, undignified king, too familiar with those around him, whose narrow jaw caused him to drool, and whose homosexual affection for favorites caused him to paw them in public. "Anyone may enter the King's presence while he is at dinner," wrote Sir Henry Wotton, "and as he eats he converses with those about him. . . . With his domestics and with gentlemen of the chamber he is extremely familiar." Noted the Frenchman Fontenay, "In speaking and eating, in his dress and in his sports, in his conversation in the presence of women, his manners are crude and uncivil and display a lack of proper instruction. . . . His voice is loud and his words grave and sententious." Paradoxically, at least to us, it did not help James' reputation that he was as funny as he was familiar. When his wife, Anne of Denmark, accidently killed a hunting dog that James loved, the king took the occasion to write a note of forgiveness, in which he enclosed a handsome sum, tongue-in-cheek, as the dog's legacy. James would lose temper and dignity by kicking a servant, and then make himself more ridiculous to his subjects by apologizing for it. "Dear Dad and Gossip": this is how one favorite was allowed to address letters to King James I of England. He shambled through life, this unimpressive, often jester-like king.

Portrait of James I. Daniel Mytens
Courtesy of the National Portrait Gallery, London.

Unkingly behavior was always compounded by James' thoroughly unkingly appearance. Not tall, sporting a scraggly beard, and with a fear of assassination, James chose to wear padded doublets, making his moderate, bandy-legged stature appear even more corpulent and ungraceful. James, while no dirtier than most of his subjects, was certainly no cleaner, and for this historians have never forgiven him. "By his good will he would never change his clothes until worn out to the very rags," wrote Sir Anthony Welldon. "His beard was very thin," Sir Anthony continued, "his tongue too large for his mouth, which made him drink very uncomely, as if eating it."

Contemporaries, and subsequent generations of historians, were also horrified and fascinated by James' homosexuality. According to Sir John Oglander, James "loved young men, his favourites, better than women, loving them beyond the love of men to women." "The king leaneth on his arm," it was said of one of James' favorites, and it was noted with disapproval that the king, "pinches his cheek, smooths his ruffled garments. . . ." Undignified, condemned by some contemporaries and many historians for his preference for men, James' sexual preferences and physical shortcomings have been unfairly seen as evidences of weakness of will and character. The illogic and injudiciousness of this attitude has been satirized by the authors of *1066 And All That* who wrote, "King James slobbered at the mouth and had favorites; he was, thus, a Bad King."

James and his Stuart successors also suffer by comparison with their Tudor predecessors, particularly Queen Elizabeth I. The Tudors, because they were on friendlier terms, at least apparently, with their Parliaments, have been roundly praised by the Whig historians and their successors, while the Stuarts, who quarreled with theirs, have been viewed as reactionary obstructionists. On the available facts it is sometimes hard to see why they have been treated so differently. Elizabeth I possessed at the end of her reign a visage nearly as ridiculous as James'. Teeth blackened by sweets, affecting absurd whigs and ruffs, her hair a bright orange, Elizabeth was as wrinkled and worn as she was vain. She quarreled with her last Parliament, and she took a bath no more than once a month, but nonetheless to many contemporaries and subsequent generations she has remained "Gloriana" and "Good Queen Bess." The Stuarts, who had the bad luck to succeed her in difficult circumstances, are left with little but bad memory.

James' political errors, and he made them to be sure, have little to do with the way he looked, or with his preference for young men. The roots of his policy decisions should be sought instead in certain of his life experiences, and the decisions themselves must be studied in the political and economic situation that James found when he came to the throne of England in 1603.

James had been born in Edinburgh Castle on June 19, 1566, the only son of Mary Queen of Scots and her second husband, Henry Stewart, Lord Darnley. Even before James' birth there were rumors that James was not Darnley's son, that he was perhaps the illicit offspring of his mother and the court musician David Rizzio. This rumor so maddened Darnley, a diseased and odious voluptuary, that he and his henchmen dragged the hapless musician from the presence of the horrified Mary Queen of Scots and did him to death with knives. It was believed by some, including Mary Queen of Scots, that Darnley's intention had been to kill her as well, or at least to force her to miscarry the child within her. It is unclear whether James was ever to believe that this was his father's intention, but rumors of the questionable nature of his birth, and of his mothers alleged sexual misconduct, followed him all the rest of his life. "Solomon, the son of David" was a common jeer, and in 1604, with James on the English throne only one year, it was reported to the Lord Mayor of London by an informant that "On Wednesday last one Alice Wells said in my hearing that our king's mother was a whore and our king a bastard and no lawful heir to the Crown of England."

Further, James was less than a year old when his avowed father Lord Darnley was murdered at the manor house of Kirk o' Field, quite possibly at the instigation of Mary Queen of Scots and James Hepburn, Earl of Bothwell, a man rumored to be her lover and whom she hastily married. Vilified as a witch and a Catholic, accused of whorishness and incompetence by her rebellious Calvinist subjects, Mary was defeated in battle and forced to abdicate in May 1567, an act which made her infant son James VI of Scotland. When she fled the kingdom less than ten months later the new king, already taken from her, was left behind in the hands of Protestant lords. He never saw his mother again.

What little and lingering respect James might have had for his mother, and by implication for the sex she represented, was quickly dissipated as he grew up under the tutelage of four regents, successively the earls of Moray, Lennox, Mar, and Morton. It was a largely masculine world and, even in a period where the fracturing of families was not unusual, an insecure and cruel one. The infant James was, as custom and circumstance of the time dictated, put out to wet-nurse; not uncommonly as well, this had an unhappy result. James was put in the charge of a woman incompetent and possibly drunken, and he contracted rickets—the malady probably responsible for his bandy-legged appearance and wandering gait.

As the infant king grew into adolescence, he was given an excellent education, if a narrow one. James knew his Old Testament, and the French, Greek, and Latin languages. His tutors George Buchanan and Peter Young assembled a fine library for him, and his mother's hurried departure left him heir to a collection of French poetry. Nonetheless, this education was laid on with Calvinist rigor and occasional brutality. As a man, James would value this education, so painfully gained, as a positive accomplishment in a youth that was otherwise bleak and unhappy. In consequence, James used book-learning as a bulwark against the world, as proof of his competence and superiority against those who sniggered at his inadequacies and doubted his legitimacy. "He had much uncommon knowledge," remarked the historian Wallace Notestein in a subtle observation, "but no common sense." While this judgment is a harsh one, it is true that James at times used his education and opinions as vehicles for ignoring problems, as substitutes for common sense rather than assets to it. Priding himself on wit, on judgment, and on a capacity for debate, James thoroughly believed that everyone was entitled to his opinion, wrote tracts on everything from the evils of tobacco to the prerogatives of monarchy, but despite contemporary assertions to the contrary too often failed to hear good counsel. "I would wish that my master read fewer books than he doth"—so said Robert Cecil, one of James' state servants.

Domestic cruelty and instability in James' youth was reinforced by the violence of Scottish politics. The young king was pulled from one faction of the nobility to another, as their retainers went "riding and ganging on horss and on fuit in Heland and Lowland." In this political morass, James was dominated by four regents in twelve years. The first of these, the Earl of Moray, lasted until 1570, when he was shot to death as he rode down a city street. There followed the regency of James' grandfather Lennox, mortally wounded through the entrails during a palace revolt in 1572. The successor of Lennox, Mar, died within a year of his appointment—of exhaustion, unhappiness, and possibly poison. Only the last, the Earl of Morton, a rigorous Calvinist and an avowed hater of James' mother, lasted for any length of time.

In this company James received little but his prized education and a love for hunting, which stayed with him all of his life as well. During this time, James also developed the homosexual leanings for which he endured so much scorn. In his youth, James loved two others: Esmé Stuart, seigneur of Aubigny, whom he made duke of Lennox and James Stewart, Earl of Arran. Esmé Stuart, "of comely proportion, civil behaviour, red-bearded, honest in conversation, well-liked by the King and part of the nobility," aroused the jealousy of other kingmakers around James. In 1582, at Ruthven Castle, the sixteen-year old James was surrounded while in his bed by a pack of suspicious Protestant lords, who forced him to drive his favorites from court. Angered, powerless, and frightened, James burst into tears as his captors mockingly called for a rocking horse for the king. In 1600 another plot, the so-called Gowrie conspiracy, an event still puzzled over by historians, may have threatened James' life. Such experiences were not likely to breed in James a trust of others, or encourage patience with those who attempted to deny him his royal rights.

Though James could be amiable and familiar, he was, paradoxically, a man uncomfortable in the presence of others. This tendency was accentuated when he was with women, whom experience had taught him to suspect and mistrust. "To make a woman learned and foxes tame had the same effect," James commented later in life, "to make them cunning." In August 1589 James married Anne, the daughter of Frederick II of Denmark, but though he had sexual relations with her, and fathered several children, the couple seemed to live most amiably when they were apart. Wrote James in *Basilikon Doron,* the commentary on kingship composed for his son: "Marriage is the greatest earthly felicity or misery . . . according as it pleaseth God to bless or curse the same." The troubled union of James and Anne of Denmark was made even more distant by the death of several of their children. The princesses Margaret, Mary, and Sophia died in infancy or early childhood, respectively in 1598, 1605, and 1606. "The little Lady Mary," wrote John Chamberlain, ". . . died yesterday morning at Stanwell. . . . She was aged 2 years and 5 months. . . . She will be buried on the 21st but without any solemnity or funeral." More important to James was the death of Prince Henry, his eldest son and heir, at the age of eighteen. Perhaps the only woman who James ever cared for deeply was his daughter Elizabeth, whom he later married off to the Elector Frederick of the Palatinate.

Personal experiences like these, as well as the temper of the times, made James fear the biological results of illicit or extramarital sex, and he endeavored to discourage his heir from "the filthy vice of adulterie." Surely James owed his own mother nothing. When Mary Queen of Scots was executed for plotting against Queen Elizabeth while in exile in England, he lodged only the most formal protest. He has often been condemned for doing nothing more, but it is hard to see what else James could have done for an adulterous mother for whom he had little affection, and who had left him in infancy. Suspicious of women, and knowing that he might one day inherit the English throne from the childless Elizabeth, it was not hard for James to tolerate the death of his mother and to await the demise of her barren rival.

Dislike for women and perhaps remembrance of the plots that troubled his youth fused in James' fascination with witchcraft.

When Reginald Scot published his skeptical *Discoverie of Witchcraft,* James countered with a restatement of traditional witchcraft belief in his *Daemonologie,* published in 1597, and ordered Scot's book burned. As king of England, James encouraged Parliament to pass an act making witchcraft practices capital felonies. Biased and scarred from his boyhood, James was easily predisposed to participate in the "witchcraft craze" of the times.

It has sometimes been forgotten that James, after attaining personal control over Scottish affairs in 1587, accomplished much as the sovereign of that country. With the assistance of the able Sir John Maitland, he endeavored to enforce respect for law, limit the use of guns and other weapons, and reduce the unjust authority of the powerful over the poor. James prided himself, with some reason, on his sense of justice. "In giving pardons," he once wrote, "I doe allways suppose my selfe in the offender, and then judge how far the like occasion might have tempted me." He advised his son to "embrace the quarrel of the poore and distressed, as your own particular" and to "teach your Nobility to keep your lawes as precisely as the meanest." James also gained a measure of control over the crown finances and the fractious Scots Presbyterian church. In these actions, and on the pages of *Basilikon Doron,* James revealed what he had become: a sovereign who had met success by asserting his authority, a law giver and philosopher-king who recognized the need to control crown finance and the church, a mature man conditioned by experience and inclination to suspect opposition and to emphasize his own authority.

In 1603 the son of Mary Queen of Scots obtained his great ambition: James VI of Scotland became also James I of England. In that year James was a man approaching an inflexible middle age, the product of a background that taught him everything about the deceitfulness of men and especially of women and convinced him of the virtues of peace and order, but that left him ill-prepared and unwilling to share power with institutions like the English Parliament. Without a moment's hesitation James and his Scots retainers poured south, so anxious to reach London that James rode on in pain with a broken collar bone. They seemed to fall like locusts on a realm that, if not rich, was richer than the one they left. Unknowingly, James confronted the greatest of dilemmas: that of an experienced man whose very experiences ill-fitted him to rule successfully over his new realm. Awaiting him at Westminster was his own "High Court of Parliament," its members very conscious of their own privileges, as high-minded and histrionic as the man who came to meet them.

C. The Struggle of Crown and Parliament: Prerogative versus Privilege, 1485-1625

The Whig historians robed the English Parliament in historic majesty, and some of its seventeenth-century members strongly asserted its status as an independent legislative body, but in truth its origins were probably neither glorious nor free. Parliament was an old institution, with roots deep in the soil of medieval England, but the best scholarship on its beginnings asserts that Parliament was traditionally a court of the English sovereigns, assembled and dissolved at their command. Monarchs had initially called Parliaments to consult with them on state matters, but as time passed members of Parliament were asked to give their assent to taxation and to certain proposed items of legislation called bills. If Parliament gave its assent to the bill, generally proposed by the monarch and his ministers, the measure became law, or statute.

In time, Parliament came to be divided for convenience into two bodies, the House of Lords and the House of Commons. To the Lords came the titled nobility and the high churchmen; to the Commons came, despite what the name implies, substantial and propertied yeoman and gentry as representatives from the counties or shires, and well-to-do merchants chosen by their fellows in the boroughs or towns. Sir Thomas Smith, writing in the mid-sixteenth century, described the organization and powers in these terms:

> The most high and absolute power of the realm of England consisteth in the Parliament. For as in war, where the King himself in person, the nobility, the rest of the gentility and nobility are, is the force and power of England: so in peace and consultation where the prince is to give life and the highest and last commandment, the barony for the nobility and higher, the knights, esquires, gentlemen and commons for the lower part of the commonwealth, and to consult together and upon mature deliberation (every bill or law being thrice read and disputed upon in either House) the other two parts first each part and after the prince himself in presence of both the parts both consent to and alloweth. That is the prince's and whole realm's deed.... That which is done by this consent is called firm, stable and *sanctum*, and is taken for law....

The important thing to notice in Smith's and other contemporary accounts is their assertion of the doctrine of "king in Parliament"—the idea that when Parliament was assembled at the command of the monarch, and met together with the sovereign, it was the foundation of law and government, the expression of the will of the whole English commonwealth. "The Parliament of England," wrote Richard Hooker in 1595, ". . . is that whereupon the very essence of all government within the kingdom doth depend: it is even the body of the whole realm; it consisteth of the king and all that within the land are subject unto him. . . ."

Thus, by the sixteenth century, Parliament had become an important body, though still not necessarily an independent one. It was still called and dissolved at the whim of the sovereign; it was the king or queen who gave it authority and guaranteed its privileges; it was the consent of the monarch, who was in a sense the most important part of it, that gave its work the force of law; and it was the sovereign who chose the Speaker of the Commons and created new nobility to sit in the House of Lords. This distinction between the greater powers of the monarch and the lesser authority of Parliament was a subtle one, but one that many English subjects understood. At the same time, in the period before James came to the English throne, certain events and trends, and certain actions of James' Tudor predecessors, muddied this distinction, thereby setting off a struggle for power between crown and Parliament.

The Tudors, who ruled England from 1485 until 1603, had used Parliament increasingly to give their royal decisions the consent of "the body of the whole realm." Henry VII, the first of the Tudors, used Parliament to legalize his violent seizure of the throne and to oulaw livery and maintenance, by which the English nobility had traditionally raised private armies. In the reign of Henry VIII, the English Reformation was legitimized by parliamentary statute, as were many of the religious policies of Elizabeth I.

To enable Parliament to do the work of the realm efficiently, the Tudors granted the body certain privileges. In Ferrer's Case (1543) Henry VIII declared that members of Parliament, as his servants, were to be free from arrest during parliamentary sessions. Other privileges, such as freedom of access to the sovereign, and freedom of speech and debate, were often granted to Parliament when it petitioned the monarch at the beginning of parliamentary sessions. In the Norfolk election case of 1586, the House of Commons asserted its power to decide disputed elections. At the same time, by developing committees and secrecy of proceedings the Commons made itself increasingly capable of opposing royal bills and even of writing legislation of its own.

By the time of Queen Elizabeth, Commons felt secure enough to question royal policy itself. In 1576 the strenuous Puritan Peter Wentworth rose in Commons to denounce instructions from the queen not to debate religious issues. "Surely this was a doleful message," Wentworth ranted, "for it was as much as to say, Sirs, ye shall not deal in God's causes. . . ." A decade later Wentworth was again on his feet asserting his privilege of free speech, arrogantly demanding to know "whether the prince and state can be maintained without this Court of Parliament."

Agitated by the failure to achieve what it considered a godly religious settlement, worried over Elizabeth's failure to provide a clear, and Protestant, succession, members of Parliament endured sporadic intimidation and arrest to express to the old queen their unwelcome views. Elizabeth fumed, but she did not crush her fractious Commons, for she had come to know the answer to Peter Wentworth's last question. Through habit, as well as financial and administrative need, "the prince and the state" had indeed grown used to relying on its "Court of Parliament." From Parliament came the legislation to legitimize royal actions, and the grants of supply and taxes to counter the ever-rising costs of government; from the Lords and Commons, and from their brethren in towns and counties, came the justices of the peace and lord lieutenants who formed the unpaid backbone of English local government. In the last years of her reign, when Parliament debated "unjust" monopolies granted by the crown, Elizabeth, knowing these things, compromised, and backed away from confrontation with her Commons.

Over against the encroachments of Parliament and its privileges stood the more traditional prerogatives of the English monarchy. "*Prerogativa* is . . . a privilege or preeminence that any person hath before another," so the Englishman William Stanford wrote in 1548, "which, as it is tolerable to some, so it is most to be permitted and allowed in a prince or a sovereign governor of a realm." Among the crown prerogatives mentioned by Sir Thomas Smith were making war and peace, coining money, suspending and dispensing with unjust laws, granting pardons, and appointing high officers of church and state. "To be short," Smith concluded, "the prince is the life, the head and authority of all things that be done in the realm of England."

When James acceded to the English throne in 1603, Parliamentary privilege and prerogative royal were on a collision course. Parliament, increasingly asserting that it was the supreme arbiter of the law, had begun to view its traditional privileges almost as rights. But Parliament could grow in authority only by challenging the prerogatives that were the preserve of the monarch. James I, believing himself the fountainhead of justice and law, distrustful of the claims of a parliamentary system that he probably never completely understood, was bound to assert royal prerogative more strongly.

As James took up his duties as king of England, it became clear that the financial difficulties of the monarchy might give Parliament the opportunity to press its claims. Reporting home to his government the Venetian ambassador noted that

> ... it is the common opinion that the king has not a sou, for the late Queen sank a great deal of money in her wars with Ireland and Spain, and it is a wonder that she did not leave debts rather than cash. Then the present king was obliged to spend a large amount on his succession and to make many presents, especially to those who had served him so long in Scotland, where the poverty of the kingdom had forbidden him to do so. When he came to the throne of England he showed the liberality of his nature. It is commonly calculated that ... he must have given away two millions....

Inheriting a debt of some £100,000, James to his credit did take several measures to alleviate the financial problem. Fortunately for James the expensive Irish rebellion ended in 1603, but he showed great wisdom by ending the long-lived Spanish war in 1604, with good diplomatic and financial results. Under the guidance of Robert Cecil, the economic position of the crown was further improved by increasing tariffs, farming the customs, raising rents on crown lands, and increasing the profits of the Court of Wards.

James has often been accused of being a spender who rewarded his servants with expensive presents, but in this regard he was no different from his predecessors, and he was bound by the practices of his time. Needing the services of servants and officials in order to govern, but lacking the financial means to reward them with regular salaries, James and his predecessors rewarded them instead with occasional and expensive gifts, or bestowed upon them monopolies, titles, and grants of crown lands. Such clumsy expedients, particularly the latter ones, for rewarding servants had the tragic consequence of diminishing the finances and reputation of the crown still further. The granting of monopolies angered those who were excluded from them, the bestowing of titles enraged nobility against those they considered upstarts, and the granting of crown lands honored and enriched state servants but lessened the income and wealth of the crown.

Such expedients aroused the anger of Parliament and created self-interested groups of courtiers anxious only to preserve the system. In 1610 Robert Cecil tried to solve James' financial problems once and for all in the so-called "Great Contract." He proposed to Parliament that it grant James an income of £200,000 per year in return for the abolition of the feudal crown privileges of wardship and purveyance. Unfortunately for James a combination of House of Commons men anxious to keep him in their debt, and courtiers anxious to preserve their rewards, forced the abandonment of the Great Contract, and the able Cecil was hounded from office. Cecil's successor as Lord Treasurer announced the triumph of the old system by expropriating some £60,000 in state revenue. In 1621 when the new Lord Treasurer, Lionel Cranfield, tried to force economies in government, he too was attacked and forced to resign. Strangled by corruption, poverty, and inefficiency, the crown adopted the doubtful expedient of selling the title of baronet, from which it reaped £100,000 but gained the disgust of the old landed classes on whom it depended. The same can be said of the forced loans that the crown imposed on the wealthy and powerful.

Troubled by his financial problems, James made, or was obliged to make, decisions that brought unfortunate political consequences. Even when the decisions were good ones, it seemed that the political costs were high. The ending of the Spanish war, a sound decision in terms of diplomacy and expenditure, angered influential people in commons and country for whom Spain was the incarnation of the Catholic menace. The Puritans in Parliament, taking heart from James' Presbyterian upbringing, presented the new king with the Millenary Petition calling for moderate church reform. James responded by condemning what he later called "the humors of Puritanes, and rash-headie Preachers, that think it their honour to contend with kings, and perturbe whole kingdomes." He allied with the bishops against the uncontrolled Puritan lecturers, telling their representatives at the Hampton Court Conference of 1604 that they must conform or he would "harry them out of the land." In James' defense he realized that to control his kingdom he had to control the propaganda of its preachers, but he underestimated the strength of the proud Puritans whom he had inherited from Elizabeth.

James was used to expressing his beliefs openly and with vigor, but in so doing he antagonized his people. "As the king had no standing army," commented the Whig historian Lord Macaulay, ". . . it would have been wise in him to avoid any conflict with his people. But such was his indiscretion that . . . he constantly put forward, in the most offensive form, claims of which none of his predecessors had ever dreamed." In this, Macaulay was partly right and partly wrong. James' ideas on royal prerogative were not new, and the conflict between sovereign and Commons did not begin with him, but his assertions did offend many by their very boldness. "The state of monarchy is the supremest thing on earth"; James lectured his Parliament in 1610, "for kings are not only God's lieutenants on earth, and sit upon God's throne, but even by God himself they are called gods." Warming to his subject, James added that sovereigns "make and unmake their subjects; they have power of raising, and casting down; of life, and of death, ... They have power to exalt low things, and abase high things, and make of their subjects like men of the chess. . . ."

The combination of obstreperous Parliaments and James' own attitudes insured a difficult reign. Early on, Parliament rejected James' plan for a union between Scotland and England, and a quarrel over disputed elections caused the Commons to declare that their privileges were inherited by right, not by gift of the king. In 1614, what has come to be called the "Addled Parliament" was dissolved by James after only a few weeks because of its ambition and rancor, and well before it voted him any money. The Parliament of 1621 impeached Lord Chancellor Bacon, one of James' most able servants, for bribery, and, in 1622, when the Commons tried to tie its grant of subsidy to renewal of the Spanish war, James had to dissolve it once again without obtaining supply.

James soon found himself an unpopular sovereign. "He does not caress the people and make them that good cheer the late Queen did"—so remarked the Venetian ambassador, adding that ". . . this king manifests no taste for them but rather contempt and dislike." In 1604 there was an alleged plot to put Arabella Stuart on the throne, which led to the imprisonment and eventual execution of the popular adventurer and explorer Sir Walter Raleigh. This episode was followed a year later by the Guy Fawkes conspiracy to blow up both James and his Parliament, and in 1606 a rumor spread that James had been assassinated. Resentment was heightened when James, though in many ways a man of simple tastes, began to spend money on masques and balls, hunts, and presents to courtiers. On the wedding of his daughter Elizabeth to the Elector Palatine, it was noted disapprovingly that James had spent £6,000.

Especially loathsome to some of James' subjects, who regarded any form of sexual deviance with biblical horror, was his continued use of male favorites. "I wonder not so much that women paint themselves," James declared with his usual candor and carelessness, "as that when they are painted men can love them." Such attitudes might have been overlooked if they had been kept private, but James flaunted his favorites as much as he flaunted his claims of prerogative. James' sexual preferences did not make him a bad king, but the revulsion of his subjects lessened his prestige. As James grew older, and this was much more serious, James seemed not only to fawn on his favorites, but actually to rule through them. The first of James' favorites, Robert Carr, Earl of Somerset, disgraced James all the more because he became involved in a divorce scandal involving the estranged wife of the Earl of Essex, and was then implicated with his new wife in the poisoning of Sir Thomas Overbury. Succeeding Somerset in James' affections was George Villiers, who James made Duke of Buckingham and showered with powers and favors. "No one danced better, no man runs or jumps better," wrote Arthur Wilson sardonically of this new favorite: "Indeed he jumped higher than ever an Englishman did, from a private gentleman to a dukedom."

By 1616 James reached the beginning of his fifth decade, an advanced age for the seventeenth century, and he suffered from the effects of a daunting variety of ailments: nephritis, gout, dysentery, arthritis, fevers, and perhaps even premature senility. The man who asserted his sovereign rights so strongly began to lose his physical powers, and the task of policy-making fell into greedy and dangerous hands. James' peace-making foreign policy, of which he was so proud, collapsed in shambles in 1618 when James' son-in-law, the Elector Palatine, was elected king of Bohemia in place of the Hapsburg Holy Roman Emperor, thus beginning the Thirty Year's War in Europe. Only with difficulty did James put off the hotheads in Parliament who wanted to go to war to save the throne of his soon-deposed son-in-law. In the early 1620s James' son Charles, in the company of Buckingham, journeyed to Spain with the ill-conceived objective of winning for the former the hand of the Infanta, the heiress to the Spanish throne. When the match failed, the anti-Spanish and anti-Catholic English were delighted, and in 1624 Charles and Buckingham obtained grants from Parliament for a new war with Spain.

In 1625 James finally succumbed to his many afflictions. A day or two before he died, James' fevered body suffered a stroke that loosened the muscles of his face. In bitter irony and caricature, the old king's tongue grew too swollen for him to speak, and he nearly choked to death on his own phlegm. But there was a final indignity in the form of the violent attack of dysentery which carried him away. An autopsy was conducted, and it would have pleased James to know that his skull was found to be "so full of braynes that they could not upon the opening keep them from spilling, a great marke of his infinite judgement."

Despite such findings, James' greatest failure was in the area of that "judgement" of which he was so proud. Though a friend to the Royal College of Physicians, a patron of an enlightened scheme to bring running water to London, and a well-read writer of tracts and polemics, James possessed an intellect that was in the end inflexible, and which could not save him from impolitic errors. James' mind compassed perfectly an ideal of philosopher-kingship, but it could not seem to comprehend the realities and nuances of English politics. James often acted as if he believed that his subjects would follow him in every circumstance. He overestimated their loyalty and underestimated his ability to offend them. The man who proposed to be the father of his people often could not abide those he ruled, and railed at the crowds of petitioners who pressed upon him. In fairness to James it must be said that tolerance of opposition was not a skill that his Scottish background taught him.

Courage and candor James had in abundance. When he stood on his royal prerogative he did so honestly and openly, out of genuine belief, and no one who heard him could doubt his sincerity. Such an impolitic man needed the best of servants and ministers, and James had some—Cecil, Bacon, Cranfield—but the jealousies of favorites, courtiers, and Parliaments stripped them away. In consequence, the financial problem, the running sore that sapped the strength of the state, went undoctored, and James was left with a governing bureaucracy that creaked with inefficiency, and an unmanaged, fractious Parliament that questioned his authority. Local government, in the hands of unpaid gentry who reveled in their independence and despised the court and many of its policies, was simply beyond James' control. In such a situation, even James realized that he might be sitting on an unstable throne. "So you are of the opinion that subjects can dispossess their kings?" With this question James challenged the ambassador of the Elector Palatine, who had recently seized the throne of Bohemia. "You are come in good time to England," James continued in grim jest, "to spread these opinions among the people, that my subjects might drive me away, and place another in my room."

D. Charles I, Henrietta Maria, and the Onset of the Civil War, 1625-1649

"King James in the end of March 1625 died, leaving his Majesty that now is, engaged in a war with Spain, but unprovided with money to manage it; though it was undertaken by the consent and advice of Parliament." In this way Edward Hyde, Earl of Clarendon, loyal servant to the Stuart monarchs, described the state of affairs at the accession of Charles I. It was a grim inheritance. Old debts were presented to the new king, and the funeral of his father cost Charles £50,000; finances were in a shambles; Barbary corsairs, it was said, raided the coasts, outraging women and enslaving men; the plague renewed itself and began to kill scores, than hundreds, in London each week. Charles ordered a fast of repentence, distributed alms for the poor, and fled to the safety of Woodstock as his reign began, ill-starred and bad-omened.

The man who inherited the English throne was never intended, either by circumstance or temperament, to rule. Charles I became the heir-apparent only after the unexpected death of his elder brother Prince Henry, a resolute and hearty youth, extroverted, a player at billiards, a golfer and a swimmer, who had endeared himself to some of his countrymen by belaboring Robert Carr, his father's grasping favorite, with a tennis racket.

In marked contrast to his brother, Charles I had physical problems that scarred his early life, and left unfortunate marks on his personality. Born nearly crippled in the bleakness of Dumferlinge Palace in November 1600, Charles' entry into the world was confirmed in its grim unhappiness by the nearly simultaneous execution and ritual dismemberment of the Earl of Gowrie and his brother for allegedly plotting against King James. Terrible weakness in the legs, especially in the ankles, testified that the infant had inherited his father's weak limbs. In addition, the boy soon proved a stutterer. After contemplating his son's condition, James, exhibiting a shocking and obtuse practicality, was barely dissuaded from putting Charles in leg-irons to improve his gait, and from employing a surgeon to cut the boy's tongue to improve his speech. Charles, who did not talk until he was four, was ever after, in ironic contrast to his father, troubled by a shyness and hesitation which hampered his performance as king, and which was only partly overcome by eloquence in written expression. "When he was warm in discourse," said Sir Anthony Welwood of Charles I, "he was inclinable to stammer."

In his appearance Charles was little more fortunate. He inherited the Stuart shortness of stature, though not the slovenliness of his father, so he grew into a neat but not regal man. "The prince is now thirteen years of age," wrote John Ernest of Saxe-Weimar in 1613, "and to all appearance is not of a strong constitution." John Ernest did not realize how hard Charles had worked to attain even modest health and physical mobility. Four years after his birth the young Prince Charles had been seen dragging himself along, at first with a staff and then unaided, up and down the great chamber at Dumferlinge "like a gallant soldier all alone." Thereafter Charles bullied and punished his feeble body until it was fit for riding and the hunt, and he soon loved the latter pursuit as much as his father did. Smallness of size and hesitation in speech masked a physical courage that was often remarkable.

As if in reaction to his father, Charles grew into a moral, and sternly heterosexual, man. "King Charles was temperate, chaste, and serious; so that the fools and bawds, mimics and catamites of the former court grew out of fashion; and the nobility and the courtiers, who did not quite abandon their debaucheries, had yet the reverence for the king as to retire into corners to practice them." In this way Lucy Hutchinson remembered the court of the second Stuart.

"If I cannot live as a king," Charles once said, "I will die as a gentleman." A notable patron of art, Charles at one time or other owned or commissioned works by Titian, Mantegna, Bernini, Tintoretto, Corregio, Raphael, Rubens, Van Dyck, Mytens, Honthorst, and Hollar, as well as paintings by Orazio Gentileschi and his gifted daughter Artemisia. He also favored Theodore de Mayerne, one of the fathers of clinical medicine in England, and William Harvey, known for his work on the circulation of the blood. "Whereas we understand that an excellent collection of paintings is to be sold in Venice . . . we are desirous that our beloved servant, Mr. William Petty, should go thither to make a bargain for them." So wrote the dignified and often extravagant sovereign of an unstable and indigent state.

Circumstance and experience left Charles a mirror of contradictions, at once inflexible and vacillating, assertive and hesitating, principled and mendacious. Such a combination has earned Charles a historical reputation, not entirely undeserved, for weakness and dishonesty. A formal sovereign, perhaps the only one in Europe who required all in his service save his wife to stand or kneel before him, Charles was nonetheless troubled with self-doubt. "He was very fearless in his person"; wrote Lord Clarendon, "but not very enterprising. He had an excellent understanding, but was not confident enough of it; which made him oftentimes change his opinions for a worse, and follow the advice of men who did not judge so well as himself. This made him more irresolute than the conjuncture of his affairs would permit; if he had been of a rougher and more imperious nature, he would have found more respect and duty." Time after time, Charles would face events with seeming resolution then, with cause and resolution crumbling away, he would retreat not with a politic and kingly grace but with an impotent sadness and anger, at times abandoning allies and friends. Charles never realized that capitulation was less dignified than an early and respectable compromise. "It was King Charles' perpetual fault to grant the people's desires by bits and so late he ever lost his thanks"—so remarked the contemporary, Robert Baillie.

It was left to this quiet, indecisive, and gentle man to deal with unquiet Parliaments that were, in the words of Sir James Harrington, "running to popularity of government like a bowl down a hill: not so much . . . of malice . . . as of natural instinct. . . ." Charles did not seem to grasp that realities were changing, that there was little stability, and that a combination of high words and irresolute actions could destroy him. Believing not so much in the absolutism of which he has so often been accused as in a medieval ideal of kingship in which the sovereign was at the apex of a stable social order, where the "authority of a king is the keystone which closeth up the arch of government," Charles felt bound by principle to assert the royal prerogative. "There remained nothing to the destruction of a monarchy," Harrington continued, "more than a prince who by contending should make the people feel those advantages which they could not see... who, too secure in the undoubted right whereby he was advanced to a throne, which had no foundation, dared to put this to an unseasonable trial...." The man whom Archbishop Laud described as "a mild and gracious prince who knew not how to be or be made great" was eventually crushed by events and went down to his death a martyr for monarchy.

What strength of character Charles possessed was reinforced by the woman he made his queen. This was the princess Henrietta Maria of France, the daughter and sixth child of Henry IV and Marie de Medici. Henrietta Maria's childhood, like that of her husband, must have given her a horror of disorder and profligacy, as well as a respect for royal legitimacy. Born to a father who flaunted his masculinity, mistresses, and illegitimate progeny as much as James had his favorites, Henrietta Maria lost one parent to an assassin, while the other, her mother, was temporarily exiled for meddling in the affairs of her son, Louis XIII. Thus, as with many royal princesses in the seventeenth century, Henrietta Maria's childhood was a hard school that placed iron in the soul of the young woman who survived it. When, in 1624 at the age of fourteen, she was committed by her elders to marry the then Prince Charles of England, a man nine years her senior, she was more than his equal in character.

Though the marriage was temporarily delayed by the folly of the "Spanish match," the failure of Charles and Buckingham to woo the Spanish Infanta caused both to reopen negotiations with France, hoping thereby to find an ally against the Spanish who had humiliated them. The French, sensing the anxiety of the English, were thus able to extract strong terms, and stopped short of committing themselves to a military alliance against Spain. Even so, the negotiations proceeded, and Buckingham was sent to France to fetch Henrietta Maria. On May 23, 1625, the French princess, who by then had seen her fifteenth birthday, began the long progress to England.

It must have been an interesting journey. Buckingham, who had already called attention to himself by his bejewelled and foppish attire, at once began to pay court to the French queen. During a moonlit walk at Amiens, he pressed his ardor with such distressing vigor that the lady screamed. Thereafter Buckingham sulked. With tempers frayed, no doubt upset at the strange ways of the English, the marriage party of Henrietta Maria wended its way to the port of Boulogne, where the young princess took ship for Dover.

In addition to the burden of inexperience and the inability to speak English, Henrietta Maria carried into England a deeply-felt Catholicism that had to be troubling to her new subjects. To her, and to many of the French, the English were still Protestant heretics, and

Portrait of Charles I. Unknown Artist
Courtesy of Special Collections, University of Minnesota Libraries.

because of this the marriage treaty contained many provisions allowing Henrietta Maria freedom to practice her faith—as well as to propagate it among the English. The French had required a special bull of dispensation from the pope before the wedding ceremony could proceed, and in France the marriage had been celebrated by proxy—not inside the great Cathedral of Notre Dame, but on its steps. The English were also required to assist Louis XIII of France in suppressing the Huguenot city of La Rochelle, an anti-Protestant move that angered English Puritans. The terms of the marriage treaty itself allowed Henrietta Maria to have twenty-eight Catholic priests in her household, a domestic staff entirely French and Catholic, and a bishop for her almoner. The English had to promise, in addition, never to attempt to persuade Henrietta Maria to abandon her faith, to provide chapels accessible to the Catholic faithful in all royal residences, and to allow Henrietta Maria control of any children until they were thirteen. In these ways, the French sought to protect Henrietta Maria in the practice of her faith, but in so doing humiliated the English and weakened her reputation among Anglicans and Puritans alike.

Whig historians have condemned Henrietta Maria for her Catholicism, but this is little else than an exercise in historical bias, in which Catholicism is falsely seen as a reactionary counterpart to a

Queen Henrietta Maria and her Dwarf.
Sir Anthony Van Dyck
*Courtesy of the National Gallery of Art,
Washington. Samuel H. Kress Collection.*

supposedly progressive Protestantism. "Strange injustice!", commented Thomas Hobbes in his *Behemoth,* "the Queen was a Catholic by profession, and therefore could not but endeavour to do the Catholics all the good she could: she had not else been truly that which she professed to be." The honesty of Henrietta Maria's religious idealism has been ignored; her failure to make compromises in religion has been condemned because of the failure to admit the legitimacy of the Catholic faith which motivated it.

Wearing her Catholicism like a banner, perhaps persuaded by her monks and elders that she could bring about a renewal of the Catholic faith in England, Henrietta Maria had to confront thousands of turbulent subjects for whom the Protestant Reformation was a fact and the Pope the Antichrist. Her religious beliefs were unhypocritical and honest, but for those very reasons they were impolitic. Because of his willingness to tolerate the Catholicism of his new wife, Charles was falsely accused of professing the same faith, and this further eroded the political position of the monarchy. Not since the time of Mary Tudor had the religious professions of an English queen, no matter how honestly arrived at, placed the monarchy in such jeopardy from internal dissent.

All of this was in the future, however, when the French princess landed at Dover on June 12. For Henrietta Maria the immediate problems of making adjustments to the English and to her new husband proved painful enough. At Dover she was treated to filthy and uncomfortable sleeping accommodations, and the first meeting with Charles was awkward. Sensitive about his short stature, Charles indicated that Henrietta Maria was too close to him in height, and that she ought not in the future wear high shoes. Henrietta Maria replied with the spirit and directness that always characterized her. "Sir," she said in translation from the French, "I stand upon mine own feet. I have no helps by art. Thus I am, and am neither higher nor lower."

For the moment, this strong answer induced Charles only to try to assert control over his new bride. He clumsily attempted to remove Madame de Saint-Georges, his wife's most trusted attendant, from the coach as the couple set out for Canterbury. Once there, Henrietta Maria found housing more terrible than at Dover, and had to deal with a determined husband whose ardor caused him to bolt all her servants out of the chambers. The next morning, the happiness of Charles contrasted markedly with the moroseness of his wife.

The personal difficulties of the couple were heightened by the jealousies of Buckingham, and by the actions of Madame de Saint-Georges and the Capucin monks who accompanied Henrietta Maria virtually wherever she went. Buckingham, anxious to dominate Charles as completely after his marriage as he had before it, pointedly warned Henrietta Maria "that there had been queens of England who had lost their heads." Once, with her attendants, Henrietta Maria interrupted a Church of England service with laughter and giggling, perhaps accidently, perhaps not. Madame de Saint-Georges further offended the English by indulging in the eccentricity of swimming in the Thames and by throwing her English breakfast out the window and into the Strand, thus causing the formation of a howling, anti-Catholic mob to gather on the streets below.

Some English proferred clumsy efforts to help, others only disapproval. Sir George Goring, in violation of the marriage treaty, sent Henrietta Maria translations of Protestant prayer books. Others, more grimly moralistic, voiced their disapproval of Henrietta Maria's female attendants. "The queen hath brought, they say," John Chamberlain sneered, "such a poor, pitiful sort of women, that there is not one worth the looking after, saving herself and the Duchess of Chevreuse, who, though she be fair, yet paints foully." Discontent began to surface about this strange queen, French and foreign, surrounded by even stranger hangers-on, who failed to attend her husband's coronation, opened her chapels to Catholic malcontents, threw things in rages at windows, refused to learn English, and possibly prayed with her priests at the sites of Catholic martyrdom.

Charles himself was less than happy with his new wife, and confided his discontent to the gleeful Buckingham. "Many little neglects I will not take the pains to set down"; in this high-minded way Charles began a letter to Buckingham. Then, dispensing with these self-imposed restrictions, he spent the the rest of the missive complaining bitterly of a wife who "eschewing to be in my company," communicated to him only through her servants and who neglected her duties to her husband and even to the nation.

Finally Charles stopped complaining, and took action. In violation of the marriage treaty, and braving the rages of Henrietta Maria, he packed off a portion of his wife's Catholic retinue, and replaced them with English servants. At the same time, events also conspired to rid Henrietta Maria of her rival, Buckingham. In 1626 the Commons, under the leadership of Sir John Eliot, went on the attack. Speaking in Parliament, Sir Dudley Digges compared Buckingham to a comet, "exhaled out of base and putrid matter." Charles was forced to dissolve Parliament before it could vote him supplies, including the vital customs duties called tunnage and poundage. Buckingham, as if playing into the hands of his enemies, took steps that further compromised his reputation. Though England was still at war with Spain, Buckingham, disappointed in his dealings for a binding military alliance with the French, went to war with France as well. Then, with the financial pressures on the monarchy growing because of his policies, the unpopular Buckingham was murdered by an assassin.

The loss of Buckingham did little to relieve the crises of the monarchy, but it markedly improved the marriage of Charles and Henrietta Maria, and the latter flowed into the vacuum left by Buckingham to become a political force in her own right. "The Queen of England was one of the people who gained most by Buckingham's death." So wrote a French observer with unsympathetic directness.

The Queen who assumed such responsibilities was no more physically prepossessing than her husband. On her arrival in England an acute observer had described Henrietta Maria as "nimble and quick, black-eyes, brown-haired, though perhaps a little touched with the green sickness." Though the beautiful eyes always remained, and a strong will overcame the anemia and questionable health of her petite body, Henrietta Maria quickly lost what looks she had to frequent pregnancy and fatigue. Crooked-spined and long-armed, she became an intense, wraith-like woman, the less impressive for the teeth that stuck out of her mouth, according to one source, "like guns from a fortress."

Henrietta Maria, following the nearly sacrificial standards of childbearing typical of the seventeenth century, was delivered of children nine times, always with considerable pain. In 1628 fright or strenuous exercise forced Henrietta Maria into premature labor at Greenwich. When the local midwife fainted in the royal presence, the Chamberlens, the noted family of midwives, were called in, "at which time the queen did suffer great pain, because the child was turned overthwart in her belly." The infant, called Charles, died within hours of delivery. A year later, in May 1629, one of the Queen's priests reported that "a bad lying-in had placed her Majesty in evident danger of death." The result was a stillborn male child. Through such ordeals, Henrietta Maria exhibited a singular toughness. "As to my loss," she remarked after the second tragedy, "I wish to forget it." She went on to conceive and bear seven more children, all of them successfully.

Possibly because he saw in Henrietta Maria's physical shortcomings reflections of his own, possibly because he was more sensitive than many men of his time to his wife's sacrifices in childbed, possibly because he saw in Henrietta Maria's character elements lacking in his own, Charles came to adore his headstrong wife, and she him. When Charles contracted a mild case of smallpox, Henrietta Maria stayed with him, nursed him, shared his bed. "I was the happiest and most fortunate of queens . . . ;" Henrietta Maria once said simply, "I had a husband who adored me." In the midst of the Civil War, learning that his wife was once again in labor, Charles urged his physician with a cryptic and concerned message: "Mayerne, for the love of me, go to my wife." Left to their own devices, Charles and his queen made a marriage strong by any standard, and extraordinary by those of the seventeenth century. Girding themselves against the outside world, living a life pleasant and isolated from political realities, the royal couple sustained themselves but grew apart from their subjects.

Though the bonds of their marriage strengthened, Charles and Henrietta Maria seemed less and less capable of dealing with a realm on the verge of dissolution. Charles began to collect his taxes without the consent of his tumultuous Parliament, and he angered the gentry further by collecting forced loans and by using the hated prerogative courts of High Commission and Star Chamber to intimidate and imprison his opponents. Refusals to pay the forced loans, and consequent jailings by the king, led to the Five Knight's Case in 1627. In their decision, the judges reaffirmed the royal prerogative, declaring that the king had the right to commit men to prison without cause shown.

Though the prerogative was upheld, the result was disastrous for the monarchy. The Five Knight's Case infuriated many members of Parliament, and when they met again in 1628-1629, they drafted and issued the Petition of Right. This petition, which is considered a landmark in the development of the English constitution, declared against key elements of the royal prerogative. The petitioners asserted that it was illegal for the king or anyone else to imprison without cause, to tax without the consent of Parliament, to declare martial law, or to allow the billeting of soldiers in English households. Soon after the drafting of the Petition of Right Charles sent Parliament home once again, beginning a period of personal rule lasting eleven years.

In this period, Charles turned to two men for support. The first of these was William Laud, Archbishop of Canterbury, the second, Thomas Wentworth, later Earl of Strafford. Laud, working through the Court of High Commission, and Strafford, in his capacity as Lord Deputy of Ireland, cooperated in the policy called "thorough," which some, though not all, historians have seen as an attempt to make royal administration more efficient, and perhaps even absolutist. Whatever the intent, the policy of thorough irritated and frightened Puritans and gentry in the House of Commons. Laud's Court of High Commission harried Puritan lecturers without really controlling them, and Laud himself was accused of Arminianism by his enemies. For a Puritan no epithet could have been stronger, for to them an Arminian was the worst type of backslider, one who dared to assert, in contradiction to the Reformation ideas of predestination and justification by faith, that individuals could in some way contribute to their own salvation. At the same time, members of the Commons noted with fear, real or feigned, that Strafford was organizing an army in Ireland, possibly to be used to overawe Parliament.

Desperate for money, Charles began to use, and extend, an old tax known as Ship Money. Ship Money grew out of that part of the royal prerogative which made the sovereign responsible for defending the realm in time of war. Traditionally, in times of crisis, the English monarchy had levied Ship Money on the seaport towns and cities, but in 1635 Charles extended the tax to inland towns. His parliamentary opponents, led by John Hampden and Lord Saye and Sele, countered with a test case in the courts. As they had earlier in the Five Knight's Case, the judges found for the king, declaring that Ship Money was a legitimate part of the prerogative royal. Charles had once again been vindicated at law, but the price was increased political isolation. The gentry sulked and grumbled in their country houses, and English gentlemen continued to appear before Star Chamber and High Commission for refusing to pay their assessments, or for thumbing their noses at the Laudian Church.

Henrietta Maria, in her direct, strong-willed way, compounded her husband's difficulties. Her Catholicism, which Charles had vainly tried to moderate for political reasons, became more overt. Puritan publicists responded in kind. In 1633, William Prynne attacked the Queen's love for the drama in his *Histriomastix*. Writing under the heading "Women actors notorious whores," revealing many of the contemporary biases against women, Prynne inveighed against women who were "whorishly impudent" enough "as to act, to speak publicly on a stage . . . in the presence of sundry men and women." "Lord, open her eyes," said a Puritan lecturer in reference to Henrietta Maria, "that she may see her Saviour, whom she hath pierced with her superstition and idolatry." At the Stuart court such demands were ignored, ridiculed, or attacked. The recusancy laws against Catholics were not enforced; the curious and the faithful prayed in Henrietta Maria's chapels; a papal emissary, George Con, was received at a court where Catholicism became increasingly fashionable. Pointed jokes were made about a king who appeared to be governed by his wife: "for according to the example of our gratious sovereign," Sir Ralph Verney jested to friends, "I must obey my wife, and she commands my presence on the 26th." In 1637 William Prynne and his compatriots, the clergyman Henry Burton and Dr. John Bastwick, were multilated, fined, and cast into prison for their noisome opinions. The division between court and country, between Anglican and Puritan, maneuvered England in the direction of disaster.

Yet, in the end, it was the nagging problem of governmental finance, combined with ill-conceived policy, that brought the country to the Great Rebellion. Charles, like most monarchs of his time, believed that control of the Church throughout his dominions was an essential part of his power and prerogative. In 1646 Charles observed that "people are governed by the pulpit more than the sword in time of peace." Convinced of the need to control the religious life of all of his subjects, knowing that control of the pulpits gave him the power to propagandize his people, Charles had already caused Laud to try to impose Anglican uniformity in England. Now, in 1637, with the blind adherence to principle and uniformity that often characterized him, Charles ordered that a modified version of the Anglican Prayer Book be imposed upon his fractious, and Calvinist, Scots subjects. "I have no more power in Scotland than a Duke of Venice," Charles complained, "which I will rather die than suffer."

The Scots responded to this ungodly intrusion with rebellion. At the great Kirk in Edinburgh, furniture was thrown at the divine who dared to read the Anglican service. By the end of 1638, drawing on a native tradition of political violence and the Calvinist doctrine of the right of resistance to unholy authority, the Scots Presbyterians had signed a National Covenant and raised an army. With the new year the Scots, already in contact with Charles' opposition in England, poured over the River Tweed, and Charles had neither the money nor the troops to stop them. Charles was obliged to call Parliament to provide funds for English resistance, but its members used the occasion to castigate the king, and this "Short Parliament" was dissolved after only three weeks. The Church granted Charles £20,000, but the wary London merchants refused to agree to a loan. Backed to the wall, Charles had to make peace with the Scots at Ripon in October 1640, but the terms only compounded his problems. The treaty required Charles to maintain the Scots army at a cost of £850 per day. Once again, in November, Charles had to call back the members of Parliament for whom he had such loathing and contempt. Even Laud was worried. "It is not the Scottish business alone that I look upon," he fretted, "but the whole frame of things at home and abroad, with vast expenses out of little treasure, and my misgiving soul is deeply apprehensive of no small evils coming on. . . . I can see no cure without a miracle."

This new meeting of Parliament, known as the Long Parliament because it met intermittently for the next twenty years, proved even more hostile to the king than its predecessors, and its members moved quickly to the attack. Laud, hated by the Puritans for his persecutions and Arminianism, suffered impeachment. The Commons then turned on Strafford, feared for his efficiency and administrative abilities. As late as April 1641 Charles promised Strafford "upon the word of a king" that he would "not suffer in life, honour, or fortune," but Parliament was implacable, and framed a bill of attainder calling for Strafford's death. Then Strafford, in an act of singular loyalty and courage, urged Charles to allow the bill to pass and the execution to take place "for the prevention of evils which may happen by your refusal. . . ." Charles, heartsick, irresolute, fearing for the safety of Henrietta Maria and their children, reluctantly agreed. After trying, and failing, to persuade Parliament to commute the death sentence to close imprisonment, Charles had to acquiesce to Strafford's beheading in May. "I sinned against my conscience," Charles later wrote to his wife. "It was a base sinful concession."

"Take not this as a threatening," Charles had told the Parliament of 1628, "for I scorn to threaten any but my equals." Thirteen years later, Parliament strove to become his superior. With Strafford gone, and the royal finances in shambles, a flood of legislation testified to the triumph of Parliament over prerogative. By a Triennial Act, regular meetings of Parliament were assured; another act prevented the Long Parliament from being dissolved; several measures forbade the collecting of any tax, including Ship Money, without parliamentary consent. The prerogative courts of High Commission, Star Chamber, and the Council of the North were abolished. In September 1641, Commons passed the "Root and Branch" bill, which was to abolish episcopacy, or rule by bishops, over the Church of England. It was a calculated insult, aimed at the royal control over the English church that Charles valued so highly. The Commons, under the brilliant leadership of John Pym and others, rode roughshod over the feelings of their proud sovereign, while Henrietta Maria and her ladies-in-waiting hid in the royal apartments, confessing their sins and shaking with fear, expecting to hear the London mob on the streets below.

In November 1640 a rebellion in Ireland once again created the need for an army, and with it a controversy over who was to control it. Suspecting that Charles was behind the Irish rebellion, and unwilling to place armed men under the king's command, Parliament temporized and accused. Its leaders issued the Grand Remonstrance, a generalized propaganda barrage against all of Charles' policies. At last, Charles reacted. Abandoning his irresolution temporarily and too late, Charles organized a group of armed men in January 1642 to arrest the five members of Parliament who had led the opposition. Henrietta Maria was one who urged him to action, lashing him with strong words: "Go, you poltroon!", she is reputed to have said. "Go and pull those rogues out by the ears, or never see my face again." But, in the end, nothing was accomplished. The five members, amply forewarned, had fled, and Charles was left to pad about the empty Commons chamber, posturing to hide his embarrassment.

Humiliated, Charles acknowledged that he had lost control of this capitol by leaving the city. While Parliament and London lionized the returning five members, Charles was left to wander about the countryside and to assent to more legislative limitation on his prerogative. Bishops were excluded from the House of Lords, as Parliament once again lashed out at the Laudian church. Early in February Parliament passed the Militia Bill, which would have required Charles to subject all military and naval appointments to parliamentary inspection. Forced to the limit, Charles refused to surrender this last shred of prerogative, and his reply, for once, was firm: "By God, not for an hour! What you have asked me in this, was never asked of a king. . . ."

But, having gained so much, Parliament was loathe to give up its tactic of pressure. In June 1642 it sent Charles the Nineteen

Propositions, in which it was demanded that the king surrender or share with Parliament his prerogative rights to appoint ministers of state, control the army, order religion, arrange the marriages of royal children, and conduct foreign affairs. Seeing that the Nineteen Propositions would make him nothing "but the outside, but the picture, but the sign of a king," Charles resolved to fight and set up his standard outside the city of Nottingham. Charles' banner was erected, Clarendon remembered, "about six of the clock in the evening of a very stormy and tempestuous day. . . . with little other ceremony than the sound of drums and trumpets. . . ." "God save King Charles and hang up the Roundheads." With this gibe at the short haircuts of their foes in Parliament and pulpit, the Cavaliers, the followers of Charles I, began the English Civil War. Some time later in the night, the ceremonies over, "a very strong and unruly wind," in apparent ill-omen, cast the royal standard to the earth.

Henrietta Maria was not at Nottingham to witness this melancholy ceremony. Months before, on pretext of poor health, with coffers full of plate and jewels, she had fled abroad to pawn and sell the wealth of the Stuarts in support of her husband. When Parliament made threats and protested the journey, the Queen thanked its members sardonically for their concern for her health, and proceeded with her business. The Dutch dealers she approached drove a hard bargain. "You may judge how, when they know we want money," she wrote home, "they keep their foot on our throat." With the £3000 in proceeds, far less than she had hoped, Henrietta Maria fell to buying firelocks, carbines, pistols, powder, cannon. Ranging over Europe, the "she-generalissima" sought loans and support from the Danes, the French, and the Prince of Orange. All the while, she wrote letters to her husband urging him to be strong, pressing him to allow her to return to England: "Tell me now by what road I may come to join you."

In 1643, Henrietta Maria finally obtained her wish. After an initial attempt in which two ships were lost, Henrietta Maria returned to England by means of an arduous nine-day crossing. Soon after landing, while she lay in a house by the sea, shot from a parliamentary cannon entered her chamber, and the Queen had to flee to the fields. But she was still high-spirited when she rejoined Charles at Oxford, and brought with her two thousand foot, and a thousand of horse, as well as cannon, mortars, and more than a hundred wagons. Cajoling and haranguing, keeping a court at Oxford that some said was too expensive, Henrietta Maria became immersed once again in politics and strategy. By the spring of 1644 Henrietta Maria was pregnant with her ninth child and was suffering simultaneously from rheumatic fever. Nonetheless, as more money was needed, the Queen prepared to go abroad once again. After another agonizing birth in June 1644, Henrietta Maria left her infant daughter and took ship for France from the blockaded harbor of Falmouth. Dogged by ill-health—swollen stomach, abscessed breasts that required lancing, possibly measles—Henrietta Maria plunged into a new round of seeking alliances, money, and supplies.

In England, things began to go badly, then tragically, for the Royalists. In September of 1643, Parliament signed the Solemn League and Covenant, allying themselves with the Scots, and with the new year Scots troops once again marched southward. In July the fruits of the alliance were seen at Marston Moor, where the combined armies of the Scots and the English defeated the Royalists and won control of the English north. Thereafter, under the guidance of Oliver Cromwell and others, the parliamentary armies were reorganized, and at the Battle of Naseby, in June 1645, the Royalists were routed. A year later, Charles surrendered himself to the Scots, and the Cavalier stronghold of Oxford fell.

Separated from his wife and family, Charles was given over by the Scots to the keeping of Parliament, but in 1647 the army, growing more assertive and radical through religious agitation and lack of pay, seized him. Charles, once so proud of his prerogative and his regality, had become a pawn in an emerging struggle for power between the English Parliament and the restive army that it had called into being but could not control. Seeking to regain his authority by dividing his opposition, Charles attempted to negotiate terms with the Scots, with Parliament, and with the army generals. From abroad, Henrietta Maria urged him not to give away too much, and not to feel bound by agreements made with traitors. By the summer of 1648, Charles had managed to escape to the Isle of Wight, and to arrange for a Scots invasion of England on his behalf, but Cromwell was able to defeat the force at Preston. Charles, by now mistrusted by the army, blamed for the renewal of war, tried to resume negotiations with Parliament, by now anxious to curb the power of the generals. Discovering this, the army leaders determined that Parliament had to be muzzled, and that Charles had to die. Colonel Pride was quickly dispatched to London, and in 1648, in an action thereafter known as Pride's Purge, excluded from Parliament all those suspected of disloyalty to the army. The acquiescent members of Parliament who remained were derisively designated as "the Rump." All that was left to threaten the power of the generals was the monarch they had come to despise.

Knowing that his opponents meant to kill him, and that vacillation and compromise would avail him nothing, Charles carried out his vow to die as a gentleman. At his trial Charles refused to plead, laughed at the charges, feigned disinterest in the proceedings, and when given leave to speak, he said this: "It is not my case alone

... it is the freedom and liberty of the people of England; and do you pretend what you will, I stand more for their liberties. For if power without law may make laws, may alter the fundamental laws of the kingdom, I do not know what subject he is in England that can be sure of his life, or anything that he calls his own." Thus declaring himself a defender of the law that the army had usurped, and a martyr for his people, Charles listened with contempt as the judges he refused to recognize found him guilty of treason.

The Trial of King Charles I.
Courtesy of the Prints Division, New York Public Library. Astor, Lenox, and Tilden Foundations.

On January 30, 1649, after having donned two shirts so that witnesses would not confuse shivering with fear, Charles stepped from a window in Whitehall Palace onto a specially-built scaffold. He urged the executioner, very calmly, not to put him in too much pain. "I go from a corruptible to an incorruptible crown," he said with certainty, "where not disturbance can be, no disturbance at all." Soon after, the axe plunged downward. "I remember well," said one witness, "there was such a great grone by the Thousands then present as I never heard before and desire I may never hear again." Some surged forward to dip handkerchiefs in Charles' blood, and the corpse was quickly taken away. Later, when the body was taken out of St. George's Hall for burial, the clear skies darkened, snow came, "and fell so fast, as by the time they came to the west end of the royal chapel, the black velvet pall was all white, being thick covered with snow."

Henrietta Maria, far away in France, did not hear of Charles' death until a week later. When the news was brought to her in the Louvre, she fell into a kind of stupor, then wept, and took to her bed. Though the death did not crush her, the last years of her life were clouded with unhappiness. "A principal part of your honour will consist in deferring all respect, love and protection to your mother, my wife." With these words, Charles I before his death had admonished his son and namesake. Political considerations, however, flew in the face of Charles' last wishes. The young Charles II, in exile and short of money, turned to the Earl of Clarendon rather than his mother for advice, and his brother James offended Henrietta Maria nearly as much by his boorishness and whoring. A beloved daughter, Elizabeth, died at fourteen in 1650. A son, Henry, succumbed to smallpox. A combination of penury and religiosity encouraged Henrietta Maria to retreat with regularity into convents, and she struggled enthusiastically but unsuccessfully to bring her two eldest sons to a public profession of Catholicism. Still, Henrietta Maria had some successes. She managed to wed her daughter Henrietta Anne to the brother of Louis XIV, and she saw her eldest son restored to the throne of England in 1660. Relations with Charles II remained strained nonetheless. Thus it was in Paris that Henrietta Maria died in 1669, the victim of an overdose of opiates prescribed by an inept physician.

The execution of Charles I confirmed the fact of the Great Rebellion, but it also prepared the way for the restoration of the monarchy if the rule of the generals failed. By demanding the life of the king, the army created a stage on which Charles I, by showing resolution, courage, and principle, might expiate and atone for the indecisiveness and errors of his past. The sovereign who seemed so incapable of greatness in life attained martyrdom in death; the impolitic man who wanted so to live for principle and prerogative was given the chance to die for both. In one stroke, Charles I restored the monarchy to respectability, even majesty. At the same time, the revolutionaries who took his place inherited only problems of state and their attendant woes. Henrietta Maria, with her appreciation of masque and theater, would have appreciated the way her beloved husband, who had so often disappointed her through irresolution, had staged the last drama of his life. The English had made a rebellion, and by means abhorrent to many in the seventeenth century, had toppled and executed their king. They now faced the far more difficult task of finding the individuals and institutions to replace him.

E. Oliver Cromwell and the Rule of the Generals

The individual who did the most to protect the accomplishments of the Great Rebellion, and to move the tender consciences of the revolutionary godly in the direction of pragmatic government, had been born into the ranks of the Huntingdonshire gentry fifty years before the execution of Charles I. His name was Oliver Cromwell, the fifth but sole-surviving son of the squire Richard Cromwell and his once-widowed wife Elizabeth. The precious baby boy eventually grew into that nearly indefinable phenomenon so embarrassing to historians of the twentieth century—the "great man." Modern historians do not quite know what to do with Oliver Cromwell, the leader described by the poet John Milton as "our chief of men," and by another scholar as a "puzzled Atlas," an individual who possessed, in the words of a rival, "a great spirit, an admirable circumspection and sagacity, and a most magnaminious resolution." "What brave things he did," wrote even the critical Pepys, "and made all the neighbour princes fear him."

The twentieth, moreover, is not the only century uncomfortable with Cromwell. If Wilbur Cortez Abbot saw Cromwell as the prototype of a twentieth-century totalitarian dictator, nineteenth-century Whig historians, self-appointed apostles of orderly progress and representative government, were sometimes troubled by the bluff soldier in Cromwell that was contemptuous of Parliaments, the man who sent the major-generals to rule the English counties with an iron hand. To some of his seventeenth-century contemporaries, and to some of their rationalist successors writing during the Enlightenment a century after, Cromwell was indeed a "man of blood," the irrational Calvinist revolutionary who had carried out his dark threat to chop off the head of Charles I "with the crown on it," and who had then hypocritically indulged in the same high-handed policies for which his royal predecessor went to the block. Royalists in all ages, and in all places, have loathed Cromwell's memory, and for obvious reasons. Marxist historians, and others devoted to an economic interpretation of the English Civil War, have attributed much of Cromwell's behavior to his membership in the gentry class, and to its rising or declining status.

Cromwell, finally, is even a puzzlement and frustration to those very few historians still loyal to the "great man" theory of history. Indeed, Cromwell's career is a reproach to all those who believe that greatness is necessarily a constant or consistent quality. He did not even enter the mainstream of public life until his fourth decade, and he was the unchallenged ruler of England for only five years. During his short career Cromwell accomplished much, but certain of his actions, particularly during his brutal Irish campaign, tarnish the image of greatness. Cromwell helped kill a king, only to become one in everything but name. He was an advocate of Parliament who nonetheless broke Parliaments and ruled with the backing of an army; a witness for religious toleration who massacred Catholics and mistrusted Protestant sectaries; a disciple of the ideal of Protestant unity who went to war with Dutch Protestants; a believer in people's innate abilities who tried to create a new aristocracy; a man of action who seemed to wait on events and paper over differences; a crude, harsh-voiced soldier who could summon up, when they were needed, masses of majesty and plain eloquence; a man of God who, despite Clarendon's assurances, was in truth a man of blood as well. Perhaps, as Christopher Hill has suggested, Cromwell mirrors the contradictions, the suddenness, the fits and starts of the English Revolution itself. Cromwell was metamorphised out of his unnoticed, unremarkable gentry ruralism by the English Civil War, in the middle of his life, to participate in the remarkable events of his time. As the Venetian ambassador observed in 1656, all of Cromwell's abilities would "have served him for nothing if circumstances had not opened the way to greatness."

"I was by birth a gentleman," Cromwell related years later, "living neither in any considerable height, nor yet in obscurity." Oliver Cromwell owed his surname to Thomas Cromwell, the minister of King Henry VIII and architect of the dissolution of the monasteries, whose sister Katherine had married one Morgan Williams, a brewer of Putney, in 1494. Katherine's eldest son Richard was evidently a man on the make, for he adopted the surname of his powerful uncle, serving both under him and Henry VIII, obtaining in spoil and reward the Benedictine priory of Hinchinbrook and the site of Ramsey Abbey, also a Benedictine establishment. Alienated monastic lands became the basis for wealth and power. Thus the Cromwell family had a vested interest in the English Reformation and Protestantism.

After the first Richard Cromwell died in 1546, leaving both lands and honor, his son Henry piloted the family firmly into the ranks of the gentry. A manor-house was quickly under construction at Hinchinbrook, and Henry Cromwell was knighted by Queen Elizabeth I. Known as the "golden knight" because of his prestige and wealth, Henry Cromwell served his class and crown several times as sheriff of Huntingdonshire.

Fortune was not to smile so brightly on Henry Cromwell's second son Robert. As a younger son, Robert could hope for relatively little in terms of inheritance. The manor house at Hinchinbrook went to his elder brother Oliver, and it was thus necessary for Robert Cromwell to seek a wife with a fortune. He was successful in marrying an eligible widow, Elizabeth Lynn, whose family connection to the Dean of Ely Cathedral created sufficient wealth to bring a marriage jointure of £60 per year, not a small sum in the seventeenth century. The fragile human biology so typical of the times, however, used the couple harshly. No fewer than four of Robert Cromwell's sons died in infancy, and he was carried away himself before his surviving son Oliver was eighteen.

Still, Robert Cromwell had managed to do some good things for his son. After a smattering of education under a local Puritan schoolmaster, Oliver Cromwell was sent to Sidney Sussex College, Cambridge, thought by Archbishop Laud to be a hotbed of Puritan sectarianism. Though his education was temporarily interrupted by his father's death and a return to Huntingdon to manage the estate, it is possible that the young Cromwell also went to Lincoln's Inn in London to learn the Common Law thought beneficial to the English country gentleman. By the standards of his time, Oliver Cromwell could be considered well and properly educated.

As two-thirds of his father's estate was settled on his mother, Cromwell may have had little money as a young man. This has caused at least one historian to dismiss him as a "country-house radical," a gentryman made more obstreperous in his Puritanism and political ideas by financial reverses. There is, perhaps, some merit in this view. Oliver Cromwell's uncle, the heir to the Cromwell fortune, was obliged to sell off Hinchinbrook manor and retire to Ramsey. There was talk in the Cromwell family of immigration to the New World, and some accounts refer to Oliver Cromwell as "lord of the fens" for his defense of the people of that low-lying area from the rapacities of speculators and developers determined to drain it. It is also possible that by emphasizing these details, some scholars have exaggerated their importance. In 1621, Oliver Cromwell married Elizabeth Bourchier, the well-dowered daughter of a London merchant. He was also the designated heir to his maternal uncle, a substantial man, and inherited property at Huntingdon from another uncle. That Oliver Cromwell was considered stable and responsible, irrespective of the fortunes of some of the rest of his family, was demonstrated by his election to Parliament from Huntingdonshire in February 1628.

This was the very same Parliament that tied its vote of supplies to redress of grievances, issued the Petition of Right, and vented its spleen against the Arminianism of Laud. Disgust at royal policy, and disgust with the corruption of the Court of Wards, where he had labored, caused Cromwell's contemporary John Winthrop to sell off earthly goods and lead a migration to Massachusetts Bay. Though Cromwell was at least tempted to the same, in the end he chose a different course. Stirred by the political and religious issues debated at Westminster, Cromwell could only have been affronted when Charles I dissolved Parliament in 1629 and began his personal government.

Frustrated politically, Cromwell used the eleven-year period of personal government to mature. He saw to his land and estates, and he involved himself with local political issues. He resisted royal efforts to tamper with the borough government of Huntingdon, helped to maintain a Puritan lectureship, was prosecuted for refusing to go through the ceremony of knighthood, paid, but undoubtedly grumbled over, Ship Money. He became fascinated with the conduct of the Thirty Years' War in Germany, which he saw as a divinely-ordained struggle between Catholic and Protestant. Significantly, also during this period, he underwent the conversion experience, that intense yet undefinable awareness of God's presence, which made him a Puritan in being as well as in background.

It was thus a revivified and stronger man who returned to Westminster on the heels of the Scottish invasion as a member of the Long Parliament. Because he still sat on the back benches, Cromwell's emerging talents were recognized only by a few. One of these was John Hampden, Cromwell's brother-in-law and one of the instigators of the Ship Money Case. "That slovenly fellow which you see before us," he told a colleague in reference to Cromwell, "who hath no ornament in his speech; I say that sloven, if we should ever come to have a breach with the king . . . will be one of the greatest men of England." Sir Philip Warwick, a Royalist member of Parliament, remembered his first sight of Cromwell at about the same time. He was dressed in a suit seemingly "made by an ill country tailor," wearing linen "plain, and not very clean," a man of good size, "his countenance swollen and reddish, his voice sharp and untunable, and his eloquence full of fervour. . . ." Some years later, as a prisoner of the army of Parliament, Warwick saw Cromwell again, this time near the height of his power, a man who could now afford much better clothes, appearing "of great and majestic deportment and comely presence," a man clearly "extraordinarily designed for these extraordinary things. . . ."

It was a transformation indeed wrought by an exceptional character, and one reacting to exceptional times. As events moved toward the Civil War, Cromwell began to show his gifts as a leader of men and military organizer. By July of 1642, he was mustering militia in Cambridge; a month later, at about the same time Charles set up his standard at Nottingham, Cromwell prevented the plate of Cambridge University from being given over to Charles; in October he joined the army of Parliament under the Earl of Essex and, as a captain, he fought in a defeat of the forces of Parliament at Edgehill.

X—Key Battles

The Great Rebellion in England, 1642-1649

By February 1643 Roundheads and Royalists had exchanged strings of victories, and Cromwell had risen to the rank of colonel. In November 1642, at Turnham Green, Essex and the trained bands faced down the Royalists, and Charles was turned from his objective of London. In December, at the Battle of Tadcaster, Sir William Waller led the forces of Parliament to victory, and later in the month Winchester fell to the Parliament-men.

The Royalists countered bravely and successfully. In February 1643 Prince Rupert stormed Cirencester and Henrietta Maria landed at Bridlington. Royalist victories followed in March at Seacroft Moor and in April at Ripple Field. In June came further Royalist successes at Chalgrove Field and Adwalton Moor. At the first of these engagements John Hampden was slain; at the second, the parliamentary army of Sir Thomas Fairfax was routed. In July, the forces of the king fell upon Sir William Waller's forces at Landsdown and Roundway Down, defeating and destroying them, and the key port city of Bristol fell to the besieging Royalists under Prince Rupert.

By this time, like other parliamentary commanders, Cromwell had been well-blooded, but unlike most of the others, he had not suffered a personal defeat in battle. In May of 1643, at Grantham, Cromwell had met and defeated the Royalists under Cavendish. Serving in the eastern counties that he knew so well, Cromwell became known as a superb leader of men. In the troops he chose, Cromwell valued competance and godliness, and saw a relationship between the two. "If you choose godly, honest men to be captains of horse," he wrote with eloquent confidence, "honest men will follow them; and they will be careful to mount such. . . . I had rather have a plain russet-coated captain that knows what he fights for, and loves what he knows, than that which you call a gentleman and is nothing else." "I raised such men as had the fear of God before them," he noted on another occasion, "and made some conscience of what they did; and from that day forward . . . they were never beaten."

Partly for military reasons, partly because he saw the risks involved in offending the civilian population in time of war, Cromwell disciplined his men stringently, and denied them the privilege of looting. In this regard, Cromwell's cavalry formed a marked contrast to the cavalry of the royalist commander Prince Rupert, known to the populace as "Prince Robber, Duke of Plunderland." Cromwell also knew and valued his soldiers, and, despite the discipline, they followed him in battle because they knew and respected him. Cromwell's respect for his men, and his religious faith, animate the simple words written to the father of a trooper, newly dead in battle:

> Sir, God hath taken away your eldest son by a cannon-shot. It brake his leg. We were necessitated to cut it off, whereof

he died. . . . There is your precious child full of glory, to know sin nor sorrow any more. He was a gallant young man, exceeding gracious. . . . He is a glorious Saint in Heaven, wherein you ought exceedingly to rejoice. Let this drink up your sorrow; seeing these are not feigned words to comfort you, but the thing is so real and so undoubted a truth.

While Cromwell was probably not a military tactician on the grand scale, he did grasp the key to victory in cavalry engagements. While the horse of Prince Rupert tended to pursue and scatter after a charge, Cromwell's men were disciplined to regroup to mount another assault. With the help of such tactics, Cromwell defeated and killed the royalist commander Cavendish at Gainsborough in July 1643, this at a time when other parliamentary commanders suffered defeats. In October, at Winceby, Cromwell joined Manchester and Fairfax in another victory over the Royalists. There, as he led his Psalm-singing troopers in a charge, Cromwell's horse was shot from under him, but he was able to seize another mount, and he pressed on. "Truly," wrote an observer, "this first charge was so home given and performed with such admirable courage and resolution . . . that the Enemy stood not another."

The prestige that Cromwell gained on the field made him more persuasive in the Commons, where he pressed for the creation of a new army, a superior force which would move Parliament from a defensive position to the attack. At Cromwell's urging, the Earl of Manchester was appointed commander of the new force, and Cromwell became his Lieutenant-General. Manchester, described by Robert Baillie as "a sweet, meek man" gave Cromwell great freedom, and men flocked to put themselves under his command. As with many who are able and ambitious, Cromwell was not slow to criticize his fellow-commanders in the Commons.

Cromwell used his political and military positions adroitly to gain ever greater power. Five months after the Solemn League and Covenant was signed between Parliament and the Scots in September 1643, a Scots army moved southward to assist Parliament against the King. With the balance of the war now swinging toward Parliament, Cromwell was quick to gain membership on the Committee of Both Kingdoms, the body designed to coordinate Scots and English operations. In early May 1644, Lincoln fell to Manchester, and in July came the great parliamentary victory at Marston Moor. Here Cromwell fought gallantly again, taking a pistol shot near enough to his eyes to be temporarily blinded. Later on in the same month York fell, and the English north belonged to Parliament.

But the Royalists rallied, creating the need for a further military reorganization. In August of 1644 the Earl of Essex was defeated by Charles I at Beacon Hill. This was followed ten days later by another defeat at Castle Dore, after which Essex fled by sea, leaving his army to surrender. In September the Scots Covenanters, the allies of Parliament, lost at Tippermuir and Aberdeen, and, in October at the Second Battle of Newbury, Charles I held off a superior parliamentary force led by Manchester and Waller.

Fearing that the drawn-out struggle would make the English Revolution unpopular, and taking advantage of a fortuitous opportunity, Cromwell used his seat in Parliament to attack the military policies of Manchester, the man who had raised him to Lieutenant-General. This opposition cost Cromwell in reputation, and Manchester countered Cromwell's attacks from the House of Lords, but in the end Cromwell's political gamble succeeded. "Without a more speedy, vigorous, and effectual prosecution of the war," Cromwell warned his colleagues in commons, "we shall make the kingdom weary of us, and make it hate the name of a Parliament. . . . If the army be not put into another method and the war more vigorously prosecuted, the people can bear the war no longer, and will enforce you to a dishonourable peace." In December 1644 Cromwell proposed a "Self-Denying Ordinance," a measure that passed the House of Lords in April 1645 and that prohibited members of Parliament from serving in the army. At a stroke the three men that Cromwell had vilified as incompetents—Manchester, Essex, and Waller—were forced to resign their commissions. Out of the remains of their armies a "New Model Army" of the godly, under the command of Sir Thomas Fairfax, was formed.

With the passage of the Self-Denying Ordinance, a momentous step had been taken. The army, itself a creation of Parliament, had been made independent of the institution that had given it birth. Increasingly beyond Parliament's control, irregularly paid, the army began to emerge as yet another political force in an arena that already contained Charles I, Parliament itself, and the Scots.

At first it seemed that Cromwell had suffered the same fate as his opponents. The Self-Denying Ordinance excluded him from command as well, but, as events proved, he lost his commission for only a few months. Fairfax turned out to be most obliging; he left a senior command open, and Cromwell, in the summer in 1645, in apparent disobedience to the Self-Denying Ordinance, was named second-in-command to Fairfax. Cromwell had succeeded in another calculated risk and was soon given the opportunity to enhance his military reputation yet again. At Naseby, in June 1645, Fairfax and Cromwell inflicted a severe defeat on the forces of Charles I. Later, in July, Leicester fell, and at Langport Charles' last field army was surrendered by Goring. In January 1646 a grateful Commons voted Cromwell £2500 per year in confiscated royalist lands, and extended his commission. When, in June of 1646, the King's stronghold at Oxford fell, Cromwell was there to savor the triumph.

With the war concluded, the moderates in Parliament began to fear the power of the army they had called into being. Badly paid, led by commanders who had grown used to power and to decisive action, its ranks filled with unquiet spirits and contentious religious sectaries, its men continually stirred by the preaching of radical chaplains, the army seemed capable of forcing a much more severe rebellion than the Parliament desired. While members of Parliament talked of a constitutional monarchy, with the King's powers limited and the gentry firmly in control, some army men listened to calls for a genuine revolution, involving social as well as political changes.

Fearing its fractious army, Parliament moved to disband it quickly, and at low cost. Cromwell, warning that such actions would only embitter and antagonize the soldiers, tried to mediate a solution acceptable to both sides, but, when Parliament temporized, he sided with the army. There followed a period of maneuver and mediation, in which the King, the army, the Parliament, and the Scots, tried to arrange accommodations and cabals. Instability reigned, and radical revolution seemed to threaten.

In the Heads of Proposals the army generals and the King discussed the possibility of constitutional monarchy. The King also had discussions with Parliament and the Scots. The army radicals in the ranks, under leaders called Agitators, drafted in response a far more democratic document called the Agreement of the People. At Putney, discussions were held to resolve the differences in political views between the army officers and some of their men. The result was a stand-off, after which Cromwell forcibly terminated the Putney debates. All of the Agitators were ordered back to their regiments, and one was shot. Cromwell, seemingly, had shown himself to be no radical. Nonetheless, radicalism proliferated, as religious and political themes combined. There emerged the Levellers of John Lilburne and the early Quakers of George Foxe; the revolutionary Diggers cultivated land within cities and advocated a kind of agrarian communism; the Fifth Monarchy Men awaited the millenium; sects with strange names like Ranters and Seekers were said to practice free love, and heard women preachers. Radicals like Henry Denne threatened "to turn the world upside down," setting "in the bottom which others make the top of a building, and to set that upon the roof which others lay for a foundation."

While the radicals debated and planned, Charles I, continually scheming to divide his enemies, worsened matters more by escaping from house arrest at Hampton Court, fleeing to the Isle of Wight, and arranging an alliance with the Scots, the so-called Engagement. Thus he caused the renewal of fighting that has been called the Second Civil War. Labeling the King "an obstinate man," feeling betrayed by the sovereign with whom he had negotiated for the army, Cromwell found himself once again at war. He led his troopers northward into Lancashire against Royalists and Scots Covenanters. In August 1648, at Preston, Cromwell routed the Duke of Hamilton's Scots.

As Cromwell moved into Scotland in October, and began a six-week siege of Pontrefact, the struggle between army and Parliament was resolved in London. In November the radical commander Henry Ireton drafted a remonstrance calling for the death of the King who had revived the Civil War. In December Colonel Thomas Pride, who had been a brewer's man before the Revolution, forcibly purged Parliament of the army's enemies, leaving behind an emasculated body of men contemptuously known as the Rump. By the end of the next month, Charles I, once again in custody, had been tried and executed with the support and urging of Cromwell and his colleagues. The army had eliminated and defeated its rivals. King, Parliament, and Scots had been brought to heel.

Cromwell's Scotland and Ireland

The revolution that took place, if indeed this is an appropriate term, was thus a revolution with limits, and the limits were set by an army determined to maintain order. While the House of Lords and the monarchy were abolished, and a republic, the Commonwealth, was born, the democratic reforms that some Levellers had hoped for were not forthcoming. Leveller leaders were cast into prison, and a rebellion of radical army men at Burford was crushed.

Under Cromwell the army moved to crush what was left of royalist rebelliousness in Ireland and Scotland. Sent to Ireland first, Cromwell laid siege to the towns of Drogheda and Wexford. Both garrisons, after being warned of the mortal consequences of further resistance, chose to fight, and Cromwell stormed both cities and put their defenders to the sword. The English conquest of Ireland was as complete as it was cruel. By the Act of Settlement of 1652, all but a third of the land of Ireland was seized, and much of that turned over to English soldiers and merchants who had supported the Civil War. Most of the Irish population of County Connaught was forcibly resettled, as the English "planted" Ireland with Protestants in an effort to keep it loyal. Thereby, a legacy of bitterness was created which troubles Ireland down to the present day.

Scotland also suffered conquest. At the Battle of Dunbar in September 1650, the invading English under Cromwell crushed a Scots army. A year later, at Worcester, an invading Scots force under the youthful Stuart heir, Charles II, was routed. By Cromwell's efforts, Scotland and Ireland had been united to England more closely than ever before. Aggressive externally as well, the Commonwealth government moved quickly to secure the English colonies, passed two navigation Acts, in 1650 and 1651, to challenge the Dutch shipping monopoly, and, in 1652, began the first of a series of Dutch wars.

Such aggressiveness seemingly mirrored Cromwell's own ambitions. From his position as chairman of the Council of State, the committee of the tamed Rump Parliament charged with administration, Cromwell maintained a political presence as he waged his military campaigns. In 1653, reflecting the army's distaste for scheming Parliaments, Cromwell tired even of the Rump and sent his musketeers to dissolve it, declaring it full of "corrupt and unjust men" who were "scandalous to the profession of the Gospel." The handpicked body that succeeded the Rump, sneeringly called the "Barebones Parliament," pleased no more than its predecessor. It too was dissolved, and in 1653 the army produced a new constitution, the Instrument of Government, under which Cromwell was made "Lord Protector." Though the Instrument provided that Cromwell was to rule in conjunction with a reconstituted Parliament, the new Lord Protector made short work of it. In 1655, Cromwell once again dissolved Parliament when it refused to bow to army rule and persisted in writing a new constitution. On the excuse of a minor Royalist rebellion, Penruddock's Rising, England was divided into ten military districts, each under a major-general.

As Lord Protector, Cromwell followed a foreign policy brilliant and successful. He established friendship with Sweden, then the greatest state in northern Europe, and ended the first Dutch War in 1654 on terms favorable to the English. He dispatched an expedition to attack the Spanish West Indies, and it brought Jamaica under the English flag by 1655. Not since the time of Elizabeth had the hatred of Englishmen for the Spanish been played upon so successfully. Once again Spanish treasure fleets were intercepted, and a revivified navy under Admiral Blake bested a Spanish fleet off Santa Cruz in 1657. Such a policy lead to a series of understandings with Spain's arch-enemy France, much to England's benefit. In 1655 Cromwell's agents arranged an agreement that saw the exiled Stuarts expelled from the French court, and in 1658 English mercenaries joined French troops in the siege of Dunkirk. After the joint victory over the Spanish known as the Battle of the Dunes, Dunkirk itself was placed in English hands.

Though Cromwell once justified the Great Rebellion in terms of the maintenance of parliamentary rights, Cromwell the soldier had broken Parliaments, and Cromwell the Lord Protector did likewise. When yet another Parliament met in 1656, Cromwell was confronted with yet another unruly body. Its members mocked at his policy of religious toleration by ordering the Quaker James Nayler branded, flogged, and bored through the tongue, and, in 1657, they rejected the Militia Bill, framed to continue the militia under the hated major-generals. This stand-off brought yet another debate on the powers of Protector and Parliament, and a compromise constitution, The Humble Petition and Advice, was the result. By its provisions a new two-house Parliament was given control of the executive, but Cromwell was guaranteed financial independence by an annual revenue grant of £1,300,000, given the right to appoint his successor, and even offered the crown. Only the opposition of the army, by now growing wary of Cromwell's pretensions, led him to refuse the throne, but he accepted much of the rest. Even this fragile compromise did not last. The Parliament of 1658 was captured by Cromwell's opponents, and the Lord Protector sent its recalcitrant members home.

This opposition angered and frustrated a man who was in many ways a reformer. Cromwell opposed monopolies, the despised legacies of Elizabeth I and the early Stuarts, and opened up East India trade to all merchants. Within certain limits, Cromwell was far more friendly to the idea of religious toleration than many of his contemporaries. Genuinely interested in legal and administrative reform, he favored improvements in the creaking mechanisms of the Court of Chancery, urged the mitigation of the harsh laws governing debt, advocated the reduction of the many and extreme criminal penalties of the Common Law, and actively disliked the corruption of officials and the sale of offices. His desire to appoint honest judges impressed even the royalist cleric and historian, Bishop Burnet. "To hang a man for a trifle and pardon murder," Cromwell bluntly told one of his Parliaments, "is the ministration of the law through the ill-framing of it.... And to come and see men lose their lives for petty matters: this is a thing God will reckon for. And I wish it may not lie upon this nation a day longer than you have the opportunity to give a remedy." Sadly, few of the remedies proposed went into effect. The law went substantially unreformed until the nineteenth century, and Cromwell himself, needing money, granted the East India Company a new monopoly in 1657 in return for a financial infusion.

Portrait of Oliver Cromwell.
Unknown Artist
Courtesy of Special Collections, University of Minnesota Libraries.

In August of 1658 the ravages of a tertian fever carried off Cromwell's beloved daughter Elizabeth. Already weakened by the common maladies of the stone and gout, Cromwell's constitution could not stand the assaults of the dreaded tertian, which killed him less than a month after it had claimed his daughter. The man who had fought and helped to execute a king only to be styled as "his highness," received a state funeral worthy of a monarch. From Somerset House his body was drawn on a velvet bed of state by six horses, escorted by the new nobility he had so recently created. Robed, bearing sceptre and globe, Cromwell's funeral effigy was seen to wear the crown of a king, and it was surrounded by guidons, banners, soldiers, heralds, even a knight of honor. "In this equipage," wrote the gloating royalist Samuel Pepys, "they proceeded to Westminster: but it was the most joyous funeral I ever saw; for there were none that cried but dogs, which the soldiers hooted away with barbarous noise, drinking and taking tobacco in the streets as they went."

The English had simply tired of Cromwell, and especially Cromwell's army. The major-generals, whom Lucy Hutchinson described as "silly, mean fellows" had antagonized the gentry in the counties as thoroughly as had the agents of Charles I. What the landed and powerful had always taken to be the natural order of things had been disturbed by too much violence, too many strenuous preachers and unruly sectaries, too many upstart Cromwellian lords with their "mock titles," too many soldiers. Having bid goodby to their Lord Protector, the English soon rid themselves of his heir and his legacy. Cromwell's son and heir Richard, more suited by inclination and ability to be a gentleman farmer than a head of state, proved not a fit replacement for his father, and was mistrusted by the army. In 1659, General George Monck, commanding the English army in Scotland, descended upon England and made short work of "Tumble-Down Dick." Long underpaid, many of the soldiers sent to oppose Monck decided instead to join him, and London opened its gates. The same army that had once purged the Long Parliament now called it back into being. The rule of the generals was over. General Monck summoned to Westminster the aging remnants of the Long Parliament, and that body, after receiving assurances, invited the son of the martyred Charles I to return to England and restore the Stuart line.

F. Charles II and the Restoration

The return of Charles II was speedily accomplished. On the day of his arrival in London the new king turned thirty-one, and the capitol responded with a procession no less opulent, and far more sincere, than the one that had buried Cromwell a few months before. John Evelyn, a royalist who was almost beside himself with glee, wrote of "a Triumph of above 2000 horse & foote, brandishing their swords and shouting with unexpressable joy: The wayes straw'd with flowers, the bells ringing, the streetes hung with Tapissry, fountaines running with wine: the Mayor, Aldermen, all the Companies in their livers, Chaines of Gold, banners; Lords & nobles, Cloth of Silver, gold & vellvet every body clad in, the windos & balconies all set with Ladys, Trumpets, Musick, & myriards of people flocking the streetes & was as far as *Rochester*." From seventeen years of penurious exile Charles II returned to a realm that, in the greatest of birthday presents, had seemingly given itself back to him. For miles and miles the triumphal procession filled the eye. The Restoration had begun, and in a mood of rapture and celebration.

Exactly what had been restored to the monarchy, however, was far from clear, and it was politic for the new king to proceed cautiously. It was Parliament after all that summoned Charles back to the throne, in fact the remnants of the same Parliament that had rebelled against his father twenty years before. Some of the people who cheered Charles II through the London streets had also seen Charles I beheaded. The Puritans were silent, but not absent, and many English still despised the Catholicism associated with the Stuarts. Unpaid and disorderly soldiers still skulked about, a potential danger to monarchy and state.

Charles had begun well. Even before returning to England he had issued, in April 1660, the Declaration of Breda, in which he urged, subject to the approval of Parliament, a pardon for most of those who had rebelled against his father, religious toleration, the payment of overdue wages to the army, and the amicable settlement of the many land disputes growing out of the Interregnum. Many of these goals appeared in the so-called "Restoration settlement," a series of acts passed by Charles' first Parliament. Only fifty-seven people were exempted from pardon for being rebels, and only eleven were actually executed for the crime of regicide. The bodies of Cromwell and other deceased regicides were disinterred, hanged grotesquely in their burial shrouds, and reburied in obscurity, but little else was done to expunge the reality of rebellion. Parliament, on Charles' urging, granted nearly £1,000,000 to pay off the potentially rebellious soldiers. In return for giving up some of the traditional sources of royal revenue, Parliament granted Charles a yearly income of £100,000, to be paid from an excise on beer, cider, and tea. Less credibly, Charles acquiesced in the loss of lands suffered by Irish Catholics and some English Royalists during the time of Cromwell, and Parliament refused to pass a statute recognizing the religious toleration promised by Charles II at Breda. The Restoration Settlement was thus a compound of forbearance and expediency, a compromise agreed to by Charles and a Parliament of conservative, and Anglican, landed gentlemen.

While Charles' actions at Breda and during his first Parliament showed political wisdom, other facets of Charles' personality made it difficult for him to become a truly successful ruler. Engaging and affable, Charles was living proof that neither quality necessarily makes for good leadership.

Tall with a large nose and affecting masses of dark, curly hair, Charles was also remarkable for a dark complexion that embarassed even his mother. In an age when "blackness" of visage or skin was equated with innate sinfulness, and the newly-discovered Africans were wrongly reviled by Europeans as beasts, Charles was regarded as quite ugly—a fact which Charles, with an ingratiating if unregal candor, cheerfully admitted. A familiar man impatient with the rituals and solemnities of royalty, Charles was at his happiest when telling stories to his courtiers, mixing at cockfights with the crowds at Newmarket, watching the nursing spaniels that had the run of his chamber, or enjoying one of the many children he had fathered by several mistresses.

Charles, at times, has been too easily written off as an empty-headed and libidinous womanizer. The second part of this assertion is true, the first doubtful. Imbued with a healthy sexuality, Charles, like many men of power in the period, certainly enjoyed the favors of many women. To Bishop Burnet, Charles once said that "he could not think God would make a man miserable only for taking a little pleasure out of the way." But for Charles this was heroic understatement. By various mistresses he produced fourteen royal bastards. Unlike some of his contemporaries, however, Charles adored and acknowledged most of his illegitimate offspring. Seven of his eight sons, "graces by the grace of such mothers who brightened the bed of King Charles," received titles of nobility, and the illegitimate daughters were dowered and loved.

As a group, most significantly, his mistresses fared less well. While two were created duchesses, the others were pensioned off with greater or lesser generosity. It does not appear that Charles developed a permanent bond with any of his paramours, and it is unlikely that he was deeply influenced by any. The same may be said with regard to Charles' Portuguese queen, Catherine of Braganza, a quiet, sheltered, and most Catholic princess who was much less handsome than the dowry she brought with her. Unremarkable in physical appearance save for "teeth wronging her mouth by sticking a little too far out," Charles was doubtless bored by her, forcing her to accept his mistress Lady Castlemaine as a lady of the bedchamber, and ungenerously noting that his queen did not have "anything in her face that in the least degree can shoque one." With regard to Charles feelings for women, Halifax once remarked that "I am apt to think his stayed as much as any man's ever did in the lower regions."

Much the same attitude characterized Charles' approach to politics and affairs of state. Noted Halifax again, Charles "lived with his ministers as he did with his mistresses; he used them, but he was not in love with them." When he was irritated with those who served him, he cast them off quite easily and quite forgot about them. Edward Hyde, Earl of Clarendon, who had served Charles II as loyally as he had Charles I, was dismissed, fled the country to avoid impeachment, and died in exile. Another minister, Lord Danby, fell afoul of Charles' enemies in Parliament and was allowed to languish in the Tower for five years.

While Charles was too pleasure-loving and familiar to be a forceful or regal king, he was no simple voluptuary and was never controlled by his passions. He required little sleep, awoke early, and "alloted his time exactly." Charles was likewise never the ignorant monarch that some have thought him. Though badly read in the classics and, significantly, history, Charles was a good enough linguist to understand Spanish, Italian, and French, and had a lively interest in mathematics and science. A founder of the Royal Society, Charles possessed a laboratory of his own and a love for all things mechanical, technical, and military.

Charles' real deficiencies of character, and he had them to be sure, are sometimes overlooked by those fascinated with his personal life. He was a poor, and badly prepared, public speaker, which put him at a disadvantage when dealing with his Parliament and people. In addition to occasional ingratitude, Charles also had a reputation for lying and dissimulation. "If he dissembled," wrote the cynical Halifax, "let us remember first, that he was a king, and that dissimulation is a jewel of the crown." In sum, Charles' was a character subtle and complex, a man for whom the label "Merry Monarch" hid as much as it revealed. Charles possessed the intelligence and dissimulation to use and manipulate people, but wanted the steady application to manage events and the determination to master them.

On May 8, 1661, Charles' second Parliament, known as the "Cavalier" or "Pensioner" Parliament, met. It was to last for eighteen years. Among its first acts were four laws known commonly but inaccurately as the "Clarendon Code," which together were designed to exclude religious dissenters of any kind, Catholic or Protestant, from participation in national life. By the first of these measures, the Corporation Act of 1661, dissenters were banned from serving in local government. The Act of Uniformity of 1662 required all clergy to swear their assent and loyalty to the Church of England, or Anglican Church, and to the order of service prescribed in the Book of Common Prayer. The Conventicle Act of 1664 fined any who attended conventicles, defined as a dissenting religious meeting of more than four persons. The Five Mile Act of 1665 prohibited dissenting preachers from coming within five miles of towns. Parliament in other actions also restored most of the church courts and, in the Triennial Act of 1664, demanded that future Parliaments meet at least every three years. It seemed that the Great Rebellion was truly over, and that a leadership at once conservative, intolerant, and Anglican dominated Parliament, king, and country.

Foreign wars, domestic problems, and politically inept decisions soon separated Charles from the Parliament and people that had once embraced him so warmly. The Second Dutch War (1665-1667) brought England much humiliation and little success, and to it were quickly joined the dual disasters of the Great Plague of 1665 and the Great Fire of London of 1666. On the heels of the destruction of several English ships in the Thames by an audacious Dutch navy, England was obliged to sue for peace. Clarendon, despite the fact that he had opposed the war, was made its scapegoat and victim. Impeached and forced into exile, Clarendon found himself cast off by a monarch happy enough to use the occasion to rid himself of blame, and to dispose of a servant who had come to irritate him.

Thereafter Charles tried to rule through a group of five ministers—Clifford, Arlington, Buckingham, Ashley, and Lauderdale—collectively known as the Cabal, a word which was made up of the first letter of their last names. Through these men Charles pursued an unprincipled foreign policy and an unwise domestic one. In 1668 a Triple Alliance was formed with the Dutch and the Swedes, a move popular in Parliament and in the country because it was aimed at the hated and Catholic French. Two years later, as relations between monarchy and Parliament worsened, Charles concluded the secret Treaty of Dover with Louis XIV of France. For this alliance Charles received a handsome French pension, which made him more independent of Parliament, but it also committed Charles to a religious policy ruinous to his political position in England. In return for his pension Charles had to promise to declare himself a Catholic when affairs in England permitted. Though the terms of the Treaty of Dover remained for a time unknown to his countrymen, Charles angered many by a far more public act. In 1673, and despite the precarious nature of state finance, Charles embarked upon the Third Dutch War, in which England fought Dutch Protestants in alliance with Catholic France. Virtually simultaneously Charles issued a Declaration of Indulgence, lessening the penalties and restrictions placed on Catholic and Protestant dissenters by Parliament. Some historians have seen this act as a principled one, reflecting the ideals of a monarch who genuinely believed in religious toleration. Others, more hostile, have seen the Declaration of Indulgence as an act of dissembling expediency, and an attempt to bring about what had been promised in the Treaty of Dover.

Whatever the motivation, the Declaration of Indulgence proved to be politically unwise, and Parliament reacted severely. In

1673 it passed a Test Act which required that any officer-holder, civil or military, should be obliged to take the sacrament according to the Anglican rite, declare against the dogma of the Catholic mass, and swear an oath of supremacy and allegiance. As a result, Catholics were once again excluded from office. James, Duke of York, Charles' Catholic brother and the presumptive heir to the throne, was forced to resign his position as Lord High Admiral. The Cabal dissolved.

Frustrated, Charles turned to Thomas Osborne, Earl of Danby, as his chief minister. Parliament met infrequently, but when it did, Danby, a master-politician, maintained control by corruption and the distribution of favors. The contradictions in foreign policy remained, with Charles still receiving subsidies from Louis XIV and Danby arranging a marriage treaty involving Mary, the daughter of James, Duke of York and Anne Hyde, and William of Orange, ruler of the Netherlands and Louis' greatest enemy.

Then, as Charles found himself increasingly dependent on French subsidies, a new round of anti-Catholic hysteria broke out in England. The fear of Catholic conspiracy, a part of the English soul ever since the time of Henry VIII, had been reawakened by the Declaration of Indulgence and emerged full-blown in 1678 with the revelation of an alleged "Popish Plot" by one Titus Oates. The elements of the conspiracy, according to Oates, included the assassination of Charles II, the invasion of Ireland by the French, and the mass murder of Protestants. The fear was promptly exploited by Charles' enemies in Parliament. The secret French subsidies were revealed, leading to the impeachment of Danby and the introduction of the first Exclusion Bill, which was designed to remove the Catholic James from the succession to the throne and to replace him with Charles' illegitimate son, the Duke of Monmouth. These actions forced the hand of Charles II. In rapid succession both James and Monmouth went into voluntary but temporary exile, and the uncontrollable Parliament was prorogued and then dismissed.

Another Parliament met in early 1681, but it proved equally obstreperous, passing another Exclusion Bill that was vetoed only through the intervention of the House of Lords. The House of Commons then declared that it would cut off all subsidies to the crown and government until an Exclusion Bill was passed, and Charles was once again obliged to move for a dissolution. During this time of controversy, political labels began to be used in Parliament. Those who were for the Exclusion Bill and who petitioned against the dissolution of Parliament by the king were known as "Petitioners" and later as Whigs. Their opponents, known as "Abhorrers" because they abhorred such petitions and supported the king, came to be known as Tories. The term "Whig" was derived from "Whiggamore," the insulting name given to the Scots Covenanters who had moved south to participate in the revolt against Charles I at the beginning of the Great Rebellion. The origin of the term "Tory" was little better, and was the appellation originally given to a group of Irish Catholics who committed agrarian outrages and highway robberies for a living.

Portrait of Charles II. Studio of James M. Wright
Courtesy of the National Portrait Gallery, London.

Charles spent his declining years struggling against the poisonous political and religious hatreds that he had mistakenly reawakened. In the greatest of ironies, fearing the alleged Catholic plotting and absolutist tendencies of the later Stuarts, Parliament, by forcing Charles to dissolve it and by refusing subsidies even when it was in session, drove the king to seek ever more support from the despised French. The Parliament of March 1681, purposely called to meet in the royalist stronghold of Oxford, brought in another Exclusion bill nonetheless, and had to be dissolved. Resolving to call no more uncontrollable Parliaments, Charles forced boroughs to surrender their charters for "remodelling," in order to make possible the election of more manageable members. Whigs were driven into hiding and their leader, Shaftesbury, into exile. In 1683 a Whig-instigated scheme to seize the king, the Rye House plot, was discovered, and the court used it as an excuse to try and execute what was left of the Whig leadership.

Besieged by troubles, Charles had "a convulsion fit" one morning in 1685 while dressing "and gave a greate scream and fell into his chaire." As the fits continued, Charles was subjected to the usual and loathsome medical expedients of his day. He was bled, and hot pans were applied to his head together with "strong spirrits"; an antimony cup was also administered, as were glisters, purges, and "severall blistering plasters of cantharides." Because of such heroic efforts to repel the "humors" in his head, Charles slept badly, and awoke only to have another convulsion. His mouth and tongue inflamed by hot medicine, Charles then suffered from worsening fits and no doubt from the effects of continuous bleedings. As his breathing grew labored, Charles apparently accepted the nearness of his death, retired to bed, declared himself a Catholic, and quietly passed away.

G. The Glorious Revolution and its Legacy: James II, William and Mary, and Queen Anne

Though many English were suspicious of his avowed Catholicism, James of York was allowed to succeed his elder brother peacefully and became James II. Of mature years when he ascended the throne, James was described some years later as "something above the middle stature, well-shaped, very nervous and strong; his face rather long, his countenance engaging, his outward carriage . . . a little stiff and constrained." James had a reputation for inflexibility, and over this his brother had worried. "I am weary of travelling,"

Charles wrote in an ironic vein, "and am resolved to go abroad no more. But when I am dead and gone, I know now what my brother will do: I am much afraid that when he comes to wear the crown he will be obliged to travel again." Nonetheless, James' subjects at least initially resolved to put up with him, convinced that he was too old to father a male heir and that his reign would be a short one. Disturbed yet resigned, they comforted themselves with mocking verse:

> Here you may see Great James the Second,
> (The greatest of our kings he reckoned!) . . .
> His other Gifts we need but name,
> They are so spread abroad by Fame;
> His Faith, his Zeal, his Constancy
> Aversion to all Bigotry! . . .

James began with a brief run of good fortune. His first Parliament granted him an annual subsidy of £2,000,000, and the dual rebellions of the Earl of Argyll and the Duke of Monmouth were promptly put down. Unfortunately, in the wake of Monmouth's defeat at Sedgmoor, James took the first in a series of decisions that proved his inflexibility and that in the end weakened his political position. A vengeful royalist judge, George Jeffreys, was dispatched to the seat of rebellion in the English southwest, and there, as a result of a series of questionable judicial proceedings known as the "Bloody Assizes," savage penalties were exacted on the bodies of real and suspected rebels. Once again there seemed to be a sovereign on the English throne more concerned with underlining the powers and prerogatives of the monarchy than with upholding the English common law. This was a distinction that few English, and particularly those who had lived through the Great Rebellion, could not fail to notice. Also troubling to some was the fact that Monmouth and his followers, though rebels, were Protestants and Anglicans, while the king who wreaked his vengeance on them was a thoroughgoing Catholic.

James compounded these fears by demanding a permanent standing army under royal control. Though the rebellions of Argyll and Monmouth in a sense made this request understandable, James should have also understood that it only served to undermine his credibility with his subjects. The memory of the Great Rebellion, of rule by the major-generals, of disorderly bands of soldiers who scoffed at peace and order, still troubled James' people, and they began to suspect the ambitions of their Catholic king. These suspicions were voiced all the more strongly when James urged the repeal of the Test and Corporation acts, placed known Catholics in positions of leadership in the state and armed forces, purged local governments of those who disagreed with him, received papal diplomats at court, refounded monastic houses in London, and created a new church court that reminded many of the hated, and abolished, Court of High Commission. In the unpopular Godden versus Hales legal decision, James' power to dispense with the Test Act, and thus with all laws, was reaffirmed, and, in 1687 and again in 1688, James issued Declarations of Indulgence granting liberty of public worship to Protestant and Catholic dissenters, thus flaunting his prerogative to suspend laws that Parliament had made. Finally, in an effort to remove his enemies at Oxford University, James seized Magdalen College, threatening the sanctity of private property in a state where it was an article of faith.

In the midst of these unpopular actions, and as suspicions of a Stuart absolutism grew, James' second wife, Mary of Modena, presented him with a son and heir, and thereby increased fears that James would continue an unpopular, and Catholic, line. This fear was thrown into bold relief when Louis XIV of France, the most feared and absolutist of the Catholic rulers of Europe, almost simultaneously revoked the Edict of Nantes, which had preserved the privileges of the Huguenots, the leading French Protestant minority.

Seemingly unaware of the growing restiveness among his subjects, James plunged ahead. He ordered the reading of the Declaration of Indulgence from Anglican pulpits, and when seven bishops, including the Archbishop of Canterbury, petitioned James to rescind the order, they were imprisoned and brought to trial on a charge of seditious libel. It was this trial, the Seven Bishop's Case, that finally galvanized the country to action. The judges, despite pressure from the court, found for the bishops. In the wake of their decision, seven prominent Englishmen invited William of Orange, the Protestant Stadholder of the Netherlands, and the husband of James' eldest daughter by his first wife, to invade England.

At last awaking to the danger his own actions had placed him in, James tried to rescind the most offensive of his actions and even to treat with William, but by early November 1688 the invasion fleet had put in at Torbay. The series of events that have been somewhat incongruously called the "Glorious Revolution" had begun. Having destroyed his position through inflexibility and stupidity, James exited with a singular lack of grace. His ineptness dogging him to the end; James failed even in his first attempt to flee. On December 11, after peevishly throwing the Great Seal into the Thames, James tried to follow his wife and infant son into a French exile, only to be captured by a group of fisherman on the coast and returned to London. There, some wisely determined that the change of power should be bloodless and that the Royalists should be without a martyr and made it convenient for James to escape again. With this assistance, James was successful, and he became a pensioner of Louis XIV in France.

With James conveniently absent, a Convention Parliament soon met. Its members declared that James had broken "the Original Contract between the King and the People," and that James "having withdrawn himself out of the kingdom . . . has abdicated the Government." With the throne thus found legally vacant, it could be offered to another. At first some thought that the crown should be bestowed on Mary alone, but when William made it known through an intermediary that he "would not like to be his wife's gentleman usher," the crown was offered to both as dual sovereigns.

Their reign began in genuine partnership. Mary, cheerful and familiar, moved directly into the rooms occupied by her predecessor, proceeding with a quiet, calm routine, showing herself to the people, playing at cards, and acting as if nothing untoward had happened. William, grave, taciturn, and "ill-shaped," worn down by a lifetime of struggles against Louis XIV, at first ingratiated himself less, but used his military skills successfully against James II in Ireland, which the latter had invaded with French assistance in 1689. At the Battle of the Boyne in 1690, William inflicted a crushing defeat on the forces of James II. This victory, and his subsequent subjugation of Ireland, accomplished with the same brutality as Cromwell's, are celebrated to this day by the Protestants of Ulster, or Northern Ireland, who still call themselves "Orangemen."

Of even greater consequence were the limitations on their power that William and Mary accepted in return for the throne. The documents and acts of this so-called "revolutionary settlement" established, first, that the English landed classes, through their representatives in Parliament, would hold the dominant position in the English state and, second, that the English people had certain liberties and privileges that were never to be abridged. In this sense the events of 1688-1689 do deserve the title of "Glorious," for several pieces of parliamentary legislation from these years stand as fundamental parts of the English Constitution, which, unlike the constitutions of some other states, consists of a whole body of laws, acts, and customs.

The English Bill of Rights of 1689, the centerpiece of the settlement, formed a model for the American Bill of Rights a century later and is a landmark in the history of democratic institutions. At the same time it should not be forgotten that the English Bill of Rights was originally designed more to reinforce the powers of Parliament and the conservative, Anglican aristocrats who controlled it, than to guarantee individual rights. Under its terms, the right of the

English monarchy to suspend and dispense with laws was declared illegal, as was its privilege of raising money by royal prerogative, its use of special courts outside the scope of the common law, and its raising or keeping of standing armies without parliamentary consent. English subjects were guaranteed the right to petition their sovereign, to be free from excessive bail, fines, and "cruel and unusual punishment," to be tried by a jury, and, if they were Protestants, to bear arms. Parliament was assured in its right to freedom of speech, to control taxation and revenue, to free elections, and to frequent meetings or sessions. Parliament's supremacy was reaffirmed in the Coronation Oath Act, under which William and Mary were to promise to govern "according to the statutes in parliament agreed on and the laws and customs of the same." The Toleration Act of 1689 stated that all Protestant dissenters would be free from religious persecution, but dissenters were not exempted from the Test and Corporation Acts, and this meant that all dissenters, Protestant and Catholic, were denied the political rights that now became an Anglican monopoly. A Mutiny Act of the same year, in which Parliament granted to military commanders the right to discipline their troops for only six months at a time, reflected the English fear of standing armies and Parliament's determination to control the military.

Mary died in 1694, but William continued on the throne until his death in 1702. William III, by drawing England into the long-lived Dutch struggle against Louis XIV, drew his realm into successful competition with the greatest of European powers of the time. Under the pressure of war, the need for money, and thus for Parliaments to vote it, served to underline its growing dominance, a dominance reinforced by additional legislation. By the Triennial Act of 1694, Parliament sought again to guarantee a new election every three years; by the Act of Settlement of 1701, Parliament asserted its right to determine the succession to the English throne, declared that none but Anglicans could sit on it, and placed the appointment of judges in its own hands.

During the reign of Queen Anne the wars and the trend toward aristocratic and parliamentary power continued. Anne's reign began in 1702, the same year in which the War of the Spanish Succession was joined, and ended in 1714, the year after England and her allies made a victorious peace with the French at Utrecht. Anne was the last, unhappiest, and most distracted Stuart to occupy the English throne. Made corpulent by overindulgence and childbearing, griefstricken by the early deaths of the many children she bore, careless in dress, married to a Danish prince thought by many to be a fool, afflicted by gout, and called "Brandy Nan" for an alleged overfondness for drink, Anne's reputation became the plaything of sniggering wags as she sought solace with several female favorites,

Sarah, Duchess of Marlborough, and Abigail Masham. "There is nothing insolent or overbearing," Dr. Samuel Johnson wrote of the queen who had "touched" him in his youth as a cure for scrofula, "but then there is nothing great or firm or regal, nothing that enforces obedience or respect or which does not rather invite opposition and petulance." Wrote a contemporary wit:

> King William thinks all,
> Queen Mary talks all,
> Prince George drinks all,
> And Princess Anne eats all.

The sad and pathetic nature of the queen, the political ambitions of her favorites, the pressures of war, and Anne's own Tory sentiments produced a political atmosphere heavy with partisanship and intrigue, from which Parliament and its masters again reaped benefits. By the Place Act of 1707, Parliament sought to limit the influence of the monarchy in the House of Commons by excluding as members all who held "places," or offices in the royal household. By the Property Qualification Act of 1710 no man could hold a seat in Commons unless he held a county estate worth £600 annually or city property worth £300 per year. Anne's death brought even greater opportunities to the great landed politicians who dominated the Parliament. A new dynasty, from the tiny German state of Hanover, succeeded the heirless Anne. The Hanoverians, at first confused by the English language and the niceties of English politics, in the end proved incapable of ruling strongly. Into the vacuum of leadership moved the Whig politicians and their followers in Parliament.

H. The Meaning of a Century of Rebellion

What the events of 1640-1660 had begun, wars and weak monarchs, the events of 1688-1714 seemed to confirm. Parliament, not the monarchy, was to be the paramount power in the English state. By 1715 parliamentary dominance, but not parliamentary rule, was an established fact, and after that date English politicians, not English monarchs, dominate events. The great Whig politicians who managed the votes of their followers in the House of Commons had the power to influence, through the "power of the purse," many of the functions of government. But influence does not mean the same thing as control, and it is instructive that words like "influence" and "interest" come into common usage in eighteenth-century English politics.

At the beginning of the eighteenth century, Parliament, and the conservative and landed nobility that dominated it, had not yet fully developed the means to manage the state completely or exploit their power. There was as yet no office of prime minister, and no cabinet government in the modern sense. There were political groups—the Tories and especially the Whigs—but neither of these, as the researches of Sir Lewis Namier remind us, were structured like modern political parties. Each of them was rather subdivided into factions or interests, which were in turn dominated by some powerful man who controlled his followers by means of family connection, judicious arranged marriages, personal magnetism, patronage, or even outright corruption. Parliamentary seats were controlled by the landed classes, filled with followers, and even bought and sold. When one or another of these great politicians or magnates, alone or in alliance with others, was able to control a majority in the House of Commons, he was asked by the monarch to govern the country.

To remember the latter fact is to recognize something very important about the century of rebellion. The Revolution of 1688 had tipped the balance in favor of Parliament, but it had not dispensed with the monarchy. After 1715, in the confusion of factions, and in the absence of anything like party discipline, the role of the monarch was no longer dominant, but it was still crucial. It was the sovereign who asked men to form governments to run the country, and who received the resignations of those who could no longer do so. Despite legislation like the Place Act, English sovereigns competed for votes and influence in the House of Commons with other factions and interests, meddled in elections, and made alliances with powerful politicians. England was ruled in this rather unique way at least until the nineteenth century.

The Great Rebellion was thus no great revolution, at least in the popular conception of the term. To many, a revolution implies social and economic changes as well as political ones. In 1715 no new social class had seized power, and groups that had advocated genuine social and economic change, the Levellers, the Diggers, the Fifth Monarchists, the radical women who had preached and demanded equality of status earlier in the century, had all but disappeared. What the Great Rebellion in fact witnessed, as J. H. Hexter has perceptively written, was not the emergence of a new ruling class, but the reassertion of power by an old one. The English landed nobility which had once dominated medieval society through feudal and military power, reappeared with a vengeance and in a new guise, using their land and wealth to purchase and control seats in Parliament, as they had once used them to reward and control their knights and vassals. The struggle of nobility and monarchy for political mastery, a recurrent theme in English and European history, had been resolved in England, at least for the moment, in favor of the former.

All this does not mean however that the century of rebellion did not have important consequences, both for England and for Europe. Its results were in fact significant for both. By participating in Parliament, by paying taxes, the English landed classes came to support their monarchy and their governing institutions rather than to oppose them. In later centuries, some of the ideas and assertions of the Great Rebellion, especially those expressed in the Bill of Rights, took on new meanings as their principles were adopted by other societies more open and more free. In England a successful but at times uneasy alliance of sovereign, Parliament, and the landed, Whig politicians moved England through the eighteenth century, preserving social inequality as it guaranteed social and political stability. It was this stability, combined with military success and economic growth, that was to make England a dominant power in Europe and the world.

Portfolio: Women, 1600-1815—Family, Mortality, Sexuality, Individuality— And the Changing Images of Children

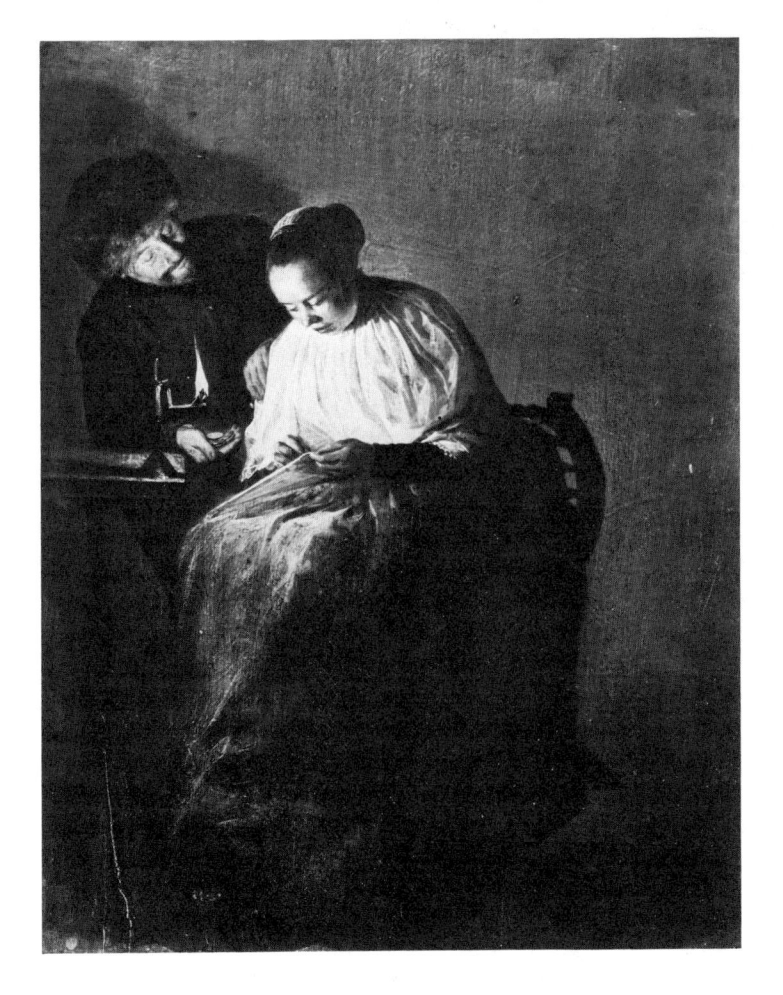

The Proposition. Judith Leyster
In this painting by a woman artist a boor tries to purchase the sexual favors of a young woman, who, in turn, attempts to ignore him by concentrating on her needlework. Women were not always portrayed as resistant to such propositions, and were often viewed as having an aggressive sexuality dangerous to men. *Courtesy Mauritshuis Museum, The Hague.*

A Girl and Her Duenna. Bartolomé Esteban Murillo
In Spain, and in other parts of Europe during this period, young women of the upper classes were often chaperoned. *Courtesy National Gallery of Art, Washington. Widener Collection.*

Mistress and Servant. Attr. Willem van Mieris
In many upper-class families of the time, servants, nurses, and valets were closer to their charges, masters, or mistresses than family members were to one another. *Courtesy Memorial Art Gallery of the University of Rochester. Bertha Buswell Bequest.*

The Wedding of Kloris and Roosje. **Top.** Cornelius Troost
The simplicity of this country wedding contrasts with the image of marriage among the merchant and landed classes, for whom it was a serious business in which property, inheritance and family position were the paramount considerations. *Courtesy the Mauritshuis Museum, The Hague.*

The First Lesson of Fraternal Friendship. Etienne Aubry
The ideals of equality and fraternity put forward during the French Revolution are here made manifest in an encounter between the offspring of a noble and a peasant family. *Courtesy Nelson Gallery of Art/Atkins Museum, Kansas City. Nelson Fund.*

Sir Thomas Aston at the Deathbed of his Wife. **Top.** John Souch
Courtesy City Art Gallery, Manchester, England.

The Saltonstall Family. David des Granges
Courtesy Tate Gallery, London.

These two paintings are remarkable in their portrayal of the effects of death in childbirth and infant mortality on the stability of families in the seventeenth and eighteenth centuries. In both cases, the male head of household stands over the deathbed of his wife and, in the former painting, a shrouded cradle and skull testify at once to the fragility of infant life and the sacrificial nature of childbirth itself.

Portrait of Saskia van Uilenburgh. The Wife of the Artist. Rembrandt van Rijn
Saskia van Uilenburgh was the leading passion of Rembrandt's life, and appears in many of his works. *Courtesy National Gallery of Art, Washington. Widener Collection.*

Portrait of Elizabeth van der Meeren. **Top.** Frans Hals
Courtesy of The Museum of Fine Arts, Houston. Gift of Mrs. Sarah C. Blaffer.

The Lady Governors of the Old Men's Home at Haarlem. Frans Hals
Courtesy Frans Halsmuseum, Haarlem.

These two Dutch portrayals of mature women seem to celebrate the strength, character, and wisdom of the painter's subjects.

Miss Catherine Tatton, **Left,** and *The Honorable Mrs. Graham,* **Right.** Thomas Gainsborough
Gainsborough's vibrant portraits of young women are among the finest examples of the British school of portraiture that flourished in the eighteenth century. *Courtesy National Gallery of Art, Washington. Widener Collection.*

Portrait of Miss Hoare, **Left.** Sir Joshua Reynolds
Courtesy Memorial Art Gallery of the University of Rochester. George Eastman Collection.

Mrs. Renny Strachan, **Right.** Sir Henry Raeburn
Courtesy of the Worcester Art Museum, Worcester, Massachusetts. Gift of Mrs. Hester Newton Wetherell.

Reynolds and Raeburn were major artists of the eighteenth-century British school.

135

An Old Woman at Prayer. Nicolaes Maes
Courtesy of the Worcester Art Museum, Worcester, Massachusetts.

During the period between 1600 and 1815 children and childhood as we know them began to emerge in the imperfect record of western art. Children are still, at times, portrayed as adults, performing adult acts, but for many artists they have become beloved individuals, clutching toys, breaking the decorum of formal poses with childlike actions, becoming the profound concern of parents and others around them. Slowly, children are recognized as special human beings, and childhood as a special period in human life.

The Twins Clara and Albert de Bray. Salomon de Bray
The artist's love for these twin children suffuses this elegant, and realistic, drawing, which portrays infants as they really are. *Courtesy of the Pierpont Morgan Library, New York.*

Portrait of Clelia Cattaneo, Daughter of Marchesa Elena Grimaldi. **Left.** Sir Anthony van Dyck
This child is portrayed alone, and virtually as a small adult. *Courtesy of the National Gallery of Art, Washington. Widener Collection.*

Girl with a Broom. **Right.** Rembrandt van Rijn
Hard work was expected of children in the preindustrial household and the distinction between childhood and adulthood was, in this sense, sometimes unclear. *Courtesy of the National Gallery of Art, Washington. Andrew W. Mellon Collection.*

Young Girl Plucking a Duck. **Left.** Barent Fabritius
Courtesy of the Dallas Museum of Fine Arts, anonymous gift.

Child with Cherries. **Right.** Salomon de Bray
Courtesy of the Memorial Art Gallery of the University of Rochester. Bertha Buswell Bequest.

The Sick Child. Gabriel Metsu
Metsu's brush has captured both the loving concern of the mother and the wrenching vulnerability so often recognizable in sick children. The child and the mother are bound together in mutual need. *Courtesy of the Rijksmuseum, Amsterdam.*

Kinder spel gheduydet tot Sinne-beelden ende Leere der Seden.
EX NVGIS SERIA.

The Dancing Couple. **Opposite, top.** Jan Steen
In this scene children are portrayed with toys and one of them, amid the noisy gathering, is the object of a mother's undivided attention. *Courtesy of the National Gallery of Art, Washington. Widener Collection.*

Illustration from J. Cats, *Silenus Alcibiadia Sive Proteus* . . . (1618) **Opposite, bottom.**
An astounding number of childhood games are portrayed in this early seventeenth-century print, but the children who are playing them are dressed like, and have the stiffness of, adults.

The Bedroom. Pieter de Hooch
The comfortable, intimate communication between mother and child visible in this painting requires no exchange of words between them, and is familiar to many of us. *Courtesy of the National Gallery of Art, Washington. Widener Collection.*

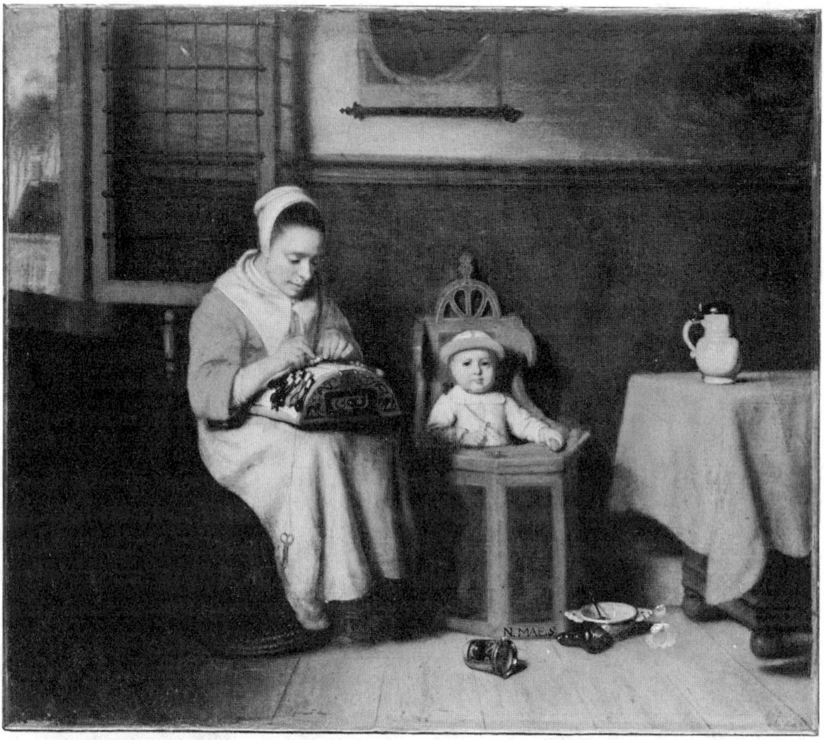
N.MAES

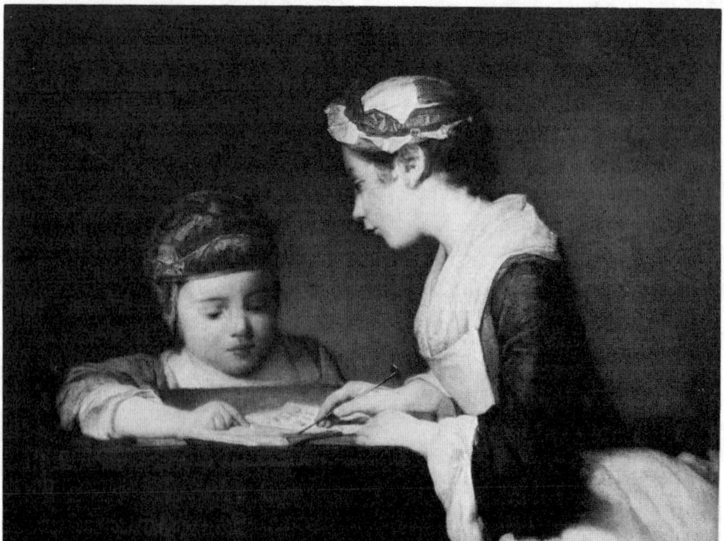

The Lacemaker. **Opposite, top.** Nicholaes Maes
The mother makes lace, and the infant is close by in a seventeenth century version of a high chair, in a scene that can be associated with much more modern times. *Courtesy of the Metropolitan Museum of Art. Bequest of Michael Friedsam.*

The Young Governess. **Opposite, bottom.** Jean-Baptiste-Simeon Chardin
Governesses, often not much older than children themselves, were employed by families of means to provide rudimentary education and support for the children of the household. Governesses and tutors were often utilized as alternatives to schools. *Courtesy of the National Gallery of Art, Washington. Andrew W. Mellon Collection.*

Las Meninas, or the Family of Philip IV. Diego Velázquez y Silva
The artist has contrived to make the disorder and action of childhood burst upon what was supposedly a carefully posed scene. Children literally rush in, and one of them, very typically, pesters the dog. *Courtesy of the Museo del Prado, Madrid.*

The Hoppner Children. John Hoppner
In this group portrait a British artist of the late eighteenth century sets an idealized country scene, yet makes his children special and real. *Courtesy of the National Gallery of Art, Washington.*

Chapter III

Great Wars and Great Powers in Central and Northern Europe, 1618-1721: Cardinal Richelieu of France, Gustavus Adolphus and Christina of Sweden, and Peter the Great of Russia

> Private miseries admit of remedies and are not so deplorable because they are limited. . . . But when they prove public and general they scorn restraints and, as violent streams, break down all before them. These are as comets, never seen but with amazement; and whose effects, as theirs, produce ruins to whole states and nations. . . . Take notice of the fearful issues and effects of war, what lamentable conclusions the sword makes; whose beginnings are blood, whose proceedings are fire and famine, whose upshot is utter destruction and desolation. . . .
> —the *Tears of Germany,* 1638

> . . . and the Effects of that Comet . . . still working in the prodigious revolutions now beginning in Europe, especially in Germany, whose sad Commotions sprung from the Bohemians defection from the Emperor Mathias, upon which quarell the Sweds brake in, giving umbrage to the rest of the Princes, and the whole Christian world, cause to deplore it. . . .
> —John Evelyn on the Thirty Years' War

> Always *allegro* and *courageux,* as though he had not a care in the world.
> —a contemporary comment on Gustavus Adolphus

He died at length prematurely, and in the midst of all these turmoils, leaving all his schemes incomplete and his name powerful and feared, rather than revered and loved.
—Voltaire on Cardinal Richelieu

I had a mortal hatred for the long and frequent sermons of the Lutherans.
—Christina of Sweden

He is a man of very hot temper, and very brutal in his passion. . . .
—Bishop Burnet on Peter the Great

Oval Medallion depicting Peter the Great and his family. Courtesy of the Walters Art Gallery, Baltimore.

A. The Struggle for European Hegemony: The Thirty Years' War and Beyond

In 1618, so the story goes, in Prague, then the capital of the kingdom of Bohemia, two royal governors, together with a hapless secretary, were cast from a window of Hradĉany Palace, and fell some seventy feet through space to land ignominiously on a dunghill. Those who landed, outraged but alive, in the filth and offal were the loyal servants of Ferdinand of Hapsburg, recently elected to the throne of Bohemia. Those in the chamber above who directed Ferdinand's representatives downward, it would seem, had decided that they did not care for Ferdinand, his Catholic religion, or his policies. It is hard to see how they could have made their opposition more clear.

With this event, which has been labeled with a certain nicety as the "Defenestration of Prague," the Thirty Years' War, one of the great conflicts of European history, was said to begin. This struggle has exercised historians as much as it appalled contemporaries. The former, armed with their favorite facts and versions of events, have for years warred over their respective interpretations. A historiographical debate has thus been superimposed on a protracted and complex conflict, creating both greater clarity and greater confusion. Contributing to the predicament are the myriad works of contemporary artists, dramatic and literary, of patriots of various nationalistic persuasions, and of religious partisans, both Catholic and Protestant. As one historian of the Thirty Years' War remarked in some discouragement several years ago, ". . . it will take time and patience to uproot the prejudices and misconceptions of historians which have been strongly backed by playwrights, novelists, and poets."

Because the battleground of the Thirty Years' War was Germany, and because the conflict has often been written about by Germans, it is a war often seen as a German tragedy, a great civil war that ended in the destruction of what was left of the Holy Roman Empire. To this sense of tragedy C. V. Wedgwood, an English historian imbued with all the pessimism of the twentieth century, has added a sense of disillusionment and futility and has written of a conflict as useless as it was horrible: "Morally subversive, economically destructive, socially degrading, confused in its causes, devious in its course, futile in its results. . . ." In its essential destructiveness and evil, the Thirty Years' War almost becomes a metaphor for the darkness in the German and European spirit, a precursor of the world wars of the twentieth century.

Other historians, like Anton Gindely and Carl Friedrich, have argued that religion was the prime mover in the Thirty Years'

War, and have called the conflict the last of the European religious wars. There is much to support their thesis. Certainly the Peace of Augsburg of 1555, which legitimized Luther's Reformation in the German states, also made future religious conflicts in Germany more likely. At Augsburg only Lutheranism and Catholicism were recognized as legitimate creeds within Germany, and the choice of religion was left not to individual consciences but to the rulers of the princely states, who selected the faith they deemed most suitable both for themselves and for their subjects. Furthermore, it was a peace in which few believed. Many of the signers of the Peace of Augsburg, including Charles V, Holy Roman Emperor and champion of the Catholic cause, saw in its terms less a treaty than a truce, allowing time for the forces of Catholicism to gather strength before driving the Lutheran heresy from Germany and the Empire. Finally, the Peace of Augsburg not only guaranteed future conflicts between Catholics and Lutherans, but also refused to accept the existence of other forms of Protestantism. Under its terms, Calvinism, a variety of Protestantism that became stronger and more aggressive as the years passed, could not be practiced in Germany. It is thus no surprise that the Thirty Years' War took on religious hues as Protestant leaders like King Christian IV of Denmark and Gustavus Adolphus of Sweden went to war with the Catholic Hapsburgs and their generals.

Other historians, like Franz Mehring, have argued forcefully for an economic interpretation of the Thirty Years' War. Inflation in the Holy Roman Empire in the years before the war certainly undermined the position of the Emperor, the rulers of the princely states, the imperial free knights, and the peasants, who bore the exactions of their social superiors. The Peace of Augsburg, by allowing the German princes to despoil the wealth of the Church on the excuse of conversion to Lutheranism, touched off a scramble for ecclesiastical property and lands. The work of J. V. Polišenský, who has studied contemporary economic and social changes at the local level, has been a valuable asset in the understanding of this aspect of the Thirty Years' War.

More recent scholarship on the Thirty Years' War has demonstrated a broadening both in geography and time. It is a conflict that cannot be called exclusively German, argues a newer group of historians, because it involved at various times the Danes, the Swedes, the Dutch, the French, and the Czechs. The Thirty Years' War is thus inseparable from the several peoples, rulers, and dynasties that, for a considerable variety of reasons, participated in it. It is in fact, in the felicitous phrase of H. G. Koenigsberger, a "European Civil War," as well as a German one. The antagonisms of many of the participants began long before 1618. The Thirty Years' War was a new opportunity for the French house of Bourbon to weaken their Hapsburg foes. It was also an opportunity for the Dutch to free themselves finally from Hapsburg domination. For the Danish king and for Gustavus Adolphus and the Swedish house of Vasa it was an opportunity to enlarge their realms, protect their vital interests, and perhaps even to dominate the Baltic and northern Europe.

Nowhere has the widening of the bounds of the Thirty Years' War been carried out with more vigor than in the work of S. H. Steinberg, who viewed the conflict as a struggle for dominance between Bourbon and Hapsburg, a struggle that lasted not merely for the thirty years between 1618 and 1648 but for the half century between 1600 and 1660. By the latter date the French succeeded in breaking out of the near encirclement of the Spanish and German Hapsburgs, and in becoming the paramount power in western Europe. In this quarrel dynastic considerations, far more than religious or economic ones, were the prime movers as the Catholic house of Bourbon supported Protestant German princes in order to weaken their Catholic Hapsburg overlords.

Indeed, even Steinberg's interpretation can be accused of a certain narrowness because it tends to focus solely on western Europe. To see the struggle solely as one between Bourbon and Hapsburg is to ignore the rise of the Swedish house of Vasa, and its participation in the Thirty Years' War, a participation that was part of a larger bid for dominance in northern Europe, and that brought Sweden into long-term conflict with both Poland and Russia. Seen from the perspective of western Europe, the Thirty Years' War can indeed be viewed as a dynastic struggle between Bourbon and Hapsburg that perhaps ended when the two dynasties agreed to the Peace of the Pyrenees in 1659. For northern Europe, in contrast, the Thirty Years' War is part of a larger and longer struggle that did not end until 1721 with the Peace of Nystadt, in which Peter the Great, Tsar of all the Russias, ended the Great Northern War, humiliated the house of Vasa, and led Russia into the ranks of major European powers.

The Thirty Years' War is thus a conflict unto itself, and an episode in even longer-lived struggles. It is at once a German civil war fought between fractious German princes and their nominal overlord, the Holy Roman Emperor; a religious struggle between Catholic and Protestant; a dynastic war between Hapsburg and Bourbon; a war for recognition and independence fought by people like the Dutch and the Czechs of Bohemia; and a conflict joined by northern European dynasties like those of Denmark and Sweden for their own complex and arguable objectives. Because it involves these many aspects, the Thirty Years' War and the conflicts that followed it emerge as the cardinal struggle of seventeenth-century Europe, and one worthy of the most careful study.

Spanish Hapsburg Lands

..... Boundary of the Holy Roman Empire

Austrian Hapsburg Lands

Hapsburg Dominance: The Holy Roman Empire in 1600

B. Gustavus Adolphus and the Growth of Swedish Hegemony

"In the year 1594, On December 9, my son Gustaf Adolf was born in Stockholm Castle. God the almighty grant that he may live his life with praise, glory, and honor and to the satisfaction of his parents." With these words, reflecting the demands that seventeenth-century European society placed upon its youthful members, Duke Charles of Södermanland, later king of Sweden, welcomed his son into the world. It is safe to conclude that the new prince eventually exceeded even his father's expectations.

At the same time, again reflecting the constricted realities of the time, important commitments regarding the future of the infant had been made even before his birth, commitments against which it would have been unthinkable for him to argue and which he would honor throughout his life. The first commitment was to his family—the house of Vasa—and to its dynastic ambition; the second was the commitment made by the Vasas to the Protestantism of the Reformation.

Since its first member acceded to the Swedish throne in 1523, the Vasa dynasty had been preoccupied with becoming a dominant power on the Baltic shores and in northern Europe. In that year King Gustavus I of Sweden went to war with Lübeck, one of the premier members of the Hanseatic League, that grouping of medieval German cities which had traditionally dominated trade and commerce in the waters of the Baltic. Almost simultaneously, decisions reached at the *Riksdag* of Västeras in 1527, and at the Synod of Örebro in 1529, brought the Swedish church into the Protestant, and Lutheran, fold.

The brief reign of Eric XIV (1560-1568), though prematurely ended by his own debilitating insanity, saw the acquisition of the port of Reval in 1561, and thus a continuation of Sweden's preoccupation with the Baltic shore. John III, Eric's brother and heir, and John's son Sigismund, king of Poland as well as Sweden, victimized a divided Russia in the Livonian Wars, in which the Swedes won a great victory at Wenden in 1578, and the port of Narva and the whole of Estonia by the Treaty of Teusina.

When King Sigismund, an avowed Catholic, attempted to restore the old religion to Sweden in 1593, the Convention of Uppsala reaffirmed the Lutheran Confession of Augsburg. Six years later when a rebellion broke out against Sigismund, Charles of Södermanland was its eventual beneficiary, becoming king of Sweden in 1604 as Charles IX.

The welfare of the house of Vasa, the protection of the Protestant faith, incipient warfare, territorial security, and expansionism—all of these were inextricably linked in the inheritance of Charles' son Gustavus Adolphus. "We strictly command you to keep God before your eyes," Charles instructed his son. Gustavus Adolphus followed his advice. He went to church twice on Sundays, heard two sermons a week, and apparently enjoyed singing hymns in a rather raucous voice. Years later when the forces of the hated and Catholic Hapsburgs seemed poised to win all of Germany, Gustavus Adolphus was seen by some Protestants as the "Lion of the North," the fulfiller of a Biblical prophecy, sent by God to wreak judgment on the Catholic Babylon to the south. Wrote the Englishman John Durye, "I make account of Your Majesty as an angel of God." While Gustavus Adolphus probably intervened in the Thirty Years' War to keep the Baltic shore out of Hapsburg hands, the religious motive was nonetheless present, although it is unknown whether he saw himself as the object of prophecy. Axel Oxenstierna, Chancellor of Sweden, put it succinctly in 1636 when he remarked that the Lutheran religion was comprehended in Sweden's quest for territorial security. For Gustavus Adolphus, as for Cromwell and other leaders of the seventeenth century, religious and political issues were but two sides of the same coin.

As with his religious experience, Gustavus Adolphus' military training dated from his youth. Charles IX saw to it that his son grew up in a distinctly masculine world, and his education was closely supervised by his father. Women never seemed to play much of a part in the life of Gustavus Adolphus.

When Gustavus Adolphus grew to manhood he had several relationships with women, and fathered an illegitimate son, but these encounters, not unusual for the time, apparently left little emotional mark. His marriage to Maria Eleonora of Brandenburg was scarred by its failure to produce a male heir. One child, a daughter named Christina, died when only twelve months old; another, also called Christina, born covered with a caul, was at first thought to be a boy, and general disappointment greeted the discovery of her true gender. The thought of leaving no male heir disturbed Gustavus Adolphus. "If anything happens to me, my family will merit your pity," he wrote plaintively to Oxenstierna. "They are womenfolk," he continued, "the mother lacking in common sense, the daughter a minor—hopeless if they rule, and dangerous if others come to rule over them." In his perception and experience of women, Gustavus Adolphus seems to have been no better than most of his contemporaries.

Nonetheless, despite their seeming narrowness, Gustavus' education and environment fitted him admirably to be both sovereign and soldier. According to Oxensteirna, he spoke Latin, German, Dutch, French, and Italian fluently, and understood Spanish and English, as well as some Russian and Polish. His tutor John Skytte drubbed the Latin classics into the head of his young charge, as well as some Greek ones. Gustavus Adolphus was also immersed in the heroic history of Sweden's past—a compound of myth and legend. At the same time, he was interested enough in his own times to write a contemporary history. Trained as well to be an effective public speaker, he could summon up effective oratory when it was required. Practical experience played a part from the beginning. At ten he was attending meetings of the royal council, and at twelve he was hearing the petitions of subjects.

A military man to his fingertips, Gustavus Adolphus grew to a physical stature greater than most of his contemporaries. Eschewing the feathers, wigs, chains, rings, and jewelry of the mass of seventeenth-century royalty, he preferred to dress like the men he led. Terribly strong, possessing a massive head set off by a reddish-blond goatee, quick to anger or to laughter, confident in his self-righteousness, abilities, and destiny, he must have been a leader unwise to cross. Like many military commanders, Gustavus Adolphus seems to have thought himself indestructible and was happiest as a man of action. "He thinks the ship cannot sink that carries him," wrote the English ambassador. "And so," Gustavus Adolphus himself wrote, "what I mean to do, I will give proof rather by deeds than upon paper."

Gustavus Adolphus was, beyond all else, well-schooled in military science and in this area made contributions that were truly innovative. John Skytte introduced his pupil to the ancient authorities on military tactics, as well as to the more modern theories of Maurice of Nassau. These newer Dutch tactics were probably modeled for Gustavus Adolphus by John of Orange and Jakob de la Gardie, who commanded in succession the Swedish armies in Livonia.

Prince Maurice of Nassau had revolutionized the military thinking of the times. His ideas revolved around the use of relatively small forces of highly-drilled and disciplined infantry and cavalry. Infantry battalions, according to Prince Maurice, should be no larger than one regiment (500 to 1,000 men), cavalry squadrons no larger than one company. Battle formations were to be well-organized; infantry, including pikemen, artillery, and musketeers, should occupy three lines in the center, with cavalry on the wings. Firing at the enemy was to take place by rank, each rank retiring to the rear of the formation to reload after firing, while the next rank moved forward to fire. In this way a constant "rolling fire" was maintained against the enemy.

Portrait of Gustavus Adolphus of Sweden.
M. Merian
Courtesy of Svenska Portrattarkivet, Stockholm.

Gustavus Adolphus modified and improved upon the ideas of Prince Maurice. He devised what was close to a national army, which allowed him to dispense with at least some of the mercenaries that dominated other forces. This Swedish army was stationed in designated regimental districts throughout the kingdom. Each unit drew recruits from its districts on the basis of the then-revolutionary idea of compulsory military service. To the infantry, Gustavus Adolphus introduced a lighter musket that did not require the cumbersome forked supports of earlier models, and achieved a more rapid rate of fire. This, in turn, allowed him to reduce the number of ranks in infantry formations further, thus increasing maneuverability. The pike, the weapon still carried by infantrymen, was shortened and became easier to use. To facilitate organization and concentrate military power, Gustavus Adolphus introduced the brigade, each of which consisted of four battalions. He added as well a genuine field artillery, largely made up of three pound cannon, easier to move than heavier pieces, and primed to fire deadly grapeshot.

Gustavus' theories were hardened and applied on the battlefield. After succeeding his father as king in 1611, he found himself committed to war with Denmark. Once the succession was settled, Gustavus repaired to the front in a sleigh covered with the black of mourning. Bad news awaited him. The port of Kalmar had fallen, Sweden had lost twenty ships, and the kingdom itself was open and undefended. It was all Gustavus Adolphus could do to prevent Christian IV from reconquering Sweden for Denmark. Assisted by the mediation of James I, the War of Kalmar came to an end with the Peace of Knared in 1613, leaving Sweden humiliated but whole.

The end of the War of Kalmar enabled Gustavus Adolphus to form an alliance with the Dutch, and to prosecute the ongoing Russian war with greater vigor. Here as well Gustavus found the Swedish position grim. Russia and its autocratic government had, since 1604, been victimized by a series of disputes over political succession known as the Time of Troubles, and both Sweden and Poland had intervened to exploit the situation to their own advantage. The Poles, the inveterate enemies of Sweden, dreamed of a union of the Polish and Russian states, while Sweden, determined at all cost to prevent it, allied itself with one of a series of claimants to the Russian throne, Vasilii Shuisky, in return for the cession of the province of Karelia. In 1610 the Swedes, together with their Russian allies, were decisively defeated at the Battle of Klusino, and the way was open for a Polish-backed tsar. Here again, Gustavus Adolphus was able to save the situation from apparent disaster. In this fortune played a part. In 1613 the Russians elected Michael Romanov tsar, dashing Polish hopes for a union of the two states, ending the Time of Troubles, and allowing the Swedes once again to pursue their territorial ambitions. In 1617, by the Peace of Stolbova, the house of Vasa was able to come away with eastern Karelia and Ingria. As a result Russia was cut off from the Baltic Sea, the Gulf of Finland became a Swedish lake, and the threat of Polish expansion was thwarted.

Not content with these gains, Gustavus Adolphus turned directly on the last of his rivals in northern Europe: the Empire of Poland. The war began in earnest in 1621 and lasted for nine years, but in the end Sweden triumphed. By the Peace of Altmark of 1629 Sweden was confirmed in her conquest of Livonia. The house of Vasa now presided over the most powerful state in northern Europe.

While he had prosecuted his wars Gustavus Adolphus had also concilliated and strengthened Sweden's internal political structure. In his Accession Charter of 1611 Gustavus Adolphus healed the conflicts that Charles IX had had with the aristocracy. In the charter he promised a limitation of royal authority and the rule of law; the Council (*riksrad*) and estates of the realm, which met in the

Riksdag, were given a voice in legislative affairs and the veto in matters of war and peace. In return for such concessions, Gustavus Adolphus and his chancellor, Oxenstierna, gained the cooperation of the powerful men of the realm, and in the practical sense lost little control over policy. At the same time both men saw to it that the administration and the courts were modernized, trade and commerce strengthened, immigration and education encouraged. By 1629 Gustavus Adolphus had indeed become the Lion of the North, determined and able to defend, and extend, his realm as opportunity arose.

The opportunity came in the form of the ongoing Thirty Years' War. This conflict, which began in 1618 soon after the Defenestration of Prague, is divided by historians into four phases: the Bohemian, 1618-1625; the Danish, 1625-1629; the Swedish, 1630-1635 and the Swedish-French, 1635-1648. During the first two phases, Gustavus, preoccupied with other matters, was an interested spectator, and the cause of the Protestant German states suffered. Initially the Protestant German states were led by Frederick of the Palatinate, elected by the Bohemians as their king and styled Frederick V. The Hapsburgs, under the newly-elected Emperor Ferdinand II, allied with Maximilian, Duke of Bavaria, and formed the Catholic League. The Hapsburg forces made short work of Frederick V, and in 1620 the forces of Frederick were defeated by the Catholic League at the Battle of White Mountain. Thereafter Frederick V, sneeringly styled as the "Winter King" for his short rule over Bohemia, was forced into exile. The Protestant Union was dissolved, and Bohemia restored to the Hapsburgs.

In 1625 Christian IV of Denmark, the old antagonist of Gustavus Adolphus, assumed the leadership of the Protestant cause against the Hapsburgs. There were, however, motives besides religious ones that caused Christian to intervene in Germany. The King of Denmark was also Duke of Holstein, a state in the extreme north of Germany, and perhaps dreamed of carving a Danish empire out of German Hapsburg lands.

Unfortunately for the Protestant cause as well as his own, Christian was no more successful than Frederick had been. Christian and his allies were successively defeated in 1626 by the Hapsburg generals Wallenstein and Tilly at Dessau and Lütner-am-Barenberge. By the end of 1627 Imperial forces had taken Holstein from Christian, and by 1629 the victory of the Hapsburg and Catholic cause was affirmed in the Edict of Restitution, in which many of the bishoprics and monasteries seized by the Protestants were restored to the Catholic Church. In addition, the Edict ordered that only Lutherans and Catholics were allowed free practice of their religions, and all other Protestant sects were proscribed. Later in the same year Christian IV agreed to the Treaty of Lübeck. In return for the restitution of his lands, Christian promised not to interfere in German affairs, and abjectly abandoned his Protestant German allies.

It was now time for Gustavus Adolphus to consider intervention in Germany, and, as he did so, a number of motivations came into play. The Swedish intervention is comprehensible at least in part as a continuation of the traditional policy of the Vasas to become the paramount power in northern Europe. Dynastic relationships with several German states were also involved. Gustavus' father had married successively into the ruling houses of the states of Holstein and the Palatinate, and Gustavus himself had married Maria Eleonora of Brandenburg. Moreover, the forces of the Catholic League had overawed or threatened the Duchy of Mecklenberg, as well as Prussia and Pomerania. The dukes of Mecklenberg were related to the house of Vasa by marriage, and Gustavus Adolphus feared that the Hapsburgs might develop a naval presence in the ports of Pomerania and Mecklenburg, and thus undermine Swedish preeminence over the Baltic shore. Conversely, if Prussia and Pomerania could be controlled by Sweden, the Baltic shores would be completely in the hands of the house of Vasa. Dynastic ambitions, questions of security, religious motivations—all of these combined with the opportunism of the moment to make intervention an undeniable temptation. On July 6, 1630, Gustavus Adolphus, thirty-five years old and at the height of his powers, landed with his invasion force on the Baltic shore at Peenemünde.

Gustavus' invasion was given financial support when he signed the Treaty of Bärwalde in early 1631 with Cardinal Richelieu of France. Richelieu, representing the French house of Bourbon, was anxious to weaken the Hapsburgs, traditionally the enemies of France, at all costs, and in the treaty Richelieu agreed to subsidize the Swedes at the rate of one million French *livres* a year. To the French, it must have seemed a sound investment, for already Gustavus Adolphus had won striking victories at Greifenhagen and Gartz, and had driven Hapsburg forces from Pomeranian territory.

In May 1631 Imperial forces captured Magdeburg, but Gustavus Adolphus countered by storming Griefswold, a key Hapsburg fortress and by overrunning Mecklenberg and restoring its Protestant ducal house. After arranging an alliance with the very reluctant Duke George of Saxony, Gustavus led 24,000 of his tired troops and 18,000 Saxons to meet 35,000 Imperial troops under Tilly at Breitenfield. There, despite the fact that the Saxons fled, the Swedish troops won the field after five hours of vicious fighting, their courage combining with the brilliant tactics of the Swedish king to produce 20,000 enemy casualties and 3,000 captives. The Swedish squares had stood solidly against repeated charges of Tilly's cavalry and hot gusts of wind, which had harassed the Swedes early in the battle, turned into the faces of the Imperialists just as Gustavus Adolphus led the charge that broke the enemy.

Shortly afterward, the Swedish armies, now being supported by alliances and troops from the Protestant German states, began a triumphal march through the heart of Catholic Germany to the Rhine. Wurzburg capitulated, then Frankfurt-am-Maine. After crossing the Rhine at Oppenheim and bloodying a Spanish Hapsburg force defending it, Gustavus Adolphus fell upon Mainz, taking it late in December.

Making Mainz the center of his administration of Germany, the Swedish king began his rule with enlightened policies. Though he seized Catholic church lands, he allowed Catholics and Lutherans alike freedom of worship. Nonetheless, there were problems. The French allies of Gustavus Adolphus, who had at first been eager enough to encourage Swedish intervention in Germany, were alarmed that a Swedish army now stood on the Rhine, a potential check on French ambitions on Germany's western borderlands.

The Hapsburgs were forced to respond as well. Wallenstein, the able and perfidious Hapsburg general, was brought out of forced retirement to face the Swedes. Tilly likewise was active and harassed the Swedish army, and the treacherous Duke George of Saxony began to treat with the Hapsburgs.

In March 1632 Gustavus Adolphus led an army out of Mainz to meet Tilly. On April 15 the King of Sweden stormed Tilly's forces at the River Lech, floating his army across the stream to win a brilliant victory and mortally wound his old foe. Two weeks later Tilly died of his wounds, despite the ministrations of a surgeon gallantly sent by his old enemy.

Only one Imperial general—Wallenstein—was left between Gustavus Adolphus and dominance over Germany, but Wallenstein proved himself troublesome. As Gustavus Adolphus set plans in motion to proceed from Bavaria down the Danube to the Hapsburg hereditary lands in Austria, Wallenstein upset the timetable by threatening Saxony. In September 1632 Wallenstein's forces repulsed those of Gustavus Adolphus at the fortress of the Alte Veste, near the strategic city of Nuremberg. For the first time, a Swedish army had lost an important battle in Germany. As desertion and disease weakened his army, Gustavus Adolphus was compelled to abandon Nuremberg, and Wallenstein invaded Saxony and captured Leipzig.

In mid-November, hearing that Wallenstein was dispersing his army to winter quarters, Gustavus Adolphus, seeing in the opportunity the hand of God, resolved to destroy his enemy. On the morning of November 16, the King of Sweden encountered the forces of Wallenstein in the mists near Lützen. After praying before his army according to his custom, Gustavus Adolphus fought his last battle. At midday the horse of the Swedish king was seen riderless on the field. Fighting desperation and anguish as well as the enemy, subordinates took command of the Swedish army and drove Wallenstein's forces from their positions, forcing him to withdraw. It was not until nightfall, according to some contemporary accounts, that the corpse of Gustavus Adolphus was found just beyond a strategic ditch, naked, his great body torn by as many as ten wounds, apparently struck down while leading a cavalry charge on the right wing.

The death of Gustavus Adolphus was followed by the death of other leaders, and the eventual betrayal of his cause. Two weeks after Lützen, Frederick V, the ill-fated Winter King, who had been the first Protestant champion, succumbed to plague and a broken heart at the age of thirty-six. Wallenstein, perhaps the most successful of Hapsburg commanders, was assassinated not long afterward, abandoned by the Emperor he had helped to save, suspected of treating with the enemy, envied and feared by others for his success and ambition. Bernard of Saxe-Weimar, who had courageously rallied Swedish forces at the victory at Lützen, went on to seize Franconia, part of the Palatinate, and the city of Regensburg, but in 1634, at the Battle of Nördlingen, the Imperialists and their Bavarian allies defeated the armies of Sweden. In May 1635 the Treaty of Prague was concluded between the Emperor and the Elector of Saxony. In return for some territorial gains, an amnesty, and a guarantee of freedom of worship for Lutherans, the Elector treacherously agreed to make common cause with the Hapsburgs against Sweden. Most other Protestant states accepted the peace.

It would be a mistake nonetheless to conclude that the campaigns of Gustavus Adolphus in Germany accomplished nothing. For the Swedish king, the protection of Protestantism and the strategic interests of his empire were one and the same, and both were given continued life through his efforts. He had kept Imperial forces from the Baltic shore, safeguarded Swedish dominance in northern Europe, and prevented the destruction of the Protestant cause in Germany. In accomplishing this he had exploited all the opportunities that had come to him, and he had made his house of Vasa a force to be reckoned with throughout Europe. It fell to Oxenstierna and the heirs of Gustavus Adolphus to make or mar what he had begun.

C. Cardinal Richelieu and the Rise of France

On September 9, 1585, perhaps on the family lands in Poitou, perhaps in Paris, a son was born to Suzanne de la Porte, daughter of a counselor of the Parlement of Paris, and to her husband Armand du Plessis, a member of the petty feudal nobility. This boy, christened Armand-Jean du Plessis de Richelieu, grew into the intense, brilliant man who, as prince of the church and first minister of France, was more responsible than any other for making the French monarchy the paramount power of western Europe.

Historians have made much of the family background of Richelieu's mother, seeing in the bourgeois, or allegedly "middle class" origins of her line, a rather strained class explanation for some of the later administrative gifts of her son. Such assumptions cannot be demonstrated or even implied. Much later, as both cardinal and statesman, Richelieu used his wealth and position to enrich himself and his relatives, to become a patron of the arts, and to erect sumptuous residences and to live opulently within them. Such actions bespeak a man whose ideals were aristocratic, not middle class. Pale, slender, with eyes looking arrogantly out over an aquiline nose and thin lips, "goatee and moustache in cavalry style," dressed in the red of a cardinal, the Richelieu the artist painted is a man aristocratic in his nature if not consistently in his background.

Richelieu, in keeping with the customs of his age, drew his values and frame of reference from his father more than his mother, and these tied him firmly to arms and the land. The family name "Plessis" means "bailey," the central defensive tower of the medieval castle, and on his father's side Richelieu had his share of roguish and violent antecedents. One of these, Antoine "the Monk," had refused the gift of an abbey to enthusiastically join in the murdering of French Protestants during the religious wars, and was himself murdered in a Paris brawl in 1576. Another relative murdered an opponent in rather imaginative style by supposedly first casting a cartwheel at his enemy while the unfortunate was crossing a stream on horseback, and then belaboring the victim to death as he struggled in the water.

Had poor health and family demands not intervened, Richelieu might have lived a military life. When an elder brother refused the bishopric of Luçon, a position which had traditionally been held by members of his line, the family began to groom Richelieu for the Church. As his father had died when he was quite young, and as the family fortunes had declined, it was a grim necessity for Luçon to remain in family hands. Obedience, however, was a quality that always characterized Richelieu, and one that, years later, he mercilessly demanded of others.

It was probably a fortunate decision. Even in a society infamous for chronic sickness, Richelieu was conspicuously unhealthy. He suffered from migraines, and perhaps epilepsy, as well as intestinal pains, boils, ulcers, hemorrhoids, and tumors. When the young man entered the College de Calvi to study theology, he did so with the support of his family, probably aware that his health made soldiering impossible, knowing full well that the Church was the only avenue of advancement left open to him. Ever after, again following the practice of the time, Richelieu responded by using the prestige of his church offices to enrich his relations.

Because of some of his later actions, many have denied the genuineness of Richelieu's religious calling, and see him as either unprincipled or hypocritical. There is an overwhelming temptation to view Richelieu as a *politique*—as the kind of man who could subordinate religious or other morality to the needs of politics or the state. The common image of Richelieu is that of a cynical and remote man, stroking one of his fourteen cats, veiled by duplicity and capable of the most unspeakable cruelties in the pursuit of his ends. What is most interesting about Richelieu, however, over and above the strange turns of his character, is how he understood, rationalized, and justified his own behavior. When these things are comprehended Richelieu emerges as a man imbued, for all his brilliance, with the ordinary values and conventions of his time.

There is no denying that some of the less edifying of human characteristics emerged in Richelieu's character. Richelieu once remarked that France had two diseases, heresy and liberty. To such apparent cynicism, Richelieu often added force. Remembered by one contemporary as "harsh Richelieu" who "had blasted men rather than governed them," and by another as one who debased the king and brought honour to the reign"; there indeed is something in Richelieu's public acts of ends justifying the means. If peasants refused to pay the taxes required by the state, fusiliers were sent to aid the tax collectors in their persuasions; when a recalcitrant Parlement refused the Cardinal's instructions, Richelieu informed its president that "I will clip your nails so close that your flesh will suffer from it." Those of Richelieu's enemies unlucky enough to be caught mouldered in jail or succumbed on the block; the heads of Huguenots rotted on pikes before the rebellious city of La Rochelle. "He does not do what he says and he does not say what he does"—so went a comment on Richelieu's duplicity. "One must sleep like a lion," Richelieu once said with elegant menace, "with open eyes."

While such a portrait is intriguing, even arresting, it is nonetheless incomplete. With Richelieu, as with many in the seventeenth century, hypocrisy, religious or otherwise, was more apparent than real. Richelieu lived when government was still intensely personal, and when religion and politics were seldom separated. Richelieu's was a personality attuned to his age: reverent to the ideas of obedience and authority, respectful of privilege but not of liberty, horrified by heresy and civil disorder, recognizing the importance of groups and institutions but not the individuals who comprised them. For Richelieu there was no clear distinction between service to church or state, to sovereign or God. The study of theology, to which Richelieu early devoted himself, carried with it an assumption of divine authority, an authority which he easily transferred to the monarchy and the state. From this it is but a short step to the theory of divinely-ordained royal absolutism elaborated by Bishop Bossuet not many years later. "I shall have no greater happiness in the world," Richelieu once assured King Louis XIII, "than in making known to Your Majesty by ever-increasing proofs that I am the most devoted subject and the most zealous servant that ever king or master had in this world."

Richelieu never was, as some have asserted, unconcerned with theology or religion. None who lived in his times could have been. "He feared hell and loved theology," so wrote one commentator, "he was not indifferent to the things of God, but his kingdom was of this world." Though Richelieu was ordained priest and consecrated bishop on the same day in rather indecent haste, and though a papal dispensation was required because Richelieu was considered too young to even be a bishop, it is wrong to conclude that he did not take his episcopal duties seriously. Richelieu arrived in his diocese to find it poor and contentious, and poor enough himself to require a loan to purchase his bishop's vestments, but before long Luçon was both reformed and reduced to obedience. To his benefice Richelieu introduced the reforms of the Council of Trent—the first bishop in France to do so. He was likewise the first French theologian to write in the language of the people, and his works, particularly his written catechism, were popular with contemporaries.

For Richelieu church and state were but two aspects of the same kingdom of God, related links in the same great chain of being. He once argued, in a rather self-serving apology to the king, that churchmen made superior servants of state because they were "more divested than any others of those personal interests which so often ruin public affairs, seeing that, celibate as they are, nothing remains to them except their souls."

In the ideal, Richelieu believed in reason and persuasion, but in fact he often found it easier to resort to force. "Authority constrains to obedience," he wrote, "but reason persuades to it. It is distinctly more sensible to govern by means which win over their wills than by those which, as a rule, drive them to action instead of leading them on." Nonetheless, despite great personal charm, Richelieu found it difficult to deal with those who most needed to be persuaded. Partly because of his many physical infirmities, partly because of the pressure of work, partly because those immediately around him were very difficult to manage, Richelieu made himself remote from many of those whose very lives were affected by his decisions. One has the impression of a man who because of his own shortcomings was impatient with those of others. "These animals," he wrote in reference to women, "are strange. Sometimes they seem incapable of doing harm because they cannot do any good, but I maintain in all good faith that there is nothing more capable of ruining a kingdom." "If an insect has bitten you," he added in reference to the troublesome in general, "you must kill it and not let others feel its sting." A victim of anxiety as well as illness, emotional, easily distraught ("He cries whenever he feels like it," wrote the Queen Mother of France), Richelieu avoided people, and by his isolation gave his acts a coldness that they might not otherwise have had.

When reason and persuasion failed, and they often did, Richelieu took refuge easily in authority and absolutism; the ultimate example of both was defined as "reason of state," which in apparent paradox did not require reason to defend it, but might well require force. Kings especially were justified in using force in pursuit of the security and peace of their states. With the monarchy thus established as the highest moral good, a king or his deputy was radically free to take whatever practical steps necessary to defend it. "In politics," Richelieu remarked, "you are impelled far more by the necessity of things than by a pre-established will." "Better than any man in the world, he distinguished between the bad and the worse, between the good and the better," so wrote Richelieu's mentor and ally Father Joseph du Tremblay. For Richelieu, the ideal minister of state could not be limited by "a cringing and scrupulous conscience," but should "pursue great things with ardour." "In Richelieu" concluded the historian David Ogg, "there was a concentration that cut through every opposition and generally reached its mark with unerring aim."

It is beyond doubt that many of Richelieu's attitudes were formed and many of his policies tempered in the difficult environment in which he rose to power. Richelieu matured in a France where the memory of the Catholic-Huguenot religious wars gave all in authority a reason to fear disorder. This fear was only partly allayed during the reign of Henry IV (1589-1610), a reign that was ended by assassination just as religious tensions were beginning to be stabilized.

Henry left a young son—Louis XIII—and a regency was set up under the control of the Queen Mother, Marie de Medici. Indolent, given to plots, the Queen Mother was herself under the control of favorites. First among them was one Concini, whose wife, the Italian Leonora Galagai, was the Queen Mother's closest friend.

Increasingly resentful over the domination of Concini and his mother, jealous that the latter loved his brother Gaston, Duke of Orléans, more than himself, King Louis XIII grew into a man of difficult disposition. Starved of affection, regularly whipped by servants on instructions of his parents, and exposed to the gross sexuality of the French court even as a young child, Louis grew from a lonely youth into an even lonelier man. He was given to bursts of sadism, as when he crushed the heads of sparrows in his hands or rode horses to death during his beloved hunts. Louis loved war and the chase; he loathed women and the court. Not unintelligent, Louis nonetheless appeared to be so, possessing a loose jaw and perpetually vacant expression that occasioned more ridicule than sympathy. The former impression was strengthened by some of his acts. On hearing of the death of Concini and thus the end of his minority, Louis proclaimed his kingship from atop a billiard table.

Likewise troubled was Anne of Austria, whose poor fortune it was to become Louis XIII's wife. Despite a variety of inveiglements and inducements, Louis could not be persuaded for years to enter his wife's bed. Denied the heir that would give her power, Anne joined in the plotting that ran rampant through the court.

Finally, there was Gaston of Orléans. Gaston was given to conspiracies and rebellions against his brother, and he indulged this penchant with some frequency. He survived nonetheless, protected from the brother he hated by the Queen Mother who adored him. In and out of exile, his appetite for the throne whetted by his brother's determined childlessness, Gaston inevitably became the focus for factions in the nobility seeking freedom from royal authority.

Difficult though these personalities were, they were perhaps less significant than the religious and political forces that swept across France. First among these were the nobility, a perpetually rebellious group, exempt from state service and taxation, hostile to the idea of a strong monarchy. Restive as well were the Huguenots, the French Calvinists who had been guaranteed their religious privileges under the Edict of Nantes. Obstreperous and militarily powerful, they skulked behind the walls of their fortified towns, arousing the jealousy and fear of the French Catholic majority.

Even among the Catholics there was the potential for disorder. Among the disparate groups within French Catholicism there were several that experienced a strong religious revival in the early years of the seventeenth century. While on one level this revival was humane and gentle, distinguished by the participation of accomplished women and encouraged by the efforts of leaders like St. Francois de Sales, it also had its more political aspects.

Ironically, Henry IV, despite the fact that he had been born a Huguenot, and despite the fact that Jesuit priests tried to murder him in 1595, converted to Catholicism for political reasons and readmitted the exiled Jesuits to France. In the years thereafter he allowed Jesuit colleges to be founded, and even endowed one himself. The Edict of Nantes, which guaranteed the Huguenots full religious and civil privileges, was balanced by the Edict of Rouen, which allowed the Jesuits full access to France. Henry hoped that such a balanced policy would end the religious animosity that had brought on years of civil war, but in the end he made both Catholics and Huguenots more dangerous. The Huguenots fortified the towns promised them in the Edict of Nantes. The Jesuits preached Ultramontanism, the idea that the pope was supreme in all matters, hence they gave encouragement to yet another Catholic faction, called the *devôts,* who believed in applying Catholic principles to political problems. In their zeal, the *devôts* affected French policy internally and externally, demanding suppression of the Huguenots on the one hand and friendship with the Catholic Hapsburgs on the other. The latter policy horrified other Frenchmen, more used to viewing the Spanish and German Hapsburgs as enemies and worried over Hapsburg armies to the south and to the east.

Through all of these restive personalities and groups, Richelieu threaded his way to power. After proving himself a model bishop at Luçon, Richelieu emerged as the champion of the French clergy, known as the First Estate, and acquired the powerful friendship of Father Joseph du Tremblay, a leading figure in French Catholicism. The young bishop also increased his popularity with the *devôts* by advocating anti-Huguenot policies. Richelieu next began to flatter the Queen Mother, praising her government and supporting her Spanish marriage policy; he also attached himself to Concini, her foppish favorite. His rise was rapid. In February of 1615 Richelieu gave the final address for the First Estate at the meeting of the *Estates-General.* Early in the next year he was made chaplain to Anne of Austria, and then secretary of state.

Richelieu's tenure as secretary coincided with a war between Spain and Venice, the latter an ally of France. The struggle played a large part in the development of Richelieu's ideas on foreign policy. He learned for the first time the dangers of Hapsburg encirclement, and thus the need to oppose Hapsburg policy at every opportunity.

Such lessons were interrupted by the actions of Louis XIII who, in a palace revolution in April 1617, proclaimed himself king in fact as well as in name. Concini was shot dead on Louis' instructions, and the king dealt with the rest of the opposition with real, if temporary, thoroughness. Concini's wife, the Queen Mother's best friend, was tried as a witch, while Marie de Medici and Richelieu were banished to separate exiles.

The fall from grace, fortunately for Richelieu, was comparatively short-lived. When Marie de Medici became the focus of noble plots against him in 1619, Louis XIII bid Richelieu to rejoin her court as a moderating influence. During the next years, Richelieu benefited from the largess of the Queen Mother as well as her royal son, obtaining both the red hat of the cardinal and increasing influence in the king's councils.

In 1624 another diplomatic crisis, the Valtellina Affair, gave Richelieu opportunity for further advancement, and he was propelled to the secretaryship for commerce and marine affairs, and to the first seat on the royal council. Valtellina was a strategic valley lying within the Swiss cantons, or states, which was coveted by the Spanish Hapsburgs. One of these cantons, Grisons, appealed for French aid against the Spanish. At this point the Valtellina affair became a case study of how foreign relations can affect the internal politics of states. The French Huguenots sided with Grisons, while the *devóts* voiced their opposition to any French action against the Hapsburgs. Richelieu, appalled that this foreign crisis might aggravate internal tensions, his convictions reinforced as to the reality of the Hapsburg threat, and realizing that inaction would please neither the *devóts* nor the Huguenots, promptly dispatched French troops to the Valtellina and routed the Hapsburgs. The Valtellina Affair became the model for Richelieu's future policy. For Richelieu, Huguenot and Hapsburg became as two sides of the same coin: alike in the sense that both threatened the security of the French state. Furthermore, at least to Richelieu, the solution of one problem simplified the solution of the other. "So long as they have a foothold in France," Richelieu wrote of the Huguenots, "the king will not be master in his own house *and will be unable to undertake any great enterprise abroad.*" The Huguenots and the Hapsburgs stood in the way of France; accordingly, both would be attacked. Richelieu thus proceeded to "unstring the Spanish rosary" abroad while he proscribed the Huguenots at home.

When in 1627 the Huguenot city of La Rochelle revolted against the monarchy and sought help from the English, Richelieu saw it as a heaven-sent justification for breaking Huguenot power in France. As Richelieu's troops laid seige to the city, the Hapsburgs took advantage of French preoccupations and seized the fortress of Casale in northern Italy. When La Rochelle fell, Richelieu sent his troops southward to check the Hapsburg advances, and the Hapsburgs for their part sent their troops into Lorraine, claimed by the French as a royal fief.

With La Rochelle humbled, Richelieu forced upon the Huguenots the Grace of Ales, which preserved their religious privileges but denied them the military and political powers granted by the Edict of Nantes. Angered by what she thought was a moderating policy toward the Huguenots, jealous of the growing power of her former protégé, Marie de Medici turned on Richelieu and became the focus of opposition to him. In a curious episode called the "Day of Dupes," she locked the bemused Louis XIII in a room in Luxembourg Palace and used all of her powers of persuasion to destroy Richelieu's position. Apprised of what the Queen Mother was doing, Richelieu found his way into the chamber by an unguarded back stair. In his presence, the Queen Mother lost her temper and lost her case. Soon after, Marillac, the royal favorite who was an obstacle to Richelieu's further advancement, fell from grace, and by 1632 both Marie de Medici and the rebellious Gaston of Orléans were in exile. Richelieu was without peer in power, answering only to the king.

Richelieu then turned on the Hapsburgs with full concentration. In this aim, he conjured up the precedent of the old Roman province of Gaul, arguing that France's borders should be congruent with it, and should reach the Alps, the Rhine, and the Pyrenees. "I wished to restore to Gaul the limit which nature designed for her," he wrote, ". . . to identify Gaul with France." The Thirty Years' War gave Richelieu the opportunity to weaken the Hapsburgs and attempt to extend French borders. He allied with the Protestant German states against their Hapsburg emperor, and he signed treaties in which he subsidized the military adventures of Gustavus Adolphus. After the death of the Swedish king at Lützen, Richelieu found a new champion in Bernhard of Saxe-Weimar. After Bernhard's death the French took over his army directly.

While he fought the Hapsburgs, Richelieu enjoyed limited success in other areas. In economic matters Richelieu was unoriginal, following the mercantilist theory of the time. Mercantilists believed that economies should be organized by the state, that states should export more than they import, maintain their defenses and currencies by keeping large reserves of precious metals, found colonies to guarantee the availability of raw materials for manufacturing, and maintain full employment to insure economic health and political stability. Accordingly Richelieu set up manufacturing enterprises of various kinds: for glass, for silk, for fine carpets. Richelieu believed in sea power, and he can rightly be called the father of the French navy and merchant marine. Believing that colonies were important, he fostered the growth of colonies in Canada and the West Indies. Richelieu did much else: he organized a postal service and tried to proscribe the senseless and violent pastime of dueling; he spent much of his substance on art and architecture, music and literature, religious foundations and the work of saints. A far-reaching system of laws, the *Code Michaud,* which attempted to regulate everything from the Church to weights and measures, came into use during his tenure. Finally, Richelieu founded the French Academy, one of the cornerstones of French culture.

Richelieu did not live to see the fruits of what he had begun. Burdened by his many physical afflictions, he survived the last of several conspiracies against him, that of his former favorite, Cinq-Mars, but died in 1642. In the weeks before the end, Richelieu grew frail and had to be carried from place to place. Louis XIII, perhaps realizing what he owed his minister, fed the enfeebled cardinal the yoke of an egg in the days before he died. After confessing that he had no enemies save those who had opposed the state, Richelieu died a firm Catholic, having designated Mazarin, another churchman and diplomat, his successor.

"He died at length prematurely, and in the midst of all these turmoils," Voltaire wrote, "leaving all his schemes incomplete and his name powerful and feared, rather than revered and loved." For Richelieu, participation in the Thirty Years' War had been but part of a larger effort to check Hapsburg dominance. This ambition, in turn, was rooted at the center of Richelieu's policy of state: the protection and enlargement of the French monarchy. In time, the work of Richelieu succeeded handsomely. By the Peace of Westphalia of 1648 the states of Germany were freed from effective Hapsburg control and France gained territory on her eastern borderlands: Richelieu had marched French troops into Lorraine in 1634, now other territory, including most of Alsace, was added to it. In 1659 Richelieu's disciple Mazarin negotiated the Peace of the Pyrenees, adding to France Artois in the north and Cerdagne and Roussilon in the south. French power extended toward the Rhine; the Hapsburg threat was ended. Little surprise that an Englishman called Richelieu the "torment and the ornament of his age" and wondered how in death he could be "shut up . . . in so small a place, whom living, the whole earth could not contain."

D. Queen Christina and Her Successors: Abdication and Expansionism in Sweden

As Richelieu was making his way to power in France, Gustavus Adolphus and his wife Maria Eleonora of Brandenburg anxiously awaited the birth of what the astrologers assured them would be a son. They had been disappointed before, and would be again. Two years earlier, in 1624, Maria Eleonora, big with child, had undertaken a sea voyage, and the violence of a sudden storm had caused her to miscarry. "Jesus," Maria Eleonora had been said to lament, "I cannot feel my child." The result, as if in punishment for the curse, had been a son born dead. Thereafter Maria Eleonora walked on the edge of hysteria, paradoxically growing more attached to the husband who, put off by her simpering and her failure to give birth to a living heir, sought solace in long absences and in war.

Then, in 1626, there had come another chance. At first, in testimony to the tension surrounding the birth, the child, born covered with hair and a caul, screaming and ugly, was thought to be a boy. Then came the horrible realization that the infant was a girl. Fearing the king's rage, the midwives refused to carry the infant out of the birth chamber. Finally, one of the child's aunts bore the baby to Gustavus Adolphus, and held the child speechlessly before him, so he could discover the gender for himself. Maria Eleonora, weakened from the labor, was not told for a while longer, because of fears that the woman might reject her child or leap into madness.

It is of importance that this child, named Christina as was a sister who had died in infancy, was never genuinely accepted by either parent. Even under the best of circumstances it might have been expected that Christina, like most royal children of her times, would have been sent out to wet-nurse and then maintained in a separate household; but separation is not the same as rejection, and Christina was made to feel both.

At first Gustavus Adolphus, contrary to the fears of the royal household, seemed to accept, even jest about, the gender of his child. "She will undoubtedly be a clever woman," he remarked, playing on the popular prejudice that woman were naturally conniving, "for even at her birth she has succeeded in deceiving us all." In fact, however, he insisted that the little girl, when older, be educated exactly as if she were a prince. Christina's tutors were hand-picked by her father, and she learned tactics, fencing, shooting, and what today would pass for political science.

Christina's identification with traditionally masculine occupations was enhanced by the mixture of contempt and pity with which her father regarded her mother, and by her fascination with the father who was so often absent on long campaigns. "He subjected every one and every thing . . . ," she wrote in envy years later. "His ambition was even greater than his strength . . . but not greater than his good fortune."

Portrait of Queen Christina of Sweden.
David Beck
Courtesy of Svenska Portrattarkivet, Stockholm.

To Christina, a large part of her father's good fortune must have been in being born a man, away from and free of the life she knew with Maria Eleonora. For the mother who rejected her, yet smothered her with her presence and disapproval, she developed a quiet loathing. "The Queen, my mother," Christina wrote in her autobiography, "who, apart from the virtues of her sex, had all the vices of it as well, was unconsolable at my birth. She could not bear me, for I was a daughter and ugly." Of her physical unattractiveness Christina became early convinced, describing herself at birth in the racist style of the time as "dark as a little Moor." Later on, she referred to herself as the ugliest girl at court. This conviction was strengthened by several unfortunate accidents. While still an infant, she was dropped on the floor, a mishap that crushed her shoulder. The slight disfigurement that resulted caused her as an adult to cover the marred shoulder with cumbersome and unbecoming clothes. This accident, as well as another, in which a beam fell from the ceiling and barely missed the cradle in which the infant Christina was sleeping, convinced her when older that her mother might have wished her dead.

While she was still a child, Christina lost her father when he fell at the Battle of Lützen. His early death reduced Maria Eleonora to paroxysms of grief, morbidity, and hysteria. Queen Eleonora promptly departed to fetch her husband's body, and, on her orders or those of others, the heart of Gustavus Adolphus was taken from the corpse, embalmed, and placed in a gold casket. This, in turn, was suspended from the ceiling in the royal chamber, immediately above the bed which Christina was then forced to share with her grieving mother. Possessing full measures of the morbidity and fascination with the grotesque that characterized the seventeenth century, Maria Eleonora for days refused to bury her husband's body, and for years afterward had her rooms darkened and draped in black. Through these palled chambers moved not only Maria Eleonora's hushed servants, but also her coterie of dwarfs. It was to this unearthly environment that Maria Eleonora summoned her daughter, insistent that the child she had refused to accept join her in her mourning.

It is not surprising that Christina's mother excited little in her daughter but rebellion. There must have been a deeply-felt need to reject the mother who rejected her. This, in turn, dovetailed nicely with Christina's interests and abilities, which lay well outside the traditional "women's sphere." ". . . I had an unconquerable aversion . . . to everything women do or talk about," she wrote later. "I was so awkward with needlework that I could never learn to do it properly. But when I was only fourteen years old . . . I showed a marked talent for science and physical exercises and games of all sorts."

The academic study on which Gustavus Adolphus had insisted became for Christina a means of escape: ". . . my studies were an excuse to leave my mother," Christina later wrote, "and to get away from her depressing apartments. . . ." For many, the thought of studying for up to six hours a day, which was Christina's norm, would be appalling, but for Christina the long hours of tutoring became associated with freedom and independence, a sphere in which she could demonstrate her superiority over her childhood peers and enter a realm usually reserved only for men.

As she grew older, Christina's energy became even more astounding. She existed on as little as three hours of sleep a night, and on sporadic and incomplete meals. As a queen she horrified the English envoy Bulstrode Whitelocke when she kept a newly-married couple from their wedding night, forcing them to dance and feast until dawn. The French mathematician Descartes, summoned to Sweden at Christina's insistence, was driven to distraction, and possibly to his death from pneumonia, by several royal summons to Christina's frigid chambers at five o'clock in the morning, there to discuss philosophy. The French ambassador, likewise obliged to come to court, was treated to a medley of obscene French songs by Christina's ladies-in-waiting, who had been tutored by their uncontrollable mistress. Horses fared no better. On hunts, Christina could remain in the saddle for ten hours at a time. Neither in the realm of thought or action was Christina prepared to defer to men. But her health often broke; she suffered from recurrent fevers, pleurisy, headaches, colitis, fainting and convulsions, and measles and chicken pox scarred her body.

Confusion reigns as to Christina's true sexual identity, and it is possible that it puzzled even her. Made to feel ashamed at being born unattractive and female, yet criticized for her purportedly "masculine" nature; brought up like a man, but expected to be womanly, Christina was bound to experience confusion as to her real relationship to either sex. Her subsequent behavior raises as many questions as it has answered.

Some have concluded that Christina was a lesbian. Bulstrode Whitelocke, the English envoy to Sweden, recounted being introduced to the Countess Ebba Sparre by the Queen, who admonished him to "Discourse with this lady, my bedfellow, and tell me if her inside be not as beautiful as her outside." Other sources emphasize, in contrast, Christina's close relationship to Magnus de la Gardie, the scion of a French family that had settled in Sweden, whom she made a royal favorite, showered with gifts, and sent abroad as ambassador to France.

One suspects that the accusations of homosexuality made against Christina are due as much to her intellectual interests and dress as to the testimony of men like Whitelocke. "There is nothing feminine about her except her sex . . . ," wrote one contemporary of Christina, "her voice, her manner of speaking, her walk, her style, her ways are all quite masculine." Another witness wrote of the Swedish Queen that "science is to her what needle and thread are to other women." It is questionable, however, whether mannerisms or intellectual interests should be an infallible guide to sexual preference. What seemed to cause the most resentment of Christina, whatever the truth regarding her sexual nature, was that she consistently violated the social conventions thought appropriate to her time and sex.

It is true that Christina fled from marriage, but in the seventeenth century especially this should not necessarily be considered evidence of lesbianism. In an age when very many woman died of childbirth or its consequences it is not outrageous to believe that an independent woman, and a queen, could assert as Christina did "that she would never submit to be treated the way a peasant treats his field when planting seeds." For Christina to say that she "would rather choose death than a man" should not be surprising in an era when marriage and female mortality were so closely connected. There was as well an ample precedent for Christina's refusal of marriage. Queen Elizabeth I of England, of whom Christina read as a child, had done precisely the same thing a century before.

What emerges most strongly about Christina is lack of confidence and comfort in other human beings, regardless of their sex. "It is as dangerous to be good to people as it is to caress wild animals," she noted in an aphorism. "Men would not be fruitless and deceiving if they were not weak and stupid," she added on another occasion. Unsure of her own role, Christina suspected the motives of others. A disturbing cynicism about human motivation characterized Christina. She once remarked that "children who await the succession to a crown are easily consoled for the loss of a father."

Mistrust of others made the ideal of royal absolutism, the prevailing political theory of seventeenth-century Europe, seem doubly attractive to Christina. "Only kings should direct," she admonished, "all others should obey and carry out their orders." Writing of Christina's subjects, Whitelocke added, "They seldom differ or dissent from what the Queen proposes, so great is her influence over them." Impressed by the example of Cardinal Richelieu and his successor Mazarin, Christina also perceived the advantage of connecting royal sovereign power with spiritual authority. This, in turn, led the daughter of the Protestant champion Gustavus Adolphus to convert in secret to the Roman Catholic faith.

"I had a mortal hatred for the long and frequent sermons of the Lutherans." In this way Christina summed up her attitude to the religion of her parents and of her state. As a woman who loved philosophy, she found the philosophical-theological bent of Catholicism attractive; as a human being who had experienced rejection and doubts as to who she really was, it was an ultimate certainty. Her conversion was also the ultimate act of freedom; an act of rejection against those who had rejected her. To accept the Roman Catholic faith, as Christina well knew, would make her abdication to the Swedish throne inevitable. A Catholic sovereign could not rule over such a staunchly Lutheran land. Slowly, in Christina's mind, there emerged a plan to convert and abdicate, and to do both in such a way as to leave her land with enough wealth to support her for the rest of her life.

Christina's refusal to marry, and her plans to abdicate, were thus closely linked and long-lived; both constituted a refusal of roles that society had placed upon her. Finally, and most importantly, both served to confound the aims of Swedish foreign policy toward Germany and to reorient that policy toward northern Europe.

As early as 1647 Christina told her cousin Charles Gustavus, who most considered to be her probable husband, that she would marry him only if made to do so by reasons of state. Had she married Charles, at once the son of a sister of Gustavus Adolphus, a scion of the German noble house of Wittelsbach, and a descendent of no less than four Holy Roman Emperors, Sweden's involvement in Germany, begun so boldly by Christina's father, might have continued. Had this or another mooted marriage, that between Christina and the electoral prince of Brandenburg, in fact taken place, Sweden might have become the most powerful state in Europe, straddling the Baltic, dominating Germany, challenging France, even controlling elections to the Imperial throne itself.

Christina, by her refusal of matrimony, made all of this unlikely; she made it even more impossible by two other actions: her persistent extravagance and her insistence on making peace with the Hapsburgs in Germany. Before Christina came to the throne the expenses of the Swedish court amounted to 3.1 percent of the national income. By the end of her reign they had quadrupled. When her expenses were combined with those of Charles Gustavus and the Queen Mother, they amounted to fully 20 percent of the national income. Christina showered largesse on poets and painters, philosophers and favorites. By the end of her reign, half of the crown lands had been given away.

This kind of extravagance, combined with the expense of years of war and Christina's conversion to Catholicism, moved her to encourage peace between the Hapsburgs and the house of Vasa. Negotiations to that effect had begun as early as 1643, before Christina had grown old enough to assume full royal power, but it was only in 1648, by the Peace of Westphalia, that the war in Germany was ended. Christina used all of her influence on the side of peace, irritating the Chancellor of Sweden, Oxenstierna, with what he saw as unpardonable interference.

Under the terms of the several treaties that made up the Peace of Westphalia, the Hapsburgs made peace with both France and Sweden, and the two latter powers made gains in territory. France received the bishoprics and cities of Metz, Toul, and Verdun in Lorraine, as well as the Pignerol, the city of Breisach, and much of

Alsace. Sweden received the bishoprics of Bremen and Verden, and the western part of Pomerania, including the city of Stettin.

The real significance of the treaties of Westphalia, however, lay in the virtual destruction of the Holy Roman Empire, the complex ruling institution that the Hapsburgs had used to dominate Germany for centuries. From this France gained much, and Sweden much less. The individual German states within the Holy Roman Empire became sovereign powers, and two of them, Brandenburg and Bavaria, gained greatly in prestige. The Dutch provinces and the Swiss Cantons, long reluctant members of the Holy Roman Empire, were granted sovereign status. Among such divisions, it was difficult if not impossible for Sweden or any other power to dominate Germany any time in the future.

To ensure the destruction of the Holy Roman Empire as an economic entity, the river mouths leading out of Germany were placed in non-German hands. The Scheldt went to the Dutch; the Oder, Elbe, and Weser to Sweden.

The last remaining bond of the Holy Roman Empire—that of the Catholic religion—was also irrevocably broken at Westphalia. The terms of the Peace of Augsburg of 1555, which had granted status to Lutherans in the Holy Roman Empire, were reaffirmed and extended: Calvinism was added to Catholicism and Lutheranism as a legitimate faith. The Pope and his emissaries were ignored in all the treaty negotiations, and the terms of the treaties themselves marked the demise of the Catholic Reformation in Germany.

No German Hapsburg could now check French designs in western or central Europe, and the house of Bourbon could now concentrate its attention on the Spanish Hapsburgs to the south. While Sweden's territorial gains were significant at Westphalia, they lay on the Baltic shore, thus predisposing Sweden to pursue her more traditional ambitions in northern Europe and the Baltic, rather than to poke about in the ruins of the Holy Roman Empire. Though both were long dead, it was the policy of the diplomat Richelieu, not that of the conqueror Gustavus Adolphus, that triumphed at Westphalia.

With the treaties of Westphalia signed, Christina turned to a realm divided by war and conflict. The traditional alliance between the house of Vasa and the Swedish nobility, symbolized in the partnership between Gustavus Adolphus and Oxenstierna, strained by constant war and Christina's extravagance, lay in ruins. In 1649, she obliged the nobility to accept Charles Gustavus as her heir by using the threat of a "reduction," or reassumption of lands by the crown. In the summer of 1654, assured of a handsome income by the Swedish government, she abdicated her throne and left her country in secret.

Thereafter, Christina traveled through Antwerp, Brussels, eventually making her way to Rome. At Innsbrück, on the borders of Italy, she abjured Lutheranism and declared her conversion to Roman Catholicism. During the many years afterward, she led a life at once urbane and coarse, serious and frivolous. She patronized the likes of the architect Bernini and the composers Alessandro Scarlatti and Arcangelo Corelli; she intrigued for the thrones of Naples and Poland; she traveled to France and wore out her welcome by having a treasonous servant stabbed to death in her presence; she returned to Sweden twice, to see to her economic interests and, one suspects, to scheme. Insistent at once on her queenly dignity and her freedom to wear men's clothes, Christina bothered, offended, awed, or bewildered all who came into contact with her. A meeting with Christina, it seems, was not easily forgotten. "She knows more than our Academy with the Sorbonne added"—so wrote an admiring French nobleman. A Roman cardinal, more bemused, fell in love with her. When her income from Sweden was temporarily cut off, she threatened to lead an army against King Charles XI, the son of the man she had made heir to her throne, and was dissuaded only by a papal pension. A fascinating figure to the last, a refugee from the conventions and obligations imposed by her time, and the duties of her rank and sex, Christina died in Rome at the age of sixty-three in 1689. The daughter of Gustavus Adolphus was interred in St. Peter's Basilica.

Christina's reign and personality forced Swedish foreign policy back into traditional grooves as her successors focused Swedish expansionism once again on northern Europe and the Baltic. The reign of Charles X (1654-1660), Christina's cousin and heir, was marked by the First Northern War, in which Swedish forces, in alliance with those of Brandenburg, pressed deeply into Poland and won a great victory before Warsaw.

Frightened by Swedish success, the Russians and the Danes allied against Charles. Brandenburg was wooed away by the promise of Polish recognition of her sovereignty over East Prussia, and Sweden found herself virtually isolated. Thereafter came a series of expensive and bloody campaigns in which the Swedes were forced to retreat from Poland, and Denmark was twice invaded. Peace was restored only after Charles' death by the Treaty of Oliva (1660). Under its terms Poland ceded Livonia to Sweden. In 1661, by the Treaty of Copenhagen, Sweden obtained the southern part of the Scandinavian peninsula, and in the same year, at Kardis, the Swedes made a treaty with the Russians on the basis of the *status quo ante bellum.*

Charles' son and namesake continued the policy of northern expansionism that his father had resumed. He also established the kind of royal absolutism that Christina had found so attractive. When Louis XIV undertook the first of his wars with the Dutch in 1672, Charles XI allied with the French and attacked the old Swedish ally of Brandenburg. In 1675 the forces of the Elector of Brandenburg inflicted a major defeat on the Swedes at Fahrbellin and thereafter captured much of the territory that Sweden had obtained at Westphalia. Only the aid and diplomatic support of the French enabled Sweden to recover her lost Pomeranian lands in the Treaty of St. Germain-en-Laye.

By the time of the death of Charles XI in 1697, Sweden appeared to be the most powerful state in northern Europe. Denmark and Poland had been weakened by years of conflict, and Russia seemed wrapped in a cloak of ignorance and barbarism. Despite the immense cost of nearly a century of war, it seemed that nothing could halt continued Swedish expansion in northern Europe.

E. Russia in Europe: Autocracy, Orthodoxy, and Peter the Great

With fear, fascination, and misunderstanding, western Europeans contemplated the vast lands of Russia to the east. Indeed, out of a monumental arrogance and unfairness, many Europeans saw Russia, quite wrongly, as outside the sphere of Europe altogether. As for Russia's Slavic majority, western Europeans likewise had little positive or knowledgeable to say. Russia, quite simply, was another world, inhabited by a people considered barbarous and brutish, steeped in superstition, erratically guided by a form of Christianity that few in the west could comprehend, grudgingly admired only for their endurance and their occasional bravery in battle. The Russians returned this contempt and ignorance in kind. In Russia, all westerners, regardless of geographic origin, were referred to as "Germans," or *nemtsy* ("dumb ones").

In fact, Russia's connection to the rest of Europe, despite this sense of mutual separateness, lies in common experiences running deep into the past. By the seventh century the Vikings, that kindred group of peoples from Scandinavia who did so much to alter the histories of early Britain and France, had found their way eastward to the lands of the eastern Slavs. These conquerors, known as Varangians in Russian history, penetrated into the river systems of what we now know as Russia, establishing trading settlements and forcing their authority on Slav settlements like Novgorod. In so doing, they gave Russia its English name: ". . . these particular Varangians were known as *Rus.*" Thus runs an early source, the *Primary Chronicle.* The word *Rus,* derived perhaps from a Finnish word meaning "those who rowed," came to refer to all the land occupied or claimed by the eastern Slavs. In 862, according to the chronicles, the Varangian prince, Rurik, became ruler of the eastern Slavs on the banks of the Dneiper River, making Novgorod his capital.

The land over which Rurik and his successors ruled was in no sense a unified state. Various parts of *Rus* fell under the sway of princes of powerful cities—Kiev and Pskov, Novgorod and Suzdal and, finally, Moscow. Finns, Lithuanians, Poles, and Germans pushed into *Rus* at various times, and with various results. As these cities and peoples competed and traded, waxed and waned, they were affected by forces that would help fuse *Rus* into something like a unity.

One of these forces was Christianity. In 988 Vladimir, Grand Prince of Kiev, then the most powerful ruler in *Rus,* was converted to Greek Orthodox Christianity. His people were converted *en masse* and immediately, according to one source, "wept for joy." Thereafter, Orthodoxy cut a swath of conversion throughout all *Rus.* Vladimir's choice of Orthodox Christianity was significant. Centered at Constantinople, Greek Orthodoxy was the state religion of the Byzantine Empire or, as it is sometimes known, the Roman Empire in the East. The Byzantine Emperors had established a unique relationship between Orthodoxy and themselves, between church and state. Unlike the popes and bishops of the Roman Catholic Church, who asserted their independence of, and superiority to, secular rulers, the patriarchs and metropolitans of Orthodoxy were expected to defer to the authority of the ultimate secular ruler, the Byzantine emperor. This idea of state dominance over the Church is known as *caesaropapism,* and the concept sparked the imaginations of the princes of *Rus.*

This was especially true of the grand dukes of Moscow, who had been competing with the rulers of other cities for the dominance of *Rus.* In 1396 the Orthodox Church in Russia was persuaded to move from Kiev to Moscow, making it possible for the latter city to claim that it was the religious capital of all Russia. It was a symbolic step in the political aggrandizement of the grand dukes of Moscow.

Orthodoxy was an important symbol for unity precisely because after 1240 Russia experienced another great invasion. In that year the Golden Horde of the Tatars swept into *Rus,* conquered Kiev, and established a tribute-paying "yoke" on most of the other cities, extorting money and deference.

The massive Tatar invasion, combined with the great Schism of 1054, which irrevocably divided Orthodox and Catholic Christians, served to isolate Russia from the west and to heighten Russian suspicion and ignorance of the peoples beyond their western frontiers. Russian suspicion turned to violent resistance when the rulers of Catholic Poland and Sweden seized Russian borderlands, and German religious orders like the Teutonic and Livonian knights, given sanction to do violence to non-Catholics by papal dispensation, began their *drang nach osten,* their "drive to the east," into the lands of Russia. In 1242 the first legitimate Russian hero, Alexander Nevsky, defeated the Teutonic Knights at Lake Peipus.

Resistance to the outsider thus formed an impetus to Russian unity. Here, as with the religious issue, the grand dukes of Moscow proved apt pupils, and they manipulated both in a successful bid to dominate all Russia. By the 1440s the grand dukes of Moscow were installing their own candidates as head of the Russian Orthodox Church, doing so without the approval of either the Roman Emperor in the East or the Orthodox Patriarch in Constantinople. When, in 1453, the Turks conquered Constantinople itself, leaving Orthodox Christianity without a center and destroying the Byzantine Empire, Moscow proclaimed itself the "Third Rome," and in so doing declared its rulers to be heirs to the Caesars and the overlords of Orthodox Christians everywhere. Moscow thus became the arbiter of Orthodoxy or *pravoslavie,* the latter term literally translated as "the right praising of God." The process was completed when Ivan III of Moscow married Zoe, the niece of the last Roman Emperor in the East, took the title of *Tsar* (from the Latin "Caesar"), and adopted the bicapitate eagle, the insignia of the ancient Roman legions, as the seal of state.

Ivan III and his successors backed their imperial pretensions with conquests over foreign and domestic foes. By 1480 Ivan III had thrown off the hated Tatar yoke. Even before this, an obliging Metropolitan of Moscow had proclaimed a religious crusade against the rival city of Novgorod, and in 1471 its proud rulers had to sue for peace. Ivan's son and successor, Vasily III, seized Pskov, Ryazan, and Smolensk, incorporating them into Muscovy.

It fell to Ivan IV, the next tsar, who took power in 1547, to push the powers of Moscow, and of the tsarist autocracy itself, to new limits. Ivan IV, sometimes known by the appellation "the Terrible," allowed no opposition to his rule. While his predecessors had been obliged to share power with the *boyars,* the great nobles who controlled the mass of the land, Ivan the Terrible attacked their prerogatives and powers, and confiscated their estates for his own. The lesser landowners, the "sons of boyars" and the *dvoriane,* were enlisted by Ivan IV as allies against their social and economic superiors. From the *oprichnina,* those lands confiscated by the tsar and controlled personally by him, issued scores of Ivan's loyal henchmen, the *oprichniki.* Known as the "Black Hundreds" because of their black mounts and uniforms, wearing the sign of the dog's head and bearing symbolic brooms to "sweep treason from the land," the *oprichniki* unleashed a reign of terror and quelled all opposition.

Hating the boyars because they had treated him with contempt in his minority, Ivan began to order their deaths as early as his thirteenth year. Thereafter, recalcitrant boyars were liable to find themselves beheaded or impaled upon stakes. Nor was operation from the church hierarchy or the ruling family tolerated. The Orthodox Metropolitan of Moscow was murdered on Ivan's orders, and the tsar himself battered his son to death with his staff. Thus was laid the foundation for the absolute rule of the tsar—the autocracy—that characterized Russia down to 1917.

Ivan IV also expanded his empire and opened Russia to the west, and, by his actions, helped set the direction of Russian foreign policy for centuries to come. Ivan founded the port of Archangel on the White Sea to encourage trade. He seized the khanates of Kazan and Astrakhan, extending the power of Moscow toward the Caspian and Black seas. Less successfully, Ivan tried to capture a part of the Baltic shore by picking a quarrel with the Livonian Knights. Though Ivan's forces temporarily captured the key port of Narva, they did so only at the cost of involving Russia in a war with Sweden, Lithuania, and Denmark. Ivan had to sue for peace, and watched Estonia pass to Sweden, Ösel to Denmark, and Livonia to Lithuania. Nonetheless, the Russian quest for the Baltic shore had begun, a quest that would continue under Ivan's successors. Finally, under careful state control, trading agreements were made between Russia and companies of English and Dutch traders. Ivan himself even proposed marriage, quite unsuccessfully, to his sixteenth-century contemporary, Elizabeth I of England.

While the rulers of Moscow consolidated their power and expanded their domains, relationships upon the land also changed as the *smerd,* the Russian free peasant of old, was reduced to a bound chattel in the emerging institution of serfdom. Ivan and his successors contributed to this long-term development by decreeing that during certain "forbidden years" peasants could not move from the estates on which they labored. Ivan, following the lead of his predecessors, and setting a precedent for his successors, helped transform the Russian peasant from a free laborer into a virtual slave, completely controlled by those on whose lands they labored. Left alone by the autocracy to work their will on the serfs on their own estates, the landowning classes proved less and less likely to interfere with the prerogatives of the tsar. A bargain was thus struck, for which the Russian peasant, reduced to a bound laborer, paid the price. "The sovereign is the father, the earth the mother." So runs the Russian proverb, descriptive of the plight of the serf who was subordinate both to the tsar and the soil of the great estates.

By the time of Ivan's death in 1584 the three bases of the Russian state—the autocracy, serfdom, and Orthodoxy—had been firmly established. Under Ivan's immediate successors, however, the boyars were able to reassert power. One of these nobles was Nikita Romanov, whose sister Anastasia had been Ivan's wife; another was Boris Godunov, whose sister had married Ivan's son, Tsar Fedor I, and who became tsar in his own right in 1598. In 1605, rival claims for the throne and external intervention led to the disorders of the Time of Troubles, which ended when Michael Romanov, a descendant of the wife of Ivan the Terrible, became tsar. Thereafter, all the tsars of Russia would be of the house of Romanov.

This was to be the inheritance of the infant child called Peter, born in 1672 as the only son of the second marriage of Tsar Alexis I. At the moment of Peter's birth, however, the possibility that the child, proudly named for the Apostle, would become tsar was at best problematical. Tsar Alexis had already fathered fourteen children, including five sons, by his first wife Maria Miloslavskaya. As she was giving birth to the last, Maria herself had died. Within the year, as a result of the horrible mortality of the times, only two of her sons were left alive to claim Alexis' inheritance. Around these two boys, the frail Fedor and the half-sighted and half-witted Ivan, gathered the Miloslavsky family, the relatives of Alexis' late wife, ruthless, grasping, protective, determined to keep the power that Maria Miloslavskaya had purchased for them with her fertility. Anyone who claimed the throne as Alexis' successor, even if he proved himself the superior to Fedor and Ivan, would have to contend with the wrath of the Miloslavskys.

Alexis lived just long enough to complicate his succession and create the circumstances for a power struggle. Intelligent and conscientious, no doubt worrying over the health and capacities of his two weak sons, Alexis determined to marry again. He fell in love with the lively-eyed Natalia Naryshkina, the ward of Artamon Matveyev, a powerful minister of state who awed and horrified his countrymen by furnishing his house in western-European fashion and by allowing his wife and his ward far greater freedom than was customary for Russian women. Russian women of the upper classes were normally secluded in the *terem,* generally located in the remotest part of Russian homes, forbidden contact with the outside world until they either married or died. It was the remarkable Natalia Naryshkina, strong-willed and used to freedom, who became Peter's mother.

Within three years of her marriage in 1670, Natalia had given birth to Peter and his sister Natasha, and her Naryshkin relatives had come flooding into the court, threatening the positions of the angry Miloslavskys. Despite the undercurrents of rivalry, these early years were happy ones for Peter. From the moment of birth, Peter was a large and precocious child, noticeably stronger than his half-brothers. Peter walked within seven months. Soon he was served by an entire household staff of dwarfs, and he was dressed in clothes cut from rich fabrics and decorated with pearls and emeralds.

Much of this opulence was cut off when Tsar Alexis died suddenly in 1676. He was succeeded by the simple-minded Fedor, and the victorious Miloslavskys returned gleefully to influence. Peter and his mother were shunted aside as the hapless and innocent Fedor was married off in the hopes that he would produce an heir. This was not to be. Fedor's first wife died in childbirth, and a second, high-spirited and sexually active, was simply too much for Fedor. He died in 1682.

Fedor's death reawakened the Naryshkin-Miloslavsky feud, with the Naryshkins arguing for the succession of Peter and the Miloslavskys for that of his half-brother Ivan. At first the supporters of Peter seemed to win out. At a meeting of a *Zemsky Sobor,* an "assembly of the land," Peter, healthy and strapping, was chosen tsar over the half-blind and feeble Ivan.

The Miloslavskys, however were not to be denied. They fell to plotting, and a fortuitous opportunity soon presented itself in the form of a revolt of the *streltsi.* The *streltsi,* literally translated as "shooters," formed the palace guard in Moscow. Twenty-thousand strong, dressed in caftans of vivid red, green, or purple and armed with a frightening array of swords, muskets, and pikes, chronically underpaid and mistreated by their corrupt boyar commanders, the *streltsi* constituted a formidable and volatile force at the very center of power.

In 1682 the *streltsi,* angered by grievances against their officers, egged on by deftly-planted rumors that Ivan had been murdered by the Naryshkins, stormed the fortress of the Kremlin and made for the tsar's apartments. On their way, upon a staircase, they were met by a courageous Natalia Naryshkina, who hand in hand with Peter and Ivan, demonstrated to the mob that Ivan was in fact alive. At first soothing words seemed to calm the *streltsi,* but then abusive commands from a boyar officer goaded them to renewed action. Peter, still very much a child, must have watched in horror as Artamon Matveyev and others of his friends and family were lifted bodily to spin crazily upon the upraised and pummeling hands of the enraged *streltsi,* passed hand-to-hand to a balustrade, and then dropped on the pikes of other *streltsi* who were standing on the floor below. Thus began an orgy of blood and violence that lasted for days. Naryshkins and boyars were hunted throughout the palace, subjected to the most hideous torments, and then hacked to pieces in the halls and courtyards. Ivan Naryshkin, Peter's uncle, demanded by the *streltsi* as a blood-sacrifice in exchange for ending the revolt, calmly took communion, surrendered himself to the enraged musketeers, and perished after extremes of torture. Peter and his mother survived, but it was the Miloslavskys who triumphed. Ivan and Peter were made co-tsars under a regency headed by the Tsarevna Sophia, the strong and intelligent daughter of Maria Miloslavsky. Thereafter, Peter and his mother were dispatched to exile in the countryside.

After the horror and the reek of death at the Kremlin, the village of Preobrazhenskoye must have seemed like heaven to Peter. While Sophia ruled, Peter played, and the games he played were imaginative, self-instructive, strenuous, and sometimes cruel. Already such a large boy that, at the age of eleven, he was thought by the Swedish ambassador to be at least sixteen, Peter was by nature hyperactive and energetic. Like many boys, Peter loved war games; unlike his fellows, however, Peter was allowed to play war with real muskets, cannon, and uniforms drawn from state arsenals. Out of these childhood pursuits emerged two regiments of guards—the Preobrazhensky and the Semyonovsky—which in turn formed the model for a new Russian army.

Ceaselessly active, unconfined by palaces and the trappings of monarchy, given little education aside from reading lessons by an ingratiating tutor, Peter broke things and built things. He blacksmithed and he printed, he carpentered and joined. Peter also spent much time with the "Germans" at a nearby *vemetskaya sloboda,* a specialized settlement set up to house non-Russians. With Peter, one activity led to another; one discovery to a host of them. Beginning with a whim, or a gift, Peter spun off in all directions and acquired an immense amount of practical knowledge. The discovery of a sailboat in a shed created in Peter the necessity to learn how to sail. This, as at least one historian has observed, led in turn, to boat-building, to the discovery of the sea, to the gift of an astrolabe by a diplomat, to the need to learn navigation. Restless and impatient, his rooms littered with models and his simple clothes besmirched with grease and grime, Peter's intellect grew with his stature.

Having found a lover in the enlightened boyar Prince Vasily Golitsyn, Peter's half-sister Sophia ruled Russia with imagination and zest. "She is immensely fat with a head as large as a bushel, hairs on her face, and tumors on her legs. . . ." So remarked the French ambassador ungallantly of Russia's regent. He was careful, however, to note as well that "her mind is shrewd, unprejudiced and full of policy." During her short regency, Sophia opened diplomatic relations with much of Europe and signed the Treaty of Nerchinsk with the Chinese in 1689—the first European ruler to sign an agreement with the Middle Kingdom. For his part, the erudite and westernized Golitsyn sent Russians abroad for education and even tried to better the lot of the serfs.

But not even Sophia and her consort could keep Peter from growing up. In 1689 Peter, at seventeen, was married off by his mother as a demonstration that he was of age. Peter loathed his conservative and uneducated boyar bride, but he slept with her, and she gave him a son within the year. Thereafter, Peter ignored her, and in 1698 he had her placed in a convent. The unfortunate woman—Eudoxia Lopukhina—had long since served her purpose. She had produced an heir, and she had proven that Peter was at least biologically a man.

The significance of Peter's marriage was not lost on the Miloslavskys. In August of 1689, rumors reached Peter of another *streltsi* revolt. Terrified lest he might share the fate of his unfortunate uncle, Peter fled on a horse at night clad in nothing but a shirt. Soon safe behind the walls of a monastery, Peter regained his composure and rallied support. With time, Sophia's supporters deserted her. Helpless, but still defiant, Sophia frightened Peter to the day of her death, even after she was relegated to a convent. Peter was now tsar in fact. Significantly Peter did no violence to the simple-minded Ivan, and he remained nominal co-tsar until his death in 1696.

At the center of power for the first time, Peter gave full vent to his curiosity, restlessness, and talent. Some scholars, in fact, have called him a revolutionary, a transformer of Russian society. "He resolved to be a man, to command men, and to create a new nation." Thus wrote Voltaire with admiration. Other scholars have treated Peter's accomplishments with more caution and less hyperbole, regarding Peter as at best a reformer, and one who was often guided by the actions and policies of his tsarist predecessors.

This was almost certainly true in the case of Peter's first military initiative: the Azov campaign, begun in 1695. The objective was a Turkish fortress on the Sea of Azov, a fortress which also commanded the entrance to the Black Sea. This Russian quest for a warm-water port and for access to the sea certainly antedated Peter's reign. As early as 1637 Russian pioneers had reached the Pacific, and in the same year the Cossacks had conquered Azov, offering it to Peter's predecessor, Michael Romanov. Tsar Michael, however, feared Turkish anger, doubted the ability of Russia to defend it, and the fortress eventually found its way into the hands of the Turks. Building on such precedents, making much of the fact that Russia had been committed to an anti-Turkish "Holy League" by Sophia, Peter launched a land-based attack on Azov in 1695 that failed ignominiously. Typically, Peter remained undiscouraged and threw all his energy into the building of a fleet. In 1696 Peter's new navy sailed down the Don and captured Azov. A Russian presence on the Black Sea had been initiated. By the treaty of Adrianople (1713), the Russians were forced to cede their gains around the Black Sea to the Ottoman Empire, but Peter had made a naval presence there a cornerstone of Russian policy.

Peter the Great obtained a temporary foothold on the Black Sea shore, but he was forced to cede Taganrog and Azov to the Ottoman Empire by the Treaty of Adrianople (1713). Nonetheless, Peter's successors succeeded where he had failed, and control of the Crimean Peninsula and the Black Sea became a consistent goal of Russian foreign policy.

The Azov Campaign: Peter's Struggle to Reach the Black Sea

Not content to glory in his victory, Peter promptly set about planning a project of which none of his predecessors would have dreamed. This was the great embassy to western Europe. While Peter's journey west has captured the imaginations of many historians, his motives in undertaking it have often been misunderstood. Those who have considered Peter a revolutionary, or who have thought smugly that Peter desired only to bring what he considered to be a superior culture to backward Russia, have failed to comprehend what Peter was about. His motives were at once simple and subtle. Peter was, at the most basic level, curious about the west, but he was also in search of the expertise and technology that he felt was necessary to strengthen his dynasty and his state.

Thus it was that Peter's "Grand Embassy" criss-crossed Europe in 1697-1698. Characteristically, Peter wanted to see everything. In France he did not hesitate to steal a noblewoman's carriage, the better to reach a destination. In the Netherlands and in England he worked for a time in the dockyards as a laborer to learn the techniques of shipbuilding. In the latter country he was everywhere, turning up as a visitor at Parliament and at the Tower, "an uncouth figure in a long black wig, with dirty scratched hands." Peter also, as was his hallmark, played hard. Sayes Court, his place of residence in England, suffered three hundred broken windowpanes, twenty damaged pictures, and fifty broken chairs. Ink and grease bespattered the mansion's floors; its lawns were runneled by various conveyances; its gardens given over to weeds.

By this time Peter was in all senses an adult, and one who at once menaced and fascinated. Close to seven feet tall, strong enough to straighten a horseshoe or to turn a silver platter into a delicate scroll with his bare hands, possessing sufficient dexterity to cut a tossed napkin cleanly in half before it hit the floor, Peter was a man few forgot. The Duke of Saint-Simon remarked on Peter's "good black eyes, large, bright, piercing and well open, his look majestic and gracious when he liked." Saint-Simon also noted how anger and drink could alter Peter's features in a frightening way. His eyes would roll, and his face would contort and twitch.

Unfortunately for his companions and underlings, Peter ate and drank often and to excess. "He is a man of very hot temper," wrote the English ecclesiastic Bishop Burnet, "and very brutal in his passion; he raises his natural heat by drinking much brandy." When hungry, Peter would dispense with the then new-fangled knives and forks, go to the sideboard, pick up a whole roast in his hands, and gobble.

Whatever Peter did, his compatriots and guests were obliged to do as well. Peter's receptions were sometimes surrounded by troops, as a guarantee that no guests would leave too early. Extreme in his hospitality, Peter's expectations of others often passed over into cruelty. Guests were made to drink so much corn brandy, brought in by servants by the bucket-full, that they could only be revived with sluices of water and massage. On one occasion, a wedding, Peter, discovering that the father of the bride liked jelly-sweets, forced the unfortunate's mouth open and jammed sweet after sweet down his throat; on another, he forced salad and vinegar down the nose and throat of a hapless boyar until the blood flowed. Even more strenuous were the strange, inebriated rites of Peter's "Most Drunken Synod of Fools and Jesters." On one occasion, when a participant arrived late at one of the Synod's entertainments, he was staked out naked on the ice of a river. He died of the consequences.

Peter's childhood memories merged with his capacity for cruelty when he heard, in the midst of his tour of Europe, that the *streltsi* had once again revolted. Embarrassed, with horrible memories of earlier *streltsi* uprisings spinning through his head, Peter hurried home in 1698 to exact a terrible retribution. Anxious to expose what he thought was Sophia's involvement, Peter ordered the revolt's ringleaders to be tortured by alternate floggings and roastings of their living flesh. Physicians were kept in attendance to keep the victims from dying. Fourteen torture chambers were speedily constructed, and over twelve hundred *streltsi* were put to the knout, the fire, and the rack. Hundreds of *streltsi* were hanged, some in front of the convent where Sophia resided, others from the battlements of the Kremlin and in the squares. Others were broken on wheels, impaled on stakes, or beheaded, their bodies left to rot and decompose in the open air. Clergy suspected of involvement with the *streltsi* were executed in a group ceremony presided over by a mocking dwarf wearing priest's robes. Others of the *streltsi* were exiled, some of them with their noses and ears cut off. Clear evidence of Sophia's complicity was never found, but the *streltsi* ceased to exist. Only with the spring thaw had Peter's rage diminished sufficiently to allow the corpses to be buried.

With the *streltsi* destroyed, Peter was free to embark on the most ambitious enterprise of his career. With all his determination, Peter planned to challenge Sweden for supremacy over the Baltic shore. Imperial Sweden, ruled by the general-king Charles XII, controlled Karelia, Ingria, Estonia, and Livonia, blocking the Russian advance to the Baltic. By 1700, events and alliances had opened the way for Peter to revive Ivan the Terrible's dream for a foothold on the Baltic. With many of the western European powers preoccupied with the war of the Spanish Succession. Peter guaranteed Turkish neutrality by arranging the Peace of Constantinople (1700). Thereafter, Peter cobbled together yet another alliance, this time directly against Sweden, comprising Russia, Saxony, and Denmark.

With this, the Great Northern War began, and it was to last twenty-one years. Despite Peter's well-laid plans, Charles XII proved a difficult and cunning adversary. Though the Danes pushed into the Swedish client-state of Schleswig, and the Saxons penetrated into Livonia and laid siege to Riga, the Swedish king responded with tactical brilliance. He effected a landing in Zeeland, marched on Copenhagen, and forced the Danes to declare their neutrality in the Treaty of Ravendal (1700). With Denmark so quickly out of the war, Charles turned abruptly on Russia. In November 1700 he landed at Narva with eight thousand men, and there inflicted a terrible defeat on a massive but undisciplined Russian army. Charles was then free to wheel on Saxony. By the following summer he had relieved Riga and invaded Poland, taking vengeance on Augustus of Saxony, who was also the elective Polish monarch.

In embarking on his Polish campaign, Charles inadvertantly gave Peter the opportunity to recover. As Peter put it: "necessity drove away sloth and forced me to work night and day." While

Charles spent six years in Poland chasing the armies of Augustus, Peter rebuilt his army along western European lines. It was not until 1706, in the Treaty of Altranstadt, that Charles was able to force Augustus off the Polish throne and Saxony out of the war. By then Peter had laid siege to Narva, recovering it in 1704, and his forces were ready for a renewed Swedish challenge. After an initial loss at the Battle of Lesnaya (1708), the Swedes suffered a catastrophic defeat at Poltava (1709). There Russian earthworks, brilliantly designed by Peter's engineers, broke the ranks of Charles' wonderful but exhausted army into doomed, ragged groups. In 1714 there occurred a major Russian naval victory at Hangö. Anticipating his final victory, Peter began to construct a new Russian city on the Gulf of Finland in 1703. He called it St. Petersburg, after the apostle for whom he was named, and it became Russia's capital in 1712. Russia's fitful surge toward the Baltic shore, begun under Ivan the Terrible, had been realized under his successor.

Peter the Great as the Founder of the Russian Navy. L. Caravak
Courtesy of the Central Naval Museum, Leningrad.

After the disaster at Poltava, Charles XII escaped to the territory of the Ottoman Empire and persuaded the Sultan to declare war on Russia. By 1711 Peter had been obliged to make peace with the Turks, return Azov, and allow Charles XII free passage to Sweden, but Charles, angry over the treaty terms, refused to leave. Deprived of his leadership, Sweden suffered continued reverses. The Saxons drove Stanislaus Lesynski, a puppet of Sweden, off the Polish throne, and the Danes at last took Schleswig and pressed into the Swedish holdings of Bremen and Verden, selling the latter holdings to Hanover in return for an anti-Swedish alliance. Peter's forces seized all of the Swedish provinces along the Baltic shore. In 1718 Charles, who had finally returned to Sweden, fell in battle in Norway and was succeeded by his sister Ulrika Eleanora, who conceded constitutional privileges to the clergy and nobility. Exhausted by years of war, Sweden sued for peace. In 1721 by the Treaties of Stockholm, Sweden made peace with Saxony and Poland on the basis of the *status quo ante bellum,* and by the Peace of Nystadt of the same year ceded Livonia, Estonia, Ingermanland, and Karelia—the whole of the eastern Baltic shore—to Russia.

In November 1721 Peter's title was changed from tsar to "emperor of all the Russias," a move that recognized both his territorial conquests and his strengthening of the autocracy at home. In the latter area, Peter was also a student of his predecessors. Serfdom deepened, and several serf rebellions were violently put down. Administrative provinces and districts were formed throughout Russia, run by appointed bureaucrats responsible to Peter himself. Overlapping these administrative districts were regimental districts, each with a garrison under the command of a military officer. At the level of the central government, the old Boyar Duma was replaced by a more efficient, and efficiently controlled, Senate, and a system of administrative "colleges."

Peter expected the landed classes to perform state service in return for their privileges on the land. Compulsory education was required for the sons of nobility, and a "Table of Ranks" ordered virtually all of civil society on a military basis. Not even the Orthodox Church escaped, being put under a Procurator of the Holy Synod responsible to Peter alone. The same control extended to Peter's family. Alexis, Peter's son, disloyal, stupid, and a dupe of his mistress, was imprisoned and tortured by his father's orders and died under mysterious circumstances. The Military Service Regulations of 1716 defined the extent of Peter's power quite simply: "His Majesty is an autocratic monarch who is not obliged to answer for his acts to anyone in the world. . . ."

By the mid-1720s Peter had embarked on yet another campaign, this time in Persia, in which he succeeded in wresting away the western and southern shores of the Caspian Sea. For this he paid the ultimate price. The Persian war put an untolerable strain on a constitution already compromised by overwork and alcoholic excess. In the autumn of 1724, seeing that some of his men had fallen into the water from a ship gone aground, Peter plunged in after them. Thereafter not even the Empress Catherine, that hardy woman of peasant extraction who had been Peter's mistress and then his wife, could quiet the convulsive fits that with increasing frequency racked Peter's body. Leaving an empire that stretched from the Baltic to the Caspian, and eastward as far as the Pacific, Peter died at his new capital in February, 1725.

Peter died not as a blind imposer of western values, but as the autocrat of all the Russias. Voltaire might have seen him as a prototype of an enlightened monarch, bringing civilization and culture to a backward land, but few of his actions would have been incomprehensible to his predecessors, like Ivan the Terrible who also looked westward for expertise and who also drove Russia to the sea. Neither the creation of St. Petersburg, the "window on the west," or the symbolic shaving of long boyar beards by English barbers, an event that has impressed many as a sign of Peter's modernism, alters the fact that Peter was a thoroughly Russian sovereign, following long-lived policies, presiding over an autocratic peasant empire. Peter's contribution was that he made Russia a stronger and greater empire than it had ever been before, so large and so powerful that the rest of Europe, however much it tried, could ignore it only at peril. The traditional tripod of authority—the autocracy, the Orthodox Church, and the institution of serfdom—remained in place. Peter did admire western technology and some of western culture, as did other Russians, and in his restless borrowing of expertise and technique he was indeed a "westernizer."

Throughout Russian history there has been a creative tension between westernizers like Peter, those who have wished to borrow whatever was good and useful from the west to make Russia better and stronger, and the "slavophiles," who have looked inward and sought to preserve Slavic uniqueness and identity. Peter's reign constituted an early, and intense, chapter in a controversy that continues still.

F. Conclusion: Central and Northern Europe in 1721

The Thirty Years' War was part of a larger and longer struggle for power in all parts of Europe. Before the conflict began the

Hapsburgs, from their bases in Spain and Germany, threatened to overawe all of Europe. This was a possibility that neither France, virtually surrounded by Hapsburg power, nor Sweden, out of a concern for her growing empire in northern Europe and the Baltic, could allow. Thus, central Europe and Germany, already a seed-bed of religious conflict and anti-imperial sentiment, became a battleground involving powers whose real interests lay in the western and northern borderlands. In 1648 and again in 1659, France emerged victorious over the Hapsburgs, becoming almost for the next sixty years the dominant power in western Europe. For such pretensions France, too, would be challenged, and that is a subject for a later chapter.

The same treaty, that of Westphalia, that did so much for France, only complicated matters for Sweden. Gustavus Adolphus had entered the Thirty Years' War, at least in part, to protect and extend Sweden's Baltic Empire, but Sweden emerged at Westphalia in some respects a German landlord, her resources strained and overextended, required to defend her massive holdings with almost constant warfare. Queen Christina, by her Catholic predilections and by her refusal to marry, did much to lessen Swedish involvement in Germany, but her internal policies and extravagance rendered her successors less able to defend Sweden's northern empire. After her abdication, Swedish foreign policy fell into familiar grooves as the Swedes resumed warfare with old enemies: Denmark, Poland, and Russia. After years of valiant struggle under brilliant military leadership, it was Sweden's tragedy to emerge from the negotiations at Nystadt stripped of her empire and reduced to the status of a second-rank power. Russia, not Sweden, had inherited the Baltic shore.

Within Germany itself the Holy Roman Empire, for practical purposes, no longer existed, and the resulting power vacuum in Germany allowed new powers and dynasties to emerge—Saxony, the Prussia of the Hohenzollerns, the Bavaria of the Wittelsbachs. The German Hapsburgs, thrown back on their ancestral lands in Austria, experienced a miraculous change of fortune, eventually creating out of Austria and Hungary a new empire that lasted until the end of World War I.

Portfolio: Louis XIV—Art, Propaganda, and the Pursuit of Absolutism

Bust of Louis XIV. French School (After Bernini).
Courtesy National Gallery of Art, Washington. Samuel H. Kress Collection.

Louis XIV in Costume. Joseph Werner
Louis delighted in balls, masques, plays, and theatricals, using these opulent diversions as a way to glorify himself and to force expenditures on his nobility, which not incidently had the effect of weakening them as a class and thus enhancing Louis' power. Another artistic medium dear to Louis was ballet, and he can be considered one of its founding patrons. Ballet, with its discipline, order, harmony, and elegance was, for Louis, as were all the arts, a means to propagandize the supposed virtues of royal absolutism.
Courtesy Norton Simon Museum of Art, Pasadena.

Mademoiselle de la Vallière in Costume. Joseph Werner
Mlle. de la Vallière was one of Louis' favorite mistresses. All of those who were close to the king, or who wanted to be so, were expected to participate in court rituals and entertainments, and often competed to be able to do so. *Courtesy Norton Simon Museum of Art, Pasadena.*

The Family of Louis XIV. Attributed to Nicholas de Largillière Louis is here pictured with his son the Grand Dauphin, his grandson the Duke of Burgundy, and his great-grandson the Duke of Brittany. A governess tends the latter by means of a restraining cord. Of those portrayed, only the Duke of Brittany, who succeeded to the French throne in 1715 at the age of five, survived the vigorous Louis XIV. *Courtesy of the Trustees of the Wallace Collection, London.*

Chapter IV

The Play of the Balance of Power in Western Europe, 1648-1715: Louis XIV, The Dutch Republic and the House of Orange, Carlos II of Spain, and The Duke and Duchess of Marlborough

> He was a fortunate prince in that he was a unique figure of his time, a pillar of strength, with almost uninterrupted good health.
> —Saint Simon on Louis XIV

> The man of God's right hand, whom He made strong for Himself.
> —Bishop Burnet on William III

> This prince has passed his life in profound ignorance.
> —Louis XIV on Carlos II

> I have a great mind to believe that kings' and first ministers' souls, when they die, go into chimney-sweeps'.
> —Sarah, Duchess of Marlborough

The Estates General, 1614. Jean Ziarnko
The Estates General, a fractious, independent body, was one of the few expressions of Dutch unity. *Courtesy of the National Gallery of Art, Washington. Rosenwald Collection.*

A. Introduction: The Play of the European Balance of Power

From the time of Charles V to the framing of the Peace of Westphalia in 1648, the states of Europe had been overawed by the power of the Hapsburgs, both Austrian and Spanish. Between 1648 and 1715 the France of Louis XIV emerged as Europe's paramount power, threatening all of western Europe with its wars as it tried to gobble up the remnants of the Spanish Hapsburg empire in Europe.

Because no single European state could stand alone against the might of Louis' armies, the crowned heads of Europe in the latter part of the century began to combine in a series of alliances and alignments to contain or defeat him. Thus was inaugurated, as John B. Wolfe and other scholars have observed, the idea of "the balance of power," one of the most durable and long-lived concepts in European history.

According to the theory of the balance of power, the security and independence of *individual* states was possible only if the power of *all* the states collectively was in equilibrium, or balance. This meant, in practice, that if a single European state, or group of states, grew too powerful, other states had to combine in alliances to maintain the balance of power. Thus, the balance of power idea implied a system of alliances and alignments.

Though the balance of power idea originated out of a need for security and independence on the part of individual states and was often intended to maintain peace and check aggression, it sometimes has had opposite and contradictory effects. In the negative sense, if a state declined or collapsed, its territories, instead of being protected, might be carved up and distributed among other states on the excuse of "maintaining" the balance. Also, a state was said to "hold" the balance of power if it could act to maintain or disturb the peace and equilibrium of other states. As alliance systems became more complex this has meant that smaller, aggressive states could have an influence out of proportion to their actual strength, and even cause a serious war.

Productive of both peace and conflict, security and aggression, the idea of the balance of power has had an incalculable effect on European, and world, history.

B. Louis XIV and the French Monarchy

September 5, 1638, was a long day for Gaston, Duke of Orléans, brother to King Louis XIII and heir presumptive to the

French throne. On that day, Gaston, who had spent his life alternately rebelling against his royal brother and waiting for him to die without issue, had been informed that Louis XIII had at last fathered a boy-child. Accordingly, Gaston repaired to his apartments and burst into tears.

Anyone who understood Louis' unique personality would have understood as well the depth of Gaston's frustration. For years Louis XIII had refused to cohabit with his wife, the Spanish princess Anne of Austria. Gaston had every reason to expect that Anne, humiliated, suspected by the court of being a Hapsburg agent, increasingly fond of gambling and other frivolities, would grow ever more estranged from a husband who liked horses and hunting dogs far better than he liked women.

Then, for some reason, Louis had changed his mind. Perhaps he had at last yielded to the persuasions of his minister, Cardinal Richelieu, or his successor Mazarin, to produce an heir; perhaps he himself decided that he had to fulfill his dynastic duties. Whatever the reason, vowing to dedicate his country to the Virgin if a male child was born, Louis had reluctantly climbed into bed with his wife. The child that resulted was greeted with rejoicing as Louis *le Dieudonné*—Louis the Gift of God.

This Louis was a beautiful child, and he enjoyed excellent health almost until his death seventy-seven years later. For seventy-two of them, as Louis XIV, he was king of France. Known, appropriately enough, as the "Sun King," he presided over his monarchy and state, and blinded and bemused Europe by his presence. Seemingly secure in his magnificence, never doubting his right to do so, Louis freely spent of the vast substance of French society on his palaces and on his wars. Mesmerized, the crowned heads of Europe allowed themselves to be led around by the nose for more than half a century. All the courts of Europe strove to emulate Louis' at Versailles. Louis' contemporaries pirouetted to French dances and sniggered at French masques and operas; they wore French wigs and clothing of French cut; they copied French absolutism; they ate French cuisine and drank French wine; they read French books; all the while they awaited the impact of Louis' next diplomatic decision, or the news of his next war. There was no doubt at all that the Sun King would in some way influence them.

Such a sovereign has excited many into writing of his life and reign, and the historiography of Louis XIV has taken many twists and turns. To the aristocratic memorialist, the Duke of Saint-Simon, who loathed the Sun King for his attack on the power of the old nobility, Louis was at best an imperfect king, vain, lacking in intelligence, petty, prone to flattery. To the eighteenth-century French philosopher Voltaire, that admirer of enlightened despotism, both

Louis and his reign were glorious, as they laid the groundwork for French culture and civilization.

With the French Revolution, the historiography of Louis XIV reached a new level of criticism. Louis' absolutism, so admired by Voltaire, was not so attractive to the revolutionary generation of 1789.

In the early nineteenth century Pierre-Edouard Lemontey turned the tables on the revolutionaries by proclaiming that Louis' reorganization of the monarchy was in itself a truly revolutionary act. As the nineteenth century progressed, liberal historians, imbued with the idea of inevitable improvement, saw Louis' reign, for all of its absolutism, in a positive light.

Since World War II the *Annales* School, consisting of a group of social historians who have applied statistics and the computer to their researches, has emphasized not Louis XIV but the people he ruled, and have concluded that his *grandeur* and policies did not always influence the lives of ordinary people. John B. Wolfe's recent biography of Louis XIV portrays a sovereign who, despite his wealth and *gloire,* acted much like an ordinary man, making mistakes, experiencing doubts, and often being the victim of bad advice. Other scholars, having probed the reality of Louis' powers at the local or regional level, have concluded that French absolutism, for all of its assertions, was far from complete.

The extent of Louis' power is incomprehensible without understanding the land over which he ruled, and the nature of its society and economy. As king of France, Louis inherited an extensive, and Catholic, agricultural peasant empire, and his *gloire* and power is not explained by the magnificence of his court, the achievements of his bankers and bourgeoisie, the extensive French colonies overseas, the economic policies of his finance minister Colbert, or the might of his armies. All of these things had their place, but they all owed their origin to the vastness and variety of the French agricultural landscape and to the peasants who labored upon it.

From the fruit of the earth, and their grinding effort, the peasantry produced the wealth of France and the taxes to support Louis' court and armies, the prelates of the French church, the bulk of the French nobility, and local institutions without number. Of all the exactions, the taxes of the king were both the most numerous and the most onerous. First there was the *taille,* a sort of primitive income tax. Then came the *gabelle,* the tax on salt. Peasants were also obliged to pay the *aides,* the despised indirect taxes on consumer goods and liquor. There were also taxes peculiar to certain provinces, such as the *Equivalent* in Languedoc. Still other taxes—the *Fermes unies, the Édit du Toisé,* the *Dixième*—were imposed at various times during Louis' reign. Many peasants were further vic-

Portrait of Jean Baptiste Colbert.
Philippe de Champagne
Courtesy of the Metropolitan Museum of Art, New York. Gift of the Wildenstein Foundation.

timized by the *Corvées,* the system of compulsory manual labor required by landlords, and by the *Métairies,* a sharecropping system whereby the profits of agricultural labor had to be divided between a peasant-tenant and an exploiting *seigneur*. From most of these taxes the nobility and clergy were almost entirely exempt. It was the French peasantry, many millions strong, who supported the mammoth expenditures of the French state.

Of this fact Louis remained, throughout his life, quite indifferent. This should not be surprising. Possessing unlimited good health and unlimited luxury from the day of his birth, Louis was not conditioned to recognize the limitations, physical, emotional, or financial, of others. Mazarin early on introduced him to gambling, an expensive passion that remained with him throughout his life. Mazarin also introduced Louis, at the appropriate time, to Marie Concini, one of the six buxom "Mazarinettes," the offspring of Mazarin's sister. When Louis complicated the dalliance, which was designed merely to occupy him, by falling in love, Marie was sent away and another Mazarinette thrown into Louis' arms. To these pastimes were added others—more mistresses, entertainments, armies, and buildings. As an older monarch, Louis insisted on traveling frequently from palace to palace. Into the royal coach were crammed his wife, mistresses, serving-maids, and, later, daughters-in-law. Neither pregnancy nor infirmity was sufficient excuse to beg off from one of these excursions, and, as the royal coach hurtled and rocked through the French countryside, Louis stuffed sweets and other viands into the mouths of his female charges, growing peevish if they were not witty and refusing to stop when they felt the call of nature.

Louis' family was typical of many in the seventeenth century in that it was characterized by early death and lack of strong interpersonal bonds. Of his troubled father, Louis knew little, as Louis XIII died before his son was five. Louis' mother, Anne of Austria, although undoubtedly grateful that the birth of her son enhanced her position at court, seemed to be indifferent to all things regarding her offspring save for his religious instruction. The young Louis nearly drowned in a pond because no one had been assigned to watch over him.

As he grew older, Louis must have come to know how cordially his parents had hated each other. Louis' own marriage, to Maria Theresa of Austria, the daughter of the king of Spain, was a typical, and therefore loveless, seventeenth-century political match, designed to cement the Peace of the Pyrenees. Not surprisingly, Louis' relations with his own son, the Grand Dauphin, were characterized by frustration on the part of the father and terror on the part of the son. Significantly, Louis the Grand Dauphin, described by Saint Simon as "on the tall side, and very fat without being lumpy," lived an aimless and pointless life, and predeceased his father. Louis had three mistresses of record, Louise de La Vallière, Madame de Montespan, and the Marquise de Maintenon. Though he adored his illegitimate offspring, and secretly married Maintenon after the death of his first wife, La Vallière ended her life alone in a convent, and the witty, scheming Montespan fell from grace after bearing Louis eight children.

Louis' apparent indifference to and contempt for people was perhaps given impetus by the *Fronde,* the terrible revolt of the nobles and the Parlement of Paris against the power of Mazarin and the authority of the French centralized monarchy. The *Fronde* began in 1648 when Louis was only nine, and took its name from a catapult used by children. The name was indeed apt, for once the revolt was launched by the Parlement of Paris, a law court dominated by the nobility, it quickly spread to other parts of the country and to other classes. The peasantry, maddened by years of bad harvests and mounting debts, egged on by the local nobility, rose in some parts of France, as did hungry working people in Paris, Marseilles, and Bordeaux. In the latter city in 1652, workers and petty bourgeois formed a group known as the *Ormée,* which engaged in warfare against its social betters. The Duke of Orléans and the Prince of Condé, ambitious for power, as well as Paul de Gondi, Bishop Coadjutor of Paris, who was anxious to supersede Mazarin as chief minister, eventually threw in their lot with the revolt. Turenne, the most able of the anti-*Fronde* military leaders, went over to the side of the rebels and then changed sides again. Mazarin was for a time exiled. Not put down until 1653, changing form and objectives as it increased in violence, the *Fronde* thoroughly frightened all those in power or of the blood royal.

Among these was the young Louis XIV. Years later Louis, remembering the *Fronde,* wrote of "a prince of my blood, and a very great name, at the head of the armies of our foes; many cabals in the state; the Parlement in possession of, and with a taste for, usurped authority; in my court little fidelity without personal interest...." During the revolt the young man who had known only luxury became familiar with privation; the heir to the French throne learned about fear, humiliation, and powerlessness. As an adult, Louis resolved that he would never experience such feelings again. Instead, combining personal malice with reason of state, Louis obliged the nobility, the architects of the *Fronde,* to feel all of the anxieties that the *Fronde* had forced upon him.

At Versailles, far from the hated Paris of the *Fronde,* Louis constructed a palace of immense dimensions as a fitting arena both for his own glory and for his nobility's humiliation. Around a modest lodge built by Louis' father grew a ring of gardens and stables, outbuildings and housing for workmen and the court. Work began in 1661, and went on well into the next century. Architect succeeded architect; artist succeeded artist. By 1685 some 36,000 workmen and 6,000 horses were laboring on the vast enterprise, and it was said that dead laborers, killed by disease or overwork, had to be removed from the site by the cartload. Another task force, including detachments from the French army, set to work on a ninety-mile aqueduct, named for Madame de Maintenon, which was to divert water from the River Eure to Versailles' gardens and apartments. This project was defeated only by the costs of war, and after fantastic expenditure. By 1690 the enterprise of Versailles had cost the French people at least 200,000,000 francs.

To the old hunting lodge was added chamber after chamber, gallery after gallery, in complex array. The vast rooms were peopled by the proud nobility of France. There, under the king's watchful eye, they were forced to attend upon him. They were obliged to watch Louis rise, dress, dance, eat, even defecate. If they felt the call of nature themselves, the nobles and their ladies had to crouch ignominiously in corners, behind hangings, upon stairwells. Like puppets on strings they served the insulting whims of Louis XIV, penitents in the palace of the Sun King, forbidden to leave and obliged to articulate social rituals as enervating and complicated as Versailles itself.

In the chambers themselves, under the direction of the great Le Brun, were hung Gobelin and Beauvais tapestries, elegant mirrors and crystal. Furniture of breathtaking perfection filled the apartments. On the ceiling of the famous Galerie des Glaces, Le Brun himself labored, painting a long tribute to the Sun King's reign. Louis was indeed a great patron. The sculptures of Girardon and Coysevox, the witty theatricals of Molière, the works of Corneille and Racine, the paintings of Pouissin, were encouraged by the largesse of the king.

Even so, one wonders at times how deeply the glory and culture of Louis XIV impressed even those who immediately surrounded the Sun King. To Versailles, or to Louis' retreat at Marly, or to Maintenon's palace of the Grand Trianon, came people ridiculous, grotesque, crude. There were women with wigs so elaborate and awkward that they could, and did, fall off and even catch on fire. There was the Duke of Vendôme, who earned the censure of the king for openly practicing deviant sexuality, for twice taking the mercury cure for syphilis, and for extremes of personal filth. The Duke's dogs littered his apartments and slept in his bed, but he asserted blithely that he was no dirtier than anybody else. No gourmet, Vendôme was fond of dining on rotten fish. The Duke of Orléans, Louis' dissolute nephew, denied God, engaged in elaborate debauches on holy days, and tried to establish communication with the devil. Louis' grandson, the Duke of Berry, berated his wife incessantly and publicly, on one occasion kicking her and threatening to lock her in a convent.

Around these people lurked smells strong and memorable. Bathing was for the sick or the addled, and Louis himself was bundled so heavily in pillows at night that he sweated profusely, with probable odoriferous consequences. During the mourning for the Duchess of Montpensier, the first cousin of Louis XIV, the urn containing the embalmed entrails of the corpse burst open, releasing an intolerable reek and stench throughout the surrounding apartments. Perfume, at times, was the only remedy. To such unpleasantness were added other discomforts and high mortality. During the cold winter of 1709, Saint-Simon remembered icicles falling into his glass from the mantle above as he dined in an apartment in Versailles. Death cut such a swath through the royal family that poison was several times suspected.

With the death of Mazarin in 1661, Louis XIV began his period of personal rule, devoting eight hours a day to administration. All of the business of government for the next forty-five years was routinely referred to him, and there was to be no doubt of his authority. As had Richelieu, Louis regarded the French Huguenots as potential traitors. In 1685, he withdrew the Edict of Nantes, which guaranteed Huguenots religious freedom. Severe persecution and forced conversions followed. Bishop Bossuet hammered home the theory of royal absolutism, and at daily mass the congregation faced the king, not the celebrant.

Louis could make and break his ministers at will, but during his long reign he employed only sixteen, and most of them were from three families. Louis, while certainly not brilliant himself, had a knack for choosing good men, and he generally rewarded them well. Of all of Louis' ministers, it was beyond doubt that the most able and successful was Jean Baptiste Colbert, who was charged with managing the economy of France. Colbert was a thoroughgoing mercantilist, and he aimed at making France economically self-sufficient. He built canals and roads, promulgated a commercial code, ended many of the internal tariffs that inhibited trade, established state-run manufacturing concerns, rebuilt the navy, and encouraged colonization. In the end, however, Colbert accomplished few major reforms. Particularly in the area of tax collection, Colbert at best made a bad system work better, and he could not prevent his sovereign from spending vast sums on buildings and wars.

Louis loved war. Much of the French economy was taken up with the manufacture of war material, and the king himself occasionally intervened to lead troops and control the movements of his armies. Parades and military displays also fascinated him. Military reformers were given encouragement. Martinet, Inspector-General of Infantry, introduced harsh discipline and marching in step and thereby brought the term "martinet," meaning a person who advocates strict obedience to discipline and rules, into the English language. Vauban introduced the ring bayonet and revolutionized defensive warfare. Regular uniforms were introduced to the ranks, and by 1678 the French army numbered 280,000 men. Due to the efforts of Colbert, the French navy was also well-equipped, boasting 116 men-of-war.

Louis could not resist using his armies. He dreamed of securing the French frontiers and, more than that, of even extending them to the Rhine and the Alps. Louis had his first opportunity in 1667 when his father-in-law, Philip IV of Spain, died. Citing the *droit de dévolution*, a legal principle by which property was to go to the children of the deceased, Louis laid claim to the Spanish possessions in Brabant and Flanders in the name of his wife. Though a Triple Alliance of England, Holland, and Sweden partially blocked his plans, Louis was able to gain twelve fortified towns on the border of the

Spanish Netherlands by the terms of the Treaty of Aix-la-Chapelle (1668).

In 1672, having already disengaged England from the Triple Alliance in the Treaty of Dover (1670), Louis struck directly at the Dutch. French armies crossed the Rhine and pressed into the southern provinces of the Dutch Republic. By 1678 Ghent and Ypres fell to the French, and, in the same year, by the Treaty of Nimwegen, Louis gained from the Spanish, who had joined in the war, Franche-Comté and a number of key cities on the northeastern frontier. The Dutch, who fought valiantly, received back their territories in return for neutrality.

During the next eight years, Louis refrained from war but used the Chambers of Reunion, special courts designed to decide territorial claims, to absorb the dependent territories of those cities that had come to France by treaty. In 1683-84 Louis marched his armies into the Spanish Netherlands, occupied Luxembourg and Lorraine, and seized the city of Trier. By 1686, French arms and the power of the Sun King had awed the crowned heads of Europe. Only a precise series of events, and a group of strong leaders, prevented French dominance.

C. The Dutch Republic and the House of Orange

The Dutch Republic, which was in the way of so much of the diplomacy and warfare of Louis XIV, had gained what political unity it had the century before. At that time the aggressors had been the Hapsburgs, who had sought to stamp out the Reformation and heresy in their rebellious Dutch provinces. Collectively part of the "Low Countries," which in turn were but a part of the great hereditary empire of the Holy Roman Emperor, Charles V, the Dutch provinces were welded together by the harsh anti-Calvinist measures of Charles' son and successor, Philip II of Spain.

The architect of Dutch resistance was William the Silent, Prince of the House of Orange-Nassau and Stadholder of the United Provinces. For most of his life William the Silent resisted the Spanish. Then, in 1584, as he sat at table at Delft, an assassin in Spanish pay, whom William had invited to dinner, shot him through both lungs and stomach. William died almost instantly; his assailant, very slowly. Apprehended as he tried to vault a garden wall, William's assassin was later to murmur prayers as the executioner broke his body to bits, and with such zeal that a hammer was damaged in the process. When a spectator gasped at the gory spectacle, she was nearly lynched by her vengeful fellow citizens. Thus was the tenuous Dutch unity born: in anger, in resistance to the outsider, in religious controversy, in inquisition and iconoclasm, in violence and great effusions of blood.

Such unity as there was was confirmed by commerce and seaborne trade. In this the Dutch were fabulously successful, contradicting yet tempering their Protestant principles with sound mercantile decisions. All the while that the Dutch fought the Hapsburgs, they traded with Hapsburg Spain. Dutch *fluits,* ships that were little more than floating holds, sailed southward in hundreds to be laden with Mediterranean wine and Biscay salt, English cloth and Italian silk. Turning northward again, Dutch ships passed the Sound for the Baltic, to bring back grain and timber, pitch and tar. A vast trading network, extending from Danzig to Venice, from the White Sea to the Bay of Biscay, was maintained by the merchants and captains of Amsterdam.

In the Indies and the Americas, Dutch forts and factories grew up to challenge their Portuguese and Spanish predecessors. In the east the Dutch East India Company established itself in Batavia in 1619. To this was soon added Ceylon and Malacca, the Cape of Good Hope, and Indonesia. At about the same time, agents of the Dutch West India Company established themselves in Brazil and in the Caribbean. So rich and extensive was Dutch commerce and Dutch carrying trade that the English fought three Dutch Wars (1652-1654; 1665-1667; 1672-1674) to share in the former, and passed the first of the Navigation Acts, in 1651, to check the dominance of Dutch shipping.

The wealth of the seas and all the lands that touched them, the earnings of the merchants and factors and financiers of Haarlem and Amsterdam, produced in the seventeenth century a brilliant Dutch culture. The names of Dutch artists of the time seem to roll on endlessly, and their numerous works still enrich galleries all over the world: Rembrandt von Rijn and Jan Steen, Frans Hals and Jan Vermeer, Jacob van Ruisdael and Meindert Hobbema, Thomas de Keyser and Gerard Ter Borch, Jan Rauesteyn and Bartholomeus van der Helst, Pieter Codde and Jacob Duck, Jan de Hiem and Adrien Brouwer, Adriaen van Ostade and Judith Leyster. Among these men and women were wonderful painters of humankind, with all the sensitivity to form and anatomy bequeathed to them by the Renaissance; but there were also painters of landscapes and still lifes, who inform by their subject matter that, in art, the Renaissance had given way to the Baroque, where man is no longer the central concern, and is at best part of a larger, and sometimes daunting, environment.

A sense of light and fine detail characterized the art of the Dutch, and this is no accident. Dutch painters shared with Dutch scientists a fascination with optics and with the anatomy of the world. The telescope was a Dutch preoccupation, and Christian Huyghens, perhaps the most accomplished Dutch scientist of the time, was involved in improving it. Baruch Spinoza, a Dutch-Jewish philosopher who speculated on the nature of reality, was a lens-grinder by trade. Some of his fellows developed the microscope, and others, like Leeuwenhoek and Swammerdam, used this new invention to open the microbiological world. The painter Vermeer might have used the *camera obscura,* a by-product of such optical interest, to improve his understanding of the movement of light.

Portrait of a Young Man in an Armchair.
Rembrandt van Rijn
Courtesy of the Memorial Art Gallery of the University of Rochester. George Eastman Collection.

Although the Peace of Westphalia had guaranteed the liberties and elegant culture of the Dutch United Provinces, protecting both from Hapsburg encroachment, it confirmed as well French dominance over western Europe. With the accession of Louis XIV the leaders of the seven Dutch provinces found that they had merely exchanged one threat for another.

Further, the Dutch were compromised in their response to French incursions by the incoherence and inefficiency of their government. Only the strongest of personalities, combined with the deepest of dangers, could make the suspicious Dutch burghers respond with unity and alacrity. The Estates-General, the closest thing that the Dutch had to a central governing body, was in fact a consultative assembly only, and all decisions had to be confirmed by the estates of the seven Dutch provinces. Also, the seven provinces individually elected one Stadholder as executive, and total chaos was prevented only by the happy fact that each provincial body generally chose the same man. Generally, but not always, Stadholders were selected from members of the House of Orange-Nassau. Once elected, the Stadholders had to deal with the merchant-dominated estates, which saw little need for taxation or for the military defenses for which such taxes paid. At the same time, the Dutch were unforgiving if their leaders failed. In 1672, when the armies of Louis XIV pressed into the United Provinces, the brothers De Witt, the leaders who were partially to blame for the debacle, were snatched by a mob from the jail in which they were incarcerated. They were promptly riddled with musket fire, and it was hopefully as corpses and not as living men that the two were stripped, mutilated, and hung heads downward on a gallows.

This done, the Dutch once again looked to the House of Orange for leadership. This time its head was William III, the great-grandson of that William the Silent who had been assassinated in 1584. Born in 1650 as the result of a union between William II and Mary, the daughter of Charles I of England, William III had lived one of those lonely childhoods not untypical of the time. William II, described by one historian as "a rather grubby young man," spent the majority of his young life whoring, hunting, and gambling, and succumbed to smallpox before his only legitimate son was born. His wife, scrawny and frightened, who had been first forced into bed with her husband at the age of ten with a strategically sewn nightgown as her only protection, was left pregnant and alone. When Mary's son was born, the cheers of rejoicing fell upon the echoes of earlier rejoicing over the death of her husband. For more than twenty years thereafter the Dutch burghers ruled themselves through their Estates-General, untroubled by the interference of a Stadholder from the House of Orange.

In 1672, William III was finally elected Stadholder, but had at first to deal with the opposition of the De Witts and their allies. Only the reality of war and the death of the two De Witts gave him his opportunity. It was an opportunity that William III seized with alacrity, and a responsibility that he did not relinquish until his death in 1702.

In order to better resist the French, William managed to gain the support of the Holy Roman Emperor, the King of Denmark, and the Elector of Brandenburg. For eight years William cobbled armies together to resist the French. In 1678, by the Treaty of Nimwegen, the Dutch emerged from the war without losses, though the Spanish lost Franche-Comté.

The year before Nimwegen, William had strengthened his hand, and his claim to the English throne, by marrying Mary Stuart, the Protestant daughter of James, Duke of York. This marriage paid off handsomely in 1689 when, as a result of the English Revolution of 1688, William and Mary were summoned to England as joint sovereigns.

It was as king of England, as well as Stadholder, that William faced the renewed challenge of the French in 1689. Thus began the War of the League of Augsburg, named for the anti-French alliance of the Holy Roman Emperor, the kings of Sweden and Spain, and the electors of Bavaria, Saxony, and the Palatinate that had been put together some years before. To this alliance William was able to add the English and the Dutch. In all this Louis unintentionally cooperated. By his revocation of the Edict of Nantes, and by the base persecutions and forced conversions of French Huguenots, Louis aroused the hatred of Protestant Europe and allowed William to emerge as a Protestant champion. Against French arms William and his allies suffered defeat after defeat—at Fleurus and Staffarda in 1690, at Steinkirk in 1692, at Neerwinden and Marsaglia in 1693— but William kept his armies doggedly in the field. This grinding resistance, combined with a naval victory over the French at La Hogue in 1692, the failure of a French expedition to Ireland, and the death of Luxembourg, the most capable of Louis' generals, wore the French down. Although the French were able to force Savoy, a latecomer to the anti-French alliance, out of the war, the Peace of Ryswick, concluded in 1697, left matters substantially as they were ten years before.

With the French for the moment checked, an exhausted William turned to the administration of the United Provinces and England. To the old problem of rebellious Dutch burghers was added the newer afflictions of English politicians, both Whig and Tory. Louis XIV soon renewed his assault on the European balance of power. In 1700, coveting the vacant throne of Spain, Louis again threatened war, and William was obliged to put together yet another alliance against him. In 1702 as William rode through Richmond Park, he fell from his horse and suffered a broken collarbone. To this affliction were soon added recurrent fevers and swellings of the legs. The combination killed him. His senses clear to the end, William of

Orange died in great pain. "The man of God's right hand," so Bishop Burnet described his sovereign, applying scripture, "whom He made strong for Himself." Future resistance to the ambitions of Louis XIV had to be left to others

D. King Carlos II and the Spanish Dilemma

Carlos II, the last of the Hapsburg sovereigns of Spain, was in theory one of the most powerful rulers of his day. His titles, like those of his ancestor Charles V, move in resplendent clauses and commas: King of Spain, of Jerusalem, Naples, Sicily and Sardinia, of The New World, Archduke of Austria, Duke of Luxembourg and of Milan, Count of Hapsburg, of Flanders, of the Tyrol and Barcelona, Marquess of the Holy Roman Empire, Over Lord of Asia and Africa, Knight of the Order of the Golden Fleece. Unfortunately for Carlos, for his dynasty, and for his people, neither the glory nor the reality of his responsibilities intruded much upon his consciousness. Carlos II, king of Spain for thirty-five years, was thoroughly and tragically retarded.

Portrait of Carlos II. Claudio Coello
Courtesy of the Museo Nacional del Prado, Madrid.

This misfortune of mind and body was almost certainly the product of generations of inbreeding within the house of Hapsburg. The Hapsburg dynasty had prided itself on gaining and keeping its vast domains in Spain, Austria, the Low Countries, and the Americas through judicious marriages. Such unions may have been politic, but they were, in terms of genetics, ruinous to generations to come. Their result was that when Philip IV of Spain and Doña Mariana of Austria, the eventual parents of Carlos II, married, they did so as fairly close relations, with many ancestors in common.

The scholar John Langdon-Davies has portrayed this genetic labyrinth in exacting and horrible detail. Philip IV and Mariana of Austria shared no fewer than forty-eight ancestors. Among them were the likes of Isabella of Portugal, known as "the Mad," and her stepson Henry IV, mentally deficient and sexually nongenerative. Philip II of Spain, another ancestor, had fathered one heir who predeceased him, a young man cursed by mental as well as physical ills. Also in the family tree was Juana la Loca, bluntly called "Crazy Joanna" by English-speaking historians. Juana, a daughter of Ferdinand and Isabella, had been driven into frequent paroxysms of rage by the infidelities and cruelties of her adored husband, Philip the Handsome of Austria. Then, as Juana drifted deeper and deeper into insanity, Philip was carried off by a brief illness. Maddened by grief as she had once been by jealousy, Juana bore the body of her husband back to Spain, there to rest in a coffin close by her side, to be gazed upon and embraced by his crazed spouse. Juana la Loca, daughter of Isabella the Catholic and presumptive Queen of Spain, was locked away for the rest of her life on the orders of her own father.

Of this genetic misfortune, Philip IV and Doña Mariana may even have had more personal warnings, but these came in the unclear form of infant death, a commonplace occurrence in the seventeenth century. Though Philip IV had fathered several healthy illegitimate children, no fewer than six of his offspring by Doña Mariana had died at birth or in early childhood. It might have been especially hard for Philip to make the proper connection. As he was a man who combined gargantuan sexual appetites with a delicate, and Christian, conscience, Philip may have regarded the deaths of his legitimate children as God's judgment on his frequenting of brothels and fleshpots.

Still, when Doña Mariana was brought to bed with yet another pregnancy, the couple took precautions that they regarded as efficacious. Religious relics of perceived, if dubious, validity were brought from shrines and monasteries to repose in the delivery chamber. Carlos II was born in a room cluttered with thorns from Christ's crown, nails from the true cross and fragments thereof, and

Portraits of King Philip IV and Queen Mariana of Spain. Diego Velázquez Courtesy of the Meadows Museum and Art Gallery, Southern Methodist University.

the girdles of saints. They seemed at first to do their work well. Previous births had been nearly mortal for Doña Mariana. This one was auspiciously easy. "Most beautiful in features," so went an early description of the baby boy, "large head, dark skin, and somewhat overplump."

The happy initial impression did not last long. The French ambassadors reported with malicious glee to Louis XIV, who stood to gain much if the Spanish Hapsburgs died out, that the child was sickly, with a scaly eczema on his head and a suppurating sore on his neck. Other, and later, observers noted that the child walked late, that he was borne about for years in the arms of women, that squads of wetnurses were needed to attend him because his malformed jaw would not allow him to chew food and that he was in consequence not weaned until the age of four.

Though Carlos could stand at last by the age of six, he could not walk, or ride a horse, until much later. Rickets, recurrent fevers, vertigo, rashes, foul discharges, plagued Carlos into what passed for adulthood, and his mind grew even more poorly than his body. Documents were a torture to Carlos because he could barely read and write; in consequence he made his mark on anything put in front of him. Fresh air caused his eyes to water; physical effort gave him fevers; riding in a moving coach made him sick; the inability to masticate food forced him to gulp down meals in great lumps, which gave him chronic gastritis. "He has a ravenous stomach," noted the Duke of Shrewsbury of Carlos II, "and swallows all he eats whole . . . he has a prodigious wide throat, so that a gizzard or liver of a hen passes down whole, and his weak stomach not being able to digest it, he voids in the same manner."

Despite this vast range of physical maladies, Carlos II was married off twice in the vain hope that he would somehow produce an heir. Before the arrival of his first wife, Maria Luisa of France, Carlos became so excited that he grew feverish, but he was able to do little after her arrival. Maria Luisa was left to grow fat and frustrated. Denied the children that usually gave royal women what power they had, she appalled the conservative Spanish court with her French boldness, fell to plotting, and died amid rumors of poison in 1689. After the death of Maria Luisa, the bemused Carlos was married with indecent haste to Maria Ana of Neuburg, the daughter of the Elector Palatine. Again the dreary round of rumors began: false pregnancies, sniggers about impotence and premature ejaculation. "Three virgins there are in Madrid, The Cardinal's Library, Medina Sidonia's sword, and the Queen, our lady." So ran a ditty composed by a courtier or the mob.

Surprisingly, Carlos remained calm and on the whole dutiful as he presided over the wreck of his reign. He was devoted to the bullfight and to the Inquisition, those two blood dramas thought to be evocative of the Spanish spirit. He also liked to hunt. Although usually kindly, Carlos could indulge in crass and cruel practical jokes and flashes of temper. Carlos was said to giggle at those who pinched their fingers in doors or who had been obliged to stand out in the rain. Perhaps such behavior is even understandable in a person who was daily forced to acknowledge his many limitations and who quickly became the victim of pro-French and pro-Austrian factions at the Spanish court. Little wonder that Carlos II, according to one contemporary account, wore "a melancholic and faintly surprised look" at the age of twenty-five. Little wonder as well that the Spanish people, at a loss to explain Carlos' ill health as well as his inability to reproduce and the incompetency of his reign, called him *Carlos el Hechizado*—Carlos the Bewitched.

The misery of Carlos' life and reign has been seen by many historians as a personal symbol, a living metaphor, for the decline of Imperial Spain itself. Much has been written, and with validity, about Spain's dissolution in the seventeenth century. In addition to a weakened monarchy, Spain suffered from the consequences of revolts in Catalonia and elsewhere, and from the expulsion of the *Moriscos* and *Marranos,* respectively the Muslims and Jews of Spain. To the economic effects caused by the exile of some of its most productive people, Spain almost certainly added the problems of economic stagnation, population decline, and the presence of the *hidalgo* class, a large group of petty nobility whose profession of warfare was increasingly nonproductive. At the same time, Dutch and English sea power preyed on Spanish gold fleets and enabled each state to establish competing colonial empires. In 1640 Portugal, which had been absorbed by Spain in 1580, reestablished its independence. Finally, the Battle of Rocroi (1643) and the Peace of the Pyrenees (1659) seemed to firmly establish French dominance over her neighbor to the south.

More recent research has indicated that the decline of Spain in the later seventeenth century has perhaps been overstressed. Henry Kamen, among others, has argued that Spain's economic difficulties and population decreases began to resolve themselves by mid-century, while inflation began to moderate from the 1680s. Such conclusions are in a sense paralleled by cultural evidence. It is true that the *siglo de oro,* the "golden century," synonymous with names like El Greco and Velázquez in art, and Lope de Vega and Cervantes in literature, was over by 1650. Nonetheless writers like Calderón de la Barca and painters like Murillo, Leal, and Coello worked almost until the end of the century. Spain, for all of its problems, was still a worthy enough prize to be coveted by both Louis XIV and the Austrian Hapsburgs.

In these circumstances the tragic and futile life of Carlos II assumes a paradoxical importance. Carlos stands the "great man" theory of history on its head: As a dynastic sovereign he was significant precisely because he was not sovereign; a living proof, as John Langdon-Davies observed, that the weak can influence history as much as the strong. While Carlos played his games of spillikins and suffered from his many maladies, factions of the nobility, some pro-French, others pro-Austrian, battled for control of the Spanish government and the right to control Spanish policy. In place of the deficient Carlos there grew up a government of councils presided over by a series of *validos,* powerful favorites who ruled by virtue of association with the royal family and the nobility, or *caudillos,* the "strong men." In the first category were Father John Nithard, an Austrian Jesuit, and Fernando Valenzuela, a military adventurer; in the latter were Don Juan, the illegitimate son of Philip IV, and the actress Maria Calderón.

Carlos' feebleness of mind failed the Spanish state administratively; his body failed his dynasty biologically. When it became clear that Carlos would never produce a child, both Louis XIV and the Holy Roman Emperor Leopold I, each of whom had wed sisters of Carlos to lay claim to the Spanish throne, made treaties dividing Spain's dominions between them, and impatiently waited for the feeble king to die. Not until 1700 did Carlos II oblige them. Only then did the combined effects of his many ills and his physician's efforts kill him. During Carlos' last illness dead pigeons were placed strategically on his body to counter vertigo; entrails of recently-killed animals were deposited on his stomach to keep him warm; finally, the withered remains of saints were placed in his bed to aid his recovery. All was to no avail. On November 1, Carlos II passed from this world, his death, as his life, ascribed to witchcraft.

With Carlos' death, Louis XIV resolved to make Spain a possession of the French Bourbons. *Il n'y a plus de Pyrenees,* Louis purportedly said: "The Pyrenees exist no longer." Having claimed the Spanish throne for his grandson, and thus incurring the opposition of most of the other European powers, Louis commenced the greatest of his campaigns. The War of the Spanish Succession had begun.

E. Party Politics, the Duke and Duchess of Marlborough, and the War of the Spanish Succession

With the arrival of the news that Louis XIV had claimed the Spanish throne for his grandson, the King of England and Stadholder of the Netherlands, William III, forged his last coalition against his old adversary. This grouping of states, known as the Grand Alliance, consisted of England, Portugal, the Netherlands, Austria, Prussia, and many of the other member-states of what was once the Holy Roman Empire. Louis responded by putting together an alliance of his own. France was joined by the dukes of Savoy and Mantua, and the electors of Bavaria and Cologne. The opposing alliances proved surprisingly durable, and lasted for nearly fifteen years. Only Savoy changed sides, becoming a member of the Grand Alliance in 1703.

Having involved England in a European war, William III died, and Anne, the daughter of James II, became queen. She inherited a political structure that could, with charitable understatement, be called confused. The long reign of Charles II and the far shorter one of James II had given rise to two rival political factions or "parties," the Whigs and Tories. Far less organized than modern political parties, the Whigs and Tories consisted largely of landed nobility and gentry, who sat, respectively, in the House of Lords and the House of Commons, which together made up the English Parliament. Members of the House of Lords held their seats by hereditary right; members of the House of Commons were also men of property, who were elected to their seats by other property-holders.

After the Revolution of 1688, Parliament replaced the sovereign as the dominant power in the English state. Through legislation and the agreement of the new rulers, William and Mary, the members of Parliament were guaranteed in their rights and privileges. By the Mutiny Act, renewed annually from 1689, the maintenance of an army was made legal for one year only. This made it necessary to call Parliament on a yearly basis so the Act might be renewed. Frequent Parliaments were also insured by the Triennial Act of 1694.

The basis of Parliament's power was primarily financial. After 1689, the monarchy was granted an annual income but the monarch and his ministers of state had to seek a vote of Parliament if other funds were needed. They often were. The "power of the purse" thus guaranteed that Parliament could influence government policy.

Yet this potential for Parliamentary control would have come to nothing if leadership had not emerged to manage Parliament itself. The English Revolution of the seventeenth century had at last ended the quarrel as to whether the monarchy or Parliament should be the dominant power in the state by deciding in favor of the latter; what the English Revolution had *not* decided was *how* Parliament would be managed, or how it would undertake to govern a society growing increasingly complex and troubled by war.

The problem of management was compounded by the fact that the Revolution had not stripped the monarchy of all of its power. Far from it. The king or queen still called Parliaments to assemble, and advised them to dissolve. It was the monarch as well who appointed ministers of state, and who dismissed them. The sovereign, through his or her private income and control of land, controlled also a number of seats in the House of Commons, which were usually filled with "placemen" loyal to the monarchy. Finally, it was the king or the queen who could elevate members of great families to the peerage, or nobility, thus enabling them to sit in the House of Lords, and who controlled the distribution of knighthoods and other honors in church and state readily exchangeable for political favors.

Thus any leader who proposed to control English foreign and domestic policy had to manage, and coordinate the efforts of, two institutions: the monarchy and Parliament. The monarchy proved a difficult challenge, and Parliament even more. After 1688 Parliament was packed with Whig and Tory factions, which were led in turn by the heads of landed noble families. These Whig and Tory nobles, or magnates, generally sat in the House of Lords and used the political power they possessed through the ownership of land to control the election of their followers to the House of Commons. By using every tactic from political marriages to the outright management of seats and the purchase of votes, the magnates maintained their influence and power.

For the first years of their reign William and Mary tried to rule without becoming embroiled in the political factions of Parliament. William freely chose ministers from both the Whig and Tory factions, but by the mid-1690s, when it became obvious that the Whigs were more likely to support his anti-French policies than were Tories, William had begun to choose his ministers from among the powerful Whigs who sat in Parliament. Emerging as William's link between the monarchy and Parliament was the Earl of Sunderland, a prominent Whig politician. By consenting to a predominantly Whig ministry, William gained the votes of money and supply he needed to pursue his policies. In addition, by an Act of 1694, the Bank of England was created, which proved of invaluable assistance in stabilizing the currency, funding the national debt, and financing the wars against Louis XIV.

For these gains William had to pay a price. To appease the Whigs he consented to the Triennial Act of 1694. William also gained the hatred of the Tories. The Tories, some of whom were Jacobites, or supporters of the exiled Stuart kings, were driven to oppose William's policies, forcing William to be more dependent on the Whigs and on the concept of party government.

With the death of William III in 1702, the throne passed, by the Act of Succession, to Anne, the second Protestant daughter of James II. While William had only reluctantly used the Whigs, and was suspicious of parties, Anne was by inclination an ardent Tory, believing the Tories to be the conservative party of "church and king." Though she was at least initially for prosecuting the War of the Spanish Succession, Anne also made it clear in several speeches to Parliament that she was pro-Tory. The Whigs feared loss of power and the possible abandonment, at the hands of the Tories, of the Whig war policy. To pursue the war, the Whigs had to manage a fractious Parliament and a Tory queen.

All these tasks fell, at least in part, to one of the most interesting political and personal unions in English history, that between John Churchill, Duke of Marlborough, and his Duchess, Sarah.

Portrait of John Churchill. Attr. Sir Godfrey Kneller
Courtesy of the Hudson's Bay Company, Winnepeg, Manitoba.

Born Sarah Jennings in 1660, the years of the Restoration, the girl who eventually became the Duchess of Marlborough went in her own words "extream young into the court and had the luck to be liked." In the court of Charles II, at the age of ten, she had met, and established a friendship with, the Princess Anne.

At the age of fifteen Sarah Jennings, ambitious, calculating, audacious, and tough, was married to John Churchill who, after a mediocre education at St. Paul's School, had come to court as page to Anne's father, the future James II of England. John Churchill had his court connections as well. Arabella Churchill, his elder sister, had been mistress to James, and John Churchill himself had formed a liaison with Barbara Villiers, Duchess of Cleveland, at one time mistress to King Charles II. The union between John Churchill and Sarah Jennings was a judicious, political marriage, made between two well-established court families.

Sarah brought to the match all of her ambition and physical vigor. Between 1679 and 1690, Sarah Churchill gave birth to no less than seven children, of whom four reached full, marriageable adulthood. As she raised her children Sarah also reestablished her friendship with Princess Anne, who married Prince George of Denmark in 1683. Soon after, Anne began to suffer the long and mortal round of births and miscarriages that was to scar her life. Desolate, in need of support, Anne turned to Sarah Churchill, appointing her a lady of the Bedchamber. From her position at court, Sarah Churchill sought to strengthen the position of her family through marriage. One daughter, Henrietta, was married to the son of the Earl of Godolphin, a prominent power broker and politician; another, Anne, was betrothed to the eldest son of the powerful Whig magnate and minister of William III, the Earl of Sunderland. The Churchill family was now connected both to the court and to some of the most influential parliamentary families.

At the same time John Churchill was using his connection with James to enrich his family. He served with the future king of England in Scotland, and was awarded a Scottish peerage and lands. With the coming of the Revolution of 1688, however, John Churchill abandoned his patron and sided with the victorious William. Anne, raised a Protestant, and far from close to the Catholic James II, needed little prodding from Sarah Churchill to abandon her father.

During most of the reign of William and Mary the Churchills found themselves in the political wilderness. Anne and her sister, Queen Mary, became estranged, and John Churchill, perhaps because of the family connection with Anne, perhaps because of rumored Jacobite sympathies, was deprived of his military command by King William. Anne, however, continued to be generous, and awarded Sarah a yearly pension of £1,000.

With the death of William and the accession of Anne, the Churchills came sweeping back into power. Sarah Churchill was appointed to key court offices: Groom of the Stoll, Keeper of the Privy Purse, Mistress of the Robes. Her husband was named Knight of the Garter, Captain-General, and Master of the Ordnance. John Churchill was also put in charge of English military operations against Louis XIV. Despite her conservatism, Anne could not now ignore the challenge of Louis XIV. Contrary to the Act of Succession of 1701, which had bequeathed the throne to Anne, Louis recognized the exiled Stuart "Pretender" as king of England. In such circumstances, the triumph of the Churchills and the pro-war faction seemed complete. As if to confirm this, two of Sarah's daughters were made Ladies of the Bedchamber and Godolphin, now an in-law, was named Lord Treasurer.

Though her husband was a moderate Tory who disliked the idea of party and faction, Sarah Churchill was a thoroughgoing Whig who worried over Anne's Tory sympathies, and who listened to the histrionics of her violently Whig son-in-law, the Earl of Sunderland. Together with four other Whig lords, Sunderland organized the Whig "Junto" as a counterbalance to the Tories who dominated Anne's Council of State, or Privy Council. It fell to Sarah Churchill to try to control the queen. She did so with zest, but not always with tact. In their correspondence Sarah Churchill became "Mrs. Freeman" and Anne "Mrs. Morley." Mrs. Morley often seemed pathetic, while Mrs. Freeman was petty and bullying. Underestimating Anne, Sarah Churchill unwittingly began to undermine her own position through tactlessness.

In fairness to Sarah Churchill she had reason to fear the Tories for they might have indeed undermined the political position of her husband, often abroad conducting campaigns against the French. The Parliamentary election of 1702 ushered in a solid Tory majority, but it was more fragile than it first appeared. The radical Tories made their party unpopular in 1704 when they attempted to "tack," or attach, an Occasional Conformity bill, a strongly anti-Protestant and anti-Whig measure, to another bill for financial appropriation. The attempts of the "Tackers" put the Tories in bad repute, and the Godolphin-Churchill faction was, in the 1705 elections, with the help of the Whigs, able to regain enough seats for the latter party to cut into the Tory majority. With Parliament more evenly divided, Godolphin, as the queen's chief minister, was able to manage political affairs.

The personal fortunes of the Churchills continued to wax. In 1702 Queen Anne made John Churchill Duke of Marlborough and, despite Sarah Churchill's objections that it was an honor the family could not afford, he accepted. Sarah's complaints about lack of money were more than answered by Anne, who offered the Marlboroughs a yearly income of £2000, which the new Duchess initially, and unwisely, declined as insufficient.

John Churchill more than earned his dukedom. The land forces of the Grand Alliance triumphed over those of Louis XIV. In August of 1704, the forces of Marlborough and Prince Eugene of Savoy were victorious at Blenheim. Two years later, at Ramillies, Marlborough was again successful, receiving the submission of Brussels, Antwerp, and Ghent after a successful battle. In the same year Prince Eugene defeated the French at the Battle of Turin, driving the forces of Louis XIV from Italy. In 1708 and 1709, respectively, Marlborough and Prince Eugene won again at Oudenarde and Malplaquet. In 1705, under the guidance of the accomplished architects Vanbrugh and Hawksmoor, the cornerstone of a magnificent palace, to be called Blenheim after Marlborough's great victory, was laid, the gift of a grateful nation. From the Emperor Leopold the Marlboroughs obtained the state of Mindelheim, near the Danube, and were thus, technically, prince and princess.

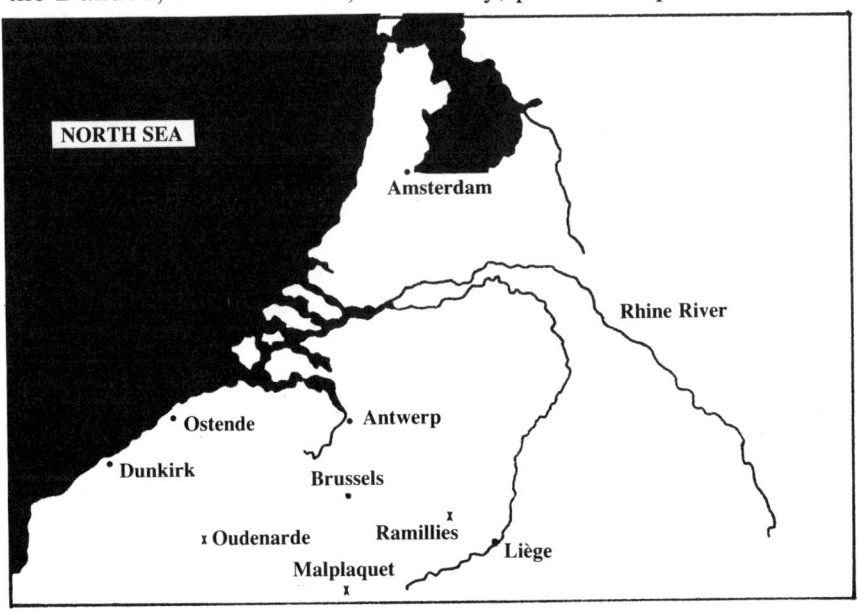

X — Battles fought by the Duke of Marlborough

This part of Europe has always been regarded by the English as strategically crucial. Wellington engaged Napoleon at the Battle of Waterloo near Brussels in 1815, and the British entered World War I on the German invasion of the same area in 1914.

Key Battles Fought by the Duke of Marlborough in the War of the Spanish Succession

It was in the midst of all these victories, ironically, that the Marlboroughs fell from grace. The Duchess of Marlborough had a relation, Abigail Masham, whom she had introduced to the court and to Queen Anne. Mrs. Masham turned out to be a wise young woman and quickly ingratiated herself with the queen. Less high-strung and less bossy than the Duchess of Marlborough, Abigail Masham cheerfully endured Anne's endless card games, her ills, and her boring conversation. In concert with a newfound ally, the Tory Sir Robert Harley, Earl of Oxford, Abigail Masham gained the queen's ear, usurped the position of her former patron at court, and lessened the influence of the Marlboroughs. The Duchess of Marlborough, outraged at what she considered betrayal and disloyalty, contributed to the demise of her fortune through high-handed actions and words.

The Marlboroughs' personal decline roughly followed a Whig reversal in Parliament. In the elections of 1708, under the leadership of Sunderland, in the wake of Marlborough's victories and the discovery of a French-Jacobite plot to invade Scotland, the Whigs swept into power. Two years later, however, largely due to the efforts of Robert Harley, the "Backstairs Dragon," in leading an anti-Whig purge at the court, the Tories were able to come back to power with a substantial majority.

In short order, the Harley ministry removed Marlborough from his command. This coincided with other events that in the end broke up the Grand alliance. With the death of the Emperor Joseph in 1711, the Archduke Charles, the Hapsburg candidate for the Spanish throne, inherited all of the Hapsburg territories in Germany. The other members of the Grand Alliance, fearing a reunion of Hapsburg Germany and Spain as much as they feared a union of France and Spain under the Bourbons, lost their zeal and unity. They sued for peace.

Reacting to the wreckage of their dreams, the Marlboroughs repaired to their still-incompleted palace at Blenheim. Their departure was accompanied by news both bad and good. As the peace negotiations progressed to end the War of the Spanish Succession, Queen Anne slipped into a final coma and died. With even more satisfaction the Duchess Sarah may have observed the demise of her political enemies. The two Tory leaders, Oxford and Bolingbroke, quarreled. This, combined with renewed charges of Jacobite activity on the part of the Tories, allowed for a complete Whig triumph after 1715.

All of this was too late for the Marlboroughs. Already saddened by the death of some of her children, the Duchess Sarah buried her husband, who succumbed after a series of strokes, in 1722. Sarah herself lived until 1744, finishing her vast house, seeing to her family interests, distributing advice, and filling paper after paper with histories and harangues. Only one of her children outlived her, but all had married well, and the Marlboroughs were established as one of the great families of England. One of Sarah's direct descendants, Sir Winston Churchill, served England with distinction as Prime Minister during the Second World War. After commenting on the death of the poet Alexander Pope, the writer Tobias Smollet noted the death of the Duchess quite baldly: ". . . the old Duchess of Marlborough resigned her breath in the 85th year of her age, immensely rich and very little regretted by her own family or by the world in general." More fitting perhaps was the comment of Arthur Maynwaring: "There is nobody like her, nor ever will be."

During the public careers of the first Marlboroughs, English politics took a form that was to last for more than a century. In order for a minister of state to run the country efficiently, he had to have the support of Parliament certainly and the sovereign usually. Above all else he had to negotiate with, and earn the support of, the landed nobles and other "interests" who controlled Parliament. To lose the support of court or Parliament, as the Marlboroughs found, was to invite disaster. The long road to responsible parliamentary government had begun.

The pressure of constant war in the period 1688-1714 also had its effect on English politics. War created the need for government finance, and to this need the English, but not the French, responded. The Bank of England was the foundation on which the stable English economy stood, and the French had no counterpart. Unlike the French nobility, the English landed classes participated in the government through their Parliament and through their pocketbooks. The union of the English government with the wealthiest segment of its population was the source of English stability and power in the eighteenth century.

F. European Realignment: The Peace of Utrecht and After

The War of the Spanish Succession finally ended with a series of agreements comprehended in the treaties of Utrecht and Rastadt of 1713 and 1714. The Treaty of Utrecht was not universally praised, popular, or lasting. So unpopular was the Treaty of Utrecht in England that the Tories had to ask the monarch to create twelve new peers to insure its passage through the House of Lords. The English did not tire of fighting the French. In fact the two powers fought intermittently for another century, until the time of the Vienna Congress in 1815.

Despite Tory peace-mongering, the English emerged very successfully from the treaty negotiations. England and Scotland, joined as Great Britain in the Act of Union of 1707, greatly extended their influence in the Americas, obtaining from the French not only Nova Scotia and Newfoundland but the vast and ill-defined mass of territory known as Hudson's Bay; the acquisition of Gibraltar and Minorca, also acquired at Utrecht, strengthened the British presence in the Mediterranean. Most valuable was the *asiento,* a trading privilege conceded by the Spaniards, allowing the British to be the chief suppliers of slaves to Spanish America. Building on the *asiento,* the British developed a lucrative trading network in the western hemisphere. Indirectly, Great Britain also profited from the exhaustion of the Dutch in the long wars with France. From the wars against Louis the Dutch gained little but the right to garrison certain barrier fortresses along the French border. The existence of the Dutch Republic was confirmed, but at the expense, over the long term, of conceding its commercial superiority to the British. Finally, the British gained a measure of political stability when the French promised at Utrecht to abandon the Stuart pretenders and recognize the Protestant succession in England and Scotland.

French might was thus balanced in western Europe with that of an emergent Great Britain. It is a mistake, however, to assume that France ceased to be a great power. French civilization continued to dominate Europe, and French economic interests continued to challenge the British in India and North America. The French, by the Peace of Utrecht, were also allowed to keep Louis XIV's conquests in Franche-Comté and Alsace. Lastly, Louis' grandson was permitted to become the first Bourbon king of Spain, on the understanding that the French and Spanish monarchies would never be ruled by the same sovereign. When Louis XIV died in 1715, he left the French government severely weakened financially and his absolutist state vulnerable to aristocratic recovery. Nonetheless, France remained a formidable power.

Other powers waxed or recovered as a result of Utrecht. Savoy was enlarged markedly by the acquisition of the large island of Sardinia in the Mediterranean, and in the nineteenth century became the nucleus around which modern Italy was unified. The small state of Prussia, eventually the center of a unified Germany, received a royal title for its ruling dynasty of Hohenzollern and acquired Spanish Guelderland. The Austrian Hapsburgs, dealt with so harshly at the Peace of Westphalia, came away with Milan, Naples, and Sicily, which had formerly belonged to Spain. Spain, though it was forced to replace its defunct Hapsburg dynasty with a French Bourbon one, was able to retain its empire in the Americas. The Bourbons gave to Spain a long-lived dynasty that lasted until 1931.

The Peace of Utrecht thus joined that of Westphalia as one of the key treaties of European history. Though an important peace, it did not prove a lasting one. The eighteenth century, like its predecessor, was one of war and revolution. The idea of the balance of power had become enshrined in the hearts and minds of European diplomats, but it was not always productive of the peace and stability which provided its major justification. Before the eighteenth century, the balance of power had been applied against single overwhelming dynastic powers—the Hapsburgs or the France of Louis XIV. After 1715, the European world grew infinitely more complex. Newer, yet substantial, European powers—Great Britain, Prussia, and Russia—took their places among, and competed for influence with, more established states. It was a situation that strained, and often overwhelmed, the skills of foreign secretaries and ambassadors.

Portfolio: The Health Professions—Physicians, Surgeons, Midwives, Anatomists, and Quacks

Title page from *The Grete Herball* . . . (London, 1526). Compendiums of herbal medicine like this one were very commonly used. *Courtesy of the History of Science Collections, University of Oklahoma Libraries.*

Title page from Andreas Vesalius, *Humani corporis fabrica Libri septum* (Basel, 1543).
The drawings in Vesalius' work, one of the landmarks in the history of anatomical research, are also splendid examples of Renaissance art. *Courtesy of the Edward G. Miner Library, University of Rochester School of Medicine and Dentistry.*

The Kopster [Cupper]. Cornelius Dusart
Humoral medicine, first enunciated by ancient physicians, required that the four bodily "humors" be in balance to maintain good health. Illness was thus often ascribed to an excess of one of them. To maintain or restore health, many practitioners in the seventeenth and eighteenth centuries prescribed purges, bloodlettings, and other harsh measures for their patients. In this scene, glass cups, in company with the heat of candles, are being used to draw "excess" blood to the skin surface. Sometimes leeches or the knives of a barber-surgeon were employed instead. *Courtesy of the Yale Medical Library, Clements C. Fry Collection.*

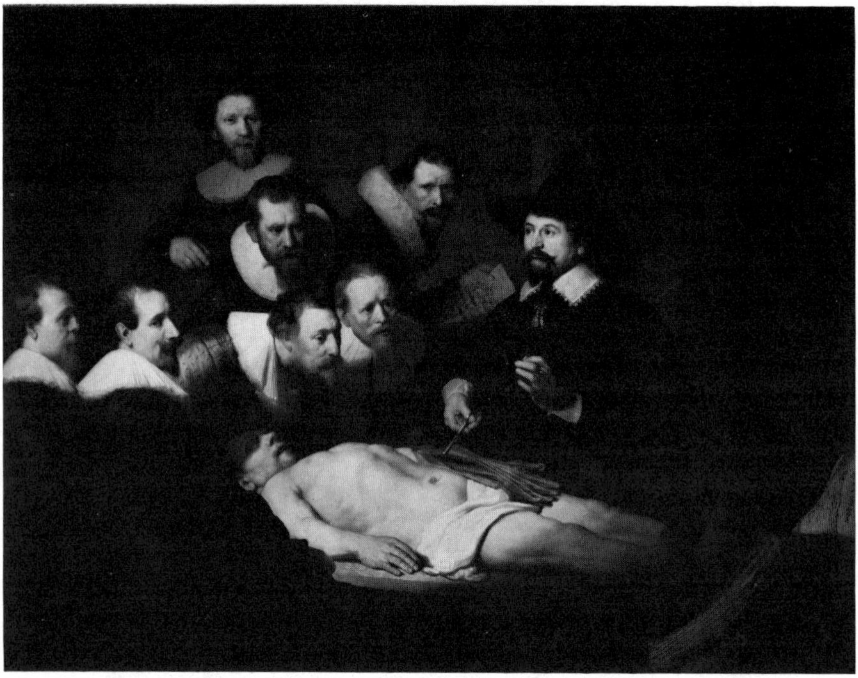

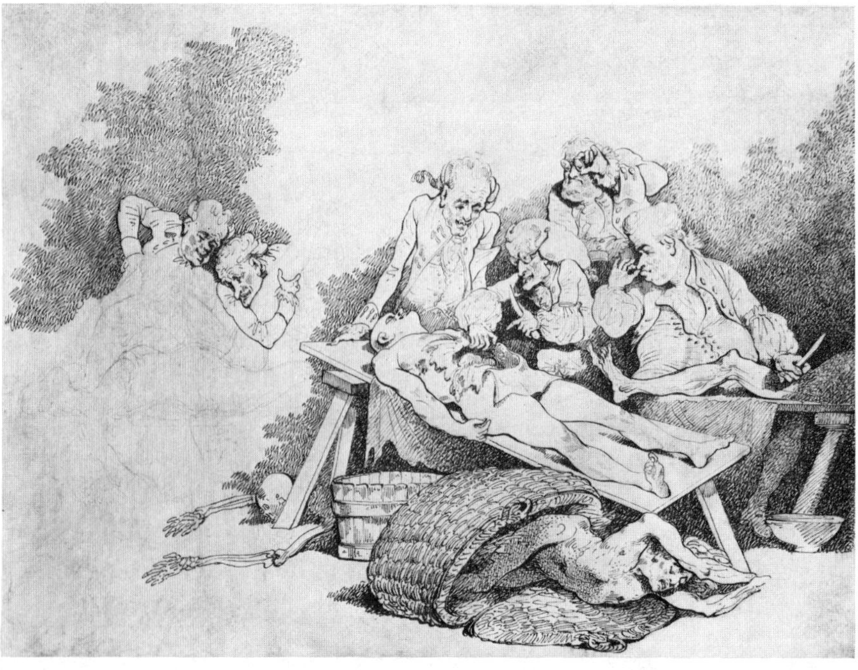

The Anatomy Lesson of Dr. Tulp. ***Opposite, top.*** Rembrandt van Rijn
This magnificent and famous painting portrays medical anatomy in an idealized fashion. *Courtesy of the Mauritshuis Museum, The Hague.*

The Dissection. ***Opposite, bottom.*** Thomas Rowlandson
Public acceptance of anatomical research was not always enthusiastic, as is demonstrated by this drawing. Public opinion, already suspicious with regard to physicians in general, could turn menacing when vivisection was concerned. Those who participated in anatomical demonstrations, and those who obtained corpses for that purpose, were reviled for their alleged ghoulishness and provoked occasional riots by their practices. *Courtesy of the Huntington Library and Art Gallery, San Marino, California.*

The Barber-Surgeons. Flemish woodcut [artist unknown]
Far from enjoying the prestige they do today, surgeons in early modern Europe were less well-regarded than physicians and were sometimes accused of quackery. In this engraving, a bevy of barber-surgeons, lampooned by being portrayed as apes, cut hair, induce vomiting, let blood, extract teeth, attend a wound, and prepare medicines. *Courtesy of the Yale Medical Library, Clements C. Fry Collection.*

234

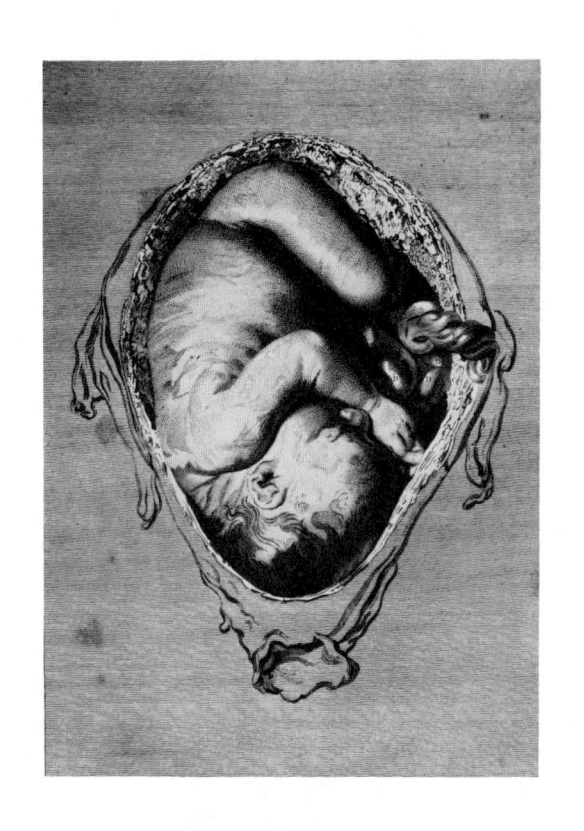

Illustration of a child in the womb, from Sir William Hunter, *The Anatomy of the Human Gravid Uterus*. (Birmingham, 1774). ***Opposite, Top.***
Hunter's marvelous, illustrated study of a fetus in the womb is an example of how human tragedy can paradoxically contribute to medical advance. "A woman died suddenly," Hunter wrote, "when very near the end of her pregnancy; the body was procured before any sensible putrefaction had begun. . . ." Taking advantage of the opportunity, and the coldness of the weather, Hunter conducted a series of dissections that were a fundamental contribution to obstetric anatomy.

The Lying-in Room. ***Opposite, bottom.*** Adriaen or Carol Dusart
In this idealized childbirth scene the mother and newborn infant are attended by midwives. Slowly but persistently male physicians and surgeons, asserting superiority in training and professionalism, replaced the midwife as the chief attendants at birth. *Courtesy of the Yale Medical Library, Clements C. Fry Collection.*

Pass-Room Bridewell. A. C. Rugin and Thomas Rowlandson
Resembling a prison more than any modern conception of a hospital, London's Bridewell was the forced residence of indigent women and prostitutes. Only in recent times have hospitals been viewed solely as sites of advanced medical treatment. In earlier centuries they were regarded as warehouses for the poor and diseased who, left unattended, might threaten the welfare of the society. *Courtesy of the Yale Medical Library. Clements C. Fry Collection.*

La Pharmacie Rustique. Gottfried Locher and Barthelemi Hubner Pharmacists, to the increasing rage of their physician-contemporaries, not only prepared medicines but gave medical advice as well. In rural areas, distant from the well-stocked shelves of the pharmacist, an unlicensed underclass practiced folk medicine and compounded the herbal remedies that were utilized by the common people. *Courtesy of the Yale Medical Library, Clements C. Fry Collection.*

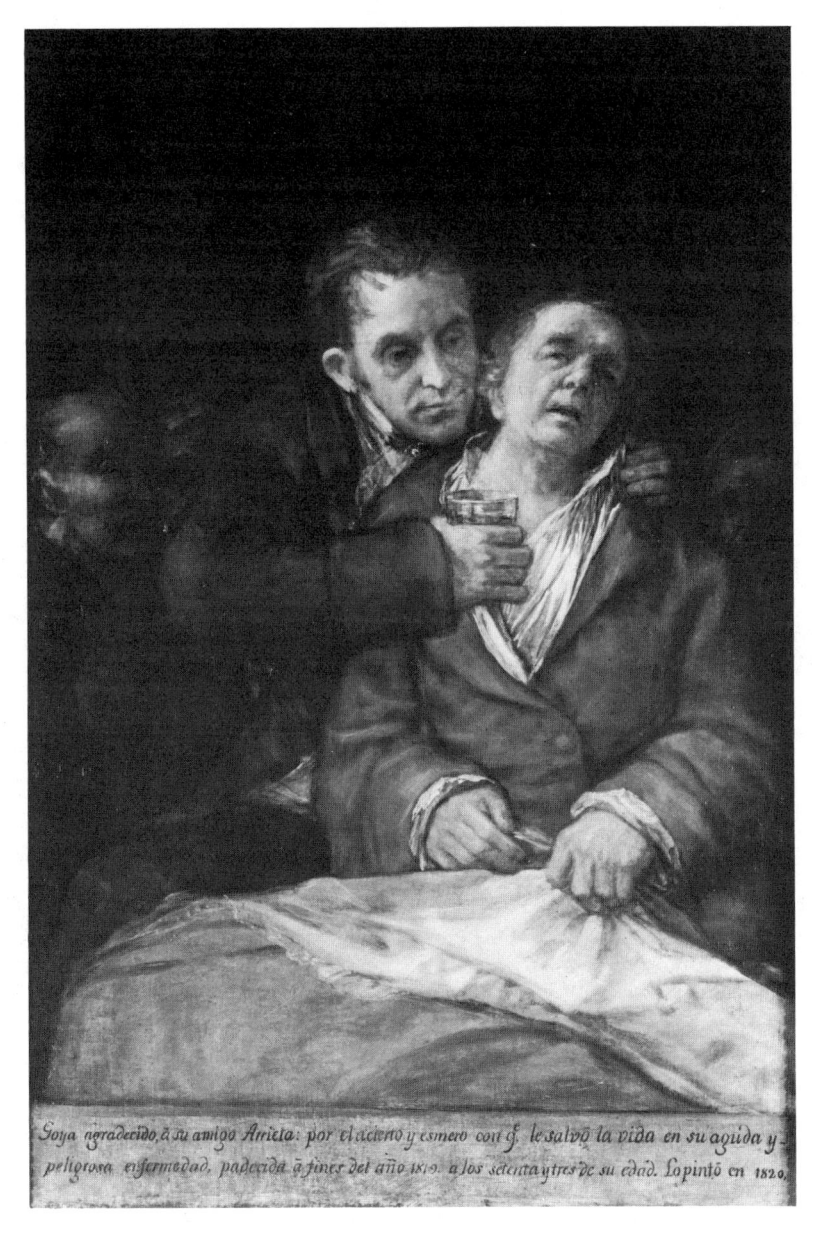

Self Portrait with Dr. Arrieta. Francisco José de Goya y Lucientes
Goya's work, painted in about 1820, testifies both to his faith in his own
physician and to the fact that some practitioners, despite a relative modesty
of medical knowledge, served and cared for their patients. *Courtesy of The
Minneapolis Institute of Arts. Ethel Morrison Van Derlip Fund.*

Madhouse at Saragossa. Francisco José de Goya y Lucientes
In this stunning painting, Goya documented the plight of the mad, incarcerated without understanding or compassion, often a form of entertainment for those willing to provide their keepers with an admission fee. *Courtesy of the Meadows Museum and Art Gallery, Southern Methodist University.*

Chapter V

The Scientific Revolution and the Enlightenment, 1600-1800: René Descartes, Galileo Galilei, Isaac Newton, William Harvey, Voltaire, and Mary Wollstonecraft

> The raising of notions and axioms by *legitimate Induction*, is doubtless the proper Remedy for removing and driving out the Idols of the Mind. . . .
> —Francis Bacon

> . . . I think, therefore I am. . . .
> —René Descartes

> Let us then suppose the mind to be, as we say, a white paper, void of all characters, without any ideas; how comes it to be furnished? . . . I answer, in one word, from experience. . . .
> —John Locke

> The toleration of religion is a law of nature. . . .
> —Voltaire

> Would men but generously snap our chains, and be content with rational fellowship instead of slavish obedience, they would find us. . . better citizens.
> —Mary Wollstonecraft

Geometry existed before the creation, is coeternal with the mind of God, is God himself. . . .

—John Kepler

We have in our age new accidents and observations, and such, that I question not in the least, but if Aristotle were now alive, they would make him change his opinion.

—Galileo Galilei

Mural Quadrant from Tycho Brahe's *Astronomiae instauratae mechanica* (1602).
Courtesy of the History of Science Collections, University of Oklahoma Libraries.

A. A Scientific Revolution?

Beginning in the late sixteenth century a noticeable number of important scientific discoveries, observations, calculations, and experiments were made. These events, in the collective, are said by some historians to constitute a "Scientific Revolution." While other scholars feel that this term implies too much, and avoid using it, there seems little doubt that the years between 1600 and 1700 witnessed the flowering of many forms of science.

The language of this "new science," if it may be so called, was mathematics, and the sixteenth and seventeenth centuries are heavy with mathematical discovery. The Italian Nicolò Tartaglia (1506-1559), the first man to prove that missiles from a cannon followed an arc trajectory, also did fundamental work in algebra. Tartaglia's work in cubic equations was amplified by Girolamo Cardano (1501-1576), who introduced negative and imaginary roots. The Englishman Robert Recorde (1510-1558) introduced the sign of equality ($=$), and the Italian Franciscus Vieta (1540-1603) began to use reduction to solve algebraic equations, alphabetic letters to denote unknown quantities, and the plus ($+$) and minus ($-$) signs.

Equally important was the work of John Napier (1550-1617). Napier's discovery of logarithms, which he may in fact share with the Swiss watchmaker Jobst Bürgi, reduced multiplication and division to addition and subtraction, and the extractions of roots to division. Napier also created a calculating machine based on a set of ivory rods inscribed with geometric squares ("Napier's bones").

The gateway to higher mathematics was now open, and seventeenth-century mathematicians surged through it. Pierre de Fermat (1601-1665) and René Descartes (1596-1650), each working independently, began to apply algebra to geometry, and in so doing invented analytic and coordinate geometry. Wilhelm Leibniz (1646-1716) and Isaac Newton (1642-1727) can be credited with the invention of calculus. Finally, intellectual interest and the fascination with gambling led to the creation of probability theory and statistics. Cardano actually wrote a handbook on games of chance, but it was Pierre de Fermat and Blaise Pascal (1623-1662) who put probability theory on a modern basis.

If mathematics became the language of the new science, observation and experiment was its creed, and measurement and the discovery of physical laws its preoccupation. At times, as the historian Roland Stromberg has observed, the mathematicians and experimenters often quarreled over the viability of their methods. Indeed, Sir Francis Bacon (1561-1626), considered the "father of inductive science," and thus of the modern scientific method, was not forward in his study of mathematics. Nonetheless, by his thoroughgoing skepticism, Bacon helped move science away from the authoritarianism of Aristotle and toward empiricism. In his *Novum Organum* (1621), Bacon urged on his contemporaries the techniques of careful observation and experimentation. Science should begin, Bacon insisted, with the observation of particular phenomena, from which axioms and hypotheses might eventually be derived.

Observation was enhanced by the utilization of new tools to aid the eye. Many of the new scientists were fascinated with optics and light. The Italian Galileo Galilei (1564-1642) applied the newly-invented telescope to the heavens, with spectacular results. Galileo's countryman Marcello Malpighi (1628-1694) made use of the new technology of the microscope to discover capillaries in human anatomy and to understand plant growth. The Dutch scientist Leeuwenhoek (1632-1723) used the same instrument to see, for the first time, bacteria, spermatozoa, and corpuscles. At about the same time Jan Swammerdam (1637-1680) abandoned his medical training to use the microscope to anatomize over three thousand species of insects.

"Physico-mechanical laws are, as it were, the telescope of our spiritual eye, which can penetrate into the deepest night of times past and to come." These words of the scientist Helmholtz describe the importance of physical laws in the new science. Utilizing mathematics and observation as tools, seventeenth-century scientists believed they had begun to discover a new universe, knowable, measurable, and amenable to laws that humankind could determine. As early as 1550 Cardano had written of a natural law unifying and supremely powerful, yet knowable through experiment and empiricism. Galileo, applying mathematics to the dynamics of falling bodies, discovered the law of inertia, which held that objects would remain in motion indefinitely if retarding forces like friction could be checked. Robert Boyle (1627-1691) discovered the law of reciprocity of volume and pressure in a gas. Pascal enumerated his law of fluid mechanics: that pressure applied to a confined fluid is transmitted equally. Fluidity and mechanics, dynamics and motion fill the notebooks of seventeenth-century scientists, reflecting their belief that the universe and everything in it moved, and moved with the elegance of a divine, yet knowable, mathematics.

Mathematics, a rigor in observing and experimenting, a belief in knowable, physical laws—these were the hallmarks of the new science, and the work of many seventeenth-century scientists can be said to embody them. Four of these scientists seem particularly representative: René Descartes, Isaac Newton, Galileo Galilei, and William Harvey.

B. René Descartes, the New Science, and Mathematics

René Descartes, mathematician and philosopher, was born into the family of a prominent French lawyer, a member of the Parlement of Rennes, in 1596. The infant boy was thus immediately a member of that privileged class, the *noblesse de robe*, which ranked above the bourgeoisie, but below the old nobility, in status.

Though they might seem unusual today, the circumstances of Descartes' birth and upbringing, which are known only in bare outline, were troubling but not unconventional for the seventeenth century. The death of Descartes' mother in childbed only a year after his own birth made his family only too typical of the time in the absence of close emotional relationships. Descartes' father married again very quickly and seems to have been away from home a good deal, and Descartes did not ingratiate himself with the rest of the family when he failed to pursue the law as a career. The lack of familial closeness no doubt explains Descartes' absence from his father's funeral and from family weddings.

At the age of eight, Descartes, whose brilliance was already impressive, was sent away to school at the Royal College of La Flèche, operated by the Jesuit Order. Thereafter, Descartes returned home seldom and as soon as possible sold off the lands of his mother's inheritance, investing the profits to insure a modest but life-long income.

Descartes apparently loved La Flèche, and his Jesuit teachers grew fond of him. Because of his fragile health, Descartes was allowed to languish in bed in the mornings, an indulgence, one suspects, not allowed to his classmates. Several of his instructors possessed first-rate minds. To this early scholastic education Descartes owed much. He knew both ancient and medieval literature and philosophy; he wrote both French and Latin with elegance; he was a master of dialectical argument. Descartes did not forget his indebtedness. Despite the fact that his later thought challenged some of the doctrines of the Catholic Church, Descartes remained loyal to the bulk of its teachings and was wedded to the idea of the existence of God and to the deductive reasoning characteristic of scholastic philosophy.

There is little doubt as well that Descartes loved the learning and books of the medieval and classical past, once remarking "that the reading of all the great books is like conversing with the best people of earlier times." He began to discover, however, that simple book-learning left him only minimal intellectual satisfaction. The more he knew, the more ignorant he felt. The only exception was mathematics. Mathematics, Descartes believed, was "because of the certainty and self-evidence of its proofs" the only discipline that might rescue him from the uncertainties and doubts that had begun to plague him.

With that germ of hope, Descartes left La Flèche, took a degree in law at Poitiers as a sop to the wishes of his family, and departed France with the unlikely ambition of serving in the mercenary armies of the Thirty Years' War.

In so doing, Descartes began a life-long journey that took him from Holland, back to France, to Germany, and back again. He found mentors and teachers on his journeys: the Dutch polymath Isaac Beeckman, who introduced him to the work of the mathematician Vieta; the French cleric Marin Mersenne, a valuable conduit to the leading intellects of the day. These travels, undertaken by Descartes to "gain experience" in the "book of the world" caused him to develop an intellectual relativism, a tolerance toward new ideas that seems very modern. Descartes had already discovered "that one cannot imagine anything so strange and unbelievable that it has been upheld by some philosophers." His travels taught him, further, "that those who held opinions contrary to ours were neither barbarians nor savages," but rather "at least as reasonable as ourselves."

At the same time, Descartes' scholastic background made it impossible for him to be really comfortable with relative truths, any more than he had been with the contradictions he found in books. In 1619, in a series of three dreams, Descartes conceived of a "universal science" that could be applied to all intellectual endeavors and that would replace contradiction and uncertainty with logical precision. The core of this "science of sciences" was to be mathematics, particularly geometry. "Those long chains of reasoning, simple and easy as they are," Descartes wrote, "of which geometricians make use in order to arrive at the most difficult demonstrations, had caused me to imagine that all things . . . might be mutually related in the same fashion. . . ."

For Descartes, it was the chain of reasoning that mattered. If one began well, and reasoned logically and analytically thereafter, all that was needed was a starting place in fact. Like Bacon, Descartes believed that one must move along a chain of reasoning in an orderly way, step by step. Beyond that, however, the two parted company. Descartes had no patience for Bacon's belief in observation and experiment; mathematics was the authoritative way to find the truth. Descartes was the systematizer of the new science, while Bacon was its first experimenter and empiricist. While Bacon emphasized inductive reasoning, Descartes' reasoning was, in the tradition of the medieval schoolmen, essentially deductive. Once a first cause was established, the rest was easy enough. "After that," Descartes wrote, in reference to such first principles," I examined what were the first and commonest effects which could be deduced from such causes."

Descartes' best-known work, *The Discourse on Method*, begins with the skepticism of the new science but ends with an optimistic universe in the hands of a rational God. In the *Discourse* Descartes propounded four major rules for the investigation of all things. The first was never to accept anything as true unless it was evidently so, in order "to avoid all precipitation and prejudgement, and to conclude nothing [unless] it presented itself so clearly and distinctly [to the mind] that there was no reason or occasion to doubt it." The second rule was to analyze every problem carefully and to break it down into its simplest components. Third, Descartes proposed to reason in an orderly manner from the simple to the complex. Fourth, Descartes insisted that he would review and reexamine all his conclusions, in order to assure himself that "nothing was omitted."

This kind of skepticism led Descartes to doubt everything except his own capacity for thought. He stated this proposition in the famous phrase, "Cogito ergo sum"—"I think, therefore I am." Relying on this certainty of self, Descartes was able to reinforce his connection to his Catholic past and infer the existence of God. Descartes argued that since he existed, and since he was able to think of rational and orderly and even perfect things, and since such thoughts could not come from his own imperfect experience, they must have come from God.

While Descartes thought he had made a place for God, some of his contemporaries condemned him for his presumption and were troubled by the rationalistic and mechanistic nature of Descartes' deity. "Consequently," Descartes had written, "it is at least as certain that God, who is this perfect Being, exists, as any theorem of geometry could possibly be." The risk in Descartes' divine geometry, certain of his critics believed, was that geometry, and not God, would be perceived as sovereign. There would be no room in Descartes' system for the unknowable, the idea of the holy, the dynamic of doubt and faith. Significantly, it was the mathematician Pascal who saw the theological dilemmas in Descartes' system. "I cannot forgive Descartes," Pascal noted with a certain bitterness. "In all his philosophy he would have been quite willing to dispense with God. . . . [Descartes] had to make Him . . . set the world in motion; beyond this, he has no further need of God."

Others of Descartes' contemporaries were less concerned with his theology than with his investigative method, and for this reason *The Discourse on Method* can be considered one of the fundamental contributions to the new science. These same thinkers were interested as well in Descartes' view of the physical universe. Like many before him, Descartes was a dualist; that is, he thought of the world as made up of two fundamentally different aspects. Descartes nonetheless gave dualism, a concept familiar enough to all Christians, a new direction. Descartes' dualism—called Cartesian dualism ever after—created a mathematician's universe, mechanistic and knowable in all of its parts and inhabitants.

According to the tenets of Cartesian dualism all substances were reduced to *res extensa* or *res cogitans,* respectively "extended" substance and "thinking" substance. Extended substance was the stuff of the physical world. Thus the universe and everything in it, according to Descartes, should be described by their "extensions," Descartes' term for their mathematically measurable length, width, and depth. Although we generally perceive and describe physical objects according to their color, relative weight, or softness, these are subjective, relative values imposed by our minds. Such things Descartes put in the category of the *res cogitans* or thinking substance. The mind and the physical universe that the mind imperfectly perceived were driven apart in Descartes' thought, with the only bridge being mathematics. The *res extensa* of the physical universe was properly knowable only by mathematics, understandable only according to physical laws.

Descartes polished and defended his ideas in a series of written works, but these brought him neither satisfaction or peace. The major treatise that Descartes planned was suppressed by Descartes himself when he heard that the Inquisition had condemned Galileo for his controversial astronomical theories. *The Discourse on Method,* for which Descartes is most widely known, was in fact an anonymous summary of this longer work that Descartes had tentatively titled *Le Monde.*

As remarkable as some of Descartes' ideas were, it is important to realize that he was not always the scientific revolutionary that he has been portrayed. Descartes was in many ways a conservative. Trained in the medieval authoritarian tradition of scholasticism, Descartes can be accused of replacing the authority of God with the authority of mathematics. In many areas Descartes can be shown to be neither innovative nor correct.

The omissions in and traditionalism of some of Descartes' theories become apparent in his physics. John Herman Randall, among others, has argued that Descartes' conception of the universe was hardly novel, and that it in fact had medieval, even ancient, roots going back beyond St. Augustine to the dualism of Plato. To Descartes, the universe and everything in it was made up of matter that moved, and true motion he defined as the displacement of one particle, or "corpuscle," of matter in relation to others. In this, Descartes was no different from Aristotle, the ancient authority challenged by other seventeenth-century scientists.

Like Aristotle before him, Descartes believed that the motion of one body must cause the motion, or displacement, of others. If no displacement occurred, there was no motion. The universe, as conceptualized by Descartes, was full of such corpuscles of matter, causing motion as they impacted on one another mechanically. There was simply no room, or need, in Descartes' mechanistic universe for vacuums, emptiness, or what other scientists had begun to call "attraction" and what is now called gravity.

Descartes conceived of a mechanical solar system that would agree with his ideas on motion. Descartes' universe was made up of what he called *tourbillons,* or vortices, set in motion by some "first cause," like Aristotle's "unmoved mover" or the Christian God. The solar system, according to Descartes, was such a vortex, moving like all the others in a whirlpool-like, centripetal motion. The heavier particles, driven to the center of the vortex, formed the sun. All the planets, including the earth, were caught in this whirling mass of matter and were dragged about the sun in orbits. In a similar sense, a smaller vortex of particles, with the earth as its center, dragged the moon around it in an orbital path. Thus centripetal pressure, not gravity, was Descartes' explanation for the orbits of the heavenly bodies.

If Descartes can be considered a founder of a scientific revolution, it must be a revolution that formed a continuity with the science of the ancients and of medieval times. Still, by the time he died in 1650 at the court of Christina of Sweden, in self-imposed exile in the "land of bears between rock and ice," Descartes had made real contributions to scientific thought and method. Descartes formulated the law of refraction, which may make him one of the fathers of modern optics; he explained the phenomenon of the rainbow; he was a founder of the science of meteorology; he was an inventor of analytic geometry. By his mechanical view of the universe, by the rigor of his investigative method, by his insistence on the importance of mathematics, and by his skepticism, he gave much to the discipline of modern science. Significantly, it was in his physics and in his conception of the solar system, the very areas where he provided hypotheses but failed to provide mathematical proofs, that he was most vulnerable to challenge. The challenge was to come, in utter irony, from the Englishman Sir Isaac Newton, a mathematician as accomplished as Descartes himself.

C. Galileo Galilei and Sir Isaac Newton: A New Universe and a New Physics

Portrait of Sir Isaac Newton. Unknown Artist
Courtesy of the National Portrait Gallery, London.

"The shape of heaven must be spherical." This statement was made, in sublime confidence, by the ancient Greek polymath Aristotle in the fourth century before Christ. Aristotle's conception of the universe, which, in turn, was based on a Greek tradition that went back to Eudoxus and Plato, was an elegant, speculative construct based on the "natural" form of the circle and the ideas of symmetry and harmony. In this system the heavens were conceived of as beautiful, transparent substances, perfect in their creation, which abided by different rules than the base and corrupt substances that made up the earth. Surrounding the earth, which was located at the center of the universe, were concentric, transparent spheres in which the orbs of the heavenly bodies were set, and in which they moved.

Though other thinkers, such as Heraclides (375-310 B.C.) and Aristarchus (310-230 B.C.) advocated a planetary system that was heliocentric, or "sun centered," the earth-centered system proposed by Aristotle was strengthened by the work of Hipparchus (140 B.C.) and Ptolemy (120 A.D.). Ptolemy, in his *Almagest,* formulated the ultimate defense for the Aristotelean theory by proposing a complex mathematical system based on epicycles, main circles and sub-circles, and varying speeds and tilts. Ptolemy's work was so impressive that the heliocentric system, sometimes called the Ptolemaic system after its great defender, was enshrined for fourteen centuries. To the Ptolemaic system the medieval Catholic Church gave its approval, its scholastic thinkers finding a system based at once on a corrupt earth, a perfect heaven, and the authority of Aristotle and Ptolemy theologically and intellectually congenial. Even Dante, who challenged the medieval order in several respects, left the Ptolemaic cosmos alone. "All things whatsoever observe a mutual order," Dante wrote, "and this the form that maketh the universe like unto God."

Not until the sixteenth century was there a substantive challenge to Ptolemy's ideas. Its agent was a Polish-German scholar named Niklas Koppernigk (1473-1543) whose name was later latinized as Copernicus. Citing the works of such classical thinkers as Heraclides as a precedent, Copernicus reintroduced the hypothesis of a heliocentric universe. More than that, contrary to Aristotle, he asserted that the earth moved.

One thinker who was converted to what was renamed the Copernican system was the Venetian Galileo Galilei. In 1609 Galileo began to use the telescope to observe the planets and the vastness of the stars and, by careful observation, began to refute the Aristotelean-Ptolemaic idea of a perfect, transparent heaven. When Galileo observed the moon he found it to be not one of Aristotle's perfect orbs, but a pock-marked planet of mountains and valleys, seemingly like the imperfect earth. Galileo's observation of the moon also forced him to conclude that the moon was brightened not only by the sun, but by reflection from the earth as well. This observation, in turn, implied that the earth must shine like other heavenly bodies, thus creating an argument for the Copernican theory. When Galileo discovered that the planet Jupiter was orbited by moons, he delivered another blow to the idea that somehow the earth and the heavens were radically different.

The telescope also enabled Galileo to answer one of the chief objections to the Copernican system, and to confute its Ptolemaic rival. If the earth moved, said Copernicus' detractors, why did not all the stars in the heavens appear to move? Copernicus had hypothesized in answer that motion was relative and that, since the stars were so far away, movement was not apparent. Galileo, noting that the planets could be observed much more clearly than the stars, concluded that such bodies must be as far away as Copernicus believed.

Further, as Galileo observed the planet Venus, he found that it was subject to phases of light and shadow, implying that it shined, not on its own, but by reflected light from the sun. If Venus traveled in an epicycle, or smaller orbit, as Ptolemy had believed, the phases of Venus should not have been observable. This pointed to the conclusion that Venus must travel in a solar orbit. Finally, in 1613, Galileo discovered spots on the surface of the sun, demonstrating that the sun was not the perfect sphere described by the ancients. Through the observation of these sunspots over time, Galileo was forced to conclude that the sun must rotate on its axis.

Galileo's telescope and Copernicus' theory had seemingly wrecked the universe constructed so carefully by Aristotle and Ptolemy. The earth, apparently, had to move, and had to move around the sun, which was at the center of the universe, and had to be composed of material no more base than that making up the planets observed in Galileo's telescope. The radical distinction between heaven and earth hypothesized by Aristotle and Ptolemy, and sanctified by Christian theology, seemed no longer to apply. These new conceptions of matter and motion created the need for a new physics that would explain them.

This new physics was given impetus by the work of two other mathematician-astronomers, Tycho Brahe (1546-1601) and John Kepler (1571-1630), as well as by Galileo himself. Brahe, never convinced of the validity of the Copernican system, demonstrated from exact observation that Copernicus' belief that the planets moved in circular orbits was invalid. Kepler, Brahe's disciple, was able to use Brahe's observations to modify and validate the Copernican theory. Kepler demonstrated mathematically that the planetary orbits were not circular, but rather elliptical. Kepler also showed that the length of time in which the planets revolve around the sun varies proportionately with their distance from the sun (the square of the time is proportional to the cube of the distance). The Copernican hypothesis, seemingly confirmed by Galileo's observations, was now confirmed, with modification, by mathematics. Aristotle's belief in orbs of perfect circles was confuted by Kepler's elliptical orbits.

While Kepler was destroying Aristotle's perfect circles, Galileo launched an attack on the principles of Aristotle's physics, which his own astronomical observations had called into question. Aristotle had believed in a motionless earth, and he had believed that the natural state of all bodies, aside from living things or objects dropped from heights, was to be motionless, or at rest, as well. In most cases, Aristotle had thought, an "unmoved mover" was needed to impart motion to anything, as when an object is thrown. Further, once the object was set in motion, it retained motion, or impetus, by air rushing to fill the vacuum behind the moving object. "Nature," the Aristoteleans firmly believed, "abhors a vacuum." In the case of falling objects, Aristotle believed that the speed of the fall would vary according to their weight or mass, divided by the resistance of the air. In sum, the heavier the object, the faster it would fall.

Galileo called these Aristotelean assumptions into question in a number of famous experiments. First, he proved that falling objects of differing weights, once allowance was made for air resistance, would hit the ground at the same time. Further, Galileo was able to demonstrate that when objects on earth fall, they fall with a speed that increases according to a mathematical formula. Further experiments convinced Galileo that motion, not its opposite, was a natural state of matter. Contrary to the old Aristotelean view, which held that an object had to have a constant mover to remain in motion, Galileo declared in his law of inertia that an object, once started in motion, would continue in motion by its own momentum.

Galileo's refutation of the Ptolemaic universe and Aristotelean physics refuted not only medieval, scholastic science, but Christian theology as well. This the Church, though it had shown a certain willingness to live with the Copernican system as a hypothesis, could not accept. Though some in the Catholic hierarchy tried to protect Galileo, as they had Kepler, the die-hard Aristoteleans in the Italian universities objected. Galileo was accused of heresy, forced to abjure his discoveries, and forced into retirement. As profound a Catholic as he was a scientist, Galileo accepted the verdict of the Holy Inquisition.

It was now left to other scientists, singly and in groups, to ponder the implications of the discoveries of Copernicus, Galileo, Kepler, and others. There were other contributions. The Englishman Gilbert, for example, began to explore magnetism and raised interesting questions about the phenomenon of "attraction" between bodies. Huyghens, a Dutch scientist, had used the pendulum to study orbital motion.

The first scientist to put all of these discoveries into a coherent system was the Englishman Sir Isaac Newton (1642-1727). Newton was born into a family of farmers, but early schooling proved him to be a brilliant boy. Accordingly, he was sent up to the University of Cambridge where he eventually became a mathematics professor. Reclusive, absent-minded, Newton seemed to work best in isolation, and he had his most arresting idea when he fled into the country to avoid the plague. As Newton was resting under a tree at Woolsthorpe, so the story goes, an apple fell and hit him on the head. This accident, or some other event, caused Newton to think that perhaps Kepler's laws of planetary motion, and Galileo's demonstrations with regard to moving and falling bodies on earth, were governed by the same phenomenon. If the earth appeared to pull an apple toward it, might not the sun pull the earth toward it in just the same manner?

This thought allowed Newton to find an explanation for a phenomenon that had puzzled other thinkers. If the planets moved around the sun, and the moon around the earth, what kept them in their orbits, kept them from spinning in a straight line, much as a moving pendulum would if its moorings broke? Newton's answer was that the orbits were preserved due to the operation of what we now call gravity. Galileo's law of falling bodies had been translated by Newton into the phenomenon of "universal gravitation." This Newton further reduced to a mathematical formula, called the inverse square law. This law states, simply, that every particle of matter attracts another with a force determined by multiplying their mass together and dividing the square of the distance between them. Newton went on to reduce the phenomenon of motion to three universal laws, publishing them in his *Mathematical Principles of Natural Philosopy* (1687).

Newton's mathematical descriptions of motion and gravity eventually confuted the vortex theory of Descartes. The universal gravitation of Newton, not the pressure-related theory of Descartes, became the mathematically demonstrable proof for the organization of the solar system. While working out his laws of motion, Newton became, with Leibniz, an inventor of differential and integral calculus, that mathematical discipline which deals with changing quantities and objects in motion. The discovery of gravity also lead to explanations for such things as tides and comets, and mathematical knowledge of the solar system proved a boon to the navigation of ships at sea. In a negative sense, calculus made possible the more precise use of artillery.

Newton, like Galileo and Descartes, was not a modern man. When Newton died in 1727 he was wealthy and honored, hardly the rewards of a man perceived to be a revolutionary. His library was stuffed with the writings of the Christian fathers, and his experiments in alchemy joined him to the medieval tradition. Nonetheless, it seemed to some that Newton, for all his modesty, reclusiveness, and dislike of controversy, had confirmed the opening of a new cosmos. Wrote the poet Alexander Pope:

> Nature and nature's laws lay hid in night;
> God said, "Let Newton be," and all was light.

D. William Harvey and the Human Universe

In astronomy and physics the new scientists had departed from the teachings of the ancients in significant ways. To Aristotle and his disciples, the so-called peripatetics, the form of the perfect circle governed the universe and everything within it. The idea of the perfect universe, circular in form, with its epicycles and orbs, persisted in theory to the time of Copernicus, only to be replaced by the observations of Galileo and the mathematics of Kepler and Newton.

Ironically, as Aristotle's perfect circle disappeared from the universe, it survived in microcosm in the brilliant work of the English physician William Harvey (1578-1657), who applied the idea of the circle to the circulation of the blood, and who can rightly be called the father of modern physiology. In the work of Harvey, the teachings of the ancients, the great traditions of the anatomists of the middle ages and the Renaissance, and the experimental and mathematical approaches of the new science existed in equal measure. Harvey's work represents continuity as well as change, a link with the ancient and medieval tradition.

Portrait of William Harvey.
Unknown Artist
Courtesy of the National Portrait Gallery, London.

William Harvey came by this position honestly and honorably enough. Born in Folkestone, Kent, in 1578, the eldest in a family of seven sons, William Harvey was considered precocious enough to be sent to Caius College, Cambridge at the age of fifteen. Significantly, Caius College was a center of Aristotelean learning with strong medieval traditions. When Harvey earned his bachelor's in 1597, he booked passage for Italy to study medicine at the University of Padua, one of the most renowned of Europe's medical schools.

Padua stood in a medical-anatomical tradition that went back deep into the medieval centuries, and it was the perfect place to learn the teachings of the ancient Greek physicians and those of more contemporary anatomists who had begun to challenge them.

Medicine and the allied sciences, as Harvey came to know them at Cambridge and Padua, were still dominated by the teachings of the ancient Greeks and Romans. Ancient medicine had been the particular province of two authorities, Hippocrates and Galen. Hippocrates, perhaps best-known for the physician's oath that bears his name, was also remarkable for his careful observation of symptoms and his advocacy of diet, baths, rest, and massage in opposition to dangerous drugs.

More importantly, Hippocrates and his successors, both ancient and medieval, had an interesting, if incorrect, idea of how the body worked. They supposed that the body contained four fluids, or humors—blood, phlegm, black bile, and yellow bile—all of which remained in a kind of balance in a healthy body. When the humors were not in balance, when an excess of one humor became obvious, disease occurred. Indeed, a surfeit of one humor could determine personality as well as affliction, and an individual psyche was said to be sanguine, phlegmatic, choleric, or melancholic on the basis of supposed humoral imbalance.

The task of the Hippocratic physician thus became one of managing and balancing the humors. Localized diseases were explained by the concept of the "flux," or the movement and concentration of a humor in a given area of the body. Injuries and inflammations were thought to be characterized by an excess of blood, and the prescribed remedy was often bloodletting. Other humoral excesses could be relieved, supposedly, by induced vomiting, dietary change, or the prescription of purges, or laxatives.

Hippocrates was no anatomist, but his successor, Galen, had a rudimentary knowledge of anatomy obtained through actual dissection. Galen elaborated on his predecessor's teaching, and developed what one scholar calls a "physiology of nutrition." To Galen, every part of the body had four "natural faculties" by which it attracted, retained, assimilated, and expelled food. Blood did not circulate, but ebbed and flowed, sometimes in a volatile way, due to the expansion and contraction of the right side of the heart. When food was digested, it passed to the liver, where "natural spirits" were extracted. The natural spirits, in turn, were carried to the heart, where they passed through openings in the septum from the right to the left side, there mixing with air from the lungs. In the heart, the air, blood, and natural spirits were converted to "vital spirits," and the vital spirits were carried by the blood to the brain. There they were transformed, in turn, into "animal spirits," which were forced by the brain through the muscles. There, movement was caused by expansion and contraction.

Knowledge of the arteries and veins was also imperfect among the ancients. Galen had believed that blood was contained in the arteries and veins, but this view was challenged by the anatomist Erasistratus, who believed that blood was naturally contained in the veins only. The damage that this latter theory would do to any notion of a circulatory system is obvious.

To this imperfect anatomical scheme ancient biology added some important caveats. Aristotle, as authoritative in biology as he was in other areas of learning, was particularly influential. Aristotle dissected numerous species of animals, and created a basic system of classification. More importantly, Aristotle believed in "purposive anatomy," the idea that animals and all their parts were perfectly adapted to perform certain functions. While Galen had emphasized the liver as much as the heart in his life-system, Aristotle saw the heart as the center, the "sun," of animal and human anatomy. Aristotle also believed that the presence of blood in an organism was evidence of a higher form of life. Having elevated the heart and the blood to positions of primary importance, Aristotle and his peripatetic followers added one more important idea: that in nature there were certain purposive circular processes that preserved and regenerated life. If the writings of Aristotle were read carefully, the germ of the idea of a circulatory system might be found.

The heritage of Hippocrates, Galen, and Aristotle persisted down to Harvey's day and beyond; but at Padua, the very university that Harvey had chosen, a series of accomplished anatomists had begun to break new ground. First among these was Andreas Vesalius (1514-1564) who in his major work, *De humani corporis fabricus libri septum*, "The Seven Books on the Structure of the Human Body" (1543), placed anatomy on a truly scientific footing. The illustrations in his marvelous treatise, prepared in the workshops of Titian, are classic examples of the Renaissance passion for anatomical detail. A teacher and anatomical demonstrator at both Padua and Bologna, Vesalius established that Galen had made fundamental errors in understanding human anatomy. Though Vesalius never completely rejected Galenic medicine, his accurate drawings inevitably raised questions among his successors. Vesalius discovered something else of real importance. When he dissected the human heart, he found that there could be no passage of blood through the septum as the Galenists claimed.

At about the same time Michael Servetus (ca. 1511-1553), a unitarian heretic who had also studied with Vesalius' teacher, Guinther of Andernach, accidentally discovered the phenomenon of pulmonary circulation, thus giving a non-Galenic explanation for the motion of the blood from the right to the left side of the heart. The conclusions of Vesalius and Servetus were supported by Realdus Colombus (1516-1559), who also lectured in anatomy at Padua. In 1599, just before Harvey arrived at the university, another Paduan professor, G. T. Minadoi, proposed that blood might move in a circuit. Another scholar, Cisalpino, who had heard Realdus Colombus when he lectured at Pisa, applied Aristotle's notion of the circle to the movement of blood, and was the first to use the term *circulatio*. Fabrius ap Aquapendente, the anatomical demonstrator at Padua when Harvey arrived, called Harvey's attention to the existence of valves in the veins, a phenomenon that suggested the circulation of the blood. Finally, Galileo was at Padua when Harvey was there, and it is tempting to suppose that the astronomer's documentation of a universe in motion might have been applied by the Paduan anatomists to the microcosm of the body.

If such a thing was not suggested to Harvey in Italy, it might well have been when he returned to England, his head crammed with the ideas of the Paduan anatomists. When Harvey arrived back in England in 1602, he found an environment at least as stimulating as the one he had left. William Gilbert, a physician best known for his treatise on magnetism, had written another work, *De Mundo,* criticizing all who would blindly follow the ancients in medicine. Convinced that a uniform, animistic, circular motion characterized all things, Gilbert was supported by the likes of the visionary John Dee and the poet John Donne. Other physicians, like Robert Fludd and Robert Browne, affirmed the primacy of the heart in the body, as Aristotle had, and the possibility of circulation.

In 1606 Harvey, after battling prejudices against his foreign medical degree, was at last admitted as a Fellow of the Royal College of Physicians, an association which he continued for the rest of his life. Through his association with the College, Harvey was swept into the midst of the crises and controversies of seventeenth-century English medicine. As Charles Webster has observed, there was indeed a "crisis of medicine" in Harvey's London, brought on by visitations of the plague and a rapidly rising population. Adding to the crisis was the fact that quacks and unlicensed physicians flocked to the beleaguered city, challenging the monopoly imperfectly enforced by the Royal College of Physicians. London bubbled with rival medical and anatomical ideas, as Galenists and peripatetics, Paracelsians and outright quacks, hawked their remedies to a population perpetually ill. Appointed by the Royal College both to advise on the plague and to examine unlicensed physicians, Harvey must have been stimulated by a variety of views.

In the midst of this shrill environment, Harvey moved with modesty and determination to investigate by dissection and observation. Certainly in this respect he stood in the tradition of Bacon and Gilbert. Appointed Lumleian Lecturer by the Royal College of Physicians in 1615, Harvey warned himself in his notes to avoid the attacks on rivals that often characterized his profession and "to learn and teach anatomy, not from books, but from dissections, not from the positions of the philosophers but from the fabric of nature." Not until 1628, after scores of dissections of both animals and humans, did Harvey publish his *Exercitatio Anatomica de Motu Cordis et Sanguinis in Animalibus* in which he demonstrated the circulation of the blood and founded the modern discipline of physiology.

Reflecting Harvey's own experience, *de Motu Cordis* evokes both ancient authority and the spirit of the new science. Galen and Aristotle, and particularly the latter, are referred to incessantly. Many of Aristotle's theories—that higher animals are distinguishable by the presence of blood, that nature does nothing in vain, that the heart is the "sun of the microcosm," that purposive circular processes might dominate the human body—pepper Harvey's greatest work. ". . . I began to think," Harvey wrote in *de Motu Cordis,* "whether there might not be a MOTION, AS IT WERE, IN A CIRCLE. . . . Which motion we may be allowed to call circular, in the same way that the air and the rain emulate the circular motion of superior bodies." Harvey seems to have attempted, amidst the swirling medical controversies of his time, to find reverence for authority compatible with some of his striking conclusions.

Still, there was to be no compromise where ancient and medieval authorities had erred. Harvey's diplomatic yet independent viewpoint is perhaps best expressed by his fellow-physician and scientist, William Gilbert. "To those men of early times," Gilbert had written in *De Mundo,* ". . . to Aristotle, Theophrastus, Ptolemy, Hippocrates, Galen, be due honour rendered ever, for from them has knowledge descended to those who have come after them: but our age has discovered and brought to light many new things which they too, were they among the living, would cheerfully adopt. Wherefore we have had no hesitation in setting forth, in hypotheses that are provable, the things that we have through a long experience discovered."

At times, there seems to be so much of the ancients in Harvey's work that some of his critics doubted that he had proposed anything new. It was also true that the idea of some sort of circulation had been propounded by Harvey's predecessors and teachers. Nonetheless, Harvey's contribution was unique and in keeping with the spirit of the new science. He proved through experiment, observation, and the use of mathematics that the circulation of blood had to be a fact.

For Harvey, the heart became, rather than the center of Galen's vital spirits, a pump, and a pump that drove blood through the great circle formed by the veins and arteries. To prove his assertion, Harvey first demonstrated that the valves of the heart were so constructed as to allow the blood to pass in only one direction. He then calculated, crudely but mathematically, how much blood flowed from the heart in a given period of time, and demonstrated that this greatly exceeded the volume of blood in the tissues, or that could be made through the digestion of food. Harvey's anatomical observations also told him that the blood in the arteries came from the aorta, which in turn obtained it from the veins. To prove that the veins and arteries were indeed part of the same system, Harvey opened arteries in living animals, an action that eventually drained the subject of blood.

While it is too optimistic to say that Harvey's discoveries were met with universal acclaim, it is also wrong to assume that he suffered at the hands of authority as Galileo did. Within the medical community, Harvey had both detractors and supporters. The medical faculty of the University of Paris attacked him, but others of his colleagues honored him, and Descartes wrote a treatise that supported Harvey's discoveries. Through it all Harvey remained a successful medical practitioner, being appointed chief physician to St. Bartholemew's Hospital and royal physician to Charles I. He benefited greatly from royal patronage, and *de Motu Cordis* was dedicated to a Stuart sovereign.

Not even the animosities of the English Civil War seemed to disturb Harvey greatly. There is a story, reported by the biographer Aubrey, that Harvey read a book under a hedge during the battle of Edgehill. Though Harvey served the Royalists until Oxford surrendered in 1646, he was allowed to return to London to practice medicine thereafter. The way Harvey glided through life astonished at least one contemporary: "the only one I know," wrote the physician and political philosopher Thomas Hobbes, "who has overcome public odium and established a new doctrine in his lifetime." While Hobbes may have claimed too much, Caius College commissioned a statue honoring their eminent graduate, and the College of Physicians unsuccessfully drafted Harvey to its presidency. In return, Harvey endowed a library and an oration at his old college, a sure sign that he had prospered. Not until the eightieth year did Harvey's full life come to a close. Struck suddenly by a paralysis in 1657, he did not linger or suffer, but died on the same day he was afflicted.

E. The Scientific Revolution and the Transition to the Enlightenment

To believe in a seventeenth-century scientific revolution is to believe, as H. F. Kearney has observed, in the importance of individuals in human experience. In this sense, the concept of the scientific revolution is but a function of the "great man" theory of history, where "men of genius" have taken their place on the historical stage with men of the cloth, the sword, and the exchange.

For this very reason the whole notion of the scientific revolution seems to some scholars to be limited in nature, flawed as a concept. How much, say the critics, did the ideas of the new science influence the intellectual climate of the time and the lives of less than extraordinary people? How much, they continue, did the scientific revolution mark a real break with the past? Harvey's discoveries did not enjoy universal acceptance, and for years his disciples competed with Paracelsians, Galenists, apothecaries, and midwives for the custom of the population. Harvey's work stood on that of his professors and predecessors, and showed the influence of Aristotle—according to some the great enemy of scientific progress. Some historians, like R. K. Merton and his disciples, have linked the scientific revolution in England to Puritanism, a religious movement that many historians have seen as unprogressive. In similar vein, Descartes always reflected his Jesuit education, and Galileo was a devoted son of the Church. Arguments for continuity as well as change, indifference as well as revolution, have their place in the discussion of seventeenth-century science.

Whatever the roots of the new science, it could not help but alter the world-view of the minority of educated men and women who lived in seventeenth-century society. The earth, once the center of a defined and perfect universe ordained by God, had been sent whirling away in an elliptical orbit that was comprehensible to mathematicians. The earth had become but another planet, constructed, it seemed, of the same base stuff as all of the others.

If there was to be a new earth so, too, there was to be a new view of humankind. In a universe explicable by physical laws, which were in turn knowable through mathematics, observation, and human reason, the role of human beings was apparently enhanced and that of God diminished. God had become more remote, a distant first cause rather than an immediate, unpredictable presence in nature. Nature, once the theater of God's revelation, had become the rational province of rational human beings.

Strangely, the new science seemed both to diminish and to exalt humanity. Christian doctrine had placed humankind at the center of the cosmos, a beloved creation of God in his own image. The new science said, in apparent contrast, that the body was a machine, the heart a pump. The Aristotelean cosmos had been ordered and comprehensible, the new universe was vast and diverse. "The eternal silence of these infinite spaces frightens me." This was the reaction of the mathematician Pascal as he sought refuge from a mechanistic universe in a mystical God. "It is the heart which experiences God," he assured himself, "and not the reason."

Nonetheless, like others of his time, Pascal was convinced, in apparent contradiction, that it was reason that affirmed what human beings were. "Man is obviously made to think," Pascal observed. "It is his whole dignity and his whole merit." "Man is but a reed," Pascal wrote in another place, "the most feeble thing in nature; but he is a thinking reed." While human beings could, like reeds, be easily crushed and destroyed, Pascal believed that reason made them more noble than the forces that could end their existence. Man was noble, in Pascal's words, "because he knows that he dies and the advantage that the universe has over him" while "the universe knows nothing of this."

This theme of the "greatness and wretchedness of man," as Franklin L. Baumer has called it, became a characteristic of seventeenth-century European thought. By the end of the century, however, it was the greatness of humankind, the optimistic idea that humans could understand their physical environment through the use of reason, that began to prevail. "Speaking broadly, we are confronted, on approaching the eighteenth century, with a steady decline in what has been called the tragic sense of life." So wrote Basil Willey of a new age that came to be called the Enlightenment.

In some respects, the eighteenth-century Enlightenment was but a broadening and a popularization of the ideas of seventeenth-century science. It followed that the first agents of the Enlightenment were not scientists and mathematicians, but a group of writers, wits, and publicists who were known as the *philosophes*. As the latter term implies, the Enlightenment was centered in France, and certain French intellectuals—Voltaire, Montesquieu, Diderot, Rousseau, Condorcet—at times seemed to dominate the whole movement. From France, the cultural and intellectual capital of Europe, the Enlightenment spread to all corners of the continent, and even to America. Germans like Holbach, English thinkers as various as John

Locke, Adam Smith, and Mary Wollstonecraft, Americans like Jefferson and Franklin can all be considered part of the Enlightenment movement.

The *philosophes* asked some important questions of the new science, and answered them in the affirmative. "Why not," one of the *philosophes* might have asked, "apply the modes of investigation and reasoning of the new science to the problems of society?" If the physical universe was understandable by mathematics and law, might it be possible that there was a "natural law" that underlay both the physical universe and human society? Should not the test of "reason" be applied to all institutions, practices, and ideas, whether governmental, political, social, or religious?

"The geometrical spirit is not so tied to geometry that it cannot be detached from it and transported to other branches of knowledge." This was the assertion of the *philosophe* Fontenelle as well as of the Englishman Sir William Petty, who expressed his sentiments in a tome called *Political Arithmetic*. What are now called the social sciences—economics, sociology, anthropology, and political science—owe much of their being to this eighteenth-century attitude of mind. Even history, that venerable humanistic discipline, was imbued with a new sense of evidence during the Enlightenment, and has become for many yet another branch of the social sciences.

Erudite and sophisticated, secular and pagan in attitude, the *philosophes* met to discuss their ideas in *salons*, or receptions, hosted by the most brilliant women in France. Imbued with all the skepticism of their seventeenth-century predecessors, the *philosophes* savaged with words any institution thought to fail the test of reason. Mockery and satire were powerful weapons in their hands, and the use of the latter by the *philosophes* is in itself instructive. Satire calls attention to wrongs and abuses, not out of despair but out of the conviction that change might be possible. Thus, for all of its vitriol, the Enlightenment was essentially an optimistic movement suffused with a strong belief in progress.

Progress was joined in the minds of several of the *philosophes* with the concept of relativism, the idea that moral and ethical truths vary according to the environments and needs of the groups holding them. Relativism, in turn, allowed the truly critical to question the claims of authority and absolute truth. An openness to the wisdom of other societies and cultures, a belief in toleration and in the right of individuals to make judgments according to their best reason—all these formed a part of the Enlightenment dogma.

Such freedom, however, was to be limited to those who were qualified to make use of it. Some *philosophes* believed that the way to progress was to place governments in the hands of so-called enlightened despots, who would rule and reform according to the tenets of reason, even if what was reasonable was unpopular. Reason was to be supplied, of course, by the *philosophes* themselves. The *philosophes* were thus progressives but not democrats, reformers but not revolutionaries.

F. Voltaire and the Founding of the Enlightenment

For very many the life and works of Voltaire define the first generation of the Enlightenment. More than that, Voltaire demands study for himself, for a more interesting man never lived. Voltaire's was a personality that yawed between contradictions. On the one hand, Voltaire could be mendacious, self-congratulatory, vindictive, obscene, vain, pessimistic, cruel, and toadying, but he could also rise to heights of eloquence in defense of the oppressed, turn a witty phrase that could make those who opposed him appear ridiculous, and affirm, despite disappointments, the capacity of humanity for decency and improvement. A terrible enemy and a good friend, a man of wealth who championed the cause of the poor, a writer who enhanced the most serious purpose by mocking the alternatives, Voltaire compels attention. "It was he," wrote one historian of Voltaire, "who taught three generations that superstition was ridiculous, sentiment absurd, fanaticism unintelligent, and oppression infamous."

Few institutions, and few contemporaries, escaped the vitriolic point of Voltaire's pen. A few examples must suffice. On the condition of Paris: "I believe Paris is only good for farmers-general, whores, and big-wigs in the *parlement*. . . ." A reply to Rousseau, who had just written a treatise on the virtues of humanity in the "natural state": "One feels like crawling on all fours after reading your work." On the stupidity of his opponents: "I have never made but one prayer to God, a very short one: 'O Lord, make my enemies ridiculous.' And God granted it." To a fellow-scholar on the perils and stupidity of censorship: "Your book is dictated by the soundest reason, You had better get out of France as quickly as you can." On chastity: "It is one of the superstitions of mankind that virginity could be a virtue." On the human condition: "It is difficult to free fools from the chains they revere," or "Men who seek happiness are like drunkards who can never find their house but are sure that they have one." On the restrictions of Lent: "Why must we ask permission of our bishop to eat eggs?. . . . What strange aversion have bishops to omelets?"

Voltaire's seeming cynicism was redeemed by his ceaseless quest for justice, his disgust at intolerance, and his willingness to spend of himself and his wealth to support the causes he thought worthy. Significantly, Voltaire used his wit not only on others, but on himself as well. "You have sent me champagne, Monsieur," an aging Voltaire wrote to a friend, "at a time when I am restricted to infusions; it is like sending a prostitute to a eunuch." "I have seen," he wrote on another occasion, "in the *Whitehall Evening Post* . . . an alleged letter from me to His Majesty the King of Prussia. It's a very stupid letter; nonetheless, I did not write it."

Voltaire. Joseph Rosset *Courtesy of the Nelson Gallery of Art/Atkins Museum, Kansas City, Missouri. Nelson Fund.*

In a life that spanned more than eight decades, Voltaire wrote scores of diatribes and dramas, composed thousands upon thousands of letters, made a personal fortune through judicious investments, and inveighed against infamy and intolerance wherever he found it. On his estate at Ferney he installed a mistress, hosted the best minds of Europe, and gave jobs to all who asked for them. Wraith-like, his thinness aggravated by self-imposed doses of physics and purges, ready to run at the first sign of official displeasure, Voltaire gleefully pounced upon what he considered the stupidity and bigotry of his times. *Ecrasez l'infâme*—"crush the infamous thing"—became the battle-cry of a man who waged war with words.

Voltaire was born François-Marie Arouet in Paris in November 1694, supposedly the son of a legal official who served the titled nobility. Voltaire, though he shared the prosperous background of most of the other *philosophes,* did not believe in the legitimacy of his birth, claiming that he was the son of a military officer. Whatever the circumstances, Voltaire apparently had little family experience, never mentioned his mother, and was far from respectful to his purported father. He spent time instead with his godfather, a free-thinking cleric. Though Voltaire was educated at the Jesuit college of Louis-le-Grand, he apparently had little interest in religion.

After defying his family by refusing to study for the law, he attached himself, as a young man, to the entourage of the French ambassador to the Netherlands. He then disgraced himself by falling in love with Olympe Denoyer, the daughter of a French national, and had to be packed off home to France.

For a time, Arouet appeased his family by working in a lawyer's office, but he was soon adopted by yet another nobleman, the Marquis de Saint Ange, who introduced him to society. Soon Arouet was attending the salons of elegant ladies and composing lampoons and epigrams against the great. He developed such a reputation for libelous wit that he was ordered to jail on a *lettre de cachet,* a royal administrative order, for an epigram he probably did not compose. From this, Arouet gained a hatred for authority and arbitrary arrest, and thereafter his attacks on the powerful became commonplace, as did sporadic official harassment.

In 1718 Arouet made his first great literary success with his tragedy *Oedipe,* and afterward changed his name to Voltaire. On the heels of the first success came another, the epic poem *Henriade,* which recounted the accomplishments of Henry IV. This earned him a royal pension, but no wisdom. Ill-advised enough to pick a quarrel with the scion of a powerful French family, Voltaire was belabored by the man's attendants and cast into prison. Then, his sense of injustice outraged anew, Voltaire was conducted to Calais and made to see that it was in his best interest to go into exile. Voltaire chose England.

Voltaire's decision was most significant for his intellectual development. While still in France, Voltaire had met the philosopher-politician Viscount Bolingbroke, himself in exile, who in turn introduced him to the writings of John Locke, the English political philosopher and scientist. Ever after, Voltaire retained the greatest admiration for Locke, and Locke's ideas contributed to his own in several areas.

Locke impressed Voltaire with his rejection of the concept of "innate ideas." Locke believed, in contrast to this notion, that there was little in the human mind that was innate. At birth, Locke argued, the mind of a human being contained nothing of significance—that it was clear of ideas, a *tabula rasa*. It followed, according to Locke, that the mind could be altered only by the senses or experience. The environment thus became more important than "nature" in determining individual character.

Voltaire and other Enlightenment thinkers pushed this concept to the limit. They reasoned that if one reformed the environment according to proper principles, it might be possible to improve the human condition. Locke's emphasis on empiricism and experience, rather than on preconceived metaphysical systems, pleased Voltaire. "The more that one reads," Voltaire wrote, "the more one discovers that these metaphysicians do not know what they are talking about, and all their works increase my esteem for Locke."

Locke, as the philosopher of the English Revolution, also influenced Voltaire's political ideas. Locke had argued in his *Two Treatises on Government* that human society revolved around a "social contract" between the government and those it governed. According to this doctrine, the governed, who were the real source of political authority, surrendered to their government part of the freedom that was theirs by natural right in exchange for the security and protection that the government would provide. Locke also believed that the social contract could be abrogated by the governed if the government acted in a tyrannical manner. The governed, or the responsible citizens of the state, had the implicit right to rebel if the government did not act responsibly.

Other thinkers pushed the concept of the social contract in new directions. Locke's countryman, Thomas Hobbes, wrote on the social contract in a conservative treatise, the *Leviathan*. Hobbes argued, in contrast to Locke, that the social contract, once made, could not be broken and that rebellion was immoral. Jean-Jacques Rousseau, a near-contemporary of Voltaire, brought the concept to the frontier of revolution. The social contract idea influenced the leaders of the American Revolution and encouraged, at least on the intellectual plane, the coming of the French Revolution of 1789. Voltaire, by popularizing the idea, contributed to the growing dissatisfaction with French royal absolutism, a system of government that seemed irrational to many Enlightenment thinkers.

Locke and other English philosophers influenced Voltaire's religious ideas as well. Already hostile to the idea of a structural Catholic Church, Voltaire was attracted to the alternative of English deism, which attempted to transform Christianity into a "reasonable" religion. In Deism, God became the "clockmaker," a remote first cause who set a perfect, mechanical universe in motion.

Voltaire's infatuation with Locke soon became a generalized reverence for other English thinkers as Voltaire became the popularizer of the ideas of the scientific revolution, attempted to apply its methods to human institutions, and acted as a conduit through which its wisdom was received in France. Voltaire wrote of Bacon as the "scaffold" on "which the edifice of the new philosophy was built," and was fulsome in his praise of Boyle and especially of Newton. Voltaire was among the first to popularize Newton's and Locke's ideas in France, and used them to bludgeon the "metaphysical" ideas of Descartes and Pascal. "Descartes was a dreamer," Voltaire assured anyone who would listen, "Newton a sage." While "Descartes was more dangerous than Aristotle, because he had the air of being more reasonable," Newton "saw and demonstrated but never substituted his imagination for the truth."

Through the writings of the scientific revolutionaries and the English empiricists Voltaire glimpsed a world where superstition and metaphysical systems would be banished, where politics could be reduced to rational science, where intolerance would be defeated by reason, where wise men like himself could improve the lot of those he thought less wise. From the time of his return to France in 1728 or 1729 to his death fifty years later, Voltaire never gave up these dreams.

"Originality is nothing but judicious imitation." So remarked Voltaire with his usual brash realism. Like most of the other *philosophes*, Voltaire was a popularizer rather than an original thinker. This was never more obvious than when Voltaire discussed political theory.

Like Locke, Voltaire believed that men were free and equal in a state of nature, that they should have the right to make their own laws, and that they should have certain civil rights. The latter should include freedom of person and the abolition of slavery, freedom of speech and the press, freedom of conscience, freedom from illegal imprisonment, and freedom to work as one chose. Locke's demand for "life, liberty and property" carried over strongly into Voltaire's thought.

Voltaire's political theories stopped short of political revolution or social upheaval. He assumed that it was to be the productive property-holders and bourgeois who should be the soul of the state. Drawing from Asian models, he favored authoritarian rule by "enlightened despots" who would rule according to right reason, and convinced himself that contemporary rulers like Frederick the Great of Prussia and Catherine II of Russia were European prototypes. Voltaire saw revolution as mainly an intellectual exercise, and one which would exclude the mass of humanity. While he called "liberty of thought" the "life of the soul," he did not favor mass education, and feared the power of the mob. "The public," he wrote, "is a ferocious beast; one must either chain it up or flee from it." All had the right to be protected in terms of liberty, property, and the law, but Voltaire could never believe that men were "equal in their stations and employments, since they are not so by their talents."

From the perspective of the twentieth century, Voltaire's political ideas seem almost tame, but they seemed dangerous enough to those who ruled France in the name of absolutism and divine right. Voltaire's insistence on the right of all to own property, to sell their skills to the highest bidder, and to be free from servitude and bondage, struck at the heart of the social system of eighteenth-century France, which was based on feudalism, noble dominance, and virtual serfdom. Even Voltaire's brand of authoritarian rule was suspect because his enlightened despots, at least in theory, derived their authority from reason rather than divine right. Though no revolutionary himself, Voltaire's thought could carry revolutionary implications in eighteenth-century France.

Voltaire also undermined the social order by criticizing the French Catholic Church. Voltaire, to be sure, was no atheist, noting that "atheists have never responded to the objection that a clock proves the existence of a clockmaker." Nonetheless, Voltaire saw the institutional Catholic Church as an amalgam of everything he loathed, as fanatical, superstitious, intolerant, and cruel. To Catherine the Great, Voltaire confided his loathing for the papacy, calling it "ridiculous and abominable." No "superstitious" religion escaped Voltaire's contempt, and he did not play favorites. Protestants and Jews as well were affected as Voltaire mocked at the Old Testament, which he saw as brutal and savage.

At the same time, it is well to remember that Voltaire's religious attacks, particularly against Christians, derived their force not from religions as we know them today, but from his memory of the violent religious struggles waged in early modern France. The French historical memory included the bitter religious wars of the sixteenth century, the hatred of Catholics for Huguenots, and of Catholic Jesuits for Catholic Jansenists, the outrages of the St.

Bartholomew's Day Massacre, and the execution of hundreds of Protestant dissenters. The quarrels between the rival Catholic groups particularly provoked Voltaire. "The Jansenists and Jesuits," Voltaire noted with bitterness, "are joining hands in the slaughter of reason and are fighting among themselves for the spoils."

Religious intolerance offended both Voltaire's reason and common sense. "There is one morality," he wrote, "as there is but one geometry." Nonetheless, Voltaire backed away from defining either morality or God. "Reason tells me that God exists," Voltaire remarked on another occasion, "but this same reason tells me that I cannot know what he is." To Voltaire, most human beings were simply too ignorant and too imperfect to know the nature of God; in that belief he was no different from many orthodox Christians; but while they fell back on faith, Voltaire fell back on tolerance. Tolerance had to be the "portion of humanity" because "we are full of weakness and errors." "The tolerance of all religions is a law of nature," Voltaire proclaimed, "stamped on the hearts of all men." The reverse of tolerance, he believed, was fanaticism, which in its active violence was worse even than atheism because it destroyed the entire social fabric rather than one individual.

Voltaire complemented his deism with a very cautious humanism. No more than Locke did he believe that human beings were complete innocents, and contemporary events like the Lisbon earthquake combined with life experience to make him suspicious of simple optimism. "We need a God who speaks to the human race," he wrote after the Lisbon disaster. "Optimism is despairing. It is a cruel philosophy under a consoling name." In his satire *Candide,* Voltaire mocked and pilloried his contemporary Leibniz, and all optimists naive enough to believe that they lived in a perfect world.

"May all men remember that they are brothers." This was the fragile phrase on which Voltaire acted, and any institution that diminished persons or made them less than they could be was his enemy. He urged reform of the law, because he believed that the law was a means to help, rather than merely to punish, humanity: "once a man is hanged," he wrote, "he is good for nothing." Cases that involved miscarriages of justice often attracted Voltaire's attention. In 1724, he intervened in the case of the Abbé Desfontaines, accused of homosexuality and seemingly destined for the flames by order of an ecclesiastical court. Some years later, Voltaire moved to save the family of the Toulouse Huguenot Jean Calas, broken on a wheel on doubtful evidence for purportedly murdering a son who defied him by turning Catholic. Then came the case of the Sirven family, also Protestant, accused by the Toulouse magistrates of murdering a daughter. Voltaire also unsuccessfully defended the Chevalier de la Barre, who eventually had his tongue ripped out and his head struck from his shoulders for anti-Catholic acts. Whenever possible, Voltaire used his pen to cause a public outcry against injustice, to raise funds for those wronged, to obtain redress. "Provided men do not persecute," he noted, "I will forgive them for anything. I would be fond of Calvin if he had not had Servetus burned."

A born publicist, Voltaire never stopped writing. He outraged no less by the way he lived than by what he wrote. He eschewed marriage, and lived with two mistresses in succession, each of whom he adored. One of them was his niece, and some of Voltaire's letters to her are marvels of the frankest sexuality. His defense of unpopular causes kept him on the move, as did his tongue, as when he publicly accused a group of noble card-players at Fountainbleau of cheating. "Philosophers," he remarked, "need to have two or three holes in the ground to escape from the dogs who chase them." Voltaire, blessed with a good income, found fashionable exile when the need arose.

Along with other contemporaries, Voltaire proposed turning the study of humankind into a science. Among other things, Voltaire was an accomplished historian, and in his hands history became less a chronicle of great deeds and more of a social science. While he wrote about great men and women, Voltaire took pains to do research and to weigh evidence. "Let us admit in physics only that which is proven," he wrote, "and in history, that which is the greatest and most recognized probability." Using such methods Voltaire wrote histories of Louis XIV, Charles XII of Sweden, and other figures. His zeal for documentation is revealed in a letter to Catherine of Russia, asking for source material on Peter the Great.

Virtually until the day of his death Voltaire wrote, declaimed, debated, and predicted. By 1778, however, he had grown tired. "I have been persecuted enough," Voltaire wrote with his usual exaggeration, "I want to die in peace." Soon after, he was dead. A nephew, the Abbé Mignot, had his remains buried in consecrated ground before the Catholic Church could prohibit it. Had he known of this, Voltaire would have been amused. In death, as in life, Voltaire managed to get the last laugh on his enemies. "One day," Voltaire had written just before his death, "there will surely be a great intellectual revolution. A man my age will not live to see it, but he will die in the hope that men will be more enlightened and gentle." It is this desire for progress, this hope for the future that saved Voltaire from simple cynicism and constitutes one of the major contributions of the Enlightenment to western thought.

Voltaire's life mirrored the complexities and contradictions of the Enlightenment. Voltaire loved humanity but distrusted the mob, insisted on civil rights but revered enlightened authority, believed that the environment was alterable by mankind but believed in educating only a few to do so, worshipped reason but defined it passionately and subjectively, advocated revolutionary ideas but shied away from rebellion, hated war but invested with munitions-makers.

Voltaire's contemporaries and successors continued in the directions that he pointed. Montesquieu (1689-1725) mocked in relativistic fashion the irrational in European civilization in his *Persian Letters* (1721), and in his *Spirit of the Laws* (1748) further developed the fledgling discipline of political science. Montesquieu, by arguing that governments should and did vary according to geography and climate, and by proposing that the best form of government was attained through the separation and balance of powers, unwittingly created a justification for both the American Revolution and the structure of the United States Constitution. The Marquis de Condorcet (1743-1794) argued, as Voltaire had, that progress toward a more decent and humane society should be the goal of all enlightened men. Denis Diderot (1713-1784) published the *Encyclopedia,* publicizing further the thought of the *philosophes,* and attacking traditional institutions. Claude Helvetius (1715-1771) argued for a utilitarian social policy based on the greatest good to the greatest number.

Other Enlightenment thinkers pushed into areas that Voltaire only mentioned, and some into realms that he would have condemned. Paul Thiry d'Holbach (1723-1789), in his *System of Nature* (1770), advocated both materialism and atheism and can be considered a precursor of Karl Marx. Adam Smith (1723-1790), in *The Wealth of Nations* (1776), began the road to modern economics. Edward Gibbon (1737-1794), by writing his monumental *Decline and Fall of the Roman Empire* (1776-1788), demonstrated the validity of the scientific approach to history at which Voltaire had hinted. Moses Mendelsshon (1729-1786) endeavored to "modernize" Judaism to make it compatible with a pluralistic world. The Englishmen John Howard and James Oglethorpe struck out at the iniquities of criminal punishment, and the former began to visualize "penitentiaries" instead of prisons and the reformation of criminals rather than their simple incarceration. The whole of human society was subjected to the test of reason by inquiring minds, or at least so it seemed.

What the *philosophes* had not considered, however, was that some, fired with the spirit of the Enlightenment and its faith in reason, would discover that the Enlightenment had its limitations as well as its virtues.

G. Mary Wollstonecraft and the Limitations of the Enlightenment: The Issue of Women's Rights

The commitment of the Enlightenment thinkers to a wide range of social and political reforms sometimes obscures the fact that the reformers had their limits. When the *philosophes* talked of reason they were usually referring to their own, and when enlightened despots spoke of rational government it was on terms definable only by them. A rationalizing of the existing order, not revolution, was the goal of most Enlightenment thinkers. Any reform that proposed to restructure the social order, or to give the disenfranchised a place within it, caused feelings of ambivalence among at least some of the *philosophes*. Ideas were one thing, actions quite another. No issue expressed the limitations of the Enlightenment more precisely than that of women's rights.

Voltaire, in all of his voluminous writings, comments very little on the position of women, their unequal treatment before the law, within the professions, or in the schools and universities. Even Montesquieu, that believer in equality and natural law, showed a certain ambivalence toward equality for women. In *The Spirit of the Laws,* female sexual corruption and disobedience was seen as a symptom of governmental decline, while female chastity is regarded as a cornerstone of an orderly republic. Utilizing the age-old assumption of female weakness and inferiority, Montesquieu argued in a rather tortured way that women were qualified to lead governments but not families. "It is contrary to reason and nature that women should reign in families," Montesquieu observed, ". . . but not that they should govern an empire. In the former case the state of their natural weakness does not permit them to have the pre-eminence; in the latter their very weakness gives them more lenity and moderation. . . ." Montesquieu also believed that incontinence among women was "contrary to the law of nature," though he said little about the same vice in men. Montesquieu did argue that women should have the right to divorce their husbands, but also believed that barrenness in women could constitute divorce grounds.

Other Enlightenment thinkers were even less supportive of equality for women, tending to glorify marriage and motherhood as women's only "natural" role. This particular group of thinkers seemed to believe that such traditional roles were more positive than the alternative of wealthy idleness presented by contemporary aristocratic women, ironically the very class that kept the *salons* the *philosophes* attended with such frequency. Perhaps this emphasis on maternal roles indicated an acceptance of bourgeois values among the *philosophes*. The reassertion of family values may also be related to the pastoral ideal, that belief in the simplicity of rural life in contrast to the decadence of urban civilization, an idea that reached full flower in the romantic movement of the nineteenth century.

Many antifeminist elements appeared in the thought of Jean Jacques Rousseau. Though Rousseau is usually classified as an Enlightenment thinker, others have seen him as a transitional figure, a precursor of the romantic movement of the next century. In many ways Rousseau stood the ideals of the early Enlightenment on their heads, and emerged as a trenchant critic of the movement as a whole. After trying to become a *philosophe* in the Voltairean style in his youth, he ended by rejecting many of Voltaire's values. While the *philosophes* emphasized reason and education, Rousseau felt more comfortable with passion and what he thought to be the innocent, virtuous ignorance of the "noble savage," or the precivilized man.

Many elements of Enlightenment thought—optimism, progress, the social contract—were reformed in the crucible of Rousseau's mind. His major work, *The Social Contract,* proposed a communal society of primitive democratic simplicity, in which everybody gave up virtually everything. In this society, decisions were to be made according to a collective "General Will" of all the citizens.

Rousseau believed strongly that all society had to be controlled by men. He found fault with the *salons*, for example, because they were controlled by women; and with the theater, because it dealt with the woman's domain of love. In the work *Emile,* Rousseau developed his antifeminist views more fully. Intellectual activity was to be denied to women, and they were to be taught to love lace- and needle-work, but not books. The role of women was simply to please and support men. Because of its pronounced nature, at least one historian has related Rousseau's antifeminism to his troubled personal psychology. Never comfortable or successful in his relations with women, Rousseau seemed to fear the power of female sexuality, and the ability of women to control their emotions and passions.

In sum, the leading male disciples of the Enlightenment, with only the fewest exceptions, were ambivalent, indifferent, or hostile to women's rights issues. Women needed their own advocate, and they found one in the Englishwoman Mary Wollstonecraft. Articulate, familiar with the Enlightenment intellect, Mary Wollstonecraft applied the Enlightenment pronouncements on human rights to the predicament of women, and in so doing was perhaps the founder of the modern women's movement.

Portrait of Mary Wollstonecraft. J. Opie
Courtesy of the National Portrait Gallery, London.

Mary Wollstonecraft was born in London in 1759, a younger child in a family of silk-weavers. Though her paternal grandfather had been a prosperous tradesman who aspired to lands and titles, her father was a failure who had moved the family half-a-dozen times in her childhood. As her father slipped into cruelty and drunkenness, and her mother into disappointment, Mary Wollstonecraft, as the eldest daughter, was left to care for the younger children and to pick up the pieces. In 1778, no doubt needing both money and an escape, she left home to become a paid companion to a woman resident in Bath.

This employment began to open her eyes to the world and convinced her that the lot of an uneducated women was a harsh one. "Few are the modes of subsistence," Wollstonecraft wrote later, "and those very humiliating." Nor did the alternative of marriage seem an attractive one. The poor marriage of her parents was one object lesson, in addition to others. In 1780 Mary Wollstonecraft had to return home to nurse her worn-out and bitter mother in her last illness. Four years later, Wollstonecraft assisted a sister, suffering the consequences of a bad marriage, to escape from the household of her husband. In 1785 she journeyed to Lisbon to nurse her best friend, Fanny Blood, who died of the effects of childbirth. It had to be obvious to an intelligent woman like Mary Wollstonecraft that the institution of marriage could be dangerous for an independent woman. This was particularly so in the eighteenth century, when women usually were obliged to surrender their property to their spouses after marriage, had few if any legal or divorce rights, and experienced the perils of pregnancy and childbirth. Marriage was often the only alternative for women, who were in the main denied access to education and employment, and it was often an unsatisfactory one.

There is every reason to believe that such experiences left their mark and strengthened Mary Wollstonecraft's belief that women had to become educated and independent to prosper. In 1784, groping to implement these convictions, she established a school for girls at Newington Green. There Wollstonecraft made contact with a group of intellectual English dissenters, including the chemist Joseph Priestley and the reforming preacher Richard Price. Sadly, the school was left in the hands of her sisters when Wollstonecraft went to Lisbon, and it soon failed. Wollstonecraft had to take another disagreeable position, that of a governess to an English family in Ireland. Though she was fond of the children, this employment also ended quickly; she was dismissed after a little more than a year.

By this time however, Mary Wollstonecraft had found a meaningful alternative to the traditional female employments. In 1786 the London publisher Joseph Johnson brought out Wollstonecraft's first work, *Thoughts on the Education of Daughters*. This short book, for which Wollstonecraft received the sum of £10, provides in capsule form what she had concluded about the dilemmas of women up to that time. She lamented the lack of occupational options for women ("The few trades that are left are now gradually falling into the hands of men, and certainly they are not very respectable."), the bankruptcy of love without respect (". . . Love, unsupported by esteem, must soon expire, or lead to depravity. . . ."), and the dangers of early marriage ("Early marriages are, in my opinion, a stop to improvement."). Wollstonecraft's corrective to these problems was, true to the spirit of the Enlightenment, the application of education and of reason: "Reason must often be called in to fill up the vacuums of life; but too many of our sex suffer theirs to lie dormant."

Wollstonecraft strove, above all, to educate herself, and here her publisher Joseph Johnson was of inestimable help. By 1787 she was working for Johnson full-time as a writer and translator and had begun to frequent the literary and intellectual circle that gathered around him. Among Johnson's friends were the revolutionary and atheist Thomas Paine, the poet-artist William Blake, the painter Henry Fuseli, the mathematician John Bonnycastle, the distinguished physician John Fordyce. Together, these men became a conduit through which Wollstonecraft's thought was strengthened. Through the books they lent her, and others that she translated, Wollstonecraft began to imbibe more of the thought of the Enlightenment.

With the coming of the French Revolution in 1789, Wollstonecraft was swept up with enthusiasm, seeing it as a struggle for human rights and full equality. Outside of her circle, however, the French Revolution generated less enthusiasm, and its violence eventually provoked a conservative reaction. This was given intellectual form by the publication of Edmund Burke's condemnatory *Reflections on the French Revolution*. This gave Wollstonecraft her first major intellectual opportunity. Again with the help of Johnson, Wollstonecraft published a bitter rejoinder to Burke, *A Vindication of the Rights of Men*. Two years later, in 1792, she followed it with *A Vindication of the Rights of Women*.

This latter work, though it was little read in her lifetime or for many years after her death, remains Mary Wollstonecraft's enduring monument. Into it she poured all of her experience as a woman, all of her hard-won knowledge, all of her skills as a writer and pamphleteer, all of her indignation at a society that robbed women of the equality she thought enjoined by a beneficent and rational God. While she admitted differences between the sexes in biological function and physical strength, she argued that most other differences were culturally conditioned, and alterable through changes in education and environment. "I here throw down my gauntlet," she wrote, "and deny the existence of sexual virtues, not excepting modesty. For man and woman ... must be the same.... Women, I allow, may have different duties to fulfil; but they are *human* duties, and the principles that regulate them must be the same." Neither sex nor class, she argued, should serve as an excuse to deny to any individual the education and opportunity to be productive. For Mary Wollstonecraft, women's rights and human rights were aspects of the same natural law.

With bitterness and skill, Wollstonecraft anatomized the tendency of writers like Rousseau to praise women for questionable "virtues" that would be considered weaknesses in men: "Gentleness, docility, and a spaniel-like affection are, on this ground, consistently recommended as the cardinal virtues of the female sex. . . . She was created to be the toy of man, his rattle, and it must jingle in his ears whenever, dismissing reason, he chooses to be amused." As much as the rest of humanity, women were entitled to strength and dignity. Society, Wollstonecraft believed, would be the better for it; human relationships would be more honest; children would be better raised by women of intelligence. "I love man as my fellow," Wollstonecraft concluded proudly, "but his scepter, real or usurped, extends not to me, unless the reason of an individual demands my homage; and even then the submission is to reason, and not to man."

For the rest of her short life, Mary Wollstonecraft tried to live her life as independently as she could, and according to her own principles. After concluding an unhappy relationship with Henry Fuseli, she departed for Paris in 1792 to observe the French Revolution. There she met the American adventurer Gilbert Imlay and by him had an illegitimate daughter. Though the break-up of this relationship drove her to attempt suicide, she survived to form a final liaison with the English intellectual William Godwin, whom she eventually married. In 1759, in her thirty-seventh year, Mary Wollstonecraft was brought to bed with child. After insisting on principle that she be attended by a midwife rather than a physician, she gave birth to her second daughter after a damaging labor. Shortly thereafter Mary Wollstonecraft died, the victim, like so many other women, of poor sepsis and imperfect medical knowledge.

Mary Godwin, the second daughter of Mary Wollstonecraft, became, as Mary Shelley, an accomplished writer and the author of the novel *Frankenstein*. William Godwin went on to further achievements and saw to the publication of much of his wife's work. For years Mary Wollstonecraft's writings escaped notice, brought to light only when the women's movement began to assert itself more strongly. Nonetheless, in her advocacy of women's rights, Mary Wollstonecraft ever remained a disciple of the eighteenth-century Enlightenment, believing that it was reason that gave human beings uniqueness, dignity, and hope:

> In what respect are we superior to the brute creation, if intellect is not allowed to be the guide of passion? Brutes hope and fear, love and hate; but without a capacity to improve, a power of turning these passions to good or evil, they neither acquire virtue nor wisdom. Why? Because the Creator has not given them reason.

H. The New Science and the New Reason: Reflections and Meanings

Both the new science and the Enlightenment are deserving of some of the criticisms leveled at them: that they were elitest, that they were limited, that they did little for the mass of contemporary people. Voltaire had no love for the common people; Rousseau affirmed the General Will, but feared freedom for women. Harvey's discoveries, as awesome as they were, did not impress all of his physician-colleagues, and physicians did not treat the mass of the people in any case. While a small group of scholars grew excited about a universe thought to be knowable, the environment of the common people as often as not stood still. While the *philosophes* set about applying reason to society in an effort to improve it, the unlettered had little knowledge of it and little hope of benefit.

Even among intellectuals, praise for the new science and new reason was far from universal. A great debate raged between the "moderns," those who advocated the new learning, and the "ancients," or those who remained unconvinced. Among the ancients were the likes of Samuel Johnson and Jonathan Swift, who employed their formidable gifts to ridicule the optimism of some of the *philosophes.* Swift's satirical classic, *A Modest Proposal,* argued that the problem of hunger in Ireland could be rationally solved if the poor could be persuaded to eat their own children. In *Gulliver's Travels,* where horses were far more noble than the run of humanity, philosophers and human society were subjected to Swift's savage and eloquent satire.

It was much the same with the witty Samuel Johnson. When asked by his confidant, James Boswell, as to what he thought of Rousseau's character, Johnson's reply was nothing if not direct. "Rousseau, Sir, is a very bad man. I would sooner sign a sentence for his transportation than that of any felon who has gone from the Old Bailey these many years." When Boswell pressed Johnson to compare Rousseau to Voltaire, he replied that it would have been "difficult to settle the proportion of iniquity between them."

An even more formidable critic was David Hume (1711-1776), a Scots intellectual who challenged the Enlightenment belief that reason was the way to knowledge. In *An Inquiry Concerning Human Understanding* and elsewhere, Hume argued from a philosophical perspective that customs, feelings, and passions play a larger role in individual lives than reason. Morality, Hume continued, cannot be demonstrated by reason. Hume believed that human beings lived in a world of assumptions and probabilities, not certainties, and that terms like "reason" and "natural law" only confirm feelings, habits, and prejudices. Finally, Hume went so far as to say, in opposition to Locke, that the human mind cannot encounter reality through the senses alone. The idea of an objective reality understandable to the human mind, the philosophical belief on which the Enlightenment stood, had been severely challenged.

The challenge was made even stronger in the work of the German philosopher Immanuel Kant (1724-1804) who in his *Critique of Pure Reason* insisted that the human mind was not the passive vessel of Locke, but an active, organizing thing that ordered, and almost created, reality. To Kant, scientific knowledge was not knowledge of ultimate reality, and thus not as significant as the new scientists had claimed.

More recently, other scholars have raised other objections to the idea that the new science and the new reason were fundamentally "new" at all. For years, most historians believed that both movements marked a sharp break with the past, and that they ushered in a "modern" way of looking at the world. "Since the rise of Christianity," Herbert Butterfield wrote, in reference to the new science, "there is no landmark in history that is worthy to be compared with this." It is now clear that this belief can be doubted, as several scholars have demonstrated the connection between seventeenth-century science and its medieval and ancient predecessors.

The same tendency has emerged in the interpretation of the Enlightenment. Some years ago Carl Becker, in a seminal series of lectures, proposed that the world-view of the *philosophes* was more akin to that of medieval times than modern ones. Reason and faith, rationalism and passion, Becker believed, were as apt to be united as opposed, and he found them united in eighteenth-century thought. For all their differences, the medieval St. Thomas Aquinas and the *philosophe* Voltaire *both* believed that reason could be employed to support their most cherished beliefs. While Becker's arguments have been ably challenged, they are still worth considering.

The abiding faith of the new scientists and the *philosophes* lay less in God and more in a small proportion of humankind and its supposed capacity to be rational. Faith in reason, in turn, translated itself into the hope and expectation of progress. The idea of progress is in itself not new, but the men and women of the age of reason gave it new meaning and transformed it. In Christian theology, the idea of progress had been associated less with humankind and more with the Kingdom of God. The new science and the new reason secularized progress and brought it into the realm of human action. Some men and women now believed that they could understand and change their environments through the use of reason. This dream, this conviction in the minds of men and women, found its first expression in the American and French revolutions, and became an important part of the western heritage.

Portfolio: Science, Cities, Commerce, Transport, and Industrial Revolution, 1600-1815

The Astronomer. Jusepe de Ribera
This painting expresses the visionary yet precise spirit of the "new science" of the seventeenth century. *Courtesy of the Worcester Art Museum, Worcester, Massachusetts.*

Experiment with the Air Pump. Joseph Wright of Derby
Wright, a founding father of the industrial revolution, was also an able painter. Here he underlines the faith of the new science in observation, experiment, and induction, themselves a bequest of Francis Bacon. *Courtesy of the Tate Gallery, London.*

Metamorphosis of a Frog. Maria Sibylla Merian
This painting by a woman artist illustrates both the observational acuity of the new science and the skills of an accomplished watercolorist. *Courtesy of the Minneapolis Institute of Arts. The Minnich Collection.*

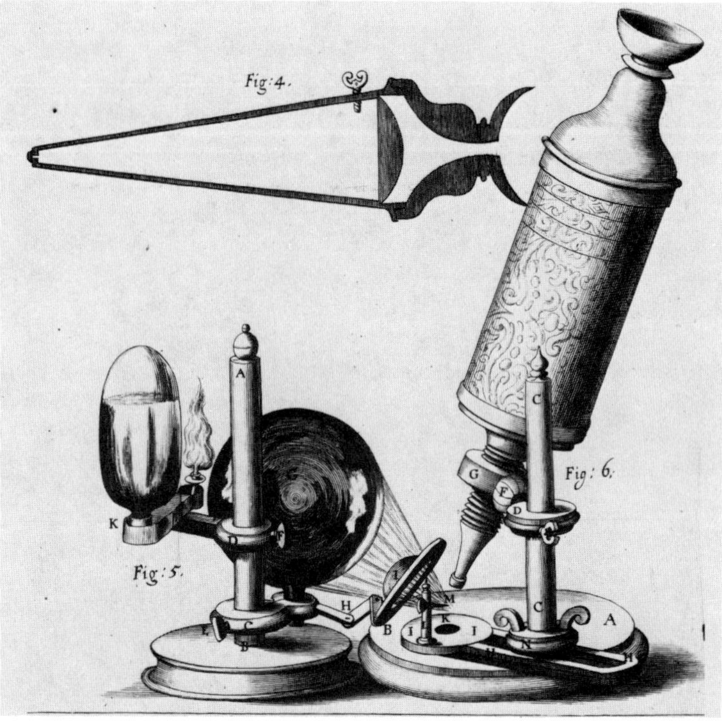
Fig: 4.
Fig: 5.
Fig: 6.

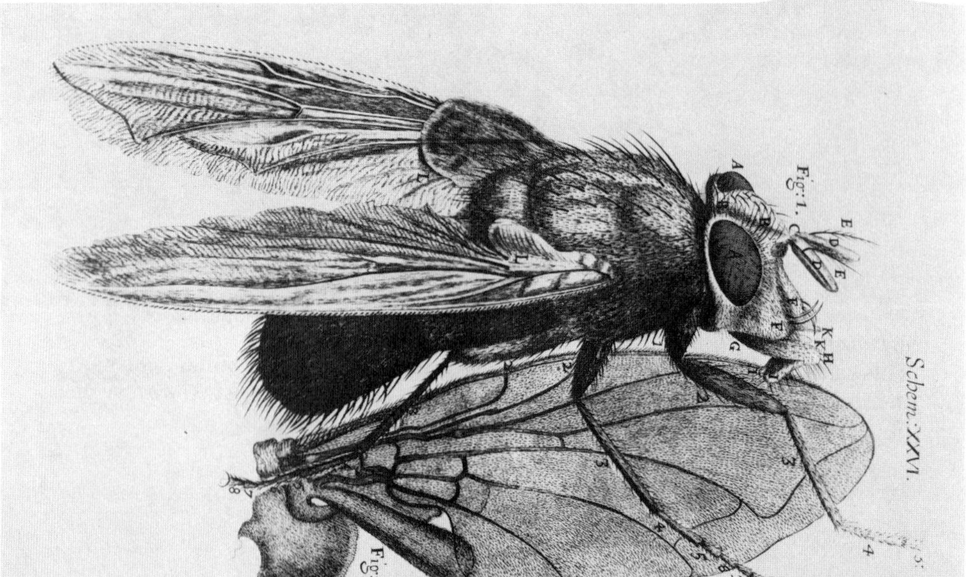
Schem: XXVI.
Fig: 1.
Fig: 2

Robert Hooke's microscope and his drawing of a fly appear in his *Micrographica* (London, 1665). ***Opposite.***
The *Micrographica* was one of the earliest full-length microscopic studies. The microscope as well as the telescope extended the observational abilities of seventeenth-century scientists, with astounding results. *Courtesy of the Edward G. Miner Library, University of Rochester School of Medicine and Dentistry.*

Nicolaus Copernicus in the Observatory in Frombork. Jan Matejko
In this idealized portrait, Copernicus is pictured with crude astronomical instruments and a diagram illustrating the heliocentric theory, which was first stated by Aristarchus. Copernicus lacked the tools and mathematical skills to demonstrate his theory, and further observational and mathematical work by Kepler, Galileo, and Newton was needed to establish its validity. *Courtesy of the Museum of the Jagellonian University, Cracow, Poland.*

Engraving of a canal and aqueduct.
By the end of the eighteenth century, canals crisscrossed England, provoking a revolution in the transport of bulk and fragile commodities which, in turn, fueled the industrial revolution. *Courtesy of Special Collections, University of Minnesota Libraries.*

The Quay of the Piazetta. **Opposite, top.** Canaletto, Venice
Courtesy of the National Gallery of Art, Washington. Gift of Mrs. Barbara Hutton.

View of Dresden from the Right Bank of the Elbe. **Opposite, bottom.** Bernardo Bellotto
The roles of watermen and boatmen in urban transport and commerce are amply illustrated here. *Courtesy of the Philbrook Art Center, Tulsa. Samuel H. Kress Collection.*

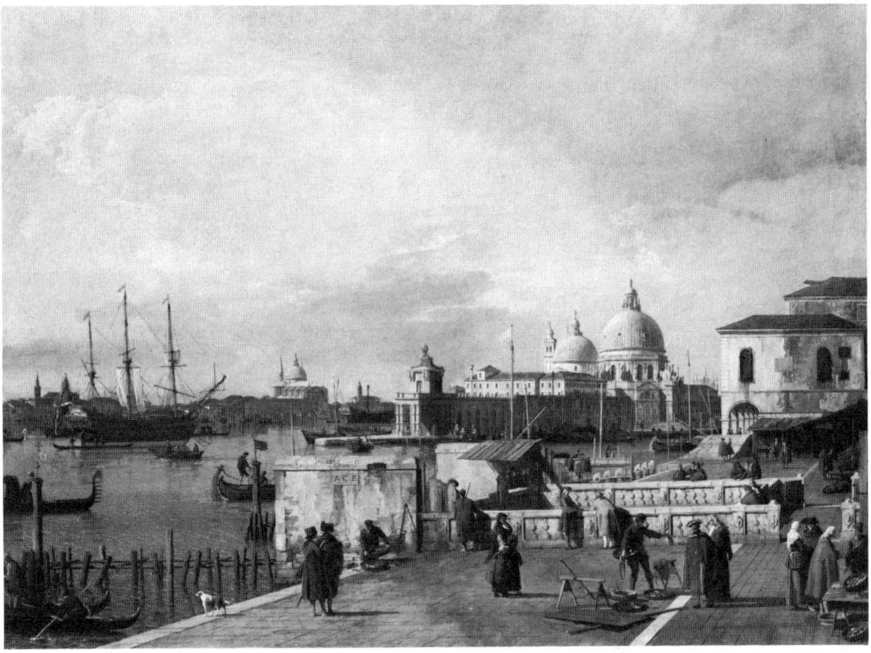

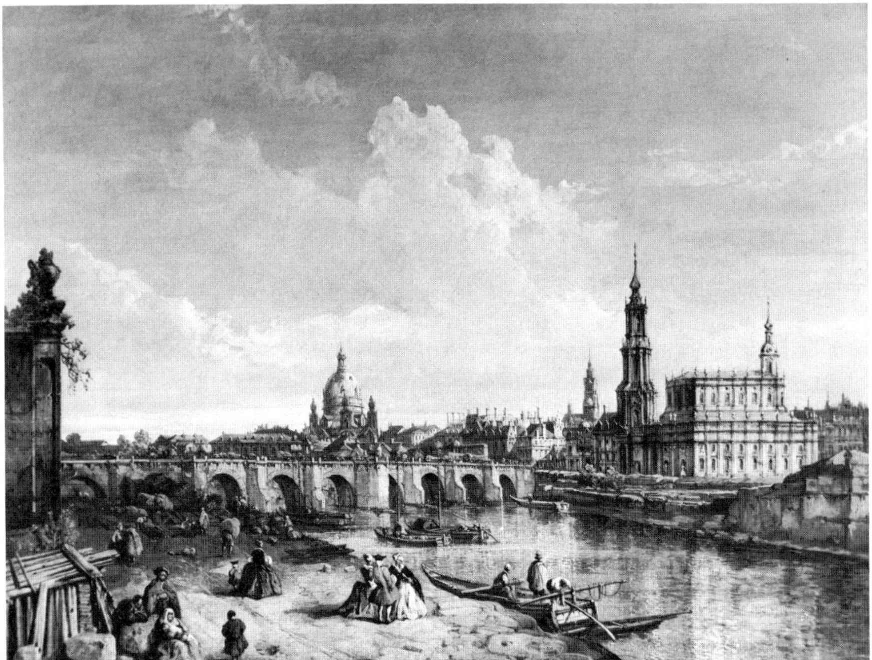

View of Amsterdam. A. J. Visscher
These views, really two parts of the same engraving, are ample illustration of the role of overseas commerce in the development of cities like Amsterdam and London. *Courtesy of the Rijksmuseum, Amsterdam.*

Chapter VI

Stability, Commerce, and Industry in Eighteenth Century Britain: The First Two Georges, Sir Robert Walpole and Caroline of Anspach, "Diamond" Pitt, Josiah Wedgwood, James Watt, and Adam Smith

> All these men have their price.
> —Sir Robert Walpole on Parliament

> I hate all Boets and Bainters.
> —George I

> It was now understood by everybody that Sir Robert was the queen's minister; that whoever he favoured, she distinguished; and whoever she distinguished the king employed.
> —Lord Hervey on the power of Walpole and Queen Caroline over George II

> He always knew what to do, and he did it.
> —A commentary on "Diamond" Pitt

> I have not time to think or write about anything, but the *immediate business* of the day. Public business I mean, for as to my private concerns I have almost forgot them, I scarcely know without a great deal of recollection whether I am a Landed Gentleman, an Engineer or a Potter. . . .
> —Josiah Wedgwood, 1765

No regulation of commerce can increase the quantity of industry in any society beyond what its capital can maintain.
—Adam Smith

The age is running mad after innovation. . . . All the business of the world is to be done in a new way: men are to be hanged in a new way: Tyburn is not safe from the fury of innovation.
—Dr. Samuel Johnson

Broad Quay, Bristol. Unknown artist
This busy English port city illustrates how foreign trade helped England grow more powerful and prosperous in the eighteenth century. Some of the wealth generated by overseas commerce provided the capital for the industrial revolution. *Courtesy of the City of Bristol Museum and Art Gallery, Bristol, England.*

A. The Process of the Industrial Revolution, 1750-1850

Beginning with the second half of the eighteenth century, a group of interlocking economic and social changes occurred in England for which historians utilize the term, "Industrial Revolution." Ironically enough, the phrase itself was not originally an English one, but rather French, and began to be used by writers in that country in the early nineteenth century. Friederich Engels, the disciple and colleague of Karl Marx, brought the term into the English language forever when he wrote his monumental work, *The Condition of the Working Classes in England* in 1845. The existence of an Industrial Revolution in English history and historiography was confirmed with the publication of Arnold Toynbee's *Lectures on the Industrial Revolution* in 1884.

Since that time, the century between 1750 and 1850 has been known as the period of the Industrial Revolution in England. As industrialization came to much of the rest of Europe, and to America, in the nineteenth century, the term and the social and economic phenomena it represented gained even wider currency. More recently, as underdeveloped countries have sought to create an industrial base of their own and thereby enter the "modern" community of nations, the older Industrial Revolution has been studied in an effort to find patterns and models to create a climate for industrialization.

The essence of the Industrial Revolution is socio-economic change, and it is in these changes that the real meaning of the term is found. The first change that the Industrial Revolution brought to England was in the area of economic emphasis. During the Industrial Revolution the English economy ceased to emphasize agriculture and commerce exclusively and began to concentrate on industrial, or factory, production. This change took place over time, and for many years farms and small shops shared the landscape with the larger factories. With the growth of the factory system came urbanization, or the growth of cities, and economic interdependence and specialization. As people began to concentrate in great numbers in cities and factory towns, they began as well to specialize in one occupation or skill. As regions and cities and the individuals within them became more specialized they were forced to depend on other regions, cities, and individuals, some of them quite far away, to provide other needed skills, services, and commodities. This kind of interdependence is called *economic integration.*

Another change brought by the Industrial Revolution was in the substitution of machine power for the work of human hands. The invention of machines and the means to power them is a reminder that an important part of the Industrial Revolution lay in innovation, the application of technological solutions to the problems of work. The adoption of machines also required the growth of two classes: a working class to operate them, and a middle class to venture the money, or capital, to build and manage the factories and to buy the machines. Machines produced more goods than had ever been produced by human hands, thus, there were more goods to sell. This, in turn, generated more capital for reinvestment in new machines and factories. In England, the old landed classes in fact joined the middle class in providing capital for industrial growth.

It is not enough, however, to understand what the changes brought by the Industrial Revolution were. It is also important to understand how, and in what sequence these changes occurred. The Industrial Revolution becomes meaningful when it is conceived as an ongoing process. This approach has in recent years been crystallized in the work of Phyllis Deane, who has seen the Industrial Revolution as the sum of several interlocking, smaller revolutions, each occurring in a precise sequence.

The first of these revolutions was in the area of demography, or population. Beginning in the 1740s the long-term population of England, which had in the past tended to stagnate, began to move decisively upward. At first the rate of increase was relatively small, three and one-half percent in the decade between 1741 and 1751, but in later decades it surged to ten percent. In the years between 1810 and 1820 the population grew at a rate of sixteen percent. Historians disagree whether this rise was due to a declining death rate or a rising birth rate, but none denies that the demographic revolution occurred. This rise in population helped create a climate for an Industrial Revolution in at least two ways. First, the rise created a demand for more goods both agricultural and manufactured, thus encouraging investment in all areas of the economy. Secondly, the demographic revolution created a pool of labor. This surplus pool of labor, eventually concentrated in the cities, provided the nucleus for an industrial working class.

The demographic revolution, in turn, benefited from two other revolutions: those in agriculture and commerce. At least one historian, Eric Kerridge, has dated the English agricultural revolution from the sixteenth century, while others have placed it later. Whenever the agricultural revolution began, the changes it wrought were important. Large tracts of land were enclosed. These larger enclosed plots, though they undoubtedly produced misery in the form of tenant eviction, improved the production of crops, milk, and meat. Production was also increased by bringing new land under the plow, by improved ditching and draining techniques, by crop rotation, by the introduction of fodder crops like turnips and clover, by selective breeding of livestock, and by the utilization of fertilizers. By the eighteenth century, English agriculture was booming. Improved agricultural output helped to encourage, and to maintain, the demographic revolution by providing the foodstuffs to support a rising population. The agricultural revolution also enriched the improving landlords and made it possible to export agricultural commodities, thus enabling them to reap high profits. The pool of capital generated by the profits of the agricultural revolution helped to finance the larger Industrial Revolution.

Capital accumulation was also a prime benefit of the commercial revolution that occurred almost simultaneously. Beginning in the mid-seventeenth century the English fought a series of wars with the Dutch as they sought predominance in seaborne trade. English aggressiveness was assisted by Dutch exhaustion in the wars against Louis XIV, by the commercial and colonial acquisitions won in the treaties of Utrecht and Paris, and by long-standing mercantilist policies applied to the English colonies. The Navigation Acts of 1651 were succeeded by other similar measures directed against the American colonies. Laws like the Hat, Iron, and Tea acts helped insure that the American Colonies remained a good market for British goods by the simple expedient of refusing to allow the Americans to create a manufacturing capacity of their own. So thorough was British penetration of the American market that it survived even the American Revolution. At the same time, the privilege of the *asiento*, gained at the Peace of Utrecht, allowed increasing English trade with the old Spanish colonies, a trade which continued unabated even after the Latin American revolutions.

During the eighteenth century both the volume and variety of English exports increased. Though by the 1750s woolen cloth was still the dominant export, it had been joined by cotton, indigo, pitch, hemp, and iron. As exports grew in variety, English dominance of the reexport and carrying trades also increased, creating yet another capital reserve. This reserve grew still larger as the commercial revolution encouraged allied and service industries, like banking, insurance, ship-building, warehousing, and processing. This last marked a significant change in the nature of British exports. Slowly, the export of primary products like grain gave way to processed commodities like sugar, or to manufactured goods like cotton cloth. To the commercial revolution the demographic revolution lent a hand, creating an available reserve of potential English sailors that was the envy of the world. Finally, the commercial revolution also encouraged the habit of taking financial risks. The merchants who participated in overseas enterprise, as well as their partners among the landed classes, grew conditioned to risking capital in the hope of profit. It was the commercial revolution that created much of the wealth that made the Industrial Revolution possible.

Much of the capital earned in the agricultural and commercial revolutions was utilized in the transportation revolution that transformed England in the eighteenth century. While the building of railroads is most generally associated with the Industrial Revolution, railroads in fact did not play a part in its early stages. Roads and canals formed the backbone of the transportation revolution and the larger Industrial Revolution. Without transportation, the economic integration and specialization that characterizes all industrial societies would not have been possible. In the eighteenth century the number of turnpike acts passed by Parliament increased as groups of investors built sound roads in the hope of turning a profit from tolls. Down these turnpikes, which were far more dependable than their muddy predecessors, flowed goods, commercial representatives, mail, investment, expertise, and labor.

Even more important than roads were canals. Canals were beautifully suited to England, an island country where no part of the interior is far from a seaport. Moreover, canals, unlike roads, could transport, albeit slowly, bulky, heavy, or fragile commodities at relatively low prices. Though canals and roads were what are termed *capital-intensive* investments, those which require vast amounts of initial funding, they saved money in the long run. As transport became cheaper and more dependable, merchants no longer had to maintain large inventories of goods, thus freeing capital for use elsewhere. Canals and railroads, because of their cost, attracted outside investment from other regions and other countries. Capital, goods, and information flowed through the arteries created by the transportation revolution.

The larger Industrial Revolution was also assisted by a revolution in innovation, or invention. Generations of students have memorized the names of the Industrial Revolution's inventors, together with their creations. Such an exercise has no meaning without considering the relationship among such inventions, or their relationship to the other processes of the Industrial Revolution. Each innovation created a demand for others. It is the pattern of innovation, not the individual invention alone, that is important. Such innovation would have been impossible without capital to build the machines, without the transportation to move the machines and the finished goods, or without the labor to run the factories. Invention, like other facets of the Industrial Revolution, is not so much a thing as a process.

The interlocking processes of the Industrial Revolution required still other ingredients: a stable government and a climate friendly to economic enterprise. In this, too, England was fortunate.

B. The First Two Georges and the Crisis of Whig Politics

As England entered the eighteenth century, Parliament, and the landed classes that controlled it, had begun to limit what remained of royal authority and to institute laws that confirmed a growing alliance between those whose wealth was based on land and those who enriched themselves through commerce. By the Act of Settlement of 1701 Parliament decided, since Queen Anne would likely be childless, that the English succession would be vested in the rulers of the German House of Hanover, who were descendents of James I through his daughter Elizabeth. In the same act, Parliament placed the dismissal of royal judges in its own hands, and declared that no royal pardon could override an impeachment by Parliament.

At the same time, a number of other Parliamentary measures strengthened the English nation as a commercial entity. The establishment of the Bank of England in 1694 was an important step in this process, and it was soon joined by others. Many of the old restrictive, monopolistic trading companies found themselves under attack by a Parliament determined to open trade. While some of these trading companies survived, they did so in an environment less hostile to interloping and unrestricted trade. The Act of Union of 1707, which joined England with Scotland in a United Kingdom of Great Britain and Ireland, created an immense free trade area, which, in turn, created markets for English merchants. In 1696 Parliament created the Board of Trade and Plantations to administer England's colonial possessions in her economic interest. Accompanying such legislation was an ever growing surge in commercial activity in London, and especially outlying ports like Bristol and Liverpool, which benefited from a profitable Portuguese trade and the privileges of the *asiento*.

To the growth of commerce and trade was joined the dominance of the Whig party. Between 1701 and 1715, due partially to skillful use of propaganda and partly to the political blunders of the Tories, the Whigs were able to send their political opponents into near-oblivion. The Peace of Utrecht, forced on the nation by the Tory allies of Queen Anne, gave the Whigs their first opportunity. By accusing the Tories of a cheap peace from which England gained too few benefits, the Whigs labeled their opponents as appeasers.

To this was soon added the charge of treason. In 1715 the Stuart claimant to the English throne attempted to recover it by an unsuccessful invasion through Scotland. The so-called "Fifteen" sent a shock through the English. Unfortunately for the Tories, some of their number were in truth "Jacobites," or supporters of the

Stuart cause. In short order the Whigs managed to taint all Tories with the charge of Jacobitism. With the Tories in the political wilderness, the Whig politicians surged into power with the new Hanoverian dynasty. For virtually the rest of the century, political power remained in the hands of the landed Whig oligarchs.

The Hanoverians confirmed the Whig domination of politics. Perhaps no other dynasty has come to the English throne less prepared to rule. The first Hanoverian monarch, George I, set the tone for his immediate successors. Short, gross, too used to the autocratic way in which he had always governed the petty German state of Hanover, George I was partly explicable in terms of what he liked and what he hated. George I liked women, especially those with opulent bosoms. He liked them even better if they were stupid. George liked war as well, because he had been raised a soldier and, one suspects, because he found giving orders, and the comparative simplicity of military life, congenial.

What was most arresting about George I, however, were the many things which did not suit him. First among them was his family, and he cordially hated most of its members, especially his wife and son, the latter the future George II. Of his wife, Sophia Dorothea, George I said little, for years before she had been heroically and publicly unfaithful to him. Witty and bright, Sophia had found George rather dull going and had sought solace in the arms of a Danish count named Königsmarck. When the infidelity was discovered, George acted with the cruelty of which he was so capable. Königsmarck simply disappeared, and his body was never found. Sophia Dorothea was divorced, defamed, and shut away in a castle for the remaining thirty-two years of her life. Lacking a queen, George I bore with him to England two German mistresses, the one predictably short and fat, the other, in an uncharacteristic alteration of taste, tall and thin. English wags promptly dubbed them, respectively, the "Elephant" and the "Maypole."

George I also brought with him a great suspicion of English politics and politicians. This was in a sense only just, because George I knew full well that some Tory politicians had sought to restore to the Stuart Pretender the throne he now occupied. But if George was entitled to his suspicions, he was also in another sense unwise in them. His suspicion and dislike led to avoidance and lack of understanding, and these made him dependent on the very politicians he loathed. Hating the English, George absented himself for months in his beloved Hanover, leaving the English government to the hated politicians. George's ignorance was heightened, finally, by his hatred for learning and culture in general and for the English language in particular. George never learned the language of his new land very well. Consequently, he lacked the verbal agility to follow the politicians, and his awkwardness in the language made him at once more isolated and more bitter. "I hate all Boets and Bainters," George once mumbled peevishly in his heavy German accent.

By their ignorance and their hatreds the first two Georges delivered themselves into the hands of the wits and the politicians. The failure to renew the Licensing Act in the late seventeenth century had created in England something like a free press. The eighteenth became a century of wits and wags, memoirs and political satires, and the Hanoverian dynasty became early grist for the mill. Portrayed by the wits as buffoons, increasingly dependent on the politicians they loathed, the monarchy under the Hanoverians inevitably lost credibility and power to Parliament and its managers.

Everywhere they went, and in everything they did, a chorus of laughter accompanied the Hanoverian sovereigns. "Good pipple, what for you abuse us? We come for all your goots." So shouted one of George's German mistresses from her coach to a crowd in the streets. "Yes," replied a wag in the audience, "and our chattels too." A courtier of George I, seeking to please his sovereign, once suggested that George's hated son and namesake, the future George II, be waylaid and conveyed to America. George II, for his part, hated *his* son Frederick, the father of the future George III, with as much thoroughness as his father hated him, and their quarrel grew so violent that Frederick's own mother wished him dead of apoplexy. To the amusement of all, George speculated publicly that his heir was not his own but a changeling who was placed in his son's cradle at infancy.

George II mirrored the father he detested in other ways. He, too, enjoyed dalliance with voluptuous mistresses. A punctual man, George II called at the houses of his concubines with regularity, would dutifully wait outside if he was early, and then repair homeward to confess his indiscretions to his hapless queen. Sharing his father's dubious taste in art as well as in women, George II once ordered the Vice-Chamberlain, Lord Hervey, to remove an elegant Van Dyck painting from the court and to replace it with a "fat Venus." Thereupon Lord Hervey, a wit who had already noted George's preference for corpulent women and his sexual estrangement from his wife, went home and gleefully penned the following: "Lord Hervey thought, though he did not dare to say, that, if His Majesty had liked his fat Venus as well as he used to do, there would have been none of these disputations." Such remarks would have been lost on George II, who shared his father's allergy to the written word. George often remarked contemptuously that booklearning was a mean exercise and far beneath him. Characteristically, when Edward Gibbon presented his noble work, *The Rise and Fall of the Roman Empire,* to the king, the latter accused him of scribbling.

The constant quarreling between Hanoverian fathers and sons gave the leaders of various Whig political factions too much opportunity. With the demise of the Tories, there was no opposition and thus no embarrassing questions of principle to divert attention from the simple pursuit of power. The leading Whig politicians, each commanding the votes of their followers in Parliament, scrambled to be chosen by the king as ministers of state. Some of these leaders, finding themselves out of favor with the Hanoverian kings, banked on the future, exploited family animosities, and conspired with the Hanoverian sons and heirs. Unfortunately, for all their venality and ambition, these politicians were not always knowledgeable or wise. Sir Spencer Compton, the first choice of George II to be chief minister, was so incompetent that he could not draft the king's accession speech. The Duke of Newcastle, one of the leading politicians of the day, had certain problems with geography. When aroused to the need to defend Annapolis, he was said to remark: "Oh—yes—yes—to be sure—Annapolis must be defended—troops must be sent to Annapolis. Pray where is Annapolis?" George II, contemplating the rival politicians who gathered at the court of his despised son, surveyed their dubious talents with his usual generosity: "There is my Lord Carnarvon, a hot-headed, passionate, half-witted coxcomb, with no more sense than his master; there is Townshend, a silent, proud, surly, wrong-headed booby; there is my Lord North, a very good poor creature, but a very weak man; there is my Lord Baltimore, who wants to be well with both courts, and is well at neither and is a little mad. . . ."

The accession of the Hanoverians, the combined presence of ignorance and ambition, the factionalizing of Whig party politics, and the family hatreds of Hanoverian fathers and sons created a situation where political management was as necessary as it was difficult. Any politician who proposed to run the government successfully would have to manage the Whig grandees and their factions in Parliament, and find favor with the suspicious and quarreling Hanoverians. He would, in sum, have to make a government work that might just as easily not have worked at all. Finally, he would have to lead a nation that, after the Peace of Utrecht, had become a commercial and world power.

C. Stability and Corruption: Sir Robert Walpole and Caroline of Anspach

The man who gained control of this political nightmare and managed it successfully emerged in the unlikely form of a Norfolk squire named Sir Robert Walpole. Gross, foul-mouthed even by the marginal standards of his day, course-grained, venal and cynical, Walpole thoroughly reflected, and understood, his times. He also understood the Hanoverians, and, despite the fact that George I and George II hated one another, served them both in succession. Though never designated Prime Minister—the term was not yet used—Walpole nonetheless dominated Parliament and the government for nearly two decades, from 1720 to 1738, and in so doing reinforced English political stability. Seldom has a politician been more precisely attuned to his times, and seldom has a politician been so successful.

Walpole's political career had begun in the early years of the eighteenth century when, as a young and promising Whig, he was appointed to the important, and lucrative, office of Paymaster of the Forces. His career, however, soon suffered a sharp reverse. When the Tories swept into power in 1710 Walpole found himself not only out of office, but in disgrace, as the vengeful Tories sent him to the Tower on charges of corruption.

When the failure of the Fifteen and the Hanoverian succession led to the disgrace of the Tories and the triumph of the Whigs, Walpole was among the beneficiaries. With Charles Townshend, Walpole organized a Whig faction, which was soon actively competing for power with another Whig group led by the Earl of Stanhope and the Earl of Sunderland. For a time Stanhope's group seemed to have the upper hand, and Stanhope, eager to compensate for the Treaty of Utrecht, which he saw as a Tory sell-out, pursued an aggressive and very expensive foreign policy that flirted with war.

In this Walpole, perceived his opportunity. Always sensitive to financial questions, Walpole was doubtless aware that the War of the Spanish Succession had created a national debt in excess of £50,000,000. Realizing this, Walpole began to enunciate what were to become guiding assumptions of his policy: that foreign wars were destructive of trade and were in potential financially disastrous; that such economic misfortunes, in turn, undermined political stability and thus the task of governing; that, finally, all of these troubles could destroy the personal security of Walpole himself. In this way Walpole compassed the public interest in self-interest.

These preoccupations made Walpole brilliant in his positive proposals and selective in his opposition. In temporary alliance with the Stanhope faction, he sought to manage the war debts that he perceived as such a threat to stability. Walpole first arranged the consolidation of the morass of war debts into one, and instituted a standard rate of interest. Having made the debt seem more comprehensible, Walpole arranged for its orderly repayment. Out of a portion of tax revenue, he established what came to be called a "Sinking Fund," a pool of money from which the debt was in theory repaid.

Walpole at a stroke defused a negative political issue, restored confidence to a country suffering the inevitable post-war economic contractions, and commended himself to those who invested and participated in commerce or trade.

Nonetheless, for Walpole's opposition to their aggressive foreign policy, Stanhope and Sunderland showed little liking or mercy. Possessing the reluctant confidence of George I and, perhaps more importantly, the cooperation of his mistresses, Stanhope could muster sufficient Parliamentary votes without the quarrelsome Walpole. Once again Walpole was driven out of office, but, to the sorrow of his Whig enemies, he formed a venomous opposition in pragmatic association with the minority Tories he had formerly attacked. In this way, Walpole made himself such a nuisance that he could not be ignored. Eventually he had to be asked to return to the ministry.

When it came, Walpole's political rehabilitation once again involved the containment of a potential economic disaster. This came in the form of a bankrupt Tory scheme known as the South Sea Company. Some years before, in 1711, the South Sea Company had been chartered by the Tories as a rival to the Whig Bank of England, itself founded in 1694 to stabilize the currency and manage the national debt. The South Sea Company's directors turned out to be an ambitious lot and, after they distributed shares of South Sea stock and other largesse to key figures in Parliament and the court, including the king's two grasping mistresses, Stanhope and Sunderland were persuaded to allow the South Sea Company to hold and, in return for a profit, reduce the national debt.

As the word spread of the connection of the South Sea Company to the court and government, the value of South Sea stock rose dynamically on a "bubble" of speculation. Then the bubble burst. Beginning in August of 1720, investors began to realize that the value of the stock bore little relation to the assets of the South Sea Company. Prices tumbled, many were ruined, and collectively the victims howled for the heads of those who, in the court, in Parliament, in the South Sea Company, even in the Sunderland ministry itself, had appealed so successfully to human greed.

Sunderland, unable to deal with the South Sea Bubble himself, needing an ally unconnected with the scandal, and perhaps hoping that he could involve his enemy Walpole in failure, invited Walpole back from the political wilderness. To Sunderland's surprise Walpole limited and contained the crisis. His presence as much as his policies calmed nerves and restored order. Knowing where power lay, Walpole ignored howls for justice and instead, through skillful management of Parliament, limited inquiry and saved the careers of many powerful men compromised by the crisis. In so doing Walpole ingratiated himself with influential people in Parliament and at court, thereby helping to guarantee his political future. To Walpole's advantage as well, possibly in consequence of the Bubble Scandal, his arch-enemy Stanhope had a fit and expired. Sunderland, for his part, was compelled to retire, to die in disgrace in 1722. There was no other alternative. George I was obliged to call for Walpole, naming him at once Chancellor of the Exchequer and First Lord of the Treasury, the leading financial offices of the realm.

Real power seemed within Walpole's grasp. He was a Whig, and Whig politicians controlled Parliament, and many of them, if not loyal to Walpole, were at least grateful to him for saving their careers. George I, largely because there was no one else, had made Walpole his minister. At the same time, Walpole knew that such power was an illusion if he could not govern and that, in order to govern, he would have to control the votes of enough of the Whigs in Parliament to pass into law the legislation, financial and otherwise, that would enable him to run the country. In sum, in order to govern, Walpole would have to manage Parliament. The question was how to do it.

For this dilemma Walpole had a ready solution, systematic corruption. In the absence of principles, Walpole understood that politics revolved around a system of rewards and punishments, and these he undertook to control. He understood, further, that every landed Whig politician commanded the votes of his small group of followers in Parliament through precisely the same kind of tactics. There were two kinds of Parliamentary seats—county seats and borough seats—and the great Whig lords controlled many of them. They were able to do this, in turn, because they controlled much of the land and people who made up the counties and boroughs, or towns, of England. The local Whig lord controlled the county seats by simply telling his tenants how to vote, and by "treating" them on election days.

Boroughs presented more complex problems, but many of them could be managed as well. Some boroughs, long since depopulated by the plague or economic catastrophe, still retained their seats in Parliament. These "rotten" and "pocket" boroughs could be controlled simply by buying up the land on which they stood. The Whig "boroughmongers" could also occasionally purchase such seats on the open market. Other boroughs, where the number of voters was small, or where the vote was confined to those who owned property, could be managed through bribery and influence.

Walpole undertook to manage the Whig leaders who controlled these blocs of votes. To accomplish this, Walpole used the resources of the government and the Crown. In the gift of the king were honors and sinecures, rewards and knighthoods. There were also offices to be had in the customs service, in the military, in the

Church. Thus, if the younger son of a powerful Whig Parliamentarian needed a position, Walpole could be obliging. If an influential boroughmonger wanted a knighthood, Walpole saw that he was placed on the honors list.

Significantly, one of Stanhope's measures stiffly and successfully opposed by Walpole had been the so-called Peerage Bill, which would have limited the king's power to grant titles of nobility. As the king's minister, Walpole used such patronage to advantage. Also significantly, in 1716, Walpole had supported another of Stanhope's Parliamentary measures, the Septennial Act, which extended the time limit between Parliamentary elections from three to seven years. Even then, Walpole perceived that corruption and control of Parliament would be made easier if elections were less frequent. Finally, Walpole exploited the Parliamentary seats controlled by the king. A great landowner himself, the king could influence elections. Walpole made sure that the "King's Friends" so elected were also his own.

Portrait of Robert Walpole, 1st Earl of Orford.
Studio of J. B. Van Loo
Courtesy of the National Portrait Gallery, London.

With his management of Parliament established, Walpole settled into a policy of his liking. Experience had taught him that foreign entanglements were costly financially and politically, so he followed a policy of peace. Peace and Parliamentary measures supported the revival and expansion of trade and commerce. Walpole saw to it that customs duties were simplified and reduced, and a real movement toward free trade began. Through a series of Parliamentary acts, the importation of raw materials as well as the warehousing and reexportation of commodities was made easier. At all times, Walpole resisted the heavier taxation that would have aroused political opposition and discouraged economic growth. Even at the risk of making enemies, he arranged the signing of the Treaty of Seville with Spain in 1729, temporarily ending the threat of a war many desired.

In 1727 Walpole faced a threat to his power when George I died. George II at first transferred his loathing of his father to the minister who had served him. Another minister was chosen. Walpole properly humbled himself and quickly became indispensable. Walpole also gained the friendship of the new queen, Caroline of Anspach. Earthy, coarse, handsome, and highly intelligent, Caroline liked Walpole and he her. Caroline read the books her husband avoided, investigated philosophy and theology, actively questioned Christianity, and drew great satisfaction from helping Walpole control the husband who bored her. Together they managed George II as thoroughly as Walpole managed Parliament. This was not always easy, because George II loved warfare as much as he hated books, and he was constantly courted by rival politicians. Though Walpole once referred, with his usual coarseness, to Queen Caroline as a "fat bitch" and on another occasion remarked of her that "I took the right sow by the ear," Walpole knew that she buttressed his power, and in his other references to her there was more than a little respect.

It was not until 1733 that Walpole made his first mortal political error. In that year, seeking to lessen the tax burden on the landed classes, Walpole proposed an Excise Tax, a luxury tax on certain trade goods. The proposal aroused extreme Parliamentary opposition that emboldened Walpole's rivals for political leadership. The opposition was strengthened when a new alliance between France and Spain, the so-called Family Compact of 1733, seemed to threaten English commercial interests.

In 1737, another crisis came with the death of Caroline of Anspach. George II, distraught at her deathbed, vowed to his wife that he would honor her memory by refusing to remarry; he said, rather obtusely, that he would have only mistresses. Despite Caroline's pain, neither her wit nor her will left her. After reminding her husband that it was quite possible to have a wife and mistresses at the same time, refusing a deathbed conversion by the Archbishop of Canterbury, and denying an interview to the son she loathed, she died. A portion of Walpole's power died with her.

Walpole managed to cling to shreds of power for five more years, but he was forced to preside over the demise of his policy of peace. War with Spain was duly declared. Walpole was not happy, and he expressed it with his usual bluntness. "They are ringing the bells now," he remarked of the patriots who sought war. "Soon they will be wringing their hands." To a Parliamentary rival he said, "It is your war, and I wish you the joy of it." The election of 1741 brought victory to Walpole's enemies. He resigned in 1742. By 1745, he was dead.

Walpole had nonetheless made his mark. He had managed to bridge the gap between Parliament and the king. That he had done so by means of patronage and corruption should not diminish the fact that he made the government work. Walpole's government had given England political and economic stability, and these in turn fostered both the commercial and industrial revolutions. By making economic interest a foundation-stone of his government, Sir Robert Walpole had taken an involuntary first step toward the transformation of English society.

D. Enterprise and the Politics of Commerce: "Diamond" Pitt and His Family

The story of "Diamond" Pitt begins not in England but in India. In the late seventeenth century an Englishman in India, William Hedges, noted in his diary the presence of a ship called the *Crown* and one "Mr. Pitts." The said Pitts had hired a house and, according to the diarist, had "carried divers chests of money ashore, and was very busy in buying of goods." Such an entry was a fitting description of the early activities of Thomas Pitt, the "Diamond" Pitt of eighteenth century England.

Hedges had not been the first person to notice the mercantile activities of Diamond Pitt, nor would he be the last. Pitt's trading practices often excited the interest of the authorities because they were quite illegal. Thomas Pitt was an "interloping" merchant; that is, a trader who violated the monopoly of trade granted by the Crown to a privileged group of merchants, generally organized into a trading company.

The monopoly in this case was that of the East India Company, and Pitt's activities occasioned its sporadic wrath. At various times the East India Company ordered Pitt to leave India, but he characteristically refused to go, or left only to return again. Pitt was once bound over not to engage in interloping for £40,000; on another occasion he was fined £1,000, but nothing shamed him and nothing worked. Thomas Pitt was always to have contempt for anything or anyone unwise enough to meddle with him. "He always knew what to do," wrote a contemporary, "and he did it."

What Pitt did in India was to make a fortune. That he was known as Diamond Pitt was no accident. He acquired an immense diamond on one occasion for £20,400, a bauble that he sold some years later to Regent of France for £135,000. On one occasion, in 1693, Pitt returned to India with no less than £60,000 in silver for purposes of trade. He also tried to make money elsewhere. During the French wars he fitted out a privateer for £8,000 to prey with profit on French shipping. Pitt also helped found the North-West Company, a concern specifically designed to challenge the monopoly of the Hudson's Bay Company in what is now Canada. Money and power poured in. Even the East India Company capitulated. Though one of its directors denounced Pitt as a "roughling immoral man," the East India Company ended by admitting Pitt as a member and eventually sent him back to India as governor of Fort St. George in Bengal.

The Company's change in attitude might have had something to do with the Whig power politics in which Thomas Pitt could now afford to indulge. Just before the Revolution of 1688, Pitt had purchased from Lord Salisbury the manor house of Stratford-under-the-Castle. With the house and outbuildings came the Parliamentary borough of Old Sarum, which Diamond Pitt used to his advantage. A supporter of William and Mary, Thomas Pitt sat in the Parliaments of 1689, 1690, 1695, and sporadically thereafter until 1715. Old Sarum, singled out later in the century by the radical John Wilkes as an egregious example of political corruption, was sold by one of Pitt's grandsons in 1749 for the sum of £3,000.

Soon other Parliamentary seats were occupied by Diamond Pitt's heirs and connections. In 1721 Thomas Pitt wrote from India to his son Robert that he and an election agent should consult as to "where the interest of my estate lies strongest for electing three or four Parliament men. . . ." Thomas Pitt, a grandson of Diamond Pitt, entered Parliament in 1727 and managed the Parliamentary elections of 1741 and 1747 for his patron Frederick, Prince of Wales. Other Pitt connections occupied at various times seats for Camelford and Okehampton. Commercial success had purchased Parliamentary power. Nonetheless, Diamond Pitt urged his heirs to be competent members. "If you are in Parliament," he wrote his son, "show yourself on all occasions a good Englishman, and a faithful servant to your country. Avoid faction . . . and vote according to your conscience and not for any sinister end whatever."

Thomas Pitt was a difficult man. From India, he wrote hectoring letters to his wife Jane and to his sons. When he returned home for the last time, his temper inflamed by gout and unaccustomed inactivity, Pitt quarreled with nearly everyone. He was not always wise in his investments, and he lost money in the South Sea Bubble. His grandson and namesake lost even more and had to flee the country for a time to avoid debt. When Diamond Pitt died in 1727, it may have come as a relief to all concerned.

The life of Diamond Pitt nonetheless illustrated several important characteristics of English society on the eve of the Industrial Revolution. As does Walpole's, Pitt's career testifies to the growing involvement of commercial interests in the affairs of the English government. It also reveals something more: the willingness of those who had made their money in trade to spend some of it to participate in, and support, affairs of state. Pitt made his fortune in India, but he spent much of it on land and politics. An interloper he might have been, but he was also something of an English patriot.

Diamond Pitt's heirs obtained peerages, participated in politics, entered the ranks of the landed classes through marriage. Because these things were possible the Pitt family, and others like them, were absorbed into the ruling classes and became bulwarks of the English state. Stability was thus maintained, discontent and revolution averted. In this England formed a notable contrast to France, where the commercial classes were denied political power and the nobililty fought the government and refused to pay taxes. Significantly France, but not England, experienced a political revolution in the eighteenth century.

Two of Diamond Pitt's direct descendants, both named William Pitt, rose to the apogee of English politics and guided the affairs of their country through difficult times. One of them, later ennobled as Lord Chatham, managed a successful war against France. This culminated in the Peace of Paris of 1763, as a result of which England increased her colonial dominions and her power. The heir of the interloper had fulfilled his grandfather's hopes.

E. Josiah Wedgwood: Industrialist and Agent of the Transportation Revolution

Three years after the death of the strenuous Diamond Pitt, Josiah Wedgwood was born to a family in the pottery district of Staffordshire. The two men form an interesting comparison. Diamond

Pitt was rough; Wedgwood was gentle. Pitt spent part of his career in India bullying his Asian charges; Wedgwood was a philanthropist who spent much of his life denouncing slavery. Pitt was a patriot whose direct descendant annexed much of North America, and a manipulator of rotten boroughs; Wedgwood was a humanist who believed that the American Revolution was a good thing and that Parliamentary elections should be reformed. Yet what they had in common was as profound as what they did not. Both had energy and imagination, and both possessed reserves of physical and entrepreneurial courage. Pitt was unmoved by the power of the East India Company; Wedgwood, bothered for most of his life with a damaged leg, calmly endured its amputation without anesthetic and then quietly went about his business.

Wedgwood's business was the same as generations of Staffordshire men before him: he was a pottery-maker. Traditionally pottery was an independent craft, utilizing ancient methods as well as materials, peopled by individuals undisciplined, unorganized, and often unprosperous. The potters did their work, not in factories, but in villages of thatched houses. Staffordshire had good clay for the kilns and the coal to fire them, but as a country it was still largely rural, served by oozing, muddy roads that made it hard to transport the heavy coal and clay to the potters' cottages, or the equally heavy and more fragile finished product to distant markets. Pottery was a cottage industry, frustrating, steeped in tradition, but to Wedgwood's vision Staffordshire and its industry was an opportunity. "I saw the field was spacious," he noted in his *Experiment Book,* "and the soil so good, as to promise an ample recompense to any who should labour diligently in its cultivation.

Armed with £20 as a bequest from his father, a modest education, and the experience of a pottery apprenticeship, Wedgwood began to experiment with the mystery of pottery-making. After ten-thousand trial pieces, Wedgwood produced the durable blue-and green-glazed jasper-ware that was to be his earliest success. In 1759, Wedgwood took out a lease on a pottery works at Burslem. He was then twenty-nine years old. Soon after, he perfected a cream-ware of elegant, neoclassical design. In 1763 the Burslem works exported 550,000 articles of pottery.

More importantly, Wedgwood forced discipline and specialization on the recalcitrant and independent potters he employed. Long a guild-craft, potters had traditionally learned their trade as apprentices and journeymen, and they were used to working in all stages of the manufacturing process. Wedgwood assigned his potters specific tasks and regular hours. The result was durable pottery, comparatively cheap, which met a constant and high standard. Impatient of men, admiring of machines, Wedgwood sought to "make such machines of men as cannot err." On a visit to Birmingham, he saw a lathe, and sought to adapt it to turn pots.

On a visit to another city, Liverpool, Wedgwood met an enlightened and cultured merchant named Thomas Bentley. Bentley became the medium through which Wedgwood was introduced to painting and sculpture, as well as to the designer Flaxman. All had their impact on Wedgwood's pottery ware.

By the 1760s Wedgwood's pottery business was still very small, but it was expanding, and Wedgwood began to perceive the importance of transportation for its growth. A turnpike to make transport of raw materials to Burslem easier, Wedgwood's first effort, was only partly successful. At about the same time, he began to see the advantages of canals.

The discovery was natural for a potter. Canals had particular virtues: they could carry very heavy loads at a comparatively low price, and they could carry goods without breakage. These things no eighteenth-century roadway could do. In 1761 the Duke of Bridgewater had opened a canal that ran from his mines at Worsley to the growing industrial city of Manchester. James Brindley, chief engineer of the Bridgewater Canal, had once worked for the Wedgwoods, and the connection excited Josiah Wedgwood's interest further. The result was the Grand Trunk Canal, designed to connect England's four major rivers—the Trent, Mersey, Thames, and Severn—into a coherent system. To the project Wedgwood contributed £6,000 and surety for another £10,000. He also helped raise the rest of the £130,000 necessary to begin the project.

Wedgwood's business expanded. An estate was purchased in 1766, and on it was built a new house and pottery works that Wedgwood called Etruria. Over the growing systems of roads and canals Wedgwood's products flowed to English and foreign markets. A London showroom, managed by Thomas Bentley, was opened with great success. The new works, situated on the banks of a canal, grew ever more efficient. When, in 1773, Catherine the Great of Russia ordered a creamware service of nearly one thousand pieces, it was filled and shipped without undue trouble. For the set Catherine paid £3,000.

By the 1780s Wedgwood's attention was devoted to public affairs and the cause of reform. He sought to organize his fellow-manufacturers against rotten boroughs, against the exploitation of Ireland, against the slave trade. When the Society for the Suppression of the Slave Trade was founded in 1787 Wedgwood was a founding member. He memorialized his concern in a cameo, which portrayed a slave in chains. On the cameo as well was an inscription reading, "Am I not a man and a brother?"

Josiah Wedgwood died at his grand pottery works at Etruria in January of 1795, full of years and accomplishment. His life illustrates the Industrial Revolution of which he was a part in several aspects. Wedgwood found an industry ancient and inefficient, and left it prosperous and competitive. While he was probably proudest of his innovation in pottery technique, his major contribution was in the organization of work. Like many of his contemporaries, Wedgwood attacked and broke down what remained of the guild-based medieval economic system and paved the way for the superior organization and productivity of the factory. Whether those changes were good or bad for those who worked in such establishments is worthy of the most strenuous historical debate.

Josiah Wedgwood was also active in the Industrial Revolution as a capitalist. As an entrepreneur, he furthered the transportation revolution that made economic integration and industrialization possible. Wedgwood spent much of his own money on canals, but his real service was in creating an investment opportunity for the landed classes who had money to spare, and for the likes of the merchants of Liverpool who made their profits in part from the slave trade that Wedgwood himself abhorred.

It is also worth remembering that for all of his autocratic organization and preference for machines, Wedgwood was a humanitarian and a reformer. For his workers he built schools; he encouraged music and culture; he sought Parliamentary reform. The Industrial Revolution had its dark side—the uprooting of families, child labor, the exploitation of women, poor living conditions, long hours, dangerous machines. In his creativity and philanthropy, Josiah Wedgwood represents the promise of industrial change.

F. James Watt and the Chain of Innovation

In 1736 in Greenock, Scotland, a sickly yet remarkable boy named James Watt was born. Watt's father was variously described as an architect, a carpenter, or a shipbuilder, but his grandfather had been a mathematician. According to an early biographer, the Victorian Samuel Smiles, the walls of Watt's childhood home were covered with portraits of the likes of Napier, the mathematician who invented logarithms, and of Newton, the founder of modern physics. Watt was thus as much a child of the scientific revolution as he was of his father, a borough treasurer and magistrate.

A creative, restless boy, Watt early on built models of machines in his father's workshop. Later he trained in London and Glasgow as a maker of scientific instruments. By a stroke of good fortune Watt eventually became instrument maker to the University of Glasgow. Though he would never be a university graduate, Watt made good use of his opportunities at Glasgow, attending lectures in chemistry, learning French, Italian, and German to master the scientific treatises available to him.

In 1763, Watt was given a working model of a crude steam engine and was asked to repair it. From that moment, steam power became the fascination of his life.

The steam engine was of course not invented by Watt. The first steam engine in Great Britain had been built by an army officer named Thomas Savery, who developed it as a pump to remove water from the copper mines in his native Cornwall. Savery's engine and a later version developed by Newcomen were simple but crude and costly to operate.

Newcomen's engine had the virtue of utilizing a piston, but it did not use steam to drive it. Steam was used instead to create a vacuum. This was accomplished by injecting steam into a cylinder, and then allowing it to condense. The vacuum thus created moved the piston; it kept moving through the alternate introduction and condensation of steam. In this there was a problem. The introduction of steam required that the cylinder be hot, while condensation required that it be cold. This meant slowness of operation at a very high cost in fuel consumption. Significantly, the model given to Watt for repair was a Newcomen steam engine.

There are several stories about how Watt learned about the properties of steam. One of them, charming but likely untrue, insists that Watt received his inspiration as a child by watching a kettle boil, discovering the phenomenon of condensation by holding a cold spoon to the spout. More likely, like many of his contemporaries, Watt was appalled by the inefficiency of the Newcomen engine. Unlike them, he found a solution. Watt designed a separate condenser *outside* the cylinder to cool and condense the steam. This would allow the cylinder to be kept warm when the steam was injected. Efficiency would thereby be increased.

Though good in theory, Watt's idea bogged down in application. Watt found a partner in John Roebuck but neither he nor Roebuck possessed sufficient capital to finance development, and Roebuck's iron-works could not make the precision parts that Watt needed.

In 1774, bankruptcy struck Roebuck. Paradoxically, it was just the stroke of luck that Watt needed. To satisfy a debt of £1200, Roebuck's share in Watt's engine was given over to Matthew Boulton, proprietor of the Soho Works in Birmingham and a successful industrialist. Boulton had inherited a prosperous metal manufacturing concern, and he had compounded his wealth by marrying an

James Watt and the Chain of Innovation

heiress. He could thus afford the £10,000 required to develop Watt's engine. The Soho works could also fashion the precision parts that Watt's engine required. Finally, John Wilkinson, a nearby ironmaster who had perfected a method for the precision boring of cannon, applied the same techniques to the boring of cylinders for Watt's steam engine.

The partnership of Watt and Boulton proved beneficial to both parties. Watt's inventiveness flourished. In 1781 Watt patented devices to give the steam engine rotary motion. Before this breakthrough, the engine had moved in a reciprocating, or "back and forth" motion, suitable for only a limited number of tasks. Rotary motion allowed the steam engine to turn machinery. Soon after came the rotative engine, which allowed steam to push both sides of the piston. In 1788 came the invention of the governor, enabling the engine to operate more smoothly. In return for such creativity Boulton used his Parliamentary influence to see that Watt's original patent of 1769, up for renewal in 1783, was extended for twenty-five years.

At one point, in the early 1780s, Watt despaired of ever turning a profit from his steam engine. In the decade of the 1770s the engine enjoyed only modest success, being introduced at a few mines in Cornwall and in the Birmingham area to pump water out of the shafts. Another, in 1779, was sent to the banks of the Seine to pump water for Paris. Boulton, unlike Watt, never stopped believing. To his despondent partner he wrote, "The people in London, Manchester and Birmingham are steam-mill mad."

Rotary motion and the renewal of the original patent made things better, much better. By the middle of the decade John Wilkinson, the iron monger who had been so helpful to Watt, bought a steam engine for his works at Coalbrookdale; by 1784, Josiah Wedgwood, an acquaintance of Boulton's, had two operating at Etruria. With this early flurry of important purchases, the dam broke. Between 1775 and 1800 Watt and Boulton set up nearly five hundred machines. Success was encouraged by creative sales and marketing techniques. Initially, Watt and Boulton charged only for the building and setting up of the machine. Thereafter, an additional charge was levied on the basis of the fuel actually saved by the operating machine, in comparison to the higher fuel costs of the Newcomen engine. In this way, the two partners underlined their faith in the efficiency of their engine. The response was overwhelming, and positive, and in 1795 Watt and Boulton had to build a new foundry to meet the demand. In 1800 there were few steam engines in Birmingham; by 1838, less than twenty years after Watt's death, there were 240.

Watt's inventive spirit was challenged in an environment where innovation was encouraged, and this should remind us that what was important about invention in the Industrial Revolution was less the individual inventions themselves than the total pattern of such inventions and the relationships among them. Beginning with the 1760s, the number of applications for patents, the process by which a government recognizes and protects an inventor's exclusive right to his invention, began to move markedly upward in England. This pattern was encouraged by organizations of manufacturers, by the transportation revolution, and especially by the presence of capital. Without the economic integration resulting from the transportation revolution, Watt's engine would have been unfeasible because it depended on a ready supply of coal. Likewise, without Boulton's capital, Watt would have given up in discouragement, far from success.

It is of note as well that one of the early purchasers of Watt's steam engine was Richard Arkwright, himself the inventor of a machine called the water frame that produced a strong cotton yarn. Arkwright understood that his machine would work more efficiently and universally if it were powered by the steam engine, rather than by water. Arkwright's machine was itself an improvement over the spinning jenny of Robert Hargreaves that could produce massive amounts of yarn, though of lower quality. In 1779 Crompton developed the "mule," a machine that combined the qualities of the previous two inventions to produce an even better yarn. Yet Hargreaves, Arkwright, and Crompton would never have invented their machines were there no demand for good cotton yarn. The demand was created by other, earlier, inventions on the weaving side of the cotton industry. The flying shuttle of John Kay and the carding machine of Lewis Paul had made weaving more efficient, thus producing the chronic shortage of yarn that Arkwright and others moved to satisfy. This pattern of invention was made possible, as Phyllis Deane and others have noted, by "bottlenecks." One set of inventions created conditions that in turn created demand for still others.

Similar patterns were visible in the iron and steel industry. During the 1780s James Watt encouraged Henry Cort who had, by inventing the "puddling and rolling process," made it possible to produce quality bar iron using coal fuel. "Cort is treated shamefully by the business people," Watt wrote in disgust, "who are ignorant asses, one and all." Little wonder that Watt saw the possibilities of Cort's invention. He knew about the iron industry because his machines depended on it. His friend John Wilkinson had used Watt's steam engines to power his blast furnaces. Wilkinson, Cort, and Watt, moreover, owed their successes to the work of earlier iron-masters: to William Wood and the Darbys of Coalbrookdale, who learned to smelt iron with coke, a coal by-product, rather than charcoal; and to Benjamin Huntsman, who used coke to make steel.

It was this pattern of innovation, the application and improvement of individual inventions, the fact that the perfection of one invention led to others, that helped make the Industrial Revolution. Through innovation, an economy that was once based on woolen cloth, wood and water and human hands, was slowly converted to one based on cotton cloth, coal, iron, steel, and steam. It was a wonder, wrote the satirist Samuel Johnson, that a new way was not found to conduct hangings.

G. Adam Smith and The Economics of "Perfect Liberty"

Like his contemporary James Watt, Adam Smith was a Scot. He was born in a small fishing village near Edinburgh in 1723 and, also like Watt, after some initial training in Glasgow journeyed southward to get his living and increase his knowledge. Both grew into brilliant men. There the similarities end.

Stories about Watt tend to emphasize a stolid pragmatism, and reveal a morose side. Anecdotes about Smith have more flair, and bear the flavor of eccentricity and absent-mindedness. As a youth, Smith was supposedly kidnapped by gypsies; as an adult it was said that he could wander for miles abroad, having forgotten that he was still wearing his dressing gown. While Watt settled among the industries of Birmingham, Smith's pilgrimage took him from the University of Glasgow to Balliol College, Oxford, back to Glasgow as a professor, through a tour of Europe as a tutor to a young nobleman. On his travels he defended himself against the friendly advances of a French noblewoman, spoke to Voltaire in horrible French, and began to write one of the few books that can legitimately be called important. It was eventually to be titled *An Inquiry Into the Nature and Causes of the Wealth of Nations.*

Smith's subject was economics, what eighteenth century men called political economy, and he came to it predictably enough. He had been lectured on the subject at Glasgow, and in the atmosphere of the Enlightenment other ideas flowered that had an influence on Smith's thought.

The seventeenth century philosopher Helvetius had some time before propounded a startling ethical theory: that the ultimate goodness was to maximize pleasure, the ultimate evil to maximize pain. This idea was transmitted to Smith through his instructor in political economy, Francis Hutcheson. Helvetius' idea also influenced the French Physiocratic philosopher Quesnay, who fashioned from it the concept of "economic man," a being who believes that the ultimate pleasure lay in the pursuit of worldly, material success. To economic man was added the idea of individualism. Philosophers as diverse as Locke, Hobbes, and, later, Rousseau had brought this idea to the fore. Locke had argued that free men could change their government. Rousseau wrote about the power of "natural" men of strong will, uncorrupted by education, law, or the trappings of civilization, who could change society at will. Finally there was Bernard Mandeville's idea, so skillfully articulated in the *Fable of the Bees*, that selfishness, far from being socially destructive, contributed to the good of mankind.

Into his great and extensive work Smith poured these ideas and his own. His view of society was on the whole developmental and optimistic. To Smith, society had moved through four stages: that of the "huntsman," where there was little property, law, or justice; that of nomadic agriculture; that of feudal society; and, finally, that of "The Commercial or Mercantile System," the kind of economic interdependence usually associated with what we now call the Industrial Revolution.

Smith confirmed and praised the ideas of the division of labor and the concentration of industry in towns, thus providing for some a justification for the creation of the factory system. "The greatest improvement in the productive powers of labour," he wrote, "... seem to have been the effects of the division of labour." He emphatically believed that the division of labor increased not only efficiency and productivity, but also the number of jobs. This he illustrated in *The Wealth of Nations* by describing the "trifling manufacture" of pin-making:

> One man draws out the wire, another straight[en]s it, a third cuts it, a fourth points it, a fifth grinds it at the top for receiving the head; to make the head requires two or three distinct operations; to put it on, is a peculiar business, to whiten the pins is another; it is even a trade by itself to put them into the paper; and the important business of making a pin is, in this manner, divided into about eighteen distinct operations. . . .

Smith also believed that a society that was truly enlightened, productive, and progressive must necessarily reward workers well. "The wages of labour are the encouragement of industry," he insisted, "which, like every other human quality, improves in proportion to the encouragement it receives." The better that workers were paid, the greater their strength, their hopes, and their productivity. Had some of the factory owners paid more heed to this part of Smith's argument, the human history of the Industrial Revolution might have been less bleak.

Slavery and every other form of servitude were intolerable to Smith because they offended his sense of the productivity and potential in every individual. Free human beings, Smith argued, were able to manage themselves; servitude forced upon society the indignity, and the expense, of keepers and overseers. Economic monopolies, according to Smith, were economically pernicious, unnaturally influencing the flow of capital and constricting opportunity. Any country, Smith pointedly concluded, that could trade with the East Indies only through the medium of a monopoly company, should simply not trade there.

Likewise, education was an important element in Smith's philosophy. Because he believed education to be beneficial to the whole society, Smith did not deny that it and certain other social services could be paid for by taxation. In all senses, Smith identified his belief in the freedom of the individual with the needs of the society as a whole, and those who emphasize only the former do an injustice to his thought.

Smith had a particular feeling for the waste of war, and heaped scorn on those who, remote from the scenes of action and destruction, regarded war as a means of entertainment to be followed in the newspapers, productive of "a thousand visionary hopes of conquest and national glory." Smith firmly believed that defense was a legitimate expense to be borne by society, but worried that warfare could lead to governmental improvidence. Wars, he argued, were expensive, and leaders and governments, instead of meeting the expense of war through an unpopular increase in taxes, might well seek to maintain their popularity by borrowing the money instead.

While some would conclude, as Locke in a sense had, that the pursuit of one's private ends would result in chaos, Smith himself had no such doubts. In pursuit of his own gain, the individual would be "led by an invisible hand to promote an end which was no part of his intention." The public interest was thus best served by individual action, by lack of government interference, by the free play of the laws of supply and demand in the marketplace.

Adam Smith in his *Wealth of Nations* provided an economic philosophy that reflected the intellectual and economic currents of his time. Others, not Smith, would call this philosophy *laissez-faire*.

It is nonetheless important to remember that Smith was never an apologist for greed or of the economic philosophy called capitalism. Individual liberty was for Smith a universal, not a justification for dominance by the powerful or a privilege for the elite. Self-interest was for him a means to an end: the production of wealth that would in the end give bounty to all. Smith protested that he preferred the simple life, and he did not particularly like merchants or manufacturers. Smith deplored the "monopolizing spirit" of both groups and wished that they might never rule mankind. He did have sympathy for the poor, and he railed at the poor-law system that kept the indigent bound to their own parishes, unable to work productively elsewhere. Smith also recognized that factory labor in all its specialization could degrade the individual, making him or her "as stupid and ignorant as it is possible for a worker to become." *The Wealth of Nations* was first published in 1776, the year of the American Revolution. In terms of Smith's idea, this has a certain justice. For Adam Smith, political economy had moral goals: the attainment of happiness and liberty. His theories, like the Industrial Revolution they compassed, have occasioned continued debate. A paradox developed from Smith's writings. While he believed that enlightened self-interest should benefit everyone, including the oppressed for whom he had such great sympathy, his philosophy was misused to serve the needs of authoritarian and predatory disciples.

Smith thus acknowledged his belief that he lived in a progressive time. His concern, as a disciple of the Enlightenment, was to make society better, its economic system more productive. This led him to attack the prevailing economic philosophy of the time, that set of state-imposed economic controls known as mercantilism. To Smith, any attempt on the part of governments to regulate or control commerce was bad: "No regulation of commerce can increase the quantity of industry in any society beyond what its capital can maintain."

For Smith, the most beneficial thing that a government could do is abandon all attempts to control or regulate economic activity. Free individuals, like Mandeville's bees, if left to their own devices and allowed to act in their self-interest, would create more wealth for the society as a whole. Faith in the individual, in economic man, in progress suffused one of the most famous of the passages of *The Wealth of Nations:*

> Every individual is continually exerting himself to find out the most advantageous employment for whatever capital he can command. It is his own advantage, indeed, and not that of society, which he has in view. But the study of his own advantage naturally, or rather necessarily, leads him to prefer that employment which is most advantageous to the society.

H. Men, Women, and the Industrial Revolution

The Industrial Revolution deserves a broader compass than it has generally been given. Every school-child associates the Industrial Revolution with invention, with machines, with the factory system, with power. It should never be forgotten that it was also about agriculture, commerce, ideas, banking, capital, population growth, political stability, and transportation. Without all of these things acting and interacting, the Industrial Revolution would never have occurred. Men would have still designed their machines, but they would have had as much chance of being built as some of those in Leonardo's notebooks.

The Industrial Revolution brought social and political change beyond doubt. In 1750 England was an agricultural country; a century later 3.5 million Britons were employed in industry, only 2 million in agriculture. This labor force was more mobile, more disciplined, more productive, and more specialized than ever before. In 1750 only sixteen percent of the population lived in towns of 5,000 or more; a century later sixty percent of the population lived in such towns and cities. Most of these towns were in the Midlands and the north, areas that had traditionally lagged behind the more populous and developed south. By 1850 the economic dominance of London had ended. This great population shift would, more slowly, bring about political changes. The manufacturers of Leeds, Manchester, and Birmingham bought and married their way to political influence. With these men, the landed classes made their peace, and dominated political life until the First World War.

A great debate rages over whether the Industrial Revolution benefited or harmed the masses of the people, and on each side stand able and persuasive economic historians, armed with tables and figures. For one group, the "Pessimists," led most recently by E. J. Hobsbawm, the Industrial Revolution was a disaster for quality of life. Men and women were torn from the land, their home-based economic ethic replaced by the insanity of the factory and the unhealthful city. Women and children were brutalized; the human spirit crushed.

Not so, say the "Optimists" under the command of R. M. Hartwell. The Industrial Revolution created jobs, sopping up the rising population and widening human horizons as they had never been before. Economic and social dislocations there were, injustices occurred, but, over the long term, a measure of the bounty trickled down to all.

Of more recent interest is the impact of the Industrial Revolution on women. Some historians have argued that the Industrial Revolution compromised the family and thus the honored position of working women in the household, that it made obsolete the traditional cottage industries that women had pursued with skill and dignity. After women were excluded from the newer, skilled occupations in the factories that required education or physical strength, so this argument goes, they were funneled into demeaning, low-paying jobs, or into "service," waiting on the families of the powerful. As men became the primary bread-winners and prosperity more real, women became confined to the household, dependent on the allowances doled out by their husbands.

Other historians of women have argued that the weakening of the traditional family structure was a good thing. In accomplishing this, the Industrial Revolution began a slow process, still unfinished, that would give women more options as individuals.

"The course was set towards the 'industry state,' but the voyage was not half over." Thus wrote J. H. Clapham about the economic state of Britain in 1851. Implicit in the statement is a tone of caution. For all of its industrial might, Britain was even in the nineteenth century a nation in which there were quiet rural corners, small villages, people untouched by the factory or the mill. As the rest of Europe followed England into the Industrial Revolution, the same truth was obvious in other places. Eugen Weber has written of a vigorous French peasantry that existed well into the nineteenth century, and Arno Mayer, in a recent study, has labeled most of Europe as "preindustrial" down to the First World War. The Industrial Revolution helped make England the most powerful state in Europe, and Europe the most influential continent in the world, but links still remained to the great continuities of the past.

Portfolio: Food, Drink, and Drunkenness, 1600-1815

The Pancake Baker. Jan Steen
Grain products, cheese, and fruit in season formed an important part of the diet of the common people. *Courtesy of the Memorial Art Gallery of the University of Rochester. Buswell-Hochstetter Bequest.*

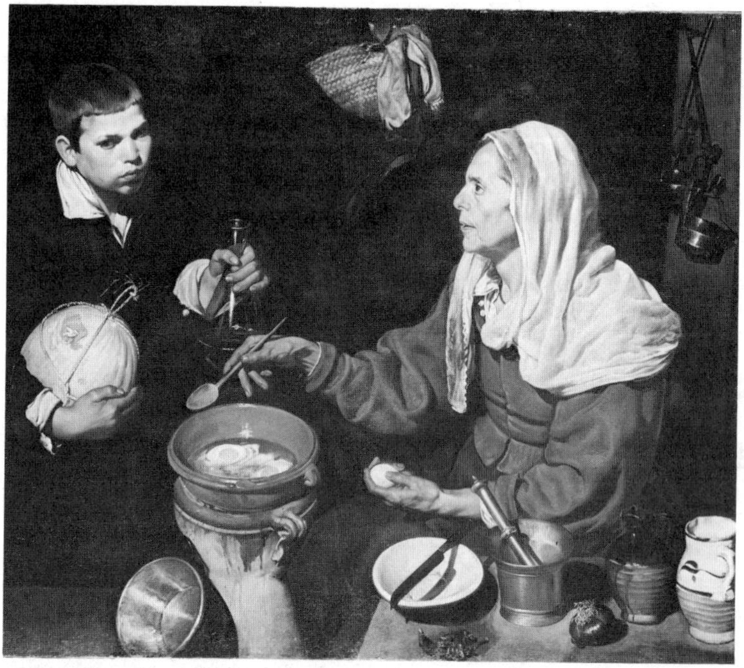

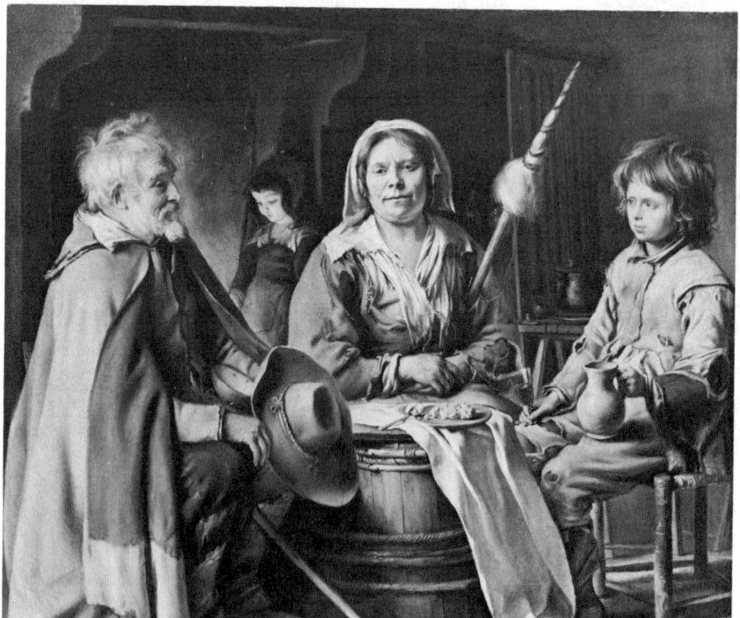

An Old Woman Cooking Eggs. **Opposite, top.** Diego Velázquez y Silva
Eggs, onions, cheese, wine, but no meat, are the ingredients of a simple meal for this woman and boy. *Courtesy of the National Galleries of Scotland.*

A Peasant Interior. **Opposite, bottom.** Louis Le Nain
This somewhat idealized portrait of a French peasant family at a meal again shows relatively simple fare—a porridge of grain products and ordinary wine. Meat was a luxury often reserved for the wealthy. *Courtesy of the National Gallery of Art, Washington. Samuel H. Kress Collection.*

Peasants Drinking. Isaac van Ostade
Drinking and gaming often went together. *Courtesy of the Pierpont Morgan Library, New York.*

Merrymakers at Shrovetide. Frans Hals
The presence of sausages and white bread at this feast is due to the prosperity of the participants and to the fact that it was a holiday occasion. *Courtesy of the Metropolitan Museum of Art. Bequest of Benjamin Altman.*

Tavern Scene. David Teniers the Younger
The earthiness of the scene testifies both to the coarseness of life at many taverns and inns as well as to the central place of spirits in the life of the people. *Courtesy of the Memorial Art Gallery of the University of Rochester. Buswell-Hochstetter Bequest.*

The Rake's Progress. **Plate III.** William Hogarth
This illustration, and the two that follow, were intended as object-lessons in the consequences of drink. In this print, the rake and his cronies, thoroughly inebriated, are entertained and victimized by a raucous group of prostitutes. In the last plate in this famous series, not pictured here, the rake is portrayed as a diseased wretch confined to a madhouse. *Courtesy of the Prints Division, New York Public Library. Astor, Lenox and Tilden Foundations.*

Wine is a Mocker. **Opposite, top.** Jan Steen
Here, a drunken woman is loaded onto a wheelbarrow to the amusement of passers-by and the leers of her male companions. The scene serves as eloquent testimony of how drink could victimize those who partook to excess. *Courtesy of the Norton Simon Museum, Pasadena, California.*

The Drunken Cobbler. **Opposite, bottom.** Jean Baptiste Greuze
The drunken head of household at once harasses, angers, and frightens his wife and family. By the eighteenth century drunkenness, already ubiquitous, had become a genuine social concern. At the same time, the availability of cheap spirits among the poorer classes could be perceived as a sign of economic prosperity, as many alcoholic beverages were brewed or fermented from excess grain.

325

The Ugly Club [Serving the Punch]. Thomas Rowlandson
Heavy drinking was a habit for all classes in the period 1600-1815. The poor had cheap wine, beer, and gin, while the rich had stronger wines, spirits, and punches. The phrase "drunk as a lord" carries with it a certain historical validity. *Courtesy of the Huntington Library and Art Gallery, San Marino, California.*

Chapter VII

Rulers and Warriors in Eighteenth Century Europe: Maria Theresa, Frederick William I and Frederick the Great, Catherine the Great, and Lord Chatham

> If anyone does not wish to obey, let him be left in peace, but let him never appear again before my eyes.
> —Maria Theresa

> Fritz, mark my words: Always keep up a large, efficient army; you cannot have a better friend, and without that friend you will not be able to survive.
> —Frederick William II

> The satisfaction of seeing my name in the gazettes and, later, in history has seduced me.
> —Frederick the Great

> The Prussian Monarchy reminds me of a vast prison, in the center of which appears a great keeper, occupied in the care of his captives.
> —The British Ambassador, Elliot, on the Prussian State

> I am his Dulcinea.
> —Frederick the Great on Tsar Peter III

> Those who are most in her society assure me that her application to business is incredible.
> —The British Ambassador on Catherine the Great

> I am sure I can save this country, and nobody else can.
> —William Pitt, Earl of Chatham

Portrait of Augustus the Strong, Elector of Saxony and King of Poland.
Nicolas de Largillière
Augustus the Strong had the dubious distinction of fathering more illegitimate children than any ruler in European history—he acknowledged more than three hundred-fifty. Not even Augustus' proffered diversions, however, could shake the determined militarism of Frederick William of Prussia. *Courtesy of Nelson Gallery of Art/Atkins Museum, Kansas City, Missouri.*

A. Introduction: The Interrelated Wars of the Eighteenth Century, 1733-1795

In the eighteenth century, the European powers began a series of wars with implications beyond Europe. Some historians, seeking to do justice to this phenomenon, have referred to this group of conflicts as an early example of a European-based "world war."

While there is merit to this view, it is perhaps more accurate to think of these conflicts not as part of one great war, but as a series of interrelated smaller ones in which there were several centers and objectives of conflict. These centers were, first, central and eastern Europe and, second, North America, Africa, and India. The wars in central and eastern Europe involved Prussia, Austria, and, at times, Russia and concerned the competition among these three powers for European territory and dominance. The wars in North America and India, in contrast, involved Great Britain and France and concerned their competition for trade, colonies, and empire. Alliances among the participants bound the respective theaters of conflict together.

It should be noted that the European and colonial wars of the mid-eighteenth century had some precedents. The War of the League of Augsburg (1688-1697) and the War of the Spanish Succession (1701-1713) were interrelated with two North American wars fought by the French and British, King William's War (1689-1697) and Queen Anne's War (1702-1713). Twenty years later conflict flared again. Central Europe was briefly engulfed in the War of the Polish Succession (1733-1735), while the British and the Spanish fought the ridiculous "War of Jenkins' Ear."

In 1740 a pattern of interrelated conflict began to assert itself even more strongly. In Europe as a whole this war went by the name of the War of the Austrian Succession (1740-1748), but in Prussia, contemporaries referred to two Silesian Wars (1740-1742; 1744-1745). These European wars of the 1740s had their counterparts in other areas of the world: King George's War in America (1744-48) and what might be called the First Anglo-French Commerical War in India (1746-1748).

In the mid-1750s, after an inconclusive period of peace, the European and colonial wars resumed. The general term used for this conflict in Europe was the Seven Years' War (1756-1763), but in eastern Europe it was known, during the same period of time, as the Third Silesian War. A parallel conflict, the French and Indian War (1754-1763), broke out in America. In India, the fighting had slowed but never really stopped, and a Second Anglo-French Commercial War (1748-1763) occurred. Though all of these conflicts were ended by treaties in 1763, the rulers of Russia continued to find new opportunities for expansion, declaring the first of several wars against the Ottoman Empire (1768-1772). In the same year that the first in this series of Russo-Turkish wars ended, Prussia and Austria joined Russia in a planned seizure of sovereign Polish territory known as the First Polish Partition.

In the mid-1770s another cycle of conflict began. The American Revolution (1775-1783), though in the Colonist's mind a struggle for independence, became as well another phase in the century-long colonial struggle between Britain and France, with the latter power taking the side of the American rebels. In India, the French provided encouragement to native princes in their resistance to the British East India Company. At about the same time, the short War of the Bavarian Succession (1778-1779) broke out in Germany, encouraged by the conflicting ambitions of Austria and Prussia. In the late 1780s a Second Russo-Turkish War (1787-1792) began, and in the next decade two other Polish Partitions (1793 and 1795) confirmed the aggressiveness of Russia, Prussia, and Austria.

By the mid-1790s the growing commercial and naval strength of Great Britain, the quarrel between Austria and Prussia, the expansionism of Russia, and the military might of a France revived by the Revolution of 1789 combined to produce the Napoleonic Wars. These, in turn, came to an end only with the Congress of Vienna in 1815.

The interrelated wars of the eighteenth century thus form a bridge between two of the cardinal peace treaties in European history: the Peace of Utrecht of 1713 and the agreements of the Congress of Vienna of 1815. Out of their midst, in 1763, came two other agreements: the Peace of Paris, which confirmed the growing might of Great Britain; and the Treaty of Hubertusburg, which confirmed the importance of Prussia. For these reasons, and for the personalities involved, the wars of the eighteenth century are deserving of study.

B. Maria Theresa: The Recovery and Stabilization of Austria

By the evening of the 10th of October, 1740, Emperor Charles VI, the heir to the Hapsburg possessions in Germany and elsewhere, was in a bad way. He had earlier partaken of a large number of mushrooms stewed in oil, and the combination induced indigestion, then vomiting. Charles was borne back to Vienna sick and fainting, his illness doubtless aggravated by the fatigue of his recent hunt, the disappointments and frustrations of thirty years of rule, and the ministrations of his physicians. The doctors were so obnoxious, in fact, that Charles told them to shut up, promising grimly that they could, after his death, perform an autopsy to ascertain its cause. If Charles' promise was kept they did not have to wait long. Ten days after consuming his strange meal, Charles VI turned to the wall and died, leaving his troubled dominions to his daughter Maria Theresa. "A pot of mushrooms changed the history of Europe." So noted the French *philosophe,* Voltaire, with his usual sense of theater.

Voltaire, to be sure, had a tendency to put things a little strongly. An admirer of Charles' daughter Maria Theresa, whom he considered to be the epitome of the "enlightened despot," Voltaire went to extremes in contrasting her with her Hapsburg predecessors. While there is some truth in Voltaire's view, Maria Theresa in fact was more like her immediate predecessors than Voltaire believed. If the means were different, the objectives were the same.

These objectives were relatively simple. After the disaster of the Peace of Westphalia in 1648, the office of Holy Roman Emperor, to which the Hapsburgs had traditionally been elected, became virtually meaningless. The German Hapsburgs, thrown back on their hereditary lands in Austria, resolved to do two things: to guarantee their continued dominance over their dynastic possessions and, if possible, to create a new imperial state in place of the virtually defunct Holy Roman Empire.

As a result of the resolution of the Thirty Years' War in the west, the Hapsburgs were able to concentrate on the eastern borders of their hereditary lands and to do battle with the Ottoman Turks who continually threatened them. Against the Ottomans the Hapsburgs were fortunate and successful, gaining prestige for their crusade against the infidel and adding to their domains the disputed territory of Hungary with its restless Magyar population.

Conflict between the Hapsburgs and the Turks began in 1663, and in the next year the imperial general Montecucculi won a major battle at St. Gotthard. This, in turn, led to a twenty years' truce, during which the Turks occupied themselves with attacking the Russians and the Poles. In 1682, with the Hapsburgs allied with the Poles, the Austro-Turkish war resumed. The immediate result was a nearly-successful Ottoman siege of Vienna, broken only by the heroics of the defenders and the action of a combined German-Polish army under Charles of Lorraine and John Sobieski.

After breaking the siege, imperial armies rolled into Hungary, to that point under Turkish overlordship. Under the generalship of Charles of Lorraine and Louis of Baden, Budapest was taken (1686), and at the Battle of Mohacs (1687) the Turks suffered a major defeat. On the heels of the victory, the Diet of Pressburg conferred the hereditary succession to the Crown of St. Stephen and the Hungarian throne to Hapsburgs. The Dual Monarchy of Austria-Hungary was thus born. Hungary was put firmly in Austrian hands when Prince Eugene of Savoy won another victory for the Hapsburgs at Zenta (1697) and the territory was formally ceded in the Treaty of Karlowitz (1699). Some years later Prince Eugene won yet another victory at Pelerwardein (1716) and thereafter captured Belgrade. Hapsburg power now pressed into the Balkans.

Under the Hapsburg Emperors Leopold I (1658-1705) and Joseph I (1705-1711), Hapsburg arms were on the whole successful. Their successor, Charles VI, was not so fortunate. Aside from Prince Eugene's capture of Belgrade, and the gaining of the Spanish Hapsburg possessions in Italy and the Netherlands at the Peace of Utrecht, Hapsburg arms produced nothing but expensive reverses. The intermittent wars with the Ottoman Empire sapped funds, and the War of the Polish Succession (1733-1735) was little short of a political disaster. As a penalty for joining Russia in backing the claims of Augustus III of Saxony for the Polish throne, Austria was forced, under the terms of the Treaty of Vienna of 1738, to cede Naples, Sicily, and Elba to Spain. Though the Hapsburgs received Parma and Piacenza from Spain to compensate them for their losses, the treaty was a humiliation. To this disgrace was added another. By the Treaty of Belgrade (1739), Austria made peace with the Turks at the cost of ceding northern Serbia and the city of Belgrade, the latter the fruit of Prince Eugene's last military victory.

Unfortunately, Charles VI had been as unlucky in the birth-chamber as he had been on the battlefield. By his wife, the beautiful Elizabeth of Brunswick, Charles had sired several children, but not the desired living male heir. Their first child, born in 1716, had indeed been a son, but he had died within hours. The next year, to general disappointment, Maria Theresa was born. When it became obvious that there would be no male heir, Charles moved to secure the succession for his beloved and beautiful daughter. In an unusual document, the Pragmatic Sanction, Charles declared that the succession to the Hapsburg dominions, failing direct male heirs, would pass into the hands of Maria Theresa. For the remaining years of his reign, Charles VI sought, and obtained, the support of most of the rulers of Europe to the terms of the Pragmatic Sanction. At best this exercise was naive. The rulers of Europe might promise obedience to the Pragmatic Sanction while Charles was alive, but they were far less likely to honor it after his death. Old Prince Eugene of Savoy remarked, bitterly and realistically, that the Pragmatic Sanction could be guaranteed only by "a full treasury and two hundred thousand fighting men."

Such practical guarantees were quite beyond Charles' grasp. When he died from his overindulgence in mushrooms he bequeathed to his daughter dominions short of money, ill-administered, and ill-defended. ". . . I found myself suddenly without either money, troops, or counsel." This was the assessment Maria Theresa made of her accession years later.

As a child Maria Theresa had obtained only a rudimentary education, and for the rest of her life spoke in a Viennese German dialect. She was, however, not completely unprepared for rule. At fourteen years old, Maria Theresa was allowed to attend meetings of the State Council, where she listened intently to the deliberations. "She admires her father's virtues," wrote a British ambassador of the young Maria Theresa, "but condemns his mismanagement and is of a temperament so formed for ruling and ambition, as to look upon him as little more than her administrator."

Upon her father's death, Maria Theresa prayed for his soul in the company of his mistress, and then set to work. This combination of piety and practicality stayed with her all of her life. "From the outset I decided and made it my principle," she wrote years later, "for my own inner guidance, to apply myself, with a pure mind and instant prayer to God, to put aside all secondary considerations, arrogance, ambition, or other passions . . . and to undertake the business of government . . . quietly and resolutely. . . ."

The new sovereign soon found herself in need of all her resolutions. Frederick the Great of Prussia analyzed the plight of his Hapsburg rival with ill-disguised glee. "The Court of Vienna was, after the death of the emperor," he noted happily, "in an untoward situation. The finances were in disorder, the army broken up and disheartened with the ill-success of the war against Turkey, and the throne was occupied by a young and inexperienced princess who had to defend a disputed succession." In clear violation of the Pragmatic Sanction, and with indecent haste, Frederick the Great invaded the rich Hapsburg province of Silesia in 1740. The Prussia invasion inaugurated both the first of the Silesian Wars and the larger War of the Austrian Succession.

Frederick's decision to attack the territiory of the Austrian Hapsburgs was an exercise in brutal logic. For all of its territories, for all of its populations, for all of its dynastic grandeur, the empire of the Hapsburgs was, in apparent contradiction, a weak institution. Behind a glorious facade, real, and unresolved, problems lingered. Immense territories there were, but they were far-flung and difficult to defend. Large populations inhabited the empire, but they were diverse and contentious. Grand the Hapsburg dynasty was, but it possessed neither the bureaucracy nor the finances to defend its quarrelsome dominions. In addition to the hereditary possessions in Austria, the Hapsburgs ruled the kingdom of Bohemia together with Silesia and Moravia, the kingdom of Hungary with Transylvania and Croatia, the Austrian Netherlands, and Milan and Parma in Italy. The Hapsburg dynasty was German, but half of their subjects were Slavs, and one-quarter were Hungarian. The defense of the central Hapsburg dominions required a strong army, while the defense of Hapsburg possessions in Italy and the Netherlands demanded either a navy or an alliance with a maritime power.

As Frederick invaded, Maria Theresa's troubles multiplied. Rival claimants for the Austrian succession presented themselves. There was Charles Albert, Elector of Bavaria, whose claim was made on the basis of his relationship to Emperor Ferdinand I. There was also Philip V of Spain, who traced his claim back to a treaty made by Charles V and his brother Ferdinand. Finally, there was Augustus III of Saxony, who based his claim on his marriage to the eldest daughter of Emperor Joseph I. Underlying all the claims were old prejudices about the unfitness of women to rule. Less than a month after the great Prussian victory at Mollwitz in 1741, Maria Theresa's rivals formed the Alliance of Nymphenburg. Under its terms France, Spain, Saxony, Bavaria, and Prussia began to take more concerted action. A French-Bavarian army marched into Austria and Bohemia; Charles Albert of Bavaria had himself proclaimed the Austrian Archduke and elected emperor as Charles VII.

Maria Theresa and her advisors rallied, and responded vigorously. Seeking support from her Hungarian nobles, she met with them at the Diet of Pressburg in 1741. Maria Theresa put on a marvelous show. As cannon sounded from the battlements Maria Theresa, dressed in white, blue, and gold, with her husband Francis of Lorraine by her side, rode in a carriage to the Diet. After donning the crown and mantle of St. Stephen, patron saint of Hungary, she addressed the Diet, turning their reluctant support to affirmation as she held her infant son Joseph before the assembled delegates. This, and her promise to exempt the Hungarian nobility from taxation, caused the Diet to proclaim her sovereign of Hungary, and to rattle their sabres in approval.

Guaranteed of Hungarian support, Maria Theresa was now able to turn on her enemies. Bavaria was overrun by an Austrian army, while another laid siege to a French force in Prague. In an effort to help her secure the Austrian Netherlands and Hapsburg lands in Italy, Maria Theresa's ministers concluded an alliance with the English. With the Bavarian threat blunted, Maria Theresa and her English allies moved to divide the other members of the Alliance of Nymphenburg. Prussia, the most mortal threat to Austria, was not defeated but neutralized. After Frederick bloodied Austrian armies two more times, Maria Theresa wisely concluded with the Prussians the Treaty of Breslau and Berlin in 1742. Under its terms, Maria Theresa was obliged to cede Upper and Lower Silesia to Prussia, but Frederick agreed to abandon the Alliance of Nymphenburg. Without a Prussian backbone, the dangerous alliance collapsed. In June of 1743, a British-Hanoverian-Hessian army, under the command of Maria Theresa's ally George II of England, humiliated the French at the Battle of Dettingen. By the end of the summer the Imperial pretender, Charles VII, was a fugitive in Frankfurt and Maria Theresa's husband claimed his place as emperor.

Maria Theresa's troubles were not over. In 1744 Frederick, concerned about Austrian success, renewed his alliance with the hapless Charles VII and with France, and began the Second Silesian War. The Austrians responded by making an alliance with Saxony, England, and Holland. In the midst of the war, Charles VII died, and his son Maximilian Joseph was quick to conclude the separate Treaty of Fussen with Austria. In exchange for ceding back Austrian conquests in Bavaria, Maria Theresa received assurances that Maximilian Joseph would end his pretensions to the imperial throne and support her husband's candidacy. In 1745 Maria Theresa's spouse was formally elected to the imperial throne. Frederick's armies punished the Austrians, and especially Maria Theresa's Saxon allies. As a result the Austrians, in 1745, concluded the Treaty of Dresden with the Prussians. Its terms included the confirmation of Frederick's old conquests of Silesia by Austria, but Frederick recognized Maria Theresa's husband as emperor. Maria Theresa had survived another Prussian challenge.

In the Austrian Netherlands and in Italy the war continued. Under Marshal Saxe, the French were successful in the Spanish Netherlands, but in Italy, where the Spaniards had joined the French in threatening Hapsburg possessions, the results were mixed. Stalemate, and the fact that the Empress Elizabeth of Russia had allied with Austria, forced the Treaty of Aix-la-Chapelle upon the European powers in 1748. Though this treaty in the main called for the restoration of conquests, the Spanish obtained Parma and Piacenza in Italy, and Prussia once again received confirmation of its conquest of Silesia. Out of all of this Maria Theresa received general recognition of the Pragmatic Sanction, and thus her right to the Austrian empire.

After the Second Silesian War ended, Maria Theresa and her advisors moved to shore up Austria's diplomatic position. Maria Theresa agreed to a treaty with Russia, which contained secret articles providing for the reunion of Silesia with Austria. Not long afterwards, in 1756, the brilliant Austrian diplomat, Count Kaunitz, arranged a treaty between Austria and her historic antagonist, France.

Also in 1756, the English King, fearing that the Prussians might overrun his hereditary German state of Hanover, obliged the British government to sign the Treaty of Westminster with Frederick the Great. Thus was accomplished the so-called "diplomatic revolution" of 1756, in which France and Britain switched alliance partners. The new state of affairs, however, did not protect Austria from Frederick the Great. Learning of the web of new alliances engineered by Austria, Frederick the Great invaded Saxony, engaged the Austrians, and began the conflict variously known as the Third Silesian War or the Seven Years' War.

This time Frederick knew humiliation as well as victory. Though Frederick was brilliant at the battles of Rossbach (1757) and Zorndoff (1758), Russian and Austrian armies bloodied his troops. In 1760 the Austrians burned his capital. Only his brilliant generalship and the sudden death of the Empress Elizabeth saved him. When the admiring Tsar Peter III pulled Russia out of the war in 1762, the alliance against Frederick the Great collapsed. Prussian victories over the Austrians at Reichenbach and Freiburg in 1762 once again forced the Austrians to the conference table. The resulting Treaty of Hubertusburg (1763), in which Frederick was yet again confirmed in his possession of Silesia, at last brought about an equilibrium between Austria and Prussia.

While Maria Theresa was disturbed that Prussia had attained great-power status, she could now be assured that her throne and what remained of her territories were secure. During the last years of her reign, Maria Theresa and the Prussians were able to resolve territorial conflicts peacefully. When the Elector of Bavaria died without heirs in 1778, a brief War of the Bavarian Succession ensued, but neither Austria or Prussia fought a pitched battle. Maria Theresa and Frederick resolved their conflicts through correspondence and mediation. The result was the Treaty of Teschen (1779), whereby Austria obtained a modest share of Bavarian territory.

Less to their credit, both Frederick and Maria Theresa were involved in the first Partition of Poland. Russian victories over the Turks had threatened to make the Russian Empire powerful enough to compromise the balance of power. Fearing this would cause a war he could ill-afford, Frederick the Great sought to satisfy all the eastern-European powers by mediating an unwarranted seizure of Polish territory. Weakened by years of war, a selfish nobility jealous of its privileges, a representative body, or Diet, that accomplished nothing, and an elective monarchy that had been corrupted by foreign ambitions, the Polish state was in no position to resist. In the first Partition, Russia acquired what came to be known as "White Russia," and all Polish territory to the Dnieper and the Dvina rivers;

Austria took Lemberg, part of Cracow, and "Red Russia"; Prussia was contented with the whole of Polish Prussia save for the cities of Danzig and Thorn. Maria Theresa protested in her correspondence against what she saw as an immoral act, bewailing her isolation, vowing that she agreed to partition only because of the threat of war with Russia and Prussia. Frederick, for his part, noted pointedly and cynically that Maria Theresa "cried, but kept on taking."

Two more partitions followed, after which Poland simply ceased to exist. While Austria did not participate in the second Partition (1792), the Hapsburgs received the remainder of Cracow in the third and last (1795). Nonetheless, Maria Theresa had reason for her original misgivings. With regard to Poland, the balance of power had been used in a way never intended. Instead of guaranteeing the integrity of a state, it had contributed to its destruction. At the same time the Polish Partitions confirmed the Hapsburg recovery that had begun in the years after the disaster of Westphalia.

Unlike her father, and other of her predecessors, Maria Theresa understood that the fate of the Hapsburg dynasty would only in part lie on the battlefield, that military success would only be possible if social, administrative, and financial reforms were made. Winning and losing battles preoccupied Maria Theresa less than undertaking the measures necessary to support her armies and the Hapsburg state itself.

To undertake the enormous task of administrative and financial reconstruction, Maria Theresa found two good ministers, Ludwig Haugwitz and Rudolf Chotek. Haugwitz declared in 1748 that the Austrian state required a standing army of 108,000 men, and that, to support it, the feudal financial structure of the disparate parts of the empire would have to be revamped. Haugwitz insisted that the long-exempt noble and clerical classes be taxed, and that tax officials reponsible to the sovereign alone collect them. He was blunt in his warnings: "If it is desired to place a country in peril, all that is necessary is to leave the Estates free to act as they choose." Maria Theresa supported Haugwitz, and in her name a series of great reforms was undertaken. A new, centralized financial directorate was established at Vienna, along with a Court Commission responsible for all administration.

Economic policy followed a similar course. Something like a ministry of commerce was established. Under Chotek's supervision the great industries of the Empire—gold, salt, linen—were encouraged and protected by tariffs from foreign competition. At the same time, internal tolls and duties were reduced, the better to encourage economic integration. The grinding injustice of serfdom was not ended, but Maria Theresa did abolish serfdom on her own dominions, and reduced noble exactions on the serfs of Hungary. A new, universal legal code, named for Maria Theresa herself, was proclaimed in 1768.

Maria Theresa always reinforced the policies of her ministers by personal example as well as official support. Though as the sovereign of her dominions Maria Theresa was often officially addressed as "king" rather than "queen," she was comfortable with the image of *landesmutter,* of being the "mother of her people." For her dynasty and for her husband, Francis of Lorraine, Maria Theresa gave birth to no less than sixteen children. Francis of Lorraine, later Emperor Francis I, was adored by his wife and pragmatically forgiven for his many infidelities. For this there was good reason, for Francis I was an excellent administrator in his own right. He founded and managed a private Hapsburg fortune, which was at times tapped to support the Austrian Empire.

Maria Theresa, because of her intelligence and her many reforms, has often been identified as an "enlightened despot"—a ruler who applied the "reason" and tolerance of the Enlightenment to her state and its problems. While such an image might suit some of her policies, it does not reflect Maria Theresa's view of the world. In her dislike of Jews, and in her edict forbidding them the freedom of Vienna, she was no better than most of her contemporaries. To her idealistic son Joseph II, who she made her co-regent in 1765, she penned letters arguing against the religious tolerance he favored. "He is no friend to humanity," fumed the Empress, ". . . who allows everyone his own thoughts." Prostitutes were pulled off the Vienna streets by female groups organized by Maria Theresa for that specific purpose. The Empress liked modest dress and simple obedience. "If anyone does not wish to obey," she once warned, "let him be left in peace, but let him never appear again before my eyes." As long as she lived, Joseph II, a true son of the Enlightenment, had little chance to make much progress or do much damage.

She died in 1780 and her end was totally in character. Joseph was kept at her bedside, one suspects to be constantly observed. Unlike others in similar circumstances, Maria Theresa actually expressed gratitude for the hand that life dealt her and for the ministers who had served her so well. She refused to sleep, saying she preferred to meet death face to face. She also summed up her life, saying that she had fought and "risked everything," that she had upheld the principles she had been taught in her youth: "the fear of God, justice, kindness and painstaking care." She closed with a note of triumph, saying that she had kept her inherited lands out of the hands of the Prussians. Shortly thereafter she slipped away, and was interred with the husband who predeceased her.

Maria Theresa's best epitaph was penned by her arch-enemy Frederick: "She put her finances in such order as her predecessors had never attained, and not only recouped by good management what she had lost by ceding provinces to the kings of Prussia and Sardinia, but she considerably augmented her revenue."

Maria Theresa's son Joseph succeeded her. A rather grim and prim man of forty, Joseph had no mistresses but hard work and Enlightenment-style idealism. The new Archduke recognized two polar opposites—good and bad—and he declared himself on the side of the former. While his mother had recognized the evil of serfdom and mitigated it, Joseph abolished it totally. Maria Theresa had been content to force her nobility to pay taxes; Joseph insisted that the noble classes be taxed on an equal basis with the peasantry. While Maria Theresa had, to her detriment, loathed Jews, Joseph granted them limited civil liberties. Other of Joseph's edicts granted religious toleration and freedom of the press.

When Joseph died in 1790, he was succeeded by his brother Leopold (Emperor 1790-1792), who, in turn, was succeeded by Francis II (Emperor 1792-1835). Both rulers had to contend with a storm of noble and clerical reaction in which much, but not all, of Joseph's reforms were lost. The coming of the French Revolution, and the wars which followed, only strengthened the reactionary bent already loose in Austria. Many of Maria Theresa's administrative reforms, which had done so much to save her empire, remained, and the Austrian Empire was a fact until 1918. What was lost was Maria Theresa's sense of conservative reform, to the eventual harm of her dynasty and empire.

The Hapsburg Dominions at the Close of the Reign of Maria Theresa

C. The Making of a Great Power: Frederick William I, Frederick the Great, the House of Hohenzollern, and Prussia

It was January 24th, 1712, a Sunday, and Elector Frederick III, also known as Frederick I, King in Prussia, was happy. Frederick was almost always happy when given the opportunity to show off and to spend money. Not without warrant is Frederick III known to German historians as "Frederick the Ostentatious." "There is not a younger scion of a minor branch who does not imagine himself to be something like Louis XIV." So wrote Frederick's greatest heir. "He builds his Versailles, has mistresses, and maintains his army." More than anything Frederick desired to be like the Sun King. As if to compensate for a weak and deformed physique, including a rather grotesque swelling on his neck, Frederick III showed an unusual desire to keep up appearances. His cellars groaned with expensive wines; he employed fifty chefs; he spent sixty thousand thalers on his royal crown.

Even funerals, because of their pageantry, excited Frederick III, and by 1712 he had joyfully, and opulently, buried two wives. His third spouse, Sophia Dorothea of Mecklenberg, lived to try Frederick's patience with her Lutheran convictions, her intelligence, and her wit. "Leibnitz lectured to me today about infinitely little," Sophia Dorothea wrote in reference to the great philosopher, "but who would know more about these things than I?" She had no illusions that her husband would miss her eccentricities if she died; he would, Sophia was sure, console himself by seeing to her funeral.

Yet on January 24th Frederick was not thinking of funerals. Quite the opposite. After two failed attempts to produce a living male heir, Frederick knew that his son Frederick William and his wife, a sister of the future George I of England, had a new infant son who looked as if he might survive. Years later this grandson would ridicule Frederick's III's memory, calling him "great in little things and little in great things," and mocking his efforts to emulate Louis XIV. This, happily for him, Frederick III never knew. He insisted that the infant, as the eventual heir of the House of Hohenzollern, be named Frederick as well. So it was. The child, outfitted in a robe heaped with diamonds and worked with silver, was appropriately christened. His godparents, represented by proxy, included Peter the Great of Russia, Emperor Charles VI of Austria, and the Elector of Hanover, later George I of England. Frederick III delighted in his fat, healthy grandchild, noting how he tugged at the breasts of his wet nurse. In just over a year, however, the proud grandfather was dead, the victim of troubled lungs.

Frederick III, his son, and his grandson were generational links in the Hohenzollern line that had ruled over Brandenburg-Prussia for centuries. Since medieval times the story of the Hohenzollerns was inseparable from the history of Brandenburg-Prussia.

The base of Hohenzollern power since 1415 had been the German state of Brandenburg, located in the eastern portion of the Holy Roman Empire, and watered by the rivers of Oder and Elbe. Brandenburg, though relatively modest in size, was influential in Germany because it was an electoral state. By the Golden Bull of 1356 the ruler, or Margrave, of Brandenburg was named as one of the seven electors who chose the Holy Roman Emperor. The Hohenzollerns, because of their warlike inclinations, also became involved in the affairs of the Teutonic Knights, that medieval religious and military order noted for spearheading the *drang nach osten,* or "drive to the east" against the pagan Slavs. Over time the Teutonic Knights carved out a sizeable state, east of Brandenburg, from the Vistula to the Niemen river, and even beyond, known as Prussia. Though the power of the Teutonic Knights eventually waned, and the order lost West Prussia, East Prussia fell into Hohenzollern hands in 1525. In that year, Albert of Brandenburg, a Hohenzollern and Grand Master of the Teutonic Order, declared himself for the Lutheran Reformation, secularized East Prussia, and arranged to hold it as a vassal of the Polish Crown. In 1618 this territory of East Prussia, also known as the Duchy of Prussia, fell into the hands of the branch of Hohenzollerns that ruled Brandenburg. In 1656, the Duchy of Prussia ceased its feudal dependence on Poland. Out of this the strange state of Brandenburg-Prussia was born.

As East Prussia was physically divided from Brandenburg, it became the objective of Hohenzollerns to expand their territory, and particularly to absorb the intervening Baltic lands between Brandenburg and the Duchy of Prussia.

Skillfully, using their emerging army, playing upon the balance of power, the Hohenzollerns added to their territories. In addition to the Duchy of Prussia, the Hohenzollerns inherited Cleves, Mark, and Ravensburg, giving the dynasty a foothold in western Germany. At the Peace of Westphalia of 1648, because both the French and the Swedes saw Brandenburg-Prussia as a counterbalance to the Hapsburgs they wanted so badly to destroy, the Hohenzollerns obtained the archbishopric of Magdeburg, the bishoprics of Halberstadt and Minden, and the large territory of Farther Pomerania. This last cession was a particularly important one because it reached eastward from Brandenburg, along the Baltic coast, toward the Duchy of Prussia. Only West Prussia, claimed by the declining Polish kingdom, remained to block the union of Brandenburg with East Prussia.

The phenomenal territorial growth of Brandenburg-Prussia in the seventeenth century was due to Frederick William "the Great Elector," who ruled from 1640 to 1688. The Great Elector had succeeded only to find his inheritance despoiled by the Thirty Years' War and divided by particularism, custom, and law. Frederick William set to work with the little he had. Educated in Holland, and married to an heiress of the Dutch House of Orange, he knew the value of organization and efficiency, and he applied both to Brandenburg's army. It was soon the envy of Europe, and gained its master respect among other rulers. The Great Elector also built canals and roads, brought in industrious Huguenot exiles from France, and began a civil service. The lesser nobility, the Junkers, were left in peace to mistreat their peasantry, so long as they agreed to serve in the army. Under the Great Elector the army became the great unifier of the disparate Hohenzollern dominions. It was a tradition his heirs continued.

When the happy Frederick III succeeded his father in 1688, he frittered away much of the modest wealth that the Great Elector had managed to accumulate, but he did make his own unique contribution to the prestige of his house. With the Elector of Saxony newly-elected King of Poland, and with the Elector of Hanover soon to be King of England, Frederick the Ostentatious did not rest until he had a crown of his own. In 1701, in return for the use of the Hohenzollern army, Emperor Leopold I granted Frederick III the less than glorious title of "King *in* Prussia." Nonetheless, Frederick had made his point, and his decision to associate the kingship with Prussia was significant. Prussia, but not Brandenburg, was outside the territory of the old Holy Roman Empire, and thus outside the Hapsburg sphere of influence. Despite the opposition of the papacy, Frederick III placed a magnificent crown on his head at Konigsberg, and styled himself King Frederick I. The Hapsburgs soon had reason to regret their generosity.

When Frederick the Ostentatious died in 1713 a marked change came over the new Hohenzollern kingship, for his son and successor, Frederick William I, was a man of vastly different stripe. Frederick William had been a hard case from earliest childhood, when he positively terrorized his governess. On one occasion, he swallowed his shoe buckle, rather than have it taken from him, and the Prussian court agonized over the state of Frederick William's bowels for days; on another, he climbed onto a window ledge and threatened to jump, all because he had been deprived of his breakfast. Frederick William bullied his tutors, and was given to fits of temper that left bystanders awed and his family cowed. In milder moments he threatened to have those in charge of his upbringing hanged or beheaded as soon as he came of age.

This strange boy grew into an even stranger man. While his father had adored fine wine, palaces, and the pastures of the intellect, Frederick William I liked beer and the barracks, coarse tobacco, and even coarser jokes. Frederick's cruelty fell on his family, his humor upon his friends, and there was little to choose between the two. Frederick William's sense of fun ran, for example, to walling up the rooms of his drinking companions, and to watching their inebriated confusion as they tried to find their way indoors. On the death of Gündling, one of the most long-suffering of his cronies, Frederick William had the poor man's corpse dressed in a court jester's uniform, and displayed on a coffin shaped like a wine cask. Frederick William had a unique sense of fun.

Frederick III had been patient and pleasure-loving, but Frederick William I was neither. As if in compensation for his father's extravagance, Frederick William I recorded every grudging expense in a book entitled an "Account of My Ducats." While Frederick III had kept a mistress, Frederick William kept none, and was apparently immune to extramarital blandishments of any kind. Not even Augustus the Strong of Saxony, a man who had experienced every kind of sexual diversion and who holds the European record for the procreation of illegitimate children, could disturb Frederick William's resolve in this regard. Frederick William's state visit to Saxony was characterized by a self-discipline that appalled his host.

Immediately after ascending his throne, Frederick William sold off his father's wines, plate, and medals to pay debts, and clapped the court jeweler in irons. Anything French and anything beautiful was sold, removed, destroyed, or whitewashed. Only the court painters were allowed to remain, the better to record Frederick William's deeds and likeness.

The latter was unimposing. Ashamed of his silky hair, Frederick William had had it nearly shorn, and had covered the wreckage with a succession of ill-fitting wigs. He eschewed court dress, opting instead for hunting habits or the uniform of his regiment, complete with an officer's baton. As he grew older Frederick William became increasingly ugly in physique and in manner. The constant use of tobacco gave him equally constant headaches; overindulgence in beer and diet added to his corpulence, aggravated his gout, and caused rather ugly blotches to appear on his face. Voltaire, never kindly to those he disliked, referred to Frederick William I as the "fat king of Prussia." Frederick William's children simply called him "stumpy," but from a distance—the baton fell on the heads of those who displeased the King.

The only thing that Frederick William I adored was the Prussian army, and particularly his Potsdam regiment of guards. Frederick William liked his grenadiers tall, and throughout Europe Prussian agents inveigled, kidnapped, impressed, or duped hundreds of tall boys to fill the ranks. Heads of state made Frederick William presents of gargantuan troopers, knowing that it would please him, and foreign ambassadors and ministers found their tables littered with appeals from young and frightened giants, citizens of their states, who had been forced into the Prussian ranks. Frederick doted on his grenadiers, drilling them constantly, building them cottages, having them bled for their health, trying to find them tall wives to produce taller offspring. It troubled him greatly that his soldiers could be unhappy, but they sometimes were. On one occasion a group of Frederick William's more reluctant recruits decided that it would be a good idea to burn down Potsdam while Frederick William was there. The plot, however, misfired, and Frederick William I lived to spend 700,000 thalers on the Potsdam regiment alone.

Even more than the Great Elector, Frederick William had made the Prussian army the soul of his state, and every resource of Brandenburg-Prussia was devoted to its maintenance. Through the expenditure of prodigious amounts of energy, constant travel, and the impassioned use of his baton, Frederick William I unified his dominions administratively. For the heart of the Prussian bureaucracy Frederick William created a unique administrative organ, the *Ober-Finanz, Kriegs, und Domanen Direktorium,* literally the "Directory over Finance, Wars, and Domains." The name was instructive.

Through this agency, sometimes called the General Directory, flowed all internal administration, excluding only matters relating to justice, eduction, and religious affairs. Justice Frederick William controlled himself, attempting to establish a common, but very brutal, standard of justice throughout his dominions. "Let justice be done," Frederick William vowed, "even if the earth perish." Frederick William was less sympathetic to education, and despised learned men. "All learned men are fools," he announced to all who would listen, and he referred to the members of the Royal Academy founded by his father as "royal buffoons." For the mass of the people Frederick decreed the barest minimum of instruction, and favored employing old soldiers as teachers. There was no doubt where Frederick William's priorities lay. When the philosopher Wolff was wrongly accused of expounding ideas that might cause the Prussian army to revolt, Frederick William had him expelled on threat of hanging.

A thoroughgoing mercantilist, Frederick William desired to build a healthy economy that could be taxed for the support of the army. He continued his grandfather's policy of attracting skilled foreign workers; industries were protected and expanded under state auspices; beggars were sent to the workhouse or given over to the army recruiters. To discourage the use of foreign styles and foreign cloth, Frederick pointedly dressed his executioners and fools in French costume and fined those who dared to dress in other than Prussian wool and linen. Little was allowed to stand in the way of a ruler who vowed to establish his throne as firmly as a "rock of bronze." "Salvation belongs to the Lord," Frederick William said with more than a touch of grimness, "everything else is my affair."

As might be expected, Frederick William was nicer to his grenadiers than he was to his family. This fact is far more than a historical footnote. It can be said with some justice that Frederick William's treatment of his eldest son and heir helped create one of the most troubled, and most successful, personalities of the eighteenth century.

Frederick William resolved to make of the fat little boy so adored by Frederick III the ideal ruler of the Prussian state. To Frederick William's consternation, the young Frederick turned out, in his estimation, to be imperfect clay. The Crown Prince was a dreamy boy, intellectual and less than perfectly obedient, and perfect obedience was what Frederick William required. To Frederick's disgust the boy liked French literature, especially the works of Racine; he also liked to play the flute, daring to play it only when Frederick William was absent. Especially enraging to the king was the boy's love for Latin, which he persuaded his tutor to teach him on the sly.

Frederick William quickly had enough of such nonsense, and resolved to humble, and break, Frederick's intelligent, and surprisingly strong, spirit. The objections of his gentle and bright wife, Sophia Dorothea of Hanover, who somehow managed to give her brutal husband fourteen children, were to no avail, and the young prince was put on a crushing regimen. The instructions to the tutors were precise. The Prince was to rise early—at six on weekdays, at seven on Sundays. Almost immediately thereafter, he was to fall on his knees and pray. These oblations, wrote Frederick William pointedly, were to be both loud and brief, and the boy was to be washed and dressed by a quarter past the hour. Thereafter, he was to busy himself learning how to write French and German in a terse and efficient way; he was also to master mathematics, artillery, agriculture, and law. "As for the Latin language," Frederick William instructed, "he is not to learn it, and I desire that no one shall even speak to me on this subject." Similarly, the only history permitted was to be that of his own times, the immediate past, and that of Hohenzollern dynasty; ancient history was to be altogether eschewed. The tutors were to impress upon the youth that only love for, and success in, the profession of arms could bring him fame, happiness, and honor. All of this Frederick William astoundingly believed would mold a character that would "love and delight in virtue and feel horror and disgust for vice." "Fritz was broken in," wrote one historian in reference to young Frederick, "not educated."

This, of course, was not all. When the young Frederick fell short of the mark, which was often, he was obliged to endure his father's beatings and contempt, to request fatherly forgiveness in letters addressed to his "Dearest Papa" that crawled with shame, and to kiss, in public, his father's boots. "He has a horror of me," wrote Frederick's father of his eldest son, "but I can bring him to heel." "I cannot stand an effeminate boy," Frederick William sneered in a missive to his son, "who has no manly tastes, who is shamefaced, who cannot ride a horse or shoot and who crowns all by not washing himself. . . ." So terrified was Frederick of his father that he once secreted himself for two hours in the commode enclosure in his mother's bedchamber, rather than have Frederick William discover him.

As Frederick grew up, he not surprisingly found these humiliations beyond endurance. In 1729, with the reluctant help of a young lieutenant named Katte, Frederick tried to run away. Unfortunately for both, the plot was discovered and the young men captured. Frederick William, suspecting that the escape might be part of a larger scheme to assassinate him, put Katte to torture and committed his own son to military prison. There, Frederick William subjected him to proceedings resembling a military court-martial, sold off his son's beloved books, ordered an innocent girl-friend of Frederick's whipped and imprisoned, and contemplated having his heir put to death. Finally, Frederick overrode the decision of his own military tribunal, and ordered Lieutenant Katte beheaded for desertion. Prince Frederick was held at a window and forced to witness Katte's death. As Katte passed, Frederick, in the grip of spiritual agony, screamed for, and obtained, Katte's forgiveness, then fainted as his friend's head thumped on the sand around the block.

Thereafter, Frederick retreated into the well-learned deviousness that was ever after to mark his character. Though he loathed most women, Frederick acceded to his father's wishes and married Princess Elizabeth of Brunswick. This gave him the excuse to live away from his father's prying eyes. On the estate of Rheinsberg, Frederick bathed himself in forbidden French culture. Works by Watteau and Fragonard lined the walls of a specially-built chateau. For seven years Frederick rusticated there, corresponding with Voltaire, reading philosophy, writing his *Considerations on the State of Europe* and *Anti-Machiavel*, evading his father. French culture became for Frederick part of his identity. In a quiet rebellion against his father Frederick thought, wrote, and preferred to speak in French. He never spoke or spelled German well.

Though she formed the pretense for his idylls, Frederick showed scant kindness to Elizabeth of Brunswick, who, tragically, adored him. Of course Frederick was not grateful to her, but then he had not been raised to be. Battered and humiliated by those he loved, Frederick returned the favor. Eventually he put her aside, and forced her to live in a separate household. "When I am dead," old Frederick William noted with brutal satisfaction, "you will say 'Well, that's the end of the old bully'—but believe me, he who is to succeed me will tell you all to go to hell." When Frederick William expired in 1740, he thought that he had done his work well.

The new king was brilliant, but not whole. Ever seeking military glory, he was never without a box of poison to be used in case of failure. Though Samuel Johnson called him "Voltaire's footboy" because of his love of French Enlightenment philosophy, Frederick wrapped even this infatuation with cynicism. "If I wished to punish a province," Frederick mocked, "I would have it governed by philosophers." Vitriol dripped from Frederick's pen. "Religion is the idol of the mob," Frederick proclaimed, "it adores everything that it does not understand." Power and military might had their attractions for Frederick ("God is always with the strongest battalions"), but in the end even these made him impatient. "Rascals," he shrieked at his Prussian guards before one of their few defeats, "would you live forever?" For the people over whom he ruled, and who had endured the privations and sacrifices of his wars, Frederick had little but contempt. On his deathbed, he remarked, "I am tired of ruling over slaves." Though his *Anti-Machiavel* rings with humanitarian idealism, Frederick justly acquired a reputation for diplomatic immorality that went beyond Machiavelli himself. "I begin by taking," Frederick noted succinctly. "I shall find scholars afterwards to demonstrate my perfect right."

Even more than his predecessors, Frederick II used the army as the vehicle by which Prussia drove to world-power status. While his grandfather had rented the army out to others, and his father had scoured Europe for tall grenadiers, Frederick II commanded the army personally and invested his budget on the minds of his officers. Officers began training in extreme youth at the *Cadettanhaus,* and the strict discipline was the byword of their lives ever after. Leaves were seldom granted; they were usually not necessary, as Frederick liked his officers celibate. Officers who failed were never promoted; they were forgotten. Those who succeeded were the king's friends and the first estate of the realm. Soldiers who raised their hands against an officer were put to death, and few officers had to justify their conduct toward their troops. All of Prussia was divided into military cantons, from which the regiments were recruited. At the apogee of the system was Frederick himself, who acted as his own commander-in-chief and chief-of-staff. Other generals waited on the whims of politicians; Frederick's moved instantly, and the politicians were obliged to react thereafter. "The question of right," Frederick wrote in contempt to his foreign secretary before the Silesian invasion, "is for you to elaborate; work it out secretly since the orders to the army have already been issued."

Frederick II managed the state precisely as he managed the army. He used his father's General Directory and bureaucracy to the full, but he was chief-of-staff over the bureaucracy as much as he was over the army. By 1750 the Prussian state had not only a balanced budget, but a surplus. Taxes were assessed off the backs of the peasants, at a rate equivalent to forty percent of their net income. No branch of government was free from Frederick's management. Foreign affairs were conducted in Frederick's own written hand; all other matters were dealt with according to a rigorous calendar kept at the king's elbow. Prussia was run by the best bureaucracy in Europe, kept in constant animation by Frederick's savage energy.

Frederick drove both bureaucracy and army nearly to the breaking point. In the First Silesian War, Frederick's troops swallowed 14,000 square miles and 1,500,000 people, but Maria Theresa fought back, and the conquest of Silesia was not really confirmed until the Peace of Hubertusburg in 1763. To keep his conquests, Frederick at one time or another fought against most of the great powers of Europe. The wars wounded Frederick's kingdom, and forced him to undertake more severe autocratic measures, particularly in the area of finance. Tobacco and coffee were made state monopolies, and taxes were increased. Frederick's armies were always outnumbered; his troops, resentful of the harsh discipline, could not be moved at night for fear of desertion; his victories were hardly ever decisive. Nonetheless, by keeping enemy forces from joining, by interdicting supply lines, by destroying the economies of his foes, Frederick drubbed his enemies into submission. The cost, to himself and to his state, was high. "My youth has been a school of adversity," Frederick once wrote, "and since then I have not escaped reverses and misfortunes. . . ."

Frederick not only survived the wars of the mid-eighteenth century, but moved his state into the ranks of the great powers. By the First Partition of Poland, Frederick obtained West Prussia, and Brandenburg and East Prussia were at last unified into a coherent state. A unified Prussian kingdom confronted the disparate possessions of the Austrian house of Hapsburg. The result was "German dualism," in which Hapsburg and Hohenzollern sought to dominate the remaining states of Germany. Frederick II died in 1786, and was given the appellation "the Great" by the subjects he despised. He left a state virtually without a bourgeois class, without parliamentary institutions, with little to unify it save a bureaucracy and an army. It was a troubled legacy.

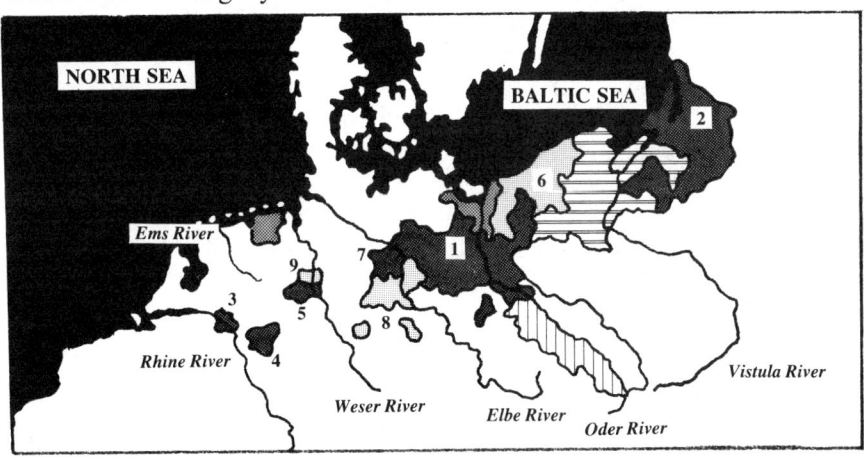

- ■ Territory held by Brandenburg—Prussia before the beginning of the Thirty Years' War
- □ Territory ceded to Brandenburg Prussia by the Peace of Westphalia, 1648
- ▨ Prussian territory at the accession of Frederick the Great
- ≡ West Prussia, added by Frederick after the First Polish Partition
- ▦ Silesia, taken from the Austrian Empire by Frederick during the War of the Austrian Succession (Silesian Wars)

1. Brandenburg
2. Prussia
3. Cleves
4. Mark
5. Ravensburg
6. Eastern Pomerania
7. Magdeburg
8. Halberstadt
9. Minden

Brandenburg—Prussia After the Peace of Westphalia, 1648, and Under Frederick the Great, 1742-1772

D. Catherine the Great and the Expansion of Russia

In the winter of 1744, in the company of her mother, a fifteen-year-old girl from a small state in Germany journeyed into Russia, there to be wed to the heir apparent to the vast domains of the ruling dynasty of Romanov. The name of this princess was Sophia-Augusta-Frederika of Anhalt-Zerbst, and she was to marry Charles-Peter-Ulrich of Holstein. It was the fondest hope of the old Russian Empress, Elizabeth I, that these two children would one day be the joint autocrats of all the Russias. In true, and historic, irony, the greatest of Slavic states was to be bequeathed to two Germans. The

Empress Elizabeth, seeking to palliate Russian sensibilities, had her heirs baptized into the Orthodox faith and renamed. Henceforth, Charles-Peter-Ulrich was to be known as the Grand Duke Peter, his future consort as Catherine.

The fact that these children were to be heirs to all Russia was attributable to a number of arranged marriages and biological misfortunes that began during the time of Peter the Great. Peter had had an heir, Alexis, but he had proven a rebellious misfit, and Peter, never one for half-measures, had him tortured to death: "The rack was applied at eleven o'clock. . . . That same day, at six o'clock in the afternoon, the Czarevich gave up his soul."

Having killed his son, Peter damaged the possibility of an orderly succession further by decreeing that the reigning Russian sovereign could choose his own heir; then he insured chaos by not naming his successor when he died in 1725. The result was a series of short reigns, accompanied by a revival of the power of the boyars, the recalcitrant noble class that Peter had tried to tame and turn into servants of the state. Peter was succeeded first by his second wife (Catherine I, Tsarina 1725-1727), then by his grandson (Peter II, Tsar 1727-1730), and finally by the daughter of his half-brother (Anne, Tsarina 1730-1740). The first two reigns were compromised by the ambitions of two noble families, the Menshikovs and Dolgurukys, the third by the presence of German favorites who antagonized powerful Russians. Though Anne was able to extend Russian influence in Poland during the War of the Polish Succession (1733-1735), her war against the Turks went badly, and at the Peace of Belgrade (1739), Russia regained Azov but was forced to renounce the right to build a Black Sea fleet.

Anne, like her immediate predecessors, died without direct heirs, and was succeeded by Ivan, her grand-nephew. His short reign (1740-1741) was quickly ended by a revolt engineered by Elizabeth, the youngest daughter of Peter the Great. Clapping a helmet on her head, she led the Imperial Guard out in a swift and successful *coup*.

As Empress, Elizabeth had her successes, and her favorites, but no children. Determined to insure and control the succession, she turned to Germany. Regardless of anti-German feelings in Russia, the move was a natural one. Years before, Peter the Great had married Elizabeth's sister to the Duke of Holstein-Gottorp. The result of the union was Charles-Peter-Ulrich, who by 1741 was the only surviving grandson of Peter the Great. Despite the fact that Charles-Peter had been raised a Lutheran and prepared to succeed his great-uncle, Charles XII, as king of Sweden, the Empress Elizabeth did not rest until she snatched the lonely and troubled boy from his Swedish tutors and brought him to Russia as her heir.

Catherine the Great

Not content to pick her successor, Elizabeth also intended to choose his consort, and for this she reached deeply into Germany and her personal past. Elizabeth, like her sister, had been betrothed as a young girl to a member of the house of Holstein-Gottorp, but her fiancé, Prince Karl-Augustus, had died before the marriage had taken place. Elizabeth, apparently, never forgot him. Years later when she sought a wife for her heir she picked the young Sophia of Anhalt-Zerbst, the daughter of Karl Augustus' sister.

Elizabeth was concerned, but not deterred, by the fact that the young couple seemed uncongenial. "I cannot say," wrote Catherine of her intended husband, "that I either liked or disliked him.... He was sixteen, quite good-looking... but small and infantile, talking of nothing but soldiers and toys."

The new Grand Duke Peter was simply no match for a young woman, healthy and sexually precocious, whose literary tastes ran to the *Annals* of Tacitus, Montesquieu's *Spirit of the Laws,* and the works of Voltaire. Peter, a near-orphan, had been raised in a harsh Lutheran environment by a Swedish tutor named Brummer, who sought to discipline his charge by making him kneel for hours on dried peas, by tying a donkey's head around his neck, and by denying him food. So terrified of Brummer was Peter that an appearance by the tutor could cause him to become physically ill.

Transported to Russia at the instigation of Elizabeth, Peter found himself in a place even more uncongenial than the one he had left. His response was to acquire a taste for drink, but he lacked the stamina to hold his liquor. Shortly after his arrival, Peter contracted smallpox which, in the words of Catherine, made him "horrid to look at." As immature physically as he was emotionally, Peter apparently was unready for a normal relationship with a woman. Nonetheless, in 1744, in a magnificient ceremony, the couple was wed.

The union was a disaster. On the wedding night, Peter kept his bride waiting for two hours, and expressed little interest thereafter. While Catherine was left to herself to read Enlightenment philosophy, Peter spent his days in the adjoining rooms sawing away on his violin, and incessantly drilling his ranks of toy soldiers. In Peter's strange world, rats were court-martialed and hanged for disobedience; and doors were bored, so the Grand Duke could spy on those inside.

"My nephew, Devil take him, is a monster." So remarked the Empress Elizabeth of the pathetic Peter. Catherine, for her part, eventually tired of the Grand Duke and began to seek physical relationships elsewhere. "I have just said," Catherine recalled with candor years later, "that I was attractive. Consequently, one-half of the road to temptation was already covered and it is only human in such situations that one should not stop half-way." While Catherine's sexual relationships have become the stuff of legend, it is well to remember that she was a young German woman alone in Russia, and that the Empress expected her to produce a male child. Accordingly, Catherine gave birth to a son, Paul, but it is unlikely that her husband was the father.

Catherine and the Grand Duke went their separate ways. Peter, unhappy in Russia, plunged more deeply into the bottle and Catherine took several lovers. Peter did eventually grow up. At the age of twenty-seven he was initiated sexually by an obliging widow named Groot, and she was succeeded by others. In 1762 when the Empress Elizabeth, diseased and dropsical, died, the Grand Duke acceded to the throne as Peter III.

Portrait of Grand Duke Peter, Catherine, and Paul.
R. M. Lisiewska
Courtesy of the Svenska Portrattarkivet, Stockholm.

As Tsar, Peter antagonized his subjects with rapidity and thoroughness. Ever entranced with all things military, Peter conceived a slavish adoration for Frederick the Great. "I am," Frederick remarked in reference to both *Don Quixote* and Peter's admiration, "his Dulcinea." Frederick, fighting for his life in the Seven Year's War, was delighted at Peter's insistence that Russian troops be withdrawn from the conflict. Peter's decision had a contrary effect on the Russian military, and he quickly compounded it by insisting that the Russian armies be trained and outfitted on the Prussian model, and by hinting that Russian troops would be used to defend his ancestral holdings in Germany.

There were other causes for antagonism. A Lutheran to his bones, Peter attacked the Russian Orthodox faith. Private chapels were banned; clergy were required to wear secular dress; icons were removed from churches. Having antagonized influential Russians in all these ways, Peter paradoxically released them from some of the constraints of autocracy. Compulsory state service for the nobility was abolished, as was the dreaded Secret Chancellory. The result was inevitable, and Peter III did not last the year. Peter was seized in a military revolt engineered by the Orlov brothers, one of whom was Catherine's lover. Placed under house arrest, Peter seemed to accept his fate, in the ungenerous words of Frederick the Great, "like a child being sent to sleep." It was, however, not so pleasant. Peter expired in a drunken brawl in rather mysterious circumstances. Word was put out that Peter died of a "hemorrhoidal colic," prompting a wag to say that this malady must indeed be risky in Russia. Peter's neglected consort, as Catherine II, took the Russian throne and held it, to the astonishment of those who believed women unfit to rule, until her death thirty years later.

Catherine was Russia's only female sovereign to attain the appellation of "the Great," and she earned it by expansionist policies and by hard work. In her prime Catherine rose at 5:00 A.M., lit her own fire, made her own coffee, and plunged into her papers. She wrote until mid-morning, then received ministers and issued ukazes, or decrees. An hour, beginning at 1:00 P.M., was allowed for dressing for dinner, which began promptly at two. Then, after family obligations, there was more work until 6:00 P.M. A short night of socializing was ended by Catherine's retirement at about 10:00 P.M. It was a work-day marked by only two meals, and these often indifferent as to quality.

"Those who are most in her society assure me that her application to business is incredible." So wrote the English ambassador, the Earl of Buckinghamshire, in one of his dispatches. "The welfare and prosperity of her subjects, the glory of her empire, are always present to her. . . ." Although the ambassador worried about her over-attention to detail and her receptivity to bad advice, he need not have done so, for Catherine followed successful policies.

This success was most striking in foreign affairs. Catherine forced the election of her former lover, Stanislaus Poniatowski, to the Polish kingship in 1763. Then in 1767, on the pretext of protecting the Polish Orthodox minority, she turned Poland into a protectorate. Frederick the Great was so afraid of Catherine's expansionist policies in the Ottoman Empire and Poland that he arranged the first Polish Partition to deflect her. Russia also obtained the lion's share of the next two partitions.

Catherine also sought territory at the expense of the declining Ottoman Empire. Her first war with the Turks began in 1770 and was brought to an unsatisfactory conclusion at the Treaty of Kuchuk Kainardji (1774), in which Russia restored to the Ottoman Empire Moldavia, Wallachia, and certain Aegean Islands. In return, however, Russia obtained the Black Sea Coast, save for the Crimean peninsula, and the right to "protect" Orthodox Christians at Constantinople.

Using these last two treaty terms as a base for intervention, Catherine concocted her "Greek Project" for the destruction of the Ottoman Empire and the establishment of a Russian presence in the Black Sea and Mediterranean. Under the pretext of protecting Orthodox Christianity, Catherine proposed to fuse the Ottoman states of Moldavia and Wallachia into the Russian protectorate of "Dacia." Two other Ottoman territories, Thrace and Macedonia, were to be directed from the old imperial city of Constantinople, which was in turn to be ruled by Catherine's grandson. Though these grandiose plans were never fulfilled, a second Turkish war led to the Treaty of Jassy (1792) in which the Ottomans acknowledged Russian control of the Black Sea Steppes and the Crimea. Not content with Poland and the Crimea, Catherine sent Gregory Shelekhov to explore the Kurile Islands and Alaska. Catherine joined Ivan the Terrible and Peter the Great as a prime author of Russian expansionism.

It is in her domestic policies that Catherine the Great has excited the most debate and controversy. Often seen as an "enlightened despot" who befriended the likes of Diderot, Catherine has also been portrayed as a hypocrite when she was less enthusiastic about implementing "enlightened" policies. It may be most useful to view Catherine as a pragmatist and realist who responded to circumstances as she found them. Like other so-called enlightened despots, Catherine was willing enough to further reform, if those reforms did not damage her position as sovereign.

One of the realities that Catherine found was the power of the nobility. For years Russia had been ruled by an implicit agreement between the autocracy and the nobility. The terms were simple. The nobility would support Russia's rulers, and the autocracy would leave the nobility free to manage their estates and serfs.

Catherine by and large continued this policy. Early in her reign, in 1667, she convoked a legislative commission of all classes, save for the serfs, for the true Enlightenment purpose of writing a new law code. The commission also gratified elements in the nobility who had been clamoring for a new constitution. The law code, however, was never promulgated.

Whatever impulse toward reform Catherine might have had was stymied by Pugachev's Rebellion, a serious revolt of serfs and Cossacks centered in southeastern Russia. The leader of the revolt, the Cossack Emilian Pugachev, claimed to be Peter III. For two years, between 1773 and 1775, much of Russia was in turmoil, and Catherine allied with the nobility to suppress the peasantry. The result, as soon as the revolt ended, was a complete governmental reorganization, which put local administration into the hands of the nobility. Local nobility were required to serve on local commissions and corporations. While Catherine opposed the extension of serfdom and took ecclesiastical peasants out of the hands of the church, she did not hesitate to hand over state serfs to her own servants, and she forbade peasants to file complaints against their noble landlords.

At the same time, Catherine avoided the dominance by nobility that characterized the reigns of her immediate predecessors. She created a bureaucracy to undertake many of the tasks of government, particularly those involving finance, and she divided the noble-dominated Senate into six departments. The country was divided into fifty-one *guberniyas,* smaller and more efficient than those established by Peter, and these in turn were put into the hands of the bureaucracy.

Still, certain of Catherine's policies could be considered enlightened. The rigors of Russian law were softened during Catherine's reign. Crimes and punishments were defined, torture and corporal punishment lessened. Catherine built up provincial school systems, favored the training of future mothers, and advanced medical education. Catherine's educational reforms buttressed her aggressive population policies. Determined to enlarge and diversify Russia's population, Catherine encouraged immigration and resettlement. Jews, by being allowed to settle in certain areas, were integrated into Russian society more completely than ever before. Tragically, there was a price. A Ukaze of 1794 decreed that Russian Jews pay double the taxes of Christians, and Catherine's policy of assimilation threatened the established structures of Jewish society. Russian Muslims were accorded toleration by edict, as Catherine's expansionism brought more Muslims into the Russian state. In the late

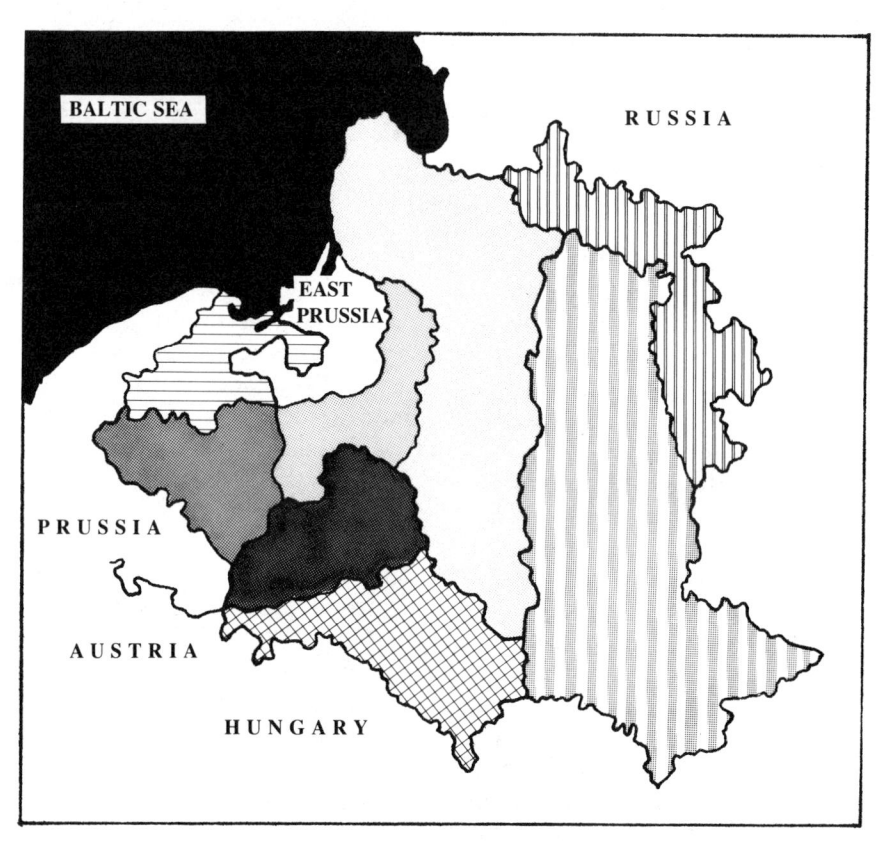

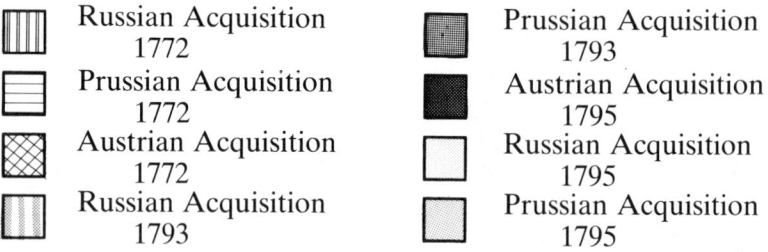

	Russian Acquisition 1772		Prussian Acquisition 1793
	Prussian Acquisition 1772		Austrian Acquisition 1795
	Austrian Acquisition 1772		Russian Acquisition 1795
	Russian Acquisition 1793		Prussian Acquisition 1795

The Destruction of Poland: The Partitions, 1772-1795

1780s a "Muslim Spiritual Assembly" was created to regulate and support Muslim communities in Russia. Catholics were less fortunate. As Russia absorbed large parts of Poland, Catherine, used to the idea of secular control over religious affairs, regulated the Catholic Church as she saw fit, without regard for the opinions of the Papacy.

In economic affairs Catherine followed a policy of moderate mercantilism. A new protective tariff was promulgated to encourage native Russian industry. Commercial relationships were extended in a number of ways, and foreign trade increased markedly during Catherine's reign. Close with finances, Catherine was able to balance the state budget in the first four years of her reign, but her expenses soon outstripped the monies gleaned from customs, state monopolies on liquor and salt, and other sources. Catherine fell back on such expedients as increasing the amount of money in circulation and the amount of foreign loans. In 1794, a new series of taxes was introduced, and the poll-tax increased. During Catherine's reign, state revenue quadrupled. Nonetheless, the Russian economy could not be considered truly healthy. To Catherine's credit, however, the percentage of the budget devoted to the military declined during her reign, while the percentage devoted to internal administration and reform actually increased.

By the time Catherine died in 1796, old, obese, with sores on her feeble legs, she had set or reaffirmed policies that characterized Russia down to very modern times. The partnership of the autocracy and nobility, made across the bodies of the serfs, remained, but Catherine's new bureaucracy strengthened the control of her successors over all aspects of Russian society. Catherine's ruthless expansionist policies, as well as those of population resettlement, were refined by Catherine's successors, both Romanov and Soviet. The same was true of Catherine's preoccupation with the Black Sea and the Mediterranean, and her interest in Poland. In her desire to make Russia great, she helped fashion the diverse yet autocratic power that has been so formidable in the affairs of the twentieth century.

E. Britain, France, and the Wars for Colonial Dominance: Lord Chatham and his Successors

In November of 1708 William Pitt was born in a house in Golden Square, London. The name of the birth-site was appropriate, for the infant was the grandson of the same "Diamond" Pitt who had grown so wealthy in the India trade. Diamond Pitt was pleased with his grandson, in marked contrast to the rest of the family, who he did not like very much. A difficult man himself, Diamond Pitt passed on the worst of his characteristics to his children, and then despised them for exhibiting them. Thomas Pitt, Diamond Pitt's second son and William Pitt's father, was the typical, but not the only, recipient of such genetic misfortune. Like his father, Thomas Pitt was cruel and violent, and given to streaks of emotional instability. While Thomas Pitt spent money superbly well, he lacked his father's knack for making it. The result was a decline in the Pitt family fortunes, personal and financial.

There was enough money, however, to send William Pitt to Eton, then as now one of the finest schools in England. Unfortunately, the boy at first showed little promise. Though he mixed with the sons of some of the great British political families, and received some academic training, William Pitt hated Eton and left early. After a short stint at Trinity College, Oxford, he entered military service as a member of the King's Own Regiment of Horse. In 1735 William Pitt, at the age of twenty-eight, entered Parliament from the safe, family-controlled borough of Old Sarum. Once there, he joined a Whig faction led by Lord Cobham and, as one of "Cobham's Cubs," fell to criticizing the peaceful policies of the First Lord of the Treasury, Sir Robert Walpole. Thus far, William Pitt had followed a career typical for a young man of his class and station.

This very quickly changed. The young Pitt, perhaps for the first time, found in the British Parliament something to get excited about, and it fired a hidden, but very healthy, ambition. Born to a family that had become powerful through trade, William Pitt and others in the Cobham faction argued that what the British Empire gained at Utrecht had to be protected and extended. Great Britain, Pitt and his faction firmly believed, was now a great power, well able to challenge France and Spain for colonial dominance. The passions of Pitt and others forced the beginning of the War of Jenkins' Ear with Spain and forced Walpole out of office. The War of Jenkins' Ear soon merged with the larger War of the Austrian Succession. The British honored the Pragmatic Sanction and sided with Maria Theresa, while the French opposed her.

Still, William Pitt was far from content. He now had his war, but he was soon discontented with the way it was prosecuted. In 1742, George II chose as his Secretary of State Sir George Cartaret, and Cartaret, to Pitt's anger and disbelief, focused the British diplomatic and war effort on the European continent, rather than on the colonies and on the seas. Driven into furious opposition by Cartaret's policies, Pitt attacked the continental emphasis of the British war effort, the sending of British subsidies to pay Hanoverian and Hessian troops, the subordination of British interests to those of ungrateful allies and the Hanoverian dynasty. With the help of Pitt's opposition, Cartaret was driven out of office in 1744. So dangerous had Pitt become to political stability that he was brought into the government as Paymaster of the Forces.

To Pitt's delight, the Seven Years' War spread to India and to America, but the news was not especially good. In India the forces of the British East India Company had been checked by those of the French East India Company under Dupleix. In this strange conflict, where each of these trading companies made alliances with native princes and hired native mercenaries, or sepoys, to fight for them, the French had managed to seize the British East India trading settlement at Madras. In America, in what was called King George's War, the results were mixed. The French settlement of Louisburg was taken, but by the Treaty of Aix-la-Chapelle, which ended the War of the Austrian Succession, Louisburg was returned to the French and Madras to the British.

Portrait of William Pitt, 1st Earl of Chatham.
After R. Brompton
Courtesy of the National Portrait Gallery, London.

In March of 1754, as Pitt was suffering from gout and depression at the seaside spa at Bath, Henry Pelham, the chief minister of the existing government, died. This meant that the ministry had to be reconstructed. It accordingly was, and initially in Pitt's favor. The Duke of Newcastle, who was named the new First Lord of the Treasury, labored under two disabilities. As a member of the House of

Lords, he could not lead the debate in the House of Commons; as a man profoundly ignorant of foreign affairs, he could not formulate foreign policy. Pitt was chosen as the leader of the House of Commons, and returned to Westminster determined to advocate his imperial foreign policy views. Newcastle, however, was not cooperative. Fearing Pitt's oratory and growing political power, Newcastle forced Pitt out of the ministry in November 1755.

Pitt's ouster from the ministry proved to be a blessing in disguise because he was not blamed, as Newcastle was, for the continuing bad news from America. In 1754, a young Virginian, George Washington, suffered a defeat attempting to seize Fort Duquesne, built by the French at the forks of the Ohio River. The French, through a network of such outposts, laid claim to the entire Ohio country, and threatened the British claim to North America. Almost as soon as the Seven Years' War broke out in Europe in 1754, its counterpart, the French and Indian War, began in America. In quick succession, British forces under General Braddock were destroyed by the French and their Indian allies as they marched on Fort Duquesne, Oswego fell, and the British island stronghold of Minorca was lost. In India, Robert Clive had successfully countered the aggressiveness of Dupleix by seizing Arcot in 1751, but a local ruler, the Nawab of Bengal, had seized Calcutta and imprisoned British residents in the infamous "Black Hole," where many perished. In November 1756, Newcastle resigned, and Pitt was asked to join the ministry of his successor, the Duke of Devonshire, as a secretary of state.

Necessity now forced the new ministry to follow the imperial policy that Pitt had always advocated. The Duke of Devonshire, as First Lord of the Treasury, was the nominal head of state, but it was Pitt who controlled the war; nor did the situation change when Pitt's old antagonist, the Duke of Newcastle, succeeded Devonshire in 1757. Pitt remained in total control until he resigned in 1761.

Pitt's war policy was a basic one, and rested on a deeply-felt sense of priorities. While Pitt was willing enough to subsidize the forces of Frederick the Great and other of his allies in Europe, he made it clear that the focus of direct British intervention would be in India and America. It was a policy that spoke at once to British trading interests and to British strength. The "wooden walls" of the Royal Navy, England's most potent military weapon, were of maximum use in a war fought in the colonies and on the sea lanes between them. With the strategy determined, Pitt left Newcastle to manage Parliament while he managed the war.

Pitt's policy paid off handsomely. After some initial setbacks, where the French under General Montcalm took and destroyed Forts Oswego and William Henry, the British countered. In 1758 the

British took Louisburg and forts Frontenac and Duquesne. Then, in 1759, on the Plains of Abraham before Quebec, the British under General Wolfe inflicted a terrible defeat on Montcalm and the French in a battle that cost both commanders their lives. In 1760 Montreal was obliged to capitulate, and all of Canada effectively passed to the British crown. Two years later a British fleet under Admiral Rodney temporarily severed the French West Indies from the French empire. In India the forces of the East India Company were also triumphant. Calcutta was retaken and Chandernagore seized. Finally, at the Battle of Plassey (1757), John Clive decisively destroyed the French position in India. On the African coast, a British task force captured Goree (Dakar), and with it access to a rich French trade in gold, ivory, slaves, and gum arabic.

By the Treaty of Paris of 1763, which was with the Treaty of Hubertusburg one of the two great diplomatic agreements of the eighteenth century, the British obtained French recognition of their control over all Canada, and America east of the Mississippi River. All territory west of the Mississippi was ceded by France to Spain, in compensation for Spanish aid in the war against the British. From the Spanish, the British received Florida in exchange for the port of Havana, which had been captured by the British during the conflict. All the French retained in North America were certain fishing rights on the Grand Banks of Newfoundland and two small islands. French diplomats did gain back the French West Indies, but it was scant comfort for the loss of a continent. In India, the Treaty of Paris served the French little better. There they retained only a few trading stations, and were limited in their use of sepoys. In 1769, the French East India Company was dissolved.

Ironically, Pitt was not happy with the Treaty of Paris, convinced as he was that Britain could have gained an even larger trading empire. In 1760 George II died, and his successor, George III, together with his advisor Lord Bute, headed calls for peace. In 1761, Pitt had resigned. He was ennobled as the Earl of Chatham in 1766.

The Treaty of Paris did not end the Anglo-French rivalry over North America, and it vastly increased the problems of British colonial administration. Chatham had won for his nation an empire in the American wilderness, but it proved an empire even harder to hold than to win. On the heels of the Treaty came the rebellion of the Ottawa Indian Chief Pontiac, and demands by restless American colonists and speculators for land in the Ohio country. To keep the frontier quiet, and to prevent violent conflicts between colonist and Indian, the British government established the Proclamation Line of 1763, which was an attempt to close white settlement west and north of streams flowing into the Atlantic Ocean. The move infuriated the

American colonists, as did the mercantilist measures foisted upon them by a succession of British ministries.

The new empire in North America required new revenues, and a succession of weak British ministries in the years after 1763 sought to obtain the money through taxation. Some of these taxes, many of them ill-advised, only antagonized the colonists further. Other measures such as the Quebec Act of 1774, which extended the Quebec boundary to the Ohio River and cut off the claims of various American colonies to western lands, led the Thirteen Colonies, in 1776, to declare their independence.

The American Revolution was thus in many respects the consequence of the Paris settlement of 1763. It was also a later chapter in the Anglo-French struggle for North America. American colonists were aided in their struggle for independence by French officers and French warships. With the help of the French, the American revolutionaries tore all of America south of Canada and east of the Mississippi from Chatham's great empire.

Nonetheless Chatham had established the basis of British foreign policy for years to come. That policy was to be grounded in an overseas empire, in a strong navy, and in trade. Only when its interests were immediately threatened would the British ever intervene on the European mainland. Through her industrial might and colonial interests, not through continental armies, Britain joined the ranks of the great powers.

F. Conclusion: The European Powers at the Close of the Eighteenth Century

In 1648 the Peace of Westphalia had produced consequences that were simple and clear. The Holy Roman Empire lay in ruins, and the house of Hapsburg had been succeeded by the French house of Bourbon as the dominant power in Europe. In contrast, the two peace treaties of 1763, signed at Paris and Hubertusburg, revealed a world more complex, where power was more variously divided. At Paris in 1763, as at Utrecht in 1715, France had been humiliated, but France remained a great power.

At Hubertusburg, Prussia, considered an upstart state only a few years previously, likewise emerged as an influential force in European affairs. Prussia, however, continued to be challenged by a revivified Hapsburg state based in Austria and Hungary, and the existence of both kept central and eastern Europe unstable for generations.

Sharing the spoils of a partitioned Poland with Austria and Prussia was an expansionist Russia, bent on forcing itself on the rest of Europe. Finally, an expansionist British empire, greatly extended by the treaties of Utrecht and Paris, was, by virtue of its economic mighty, influential in Europe even though it was a naval rather than a military power.

The overwhelming power of the Hapsburgs and the Bourbons had, by 1763, seemingly been checked, but only at the cost of creating a Europe at once more complex and more dangerous. Never had the balance of power depended on the good will of so many statesmen and crowned heads, and never had there been more crowned heads with such strong ambitions.

Portfolio: Women Artists, 1600-1815

Recent research in art history indicates that a number of women practiced successfully as painters, sculptors, and engravers in the years between 1600 and 1815. Among them was Judith Leyster, a painter of the seventeenth-century Dutch school, whose work has been at times confused with that of Frans Hals. In the late eighteenth century, a small school of woman court painters served the nobility and royalty of France but lost their positions with the coming of the French Revolution.

Mademoiselle Vigée-Lebrun and her Pupil Mademoiselle Lemoine. Marie-Victoire Lemoine
Courtesy of the Metropolitan Museum of Art, New York. Gift of Mrs. Thorneycroft Ryle.

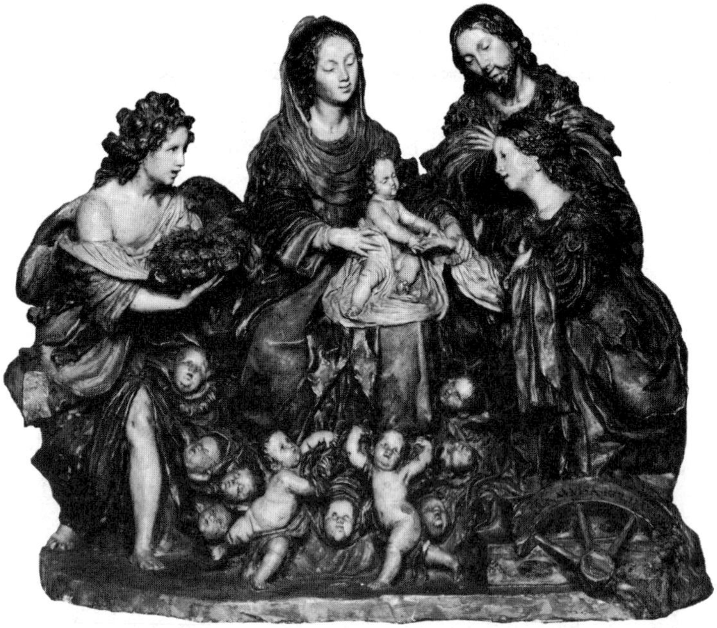

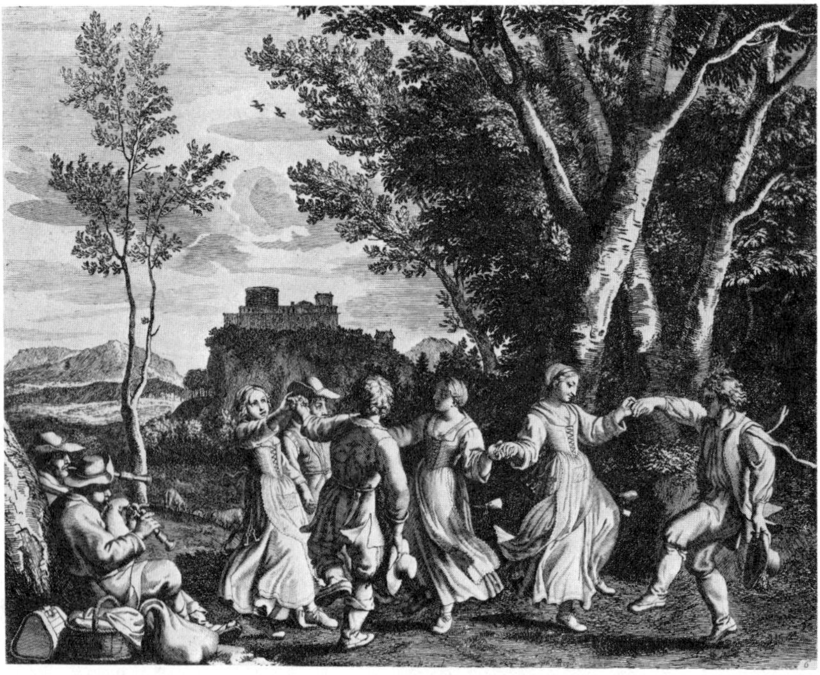

The Mystical Marriage of St. Catherine. **Opposite, top.** Luisa Roldán
Courtesy of The Hispanic Society, New York.

Danseen Branle, Pastoral #6. **Opposite, bottom.** Claudine Stella
Courtesy of the Museum of Fine Arts, Boston. Babcock Bequest.

Self-Portrait. Judith Leyster
Courtesy of the National Gallery of Art, Washington. Gift of Mr. and Mrs. Robert Woods Bliss.

The Annunciation. Suzanne de Court
Courtesy Walters Art Gallery, Baltimore.

The First Step. **Opposite, top.** Marguerite Gerard
Courtesy of Fogg Art Museum, Harvard University. Gift of Charles E. Dunlap.

The Marquise de Peze and the Marquise de Rouget with her Two Children.
Opposite, bottom. Elisabeth Vigée-Lebrun
Courtesy of the National Gallery of Art, Washington. Gift of the Bay Foundation.

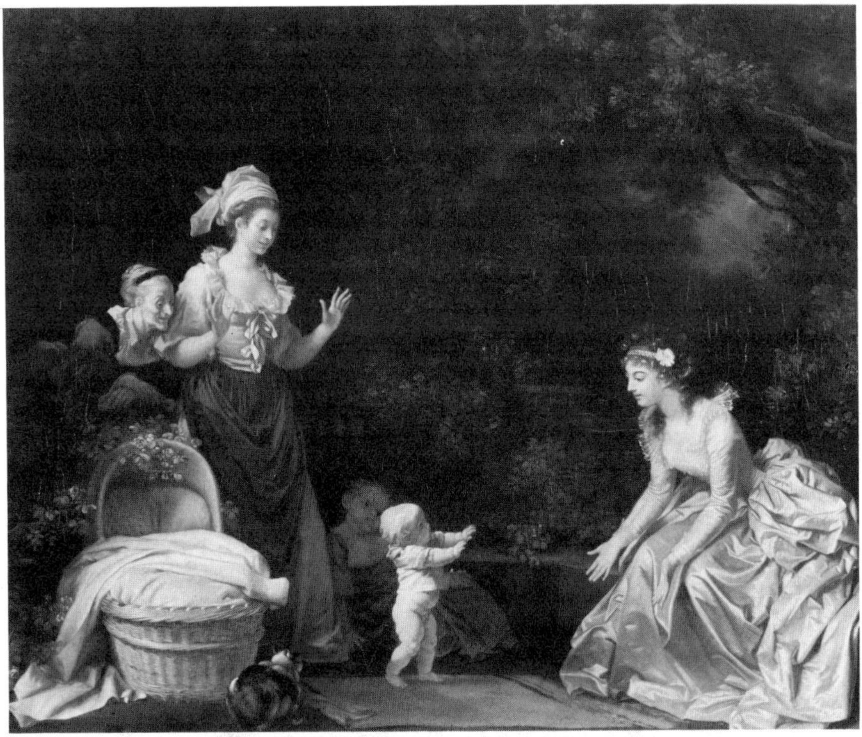

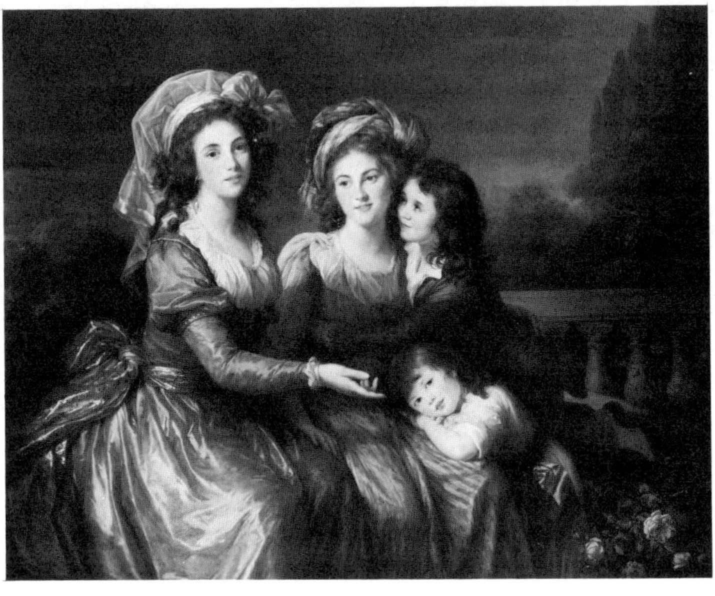

Portrait of the Artist with Two Pupils. Adelaide Labille-Guiard
Courtesy of the Metropolitan Museum of Art, New York. Gift of Julia A. Berwind.

Chapter VIII

Revolution and War in France and Europe, 1789-1815: The Marquis de Lafayette, Maximilien Robespierre, Napoleon Bonaparte, The Duke of Wellington and Prince Metternich

The Marquis was a simpleton. . . .
—Napoleon on Lafayette

The Terror is Justice—prompt, severe, inflexible.
—Robespierre

I used to say of him that his presence on the field made the difference of forty thousand men.
—The Duke of Wellington on Napoleon

I am but a man.
—The Duke of Wellington on himself

To preserve is to act. . . .
—Prince Metternich

Napoleon in His Study. Jacques-Louis David
Courtesy of the National Gallery of Art, Washington. Samuel H. Kress Collection.

A. The Era of the French Revolution, 1789-1815: History, Historiography, and Causation

The French Revolution, for many historians, was one of the great cataclysms of European history. By the time it had run its frightening, twenty-five year course, it had challenged the traditional hierarchies of Church and nobility, toppled several crowned heads, perfected the use of the mass conscript army, and provided a model against which all subsequent revolutions have been measured. Emanating from its center in France, this first "great revolution"—so-called because it produced violent social as well as political change—swept through much of the rest of Europe by conquest, defeating its armies, humiliating its monarchs and peoples, and introducing its new subjects to the disquieting notions of nationalism and revolt. Though the French Revolution was begun by moderate bourgeoisie who wanted little more than a constitutional monarchy, it quickly turned in less predictable directions, spurred by the socio-economic demands of peasants and laborers, and by a core of fanatics quite willing to use force and terror to compass their objectives. Nonetheless, the chief exporter of the French Revolution was no working-class radical, no political intellectual or simple terrorist, but a brilliant general named Napoleon Bonaparte, who nearly constructed a European-wide French empire.

Because of its historical richness, the French Revolution has produced intense scholarly debate and some elegant insights. To Karl Marx, and to a spate of historian-disciples as various as E. J. Hobsbawm, Albert Soboul, and Georges Lefebvre, the French Revolution resulted from a clash of economically-based social classes. For Lefebvre, whose work has been particularly influential in recent years, the most important cause of the Revolution was the rise of the bourgeoisie, or merchant class, who attempted to seize power from the landed nobility, the Catholic Church and the monarchy.

More recently, Lefebvre's class-centered view has been attacked by other scholars. In 1955 the English historian Alfred Cobban described Lefebvre's interpretation as a "myth" and argued that much of French feudalism had been swept away before the Revolution even began. Other scholars, including Philip Dawson, Roland Mousnier, Robert Forster, and Eleanor Barber have demonstrated in a variety of ways that a simple class interpretation of the Revolution may not work.

Another historian, Robert R. Palmer, has seen the French Revolution as but a part of a larger "Age of the Democratic Revolutions in the West." Along with the American Revolution and other struggles, the French Revolution became, for Palmer, one of the episodes that eventually resulted in modern democracy. Other experts, quite predictably, have questioned Palmer's thesis, observing that Palmer's hypothesis obscures the uniqueness of the French Revolution itself.

The French Revolution has also been the starting point for much theorizing about revolutions in general. From the time of Marx to the present day, the French Revolution has preoccupied historians and social scientists interested in developing theoretical models for revolution. In 1938, George S. Pettee began to use the term "great revolution" to describe the French Revolution and by implication any others that were characterized by social as well as political change.

In the same year, Crane Brinton published his monograph, *The Anatomy of Revolution,* in which he compared four revolutions, specifically the English, French, American, and Russian. He concluded, in a rather tentative way, that revolutions tend to follow a cyclical pattern in which the center of action moves from the more conservative political "right" toward the radical "left." Then, after a period of extreme revolutionary violence, or "terror," the revolution once again begins to move right, as if in reaction to the extremities of the terror.

Brinton also noted certain "uniformities" in all of the revolutions he discussed: that they occurred in societies on the upgrade economically; that their leaders tended to be economically secure and optimistic; that they were characterized by class antagonisms, but of a very complex kind; that they often witnessed a "transfer of allegiance of the intellectuals" to the side of the revolution; that the breakdown of an inefficient government seemed to be a precondition for revolutionary change; and that, prior to the revolution, the old landed and ruling classes lost heart, with some actually going over to the side of the revolution.

More recently, ever in pursuit of more accurate conceptual models for revolution, Chalmers Johnson has proposed no less than six specific revolutionary types. In the Johnson scheme the French Revolution becomes one of several "Jacobin Communist revolutions," a category that also includes the twentieth-century Russian and Chinese revolutions.

The French Revolution has thus contributed much to the debate about revolutions in general, but what of its own innate causes? Here, too, there is controversy. Nonetheless, certain patterns of causation have emerged out of recent scholarship. These can be grouped into several categories: demographic, social, economic, governmental, financial, and intellectual.

As Jacques Godechot observed many years ago, it is likely that the French Revolution was caused indirectly by the demographic revolution of the eighteenth century. Despite stratospheric infant mortality, the French population increased markedly in the years before 1789. From the fourteenth century to the eighteenth the total population of France had never, according to Godechot, exceeded eighteen million. In 1730, however, this began to change, and by 1789 the population had risen to twenty-six million. This dramatic population rise was not peculiar to France. England, for example, showed a significant population growth in the eighteenth century as well. The difference lay in the fact that England could absorb excess population, while France could not. The English Industrial Revolution created a demand for labor that the French agricultural economy could not match. While a new breed of French economists, the Physiocrats, emphasized the scientific cultivation of the land, it is probable that French agriculture in the eighteenth century could not meet the demands of the rising population. After 1770 excessive rainfall and heat produced famine conditions in France, and in the years before 1789 there was a shortage of bread in the cities.

The demographic crisis fertilized a growing social discontent among the masses of French poor. By any modern European standard, the social system of pre-revolutionary France was grossly inequitable, with the bulk of taxation falling on the poorest, yet most productive, segments of the population. Most peasants did not hold enough land to feed themselves, and much of what they produced was sopped up by the state in taxes. The peasantry was obliged to hire out periodically as wage-laborers, but this option was compromised in the eighteenth century by population growth. Because the rising population made labor abundant, wages in the countryside rose much more slowly than prices. To the burdens of inflation and taxation were added those of feudal dues, which may have been more rigorously collected in the eighteenth century than previously. Finally, as population increased so did pressure on available land. As agricultural plots became inevitably smaller they became less productive, making subsistence even more difficult.

Some of the same pheonomena appeared in the cities as well. By 1789 Paris was a city of perhaps 650,000 people, but of these only about twenty percent had sufficient wealth to rise above the subsistence level. In Paris, and in other cities, the poor constituted a vaguely-defined mass, but one increasingly segregated in miserable, and potentially explosive, geographic districts. According to William Doyle, as many as 100,000 poor made up a "floating population" of migrant workers who moved between Paris and the countryside, a perfect medium for spreading discontent. The price of bread and other foodstuffs grew enormously in the eighteenth century, and exceeded the amount that an urban laborer could sometimes pay. Certain taxes on goods entering cities, like the *octrois* in Paris, put the cost of life's necessities farther out of reach. As the poor flooded into Paris and other towns, overstraining municipal services, exhausting the meagre resources of charity, provoking by their violence an equally violent response from authority, they grew resentful of authority itself.

Also troubled and resentful, but for different reasons, was the bourgeoisie, that ill-defined group of French citizens who had become relatively prosperous through banking, trade, or other enterprises. Though they constituted, by one estimate, less than nine percent of the population, the bourgeoisie controlled a disproportionate, if not yet predominate, portion of the national wealth. Nonetheless, the bourgeoisie began to feel that they did not enjoy the political influence that their wealth entitled them. Some bourgeois tried to obtain prestige by buying state offices and titles of nobility. While such practices do indicate a certain lack of class consciousness, it is hard to believe that at least some bourgeoisie did not resent their lack of political privileges and the contempt with which the old nobility treated them. As a literate group, the bourgeoisie could read in justification the writers of the Enlightenment, who argued for the abolition or rationalization of traditional political institutions and the extension of political privileges.

More privileged than the bourgeoisie were the nobility. According to some studies, the nobility comprised less than one percent of the population of France, yet controlled a massive amount of its land and material wealth. In addition to certain social privileges, such as the right to wear a sword and display a coat of arms, the nobility was exempted from the mass of taxation that fell on the other legal classes. While some of the nobility served the state in military or legal capacities, some members of this class had been reared in a tradition of opposition to royal authority. For centuries the nobility had competed with the monarchy for the supreme authority in the French state. Louis XIV had successfully challenged the power of the old nobility, but the nobles had enjoyed a resurgence in power after his death. As the French monarchy, overburdened by wars, suffered from one financial crisis after another in the eighteenth century, the nobility fought off attempts to end their tax-exempt status and were irresolute or hostile in the face of appeals to rally to the king and his ministers.

Societal disaffection only complicated other problems faced by the French state—most specifically in the interrelated areas of personality, government, and finance.

French absolutism was a form of government that could only be successful if the reigning monarch was strong and vigorous. From the time of Louis XIV to the eve of the Revolution, successive French monarchs isolated themselves from those they proposed to rule. This unfortunate division between court and country was aggravated by the weak personalities of eighteenth century French monarchs. Louis XV and Louis XVI, whose reigns fill most of the years of the eighteenth century, lacked the assertiveness and knowledge to rule successfully and chose their ministers from a closed circle of churchmen, courtiers, high bureaucrats, and lawyers.

Though some of these ministers were able enough, they could not contain the long-term financial crisis that progressively hobbled the conduct of government. The long series of colonial and European wars that began with Louis XIV and continued in staccato fashion until 1815 resulted at once in increased taxation and increased indebtedness. The lack of financial solvency was worsened by waste, extravagance, corruption, and the employment of tax farmers instead of disciplined revenue officials.

The monarchy and its ministers proved unable to make the structural changes that might have alleviated the financial crisis. Short-term solutions, such as the securing of loans at high interest, papered over but did not solve the problem. Any effort at serious reform met with a hostile reaction from the nobility. René Nicolas de Maupeou, the chancellor of Louis XV, tried to reform the judiciary, end the sale of government offices, and discipline the administration, but he was opposed by the nobles in the Parlement of Paris and ill-served by his aging sovereign. On Louis' death in 1774, his grandson and successor, Louis XVI, dismissed Maupeou in order to conciliate the nobles. Louis also restored the noble-dominated parlements, the uncontrollable law courts that Maupeou had dissolved precisely because they were a threat to reform.

Louis XVI followed much the same pattern with Maupeou's successors. The first of his finance ministers was Jacques Turgot, a leading physiocratic economic thinker. Turgot abolished restrictions on grain sales, did away with the guilds that hindered economic expansion, and dispensed with the *corvée*, the much-hated custom of requiring the peasantry to perform free labor for the state. He also urged a general land tax, which would fall on all classes, including the previously exempt nobility and clergy. Louis, lacking the will to support Turgot's policies, dismissed him in 1776.

Jacques Necker, another of Maupeou's successors, was chosen at least as much for his ability to secure emergency loans as for his devotion to reform. After doing the monarchy still more damage by making public compromising financial data, Necker left the government in 1781. No stronger were the policies of Charles Alexandre Calonne, who emerged as Louis' chief minister in 1783. After beginning as a free spender, Calonne reversed himself in 1786 and revived Turgot's land tax proposal. In an attempt to get the tax reform passed, Calonne persuaded Louis XVI to summon an Assembly of Notables, thinking that a hand-picked alternative to the parlements would be amenable to reform. He was quite wrong. The proposals were rejected and Calonne dismissed. Calonne's successor, the clergyman Lomenie de Brienne, was no more successful in forcing a similar measure through the noble-dominated Parlement of Paris.

Louis XVI, belatedly realizing that his acquiescence to the nobility had gained him nothing, dissolved the Parlement of Paris and sent its members into internal exile, but the nobility continued to defy him. As riots broke out across the country and France slipped into what could be described as a pre-revolutionary situation, Louis XVI reached into the French medieval past and summoned the Estates General, the only institution that could assent to the taxes so necessary to save his government. Without knowing it, Louis had taken the step that made revolution possible.

B. A Nobleman Out of Step: Lafayette and the Failure of the Moderate Revolution

As the agricultural year of 1789 moved from the severity of winter to the shortages of spring, the people of France, with a slowness borne of lack of practice, chose their representatives to the Estates-General. The Estates-General, composed as it was of representatives from the three medieval classes or estates, was in reality not one body but three. According to tradition, each of the three estates—the clergy, the nobility, and the commonalty (by this time dominated by the bourgeoisie)—met in a different place, and this separation gave the monarchy at least a chance for control. Also in the monarchy's favor was the fact that the Estates-General had not met for years, and this lack of experience increased still more the opportunity for royal dominance.

Louis XVI, with a lack of initiative that was all too typical, failed to perceive these opportunities. He did not lead; he made no attempt to frame or present a program of reform. This combination of indifference and incompetence helped insure that initiative passed to the bourgeois-dominated third estate, who promptly urged that the estates meet together rather than separately, thus constituting a National Assembly.

In response to this alarming development the king at first took action, and then temporized. Initially, Louis sent his agents to lock up the building in which the National Assembly would meet. Then, after the third estate met on a tennis court, and its representatives swore a solemn oath not to bow to such intimidation, Louis backed down. On June 24, 1789, the three estates were given royal permission to meet together as the National Assembly. The worst possible situation for the monarchy had come to pass: the three legal classes were now in a position to combine against the ruling institution.

Other groups, not represented in the Estates-General, had also begun to express their displeasure. From March onward, even as the elections to the Estates-General were taking place, rural and urban rioting had begun. Peasants attacked the chateaux of their absentee landlords; in Paris, in the Faubourg St-Antoine, a mob stormed and burned the wallpaper works of Reveillon. Slowly pressure from the poor began to undermine moderate elements and create opportunities for emerging radical leaders. As a political revolution began in the National Assembly, the beginnings of a social revolution were emerging in the cities and the countryside.

Watching these events, and participating in some of them, was the Marquis de Lafayette. Born Marie-Joseph-Paul-Yves-Roch-Gilbert du Motier in 1757, Lafayette possessed an impeccable noble pedigree. If Lafayette's ancestry tied him to the French feudal past, the subsequent events of his life made him familiar with, even sympathetic to, the events of 1789.

Heir to an immense fortune, Lafayette compounded it when he married Adrienne, the second daughter of the Count of Ayen. As a well-connected young man, Lafayette was able to attach himself to the court of Louis XVI with ease, but royal service failed to satisfy him. The ideas of the Enlightenment were in the air, and Lafayette apparently came into contact with them. When the news of the American Revolution reached him, Lafayette, uniting a belief in social contract theory with an immodest desire for military glory, set out to assist the American colonists in their struggle against the British.

Lafayette arrived in America in 1777, well after the Revolution began. He quickly made up for lost time. He cultivated a lifelong friendship with George Washington and fought with honor on several occasions, especially at the Battle of Brandywine and during the Yorktown campaign. In the latter case, it was Lafayette's detachment that drove Cornwallis across Virginia and sealed the British forces on the Yorktown peninsula. There, with escape by sea cut off by a French fleet and with Washington's army preventing escape by land, the British suffered a final and humiliating defeat. Because he helped inflict losses on the British, a fact that gladdened every

French heart, Lafayette was lionized when he returned home in 1782. Hailed as "the Hero of Two Worlds," he was promoted to general.

What Lafayette might not have realized was that his actions in America made him suspect to some of the nobility and to the monarchy. Then, again, perhaps he did not care. Regardless of his personal feelings, Lafayette had begun a fateful process that alienated him from his class and background. In fact, Lafayette had gone to America in the teeth of a royal prohibition. Though the king punished Lafayette only lightly on his return, Louis XVI and his consort, Marie Antoinette, never fully trusted him again. Decorations Lafayette might receive at the hands of the king, but honors only seemed to reinforce Lafayette's pilgrimage from absolutism.

In the years before the French Revolution, Lafayette appeared to have a very good time. He traveled to America where he was cheered at every crossroads and visited Washington at Mount Vernon. There is little doubt that such adulation turned Lafayette's head. Jefferson noted in the Frenchman "a canine appetite for popularity and fame," but thought, quite wrongly, that he would outgrow it.

With no military campaigns left to fight, Lafayette enlisted himself, in true Enlightenment style, in the cause of domestic reform. Deciding that the Huguenots, the French Calvinists, were the "victims of an intolerable despotism," he tried to restore to them the civil rights that the French monarchy had taken away. Antislavery was Lafayette's other preoccupation. He purchased plantations, and the freedom of some forty-eight slaves, in order to create a model for "progressive emancipation."

Much to his delight, Lafayette was selected as a member of the Assembly of Notables summoned by the king to restore the financial system of the realm. During the Assembly's brief life, Lafayette pushed pro-Huguenot measures and exposed a number of state financial scandals. He then appalled monarchists and conservatives even more by calling for a National Assembly.

Lafayette may have, in fact, been formulating plans to create a constitutional monarchy. With friends like Talleyrand, Condorcet, and the Abbé Sieyès, Lafayette created a club, the "Thirty," with just such an aim. Confident, immensely popular, Lafayette may have seen himself in a role similar to that of his friend George Washington: as a leader capable of saving his country from chaos by strong leadership and moderate reform. When Lafayette's constitutional proposals failed to attract interest, he expressed his disappointment in a letter to Washington, complaining that poverty and ignorance had made the French people too sluggish and lacking in courage to improve their lot. Seldom has a leader more seriously misjudged the temper of a people.

Lafayette came to the Estates-General in 1789 as an elected representative of the nobility. Nonetheless Lafayette supported the demands of the bourgeoisie in the Third Estate to unite the Estates-General into a single body as the National Assembly. From that point on, Lafayette the aristocrat became, politically-speaking, a bourgeois.

In July of 1789 Lafayette presented to the newly-created National Assembly his "Declaration of the Rights of Man and of the Citizen." So proud was Lafayette of this document that he claimed Jefferson found it excellent enough to send on to Washington. In truth, Lafayette's Declaration, in radically revised form, became the first important document of the French Revolution. Under its sweeping provisions, the nobility surrendered their feudal privileges, all men were guaranteed civil rights, and the principle of equality before the law was enshrined. Following Rousseau, the Declaration proclaimed that the law was derived from the General Will of the people. The idea of the social contract had passed into the French political system.

While Lafayette celebrated his association with the bourgeoisie and congratulated himself on his Declaration, events on urban streets and in the countryside began to careen out of control. During the terrible time known as the "Great Fear," which occurred in the late summer of 1789, a sense of calamity troubled the country, and peasants roamed rural areas, burning the homes of their betters. The people Lafayette had once condemned for sluggishness began to move. In July the old fortress-prison of the Bastille fell to the Paris mob. Conservative nobles fled France. From exile these nobles, known as *emigrés,* plotted against the moderate revolution. In October the women of Paris marched on Versailles, obliging the king, and thus the National Assembly, to return to Paris. In Paris and other towns revolutionary communes were created, to be led by radicals organized in the political clubs that were springing up all over the country.

As if in response to the events of July, Lafayette identified himself even more closely with the bourgeoisie. One day after the fall of the Bastille, a National Guard was established in Paris. By using his popularity, Lafayette became its commander, admitting to its ranks only bourgeoisie. Lafayette now had the means to forward and protect his cherished idea of a moderate constitutional monarchy.

With Lafayette's National Guard at the ready, the National Assembly, which had renamed itself the Constituent Assembly, set about enshrining the moderate revolution into law. A new constitution set up a limited monarchy, which was to share power with a Legislative Assembly. This body was to be elected indirectly by a limited number of "active" or tax-paying citizens. The Constituent Assembly was empowered to review the king's important decisions and could, with some difficulty, override his veto. In quick succession, the Constituent Assembly also seized the lands of the Catholic Church in France, reorganized regional governments into administrative "departments," made French clergy the servants of the state and, in the Le Chapelier Law of 1791, outlawed labor unions and strikes. In sum, by the summer of 1791, the Constituent Assembly had accomplished its moderate revolution. France had become a constitutional monarchy based on liberal political principles.

All of this roughly coincided with the height of Lafayette's personal popularity. In mid-July 1790, Lafayette oversaw a "Festival of Federation" in Paris, where he received all of the adulation he could have expected. Increasingly, however, Lafayette found himself isolated both from the monarchy he had sworn to protect and reestablish on constitutional principles, and from the radicals who were organizing the people on the streets of Paris. On one visit to the court, Lafayette was publicly labeled a "Cromwell" by a noble attendant. At the same time, Louis XVI made Lafayette's defense of the monarchy more difficult. In June of 1791 Louis attempted to flee the country, but characteristically botched the job. He was caught and ignominiously returned to his palace. The "Flight to Varennes" demonstrated to all that Louis had not really accepted the idea of a constitutional monarchy, no matter how dear it was to Lafayette, and gave encouragement to the radicals.

Having identified himself with the constitutional moderates and the bourgeoisie, Lafayette found himself condemned alike by conservative elements who supported the king and radical republicans who wanted the monarchy out of government altogether. By the latter group he was described as "a rascal who plays the patriot" in order to conceal an affection for the monarchy. The radicals also mistrusted Lafayette's National Guard. It soon became obvious that they had reason. In July of 1791 Lafayette led the National Guard against a crowd of radical republicans who had gathered at the Champ de Mars to demand the abdication of the king. In a volley of shots, some fifty demonstrators lost their lives. Lafayette had irrevocably committed himself to a constitutional monarchy, and his actions alienated him from the people of Paris. A public outcry forced Lafayette to resign from the National Guard.

As Lafayette's popularity began to disintegrate, divisions between the classes became more severe, and the king temporized, which further compromised his position. The massacre of the Champ de Mars was followed by a "Tricolor Terror" directed against the republicans in Paris. In August of 1791 the Assembly voted to raise the property qualification for members of the new Legislative Assembly, which met in September. Only in the same month, after an embarrassing silence, did Louis XVI recognize the new constitution, but he made it clear he was still less than convinced. In November the king used his limited veto power under the constitution to quash decrees of the Assembly against exiled nobility. The constitutional moderates might control the Assembly, but they clearly did not control the king.

More importantly, they did not control the streets of Paris. Because it housed both the king and the Assembly, Paris had become the crucible of the Revolution, and the Parisian radicals actively sought the support of the city's volatile populace. A growing presence in Paris were the political clubs. There were the *Cordeliers,* led by Danton, Marat, Desmoulins, and Hébert; the *Feuillants,* the moderate monarchists who included Lafayette as a member; and the *Jacobins,* under Maximilien Robespierre. It was the Jacobin Club, brilliantly led, possessing connections to similar radical societies in the provinces, that posed the greatest threat to the moderate monarchists in the Assembly and appealed most successfully to the masses on the Paris streets. Jacobins also filled the Paris Commune, the revolutionary government of the city.

The Paris poor were further radicalized by interrelated international and domestic crises. In August of 1791 the rulers of Austria and Prussia issued the Declaration of Pillnitz, in which they pledged to act militarily to support the French king if other crowned heads would support them. In the spring of 1792 the Assembly declared war on the Austrian Empire. Soon France was at war with much of Europe. By summer the Duke of Brunswick, the commander of the anti-French military coalition, felt strong enough to issue a manifesto threatening the destruction of Paris.

With the war came defeat, economic dislocation, and, above all, rising food prices. All of these fell hard on the Parisian working classes and moved many of them in the direction of the Jacobins. A staccato series of counterrevolutionary uprisings and food riots infected the country, resulting in the death of at least one provincial mayor.

Ironically, the war gave Lafayette one last chance to gain control of the revolution that was now sweeping around him. By the spring of 1792 Lafayette had been placed in command of one of three revolutionary armies, hastily gathered to defend France against a formidable European coalition. In the early days of this War of the First Coalition (1792-1797), however, the poorly-trained revolutionary armies did badly, diminishing Lafayette's reputation as a military hero.

Nonetheless, with a force of 52,000 men at his disposal, Lafayette decided to gamble for power. He proposed to crush the radicals in Paris, and perhaps even hoped to rule in the name of his jealous, beleaguered king. During two fateful days in June, Lafayette tried to close down the Jacobin Club and force the Legislative Assembly to do his bidding. He failed miserably. The pressure of war, the food shortages, the cries in the streets, led to an increasing clamor for the removal of the king. On August 10 it happened. The monarchy was overthrown, and a National Convention summoned to govern in place of the Legislative Assembly. After vainly summoning his army to march on Paris, Lafayette was forced to flee. The hero of the American Revolution was now considered a traitor to revolutionary France. In August, Lafayette defected to the Austrians, who held him captive until 1797. Already a refugee from his own class, Lafayette had become a man without a country. Overestimating his power to control events, conditioned by his American experience to a vision of a moderate and constitutional revolution, Lafayette was left bemused by the radical revolution that roared by him.

Napoleon, rusticating at St. Helena in the twilight of his career, was succinct in his assessment of the reasons for Lafayette's failure: "The Marquis was a simpleton," he rather uncharitably remarked. Such an evaluation is perhaps unjust. What Lafayette's strange career demonstrates is the truth that men and women do not always control their times; that they are in fact often controlled by them. Like so many others in history, Lafayette and his supporters were men out of step, puzzled by the very events they hoped to dominate.

It must have been a comfort to Lafayette that he lived to participate in political environments which proved more congenial. Allowed by a victorious Napoleon to return to France as a landed gentleman, he survived to sit in the Chamber of Deputies that accompanied the restoration of the Bourbon monarchy in 1815. In 1830, Lafayette and the bourgeoisie were at last able to make and control a revolution to their liking. In that year, Lafayette, again the commander of the National Guard, helped engineer the overthrow of King Charles X, who was replaced by a constitutional monarch named Louis Philippe. This done, Lafayette retired. Four years later he died in Paris, the same city that had rejected him so decisively in 1792. It had taken many years but Lafayette had at last found circumstances that meshed with his ideas.

C. Robespierre and the Terror: The Radicalization of the Revolution

By the time Lafayette had fled, the Revolution had begun to reel from crisis to crisis. Fragile enough in peacetime, the French Revolution of the moderates was dissolved by the solvent of war. Hysteria and hunger fueled a continuing radicalism. In August of 1792 an "Extraordinary Tribunal" was created to judge the "enemies of the Revolution." Then, as the heat of August gave way to fall, and enemy armies gathered at the gates of France, Paris flamed into violence. In an odious display of panic and retribution, a band of cut-throats invaded the jails where alleged "counter-revolutionaries" were kept. Perhaps one thousand human beings—priests, aristocrats, Swiss Guards, plus a number of luckless thieves and prostitutes—were dragged out of the prisons and butchered in the streets. One aristocrat, the Princess de Lamballe, who had the misfortune of being well-known to Marie Antoinette, was hacked to death with sabres and pikes. Thereafter, the body was sexually mutilated, and the heart ripped from the corpse. Finally, the decapitated head was borne to a hairdresser's shop, where the hair was washed and powdered, so, the murderers claimed, it could be easily recognized by the queen. These atrocities, known as the "September Massacres," were proof that the Revolution in Paris was surging out of control.

The violence in the streets was counterpointed by the first successful military engagement of the Revolution and by a more controlled retribution. At Valmy, on September 20, French armies temporarily ended the threat of foreign invasion. Only after Valmy was there time enough to gather together the National Convention that was supposed to govern the country. Initially, however, the Convention had a more violent aim in mind. The day after it convened, the Convention ordered the arrest of Louis XVI, and by December had placed the king on trial.

For the first, and nearly the last, time in his life, Louis faced a crisis with aplomb and wisdom. Like Charles I, the English king who preceded him to the tribunal and scaffold the century before, Louis apparently did not fear death, worrying far more about his family than his fate. His trial was a farce and an indignity. Even Louis' cousin, the Duke of Orleans, known as Philip Egalité for his acceptance of the principles of the Revolution, was persuaded to vote for execution. In such an atmosphere, the verdict was a foregone conclusion.

In the days before his death Louis ate sparingly but well, and slept deeply. Early on the execution day, January 21, 1793,

Louis was borne to the Place du Temple in a coach. At the guillotine one executioner tied his hands in a way that made it difficult for him to walk; another cut his hair, pocketing it for sale later. The incessant role of drums negated Louis' efforts to make a final speech. Shortly thereafter, bound ignominiously to a plank, lying on his belly, Louis' neck was positioned under the blade. The king was decapitated almost instantly, his dripping head then displayed to the mob. The corpse was taken to the cemetery of the Madelaine where it was buried in quicklime. Marie Antoinette, Queen of France, suffered the same fate in October.

Swept up in these events was a young lawyer from Arras named Maximilien Robespierre. Robespierre was a genuine bourgeois who had characteristically followed the profession of his father. Educated early on by the Oratorian friars, the young Robespierre won a scholarship to the College of Louis-le-Grand in the capital. When he returned to Arras in 1780 with his law degree he set up housekeeping with his sister and built a prosperous practice. Soon after, he became a judge in a diocesan church court.

In spite of these apparently conservative connections, Robespierre began to exhibit republican tendencies. He joined a local intellectual society, where the ideas of the Enlightenment were undoubtedly discussed; he legally represented the poor; he wrote a prize-winning essay in which he condemned dehumanizing punishments, and another in which he attacked absolute monarchy. Then, in 1789, Robespierre was given the opportunity to translate thought into action. He was elected, as a representative of the third estate, to the Estates-General.

By the time Robespierre arrived at Versailles to join the Estates-General, he was a young man of thirty, convinced of the wrong of capital punishment, sure that the actions of men could humanize the world, a passionate believer in equality. He also believed passionately in himself. There was apparently within Robespierre a kind of perfect self-righteousness. Those who disagreed with him were, in Robespierre's mind, quite wrong. This self-righteousness, by its very intensity, had the potential to overawe even his most closely-held principles. "A lover of mankind," observed one historian of Robespierre, "he could not enter with sympathy into the minds of his own neighbors."

From the moment of its inception, Robespierre was a member of the Jacobin Club, and at times presided over its meetings. Robespierre was a persuasive speaker, and he supported the more radical ideas voiced in the National Assembly: universal suffrage, the democratization of the National Guard, all of the attacks on the powers of the church and the king. When his life was endangered by the Tricolor Terror, Robespierre took temporary refuge with a Paris cabinet-maker and merged even more completely with the growing radicalism of the city. The Jacobin Club, from which all the moderate members eventually defected, also fueled Robespierre's radicalism.

In speeches and in a newspaper he founded Robespierre continued to hammer at his powerful enemies. He attacked the king for plotting with the Austrians against the Revolution, aristocratic officers for betraying the revolutionary armies, and the Marquis de Lafayette for his bourgeois moderation.

When the conservative Legislative Assembly met, it was boycotted by Robespierre and his Jacobin colleagues, but this certainly did not remove him from public attention. He obtained the post of public prosecutor of Paris, kept up his criticisms of the army, and endeared himself to the *sans-culottes,* the urban workers who were the foot-soldiers of the radical revolution, by passionate speech-making and cries for justice. In August of 1792, when the monarchy was overthrown, Robespierre was elected to the insurrectionary Paris Commune, which served as the revolutionary government of Paris. In September he went to the National Convention at the head of the Paris delegation. Earlier in the same month, by refusing to condemn the September Massacres, Robespierre had in a sense become one with those who favored revolutionary violence.

Though it had assembled in a time of crisis, the Convention did little to alleviate it. In fact, it only made matters worse. While the execution of the king ended royalist plotting with the enemies of the Revolution, it also robbed France of a symbol of unity, authority, and tradition. These things the National Convention was in no position to replace. The peasants, restive enough under royalist taxes legitimized by centuries, chafed at the new taxes and the huge levies of young men demanded by the Convention. In March 1793 the peasants rebelled in the Vendée.

Provincial differences, largely suppressed under the monarchy, also sharpened after Louis' death. Bourgeois in the provincial cities, often more moderate than the radicals in Paris, launched a "federalist" movement, demanding an end to the dominance of the capital over other areas of France. By the summer of 1793 federalist revolts had broken out in Normandy and Bourdeaux.

The Convention complicated matters by issuing wholesale declarations of war. With France already at war with Austria and Prussia, the Convention, virtually on the heels of the execution of the king, declared war on Great Britain, Holland, and within a few months, Spain.

Faced with a crisis aggravated by its own actions, the Convention was forced to take extraordinary measures to maintain order and control; these eventually accrued to Robespierre's benefit. In a series of five steps the Convention created a Committee of General Security to police the country, empowered a Revolutionary Tribunal to attend to its enemies, authorized the creation of surveillance committees to spy out disaffection, sent out representatives to prod the army and local governments, and appointed a Committee of Public Safety. This last step, undertaken in April 1793, proved to be the most important for Robespierre.

The Committee of Public Safety, as a creation of the Convention, had to have its powers reconfirmed by that body once a month. The Committee was empowered, in the interim, to perform the administrative functions that the Convention, in its unwieldy form, could not. Initially dominated by Danton, the Committee proved no more successful than the Convention in controlling domestic or foreign affairs.

Robespierre set out to dominate both the Committee of Public Safety and the Convention that had called it into being. Robespierre, who had always opposed the export of the Revolution by warfare, profited as the wars went badly and caused food shortages in Paris. In late February 1793 food riots broke out in the capital and the convention was forced to prohibit the hoarding of food. In March the French general, Dumouriez, began to conspire with the Austrians after a massive French defeat at Neerwinden and went over to the side of the enemy. The poor performance of the army and the food shortages gave Robespierre his opportunity. As the public prosecutor of Paris, he was constantly before the masses and used his position to denounce the royalist-officered army. As the leader of the Paris Commune, the revolutionary group that had led opposition to the king and called the Convention into being, Robespierre was in an excellent position to exploit the divisions in the latter body and eventually seize control.

The Convention was split up among several loosely-aligned factions. There were, first, the Girondists. This group, the most urgently pro-war faction in the Convention, had forced through all the declarations of war but had lost popularity as the French armies failed and the food shortages worsened. Robespierre and his colleagues in the Jacobin Club dominated a rival Convention faction called the "Mountain." The Mountain, unlike the provincially-based Girondists, had massive political strength in Paris as well as in other areas of France. Aligned with neither group, but desiring to be on the winning side in any power struggle were the delegates of the faction called the "Plain."

Beginning in late May, Robespierre made his move. At his instigation, the Parisian radicals took to the streets. By June the Girondists were purged from the Convention. Robespierre had united his popularity with the *sans-culottes,* his power-base in the

Paris Commune, his position in the Jacobin Club, and his membership in the Mountain, into a successful bid for control of the Convention. Only the Committee of Public Safety eluded his grasp.

The Convention, prodded by Robespierre, drafted a new constitution in June, 1793. This document was by far the most democratic constitution that any European revolution had ever produced. It called for universal manhood suffrage, the right of revolution, the subordination of the right of property to that of the public interest, and a broad spectrum of human rights.

The new constitution, however, was never applied. Federalist revolts, military reverses, and economic hardships continued to plague the Revolution but paved the way for Robespierre's inclusion on the Committee of Public Safety. On July 10 the Convention refused to reconfirm the powers of the Committee, and Danton and his followers fell from power. Almost simultaneously Charlotte Corday, a young woman sympathetic to the Girondists, assassinated Marat, Robespierre's fellow-Mountaineer and one of his leading rivals for power. With Danton in disgrace and Marat dead, the Committee of Public Safety came into Robespierre's reach. On July 27 Robespierre became a member of the Committee of Public Safety. In less than a year, Robespierre consolidated his power by arranging the executions of Danton and his followers. Hébert, a rival in the Commune of Paris, went to the block with all of his allies at about the same time.

Robespierre was now the leader of France, but his position was a paradoxical one. Having used chaos and disorder to obtain power, he would have to end both to stay there. Without any kind of program, Robespierre resolved to use the Committee of Public Safety to enforce order. To do this, he readily sacrificed his long-avowed democratic ideals, and concluded that "one single will" was needed to save the Revolution. The tool that he chose to impose that will he called the "reign of terror."

"The Terror is Justice—prompt, severe, inflexible." This is how Robespierre described the new revolutionary weapon, which he began to use in mid-1793. Commissioners of the Convention were sent into the provinces, cooperating with the local Jacobin Clubs, and combatting uprisings with revolutionary violence. The Convention also passed the "Law of Suspects," which empowered the government to incarcerate without trial any it deemed dangerous, and perhaps half a million French citizens spent time in prison. Local officials and revolutionary committees were turned into agents of the Committee of Public Safety. A reorganization of the Revolutionary Tribunal followed. This and other revolutionary courts assessed some 17,000 death sentences, and perhaps 10,000 more were executed without trial. In spite of its viciousness, Robespierre saw the

Terror as a measure to contain even more destructive violence and used it to pacify vast areas of France that were in the grip of civil war. Perhaps as many as seventy percent of all executions under the terror occurred in areas infected by rebellion or civil war. Still, the Terror was severe. After the rebellion in the Vendée was crushed, thousands went to their deaths at Nantes. When the revolutionaries retook the rebellious city of Lyons, many of the inhabitants were massacred. By the Law of 22 Prairial, passed in June 1794, juries could convict without hearing evidence or argument, and the guillotine grew even busier in Paris.

While the Terror subdued France, other measures were passed to stabilize the food crisis and to enable France to prosecute the war. In August of 1793 the entire male population was made liable to bear arms. This *levée en masse* enabled the French to place no less than fourteen armies in the field to oppose both foreign invasion and domestic revolt. In September, the Law of the Maximum was instituted. This measure set national maximum prices for grain and other commodities, and fixed wages. Though it never worked perfectly, the Law of the Maximum did help with the provisioning of the armies and with rationing.

Nonetheless, like Lafayette before him, Robespierre overestimated his ability to control events. Overburdened by demands, Robespierre's health began to betray him, as did some of his colleagues in the Committee of Public Safety. Robespierre had inherited the Revolution by attacking the policies of those in power, but by now unpopular policies were identified with him. In response, Robespierre isolated himself from the Convention and the Committee of Public Safety. He grew aloof, failed to tend his power base, and confined his activities increasingly to the Jacobin Club. In May of 1794 fanatics attempted to assassinate him. Some revolutionaries whispered that Robespierre had gone too far; others, paradoxically, that he was too moderate. Revolutionary atheists disapproved of Robespierre's deistic cult of the Supreme Being; *sans-culottes* grew tired of continued food shortages and hardships.

On July 16, 1794, despite an impassioned speech, Robespierre lost his majority in the National Convention. Knowing by then that his power was ebbing, lacking the heart to lead an insurrection, Robespierre disheartened the last of his followers by a botched attempt at suicide. The soldiers of the National Convention found him at the Hôtel de Ville, his jaw and eloquence smashed by a self-administered pistol shot. On July 28 Robespierre led a procession of his disciples to the guillotine. The Terror he had helped to make swallowed him.

Less than twenty months separated the executions of Louis XVI and Robespierre. In the early days of the National Convention

Robespierre had risen no less than eleven times to demand the head of the king, but in the end he proved no more able to control the Revolution than his discredited monarch. Caught between his democratic, egalitarian ideals and other, more pragmatic, requirements—the need to fill hungry mouths, the need to defend his beloved Revolution against its internal and external enemies—Robespierre had chosen a path of selective violence. In the end that violence had claimed him.

In spite of its severity and destruction, the Terror made the Revolution irrevocable and able to defend itself. The Terror helped purge France from internal revolt, and enabled the Revolution to concentrate on its external enemies. The French armies, their masses of men raised and supplied by the harsh measures of the Terror, had begun at last to win victories; and it was the army and its leadership that would ultimately inherit the Revolution.

D. Revolution and War: Napoleon Bonaparte and the French Empire

"Robespierre has just died the death of traitors. His accomplices have perished with him and liberty is triumphant. *Patrie* [i.e. Country], Probity, Truth, your sacred names will no longer be sullied by lewd lips. . . ." With such contemporary comments the memory of Robespierre was hurried into oblivion. Robespierre had by his violence sought to preserve the Revolution; his successors, sometimes through similar means, sought to end it.

For all these reasons a new stage of the French Revolution has been said to begin with the execution of Robespierre. It has been called the Thermidorean Reaction. Ironically, it was Robespierre who gave this reactionary episode both its name and its force. Thermidor was a summer month in a new, revolutionary calendar created in Robespierre's period of power, and the Thermidorean Reaction itself, though it by no means ended extremism or violence, has often been seen as a period of retrenchment after the extremism of the Terror. During the Thermidorean Reaction, the older, established groups reasserted themselves and established by steps a conservative, republican government to their liking.

One of the many arrested and investigated in the wake of Robespierre's fall was a youthful military officer, Napoleon Bonaparte. It was to be a short interruption in a meteoric military career that was to last until 1815. Born not in France but on the island of Corsica in 1769, Napoleon was for much of his life a man favored by circumstances. Though he possessed noble antecedents, Napoleon's father, like Robespierre's, was a respectable bourgeois lawyer. Napoleon's father was also shrewd enough, after some initial resistance, to accept the reality of French occupation of Corsica. For his acquiescence, he received a government position for himself and the admission of his two older sons, Napoleon and Joseph, to the College d'Autun in France.

The young Napoleon was to become thoroughly French, and he was educated during the seed-time of the Revolution. Having decided on a military career, Napoleon moved from Autun, to the military school at Brienne, and finally to the Royal Military Academy at Paris. From there Napoleon graduated in 1785, with a very modest class standing, only four years before the outbreak of the French Revolution.

During those four years, Napoleon began to exhibit the contradictory tendencies that characterized the rest of his life. He trained as a royal artillery officer, indicating that he had found a home in the military; yet he soon left his regiment and returned to Corsica for an extended period, perhaps feeling a sense of apartness from the France of the Old Regime. If Napoleon felt alienated, it would not have been surprising. The officer corps of prerevolutionary France was awash with noble blood, and advancement owed something to social position and royal favor. It could not have been an easy situation for a young officer, uncomfortable in privileged society, whose reading included the works of Voltaire and Rousseau. An authoritarian by virtue of his profession, sworn to uphold the Old Regime, Napoleon nonetheless had become something of a revolutionary in his ideas.

"I was born," Napoleon once wrote, "as our country lay dying." Ambitious and opportunistic, Napoleon's career profited by the Revolution. As its successive stages swept away the old order and sought war with most of the monarchies of Europe, Napoleon could not help but benefit as officers of noble blood fell into disgrace or fled. Napoleon moved to establish his revolutionary credentials. He joined the Jacobin Club and developed a friendship with Robespierre. In 1793, due to the intervention of influential Corsicans, Napoleon received command of the National Guard artillery before the British-occupied port of Toulon. Napoleon's artillery pounded the British as they withdrew, and he became a hero in a country having too few of them. Soon thereafter, freshly wounded by a British bayonet, Napoleon became a general. He was then twenty-four years old. Years later, he protested that his rise to power owed nothing to intrigue or crime, but much "to the peculiar circumstances of the times." On the whole, this assessment is just.

Napoleon's career was interrupted, but not ended, by his Jacobin associations. He was quickly cleared of complicity in Robespierre's excesses, but for a time he languished on half-pay, turning down undesirable posts, contemplating service to the Ottoman sultan, and pursuing a mistress.

While Napoleon sulked, the French Revolution went through another metamorphosis. From July 1794 to October 1795 the Thermidorean Reaction ran its course, destroying every vestige of the Terror. The Committee of Public Safety was stripped of its power; the Jacobin Club closed down. In the economic sphere, the zeal of the Thermidoreans got the best of them. Determined to end the price controls imposed by Robespierre to feed Paris, the Thermidoreans unwittingly encouraged another round of rising food prices. To these economic woes were soon added others. Royalists became active again, and in southwestern France a vengeful "White Terror" was waged against Robespierre's disciples.

Only on the war fronts was there anything like good news. The War of the First Coalition died down as its members fell out. In Flanders the revolutionary armies proclaimed a Batavian Republic in 1795. In the same year the Prussians signed the Treaty of Basel with France on favorable terms, and two other German states, Hanover and Hesse-Cassel, followed Prussia's lead. Finally, in midsummer 1795, a British-sponsored royalist invasion was checked.

By August the military situation had stabilized sufficiently for the Convention, now dominated by moderate republicans, to proclaim yet another constitution. This document, called the Constitution of the Year III, created a republic, but on far different terms than those envisioned by Robespierre. Executive power was invested in a committee of five members, to be called the Directory. Also created was a legislature of two chambers, respectively called the Council of Ancients and the Council of Five Hundred. Initially, both bodies were to be dominated by Conventioneers. Thereafter, the two councils were to be selected by a complex system of indirect voting based on a narrow, property-holder's franchise.

The nature of the new constitution invited challenge because such a moderate settlement could please neither radicals nor royalists. The radicals, driven into hiding by the Thermidorean Reaction, did not emerge as a threat. The royalists were another matter. Assisted by the English, encouraged by a refugee nobility, the emigrés who plotted beyond the borders of France, the royalists sensed a possible victory. In their schemes the royalists were assisted, although unwittingly, by the Convention that, by insisting that its republican members dominate the Directory, had given them an issue. In October 1795, the royalists managed to raise a revolt in Paris.

The royalist revolt created a new opportunity for the unemployed General Bonaparte. The Directors, desperate for someone to quell the uprising, chose Napoleon. Relying on his artillery training, Bonaparte set cannon at the Church of St. Roche and ended the revolt with a "whiff of grapeshot." Ever after, Napoleon would put his artillery on an equality with men on the battlefield. It was a change in tactics that altered military history.

Napoleon's success in Paris allowed him to put his house in order. Awarded the command of the Army of Italy by a grateful Directory, Napoleon was well able to make a brilliant society marriage to the elegant Josephine de Beauharnais. By the spring of 1796 Napoleon was marching his army down the coast from Nice into Italy. In April he won victories at Millesimo and Mondavi, and these were merely two in a whole series of successful engagements that culminated in French control over much of the Italian peninsula. By the summer of 1797 Nice and Savoy were possessions of the French Republic; French troops garrisoned the fortresses of the Piedmont; French naval vessels moored off the Ionian Islands; and Genoa, Milan, Modena, Ferrara, Bologna, and the Romagna fell under French protection. The last four of these states were reorganized as the Cisalpine Republic, while Genoa was reborn as the Ligurian Republic. Napoleon had successfully midwifed one of the earliest dreams of the French Revolution: the export of its republican ideology abroad.

In October 1797 Napoleon's successes helped force Austria, which had quarreled with France over Italy for centuries, to come to peace terms in the Treaty of Campo Formio. In return for receiving the territory of Venice, the Austrians recognized French dominance over much of the rest of Italy, and secretly agreed to the cession of the left bank of the Rhine to France. By the stroke of a pen, Prussia was left to stand alone against the French in Europe.

In winning his victories Napoleon proved himself not only a brilliant commander but an apt pupil who had benefited from a reorientation of strategy and tactics made possible by the times in which he lived. Napoleon witnessed both a French and a military revolution, and in both he was an heir as well as a participant.

For much of the eighteenth century, warfare had been conducted by comparatively small numbers of professional soldiers, usually mercenaries, led by officers drawn from the landed classes. This elitist approach to combat was condemned by some of the *philosophes* and, with the coming of the French Revolution, became a practical impossibility. To ward off its many foes, the French revolutionary governments resorted to the *levée en masse,* the calling up of large numbers of conscripted men to create huge armies. By 1794 France had half a million men under arms.

Conscription changed the nature of warfare in revolutionary ways. In the old, elite armies, lives were expensive, as the individual soldier was highly-trained and precious. Frederick William of Prussia had doted on his tall grenadiers. The Revolution changed all that. Henceforward generals could count on having many thousands of men, each sworn to protect their motherland, whose lives could be more freely spent. As lives and bodies were lost, more men could be called up to serve and to die.

Because of the masses of men in service there was a need to revise military organization. Individual armies became too large to be commanded effectively and were broken down into smaller units called divisions. Each division had its own complement of cavalry, infantry, and, increasingly, artillery.

These smaller units could be used very creatively by a skilled commander. Divisions could be used singly, or massed in combination; one division could engage an enemy frontally while another could outflank it; one division could be used to attack an enemy while another was held in reserve to be utilized precisely at the moment when the enemy forces weakened. Napoleon became a master of these and other tactics and strategies, a genius at maneuver, at surprise, at dividing the forces of his enemies, at concentrating force against the weakness of opponents.

Napoleon also became a master of artillery, but here too he owed something to the experience of his predecessors. In the years after 1763 Jean Baptiste de Gribeauval, Inspector-General of the French army, began to standardize the production of cannon. Interchangeable parts, better gunsights, lighter and more maneuverable gun carriages all helped to make cannon a more formidable and useful weapon. Napoleon's cannoneers, many trained in the new military colleges that sprang up in the eighteenth century, were often the element of difference in his victories. A massive cannonade, Napoleon soon found, could more than balance the effect of masses of unblooded conscripts.

Napoleon possessed certain other advantages. Through the years Napoleon developed a number of experienced soldiers who functioned as an activist core in his armies. There is no doubt whatever, as accounts of some of his soldiers testify, that Napoleon could inspire men. He also found good commanders, and when he did he worked them nearly to death. At Napoleon's headquarters, staff officers slept on straw to be near a commander who waited for the last scouting report before moving his troops, or who would instantly alter battle plans to take advantage of the momentary weakness of a foe.

Napoleon, for all his able subordinates, remained his own chief-of-staff. When planning a campaign Napoleon was deliberately and usually overcautious, exaggerating the dangers he might face, but he was also able to take risks when warranted. "The impossible," Napoleon once said, "is the spectre of the timid and the refuge of a coward." Napoleon valued intelligence more than courage in his commanders, but he himself lacked neither quality. An inherent fatalism made Napoleon almost carelessly brave under fire.

While Napoleon honed his military skills, the Directory proved no more capable than its predecessors. In September 1797 the instability of the Directory was confirmed by the *Coup d'Etat* of Fructidor, which purged the government of the more reactionary Directors.

During this period Bonaparte executed one of his most daring campaigns, the Egyptian expedition. After flirting with the idea of invading Britain itself, Napoleon ruled out a cross-Channel invasion, deciding instead to weaken Britain by striking at the sea lanes to her empire. By taking Egypt, Napoleon could establish a presence in the Mediterranean, a vital connection to the British trading network.

Leaving an "army of England" concentrated around Boulogne in an effort to fool the British, Bonaparte's expeditionary force sailed for Egypt, eluding for the moment a British fleet under Admiral Nelson. In June 1798 Napoleon's forces took Malta, and, in early July, Alexandria, the gateway to the Ottoman province of Egypt, fell. By the end of July, after defeating the Ottomans at the Battle of the Pyramids, Napoleon's troops occupied Cairo.

Then, in early August, Napoleon experienced a change of fortune. Without warning, Nelson's pursuing fleet fell upon the French at Aboukir Bay. The French ships of the line, crowded into a confining harbor, had little opportunity to maneuver and were blown to pieces in the engagement known as the Battle of the Nile. Napoleon's overextended supply lines were sundered. His army was isolated in Egypt.

Napoleon's response was to fight desperately for survival. When the Ottoman Empire, in league with the British, declared war on France, Napoleon moved his forces into Syria, stormed Jaffa and invested Acre. Then, after an outbreak of the plague in his army forced a retreat back to Egypt, Napoleon turned back an Ottoman invasion at Aboukir Bay. At this point, in a politically astute decision, Napoleon left Egypt, his military reputation intact. His successor was less fortunate. The remnants of the French forces, bloodied by the British, did not return home until 1802 when the Peace of Amiens was signed.

Bonaparte returned home in secret in October 1799. Though his Egyptian campaign could hardly be called successful, he had avoided blame for the French defeats. Other French commanders, particularly in Europe, had fared little better. The French continued to take territory, making the Helvetian Republic out of Switzerland and the Ligurian Republic out of Naples, seizing Geneva and Florence, but elsewhere in Europe difficulties emerged. While Napoleon had been on his way to Egypt, the Russians and the British, in December 1798, had made a military alliance against France. To this pact other states came flying: Austria, Naples, Portugal, and the Ottoman Empire. With their adherence, the War of the Second Coalition began. In Germany, French armies suffered defeats at the hands of the Austrians and Russians, the latter under their able commander, General Suvorov. The French were able to stave off a threatened invasion from beyond the Rhine, but it was the break-up of the Second Coalition, rather than the might of French armies, that saved them from humiliation.

While others were left to fight the Second Coalition, Bonaparte played politics at home. He began to scheme with the veteran revolutionary leader, the Abbé Sieyès, to topple what remained of the Directory, which had taken the blame for war losses and rising food prices. In the *Coup d'Etat* of Brumaire, Napoleon and his allies overthrew the Directory, and on the same day, November 9, 1799, proclaimed themselves the new rulers of France. A new executive of three, called the Consulate, took over the affairs of state. Its membership consisted of Napoleon and his two fellow-conspirators. At the age of thirty, Napoleon had become one of the most powerful men in France.

"We have finished the romance of the Revolution," Napoleon wrote in 1810, "we must now begin its history." The new First Consul was physically unprepossessing and, by some standards, crudely educated. Short, thick-necked, prone to overweight, Napoleon did not enhance his appearance by having his fine dark hair cut short. Harsh barbering and a receding hairline earned him the nickname "crophead," though probably not in his presence. Napoleon's appearance was redeemed by his fine facial features and by his arresting eyes set in a massive head.

His administrative abilities honed by years of command, Napoleon was a man who quickly grasped essentials, and his awesome temper was a goad to those less able. Prince Metternich, not a man usually impressed by upstarts, found Napoleon's knowledge of particulars flawed but his understanding of causes and effects remarkable. Though Napoleon was awkward in society, his subordinates found him fascinating, intense, and often more able than they.

As First Consul, Napoleon reorganized the government on conservative, authoritarian lines. In December of 1799 a new constitutional document was presented to the French people in a plebiscite and was approved by an overwhelming margin. The new constitution left the Consulate in place, but below them it created a number of legislative bodies with very limited powers, elected at least as narrowly and indirectly as those under the Directory. These bodies included a Senate of eighty members, each chosen for life; a Tribunate of one hundred members, who could debate, but not vote on, government measures; and a Legislative Chamber, which could vote on such measures, but not debate them. The only government body with any power, other than the Consulate itself, was a Council of State, whose members were appointed by First Consul Bonaparte.

Under Napoleon's direction, the Consulate centralized government and ended much of the administrative and financial senility of the old Regime. A system of prefectures and sub-prefectures organized government at the regional and local levels. At last a much-needed reform of the tax structure was undertaken. As a military man, Napoleon knew that wars could only be prosecuted if the state was on sound financial footing. Napoleon was also helped by the fact that the Revolution had destroyed the parlements and other institutions of the Old Regime, and he could begin administrative reform with a clean slate.

Napoleon was also authoritarian in his approach to religion, police, and the press. Believing that religion cemented and preserved the social order, Napoleon reversed the anticlerical bias of the earlier periods of the Revolution and signed the Concordat of 1801 with the papacy. As a result, Catholicism was restored in France, but under government control. "Under my rule," Napoleon remarked, with a real feeling for propaganda, "freedom of the press was unnecessary." Desiring to control information, Napoleon did indeed limit press freedoms. For similar reasons, education was placed under state control. Propaganda was also instituted through architectural monuments like the Arc de Triomphe, which celebrated French military glory. "I will be master *everywhere* in France," Napoleon wrote. Propaganda helped Napoleon attain that mastery as much as administrative reorganization and the broadening of police power. It is indeed no accident that Napoleon was one of the first European rulers to create a secret police, which he placed in the hands of the merciless Fouché. For all of these reasons, Napoleon has been seen by some historians as the prototype of the modern dictator.

Napoleon also knew that military success was the key to the maintenance of political power. By the summer of 1800 Napoleon renewed the war against Austria by engaging their forces on the Italian peninsula. Bonaparte crossed the St. Bernard Pass with 40,000 men, and, at Marengo in a bloody battle, he defeated an Austrian army under Melas. The victory seemed to hearten French forces elsewhere. Another French army pressed into Germany, taking

Trumpeters of Napoleon's Imperial Guard. Theodore Gericault
Courtesy of the National Gallery of Art, Washington. Chester Dale Fund.

Munich and defeating the Austrians at Hohenlinden. In 1801, by the Treaty of Lunéville, the middle of the Rhine River became the official boundary between France and Germany, and over 25,000 square miles of German territory, and 3,500,000 Germans, passed into the hands of the French. In addition, the same treaty confirmed all French conquests and republics in Italy. Finally, Tuscany was reconstituted as the Kingdom of Etruria, and Louisiana, much to the distress of the Americans, passed from Austria's Spanish ally to France. With Austria out of the war, Prussia, allied again with Britain against France, had to abandon its treaty commitments. In 1802 the British, finding themselves isolated, were obliged to sign the Treaty of Amiens on the basis of the status quo.

Having garnered more military glory, Napoleon turned once again to the internal politics of France. By now Bonaparte regarded the French Republic, then existing in feeble form as a window-dressing for the Consulate, as nothing more than a "fancy." Sensing that the French people wanted "Glory and gratified Vanity" Napoleon gave it to them and schemed to make himself a "crowned Washington," ruler of France in name as well as in fact. In August of 1802, on the heels of the Peace of Amiens, Napoleon became "Consul for Life," with the right of appointing his successor. In 1804 Napoleon proclaimed himself Emperor of the French, laying the crown on his own head in a ceremony worthy of Charlemagne.

In 1805 the major powers of Europe, by now thoroughly alarmed at Napoleon's imperial ambitions, formed yet another coalition against him. Great Britain, Austria, Russia, Prussia, and Sweden combined against France. The War of the Third Coalition began. The allied effort seemed once again to fail. Between 1805 and 1809 Napoleon won some of his greatest victories, and France verged on the conquest of Europe. In 1805 came the great Napoleonic victory over the Austrians at Ulm. This was soon followed by the defeat of an Austro-Russian army at Austerlitz. In rapid successions the Austrians were forced to make a humiliating peace in the Treaty of Pressburg, and the Confederation of the Rhine, a union of the other German states, was formed under French auspices. France, not Austria or Prussia, had become the arbiter of German affairs.

With Austria prostrate, Napoleon turned on the Prussians and Russians. In October 1806, at the Battles of Jena and Auerstadt, the Prussians were cut to pieces. Thereafter, Napoleon occupied Berlin and there issued his famous Berlin Decree, an effort to cripple the English by closing all of Europe to British trade. In the summer of 1807, at Friedland, the Russians were not only defeated but forced out of eastern Europe. In July of the same year, having met with King Frederick William III of Prussia and Tsar Alexander I of Russia on a raft in the River Niemen, Napoleon announced the Treaties of Tilsit. Alexander agreed to peace, to substantial territorial losses, and to a secret Franco-Russian alliance against the British; Prussia agreed to similar losses and to a cash indemnity. The Third Coalition had gone the way of its predecessors, and Napoleon was nearly the master of Europe.

E. The Duke of Wellington and the Military Challenge to Napoleon

By 1808, once again, only the British stood against Napoleon. All of Europe, from the Baltic to the Pyrenees and from the edge of the English Channel to the River Niemen, was controlled by Napoleon or his clients. From his continental stronghold Napoleon issued his Milan Decree, reaffirming the closure of Europe to British trade first enunciated at Berlin. Together, the Berlin and Milan decrees constituted what came to be called the "Continental System." Europe had been officially, if not completely, closed to English merchants.

Only at sea were the British supreme, and it was at sea that they had won their few precious victories against the French. To the earlier victory in the Battle of the Nile, the British added another at Trafalgar in 1805, but purchased it dearly with the loss of their great commander, Lord Nelson. The British tried to use their seaborne supremacy to counter the Continental System, issuing Orders-in-Council forbidding neutrals to trade with France. The British policy of searches and seizures on the high seas offended potential European allies, and in America, British high-handedness and the impressment of sailors eventually led to the War of 1812. With the French dominant on land, and the British by sea, the situation approached stalemate.

While Napoleon gained control of the French Revolution by brilliant exploitation of opportunity, a British officer named Arthur Wellesley was gaining combat experience in Ireland, Holland, and India. Arthur Wellesley was almost four months older than Napoleon, and had been born into a landed family, but, curiously, his opportunities had been fewer. Wellesley was a member of that strange underclass in European landed society known as "younger sons," and this in a sense had limited his options. While the eldest sons inherited the bulk of the lands and titles, their younger siblings were left with little if any income, and parents often puzzled over how to employ and support them. The usual solutions were the purchase of a living in the church or the purchase of commissions in the army or navy.

The army had been chosen for Arthur Wellesley. "I vow to God I don't know what I shall do with my awkward son Arthur," Wellesley's mother opined of the son she feared was a dunce; "food for powder and nothing more." Like Napoleon, Wellesley was dispatched to military school in France.

Under French royalist tutelage, Wellesley grew into a conservative, capable, and acerbically witty soldier. He also became, despite a rather awesome nose, a very handsome one. Even his mother was surprised. "I do believe there is my ugly boy Arthur," his mother exclaimed in shocked surprise as she glimpsed him at the theater a few years later. Collectively pleased, the family bought Arthur Wellesley a commission in the 73rd Highland Regiment.

Wellesley became one of the most quotable soldiers to ever don the uniform, and statements made by and about him give a key to his character. The ordinary English soldier, whose training and quality Wellesley continually tried to improve, was the "scum of the earth." Of the public and the press Wellesley formed no higher opinion. "I should like very much," he once wrote, "to tell the truth; but if I did, I should be torn to pieces here and abroad." "Publish and be damned," he said on a later occasion when his mistress threatened to make compromising information public.

Wellesley was also a man of great pragmatism, and one of little fear and few illusions. "The whole art of war," he remarked in blunt counterpoint to erudite military treatises, "consists at getting at what is on the other side of the hill." Gifted with a strong constitution and regular habits, Wellesley refused to worry while other fretted. "When I throw off my clothes," he once said, "I throw off my cares, and, when I turn in my bed, it is time to turn out." Unlike some other commanders, Wellesley expected campaigns to be difficult and battle losses heavy. "Nothing except a battle lost can be half so melancholy as a battle won," he wrote in one of his dispatches from Spain. Finally, while others had come to regard Napoleon as invincible, Wellesley, though he respected Bonaparte and his troops, refused to believe it. He thought that Napoleon's massed columns could be beaten with proper tactics and that Napoleon, though a brilliant general, was in the end a man just as he was. "I don't care a two-penny damn what becomes of the ashes of Napoleon Bonaparte," Wellesley remarked in later life.

"A conqueror, like a cannon-ball, must go on; if he rebounds, his career is over." In this remark Wellesley perceived Napoleon's dilemma. In 1808 Napoleon was at the peak of his career, and he had indeed earned his reputation as a conqueror, but he had to go on conquering to preserve it. With every conquest the risks multiplied, and with every one also his empire grew more overextended and more difficult to defend. And there was no turning back. Since 1792 France had been at war, and war had become the driving force behind the French economy, as well as the organizer of its society.

Napoleon's struggle with the British had produced the Continental System, an attempt to destroy the British economy by closing off the European continent to British trade. The logic of the Continental System also pushed Napoleon to further conquest. By 1808, Napoleon controlled virtually all of western Europe except for the

Iberian peninsula, but it was there, through the ports of Portugal and Spain, that the Continental System was most openly challenged. In 1808, the need for continued conquest and the defense of the Continental System obliged Napoleon to order 100,000 French troops into Spain and Portugal. It proved to be his first major error. By putting his brother Joseph on the Spanish throne, Bonaparte provoked a nationalistic response from the Spanish people. The Iberian peninsula became a battleground, and the British had their opportunity to meet the French on land. Arthur Wellesley was dispatched to Portugal with an expeditionary force, and the long campaign known as the Peninsular Wars began.

Like Napoleon, Wellesley benefited from certain military improvements that had been put in place before he came on the scene. If the soul of Napoleon's army was the massed column and the artillery cannonade, the heart of the British infantry was the territorially-based regiment, each one with its own traditions, uniforms, and recruiting areas. Though still troubled by incompetent officers and unqualified recruits, the British army had improved under the late-eighteenth century administration of the Duke of York, who had improved training and established military and staff colleges.

To these improvements, Napoleon had added his own paradoxical contribution. His very successes had forced the British army to adopt techniques he had perfected. To counter the *levee en masse,* the British army doubled in size between 1803 and 1807, reaching a strength of 200,000. This was complemented by a growth in reserves. A partially trained militia, also of some 200,000, stood behind the front-line troops. Under Sir John Moore a light infantry brigade came into being, forming a partial response to the French *tirailleurs,* the mobile skirmishing riflemen that Napoleon had put to such good use.

By the late summer of 1808, Arthur Wellesley had landed in Portugal with over 15,000 men, most of them well trained, including an unusually high proportion of good riflemen. Wellesley's weaknesses were in cavalry and in artillery transport. Opposing Wellesley was a combined French force of somewhat larger size, but only 13,000 of these were present when the French commander, Junot, confronted the British expeditionary force at Vimiero. There, on August 21, Wellesley routed the enemy. Unfortunately, and much to Wellesley's disgust, he was forbidden to pursue the enemy by a cautious superior, and his force was withdrawn. On August 30 the British concluded the Convention of Cintra with the French, which resulted in a French withdrawal from Portugal.

Though Wellesley was disappointed, he had accomplished more than he knew. Napoleon's army, even though Napoleon had not been personally in command, had been defeated on the European continent. The victory heartened others. The Spanish, who had risen against the rule of Napoleon's brother Joseph, were encouraged to keep on fighting the French, and Napoleon was obliged to dispatch 150,000 troops to Spain, opening a massive new front with soldiers that could have been well-used elsewhere.

Napoleon was also damaged in other ways. At the Congress of Erfurt, called in September 1808 for the purpose of cementing the Franco-Russian alliance, the aristocratic French diplomat Talleyrand, who secretly hated Napoleon, schemed with the restive Tsar Alexander. The Austrians and Prussians, encouraged by events in Portugal and Spain, revived and reformed their armies and marched again against the French. Napoleon, whose forces had taken Madrid, defeated several Spanish armies, and driven a British expeditionary force out of Spain, was forced to go to Germany to retrieve the situation. While Napoleon was successful, taking Vienna, defeating the Austrians at Wagram in 1809, and forcing them to sign the humiliating Treaty of Schönbrunn in the same year, it was growing ever more clear that he was overextended militarily and that he could be weakened if the "ulcer" in the Iberian Peninsula continued to bleed.

By April 1809, reluctant British cabinet ministers had been persuaded by Wellesley and others to once again harry the French in Portugal and Spain. Another expeditionary force, of some 23,000 men, was sent off under Wellesley's command.

This time, the odds against Wellesley were greater. Of his total command, less than one-fifth had seen service in Spain or Portugal, fewer still were light infantry or riflemen. Artillery was sparse, and the horses designated to pull the guns were even poorer than before. The Spanish commander, General Cuesta, twice-defeated and jealous of Wellesley's prestige and aggressiveness, was reluctant to cooperate. The only good news for Wellesley lay in Napoleon's problems in Germany, which kept him personally out of Spain. Nonetheless, the French had a vast numerical advantage over him. A combined army of some 60,000 men confronted the British.

In late July 1809 the British and Spanish forces took up positions on a plain outside Talavera, a strategic town not far from the Tagus River. There, despite the loss of some 400 British troops in a skirmish and the headlong, panicked flight of part of Cuesta's line, Wellesley rallied his men to give battle. With 20,000 men, Wellesley defeated an army twice that size. As the French regulars marched toward Wellesley's line in massed column, British troops poured in murderous "rolling volleys" that left the valley floor covered with corpses. The French withdrew, and, as the exhausted victors watched helplessly, the field caught fire, burning to cinders the bodies of the

The Duke of Wellington 405

wounded and the dead. For this terrible triumph, Wellesley was elevated to the British peerage as Viscount Wellington of Talavera.

There was no time to reflect on the victory. With winter approaching, Wellington withdrew from his positions in Spain into Portugal. Once there, he moved his men into special defensive lines around Torres Vedras. These lines, strung between the Atlantic and the Tagus, protecting Lisbon and the quadrilateral of territory on which it stood, proved more than the equal of the French, who withdrew into Spain.

The impregnable Torres Vedras lines provided a base from which Wellington, with increasing boldness, attacked French armies and positions in Spain. It became a struggle of savagery and desperation in which the peasantry of Spain and Portugal, pillaged and raped by French troops used to living off the land, committed grievous atrocities of their own. Only the *Disasters of War,* the famous series of etchings by Goya, come close to relating the special vileness of the war in the Peninsula.

In 1811 Wellington's forces broke out and laid siege to the cities of Almeida and Badajoz and began to take the war to the French forces in Spain. In May, Wellington's troops smashed a French army under Massena at Fuentes de Onoro. Later in the same month, at Albuera, another British force under General Beresford defeated a French army under Marshal Soult. By the spring of 1812 both Badajoz and Ciudad Rodrigo had fallen to British arms. In July, Wellington's forces, after furious fighting, took Salamanca. Thereafter the French position in Spain became increasingly untenable. Joseph Bonaparte, the erstwhile king of Spain, abandoned Madrid. Though the English failed to take Burgos and retreated once again into Portugal, Wellington was drawing closer to the Pyrenees and thus to the heartland of France.

While the French position in Spain neared crisis, Napoleon became increasingly preoccupied with what he referred to as the "colossus of Russia." Under the visionary Tsar Alexander I, Russia was renewing its ambition to become a force in European affairs. Alexander, at best a reluctant French ally, had been angered by Napoleon's seizure of Poland and his creation of the Grand Duchy of Warsaw. The Duchy of Warsaw, carved out of Polish territory that Alexander regarded as a Russian sphere of influence, was an affront to Alexander's pride. Even more alarming to Alexander was Napoleon's marriage alliance with rival Austria. When Napoleon put away his first wife to marry the Austrian Archduchess Marie Louise in 1810, Alexander suspected that it formalized an anti-Russian pact. Finally, Napoleon compounded these offenses with a more personal one. He seized the territory of the Duke of Oldenburg, a close relative of Alexander's, and annexed it to France.

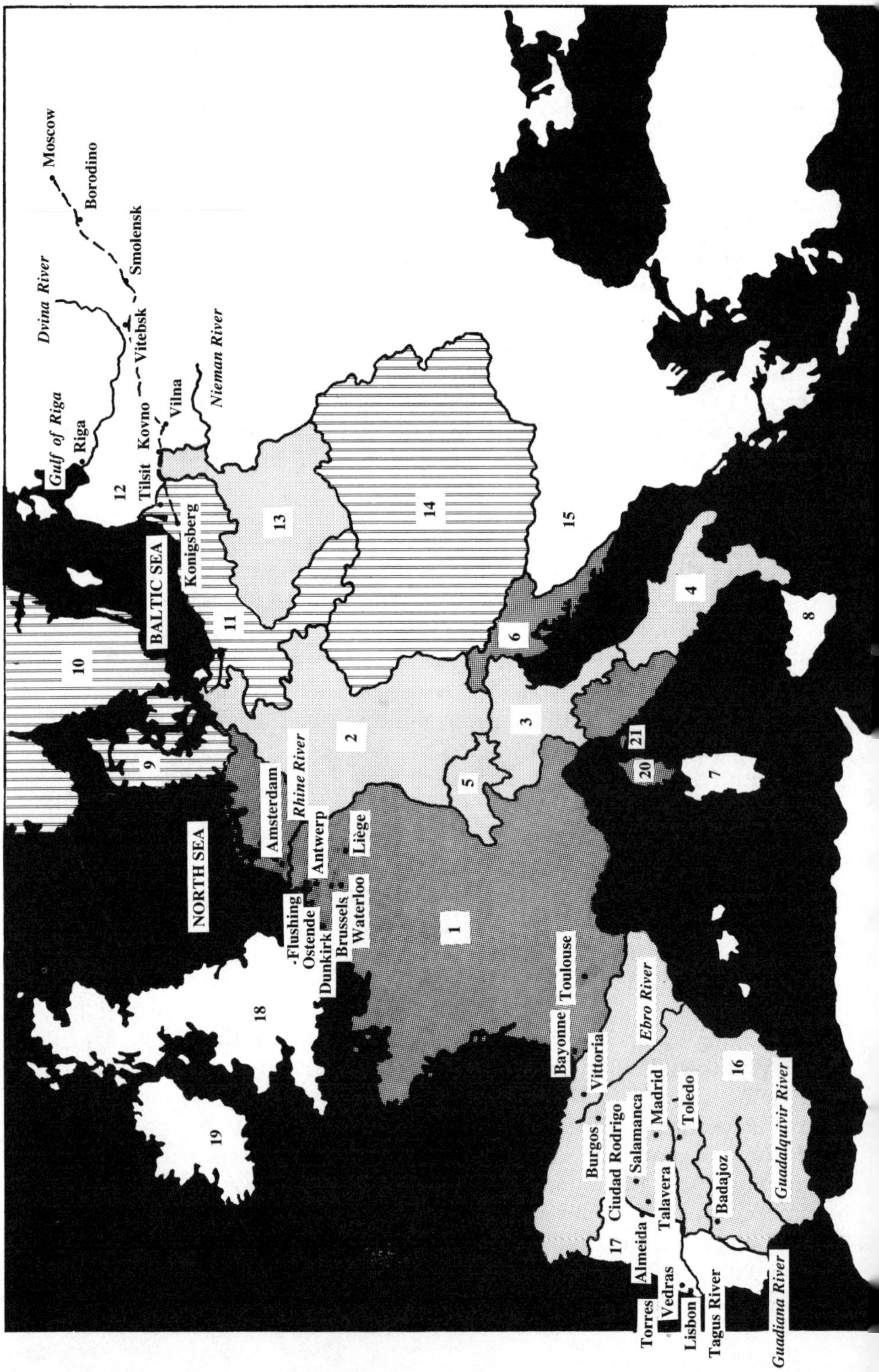
Moscow
Borodino
Smolensk
Dvina River
Vitebsk
Nieman River
Gulf of Riga
Riga
Kovno
Vilna
Tilsit
Konigsberg
BALTIC SEA
NORTH SEA
Amsterdam
Rhine River
Antwerp
Liège
Flushing
Ostende
Dunkirk
Brussels
Waterloo
Toulouse
Bayonne
Vittoria
Ebro River
Burgos
Ciudad Rodrigo
Salamanca
Madrid
Toledo
Talavera
Badajoz
Guadalquivir River
Almeida
Torres Vedras
Lisbon
Tagus River
Guadiana River
1
2
3
4
5
6
7
8
9
10
11
12
13
14
15
16
17
18
19
20
21

The Duke of Wellington 407

1. France
2. Confederation of the Rhine
3. Kingdom of Italy
4. Kingdom of Naples
5. Helvetic Republic
6. Illyrian Province
7. Kingdom of Sardinia
8. Kingdom of Sicily
9. Kingdom of Denmark
10. Kingdom of Sweden
11. Kingdom of Prussia
12. Russia (western border)
13. Duchy of Warsaw
14. Austrian Empire
15. Ottoman Empire
16. Spain
17. Portugal
18. England
19. Ireland
20. Corsica
21. Elba

■ Napoleon's Empire

□ Dependent States

▦ Allied States

Europe in 1810: The Height of Napoleonic Power

Wellington's Peninsular Campaign, 1809-1812 (lower left of map)

Between 1809 and 1812, Wellington campaigned in a northeast direction, occasionally retreating and wintering behind his lines at Torres Vedras. Eventually, the French had to give up Madrid, fearing that the Spanish capital would be cut off as Wellington pressed toward the Pyrenees and the French border. By 1812 Wellington crossed the border, and took Bayonne and Toulouse.

Waterloo, Geography and Military Strategy (center of map)

Waterloo stood on the road to Brussels, and was close to greater Germany, the Netherlands, and the ports that supplied Wellington's armies. Victory at Waterloo might have given Napoleon the opportunity to break Wellington's lines of supply, and time to divide the allies.

Napoleon's March on Moscow, 1812 ▬ ▬ ▬ ▬ ▬ (upper right of map)

Having decided that Alexander would eventually abandon France, Napoleon decided to strike first. In the midsummer of 1812, leading an international army of perhaps 600,000 men, Napoleon crossed the Niemen, occupied Vilna, and marched unopposed all the way to Smolensk. After destroying the city, the French were able to bring the Russians to battle at Borodino, where Napoleon won a costly, bloody victory. Thereafter, as the Russian fall deepened into winter, the Tsar's troops retreated into the vastness of Russia, burning anything that could sustain the invading troops, harrying Napoleon's already overextended supply lines. When Bonaparte occupied Moscow, the Russians put their capital to the torch. Early November brought the Russian winter in full force, and Napoleon's troops, hungry and suffering from frostbite, were forced to retreat. More than 30,000 baggage horses perished from the cold, and Napoleon was obliged to burn cannon and ammunition he could not move. Napoleon abandoned his army and fled to Paris to raise another. But for the Grand Army there was no escape. Less than one-fifth of the original complement of troops found their way back across the Niemen that December.

Prussia and Austria abandoned their alliances with the French and combined against France. The Confederation of the Rhine broke apart as the other German states joined the list of Napoleon's enemies. In November 1813, at the Battle of Leipzig, Napoleon's forces were crushed in a nine-hour engagement. Napoleon lost 30,000 men and was forced into full retreat as his empire crumbled.

Wellington, the general who had already contributed so much to the destruction of Napoleon's hold on the continent, benefited as the French armies in Spain were gutted by withdrawals northward. He made for the Pyrenees. In June 1813 Wellington defeated the French at Vittoria. By December Wellington had crossed the frontier and besieged Bayonne. By early spring of the new year Wellington's forces were in Bourdeaux and had defeated their old adversary Soult at the Battle of Toulouse.

By then the British Foreign Secretary, Lord Castlereagh, had negotiated with the victorious allies the Treaties of Chaumont. In these agreements, each of the victorious allies—Prussia, Russia, Austria, and Britain—pledged not to negotiate a separate peace and agreed to maintain the alliance for twenty years. At the end of March the allies marched into Paris. In April Napoleon abdicated his throne and was exiled to the island of Elba.

Believing that Napolean's exile was permanent, the victorious powers gathered at Vienna to plan the peace, but the ink was barely dry on the treaties when Napoleon effected his escape. By the spring of 1815 Napoleon was back in Paris and raising yet another army. This period of Napoleon's rule, called the "Hundred Days," terrified all Europe. Wellington, for the last time, found himself at the head of an army marching against the French. This time, however, there was a difference. For the first time in his career, Wellington stood to meet Napoleon on the field of battle.

In the summer of 1815 Napoleon moved his forces into Belgium. There, at Ligny, he met and successfully engaged a Prussian force under General Blücher, obliging it to withdraw. Almost simultaneously Napoleon's subordinate, Marshal Ney, defeated another allied force under the Prince of Orange.

Napoleon's only hope for victory lay in keeping the armies of Blücher and Wellington apart, and defeating each force in succession. Seeking to accomplish this, Napoleon ordered a French force under Grouchy to engage the Prussians, while he himself moved the bulk of the French army to Waterloo to give battle to Wellington.

The two armies were almost evenly matched at about 70,000 men each, but Wellington's troops were not all sound, and he decided to allow the French to initiate the attack. Napoleon first struck at Wellington's Foot Guards on the left of the British line, hoping to draw troops from Wellington's center, the area where he planned to strike his heaviest blow. The initial attack, however, failed, as did the later push against the British center. Wellington's regiments, organized into squares around their colors, provided a refuge for skirmishers and the wounded, as well as rolling volleys of fire to decimate Napoleon's columns and cavalry. Neither cannonade nor cavalry broke the British, and the one successful French infantry attack was negated by the arrival of the Prussians, who Grouchy had failed to hold. Fighting on two fronts against two armies, Napoleon's last attempt to break out failed when the Imperial Guard faded under the fire of the British battalions. Wellington's troops had come to the battle cold, exhausted, and hungry, but they had held together. Napoleon's army disintegrated, panicked, and was no more, pursued into oblivion by the vengeful Prussians.

Napoleon also fled, his personal treasury scattered about the roads, his coach falling into the hands of the Prussians. After vainly attempting to take ship from France, Napoleon surrendered to a British sea captain. This time, he was exiled, and for good, to the island of St. Helena. There Napoleon suffered from fevers and untreated venereal diseases, bored holes in his shutters to spy upon the populace, and shot at cows and smaller creatures who passed into his view. Sure of his place in the minds of posterity, Napoleon eventually succumbed to the Bonaparte family malady of cancer. When he died in 1821, he was only fifty-one years old.

Wellington, elevated to a dukedom, lived a longer and more honored life. "I hope to God that I have fought my last battle," Wellington remarked with his usual bluntness after Waterloo. Unlike too many others, he got his wish. He never went to war again. A hero to his countrymen, the "Iron Duke" reached the pinnacle of the political system that he so thoroughly mistrusted, becoming Prime Minister in 1828. Wellington's influence on the British army was even more profound, and his tactics, revered and perhaps obsolescent, lingered for years. He continued to enjoy good health and obtained financial security beyond dreaming. In addition to his title, Parliament voted Wellington a fortune of £500,000 and the manor of Stratfield Saye. Not until 1846 did Wellington retire from public life. When he died in 1852 his funeral was a state occasion, and his body was borne to Saint Paul's Cathedral on an iron carriage, appropriately cast from scores of cannon.

That Wellington died in peace, and Napoleon in quiet exile, owed much to the peacemakers, including Wellington himself, who gathered at Vienna in 1814. Soldiers had won the war, but it fell to the diplomats to make the peace.

F. Prince Metternich and the Restructuring of Europe: The Congress of Vienna, 1814-1815

No European diplomat has excited more comment, both contemporary and historical, than Clemens von Metternich, foreign minister and chancellor of Austria, host to the Congress of Vienna, and organizer of the post-Napoleonic peace settlements. To some contemporaries Metternich was the "god of boundaries" or the "Coachman of Europe." Others were rather more severe. "The most hated man in Europe," said one; "a society hero and nothing more," remarked the Duke of Wellington. That Metternich was good-looking, that he cut a fine figure in society, provoked the wrath of those less blessed. After all, it was hard not to dislike a man who was said to be as exquisite as "a piece of Dresden China," and as handsome as an "Adonis." Somewhat more trustworthy are the remarks of one of Metternich's mistresses, the Princess Lieven, who thought him a hypocrite, but such things mistresses are in a unique position to know.

As it was with contemporaries, so it has been with scholars. Metternich, a man who spent his life trying to stamp out both political liberalism and nationalism, has been regarded as a reactionary by historians who favor both of those ideas. A few scholars—Heinrich von Srbik, E. L. Woodward, and Henry Kissinger—have seen Metternich in a positive light. More often, however, Metternich has been portrayed as an empty opportunist, or a mindless, conservative fop. A. J. P. Taylor, a diplomatic historian of strong opinions and socialist leanings, condemned the conservative Metternich as a man whose "first thought in a crisis was to see if his skin-tight breeches fitted perfectly and the Order of the Golden Fleece was hanging rightly."

Such descriptions would have troubled Metternich, because no man ever labored harder to gain credit for his public acts, or to assure their preservation for posterity. In his manipulative egotism, Metternich virtually invites historical bias. Years ago Albert Sorel noted Metternich's fondness for the word "I," and this pronoun is sprinkled liberally throughout his writings: "I was born a cabinet minister"; "I came to Frankfurt like a Messiah"; "I have long experience of the world's affairs and I have always observed that no matter is so easily settled as that which appears to present insuperable difficulties"; "Europe will be saved, and I flatter myself that in time no small part of the credit will come to me"; "I am always above and beyond the preoccupations of most public men. . . ."

There is still more. Metternich did not read most novels because, he said, they were inferior to his own experiences; did not listen to university students because he considered them still children; did not doubt that his mistress would think of him even while she slept with her husband because he, Metternich, was so truly lovable. "I have spent my life making history," he once wrote. "I will devote my last powers to collecting materials so that the history can be written in accordance with the truth." Historians are not always kind to such men, preferring those less obvious in the art of self-promotion. Thus Metternich, the reorganizer of Europe, has fared no better in historiography than Napoleon, the man whose militarism nearly wrecked the European state system.

While Metternich's self-centeredness is indeed a hallmark of his character, it is not as important in itself as the circumstances which caused it to grow, and which nurtured his world-view. Although Metternich followed his father into the Austrian state bureaucracy, neither Metternich nor his family were Austrian by territory, experience, or culture. Metternich's family was ancient and landed, but its wealth and estates were in the Rhineland rather than Austria. His father, described ungenerously by one contemporary as "a boring babbler and a chronic liar," was a diplomat who served successively in the Rhine-Moselle region and in the Austrian Netherlands. Metternich himself was born in Coblenz in the German state of Trier but went to university in Strasbourg, an area heavily French, as well as to the more properly German University of Mainz. "In Germany you must admire German music and in France French music"; this was the advice given to the future diplomat by his mother, who added that "it is like that in most things." Metternich's upbringing was cosmopolitan, his identity established more by his membership in the landed nobility, an international caste, than by geographic region. It was, moreover, an upbringing where flattery and self-promotion were necessities in compassing political objectives. He was a diplomat to his bones.

Metternich's identity, proud but fragile, nurtured by a privileged education, reached a point of crisis with the coming of the French Revolution. If Metternich's class made him unsympathetic to strong national feelings, his education and young manhood made him a thoroughgoing conservative. Just as he entered the University of Strasbourg the French Revolution spilled into the old city. Metternich watched in horror as the city hall was vandalized, as he wrote, "by a populace out of its mind." The French Revolution obliged Metternich to interrupt his studies and flee to Mainz, but here too the revolutionaries were soon in control, and he had to take to the road again. This time he sought refuge in Brussels, where his father was posted as a diplomat. Yet Brussels too was, in Metternich's words, too soon "overflowed by the Jacobin lava." Needing employment, Metternich went on a diplomatic mission to England, leaving the continent just in time to receive word of his father's flight from Brussels to Vienna, again the result of the movement of revolutionary armies. Subsequently, Metternich's family lost their Rhineland estates to invading French forces.

The holes the French Revolution was opening in the social order were most disturbing to the young nobleman who had been educated in the harmonies of the Enlightenment. At Strasbourg, as at least one historian has noted, Metternich had been taught much about natural law, enlightened despotism, and rationalism by Christopher William Koch, the famous instructor of diplomats. At Mainz, another scholar, Nicholas Vogt, stressed the importance of history and tradition in the making of balanced institutions. The French Revolution was an affront to everything Metternich was, and everything he had learned in his lectures. It had undermined his sense of self-worth, swept away his ancestral estates, and denied the importance of the privileged class to which he belonged.

Threatened with the loss of his very identity, Metternich fell back on his egotism and his talent, battling back with an opportunism borne of simple self-preservation. In October of 1794 Metternich traveled to Vienna and rejoined his family. There he dabbled in scientific and medical studies, and saw to his prospects. These were considerably enhanced when he met and married, in a matter of months, the Countess Eleonore Kaunitz, granddaughter and heiress of the Austrian chancellor. "One marries," Metternich once remarked, "to have children and not to indulge one's inclinations."

Metternich's own marriage accomplished much more than this. It reaffirmed his station, gave him wealth, and provided access to important diplomatic posts. As a delegate at the Congress of Rastatt in 1797, Metternich helped negotiate compensation for those evicted by the French from the left bank of the Rhine, a group that included his own family. Beneath Metternich's elegant exterior there was some shallowness and not a little anxiety. "I do not wish to be quoted," he wrote candidly to his wife in 1798, "but according to my way of saying things, everything is gone to the devil and the time is come when everyone must save from the wreck what he can." This statement, though made in another context, can serve as a guide to Metternich's diplomacy.

Other opportunities followed. In 1801 Metternich was posted as minister to the court of Saxony, and in 1803 he went to Berlin in a similar capacity. Finally, in 1806, Metternich received the coveted posting to Paris and to the court of Napoleon. At these and other positions, Metternich learned his lessons in diplomacy, and he worked to ameliorate the almost constant French pressure against Austria. The survival of Austria was increasingly linked in his mind with the survival of his class. Far-flung, vulnerable and feudal, governed by a privileged aristocracy, Austria was the antithesis of the Napoleonic France that Metternich so despised. In the interest of Austria, Metternich was willing to do almost anything. In Paris, Metternich became the social rage, attending the receptions given by the new aristocracy Napoleon created, sharing the bed of Caroline Marat, Napoleon's married sister, and conniving with the traitorous Talleyrand against the Emperor himself.

In 1809, having failed to defeat Napoleon, Metternich tried to ally with the man he hated. He returned to Vienna just in time to accept the Treaty of Schönbrunn, which Napoleon forced on a prostrate Austria. It may be that, since Metternich had advised his government to renew the war with Napoleon, he bore some responsibility for the military disasters that led to Schönbrunn. Wherever the blame lay, Metternich decided that it was now necessary to give Bonaparte something he wanted. He schemed successfuly to marry the hapless Archduchess Marie Louise to Napoleon, who was childless by his first wife, Josephine. This act earned Metternich the contempt of many, both in Austria and in Europe, but it did give Austria an important respite. "A virgin of the house of Austria had to be sacrificed to appease the monster. . . ." So wrote the wife of a British diplomat on the odious match.

Believing, as he once wrote, that "peace with Napoleon is not peace," Metternich maneuvered to insure independence for Austria even while it was under Napoleon's thumb. In this, the Austro-French marriage alliance he arranged provided him with an unanticipated opportunity. When Napoleon's treaty relationship with Tsar Alexander soured and the French invaded Russia, Napoleon found he needed the support of his Austrian ally. Napoleon forced Austria to provide troops for the Russian campaign, but Metternich was able to persuade the French Emperor to let them operate as an independent unit. When Napoleon's Russian campaign collapsed, the Austrian commander, Schwarzenberg, was able to negotiate a flexible and open-ended armistice with the Russians.

At this point Metternich, to the consternation of many, did not use the Austrian troops against the retreating French. He decided instead on temporary neutrality and attempted negotiations with Bonaparte. There were some good reasons for Metternich's decision. There was still reason to fear Napoleon, Metternich reasoned, and not just for his military skill. Metternich believed that Napoleon endangered the European social fabric by his mere presence. Napoleon, nationalistic and patriotic enough himself to kiss the French flag before his assembled troops, provoked a similar response in those he attempted to subject, and nationalistic revolution was the last thing Metternich wanted to occur in the multinational and far-flung Austrian Empire. The reaction to Napoleon, Metternich perceived with his highly-developed sense of self-preservation, had become as dangerous to Austria as Napoleon himself. Even if peace negotiations ultimately failed, Metternich believed they would at least buy Austria enough time to rebuild its army, weakened and poorly armed after years of fighting. Through negotiation, Metternich hoped to persuade Napoleon to fall back on France. If Napoleon remained in power, he could not become a dangerous martyr, and if he could be persuaded to limit his ambitions, France and Austria could become the arbiters of Europe.

To force Napoleon to the bargaining table, Metternich in 1813 signed the Treaty of Reichenbach with representatives from Prussia and Russia. Under its terms Metternich promised to go to war with France if, and only if, he failed to mediate a peace with Bonaparte. With an Austrian Hapsburg already the empress of France, Austria might well gain more from peace than she could from war. The idea of a dynastic and harmonious European balance of power, a concept instilled in Metternich years before by Nicholas Vogt, seemed possible through the existing Bonaparte-Hapsburg marriage alliance. Napoleon, however, refused to compromise, believing that his hold on his throne depended on the preservation of the empire that he had won by military force. At the Marcolini Palace in Dresden, in a stormy interview, Metternich failed to move Napoleon, and a last effort, made at the Congress of Prague, also came to nothing. On August 12, Austria at last declared war on Napoleon, beginning the campaign that led to the Battle of Leipzig.

While the armies fought, Metternich hardly stopped negotiating. In 1814, under his leadership, the Congress of Vienna convened with the purpose of bringing about a permanent peace. The Vienna Congress, which was interrupted but not stopped by Napoleon's Hundred Days, was Metternich's crowning achievement. While the delegates were made bleary-eyed by a host of entertainments and receptions, Metternich accomplished what he had failed to do at Dresden. At Vienna, wrote Treitschke, Metternich "swam as happily as a fish in a glittering pool." In precisely the kind of social arena where he felt most comfortable, Metternich led negotiations for a peace that prevented a general European war for many years and enshrined the idea of the balance of power.

Some have written that the Congress of Vienna was a reactionary attempt to "turn the clock back," to recreate the states and society of Europe as they had existed in 1789. Conservative the Vienna settlement was, but Metternich followed his standard pragmatic rule of saving what could be saved, and making the best of everything else.

As Arthur May has observed, the Vienna Congress was bound by certain guidelines: previously-negotiated secret treaties, the desire to surround France by a *cordon sanitaire* of independent buffer states, and the principles of "legitimacy" and "compensation." All of these, save for the idea of legitimacy, virtually made it impossible to turn the clock back completely. At the same time, the concepts of legitimacy and compensation are the most important, and most truly reflect Metternich's pragmatic, balance-of-power approach to negotiations.

Where possible—as in Spain, Sardinia, Tuscany, Modena, and the Papal States—legitimate ruling dynasties were restored to their ancestral lands, much as the Bourbons had earlier been restored to the French throne after Napoleon's abdication. The principle of legitimacy showed Metternich at his most conservative, but it was a conservatism tempered by realism. Dynasties were brought back only when it was expedient.

Where restoration of dynasties and territories was not possible, rulers and states were compensated with territory in other areas. Metternich and the other negotiators used the principle of compensation with skill, adding to the territories of their own states and creating a system of strong states, the *cordon sanitaire,* on the borders of France. Thus Austria, in addition to much of her old territory, was compensated for the loss of the Austrian Netherlands (Belgium) by obtaining Lombardy and Venetia in Italy, and Galicia in eastern Europe. The Austrian Netherlands, in turn, was joined with the old Republic of Holland to become the Kingdom of the Netherlands. At a stroke, Metternich made Austria the second most populous state in Europe, and one of the most influential. At the same time, he created a new, strong state capable of checking the power of France. The *cordon sanitaire* against France was strengthened by recreating Switzerland as an independent republic, and Sardinia as an independent kingdom. Sardinia was further augmented by being given Genoa.

With one of his allies—Prussia—Metternich had to use great care, for Prussia was Austria's rival for the domination of Germany. So that it might block France militarily, Prussia was given almost the entire left bank of the Rhine, thus completing the *cordon sanitaire*. This meant, however, that Prussia might easily become the most powerful state in Germany. While this prospect was frightening, Metternich must have felt that he had to live with it. He did try to ameliorate Prussia's influence by preserving under a new name the Confederation of the Rhine, the loose union of smaller German states instituted by Napoleon, and by making the Austrian Emperor its president. Nonetheless, the principle of "German dualism" was enshrined at Vienna, and it eventually led to the end of Austria's preeminent position in Germany. Still, by creating a balance of power between Prussia and Austria within Germany, Metternich may have accomplished as much as was possible. Finally, the dual influence of Austria and Prussia within Germany countered the cries for nationalism and German unification, both ideas that Metternich, as the representative of an international empire, feared above all else.

Aside from Prussia, Austria's greatest military rival on the European continent was imperial Russia. Metternich could not really hope to crush or deny either power, and their aggressive diplomacy provided the gravest challenges for his idea of a European balance of power. In a diplomat's nightmare, Prussia and Russia joined together at Vienna, each supporting the other in territorial demands. Prussia, with the support of Russia, demanded the whole of the German state of Saxony; Russia, with the support of Prussia, insisted on all of Poland. Both parts of this "Polish-Saxon Question" were harmful to Austria's interests. If Russia obtained all of Poland, it would automatically become the dominant power in eastern Europe, where Metternich wanted Austria to be influential. Austria would also stand to lose the Polish territory previously gained through the Polish partitions. If Prussia obtained all of Saxony, its power in Germany would grow mightily, the balance of power would be ruined, and Prussia would share a long and difficult-to-defend frontier with Austria.

Metternich immediately set to work to compromise the threat out of existence. In this goal he found allies in the British Foreign Secretary, Viscount Castlereagh, and in the clever French diplomat

Talleyrand. Castlereagh, fearing that a strong Russia might threaten British interests in Europe, the Ottoman Empire, and the Mediterranean, favored measures for containment. Talleyrand, as the representative of the restored Bourbon monarchy, wanted to bring his defeated nation back into the mainstream of European diplomacy. On the basis of mutual self-interest, the three diplomats signed a treaty pledging that their respective governments would make war on Russia if the need arose.

With the treaty concluded, Metternich and his allies leaked the news of it to Tsar Alexander, who promptly abandoned Prussia and compromised. Alexander had to settle for only part of traditional Poland, an area roughly the size of Napoleon's now defunct Grand Duchy of Warsaw. This territory, renamed Congress Poland, became Alexander's personal kingdom. Prussia, isolated, had to be content with two-fifths of Saxony, a fact which blunted its plans for German dominance.

Great Britain, in many senses now the strongest power in the world, was Austria's only other potential rival in Europe. Metternich had, however, reached his understanding with Castlereagh. The British were well-contented to remain out of Europe, so long as they obtained recognition for the vast overseas territories they had won in the Napoleonic Wars. The Congress of Vienna accommodated them, and Britain was confirmed in its possession of St. Lucia, Trinidad, and Tobago in the West Indies; Ceylon, Mauritius, and Singapore in Asia; the Cape of Good Hope at the tip of Africa; and Malta, the Ionian Islands, and Heligoland off the coasts of Europe. The British pillage of the French and Dutch seaborne empires was happily agreed to by Metternich, and the British quickly lost interest in continental affairs.

These decisions constituted the main accomplishments of the Vienna Congress, which ended its deliberations in 1815. There were other agreements of less importance. After Napoleon had been exiled for the first time, and the Bourbons restored to the French throne, the Quadruple Alliance powers who had come together in the Treaty of Chaumont—Austria, Russia, Prussia, and Britain—signed the Treaty of Paris of 1814 with France. This treaty gave France relatively generous terms: retention of the 1792 national boundaries, rather than those of 1789, and no indemnities or reparations. Napoleon's Hundred Days, however, convinced the allies that they had been too generous. After Waterloo, in 1815, a "second" Treaty of Paris imposed on France an indemnity of 700,000,000 francs and an occupying army. The allies also entertained, and most accepted, Tsar Alexander's plan for a "Holy Alliance," in which the signatories pledged to conduct foreign relations according to Christian principles. Metternich must have been incredulous as he signed it.

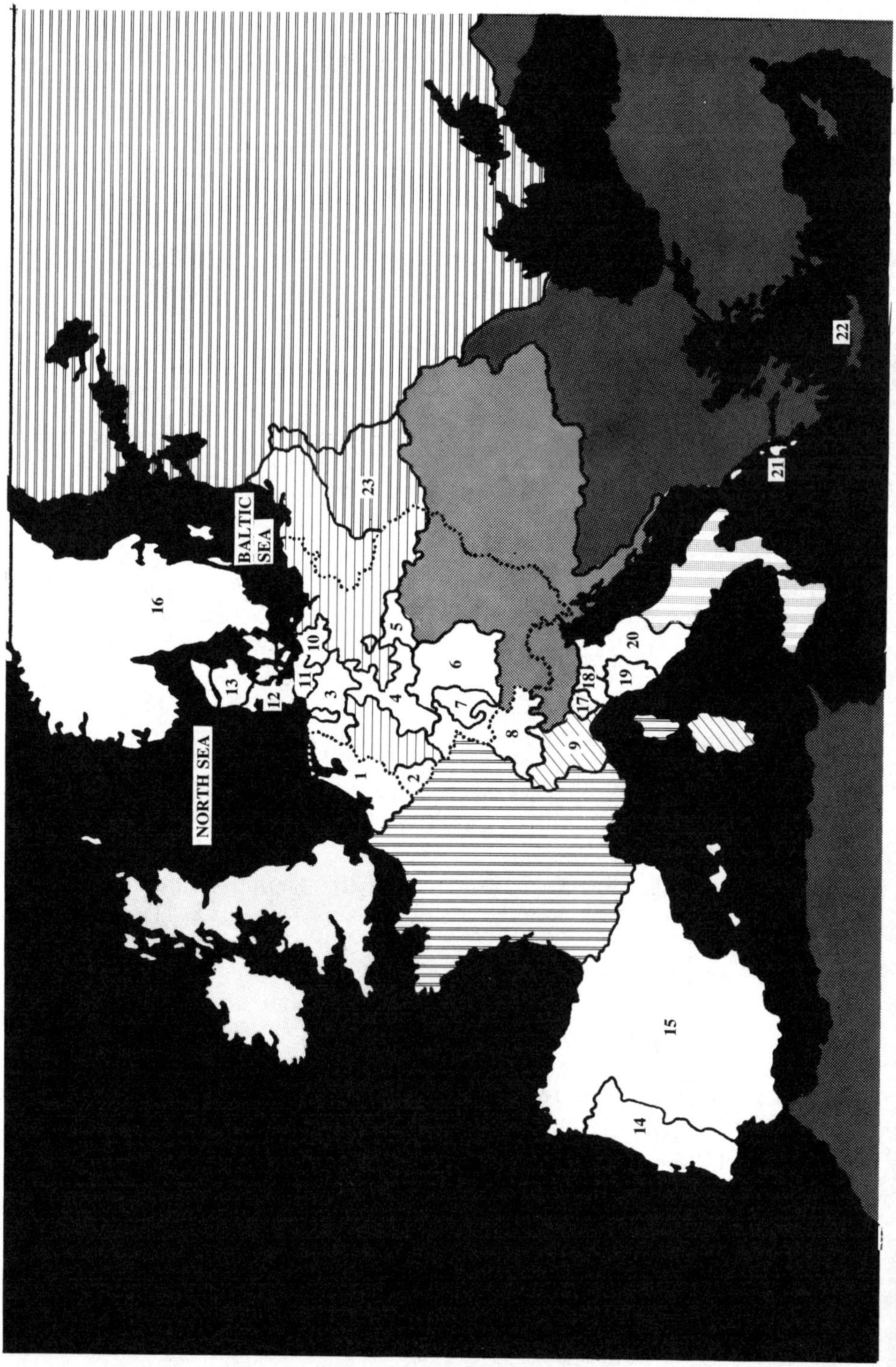
NORTH SEA
BALTIC SEA
1
2
3
4
5
6
7
8
9
10
11
12
13
14
15
16
17
18
19
20
21
22
23

1. Netherlands
2. Luxembourg
3. Hanover
4. Hesse
5. Saxony
6. Bavaria
7. Württemberg
8. Switzerland
9. Piedmont
10. Lübeck
11. Holstein
12. Schleswig
13. Denmark
14. Portugal
15. Spain
16. Kingdom of Norway and Sweden
17. Parma
18. Modena
19. Tuscany
20. Papal States
21. Ionian Islands (British)
22. Crete (Ottoman Empire)
23. Kingdom of Poland (Russia)

Kingdom of Prussia after the Congress of Vienna

Boundary of the German Confederation, 1815

Austrian Empire after the Congress of Vienna

United Kingdom of Great Britain and Ireland

Kingdom of France (Bourbons restored)

Kingdom of Sardinia

Kingdom of the Two Sicilies (Bourbon dynasty restored)

Ottoman Empire

Russian Empire

After the Congress of Vienna, Europe in 1815

The French Revolution had demonstrated the vulnerability of the European aristocracy; Metternich's Congress of Vienna proved its resiliency. Wherever possible, old institutions and crowns had been restored. A balance of power had been created in Europe with Austria, a state where the aristocracy was heavily institutionalized, as its "hinge." Nationalism and republicanism, the bugbears of aristocratic empires and the noble class, had been temporarily tamped down.

The Congress of Vienna succeeded in preventing a general war in Europe for many years, but it was less successful in preventing revolution. The powers that met at Vienna agreed to gather periodically to discuss international questions. In Metternich's hands this plan came to be known as the "Congress System," and he began to use it to attempt to crush revolutions wherever they broke out. In 1820, responding to liberal revolutions in Naples and Spain, Metternich drew up the Protocol of Troppau. This document provided for collective action against any revolution, and all the major powers except Britain accepted it. Despite this severe step, Metternich was unable to do much about the waves of revolution that broke out in Europe in 1830 and 1848. The Revolutions of 1848 struck Austria and drove Metternich from office.

The old chancellor had done much to restore the European balance of power, but, like most, he had not compassed all of his objectives. The nineteenth century, in spite of him, was to be one of revolutions, if not general war. Metternich, in a triumph of will and stamina, lived to see the frustration of much of his handiwork. He died in June of 1859, in his eighty-sixth year, proclaiming himself at the last "a rock of order."

G. Men, Women, and the Consequences of the French Revolution, 1789-1815

The French Revolution made legitimate changes in French society. By 1815 much of the feudalism of the Old Regime had disappeared. The peasants were freed from feudal dues and from church tithes; the mélange of local customs and prohibitions had begun to give way to a newer France where internal free trade was possible, and where a new legal system, the Napoleonic Code, held sway. The Revolution had once again made Paris the sole administrative center of the French state. Versailles, and the royal absolutism it represented, retreated into the past as a centralized bureaucracy took its place. At long last, something like a modern budgetary process had been devised and a modern tariff system erected. The stage was now set for the industrialization of France.

The first two estates of pre-revolutionary France—the clergy and the nobility—had suffered some setbacks, and never completely regained their former places. Although Napoleon had made his peace with the church and had created a new nobility to replace the old one, the clergy became virtual state servants and the new nobility was no real match for the old one.

Benefiting from the new order of things was the bourgeoisie. No future ruler of France, royalist or republican, could ever again afford to neglect them. They had begun a revolution, even if they had lost control over it, and no crowned head or titled noble could afford to forget that Robespierre had been a bourgeois. The revolutionary alliance between the working class and the bourgeoisie, between "mob and capital," would recur in nineteenth century Europe.

Napoleon, though far from a revolutionary at home, fostered revolution abroad. Nearly everywhere he went, Napoleon established republics and promulgated law codes, recruited armies and created bureaucracies. He changed the nature of warfare by utilizing mass conscript armies, and men who are uprooted, who move and fight and see new things, are men who are changed. More than this, Napoleon's occupation of Europe produced something else: it produced resentment. Peoples subjected by a nationalistic and patriotic French army quickly learned the lessons of nationalism and patriotism in resistance to the conqueror. In Germany, in Italy, in Spain, and elsewhere in Europe, nationalism became a means to unify against the invading French, and it lingered long after Napoleon's final defeat.

The era of the French Revolution, with its celebration of equality, also produced one of the great modern revolts against slavery. Napoleon had hoped to make the sugar-rich West Indian islands a bastion of his empire, but in Santo Domingo a courageous and articulate black slave, Pierre Dominique Toussaint L'Ouverture, claimed the ideals of the French Revolution for his own and raised a frightening revolt. It was put down only with difficulty, and the fact that it occurred sent tremors of fear through the planter aristocracy of the American antebellum south.

At the same time, it would be fallacious to say that the French Revolution established anything like the freedom, justice, and equality that it once promised. In Austria, in Prussia, and in Russia, the aristocracy remained firmly in control and the peasantry remained burdened. In England, the landed classes still dominated politics, and participation still depended on property. Metternich and his fellow-aristocrats had not turned back the clock at Vienna, but they had seen to it that their power would be conserved for some time to come.

Even in France there were continuities as well as changes. The abolition of feudal dues and the partial destruction of the old landed classes might make land available but certainly did not guarantee that the poorest peasants could buy their share. Secularization and official religious toleration there might be, but antiprotestantism and antisemitism were surely not ended. Freedom of speech, freedom of the press, and a secular school system mean relatively little as long as large portions of the population have no hope of learning to read. During the French Revolution the state had taken over many of the functions once reserved to the church—education, censorship, poor relief, marriage and divorce—but real improvement required that the new overlords be more enlightened than the old.

For those who expected a revolutionary change in French society between 1789 and 1815, there were indeed disappointments. The bourgeois instigators of the French Revolution were in the main constitutional monarchists, not democrats, and Robespierre, whatever his egalitarian ideals, succumbed to the needs of wartime emergency and to the Terror. With the coming of the Thermidorean Reaction many of the old aristocrats came out of hiding to join the new aristocracy of politicians and war profiteers in a round of receptions as opulent as any held during the Old Regime. In the provinces bourgeoisie and substantial peasants were able to buy land nationalized by the Revolution, and profited because of food shortages and the demands of Napoleon's armies, but the rural poor could buy little land and the urban poor often went hungry. Military recruiting disrupted rural life, and would have disrupted it even more had not a rising population supplied the cannon-fodder. Educational reforms there were, but their implementation was jeopardized by unevenness of application, poorly paid teachers, and the need of the poor to keep their children at home to work.

Perhaps nowhere is the incompleteness of the French Revolution better seen than through its impact on women. Under the Old Regime in France, as in much of the rest of Europe, women suffered from severe legal, economic, and social discrimination. Poorer women were denied membership in guilds and access to the more skilled crafts while their wealthier sisters were denied the opportunity for a university education and the control of their property after marriage. Marriage and divorce were in the conservative hands of the church, and women were subjected to unanswered physical and legal violence by their husbands.

To a greater or lesser extent, French women of all classes rallied to the Revolution. The concerns of literate bourgeois women were apparent in the *cahiers,* the lists of grievances that were compiled by various revolutionary groups in the months after 1789. The women who wrote in the *cahiers* urged the reform and secularization of marriage and divorce, educational opportunity as a preparation for equality, and control of their dowries and children. Other women of this class presented the Revolution with jewels and money, hosted salons, rolled bandages, and even fought.

For these reasons bourgeois women obtained a measure of what they desired. The National Assembly made marriage a civil contract, guaranteed the right of divorce, determined that women could inherit property, and that wives could share in it. Free, but separate, primary schools for girls and boys had been decreed by 1795, but war demands prevented their foundation.

Poorer women also participated in many ways, but, paradoxically, they had much to lose from the destruction of the Old Regime and were hurt by the privations of war. Food shortages fell hard on the urban poor, and women both in cities and the countryside had to cope, in addition, with the economic consequences of the conscription of their husbands. The working women of Paris and other cities lost employment when the Revolution attacked the court and the aristocracy, the traditional employers of dressmakers, lacemakers, female domestic servants, and the practitioners of luxury crafts. Bourgeois women may have harmed their poorer sisters when they called for the incarceration of prostitutes, for prostitution is inevitably a means of support for poor women when other options disappear. Finally, the revolutionary attacks on the church deprived poor women of both spiritual and charitable support in times of crisis. Significantly, the first mass female protest of the Revolution, the march to Versailles in 1791, was caused by the shortage of bread.

While poor women struggled with economic difficulties, their social betters began to agitate for political rights. Several women emerged as leaders—Théroigne de Mericourt, Olympe de Gouge, the Dutchwoman Etta Palm d'Aelders. Women organized political clubs and addressed the Convention, but women angered the radical Jacobins by associating themselves with the Girondists. Because Robespierre and his allies were influenced by the antifeminist ideas of Jean Jacques Rousseau, women who pushed for political rights were increasingly at risk. The murder of the Jacobin leader Marat by the Girondist Charlotte Corday was used as an excuse to attack political women of all kinds. By the end of 1793 the Convention had outlawed all women's clubs, and most of their leaders were either dead or disgraced. The petition for voting rights made by the most vocal of the women's clubs, the Revolutionary Republican Women, came to nothing.

Women fared no better under Napoleon. The emperor's greatest accomplishment, the Napoleonic Code, preserved or reinstated a number of legal iniquities. Women were denied the right to manage their property after marriage; female adultery was treated more harshly than its male counterpart; and no woman could seek remedy before the law without her husband's permission. Napoleon, though he talked of "careers open to talent," thought little of the academic abilities of women. In one of his letters the Emperor emphasized the need for a religious education for women because it enhanced the qualities of belief, virtue, and resignation.

For the state school for girls at Ecouen, Napoleon prescribed writing, arithmetic, rudimentary French, geography, science, and history, but no ancient or modern languages. Beyond that, the Emperor decreed that the young women should learn to make their own clothes, acquire nursing skills, and become used to manual labor. All competition and all excitement of the "passions" was to be strenuously avoided. Education, which many women saw as a means to alter their status, was used by Napoleon to reinforce traditional roles and to prepare them for marriage. Divorce, though legal under the Napoleonic Code, was difficult to obtain, and it was outlawed with the restoration of the Bourbons.

The French Revolution failed to fulfill the hopes of many who had believed in the cherished ideals of liberty, equality, and fraternity. In its social consequences as in its political ones it remained incomplete, its force dissipated by war, terror, and compromise. Ultimately, the advocates of order stepped in and put an end to its violence with violence of their own. The legacy of the French Revolution was nonetheless powerful. The vulnerability of Europe's old order had been glimpsed if not realized; egalitarian ideals had been enunciated if not fulfilled; mass action had been institutionalized in Europe's armies; a model had been provided for future revolutionary action. The guardians of order, not the advocates of revolution, had reason to fear the future.

Portfolio: Francisco de Goya y Lucientes and the Tragedy of Total War

In some respects, Napoleon can be considered the first modern general. His utilization of mass conscription, artillery, patriotism, and armies of occupation are all too familiar to those conversant with the great wars of the twentieth century. Many of the works of the artist Goya depict the horrors of modern war upon the land and people of Spain, and by implication upon humanity as a whole. Perhaps no other artist has dealt so eloquently with war's brutality, folly, and degradation. In Goya's tragic vision, both conquered and conqueror are the ultimate victims of war, and all are ultimately devoured by it.

Los Desastres de La Guerra: Number 5. "And They are Like Wild Beasts." *Courtesy Meadows Museum and Art Gallery, Southern Methodist University.*

The Third of May 1808 in Madrid. Francisco de Goya y Lucientes
Courtesy Museo Nacional del Prado, Madrid.

The Colossus. Francisco de Goya y Lucientes
Courtesy Museo Nacional del Prado Madrid.

Saturn Devouring One of His Sons. Francisco de Goya y Lucientes
Courtesy Museo Nacional del Prado, Madrid.

Epilogue: The European World in 1815

In many ways, the European world in 1815 was a vastly changed place from the Europe of 1600. For those who cherished the idea of progress, there was much that was gratifying. By 1815, gas lamps glowed softly over the streets, and in the homes, of certain select districts in London, and in the same city some of the sidewalks had even been paved. A year earlier, the English inventor George Stephenson had developed the first practical steam locomotive. In 1810, in the German city of Essen, the Krupp Works was opened, a firm that was to one day be a byword for industrial production. At the height of the French Revolution, in 1795, the metric system was adopted in France, and five years later the American Eli Whitney demonstrated that a musket could be made with interchangeable parts. Standardization and mass production, hallmarks of the industrial revolution, had begun to make their way from England to continental Europe, and to the rest of the western world. Europe was unfolding and expanding. Britain already possessed a great empire, and others would soon strive to emulate the British example, both internally and externally. Americans would soon be talking about "Manifest Destiny," and the Russians had already begun to build highways into the rich vastness of Siberia.

To the bourgeoisie, the prime beneficiaries of the industrial revolution, life was becoming an increasingly good thing. The pursuit of pleasure was becoming more frequent, and the rituals of pleasure more sedate. By 1815, golf was becoming an increasingly important game and billiard rooms had already been established in London's Covent Garden. Some Englishmen were even enjoying cricket, a legal sport since 1748. In the last years of the Napoleonic wars the waltz had conquered Europe and was accepted by the bourgeoisie and the landed classes alike. After centuries of struggle, certain professions were finally establishing themselves, giving increasing status to their members. In 1815, the English Parliament passed the Apothecaries Act, making it illegal for unqualified and unlicensed physicians to practice in England. By 1815, some of the European bourgeoisie were enjoying comfortable homes, chocolates made in factories, fountain pens, newspapers and magazines, ribbed stockings, silk hats, whist, public restaurants, water closets, cigars, and letters sent by official post.

The landed and titled, the privileged few whom the bourgoisie desired to emulate and to marry, were beginning to indulge in yachting and organized horse-racing. English aristocrats could seek out their lineages in Debrett's *Peerage* and could mix with their fellows at the Ascot Gold Cup. In most areas of Europe the landed classes still enjoyed immense political power, and in England in particular they were most adept at using it.

For those who could afford to enjoy it, European culture brought much beauty. Art moved in the period from 1600 to 1815 from the baroque, to the classical, to the romantic. Contemporary architects left monuments like Versailles and St. Paul's. In the early 1600s Rubens and Caravaggio and El Greco were still painting; Thomas Morley, John Byrd, and Orlando Gibbons were composing their madrigals; and the Gobelin family established the tapestry works that became a byword for magnificence. In Spain, artists like Velázquez and Murillo pursued their great careers. Their lives intersected with the painters of the seventeenth-century Dutch School; the composers Praetorius, Victoria, Gabrieli, and Buxtehude; the plays of Shakespeare; the poetry of Donne and Milton; the architecture of Inigo Jones and Christopher Wren; the sculpture of Bernini. Overlapping with the era of Louis XIV were the careers of the composer Lully and the architect Mansart, the painters Lorrain and Poussin, the plays of Corneille, Racine, and Molière. By the end of the seventeenth century the Theatre Royal at Drury Lane had opened, and the French horn had become a recognized orchestral instrument; opera had come to London and ballet had become the beloved ward of the French court; an Italian named Antonio Stradivari had been born and had begun to fashion violins; a literary artist named Dryden had become England's poet-laureate.

As the seventeenth-century gave way to the eighteenth, the composers Johann Sebastian Bach, George Frederick Handel, and Domenico Scarlatti grew to maturity, and the paintings of Sir Godfrey Kneller, of Watteau, and of the Italian artist known as Canaletto began to be displayed. Swift began his career in satire, and the English novel was born in the works of writers like Henry Fielding. Literate English people could enjoy the essays of Addison and Steele, and the classical poetry of Alexander Pope, while their French counterparts began to sample the wit of Voltaire and Montesquieu's political philosophy. The English publishing house of Longman's was founded in 1724, one year after the birth of Joshua Reynolds, who grew into one of the great portrait painters of the English school. A few years later the engraver and painter William Hogarth began to produce his political satires, laying down a tradition that was followed later by Rowlandson and Cruikshank. Chardin and Boucher carried on the great French tradition in painting; Vivaldi and Telemann composed. In 1740 a very young man named Joseph Haydn entered the Vienna court chapel as a choirboy. At about the same time Samuel Johnson was moving about London, often accompanied by his amanuensis, James Boswell. Female actresses and dancers had begun to appear on stage in large numbers, and they were sought after by hordes of male admirers. Goethe and Schiller, William Blake and Robert Burns, were all born in the second half of the eighteenth century. In 1762 Mozart was touring Europe as a child prodigy; he was then six. Two years later he wrote his first symphony. Some years thereafter another prodigy named Paganini traveled around Europe conquering audiences with his violin; he was eleven at the time. In the last, troubled years of the eighteenth century Schubert was born and Beethoven was working on the first of his symphonies. By the time of the Congress of Vienna, the romantic movement began to emerge in the paintings of Goya and Fragonard, and the poetry of Wordsworth and Byron. There was enough culture and art here for anyone.

The commitment to science so evident in the seventeenth century continued on into the eighteenth. Professional societies, the Industrial Revolution, and the skilled publicists of the Enlightenment all helped to make science more popular and perceived as more directly applicable to human needs. The work of von Helmont on gases in the seventeenth century pointed the way to the discoveries of Priestley, Cavendish, and Dalton in the eighteenth and nineteenth. Cavendish identified carbon dioxide and hydrogen as distinct substances and discovered that oxygen and hydrogen combined to form water. Working independently, Joseph Priestley in England and Carl Wilhelm Scheele in Sweden discovered a whole host of gases, including oxygen, chlorine, carbon monoxide, and ammonia. Dalton, for his part, laid the foundations for the modern atomic theory. These and similar discoveries overlapped with the work of Lavoisier, who discovered the true composition of air. The discovery of oxygen led, in turn, to hypotheses as to the nature of respiration and photosynthesis, laying groundwork for modern biochemistry, physiology, and the applied chemistry of the "second industrial revolution."

Medical science also made some progress. Sir William Hunter's skills as an anatomist, combined with the availability of the corpse of a pregnant woman, made it possible for him to undertake, in the late eighteenth century, a series of dissections that made a fundamental contribution to obstetric anatomy. In the same one hundred years, physicians learned how to measure blood pressure and to detect chest diseases by percussion, and Morgagni established the medical discipline of pathological anatomy. In 1800 the Royal College of Surgeons was founded in London. Nonetheless, medical care was still beyond the means and access of the mass of the people, and its efficacy was often questionable. Fundamental improvement would come only with the discoveries of Lister and Pasteur later in the nineteenth century.

Technology and industrialization, identified so often with progress, still left many in Europe unaffected and influenced some people and institutions negatively as much as positively. Vast areas of Europe still remained preindustrial in 1815. Austria, Prussia, and Russia were still essentially agrarian peasant empires, distinguished by great estates, a comparatively small bourgeois class, and masses of peasants and serfs. The French peasantry certainly survived the French Revolution, and English travelers could still move through landscapes of moors and villages untouched by industrialization.

For some Europeans, industry and technology were hardly welcome. A whole generation of nineteenth-century romantic writers celebrated rural virtues and condemned the industrial cities. In 1810 English workers, following the commands of a mythical leader known as "Ned Lud," began to attack and destroy industrial machinery in the north of England. In 1791, the workers of Hamburg staged the first general strike. There were also some signs that industrial technology could produce evil as well as good. In 1805 rockets became part of the weapons arsenal of the British army; the Krupp Works eventually specialized in the production of heavy artillery pieces. In 1814, the London *Times* was printed by a steam-operated press, a harbinger of modern mass communications. In the same years all newspapers were full of stories of blood and iron, of armies tearing each other to pieces with well-orchestrated cannonades.

The poor who poured into the industrial cities, new and old, certainly had cause to question the benefits of the new order, as they crowded into tenement housing and sought out municipal services that were either overstrained or nonexistent. London still had no formal police force in 1815, and the newfangled gas lighting did not reach the homes of the poor. There is good reason to question the positive impact of the industrial and French revolutions on women, on the condition of the less fortunate, on the family. For many Europeans, beauty and progress, insofar as they were aware of them, had in 1815 only a limited impact on their lives.

Appendix: Genealogical Tables

THE HOUSE OF BOURBON: FRANCE 1589–1830

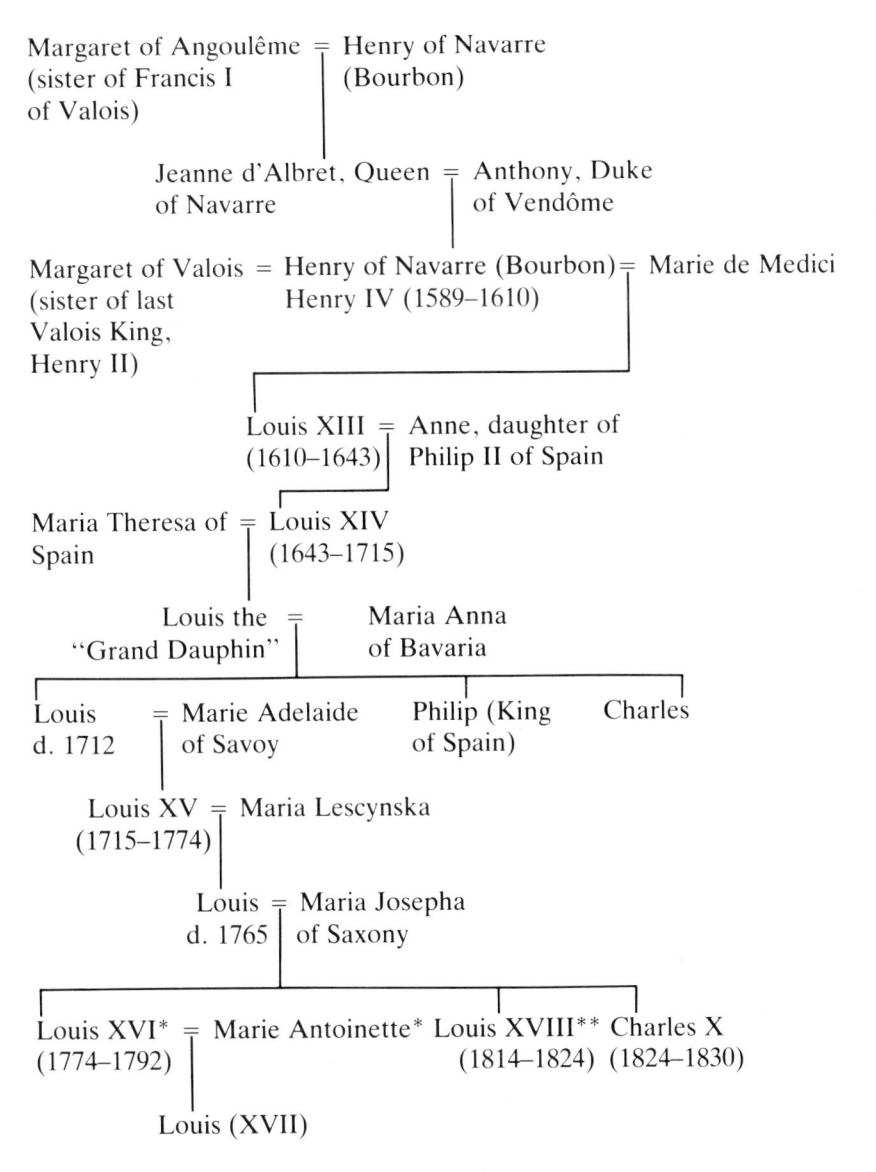

```
Margaret of Angoulême  =  Henry of Navarre
(sister of Francis I          (Bourbon)
of Valois)
                │
        Jeanne d'Albret, Queen  =  Anthony, Duke
            of Navarre                of Vendôme
                        │
Margaret of Valois  =  Henry of Navarre (Bourbon) =  Marie de Medici
(sister of last         Henry IV (1589–1610)
Valois King,
Henry II)
                        │
            Louis XIII  =  Anne, daughter of
            (1610–1643)    Philip II of Spain
                        │
Maria Theresa of  =  Louis XIV
Spain                (1643–1715)
                        │
        Louis the  =  Maria Anna
    "Grand Dauphin"   of Bavaria
                        │
    ┌───────────────────┼───────────────────┐
Louis    =  Marie Adelaide   Philip (King    Charles
d. 1712     of Savoy          of Spain)
        │
    Louis XV  =  Maria Lescynska
    (1715–1774)
            │
        Louis  =  Maria Josepha
        d. 1765   of Saxony
            │
    ┌───────────────┬───────────────┐
Louis XVI*  =  Marie Antoinette*  Louis XVIII**  Charles X
(1774–1792)                       (1814–1824)    (1824–1830)
        │
    Louis (XVII)
```

*Executed during the French Revolution
**Restored after the defeat of Napoleon

435

THE HOUSES OF STUART AND HANOVER: ENGLAND, 1603–1820

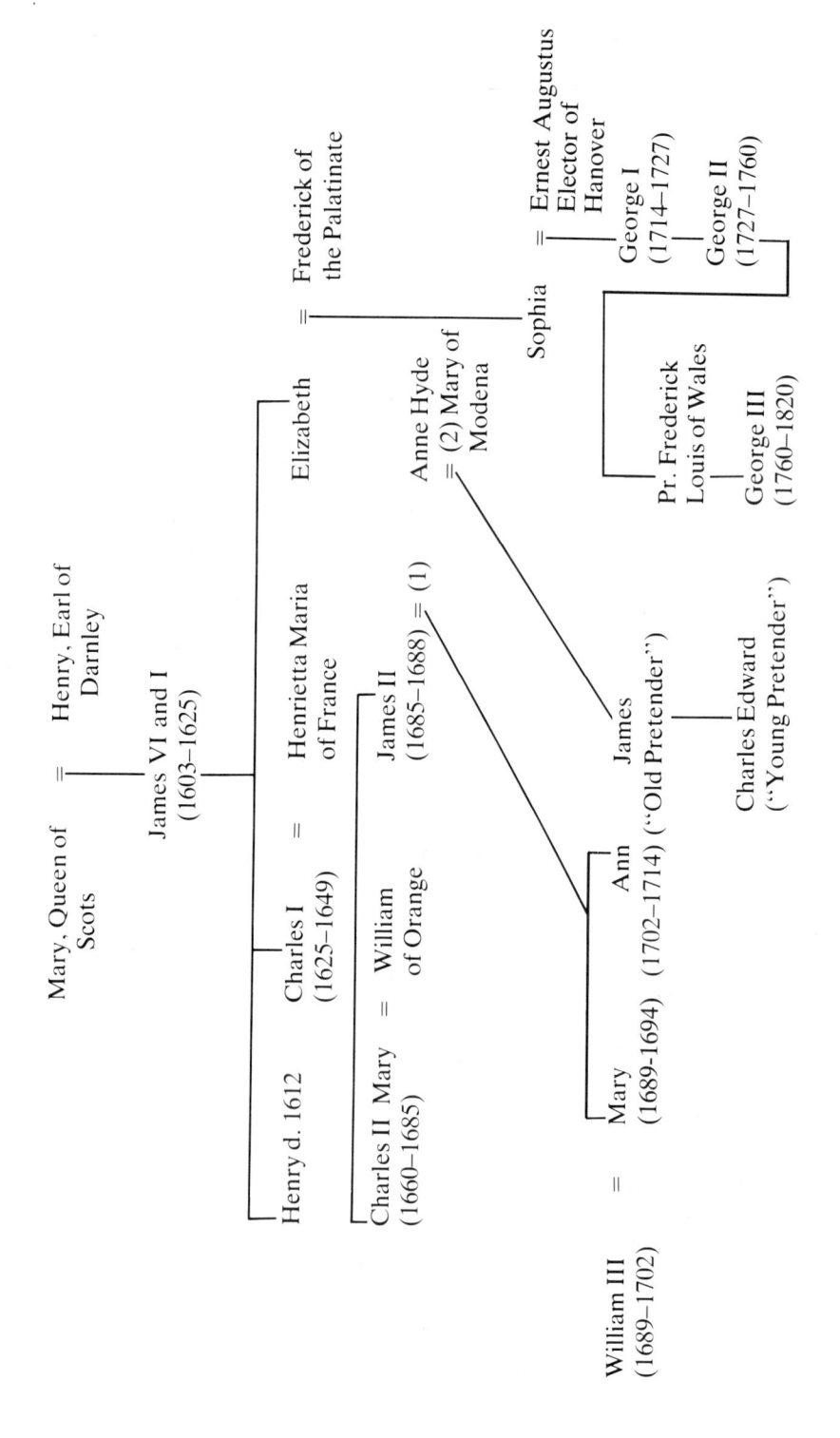

```
Mary, Queen of  =  Henry, Earl of
    Scots              Darnley
            |
       James VI and I  =  Henrietta Maria
        (1603–1625)         of France
            |
    ┌───────┼───────────────┬──────────────┐
 Henry   Charles I      Elizabeth  =  Frederick of
 d. 1612 (1625–1649)                   the Palatinate
            |                          |
            |                       Sophia  =  Ernest Augustus
            |                                   Elector of
            |                                   Hanover
            |                          |
            |                       George I
            |                       (1714–1727)
            |                          |
            |                       George II
            |                       (1727–1760)
            |                          |
            |                       Pr. Frederick
            |                       Louis of Wales
            |                          |
            |                       George III
            |                       (1760–1820)
    ┌───────┼───────────┐
 Charles II  Mary  =  William        James II      =  (1) Anne Hyde
 (1660–1685)         of Orange    (1685–1688)      =  (2) Mary of Modena
                        |              |
                        |      ┌───────┼──────┐
                        |    Mary    Ann    James
                        |  (1689–1694)(1702–1714) ("Old Pretender")
                        |                         |
                        |                      Charles Edward
                        |                      ("Young Pretender")
                        |
 William III  =  Mary
 (1689–1702)
```

436

THE HAPSBURGS: AUSTRIA, HUNGARY, AND HOLY ROMAN EMPIRE, 1556–1835

B—King of Bohemia   E—Emperor   H—King of Hungary

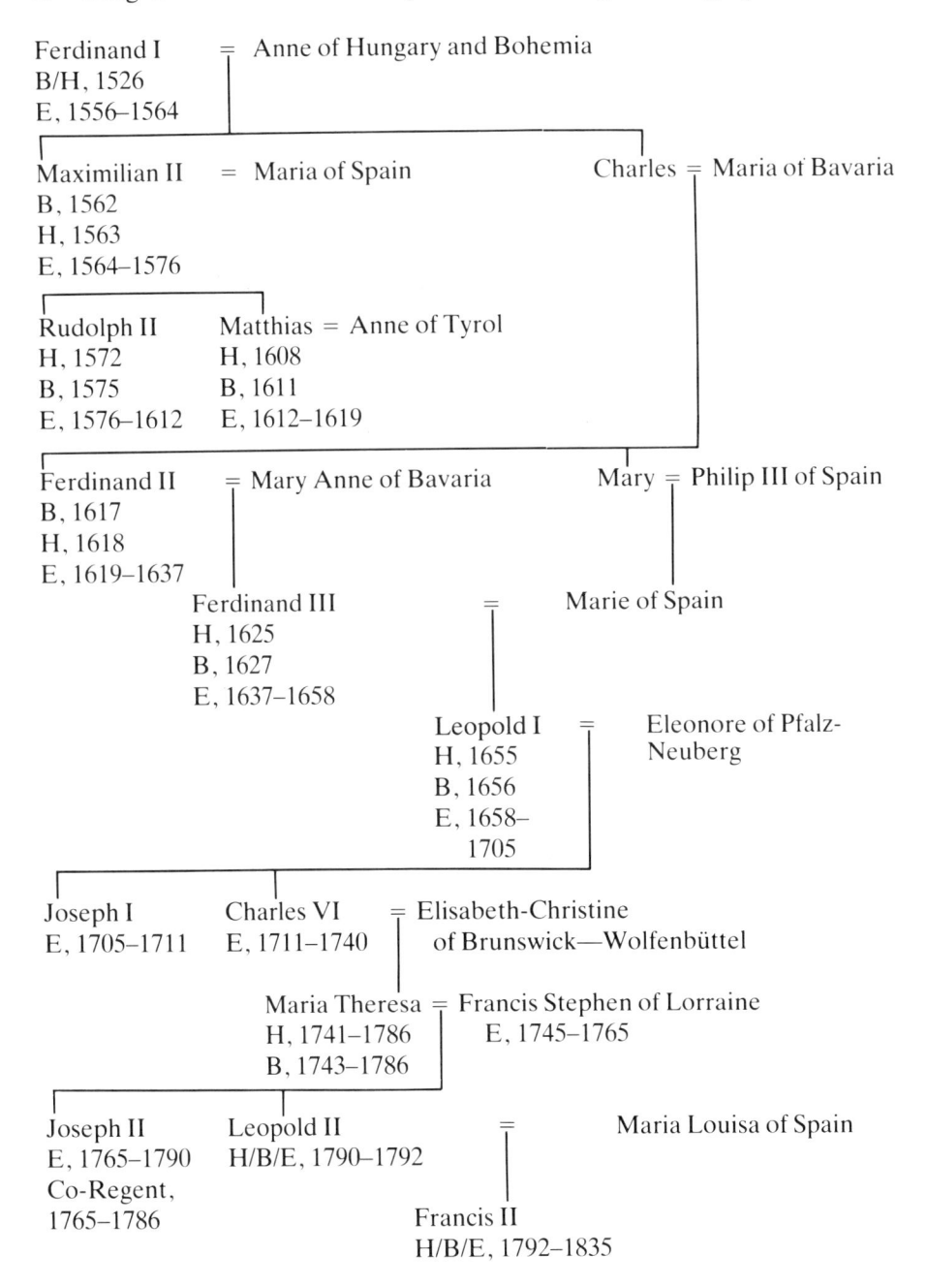

```
Ferdinand I        = Anne of Hungary and Bohemia
B/H, 1526
E, 1556–1564
    |
    |─────────────────────────────────────────────────────┐
Maximilian II    = Maria of Spain              Charles = Maria of Bavaria
B, 1562                                                     |
H, 1563                                                     |
E, 1564–1576                                                |
    |                                                       |
    |──────────────────┐                                    |
Rudolph II        Matthias = Anne of Tyrol                  |
H, 1572           H, 1608                                   |
B, 1575           B, 1611                                   |
E, 1576–1612      E, 1612–1619                              |
    |                                                       |
    |                                                       |
Ferdinand II     = Mary Anne of Bavaria      Mary = Philip III of Spain
B, 1617                  |                          |
H, 1618                  |                          |
E, 1619–1637             |                          |
                  Ferdinand III          =     Marie of Spain
                  H, 1625                          |
                  B, 1627                          |
                  E, 1637–1658                     |
                                                   |
                            Leopold I      =   Eleonore of Pfalz-
                            H, 1655            Neuberg
                            B, 1656
                            E, 1658–
                            1705
    |────────────────┬──────────────────────────────┐
Joseph I          Charles VI      = Elisabeth-Christine
E, 1705–1711      E, 1711–1740      of Brunswick—Wolfenbüttel
                            |
                    Maria Theresa  = Francis Stephen of Lorraine
                    H, 1741–1786     E, 1745–1765
                    B, 1743–1786
    |────────────────┬─────────────────────────────────┐
Joseph II         Leopold II              =    Maria Louisa of Spain
E, 1765–1790      H/B/E, 1790–1792                 |
Co-Regent,                                         |
1765–1786                              Francis II
                                       H/B/E, 1792–1835
```

437

THE HOUSE OF HOHENZOLLERN IN BRANDENBURG AND PRUSSIA 1598–1840

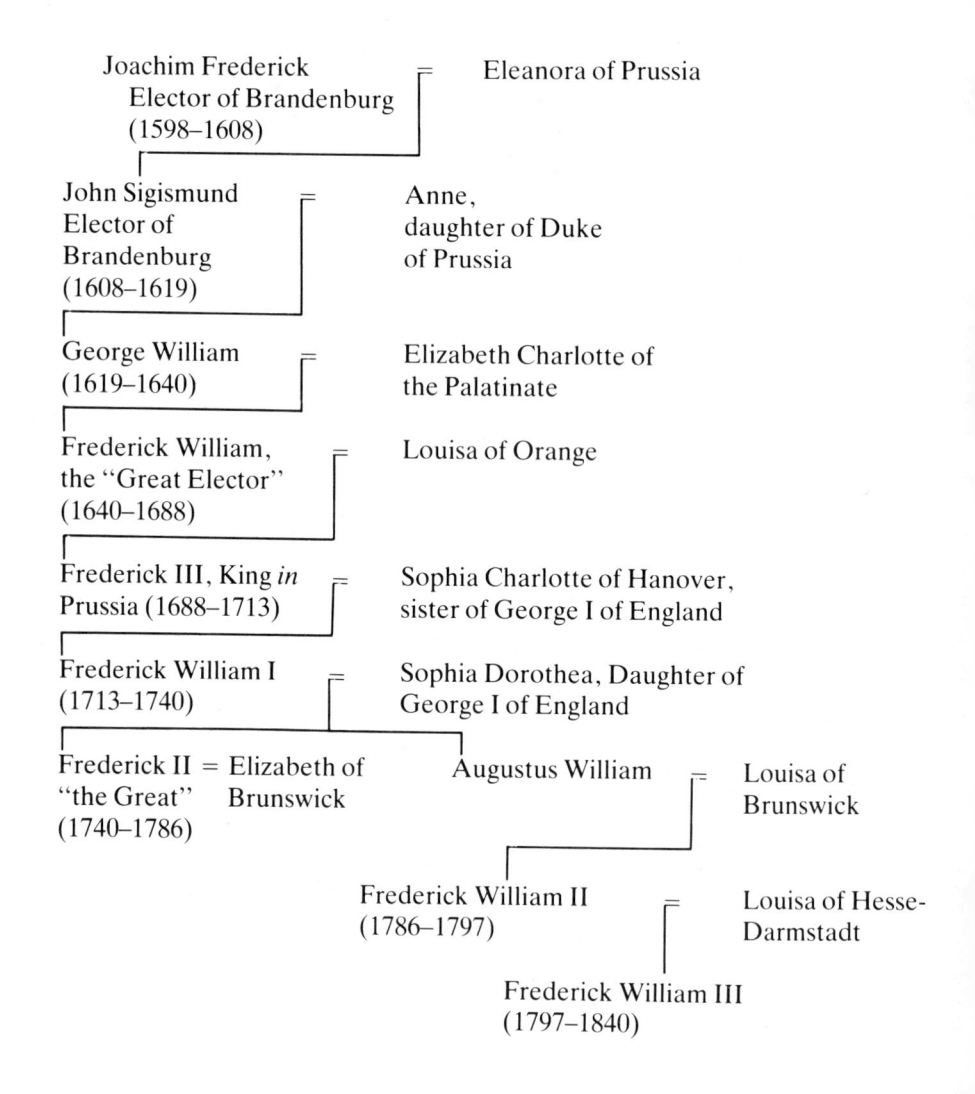

Joachim Frederick = Eleanora of Prussia
Elector of Brandenburg
(1598–1608)

John Sigismund = Anne,
Elector of   daughter of Duke
Brandenburg   of Prussia
(1608–1619)

George William = Elizabeth Charlotte of
(1619–1640)   the Palatinate

Frederick William, = Louisa of Orange
the "Great Elector"
(1640–1688)

Frederick III, King *in* = Sophia Charlotte of Hanover,
Prussia (1688–1713)   sister of George I of England

Frederick William I = Sophia Dorothea, Daughter of
(1713–1740)   George I of England

Frederick II = Elizabeth of   Augustus William = Louisa of
"the Great"   Brunswick   Brunswick
(1740–1786)

Frederick William II = Louisa of Hesse-
(1786–1797)   Darmstadt

Frederick William III
(1797–1840)

THE HOUSE OF ROMANOV: RUSSIA, 1547–1825

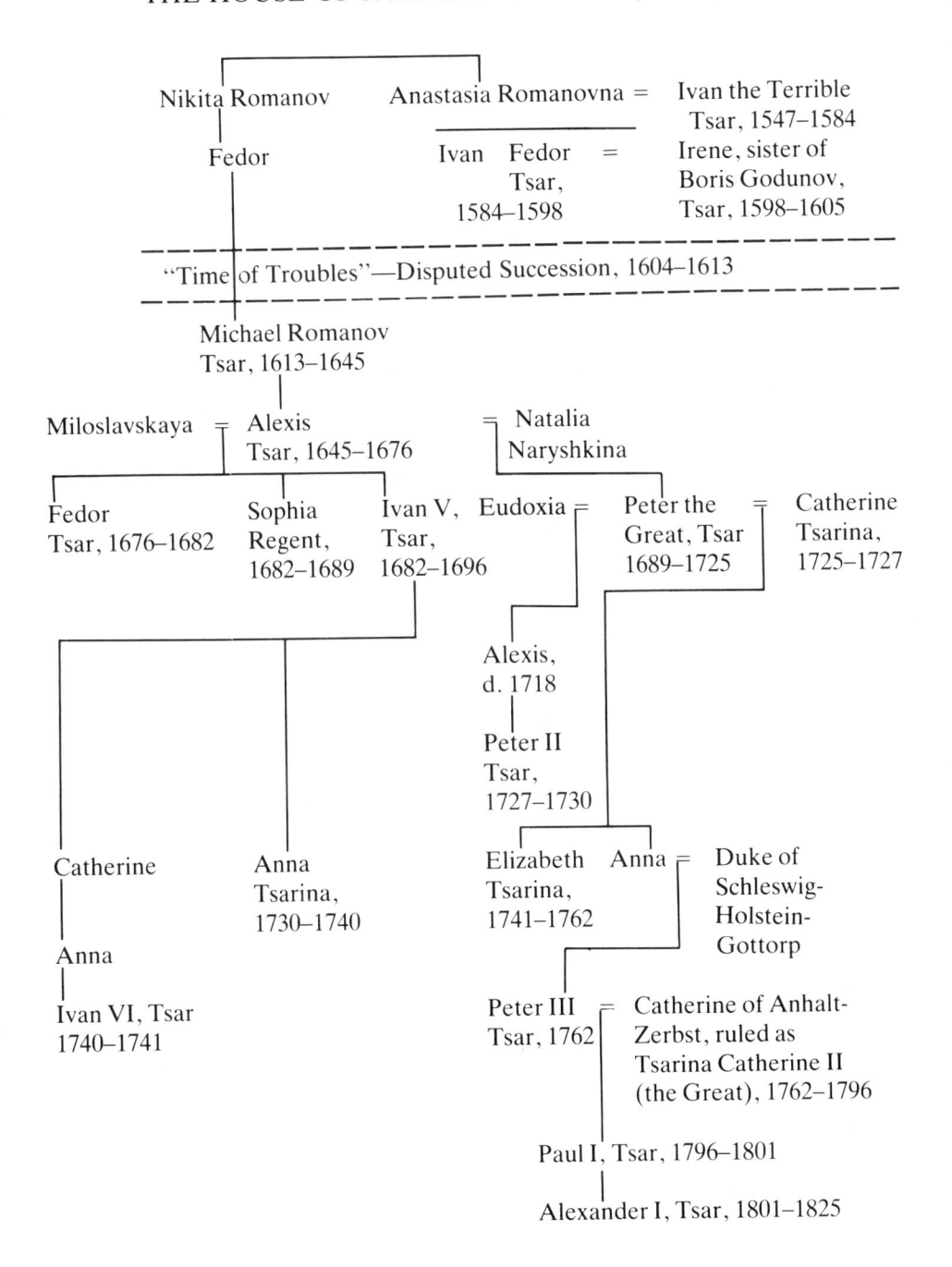

- Nikita Romanov — Anastasia Romanovna = Ivan the Terrible, Tsar, 1547–1584
  - Fedor
  - Ivan
  - Fedor = Irene, sister of Boris Godunov, Tsar, 1598–1605
  - Tsar, 1584–1598

"Time of Troubles"—Disputed Succession, 1604–1613

- Michael Romanov, Tsar, 1613–1645
  - Miloslavskaya = Alexis, Tsar, 1645–1676 = Natalia Naryshkina
    - Fedor, Tsar, 1676–1682
    - Sophia, Regent, 1682–1689
    - Ivan V, Tsar, 1682–1696
    - Eudoxia = Peter the Great, Tsar, 1689–1725 = Catherine, Tsarina, 1725–1727
      - Alexis, d. 1718
        - Peter II, Tsar, 1727–1730
    - Catherine
      - Anna
        - Ivan VI, Tsar, 1740–1741
    - Anna, Tsarina, 1730–1740
    - Elizabeth, Tsarina, 1741–1762
    - Anna = Duke of Schleswig-Holstein-Gottorp
      - Peter III, Tsar, 1762 = Catherine of Anhalt-Zerbst, ruled as Tsarina Catherine II (the Great), 1762–1796
        - Paul I, Tsar, 1796–1801
          - Alexander I, Tsar, 1801–1825

THE HOUSE OF VASA: SWEDEN 1523–1718

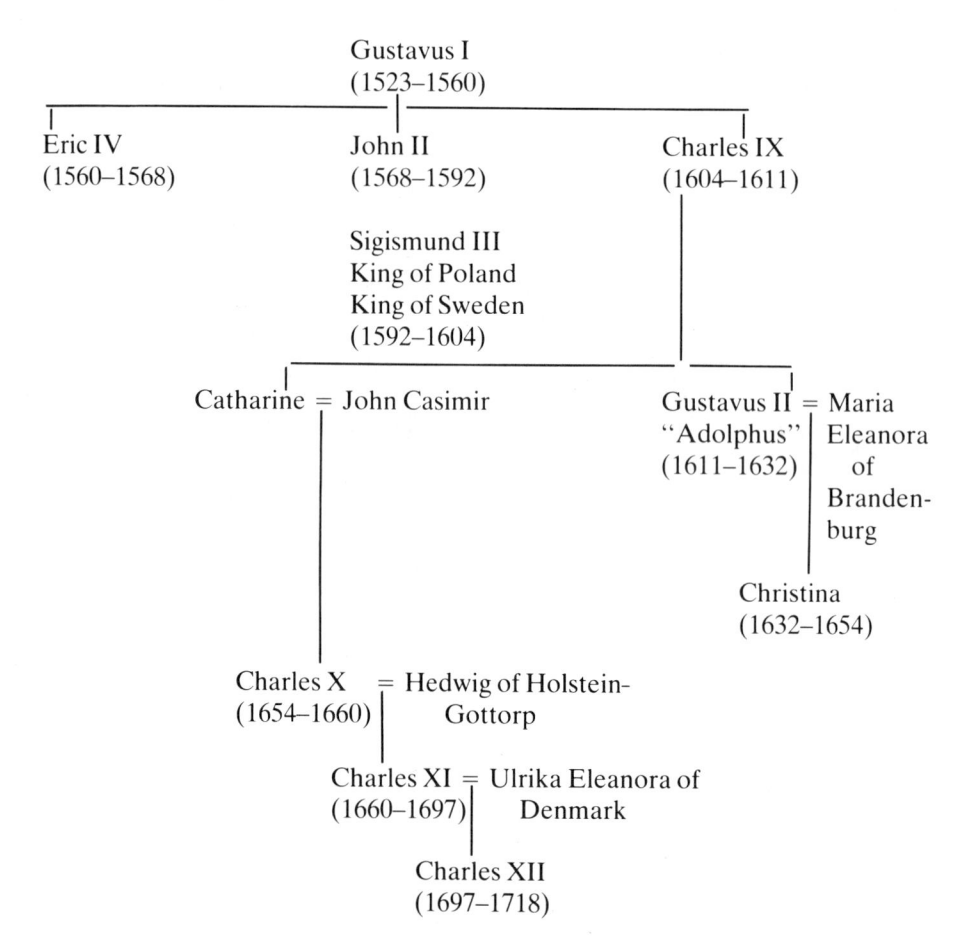

```
                        Gustavus I
                        (1523–1560)
     ┌──────────────────────┼──────────────────────┐
  Eric IV               John II                Charles IX
 (1560–1568)           (1568–1592)            (1604–1611)
                                                  
                       Sigismund III
                       King of Poland
                       King of Sweden
                       (1592–1604)
            ┌──────────────┴───────────────┬────────────────┐
       Catharine = John Casimir      Gustavus II = Maria
                                      "Adolphus"   Eleanora
                                     (1611–1632)   of
                                                   Branden-
                                                   burg
                                            
                                         Christina
                                        (1632–1654)
            │
       Charles X  = Hedwig of Holstein-
      (1654–1660)    Gottorp
                │
            Charles XI = Ulrika Eleanora of
           (1660–1697)    Denmark
                     │
                Charles XII
               (1697–1718)
```

FROM THE THE HOUSE OF HAPSBURG TO THE HOUSE OF BOURBON: SPAIN, 1598–1700

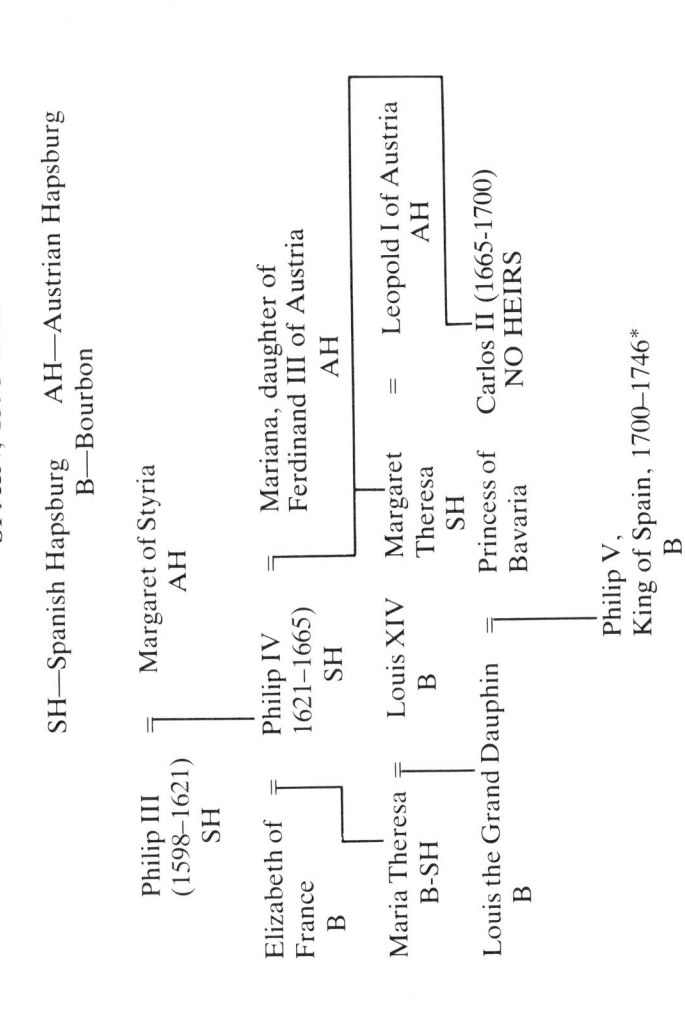

SH—Spanish Hapsburg AH—Austrian Hapsburg B—Bourbon

```
Philip III          =  Margaret of Styria
(1598–1621)            AH
SH
   |
Elizabeth of       =  Philip IV           =  Mariana, daughter of
France                1621–1665              Ferdinand III of Austria
B                     SH                     AH
   |                                              |
Maria Theresa  =  Louis XIV          Margaret   =  Leopold I of Austria
B-SH              B                  Theresa       AH
   |                                 SH
Louis the Grand Dauphin  =  Princess of      Carlos II (1665–1700)
B                           Bavaria          NO HEIRS
   |
Philip V,
King of Spain, 1700–1746*
B
```

*The dispute over the Bourbon Succession to the Spanish throne led to the War of the Spanish Succession, 1702–1713. The Bourbon claim was upheld at the Peace of Utrecht, 1713.

Bibliography

European History 1600–1815: A Bibliographic Essay

The Bibliography that appears on the following pages has been prepared with several objectives in mind: to acknowledge the debt that this textbook owes to the work of historians in many fields; to identify new directions in historical research, particularly in social history and the history of the family and of women; to provide background on various historiographical debates; and to encourage students to do extra reading on topics interesting to them. Those wishing to pursue certain topics over a longer time-period can consult the bibliography in Thomas R. Rumsey, *Men and Women of the Renaissance and Reformation 1300–1600* (Independent School Press, 1981), as a supplement to what appears here.

Chapter I

General Social History: Sources

A good starting place for source material on social history are the diaries of John Evelyn and Samuel Pepys. For the former, see E.S. de Beer, ed., *The Diary of John Evelyn*, 6 vols. (1955). *The Diary of Samuel Pepys* has been edited by S.B. Wheatley (10 vols., 1893–1899) and most recently by R. Latham and W. Mathews (1970–   ). Other valuable sources include G.P. Elliott, ed., "Diary of Sir Edward Lake . . . 1677–1678," *Camden Miscellany*, ser. 1, no. 39 (1847); G.P. Elliott, ed., "Autobiography and Anecdotes by William Taswell," *Camden Miscellany*, ser. 1, no. 55 (1853); H. Ellis, ed., *Obituary kept by Richard Smyth, 1627–1674* (1849); R. Hellie, ed., *Readings for an Introduction to Russian Civilization. Moscovite Society* (1970); E. Hockliffe, ed., *Diary of the Rev. Ralph Josselin* 1908); T.T. Lewis, ed., *Letters of the Lady Brilliana Harley* (1854); M. Lowenthal, trans., *The Memoirs of Glückel of Hameln* (1977); J.R. Marcus, ed., *The Jew in the Medieval World: A Source Book: 315–1791* (1977); N. Marlow, trans.; G. Isham, ed., *The Diary of Thomas Isham of Lamport (1658–1681). . . .* (1971); J.D. Marshall, ed., *The Autobiography of William Stout of Lancaster* (1967); J.G. Nichols, ed., *The Autobiography of Anne Lady Halkett* (1875); G. Roberts, ed., *Diary of Walter Yonge from 1604 to 1628* (1848); C. Robbins, ed., *The Diary of John Milward* (1938); W.B. Rye, ed., *England as Seen by Foreigners in the Days of Elizabeth & James the First* (repr. 1967); A.F. Scott, ed., *The Stuart Age. Commentaries of an Era* (1974); E. Thomson, ed., *The Chamberlain Letters* (1965); E.M. Thompson, ed., *Correspondence of the Family of Hatton A.D. 1601–1704* (2 vols., 1878); S. Tymms, ed., *Wills and Inventories of Bury St. Edmunds* (1850); L.B. Wright; M. Tinling, eds., *William Byrd of Virginia. The London Diary (1717–1721) and other Writings* (1958). Also worth consulting are *The Autobiography of John Brampston* (1845); John Bruce, ed., *Letters and Papers of the Verney Family to 1639* (1853); R. Caulfield, ed., *Journal of the Very Reverend Rowland Davies* (1857), and *Memoirs of the Verney Family* (1899). Many of the above are publications of the Camden Society.

General Social History: Secondary Works

For England see C. Bridenbaugh, *Vexed and Troubled Englishmen, 1590–1642* (1968); M. Coate, *Social Life in Stuart England* (repr. 1971); W.H. Dunham and S. Pargellis, *Complaint and Reform in England 1436–1714* (1968); W. Notestein, *The English People on the Eve of Colonization, 1603–1630* (1954); D. Ogg, *England in the Reign of Charles II* (2nd ed. 1956); P.S. Seaver, ed., *Seventeenth-Century England: Society in an Age of Revolution*. French society is discussed in N.Z. Davis, *Society and Culture in Early Modern France* (1975); P. Goubert, *Louis XIV and Twenty Million Frenchmen* (1972); and V.L. Tapié, *France in the Age of Louis XIII and*

Richelieu (1974). For Spain there is M. Defourneaux, *Daily Life in Spain During the Golden Age* (1979) and R. Trevor-Davies, *Spain in Decline 1621–1700* (1965). Good chapters on Russian society are found in J.H. Billington, *The Icon and the Axe* (1966); I. De Madariaga, *Russia in the Age of Catherine the Great* (1981); and L.J. Oliva, *Russia in the Era of Peter the Great* (1969). For the Low Countries, the reader should see C. Wilson, *The Dutch Republic and the Civilization of the Seventeenth Century* (1968); and especially J.L. Price, *Culture and Society in the Dutch Republic During the Seventeenth Century* (1974). A fascinating study of social customs is P. Burke, *Popular Culture in Early Modern Europe* (1978). F. Braudel, *The Structures of Everyday Life. Civilization and Capitalism 15th–18th Century* (1979) is a recent, and rich, compendium of social lore. P. Ariès, *The Hour of Our Death* (1981) surveys changing attitudes over time toward dying. See also J. McManners, *Death and the Enlightenment* (1981).

Economic History

In addition to the *Cambridge Economic History*, the best general works on the period are P. Burke, *Economy and Society in Early Modern Europe* (1972); F. Braudel, *Capitalism and Material Life 1400–1800* (1973); J. De Vries, *The Economy of Europe in an Age of Crisis, 1600–1750* (1976); and C.M. Cipolla, *Before the Industrial Revolution. European Society and Economy, 1000–1700* (1976). Cipolla has also edited two other valuable books: *The Fontana Economic History of Europe. Volume 2. The Sixteenth and Seventeenth Centuries* (1977) and *The Economic Decline of Empires* (1970). For agricultural history, see J.D. Chambers and G.E. Mingay, *The Agricultural Revolution* (1966); E.L. Jones, ed., *Agriculture and Economic Growth in England, 1650–1815* (1967); E. Kerridge, *Agrarian Problems in the Sixteenth Century and After* (1969); and J. Thirsk, ed., *The Agrarian History of England and Wales, 1500–1640* (1967). More general in scope is B.H. Slicher van Bath, *The Agrarian History of Western Europe 500–1850* (1963), and it is a good starting place. Useful for the English economy in this period are P.J. Bowden, *The Wool Trade in Tudor and Stuart England* (1962); L.A. Clarkson, *The Pre-Industrial Economy in England 1500–1750* (1972); D.C. Coleman, *The Economy of England 1450–1750* (1977); R. Davis, *The Rise of the English Shipping Industry* (1962); R. Davis, *A Commercial Revolution: English Overseas Trade in the Seventeenth and Eighteenth Centuries* (1967); N.S.B. Gras, *The Evolution of the English Corn Market* (1915); W.E. Minchinton, ed., *The Growth of English Overseas Trade in the Seventeenth and Eighteenth Centuries* (1969); B.E. Supple, *Commercial Crisis and Change in England 1600–1642* (1959); and C. Wilson, *England's Apprenticeship, 1603–1763* (1965). The Dutch trading economy is covered in C.R. Boxer, *The Dutch Seaborne Empire 1600–1800* (1965), and *The Dutch in Brazil* (1957); A.E. Christensen, *Dutch Trade to the Baltic About 1600* (1941); and K. Glamann, *Dutch-Asiatic Trade, 1620–1740*

(1958). For the history of technology there are S. Lilley, *Men, Machines and History* (1965); A.E. Musson, ed., *Science, Technology and Economic Growth in the Eighteenth Century* (1972); and C. Singer, ed., *A History of Technology* (1956). Also interesting are H.I. Bloom, *Economic Activities of the Jews of Amsterdam in the Seventeenth and Eighteenth Centuries* (1937); C.M. Cipolla, *Money, Prices, and Civilization* (1956); D. Davis, *A History of Shopping* (1966); M. Dobb, *Studies in the Development of Capitalism* (1946); and A. Tenenti, *Piracy and The Decline of Venice 1580–1615* (1946).

Travel and Transportation

There are many travel journals for the seventeenth and eighteenth centuries. A few that were particularly helpful include S.H. Baron, ed., *The Travels of Olearius in Seventeenth-Century Russia* (1967); C. Morris, ed., *The Journeys of Celia Fiennes* (1949); Fynes Moryson, *Itinerary* (1917–1918); and R.P. Stearns, ed., *A Journey to Paris in the Year 1698 by Martin Lister* (1967). Also useful are B. Penrose, *Urbane Travelers 1591–1635* (1942) and J.W. Stoye, *English Travellers Abroad 1604–1667. Their Influence on English Society and Politics* (repr. 1968). Two books that describe the difficulties and forms of travel in the pre-industrial age are V.A. La Mar, *Travel and Roads in England* (1960) and J. Parkes, *Travel in England in the Seventeenth Century* (repr. 1968).

Vagabondage, Crime, and the Social Structure

It is now accepted that the study of criminality can tell us much about a given society. A feeling for crime and punishment in the period can be gleaned from reading F. Aydelotte, *Elizabethan Rogues and Vagabonds* (1913); C. Hibbert, *The Roots of Evil: A Social History of Crime and Punishment* (1963); G. Ives, *A History of Penal Methods: Criminals, Witches, Lunatics* (repr. 1970); J. Lawrence, *A History of Capital Punishment* (1960); E. Moir, *The Justice of the Peace* (1969); L.O. Pike, *A History of Crime in England.* 2 vols. (repr. 1968); J. Pound, *Poverty and Vagrancy in Tudor England* (1971); G. Salgado, *The Elizabethan Underworld* (1978); N. Walker, *Crime and Punishment in Britain* (1965). Two excellent and recent studies of urban crime and disorder are L. Martines, *Violence and Civil Disorder in Italian Cities* (1972) and M.E. Perry, *Crime and Society in Early Modern Seville* (1980). Excellent collections of monographs on crime and punishment are found in J.S. Cockburn, ed., *Crime in England 1550–1800* (1977) and especially in Douglas Hay, et al., *Albion's Fatal Tree: Crime and Society in Eighteenth Century England* (1975). For seventeenth- and eighteenth-century attitudes toward sexual offenses, see C. Bingham, "Seventeenth Century Attitudes Toward Deviant Sex," *Journal of Interdisciplinary History* I (1971); A.N. Gilbert, "Buggery and the British Navy, 1700–1861," *Journal of Social History*, 10 (1976); and R. Trumbach, "London's Sodomites: Homosexual Behavior and Western Culture in the Eighteenth Century," *Journal of Social History* 11 (1977). J.A. Sharpe, in "Domestic Homicide in Early Modern England," *Historical Journal,* 24 (March 1981) raises some questions about women in crime. J.M. Beattie, "The Pattern of Crime in England, 1660–1800," *Past & Present,* 62 (1974) is also informative. The relationship of hunger and poverty to violence is explored in Louise A. Tilly, "The Food Riot as a Form of Political Conflict in France," *Journal of International History,* 2 (Summer, 1971). Vagrancy and beggary, which often fed into crime, is discussed in A.L. Beier, "Vagrants and the Social Order in Elizabethan England," *Past & Present,* 64 (1974) and in P.A. Slack, "Vagrants and Vagrancy in England 1598-1664," *Economic History Review,* 2nd ser., 27 (1974). Some newer studies that shed light on crime and punishment are I.A. Cameron, *Crime and Repression in the Auvergne and the Guyenne, 1720-1790* (1981); A. Macfarlane, *The Justice and the Mare's Ale: Law and Disorder in Seventeenth-Century England* (1981); P.B. Munsche, *Gentlemen and Poachers: The English Game Laws 1671—1831* (1981); and A. Wills, *Crime and Punishment in Revolutionary Paris* (1981).

Demographic History

The history of population movements, and the factors that influenced it, is an interesting and comparatively new field of history. For an introduction to the field, see C.M. Cipolla, *The Economic History of World Population,* 6th ed. (1974); the collection of articles called "Historical Population Studies," *Daedalus,* 97 (Spring 1968); D.V. Glass and D.E.C. Eversley, eds., *Population in History* (1965); and E.A. Wrigley, *An Introduction to English Historical Demography* (1966). Also useful is P. Laslett, "The History of Population and Social Structure," *International Social Science Journal,* 17 (1965). P. Goubert, "The French Peasantry of the Seventeenth Century," *Past & Present,* 10 (1956) presents a "regional example" of demographic history. Also interesting are T.H. Hollingsworth, "A Demographic Study of the British Ducal Families," *Population Studies,* 11 (1957), and P.E. Jones and A.V. Judges, "London Population in the Late Seventeenth Century," *Economic History Review,* 6 (1935–1936). The effects of climate on food supply, and thus on population, is discussed in E.L. Ladurie, *Times of Feast, Times of Famine* (trans. 1971). Food supply itself is well-covered in R. Forster and O. Ranum, eds., *Food and Drink In History* (1979); E. and R. Forster, eds., *European Diet from Preindustrial to Modern Times* (1975); E.P. Prentice, *Hunger and History* (1939); and R.M. Salaman, *The History and Social History of the Potato* (1949). Important monographs are A.B. Appleby, *Famine in Tudor and Stuart England* (1978); L.M. Cullen, "Irish History without the Potato," *Past and Present,* 40 (1968); F.J. Fisher, "The Development of the London Food Market, 1540–1640," *Economic History Review,* 5 (April 1935); J. Revel, "A Capital City's Privileges: Food

Supply in Early-Modern Rome," in *Food and Drink In History*, ed. R. Forster and O. Ranum (1979); and J. Walter and K. Wrightson, "Dearth and the Social Order in Early Modern England," *Past & Present*, 71 (May 1976). W.G. Hoskins, in "Harvest Fluctuations in England, 1620–1759," *Agricultural History Review* (1968) documents a high frequency of food shortages in England. E.L. Ladurie, in "Famine Amenorrhea (Seventeenth-Twentieth Centuries)," in *Biology of Man In History*, ed. R. Forster and O. Ranum (1975) argues that famine conditions affected the fertility of women. A feeling for the bleak lives of ordinary people in this period can be gleaned by reading R. Harvey, "Recent Research on Poverty in Tudor-Stuart England: Review and Commentary," *International Review of Social History*, 24:2 (1979); and D. Marshall, "The Old Poor Law, 1662–1795," in *Essays in Economic History*, ed., E.M. Carus-Wilson; and G.W. Oxley, *Poor Relief in England and Wales, 1603–1834*.

Urban, Regional, and Local History

The following provide introductions to the history of cities: A. Everitt, ed., *Perspectives in Urban History* (1973); G. Fox, *3000 Years of Urban Growth* (1974); M.D. Lobel, ed., *The Atlas of Historic Towns*, 2 vols. (1969, 1975); L. Mumford, *The City in History* (1966); and G. Sjoberg, *The Preindustrial City: Past and Present* (1960). W.H. McNeill, in *The Shape of European History* (1974) calls for the reorganization of European history around the great cities. As would be expected, the English cities, and particularly London, are well-covered in the period. For London, see N.G. Brett-James, *The Growth of Stuart London* (1938); W. Besant, *London in the Time of the Stuarts* (1903); G.D.H. Cole, "London One-Fifth of England," in *Persons & Periods. Studies by G.D.H. Cole* (repr. 1967); F.J. Fisher, "The Development of London as a Centre of Conspicuous Consumption," in *Essays in Economic History*, ed. E.M. Carus-Wilson, vol. II (1962); F.J. Fisher, "The Growth of London," in *The English Revolution, 1600–1660* (1968); M.D. George, *London Life in the Eighteenth Century* (repr. 1964); D. Marshall, *Dr. Johnson's London* (1968); G. Rudé, *Hanoverian London* (1971); G. Trease, *London. A Concise History* (1975); and E.A. Wrigley, "A Simple Model of London's Importance in Changing English Society and Economy, 1650–1750." *Past & Present*, 37 (1967). Aspects of the terrible "Great Fire of London" are presented in J. Bedford, *London's Burning* (1966); W.G. Bell, *The Great Fire of London in 1666* (1920); L.W. Cowie, *Plague and Fire. London 1665–1666* (1970); and T.F. Reddaway, *The Rebuilding of London After the Great Fire* (1940). Other English cities in the period are dealt with in T. Atkinson, *Elizabethan Winchester* (1963); P. Clark and P. Slack, eds., *Crisis and Order in English Towns 1500–1700* (1972); P. Clark and P. Slack, eds., *English Towns in Transition, 1500–1700* (1976); A.D. Dyer, *The City of Worcester in the Sixteenth Century* (1973); W.C. Gill, *History of Birming-*

ham, 3 vols. (1952–1974); R. Howell, Jr., *Newcastle-upon-Tyne and the Puritan Revolution* (1967); W.T. MacCaffrey, *Exeter 1540–1640. The Growth of an English County Town* (1968); V. Parker, *The Making of King's Lynn* (1971); and W.B. Stephens, *Seventeenth-Century Exeter* (1958). For the Dutch metropolis of Amsterdam, see V. Barbour, *Capitalism in Amsterdam in the Seventeenth Century* (1963), and P. Burke, *Venice and Amsterdam* (1974), which is an attempt to compare the elites of the two cities. Paris is the topic of O. Ranum, *Paris in the Age of Absolutism* (1968), a general work that can be supplemented by J. Kaplow, *The Names of Kings: The Parisian Laboring Poor in the Eighteenth Century* (1972) and O.H. Hufton, *The Poor of Eighteenth-Century France, 1750–1789* (1972). Venice has been studied by W.H. McNeill, in *Venice, The Hinge of Europe 1081–1797* (1974); P. Pullan, ed., *Crisis and Change in the Venetian Economy in the Sixteenth and Seventeenth Centuries* (1968); P. Pullan, *Rich and Poor in Renaissance Venice: The Social Institutions of a Catholic State to 1620* (1971). Other books of interest for urban history are P. Abrams & E.A. Wrigley, eds., *Towns in Societies. Essays in Economic History and Historical Sociology* (1978); P. Clark, ed., *The Early Modern Town: A Reader* (1976); and M. Walker, *German Home Towns: Community, State, and General Estate, 1648–1871* (1971). For works on the Italian cities and Seville, see the works of L. Martines and M.E. Perry above. Regional and local history in England can be explored in the following: R. Blythe, *Akenfield. Portrait of an English Village* (1969); A Everitt, *New Avenues in English Local History* (1970); W.G. Hoskins, *The Midland Peasant. The Economic and Social History of a Leicestershire Village* (1957); P. Laslett and J. Harrison, "Clayworth and Cogenhoe," in *Historical Essays 1600–1750 Presented to David Ogg* (1963); P. Laslett, *The World We Have Lost* (1965); W.K. Jordan, *The Social Institutions of Lancashire* (1962); W.K. Jordan, *The Charities of Rural England* (1961); R. Parker, *The Common Stream. Two Thousand Years of the English Village* (1975); R.C. Richardson, *Puritanism in North-West England: A Regional Study of the Diocese of Chester to 1642* (1972); M. Spufford, *Contrasting Communities: English Villagers in the Sixteenth and Seventeenth Centuries* (1974). For France, see M. Bloch, *French Rural Society* (repr. 1966); E.L. Ladurie, *The Peasants of Languedoc* (1974); and E.L. Ladurie, *Carnival in Romans* (1979). Especially stimulating is R. Mousnier's comparative study, *Peasant Uprisings in Seventeenth-Century, France, Russia and China* (1970). For the Russian peasantry see J. Blum, *Land and Peasant in Russia from the Ninth to the Nineteenth Century* (1961). For social customs in the southern Mediterranean, the reader should consult D.M. Smith, *Medieval Sicily 800–1713* (1968). Housing is discussed in E. Mercier, "The Houses of the Gentry," *Past & Present,* 5 (1954); M.J. Power, "East London Housing in the Seventeenth Century," in *Crisis and Order in English Towns, 1500–1700,* ed. P. Clark and P. Slack (1972); and C. Shammas, "The Domestic Environment in Early Modern England and America," *Journal of Social*

History, (Fall 1980). A good source-book on domestic habits and social customs is M. Harrison and O.M. Royston, eds., *How They Lived 1485–1700* (1963). Newer studies becoming available include T.J.A. Le Goff, *Vannes and Its Region: A Study of Town and Country in Eighteenth-Century France* (1981) and R. S. Neale, *Bath, 1680–1850* (1981).

Disease, Health, and the Health Professions

A good introduction to diseases and epidemics continues to be W.H. McNeill, *Plagues and Peoples* (1976), a work which can be supplemented by H. Zinnser, *Rats, Lice and History* (1957). The superstitions surrounding disease can be seen in two studies of scrofula, or the "king's evil": F. Barlow, "The King's Evil," *English Historical Review*, 45 (Jan. 1980) and M. Bloch, *The Royal Touch. Sacred Monarchy and Scrofula in England and France* (1973). Covering a range of diseases are the following: A.B. Appleby, "Nutrition and Disease: The Case of London, 1550–1750," *Journal of International History*, 6 (Summer 1975); C.M. Cipolla, *Cristofano and the Plague* (1973); C. Creighton, *A History of Epidemics in Britain* (1891–1894); L. Clarkson, *Death, Disease, and Famine in Pre-industrial England* (1975); M.K. Eshleman, "Diet During Pregnancy in the Sixteenth and Seventeenth Centuries," *Journal of the History of Medicine*, 30 (Jan. 1975); T.R. Forbes, "London Coroner's Inquests for 1590," *Journal of the History of Medicine*, 28 (Oct. 1973); T.R. Forbes, "By What Disease or Casualty: The Changing Face of Death in London," *Journal of the History of Medicine*, 31 (October 1976); K. Frost, "John Donne's Devotions: An Early Record of Epidemic Typhus," *Journal of the History of Medicine*, 31 (October 1976); B. Gastel, "Measles: A Potentially Finite History," *Journal of the History of Medicine*, 28 (Jan. 1973); R. Hare, *Pomp and Pestilence* (1954); R.E. McFarland, "The Rhetoric of Medicine: Lord Herbert's and Thomas Carew's Poems of Green Sickness," *Journal of the History of Medicine*, 30 (July 1975); H.A. Waldron, "The Devonshire Colic," *Journal of the History of Medicine*, 25 (October 1970); and F.P. Wilson, *The Plague in Shakespeare's London* (repr. 1963). John Graunt, *Naturall and political observations upon the Bills of Mortality* (1661) is an invaluable source on the health of contemporary London. Carlo M. Cipolla's *Faith, Reason, and the Plague in Seventeenth-Century Tuscany* (1981) is a powerful and suggestive essay that treats the response to the plague in a finite area of Italy, and one that questions the use of such terms as "reason" and "progress" with reference to the seventeenth century. For the medical profession, students should see C.M. Cipolla, *Public Health and the Medical Profession in the Renaissance* (1975); G. N. Clark, *A History of the Royal College of Physicians of London*, I (1964); W.C.S. Copeman, *Doctors and Disease in Tudor Times* (1960); A.G. Debus, *Medicine in Seventeenth Century England* (1974), *The English Paracelsians* (1966), *The Chemical Philosophy: Paracelsian Science and Medicine in the Sixteenth and Seventeenth*

Centuries (1977); C. Hill, "The Medical Profession and its Radical Critics," in *Change and Continuity in Seventeenth-Century England* (1975); T. Puschmann, *A History of Medical Education* (repr. 1966); H.E. Sigerest, *The Great Doctors. A Biographical History of Medicine* (1958); C. Singer and E.A. Underwood, *A Short History of Medicine*, rev. ed. (1962); J.J. Keevil, "The Seventeenth-Century English Medical Background," *Bulletin of the History of Medicine*, 31 (1957); and F.N.L. Poynter and W.J. Bishop, eds., *A Seventeenth Century Doctor and His Patients: John Symcotts, 1592?–1662* (1951). For the "tools of the trade" see E. Bennion, *Antique Medical Instruments* (1979). The then-fledgling profession of dentistry is discussed in W. Hoffman-Axthelm, *History of Dentistry* (1981). R.W. Linker and N. Womack have translated the *Ten Books of Surgery* of Ambroise Paré (1969). Interesting is J. Woodforde, *The Strange Story of False Teeth* (1970), as is E. Rosen, "The Invention of Eyeglasses," *Journal of the History of Medicine*, 11 (1956). The interrelated topics of midwifery, gynecology, and obstetrics are discussed in W.H. Allport, *Some Seventeenth Century Midwives and Their Books* (1912); J.H. Aveling, *English Midwives (*1872) and *The Chamberlens and the Midwifery Forceps* (1882); T. Cianfrani, *A Short History of Obstetrics and Gynecology* (1960); I.S. Cutter and H.R. Viets, *A Short History of Midwifery* (1964); L.V. Dill, *The Obstetrical Forceps* (1953); I.H. Flack, *Eternal Eve. The History of Gynaecology and Obstetrics* (1951); T.R. Forbes, "The Regulation of English Midwives in the Sixteenth and Seventeenth Centuries," *Medical History*, 8 (1964); and E. Gray, ed., *Man Midwife* (1946). Medicine, illustration, and art are the topics of R. Herrlinger, *History of Medical Illustration from Antiquity to 1600;* A.S. Lyons and R.J. Petrucelli, *Medicine. An Illustrated History* (1978); and J. Rouselot, et al., eds., *Medicine in Art. A Cultural History* (1967). M. MacDonald, *Mystical Bedlam: Madness, Anxiety, and Healing in Seventeenth Century England* (1981) is based on the records of a contemporary physician. R.K. McClure, *Coram's Children: The London Foundling Hospital in the Eighteenth Century* (1981) deals with Captain Coram's effort on behalf of abandoned children.

Literacy, Education, the Law, and Other Professions

For a discussion of literacy and the professions in general terms, see two monographs by C.M. Cipolla: "The Professions—The Long View," *Journal of European Economic History*, 2 (1973) and *Literacy and the Development of the West* (1969). C. Hills' article, "The Inns of Court," in *Change and Continuity in Seventeenth Century England* (1975) traces dislike of lawyers in England to the fact that they presided over transfers of property, which in turn brought about changes in social power and status. Perspectives on the importance of law in France can be found in R.L. Kagan, "Law Students and Legal Careers in Eighteenth-Century France," *Past & Present*, 68 (August 1975). For how legality permeated English landed society, see W. Prest, "Legal Education of the Gentry 1560–1640," *Past & Present*, 38 (December 1967). H.J. Graff has recently edited *Literacy and the Social Development of the West: A Reader* (1981).

Women, Children, the Family, and Sexuality

For perspectives on women in European history see P. Branca, *Woman in Europe Since 1750* (1978); V.L. Bullough, *The History of Prostitution* (1964); A. Clark, *The Working Life of Women in the Seventeenth Century* (1919); K.C. Hurd-Mead, *A History of Women in Medicine* (1938); I. Pinchbeck, *Women Workers and the Industrial Revolution* (repr. 1969); T.R. Forbes, *The Midwife and the Witch* (1966); G.E. and K.R. Fussell, *The English Countrywoman: A Farmhouse Social History* (repr. 1971); Ann Oakley, *Woman's Work. The Housewife, Past and Present* (1974); S. Rowbotham, *Hidden From History. Rediscovering Women in History From the 17th Century to the Present* (1974) and *Women, Resistance & Revolution* (1972); D.M. Stenton, *The English Woman in History* (1957); R. Thompson, *Women in Stuart England and America. A Comparative Study* (1974); L.A. Tilly and J.W. Scott, *Women, Work, and the Family* (1978); H.R. Trevor-Roper, *The European Witch-Craze of the Sixteenth and Seventeenth Centuries and Other Essays* (1969); and R. Zguta, "Witchcraft Trials in Seventeenth Century Russia," *American Historical Review*, 82 (December 1977). For a more complete bibliography on witchcraft see T.R. Rumsey, *Men and Women of the Renaissance and Reformation, 1300–1600* (1981). A good collection of articles on women in various eras is found in R. Bridenthal and K. Koonz, eds., *Becoming Visible. Women in European History* (1977). Several excellent bibliographic essays on women's history are to be found. Of particular use is R. Masek, "Women in an Age of Transition: 1485–1714," in *The Women of England from Anglo-Saxon Times to the Present. Interpretive Bibliographical Essays* (1979). See also E. Marks and I. de Coutrivon, "Histories of France and of Feminism in France," in *New French Feminisms: An Anthology* (1980). Perspectives on contraception and family limitation can be gleaned from reading P. Ariès, "On The Origins of Contraception in France," in *Popular Attitudes Toward Birth Control in Pre-Industrial France and England*, ed. O. and P. Ranum (1972); N.E. Himes, *Medical History of Contraception* (1970); J.T. Noonan, Jr., *Contraception. A History of Its Treatment By The Catholic Theologians and Canonists* (1965); J. Knodel and E. van der Walle, "Breast-Feeding, Fertility, and Infant Mortality: An Analysis of Some Early German Data," *Population Studies*, 21 (1967); and E.A. Wrigley, "Family Limitation in Pre-Industrial England," *Economic History Review*, 2nd ser. 19 (1966). H. Smith, "Gynecology and Ideology in Seventeenth-Century England," in *Liberating Women's History. Theoretical and Critical Essays*, ed. B.A. Carroll (1976) underlines the persistance of stereotypes with regard to female sexuality. Attitudes toward sexuality are discussed in

C. Fairchilds, "Female Sexual Attitudes and the Rise of Illegitimacy: A Case Study," *Journal of Interdisciplinary History*, 8 (1978); Q.R. Quaife, "The Consenting Spinster in a Peasant Society: Aspects of Premarital Sex in 'Puritan' Somerset 1645–1660," *Journal of Social History*, 11 (Winter 1977); and P. Laslett and K.O. Oosterveen, "Long-Term Trends in Bastardy in England," *Population Studies*, 27 (1973). For the study of childhood, the place to start is still P. Ariès. *Centuries of Childhood. A Social History of Family Life* (1962). Also valuable are J.R. Gillis, *Youth and History. Tradition and Change in European Age Relations 1770–Present* (1974); J.E. Illick, "Child-Rearing in Seventeenth-Century England and America," in *The History of Childhood*, ed. L. deMause (1975); E.W. Marvick, "Nature Versus Nurture: Patterns and Trends in Seventeenth-Century French Child-Rearing," in *The History of Childhood*, ed. L. deMause (1975); I. Pinchbeck and M. Hewitt, "From Tudor Times to the Eighteenth Century," in *Children in English Society*, I (1969); J.H. Plumb, "The New World of Children In Eighteenth-Century England," *Past & Present*, 67 (May 1975); A. Schorsch, *Images of Childhood. An Illustrated Social History* (1979); A. Wilson, "The Infancy of The History of Childhood: An Appraisal of Philippe Ariès," *History and Theory*, 19 (1980). Because there is extensive documentary evidence available, much interest has focused on the childhood of Louis XIII of France, whether rightly or wrongly. For this, see D. Hunt, *Parents and Children in History. The Psychology of Family Life in Early Modern France* (1970) and E.W. Marwick, "The Character of Louis XIII: The Role of His Physician," *Journal of Interdisciplinary History*, 4 (Winter 1974). Those wanting to study the history of the family should begin with E. Shorter, *The Making of the Modern Family* (1975). Awesome in scope and detail is L. Stone, *The Family, Sex, and Marriage in England 1500–1800* (1977), but he has been taken to task by some reviewers for his perceived negativism and his emphasis on the corporate nature of the family. On this, see A. Macfarlane's review in *History and Theory*, 18 (1979). An excellent collection of articles is found in *Family and Society*, ed. R. Forster and O. Ranum (1976). See in particular the article by M. Boulant, "The Scattered Family: Another Aspect of Seventeenth-Century Demography," which documents how family structure could be shattered by the death of a parent. See also R. Cole, *Human History and the Stuart Family*, 2 vols. (1959); J-L Flandrin, *Families in Former Times. Kinship, Household and Sexuality in Early Modern France* (1979); M.E. Finch, *The Wealth of Five Northamptonshire Families, 1540–1640* (1956); P. Laslett and R. Wall, eds., *Household and Family in Past Time* (1972); D. Levine, *Family Formation in an Age of Nascent Capitalism* (1977); L. Stone, *The Crisis of the Aristocracy 1558–1641* (1965); and R. Trumbach, *The Rise of the Egalitarian Family. Aristocratic Kinship and Domestic Relations in Eighteenth-Century England* (1978). Two books by A. Macfarlane are deserving of special mention: *The Family Life of Ralph Josselin. A Seventeenth-Century Clergyman* (1970) and *The Origins of English Individualism. The Family, Property, and Social Transition* (1979).

Manners, Customs, Pastimes, and Miscellaneous

On courtly and social life, see M. Coate, *Social Life in Stuart England* (1924); R. Dutton, *English Court Life From Henry VII to George II* (1963); P. Erlanger, *The Age of Courts and Kings. Manners and Morals 1558–1715* (1967); J. Laver, *The Age of Illusion. Manners and Morals 1750–1848* (1972); H.D. Trail and J.S. Mann, eds., *Social England* (1903); and J. Wildblood and P. Brinson, *The Polite World* (1965). The relationship of manners to deference and social control is explored in N. Elias, *The History of Manners* (1978) and O. Ranum, "Courtesy, Absolutism, and the Rise of the French State, 1630–1660," *Journal of Modern History*, 52 (Sept. 1980). G.Z. Thomas, *Richer than Spices* (1965) describes the impact of East India goods on English culture and society. For sports and amusements, see W.B. Boulton, *The Amusements of Old London* (1901); C. Hole, *English Sports and Pastimes* (1949); F.W. Hackwood, *Old English Sports* (1907); R. Lennard, ed., *Englishmen at Rest and Play* (1931); R.W. Malcolmson, *Popular Recreations in English Society, 1700–1850* (1973); and W.S. Scott, *Bygone Pleasures of London* (1948). For food, see J.C. Drummond and A. Wilbraham, *The Englishman's Food*, 2nd. ed. (1958); and for clothing, I. Brooke, *Dress and Undress* (1958). For rakes and rogues, the following should be consulted: E.B. Chancellor, *Lives of the Rakes* (1925); L.C. Jones, *The Clubs of the Georgian Rakes* (1942); D. McCormick, *The Hell-Fire Club* (1958); and B. Partridge, *A History of Orgies* (1958). For baths and bathrooms see, respectively, C.F. Mullett, *Public Baths and Health in England, 16th-18th Century* (1946) and L. Wright, *Clean & Decent: The Fascinating History of the Bathroom and the Water Closet* (repr. 1980). The question of social mobility in England is dealt with in articles by A. Everitt and L. Stone in *Past & Present*, 33 (1966). Various aspects of popular culture are explored in R.M. Isherwood, "Entertainment in the Parisian Fairs in the Eighteenth Century," *Journal of Modern History*, 53 (March 1981); H. Rusche, "Prophecies and Propaganda 1641 to 1651," *English Historical Review*, 84 (Oct. 1969); and G.J. Schochet, "Patriarchalism, Politics and Mass Attitudes in Stuart England," *Historical Journal*, 12 (1969). A collection of monographic articles on the subject is found in E. and S. Yeo, eds., *Popular Culture and Class Conflict, 1590–1914: Explorations in the History of Labor and Leisure* (1981).

Chapter II
Basic Sources on the "Great Rebellion" 1640–1660 and its Causes

There are some excellent primary sources on the Great Rebellion that are readily obtainable. Some of these are: Edward Hyde, Earl of Clarendon, *The History of the Great Rebellion* (published in 1888 in a 6 volume edition; excerpts printed in many other places); Lucy Hutchinson, *The Life of Colonel Hutchinson*, ed. C.H. Firth, 2 vols. (1885); and Thomas Hobbes, *Behemoth: the History of the Causes of the Civil Wars in England. . . .* (several editions). The view of the nineteenth-century Whig historians, who saw progress and virtue on the side of Parliament, is typified by T.B. Macaulay, *History of England from the Accession of James II,* I (1848). For those deeply interested in the Great Rebellion there is S.R. Gardiner's eighteen-volume *History of England, 1603–1656* (1903), which is still magisterial and wonderful. Those wanting a briefer introduction to Gardiner's work should consult *The First Two Stuarts and the Puritan Revolution* (1876). The leading modern scholar on the English Civil War and its origins is Christopher Hill. His major works include *The Century of Revolution, 1603–1714* (1961); *Puritanism and Revolution* (1968); *Society and Puritanism in Pre-Revolutionary England* (1969); *Intellectual Origins of the English Revolution* (1965); *Economic Problems of the Church* (1971); and other books and articles. Other books that cover the period of the Great Rebellion include I. Roots, *The Great Rebellion, 1642–1660* (1968) and *Commonwealth and Protectorate* (repr. 1976); J.P. Kenyon, *The Stuarts: A Study in English Kingship* (1958); G. Davies, *The Early Stuarts, 1603–1660,* 2nd ed. (1965); M. Ashley, *England in the Seventeenth Century, 1603–1714* (1952); and C.V. Wedgwood, *The King's Peace, 1637–1641* (1951) and *The King's War, 1641–1647* (1959). Wedgwood has produced several other books that enhance understanding of the atmosphere of Stuart England. Two of them are *Poetry and Politics under the Stuarts* (1960) and *The Sense of the Past* (1967). Books useful for understanding the constitutional and political issues of the time include M. Ashley, *Magna Carta in the Seventeenth Century* (1965); G.P. Gooch, *English Democratic Ideas in the Seventeenth Century,* 2nd ed. (1959); and J.R. Tanner, *English Constitutional Conflicts of the Seventeenth Century* (1928). Collections that give insights into the historiography of the Civil War are R.H. Parry, ed., *The English Civil War and After 1642–1658* (1970); L. Stone, ed., *The Causes of the English Revolution, 1529–1642* (1972) and *Social Change and Revolution in England, 1540–1640* (1965); and P.A.M. Taylor, ed., *The Origins of the English Civil War. Conspiracy, Crusade, or Class Conflict?* (1960). Those interested can enrich these with J.H. Hexter, *The Reign of King Pym* (1941) and *Reappraisals in History* (1961); L. Stone, *The Crisis of the Aristocracy* (1965); V. Pearl, *London and the Outbreak of the Puritan Revolution* (1961); D. Brunton and D.H. Pennington, *Members of the Long Parliament* (1968); D. Underdown, *Pride's Purge* (1968); and P. Zagorin, *The Court and the Country* (1969). The relationship of Puritanism to the English Civil War can be explored in two books by W. Haller: *The Rise of Puritanism* (1938) and *Liberty and Reformation in the Puritan Revolution* (1955). Religious and other radicalism can be explored in C. Hill, *The World Turned Upside Down* (1972) and M. Walzer, *The Revolution of the Saints* (1965). For women in the English Revolution see K.V. Thomas, "Women and the Civil War Sects," *Past & Present,* 13 and D. Weigall, "Women Militants in the English Civil War," *History Today,* 22 (June 1972).

James I

The political works of James I have been edited by C.H. McIlwain (repr. 1965). D.H. Willson, *King James VI & I* (1956) is usually considered the definitive biography, but there are others, including those by J. McElwee (1952), C. Williams (1934), H.R. Williamson (1935), D. Mathew (1967), S.J. Houston (1974), and A. Fraser (1975). Also valuable are A.G.R. Smith, ed., *The Reign of James VI and I* (1973); D. Mathew, *The Jacobean Age* (1938); G.P.V. Akrigg, *Jacobean Pageant. The Court of King James I* (1962); G. Parry, *The Golden Age Restor'd: The Culture of the Stuart Court* (1981); and H.G. Stafford, *King James VI of Scotland and the Throne of England (1940)*. James' troubled relations with Parliament can be understood by reading W. Notestein, "The Winning of the Initiative by the House of Commons," *Proceedings of the British Academy* (1924–1925) and *The House of Commons, 1604–1610* (1970); T.L. Moir, *The Addled Parliament of 1614* (1958); R. Zaller, *The Parliament of 1621* (1971); F.D. Wormuth, *The Royal Prerogative, 1603–1649* (1939); and D.H. Willson, *Privy Councillors in the House of Commons, 1604–1629* (1940). On James' servants, see C.D. Bowen, *The Lion and the Throne: The Life and Times of Sir Edward Coke* (1957); and M. Prestwich, *Cranfield. Politics and Profits under the Early Stuarts* (1966). On James' diplomacy there are several important works: M. Lee, *James I & Henry IV* (1970); A.J. Loomie,"Toleration and Diplomacy: The Religious Issue in Anglo-Spanish Relations 1603–1605," *Transactions of the American Philosophical Society*, New Series, vol. 53, part 6 (1963); and J.D. Mackie, "James VI and I and the Peace with Spain, 1604," *Scottish Historical Review*, 23 (1925–26). For James as king of Scotland, see G. Donaldson, *Scotland: James V-James VII* (1965).

Charles I and Henrietta Maria

Aspects of the career and personality of Charles I can be glimpsed in L. Aikin, *Memoirs of the Court of Charles I* (1833); T. Birch, *The Court and Times of Charles I* (1848); E.B. Chancellor, *Life of Charles I from 1600–1625* (1886); C.W. Coit, *The Royal Martyr* (1924); H.P. Cooke, *Charles I and his earlier Parliaments* (1939); F.M.G. Higham, *Charles I* (1932); D. Mathew, *The Age of Charles I* (1951) and *Scotland under Charles I* (1955); C. Petrie, *The Letters of King Charles I* (1935); M.B. Pickcl, *Charles I as Patron of Poetry and Drama* (1936); H. Ross-Williamson, *Charles and Cromwell* (1946) and *The Day They Killed the King* (1957); G.S. Stevenson, ed., *Charles I in Captivity* (1927); and C.V. Wedgwood, *The Trial of Charles I (1964);* C. Hibbert, *Charles I* (1968) is a pedestrian biography but contains many fine illustrations. A decent modern biography is that by J. Bowle (1975). M.J. Havran has challenged the traditional view that Stuart policy was blindly pro-Catholic in *Caroline Courtier. The Life of Lord Cottington* (1973). This biography joins other strong studies of Caroline administration and administrators, notably G.E. Aylmer, *The King's Servants:*

The Civil Service of Charles I, 1625–1642 (1961); H.R. Trevor-Roper, *Archbishop Laud*, 2nd ed. (1962); and C.V. Wedgwood, *Thomas Wentworth, First Earl of Strafford, 1593–1641: A Reevaluation* (1961). Two excellent biographies of Henrietta Maria are those by E. Hamilton (1976) and C. Oman (1936). As this book goes to press, there is news of a new biography: C. Carlton, *Charles the First. The Personal Monarch* (1983).

Oliver Cromwell and the Protectorate

Good biographies of Cromwell include those of M. Ashley (1957), J. Buchan (1934), C.H. Firth (1909), A. Fraser (1973), C. Hill (1970), J. Morley (1901), and C.V. Wedgwood (1962). For the religion and politics of the period 1640–1660 see H.F. Keaney, *The Strenuous Puritan: Hugh Peter, 1598–1660* (1954); R. Schlatter, *Richard Baxter and Puritan Politics* (1961); J.H. Hexter, *The Reign of King Pym* (1941); R.S. Capp, *The Fifth Monarchy Men* (1972); H.N. Brailsford, *The Levellers and the English Revolution* (1961); V. Snow, *Essex the Rebel* (1970); A.W. Ramey, *Henry Ireton* (1949), and G. Yule, *The Independents in the English Civil War* (1958). On Cromwell's military forces it is worthwhile to consult C.H. Firth, *Cromwell's Army* (1902) and L. Solt, *Saints in Arms: Puritanism and Democracy in Cromwell's Army* (1959). For commercial, financial, and imperial policy in the period see M. Ashley, *Financial and Commercial Policy under the Cromwellian Protectorate*, 2nd ed. (1962); C.H. Wilson, *Profit and Power: A Study of England and the Dutch Wars* (1957); C.P. Korr, *Cromwell and the New Model Foreign Policy* (1975); and R. Crabtree, "The Idea of a Protestant Foreign Policy," *Cromwell Association Handbook* (1968–1969). M. Ashley discusses the Protector's military commanders in *Cromwell's Generals* (1958). For Cromwell's utterances and letters, see W.C. Abbott, *The Writings and Speeches of Oliver Cromwell*, 14 vols. (1938–1947). Also useful in this regard is I. Roots, ed., *Cromwell: A Profile* (1973). E. Bernstein, *Cromwell and Communism* (repr. 1963) attempts to view the Protector in a revisionist Marxist light. Cromwellian policies have been most recently discussed with regard to Scotland and Ireland in F.D. Dow, *Cromwellian Scotland* (1980) and T.C. Barnard, *Cromwellian Ireland* (1975). Also valuable is J. Frank, *Cromwell's Press Agent: A Critical Biography of Marchamont Nedham, 1620–1678* (1980).

Charles II and the Restoration

A. Bryant, *Charles II*, rev. ed. (1955) is the biography that broke first with the Whig tradition, portraying the "merry monarch" in a positive light. J.P. Kenyon, among others, remains unconvinced, and his survey, *The Stuarts: A Study in English Kingship* (1958) contains a counter to Bryant. A. Fraser, *Royal Charles. Charles II and the Restoration* (1979) is sympathetic and contains an excellent bibliography. Also useful are M. Ashley, *Charles II. The Man and the Statesman* (1971); K.H.D. Haley, *Charles II. Historical*

Association Pamphlet (1966); and the biographies of J. Hayward (1933) and C. Falkus (1972). D. Ogg, *England in the Reign of Charles II*, 2nd ed. (1962) overviews the society and politics of the time. Further insight into the character of Charles II can be gained from A. Bryant, ed., *The Letters of King Charles II* (1935) and J.P. Kenyon, ed., *Halifax. Complete Works* (1969). R. Ollard, *The Escape of Charles II after the Battle of Worcester* (1966) is a discussion of a difficult period of Charles' early life. An entertaining *popular* biography of Charles is H. Pearson's *Merry Monarch. The Life and Likeness of Charles II* (1960). Charles' foreign policy can be studied in K. Feiling, *English Foreign Policy, 1660–1672*, new ed. (1968). For politics and Parliament in the period see G.R. Abernathy, The *English Puritans and the Stuart Restoration, 1648–1663* (1965); H.G. Plum, *Restoration Puritanism* (1943); M.D. Lee, *The Cabal* (1965); J.R. Jones, *The First Whigs: The Politics of the Exclusion Crisis, 1678–1683* (1961); and K.H.D. Haley, *The First Earl of Shaftesbury* (1968). A useful selection of monographic articles appear in G. Davies, *Essays on the Later Stuarts* (1958). On the transitional period that led into the Restoration see C.H. Firth, *The Last Years of the Protectorate, 1656–1658*, 2 vols. (1909); G. Davies, *The Restoration of Charles II, 1658–1660* (1955); and A.S. Turberville, *Commonwealth and Protectorate* (1936). General background can be gleaned from G.N. Clark, *The Later Stuarts, 1660–1714,* 2nd ed. (1961). A good collection of sources is A. Browning, ed., *English Historical Documents, 1660–1714* (1953). For an introduction to some of the historiographical issues of the Restoration, see the Report of the Folger Library Conference, *The Restoration of the Stuarts: Blessing or Disaster?* (1960).

The Glorious Revolution and Its Legacy

Good introductory material is found in D. Ogg, *England in the Reigns of James II and William III* (repr. 1962). For James II, see biographies by H. Belloc (repr. 1971), F.C. Turner (1948), and V. Buranelli (1962). J. Childs in *The Army, James II, and the Glorious Revolution* (1980) minimizes the role of Catholic officers in the English army prior to 1688, but found massive purging of Protestant officers from the army in Ireland. For the Glorious Revolution, see M. Ashley, *The Glorious Revolution of 1688* (1966); J.P. Kenyon, *The Nobility in the Revolution of 1688* (1963); J.R. Jones, *The Revolution of 1688 in England* (1972); T.B. Macaulay, *History of England*, ch. 4–10 (1849–1865); G.M. Straka, *Anglican Reaction to the Revolution of 1688* (1962); and G.M. Trevelyan, *The English Revolution 1688–1689*, new ed. (1968). Readers need to be cautious of the Whiggish bias of Ashley, Macaulay and Trevelyan. The career of William III is mentioned elsewhere in the text in other contexts, but for his role in the Revolution of 1688, see S.B. Baxter, *William III* (1966); D. Ogg, *William III* (1956); and L. Pinkham, *William III and the Respectable Revolution* (1954). A good biography of Mary is H.W. Chapman, *Mary II, Queen of England* (1953). J. Carswell,

The Descent on England (1969) links the Glorious Revolution to events in Europe. Useful for understanding the politics of the period are K. Feiling, *History of the Tory Party, 1640–1714* (1924); and especially J.H. Plumb, *The Origins of Political Stability. England 1675–1725* (1967). G.M. Straka, ed., *The Revolution of 1688: Whig Triumph or Palace Revolution?* (1963) is a good introduction to historiographical issues. An interesting view of the period, from the viewpoint of a prominent politician, is H. Horwitz, *Revolution Politicks. The Career of Daniel Finch, Second Earl of Nottingham, 1647–1730* (1968).

Chapter III

The Thirty Years' War

Interpretations of the conflict are anthologized in T.K. Rabb, ed., *The Thirty Years' War* (1972). S.H. Steinberg, *The Thirty Years' War and the Conflict for European Hegemony, 1600–1660* (1966) sees the war as part of a large and longer conflict. C.V. Wedgwood, *The Thirty Years' War* (repr. 1969) is a readable account that emphasizes the destructiveness of the war. This view is challenged in R. R. Ergang, *The Myth of the All-Destructive Fury of the Thirty Years' War* (1956). A Marxist account is J.V. Polisensky, *The Thirty Years' War* (trans., 1972). Also recently translated into English is G. Pages, *The Thirty Years' War* (1971). The "general crisis" theory is debated in T. Aston, ed., *Crisis in Europe, 1560–1660* (1965) and R. Forster and J.P. Greene, eds., *Preconditions of Revolution in Early Modern Europe* (1970). Particularly good illustrations are found in E.A. Beller, *Propaganda in Germany during the Thirty Years' War* (1940). Also valuable for background are B. Chudoba, *Spain and the Empire, 1519–1643* (1952); and H.G. Koenigsberger, *The Hapsburgs and Europe, 1516–1660* (1971). Two studies of Wallenstein, the mysterious Hapsburg commander, also shed light on the Thirty Years' War: G. Mann, *Wallenstein: His Life Narrated* (trans. 1976) and F. Watson, *Wallenstein: Soldier under Saturn* (1938). Fritz Redlich has produced three studies that bear on the conflict: *The German Military Enterpriser and his Work Force: a Study in European Economic and Social History*, I (1964); *De Praeda Militari: Looting and Booty, 1500–1815* (1956); and "Contributions in the Thirty Years' War," *Economic History Review* (1959).

Gustavus Adolphus, Queen Christina, and the Rise and Decline of Sweden

For seventeenth-century Sweden, the historian of note in English is Michael Roberts, and all of his works are worth reading. These include: *The Early Vasas* (1968), *Gustavus Adolphus* (2 vols., 1953–1958), and *Essays in Swedish History* (1967). Roberts has also edited an excellent collection of sources, *Sweden as A Great Power: Government, Society and For-*

eign Policy, 1611–1697 (1968), as well as *Sweden's Age of Greatness* (1973). Also valuable is N. Ahnlund, *Gustav Adolf the Great* (1940). For Gustavus' role as a general see T.N. DuPuy, *The Military Life of Gustavus Adolphus: Father of Modern War* (1969). For Christina, see M.L. Clarke, "The Making of a Queen: the Education of Christina of Sweden," *History Today*, 28 (April 1978); G. Masson, *Queen Christina* (1968); and S. Stolpe, *Christina of Sweden* (1966). For Charles XII, the great adversary of Peter the Great, see R.M. Hatton, *Charles XII of Sweden* (1969) and Voltaire, *History of Charles XII* (several editions).

Richelieu and the Rise of France

Good places to start for seventeenth-century France are W.E. Brown, *The First Bourbon Century in France* (1971); J. Lough, *An Introduction to Seventeenth-Century France* (1969); and especially G.R.R. Treasure, *Seventeenth-Century France* (1966). See also M. Prestwich, "The Making of Absolute Monarchy (1559–1683)," in *France: Government and Society*, eds. J.M. Wallace-Hadrill and J. McManners (1957). For Richelieu, there is the following: C.J. Burckhardt, *Richelieu: His Rise to Power* (repr. 1964); A.D. Lublinskaya, *French Absolutism: The Crucial Phase, 1620–1629* (trans. 1968); O. Ranum, *Richelieu and the Councillors of Louis XII* (1963); G.R.R. Treasure, *Cardinal Richelieu and the Development of Absolutism* (1972); and C.V. Wedgwood, *Richelieu and the French Monarchy* (1949). See also D.P. O'Connell, *Richelieu* (1968). The *Political Testament* of Richelieu has been translated several times. A. Huxley, *Grey Eminence* (1941) is an entertaining biography of Father Joseph, Richelieu's mysterious mentor. A valuable recent monograph is W.F. Church, *Richelieu and Reason of State* (1972). R. Bonney, *The King's Debts: Finance and Politics in France, 1589–1661* (1981) is a study of a chronic problem in French government.

Peter the Great and Russia

There are many good general histories of Russia. See in particular those by B.H. Sumner and M.T. Florinsky. On the background of the rise of Muscovy and the tsarist state, see H. von Eckhardt, *Ivan the Terrible* (1949); J. Fennell, *Ivan the Great of Moscow* (1961); I. Grey, *Ivan III and the Unification of Russia* (1965) and *Ivan the Terrible* (1964); H. Lamb, *The March of Muscovy: Ivan the Terrible and the Growth of the Russian Empire 1400–1648* (1948). For Peter the Great, see H. Lamb, *The City and the Tsar: Peter the Great and the Move to the West, 1648–1742* (1948); I. Grey, *Peter the Great* (1962); V. Kliuchevsky, *Peter the Great* (trans. 1958); L.J. Oliva, *Russia in the Era of Peter the Great* (1969); and B.H. Sumner, *Peter the Great and the Emergence of Russia* (1950). There is a good novel of Peter the Great by A. Tolstoi (trans. 1936). For Russian relations with the Turks in the time of Peter, see B.H. Sumner, *Peter the Great and the Ottoman*

Empire (1949). Dated, but still very useful, are biographies of Peter by S. Graham (1950), E. Schuyler (1884), and K. Waliszewski (1897). For historiography see M. Raeff, ed. *Peter the Great Changes Russia*, 2nd. ed. (1972). R.K. Massie, *Peter the Great: His Life and His World* (1980) is an excellent exercise in popular history. For Peter's contribution to the Russian navy, see C.A.G. Bridge, ed., "History of the Russian Fleet During the Reign of Peter the Great," *Publications of the Navy Records Society*, XV (1899). J. Perry, *The State of Russia under the Present Czar* (1716) is a good contemporary account.

Louis XIV

Louis XIV can be known through several primary sources. P. Sonnino has recently translated Louis' *Memoires* under the title of *Louis XIV: Memoires for the Instruction of the Dauphin* (1970). Also important are the memoirs of the Duke of Saint-Simon, which are available in several extracts and translations. Useful as well are the memoirs of Mme. de Sevigné and Cardinal de Retz. Louis XIV has had many biographers. The best biography in English is that by J.B. Wolfe (1968). M. Ashley, *Louis XIV and the Greatness of France* (1965) is a short introduction. Other studies available in English are those by V. Cronin (1964), A. Hassall (1895), P. Gaxotte (trans. 1970), D. Ogg, 2nd ed. (1967), and P. Erlanger (trans. 1970). For the Fronde see the study by P.R. Doolin (1935) and A.L. Moote's, *The Revolt of the Judges: The Parlement of Paris and the Fronde, 1643–1652* (1971). W.F. Church, *Louis XIV in Historical Thought* (1976) is an essay in historiography. R. Hatton has edited two important collections: *Louis XIV and Absolutism* (1976) and *Louis XIV and Europe* (1976). Hatton has also written another key study: *Europe in the Age of Louis XIV* (1969). French society under Louis is the subject of W.H. Lewis, *The Splendid Century: Life in the France of Louis XIV* (1953) and P. Goubert, *Louis XIV and Twenty Million Frenchmen* (trans. 1970). E.E. Reynolds' *Bossuet* (1963) gives insights into the architect of absolutist theory. Helpful monographic studies include C.W. Cole, *Colbert and a Century of French Mercantilism*, 2 vols. (1939); J.E. King, *Science and Rationalism in the Government of Louis XIV* (1949); E.I. Perry, *From Theology to History: Religious Controversy and the Revocation of the Edict of Nantes* (1973); L. Rothkrug, *The Opposition to Louis XIV: The Political and Social Origins of the Enlightenment* (1965); W.C. Scoville, *The Persecution of the Huguenots and French Economic Development 1680–1720* (1960); and J.H. Shennan, *Government and Society in France, 1461–1661* (1969). A good collection of documents is found in O. and P. Ranum, ed., *Europe in the Age of Louis XIV* (1972).

The Dutch Republic and the House of Orange

A good place to start is with two books by P.Geyl: *The Revolt of the Netherlands Against Spain, 1555–1609*, 2nd ed. (1958) and *Netherlands in the*

Seventeenth Century, rev. ed., 2 vols. (1961–1964). Also good on background are two works by H.H. Rowen. He has edited *The Low Countries in Early Modern Times* (1972) and written *John de Witt: Grand Pensionary of Holland, 1625–1672* (1978). Valuable as well are J. Huizinga, *Dutch Civilisation in the Seventeenth Century and Other Essays* (1949) and C.H. Wilson, *The Dutch Republic and the Civilization of the Seventeenth Century* (1968). C.V. Wedgwood's *William the Silent* (1944) is a biography of the most famous ancestor of the William of Orange who became king of England and the greatest adversary of Louis XIV. For William III see N.A. Robb, *William of Orange. A Personal Portrait*, 2 vols. (1966); S.B. Baxter, *William III* (1966); D. Ogg, *William III* (1956); G.J. Renier, *William of Orange* (1932); and H.D. Traill, *William III* (1888).

Carlos II and Spain

For the troubled background and reign of Carlos II see J. Langdon-Davies, *Carlos, The King Who Would Not Die* (1962) and J. Nada, *Carlos the Bewitched: The Last Spanish Hapsburg, 1661–1700* (1960). Something of the flavor of the "decline of Spain debate" can be sampled by reading J.H. Elliott, *The Revolt of the Catalans: A Study in the Decline of Spain, 1598–1640* (1963) and "The Decline of Spain," in *Crisis in Europe, 1560–1660*, ed. T. Aston (1965); E.J. Hamilton, "The Decline of Spain," *Economic History Review*, 8 (1938); and H. Kamen, *Spain in the Later Seventeenth Century, 1665–1700* (1980). H. Kamen, *The Spanish Inquisition* (1965) is a good introduction to the subject. Also covering the period are J.H. Elliott, *Imperial Spain, 1469–1716* (1964) and J. Lynch, *Spain under the Hapsburgs*, vol. 2 (1969). On economic matters, see J. Vicens Vives, *An Economic History of Spain* (trans. 1969).

English Party Politics, the Marlboroughs, and the War of the Spanish Succession

J.B. Wolf, *The Emergence of the Great Powers, 1685–1715* (1951) remains the best introduction to the background of the War of the Spanish Succession, which he sees as a part of a larger world war. For insights into contemporary warfare see G.N. Clark, *War and Society in the Seventeenth Century* (1958) and J.U. Nef, *War and Human Progress* (1950). The best life of John Churchill, *Duke of Marlborough* is W.S. Churchill's *Marlborough, His Life and Times*, 6 vols. (1933–1938), which is the combined work of scores of historians and researchers. For Marlborough's military career, the following are helpful: C.T. Atkinson, *Marlborough and the Rise of the British Army* (1921); D. Chandler, *Marlborough as Military Commander* (1973); and F. Taylor, *The Wars of Marlborough, 1702–1709*, 2 vols. (1921). Sarah, Duchess of Marlborough has had many biographers. The best biography is by D. Green (1967), but there are others by K. Campbell (1932), F. Chancellor (1932), and L. Kronenberger (1958). Very useful as well is S.J. Reid, *John and Sarah, Duke and Duchess of Marlborough* (1919) and A.L. Rowse, *The Early Churchills* (1956). Queen Anne's *Letters* have been edited by B.C. Brown (1935). There are biographies of Anne by N. Connell (1937), D. Green (1971), and M.R. Hopkinson (1934). For the politics and society of the period, see G.M. Trevelyan, *England under Queen Anne*, 3 vols. (1930–1934); G.E. Holmes, *British Politics in the Age of Anne* (1967); and R. Walcott, *English Politics in the Early Eighteenth Century* (1956). C.A. Petrie, *The Jacobite Movement*, 3rd. ed., 2 vols. (1959) is also important. Useful political biographies for the period include E. Hamilton, *The Backstairs Dragon: A Life of Robert Harley, Earl of Oxford* (1969) and J.P. Kenyon, *Robert Spencer, Earl of Sunderland, 1641–1702* (1958). A good collection of political sources is G.S. Holmes and W.A. Speck, eds., *The Divided Society. Parties and Politics in England 1694–1716* (1967).

Chapter V

The Scientific Revolution: History and Historiography

H. Butterfield, *The Origins of Modern Science* (1949, 1950) and A. Koestler, *The Sleepwalkers* (1959) are examples of studies that see a true revolution occurring in seventeenth-century science, constituting a major break with the past. On the other hand, other scholars emphasize the debt that the so-called "new" science owed to Aristotle and to the medieval past. On this, see M. Claggett, *The Science of Mechanics in the Middle Ages* (1959); A.C. Crombie, *Augustine to Galileo* (1952); and J.H. Randall, *The Career of Philosophy* (1962). The boundaries of this debate are explored in H.F. Kearney, "Puritanism, Capitalism and the Scientific Revolution," *Past & Present*, 28 (1964). Other works useful for the new science include E.A. Burtt, *The Metaphysical Foundations of Modern Philosophical Science* (1948); J.B. Conant, *On Understanding Science: An Historical Approach* (1947); W.C.D. Dampier, *A History of Science and its Relations with Philosophy and Religion* (1949); and A.R. Hall, *The Scientific Revolution, 1500–1800: The Formation of the Modern Scientific Attitude*, rev. ed. (1962). G. Sarton, *Introduction to the History of Science*, 3 vols. (1927–1948) and L. Thorndyke, *A History of Magic and Experimental Science*, 8 vols. (1948) are wonderful for the medieval scientific background. Shorter overviews of the history of science as a whole are A.R. Hall and M.B. Hall, *Brief History of Science* (1961); C. Singer, *A Short History of Scientific Ideas to 1900* (1959); and F.S. Taylor, *A Short History of Science and Scientific Thought* (1949). A.R. Hall has edited The Rise of Modern Science Series, and two of its volumes are useful for the period: M. Boas, *The Scientific Renaissance, 1450–1630* (1962) and A.R. Hall, *From Galileo to Newton, 1630–1720* (1963, 1982). Two good collections of documents are M.B. Hall, ed., *Nature and Nature's Laws: Documents of the Scientific Revolution* (1969) and G. Schwartz and P.W. Bishop, eds., *The Origins of Science*, 2 vols. (1958).

Descartes and Mathematics

For Descartes see L.J. Beck, *The Metaphysics of Descartes* (1965) and *The Method of Descartes* (1952); W. Doney, ed., *Descartes: A Collection of Critical Essays* (1957); K. Fischer, *Descartes and His School* (1887); A.B. Gibson, *The Philosophy of Descartes* (1932); E.S. Haldane, *Descartes: His Life and Times* (1905); A. Kenney, Descartes (1968); J. Maritain, *The Dream of Descartes* (1945); L. Roth, *Descartes' Discourse on Method* (1937); N.K. Smith, *New Studies in the Philosophy of Descartes (repr. 1963);* J.R. Vrooman, *Descartes: A Biography* (1970). See also S.H. Mellone, *The Dawn of Modern Thought: Descartes, Spinoza, Leibniz* (1930). E.T. Bell's *Men of Mathematics* (1937) has chapters on Descartes, Fermat, Pascal, Newton, and Leibniz. Also useful is M. Kline, *Mathematics in Western Culture* (1953). Two collections of sources are J.R. Newman, Ed., *Men and Numbers* (1956) and D.E. Smith, ed., *A Source Book in Mathematics* (1929). Descartes' *Discourse on Method* is available in many translations and extracts, and should be read.

Galileo and Newton: The New Universe and the New Physics

A good place to begin is with T.S. Kuhn's *The Copernican Revolution: Planetary Astronomy in the Development of Western Thought* (1957). For Galileo, see G. De Santillana, *The Crime of Galileo* (1955); S. Drake, *Discoveries and Opinions of Galileo* (1957) and *Galileo Studies* (1970); L. Geymonat, *Galileo Galilei* (1965); C.L. Golino, *Galileo Reappraised* (1966); M.F. Kaplan, ed., *Homage to Galileo* (1965); A. Koestler, *The Sleepwalkers* (1959); A Koyré, *Galileo Studies* (trans. 1978); E. McMullin, ed., *Galileo: Man of Science* (1968); F.S. Taylor, *Galileo and the Freedom of Thought* (1938); and F.R. Wegg-Prosser, *Galileo and His Judges* (1889). For Kepler, see the biography by M. Caspar (trans. 1959). The standard biography of Tycho Brahe is that of J.L.E. Dryer (1890). A good short introduction to Newton is E.N. da C. Andrade, *Sir Isaac Newton. His Life and Work* (1954). F. Manuel, *A Portrait of Newton* (1968) is an effort at historical psychology. R.S. Westfall has contributed a number of important studies on Newton. See his *Never at Rest: A Biography of Isaac Newton* (1981) and *Force in Newton's Physics* (1971). Insights into Newton's personality, and into the differences between seventeenth-century sciences and modern ones, can be gained by reading Westfall's article, "The Career of Isaac Newton. Scientific Life in the Seventeenth Century," *The American Scholar* (Summer 1981). Also useful are I.B Cohen, *Franklin and Newton* (1956); A. De Morgan, *Essays on the Life and Work of Newton* (1914); L.T. More, *Isaac Newton: A Biography* (1934); J.W. Herivel, *The Background to Newton's Principia* (1966); and A. Koyré, *Newtonian Studies* (1965).

William Harvey and the Human Universe

For an introduction to the history of anatomical medicine see C. Singer, *A Short History of Anatomy and Physiology from the Greeks to Harvey* (1957). Charles Webster and others have contributed some useful background articles under the title of *William Harvey and His Age: The Professional and Social Context of the Discovery of the Circulation of the Blood* (1979). On Harvey's life and work, see the following: K.D. Keele, *William Harvey, the Man, the Physician, the Scientist* (1965); G. Keynes, *The Life of William Harvey* (1966); W. Pagel, *William Harvey's Biological Ideas* (1967); and G. Whitteridge, *Anatomical Lectures of William Harvey* (1964).

The Enlightenment: History and Historiography

The extremes of the Enlightenment historiographical debate can be glimpsed in C. Becker, *The Heavenly City of the Eighteenth-Century Philosophers* (1932) and P. Gay, *The Enlightenment: An Interpretation*, 2 vols. (1966–1969). Becker, who has been much-criticized, argued that the Enlightenment had much more in common with the medieval view of the world than any modern one. Gay, on the other hand, saw the *philosophes* as moderns, freedom-loving and pagan in outlook, who strove to apply science to all realms of human activity. For critiques of Becker, see R. Rockwood, ed., *Carl Becker's Heavenly City Revisited* (1958). Gay has developed his views strongly in other books, such as *The Party of Humanity: Essays on the French Enlightenment* (1964). For good introductions to eighteenth-century thought, see especially E. Cassirer, *The Philosophy of the Enlightenment* (trans. 1951); N. Hampson, *A Cultural History of the Enlightenment* (1969); and F.B. Artz, *The Enlightenment in France* (1968). A good collection of sources is L.G. Crocker, ed., *The Age of Enlightenment* (1969). Interesting recent studies that add perspective are L. Krieger, *Kings and Philosophers* (1970); H. Payne, *The Philosophes and the People* (1976); F. Venturi, *Utopia and Reform in the Enlightenment* (1971); I. Wade, Intellectual *Origins of the French Enlightenment* (1971); and R.J. White, *The Anti-Philosophers* (1970). R.J. Nisbet's *History of the Idea of Progress* (1980) contributes a certain perspective by linking the idea of progress not only to the Enlightenment, but to the course of western history. B. Willey, *The Eighteenth Century Background* (1940), emphasizes England, but aids in the understanding of the transition to the Enlightenment. A. Hertzberg, in *The French Enlightenment and the Jews* (1968) argues that Enlightenment "progress" stripped Jews of traditional protections and paved the way for modern antisemitism, a paradoxical and troubling thesis.

Voltaire and the Philosophes

For Voltaire's life and thought see T. Besterman, *Voltaire*, 3rd. ed. (1976); D.B. Bien, *The Calas Affair: Persecution, Toleration and Heresy in*

Eighteenth-Century Toulouse (1960); J.H. Brumfitt, *Voltaire, Historian* (repr. 1970); P. Gay, *Voltaire's Politics: The Poet as Realist* (repr. 1965); V.W. Topazio, *Voltaire: A Critical Study of His Major Works* (1967); N.L. Torrey, *The Spirit of Voltaire* (1938); and I. Wade, *The Intellectual Development of Voltaire* (1969). There are, in addition, biographies by H. Mason (1981), J. Morley (1906), A. Noyes (1936), and J. Orieux (trans. 1979). There is a good biography of Diderot by A.M. Wilson (1972). For Montesquieu, see the life by R. Shackleton (1961). E. Cassirer, *The Question of Jean-Jacques Rousseau* (1963) is a good introduction.

Mary Wollstonecraft

The best biography is E. Flexner's *Mary Wollstonecraft* (1972), but there are others by M. George (1970) and C. Tomalin (1975). Wollstonecraft's writings, many of which have been anthologized, have been brought together and edited by B.H. Solomon and P.S. Berggren as *A Mary Wollstonecraft Reader* (1983).

Chapter VI

The Industrial Revolution in General: History and Historiography

The Industrial Revolution is both a historical period and a debate. The best introduction to the subject is P. Deane, *The First Industrial Revolution* (1965), although some would prefer the more brief work by T.S. Ashton, *The Industrial Revolution 1760–1830*, rev. ed. (1969). Essential to understanding the Industrial Revolution as historiography are the monographs of the "optimists" and the "pessimists," who are so labeled for their respective attitudes toward the effects of the Industrial Revolution on standards of living and the quality of life. For the "optimist" point of view see T.S. Ashton, "The Standard of Life of Workers in England, 1790–1830," *Journal of Economic History Supplement* (1949), and two articles by R.M. Hartwell: "The Rising Standard of Living in England 1800–1850," *Economic History Review*, 14 (1961) and "The Standard of Living during the Industrial Revolution," *Economic History Review*, 16 (1963). The neo-Marxist "pessimist" view is represented by the work of J.L. and Barbara Hammond and E.J. Hobsbawm. The Hammonds' work includes *The Village Laborer, 1760–1832* (1911); *The Skilled Laborer, 1760–1832* (1919); *The Town Laborer, 1760–1832* (1920); and *The Rise of Modern Industry* (1925). Two classic articles by Hobsbawm are "The British Standard of Living 1790–1850," *Economic History Review*, 10 (1957) and "The Standard of Living during the Industrial Revolution," *Economic History Review*, 16 (1963). Hobsbawm's views are encapsulated in a longer, and excellent, work, *Industry and Empire* (1968), which forms the third volume of The Pelican Economic History of Britain. An excellent collection of articles has been edited by R.M. Hartwell under the title *The Causes of the Industrial Revolution in England* (1967). This complements another collection edited by P.A.M. Taylor, *The Industrial Revolution in Britain. Triumph or Disaster?* (1958). An interesting attempt to develop a model for industrial change is W.W. Rostow, *The Stages of Economic Growth* (1960). J.U. Nef, in two articles, has argued for an earlier beginning to the Industrial Revolution: "The Progress of Technology and the Growth of Large-Scale Industry in Great Britain 1540–1640," in E.M. Carus-Wilson, *Essays in Economic History*, I (1954) and "The Industrial Revolution Reconsidered," *Journal of Economic History* (1943). Those deeply interested in the subject might want to look at J.H. Clapham, *An Economic History of Modern Britain*, 3 vols. (1926–38); M.W. Flinn, *Origins of the Industrial Revolution* (1966); and P. Mantoux, *The Industrial Revolution in the Eighteenth Century*, 12th ed. (1961). I. Pinchbeck, *Women Workers in the Industrial Revolution, 1750–1850* (1930) is a good beginning for this subject-area, but it should be supplemented by material cited in the bibliography for Chapter I.

The Hanoverians and Whig Politics

Introductions to eighteenth-century England are numerous and very good. Entertaining and well-written are two books by J.H. Plumb: *The First Four Georges* (1956) and *England in the Eighteenth Century* (1950). Others are V.H.H. Green, *The Hanoverians, 1714–1815* (1948); D. Jarrett, *Britain, 1688–1815* (1965); M.D. George, *England in Transition* (1953); and D. Marshall, *Eighteenth-Century England* (1962). Somewhat longer are two volumes in the Oxford History of England: B. Williams, *The Whig Supremacy, 1714–1760*, rev. ed. (1962) and S. Watson, *The Reign of George III* (1960). Monographic studies that are particularly useful are J.M. Beattie, *The English Court in the Reign of George I* (1967); K.G. Feiling, *The Second Tory Party, 1714–1732* (1959); W.T. Laprade, *Public Opinion and Politics in Eighteenth-Century England to the Fall of Walpole* (1936); L.B. Namier, *The Structure of Politics at the Accession of George III*, 2nd ed. (1957); R. Pares, *King George III and the Politicians* (1953); and P.D.G. Thomas, *The House of Commons in the Eighteenth Century* (1971).

Sir Robert Walpole and Caroline of Anspach

The best biography of Walpole is J.H. Plumb, *Sir Robert Walpole*, 2 vols. (1956–1961). S.B. Realey, *The Early Opposition of Sir Robert Walpole, 1720–1727* (1931) and R. Sedgwick, ed., *The House of Commons 1715–1754*, 2 vols. (1970) are also helpful. Walpole's fall can be documented in J.B. Owen, *The Rise of the Pelhams* (1957). The memoirs of Lord Hervey, published in several editions and extracts, are colorful on all aspects of the reign of George II. A fine, and interesting, biography of Caroline of Anspach is P. Quennell, *Caroline of England* (1939).

"Diamond" Pitt

C. Dalton, *Life of Thomas Pitt* (1915) is the standard biography, but additional material can be found in the biographies of Lord Chatham cited in the bibliography for Chapter VII. For the British experience in India see: E. Thompson and G.T. Garratt, *The Rise and Fulfillment of British Rule in India* (1934); P. Woodruff, *The Men Who Ruled India*, I (1954); M. Andrewes, *British India* (1964); P.E. Roberts, *British India* (1952); and P. Spear, *The Nabobs* (1963). The political influence of the East India Company's interests is anatomized in L. Sutherland, *The East India Company in Eighteenth Century Politics* (1952).

Josiah Wedgwood

Studies of Wedgwood's life and art include: A. Burton, *Josiah Wedgwood* (1976); W. Honey, *Wedgwood Ware* (1962); E. Meteyard, *The Life of Josiah Wedgwood*, 2 vols. (1865, 1866); H.H. Moore, *Wedgwood and His Imitators*, 2nd ed. (1978); B.W. Wedgwood and H. Wedgwood, *Wedgwood Circle, 1730–1897: Four Generations of Wedgwoods and Their Friends* (1980); and F.J. Wedgwood, *The Personal Life of Josiah Wedgwood the Potter* (1915). For the "canal mania" in which Josiah Wedgwood and others participated see A. Burton, *The Canal Builders* (1972) and C. Hadfield, *British Canals* (1959).

James Watt

Among studies of Watt and his work are the following: H.W. Dickinson, *James Watt, Craftsman and Engineer* (1936); H.W. Dickinson and H.P. Vowles, *James Watt and the Industrial Revolution* (1943); I.B. Hart, *James Watt and the History of Steam Power* (1958); and S. Smiles, *The Lives of Boulton and Watt* (1865). See also J. Lord, *Capital and Steam Power, 1750–1800* (1923). For Watt's colleague John Wilkinson, there is a biography by H.W. Dickinson (1914), which can be supplemented by T.S. Ashton, *Iron and Steel in the Industrial Revolution* (1924).

Adam Smith

R. Heilbroner's "The Wonderful World of Adam Smith" is a lively introduction and appears in his classic study, *The Worldly Philosophers* (several editions). Also useful for understanding Smith's ideas is G. Soule, *Ideas of the Great Economists* (1952). Longer studies of Smith include J. Cropsey, *Polity and Economy: An Introduction to the Principles of Adam Smith* (1957); C.R. Fay, *The World of Adam Smith* (1970); G.R. Morrow, *The Ethical and Economic Theories of Adam Smith* (repr. 1967); J. Rae, *Life of Adam Smith* (repr. 1965); and H.L. Scheider, *Adam Smith's Moral and Political Philosophy* (repr. 1970). The *Wealth of Nations* is available in many extracts and editions.

Chapter VII

Maria Theresa and the Hapsburgs

Introductions to the history of the House of Hapsburgs are V-L. Tapié, *The Rise and Fall of the Hapsburg Monarchy* (1971) and A. Wandruszka, *The House of Hapsburg* (1964). C.A. Macartney, *The Hapsburg Empire 1790–1918* (1968) has some important things to say about Maria Theresa. Macartney has also edited an excellent collection of sources, *The Hapsburg and Hohenzollern Dynasties in the Seventeenth and Eighteenth Centuries* (1970). Useful biographies of Maria Theresa include C.L. Morris, *Maria Theresa, the Last Conservative* (1937) and R. Pick, *The Empress Maria Theresa* (1966). A recent biography by Edward Crankshaw (1970) is excellent and entertainingly written. There are other studies in English by J. Bright (1897), G.P. Gooch (1965), C.A. Macartney (1969), and J.A. Mahan (1932). A good biography of Maria Theresa's son and successor is P. Bernard, *Joseph II* (1968).

The Hohenzollerns and Prussia

As introductions to the history of Prussia some of the following should be read: F.L. Carsten, *The Origins of Prussia* (1954); G.A. Craig, *The Politics of the Prussian Army, 1640–1945* (1955); and H. Rosenberg, *Bureaucracy, Aristocracy, and Autocracy: The Prussian Experience* (1958). A good biography of Prussia's first great ruler is F. Schevill, *The Great Elector* (1947). For Frederick William I, see studies by R.R. Ergang (1941) and R.A. Dorwart (repr. 1971). Heading is the list of biographies of Frederick the Great is Thomas Carlyle's adulatory *The History of Friedrich II of Prussia, Called Frederick the Great,* 6 vols. (1858–1865). Good modern biographies are P. Gaxotte, *Frederick the Great* (trans. 1942); D.B. Horn, *Frederick the Great and the Rise of Prussia* (1964); and E. Simon, *The Making of Frederick the Great* (1963). Lord Acton's essay in *Lectures on Modern History* (1906) and one in Harold Nicolson's *The Age of Reason* (1960) give valuable perspectives. Frederick the Great as a military man can be glimpsed in B.H. Liddell-Hart, *Great Captains Unveiled* (1927) and in J. Luvvas, ed., *Frederick the Great on the Art of War* (1966).

Catherine the Great and Russia

Two collections of sources can provide insights into Catherine the Great: D. Maroger, ed., *The Memoirs of Catherine the Great* (1955) and L.J. Oliva, ed., *Catherine the Great* (1971). There are biographies by K. Anthony (1925), I. Grey (1961), M. Kochan (1977), Z. Oldenburg (1971), and H. Troyat (1980). An interesting dual biography is R. Coughlin, *Elizabeth and Catherine: Empresses of all the Russias* (1974). Also useful is G.P. Gooch, *Catherine the Great and Other Studies* (1954). An excellent overview of Catherine's reign is I. de Madariaga, *Russia in the Age of Catherine the Great* (1982). The fall 1970 issue of *Canadian Slavic Studies* has some useful monographic articles on Catherine. Other monographs providing insights include J.T. Alexander, *Autocratic Politics in a National Crisis: The Imperial Russian Government and Pugachev's Revolt, 1773–1775* (1969); P. Dukes, *Catherine the Great and the Russian Nobility* (1968); and M. Raeff, "The Domestic Policies of Peter III and His Overthrow," *American Historical Review*, 75 (June 1970). On foreign affairs and expansion, see A.W. Fisher, *The Russian Annexation of the Crimea, 1772–1783* (1970); H.H. Kaplan, *The First Partition of Poland* (1962); R.H. Lord, *The Second Partition of Poland* (1915); and A. Sorel, *The Eastern Question in the Eighteenth Century* (repr. 1969). P. Longworth, *The Cossacks* (1970) has some useful information on Pugachev.

Chatham and the British Empire

The most recent first-class biography is P. Brown, *William Pitt, Earl of Chatham: the Great Commoner* (1976). Older biographies are F. Harrison, *Chatham* (1905); W.C.B. Turnstall, *William Pitt, Earl of Chatham* (1938); O.A. Sherrard, *Lord Chatham*, 3 vols., (1952–1958); and B. Williams, *The Life of William Pitt, Earl of Chatham*, 2 vols. (1915). Lord Rosebery, *Chatham: His Early Life and Connections* (1910) can be ponderous. Most readers would be content with J.H. Plumb's *Chatham* (1958). Useful for British expansion are J.S. Corbett, *England in the Seven Years' War*, 2 vols. (1907); K. Hotblack, *Chatham's Colonial Policy: A Study of the Fiscal and Economic Implications of the Colonial Policy of the Elder Pitt* (1917); and V.T. Harlow, *The Founding of the Second British Empire, 1763–1793*, 2 vols. (1952). Those wanting a concise introduction to Chatham's role in British expansion should consult C.G. Robertson, *Chatham and the British Empire* (1946, 1962).

Chapter VIII

Works on the Era of the French Revolution and Napoleon, 1789–1815

A helpful and recent introduction to the historiography and events of the French Revolution is W. Doyle, *Origins of the French Revolution* (1980). Also useful for historiography are two books by A. Cobban: *The Myth of the French Revolution* (1953) and *The Social Interpretation of the French Revolution* (1964). C. Brinton, *The Anatomy of Revolution* (1938) compares the French Revolution to three others, while R.R. Palmer, *The Age of Democratic Revolution*, 2 vols. (1959–1964) and J. Godechot, *France and the Atlantic Revolution, 1770–1799* (1965) see the French Revolution as part of a larger international movement. For the impact of Enlightenment thinking on the Revolution, see W.F. Church, ed., *The Influence of the Enlightenment on the French Revolution: Creative, Disastrous, or Non-Existent?*, rev. ed. (1972). The historiography of the Revolution can also be approached through a number of other collections. Among them are P. Amann, ed., *The Eighteenth Century Revolution: French or Western?* (1963); F.A. Kafker and M. Laux, eds., *The French Revolution: Conflicting Interpretations* (1976); J. Kaplow, ed., *New Perspectives on the History of the French Revolution: Readings in Historical Sociology* (1965); and S. Ross, ed., *The French Revolution: Conflict or Continuity?* (1971). The role of the bourgeoisie, which is much-disputed, is debated in R. Greenlaw, ed., *The Social Origins of the French Revolution: The Debate on the Role of the Middle Classes* (1975). A new book that chronicles the dissolution of the Old Regime is J. Egret, *The French Pre-Revolution, 1787–1788* (1978), but there are many other books essential for understanding the long-term causes of 1789. Among these are P.H. Beik, *A Judgement of the Old Regime* (1944); F.L. Ford, *Robe and Sword: The Regrouping of the French Aristocracy after Louis XIV* (1953); O.H. Hufton, *The Poor of Eighteenth-Century France, 1750–1789* (1974); and G.P. Gooch, *Louis XV, The Monarchy in Decline* (1956). Two primary sources are also helpful in this regard, and both have been recently reissued. These are Alexis de Tocqueville, *The Old Regime and the French Revolution* (trans., 1955) and Arthur Young, *Travels in France During the Years 1787, 1788, 1789* (1972). On the Revolution itself, there are many useful volumes. N. Hampson, *A Social History of the French Revolution* (1963) is well-written, informative, and contains a more comprehensive approach than the title would imply. A. Soboul, *The French Revolution, 1787–1799* (1975) emphasizes the role of the bourgeoisie. G. Lefebvre, *The Coming of the French Revolution* (trans. 1955) is the best short introduction, and he has also written *The Great Fear of 1789* (1973), which deals with the peasant revolution in the countryside. See also F. Furet and D. Richet, *French Revolution* (trans., 1975); A. Goodwin, *The French Revolution* (1956); J.M. Roberts, *The French Revolution* (1979); and M.J. Sydenham, *The French Revolution* (1965). A useful collection of documents is J.H. Stewart, ed., *A Documentary Survey of the French Revolution* (1951). Surveys that provide an overview of France and Europe over the whole period are E.J. Hobsbawm, *The Age of Revolution: Europe, 1789–1848* (1962) and G. Rudé, *Revolutionary Europe, 1789–1815* (1964). Also useful are two volumes in the Rise of Modern Europe Series: C. Brinton, *A Decade of Revolution, 1789–1799* (1934) and G. Bruun, *Europe and the French Imperium, 1799–1814* (1938). A recent survey of the Napoleonic period is O. Connelly, *The Epoch of Napoleon: France and Europe* (1972).

Lafayette

Biographies of Lafayette include those of H.D. Sedgwick (1928), B. Whitlock (1929) and W.E. Woodward (1938). A number of studies on Lafayette have been authored by L. Gottschalk. Among these, see especially *Lafayette Joins the American Army* (1937) and *Lafayette Between the American and French Revolutions* (1950). A. Maurois, *Adrienne: The Life of the*

Marquise de La Fayette (trans. 1961) is a biography of Lafayette's wife, but contains many insights into her husband's career.

Robespierre and the Terror

R.R. Palmer's *Twelve Who Ruled. The Year of the Terror in the French Revolution* (repr. 1970) is a masterpiece of collective biography, including Robespierre's, and a clear political history of a difficult period. There are two good recent biographies of Robespierre: N. Hampson, *The Life and Opinions of Maximilien Robespierre* (1974) and G. Rudé, *Robespierre: Portrait of a Revolutionary* (1975). See also J.M. Thompson, *Robespierre*, 2 vols. (1935). H. Belloc's *Robespierre. A Study* (1901) is a readable, but dated, popular biography. Also valuable is A. Mathiez, *The Fall of Robespierre and Other Essays* (1927). Important for background is G. Rudé, *The Crowd in the French Revolution* (1959) and A. Soboul, *The Parisian Sans-Culottes and the French Revolution* (1964). A collection of relevant readings is R. Bienvenu, ed., *The Ninth of Thermidor: The Fall of Robespierre* (1968).

Napoleon Bonaparte

As might be expected, the biographies of Napoleon are numerous. The best short introduction can be found in one of two books by F. Markham, *Napoleon and the Awakening of Europe* (1954) and *Napoleon* (1964). G. Lefebvre, *Napoleon*, 2 vols. (trans. 1969) is generally considered the best longer study. Other biographies include those of A. Castelot, *Napoleon* (trans. 1971), D. Chandler (1974), E.L. Ludwig (trans. 1926); J.H. Rose (1901), and J.M. Thompson (1952). E.V. Tarlé, *Bonaparte* (repr. 1961) is a study from a Marxist perspective. See also O. Connelly, *The Epoch of Napoleon* (1972). A dated, but still acceptable, short introduction is H.A.L. Fisher, *Napoleon* (1912). Those who savor entertaining popular history should be sure to try J.C. Herold, *The Age of Napoleon* (1963) and D. Stacton, *The Bonapartes* (1966), a witty study of the entire Bonaparte family. Those interested in Napoleon's health should consult J. Kemble, *Napoleon Immortal* (1959). For the domestic side of Napoleon's empire see L. Bergeron, *France under Napoleon* (1981); for the imperial side, see O. Connelly, *Napoleon's Satellite Kingdoms* (1965). D. Chandler, *The Campaigns of Napoleon* (1966) is an exercise in military history. P. Geyl, *Napoleon, For and Against* (1949) remains a good introduction to the historiographical debate around Napoleon. M. Hutt, ed., *Napoleon* (1972) and C. Herold, ed., *The Mind of Napoleon* (1955) contain extracts of Napoleon's letters.

The Duke of Wellington

Those seeking biographies of Wellington should see A. Bryant's *The Great Duke* (1971) and the two volumes of E. Longford, *Wellington: The Years of* the Sword (1969) and *Pillar of State* (1972). There are also older biographies by R. Aldington (1943) and P. Guedalla (1931). J. Weller has written three readable and valuable studies of phases of Wellington's career: *Wellington in the Peninsula, 1808–1814* (1962); *Wellington at Waterloo* (1967); and *Wellington in India* (1972). C.W. Oman's *History of the Peninsular War*, 7 vols. (1902–1930) is important, but of a mass useful only for the serious student. A. Brett-James, *Wellington at War, 1794–1815* (1961); M. Glover, *Wellington as Military Commander* (1968); and C.W. Oman, *Wellington's Army, 1809–1814* (1912) are, with the works of Weller above, the best introduction to Wellington as a soldier.

Prince Metternich and the Congress of Vienna

For Metternich, see G. de Bertier de Sauvigny, *Metternich and His Times* (1962) and A. Palmer, *Metternich* (1972). Also important are A. Cecil, *Metternich, 1773–1859* (1933) and H.F. Schwarz, ed., *Metternich, the Coachman of Europe* (1962). E.L. Woodward, *Three Studies in European Conservatism* (1929) contains a useful essay on Metternich. E.E. Kraehe, *Metternich's German Policy* (1963) provides insights into Metternich's education, experience, and ideas. For the Vienna Congress see G. Ferraro, *The Reconstruction of Europe: Talleyrand and the Congress of Vienna, 1814–1815* (1941); H. Kissinger, *A World Restored: Metternich, Castlereagh and the Problems of Peace, 1812–1822* (1957); H. Nicolson, *Congress of Vienna: A Study in Allied Unity* (1946); and C.K. Webster, *The Congress of Vienna, 1814–1815* (1919). See also A.J.P. Taylor, *The Hapsburg Monarchy, 1809–1918*. A. May, *The Age of Metternich, 1814–1848* (1933) is a good introduction to Metternich and his policies.

Index

Index

A

Abbot, Wilbur Cortez (historian), 100
"Abhorrers." See Tories
Absolutism, 200
Accession Charter, Swedish (1611), 155
Act of Union (1707), 295
Act of Settlement (1701), 295
"Addled Parliament," 81
Adrianople, Treaty of (1713), 185
Aelders, Etta Palm d', 423
Agitators, 108
Aides, 201
Aix-la-Chapelle, Treaty of (1668), 207; (1748), 335, 359
Alaska, 354
Albert of Brandenburg, 341
Alexander Nevsky, 179
Alexander I, Tsar, 400, 404, 414, 417
Alexis, Tsar (1645-1676), 181-182
Almeida, Siege of (1811), 405
Alte Veste, Siege of (1632)
Altmark, Peace of (1629), 155
American Revolution, 362
Amiens, Peace of (1802), 396, 400
Anastasia Romanovna, 181
Anatomy of Revolution, 374
Anglo-French Commercial Wars, 329-330
An Inquiry into the Nature and Causes of the Wealth of Nations, 313
Annales School, 201
Anne of Austria, Queen of France, 164, 200, 203
Anne of Denmark, Queen of England, 74
Anne, Queen of England (1702-1714), 124-125, 218-227 *passim*, 295
Anne, Tsarina of Russia (1730-1740), 350
Anspach, Caroline of, Queen of England, 303-304

Anti-Machiavel, 346-347
Aquapendente, Fabrius ap, 256
Apothecaries Act (1815), 429
Architecture, 430-431
Aristarchus, 248
Aristotle, 247, 248, 249, 253, 254-255
Arkwright, Richard (inventor), 312
Arouet, Francois Marie. See Voltaire
Art and artists (1600-1815), 430-431; Dutch, 208-209; Spanish, 216-217
Ashley, Maurice (historian), 65
Assembly of Notables, 380
Asiento, 295
Auerstadt, Battle of (1806), 400
Augsburg, Peace of (1555), 148, 175
Augustus III of Saxony, King of Poland, 187-188, 332
Austerlitz, Battle of (1805), 400
Austria, history of. See Hapsburgs, history of
Azov, 184-185, 350

B

Bacon, Sir Francis (English statesman and scientist), 8, 241
Badajoz, Siege of (1811-1812), 405
Balance of power, 199
Bank of England Act (1694), 219, 295
Barber, Eleanor (historian), 373
"Barebones Parliament" (1653), 110
Baroque movement, 208, 430
Bärwalde, Treaty of (1631), 157
Basel, Treaty of (1795), 393
Basilikon Doron, 75
Bastille, storming of (1789), 381
Bathing, attitudes toward (1600-1815), 36-37
Baumer, Franklin L. (historian), 260
Bayonne, Siege of (1813), 408

Becker, Carl (historian), 278
Beethoven, Ludwig von (composer), 431
Behavior, social (1600-1815), 21-24, 205
Behemoth, 63
Belgrade, Treaty of (1739), 332, 350
Berlin Decree (1806), 400
Berry, Duke of (grandson of Louis XIV), 205
Bill of Rights, English (1689), 123
Black Death, 32
"Black Hole of Calcutta," 360
"Black Hundreds," 179-180
Blake, William (English admiral), 111
Bleeding (medical treatment), 39-41
Blenheim, Battle of (1704), 223
"Bloody Assizes," 121
Blücher, Marshall (Prussian general), 409-410
Bologna, University of, 255
Board of Trade and Plantations (1696), 295
Bonaparte, Napoleon, 371, 384, 391-421 *passim*
Borodino, Battle of (1812), 408
"Bottleneck" theory, 312
Boulton, Matthew, 310-311
Bourgeoisie, 376-432 *passim*
"Boroughmongers," 301
Boyars, 179
Boyle, Robert (scientist), 242
Boyne, Battle of the (1690), 123
Braddock, General, 360
Braganza, Catherine of, Queen of England, 115
Brahe, Tycho (astronomer), 250
Breda, Declaration of (1660), 114
Breitenfeld, Battle of (1631), 157-158
Breslau and Berlin, Treaty of (1742), 335
Bridgewater, Duke of, 308
Brienne, Lomenie de (French minister), 378

Brinton, Crane (historian), 374
Buckingham, Duke of. See Villers, George.
Budapest, Siege of (1686), 331
Burford, army mutiny at, 110
Burke, Edmund, 275
Burslem Works, 307
Bute, Lord (English politican), 361
Butterfield, Herbert (historian), 278

C

Cabal, the, 117
Cadettanhaus, 347
Caesaropapism, 178
Cahiers, 422-423
Calonne, Charles Alexandre (French minister), 378
Campo Formio, Treaty of (1797), 394
Canals, 294, 308
Candide, 268
Capital intensive investments, 294
Cardano, Girolamo (mathematician), 241, 242
Carding machine, 312
Carey, Sir Robert, 3, 15, 50
Carlos II, King of Spain (1665-1700), 212-217 *passim*
Carr, Robert, Earl of Somerset (royal favorite), 80
Carteret, George (English politician), 358
Cartesian dualism, 246
Castlemaine, Lady (mistress of Charles II), 115
Castlereagh, Viscount (British statesman), 408, 416-417
Catherine I, Tsarina of Russia (1725-1727), 350
Catherine II ("the Great"), Tsarina of Russia (1762-1796), 267, 269, 327, 349-357 *passim*
"Cavalier Parliament" (1661), 116
Cavendish, William (chemist), 431

Cecil, Sir Robert (English statesman), 79
Chambers of Reunion, 207
Charles I, King of England (1625-1649), 83-100 *passim,* 258
Charles II, King of England (1660-1685), 113-120 *passim*
Charles V, Holy Roman Emperor and King of Spain, 148, 199, 207
Charles VI, Holy Roman Emperor, 330-331
Charles IX, King of Sweden (1604-1611), 151
Charles Gustavus of Sweden. See Charles X, King of Sweden
Charles X, King of Sweden (1654-1660), 175-176
Charles XI, King of Sweden (1660-1697), 176-177
Charles XII, King of Sweden (1697-1718), 176, 187-189, 269, 350
Chaumont, Treaties of (1813), 408
Childbirth and children (1600-1815), 27-30 *passim*
Chotek, Rudolf (Austrian statesman), 337
Christian IV, King of Denmark, 155, 156-157
Christina, Queen of Sweden (1632-1654), 169-177 *passim,* 191, 247
Churchill, John. See Marlborough, Duke of
Churchill, Sarah. See Marlborough, Duchess of
Cinq-Mars Conspiracy, 168
Cintra, Convention of (1808), 403
Cisalpine Republic, 394
Cities, growth of (1600-1815), 44-46
Ciudad Rodrigo, Siege of (1812)
Clapham, J.H. (historian), 318
"Clarendon Code," 116

Clive, Robert, 360-361
Cloth industry, in Industrial Revolution, 312
Clothing, 38
Cobban, Alfred (historian), 373
"Cobham's Cubs," 358
Code Michaud, 168
Colbert, Jean Baptiste (French statesman), 206
"Colleges," 189
Committee of Both Kingdoms, 106; of General Security, 388; of Public Safety, 388-391
Commune of Paris, 381, 383, 387-392
"Congress System," 420
Compton, Sir Spencer (English courtier and politician), 298
Condenser, steam, 310
Confederation of the Rhine, 400, 408
Considerations on the State of Europe, 346
Constituent Assembly. See National Assembly
Concinis, the (French royal favorites), 164, 165-166
Condition of the Working Classes in England, 291
Condorcet, Marquis de, 270, 380
Congress Poland, 417
Constantinople, Peace of (1700), 187
Constitution of the Year III, 393
Consulate (1799-1804), 397-400
"Continental System," 401-403
Conventicle Act (1664), 116
Convention. See National Convention
Copernicus (Niklas Koppernigk), 249, 253
Copenhagen, Treaty of (1661), 176
Corday, Charlotte, 423
Cordeliers, 383
cordon sanitaire, 415-416
Coronation Oath Act (1689), 124

Corvée, 202, 377
Corporation Act (1661), 116
Cort, Henry (inventor), 312
"Court and country" hypothesis, 67
Council of Ancients, 393; of Five Hundred, 393; of State, 110
Coup d'Etat of Brumaire (1799), 397; of Fructidor (1797), 396
Covent Garden, 429
Cranfield, Lionel (Lord Treasurer of England), 80
Crime and punishment (1600-1815), 15-21 *passim*
Critique of Pure Reason, 278
Crompton, Samuel (inventor), 312
Cromwell, Oliver, 94, 100-113 *passim*
Cromwell, Richard, 113
Cult of the Supreme Being, 390

D

Daemonologie (1597), 75
Dalton (chemist), 431
Danton, 383, 388, 389
Darby family (ironmasters), 313
Dawson, Philip (historian), 373
"Day of Dupes," 167
Deane, Phyllis (historian), 292, 312
Death, frequency of (1600-1815), 27-30 *passim*
Declaration of the Rights of Man and of the Citizen (1789), 381
De humani corporis fabricus libri septum, 255
Defenestration of Prague (1618), 147
Deism, 266; in French Revolution, 390
Demographic factors, 1600-1815, 27-30
De Mundo, 256, 257
Dentistry, 42
Descartes, René (mathematician), 172, 241, 242, 253, 259, 266
Desmoulins, Abbé, 383

Dessau, Battle of (1626), 156
Dettingen, Battle of (1743), 335
Deviance, attitudes toward, 18, 205
Dévots, 165
Debrett's *Peerage,* 429
De Witt brothers, 210
Diderot, Denis, 270; and Catherine II, 354
Diggers, 108
"Diplomatic Revolution" (1756), 335-336
Directory, the, 393-397
Disease (1600-1815), 30-38
Discoverie of Witchcraft, 75
Discourse on Method, 245-246
Dixième, 201
Dover, Treaty of (1670), 117, 207
Doyle, William (historian), 375
Drang nach osten, 179, 341
Dresden, Treaty of (1745), 335
Droit de devolution, 206-207
Dumouriez (French general), 388
Duquesne, Fort, 360
Duma, 189
Dunbar, Battle of (1650), 110
Dunkirk, Siege of (1658), 111
Dunes, Battle of the (1658), 111
Dupleix, 358, 360
Dutch Republic, history of, 207-212
Dutch trade, 3, 208
Dutch Wars, 110, 113, 207, 208
Dvoriane, 179

E

East India Company (British), 304-305, 330, 359-361; (French), 359-361
Eating and drinking (1600-1815), 34, 46
Economic integration, 291
"Economic man," idea of, 314
Èdit du Toise, 201
Edgehill, Battle of (1642), 104
Edict of Nantes, 164; of Restitution (1629), 157

Egyptian Campaign, 396
Elba, 408
Elizabeth I, Queen of England, 3, 71
Elizabeth I, Tsarina of Russia (1741-1762), 335, 349-353 passim
Emigrés, 381
Encomiendas, 3
Encyclopedia, 270
Engagement, the 108
Engels, Friederich, 291
England, history of. See Great Britain, history of
English Revolution (1603-1714), 62-128
Enlightened despots, 267
Enlightenment, 259-278 passim, 431
Equivalent, 201
Essex, Earl of (Parliamentary general)
Estates General, 165; in French Revolution, 378-380, 386
Erfurt, Congress of (1808), 404
Eugene of Savoy (Hapsburg general), 331-332
Evelyn, John (diarist), 7-52 passim, 62
Excise Tax, and Walpole (1733), 303
Exclusion Bill, 118
Exercitatio Anatomica de Motu Cordis et Sanquinis in Animalibus, 257-258
"Extraordinary Tribunal" (1792), 385

F

Fable of the Bees, 314
Fahrbellin, Battle of (1675), 177
Fairfax, Sir Thomas (Parliamentary general), 106-107
Families and family structure (1600-1815), 25-26
Family Compact (1733), 303
"Federalist" revolts (1793), 387
Fedor, Tsar (1676-1682), 182

Fermat, Pierre de (mathematician), 241
Fermes unies, 201
Ferrer's Case (1543), 77
"Fifteen" (1715), 295
Financial Directorate, 337
Five-Mile Act (1665), 116
Feuillants, 383
Fleurus, Battle of (1690), 211
"Flight to Varennes" (1791), 382
Fluits, 3
Fifth Monarchy Men, 108
Firth, Sir Charles (historian), 65
Fisher, F.J. (historian), 44-45
"Flux," 254
Flying shuttle, 312
Food and nutrition (1600-1815), 30-36 passim
Forster, Robert (historian), 373
Fouché, 398
Foxe, George (Quaker leader), 108
France, history of, 4, 197-228, 371-424
Francis I (of Lorraine), Emperor, 334, 338
Francis II, Emperor (1792-1835), 339
Frankenstein, 276
Frederick, Elector of the Palatinate. See Frederick V, King of Bohemia
Frederick I ("the Ostentatious"), King in Prussia (1688-1713), 341-343
Frederick II ("the Great"), King of Prussia (1740-1786), 267, 327, 333-339 passim
Frederick III, Elector of Brandenburg. See Frederick I, King in Prussia
Frederick V, King of Bohemia, 74, 156, 159
Frederick William, Elector of Brandenburg (1640-1688), 341-342
Frederick William I, King of Prussia (1713-1740), 327, 342-346

Frederick William III, King of Prussia (1797-1840), 400
Freiburg, Battle of (1762), 332
French and Indian War (1754-1763), 329, 360
French Revolution (1789-1815), 371-421 *passim*
Friedland, Battle of (1807), 400
Friedrich, Carl (historian), 147-148
Fronde, the (1649), 203-204
Fuentes de Onoro, Battle of (1811), 405
Fussen, Treaty of, 335

G

Gabelle, 200
Galen, 39, 254-259 *passim*
Galilei, Galileo (scientist), 242, 249-251, 253, 256, 258, 259
Gardiner, S.R. (historian), 65, 69
Gaston, Duke of Orleans, 164, 199-200
"General Crisis" (seventeenth century), 7
General Directory, 344
General Will, 277
"Gentry controversy," 67
George I, King of England, 296-303 *passim*
George II, King of England, 297-304 *passim*, 335
Gibbon, Edward (historian), 270, 297
Gilbert, William (scientist), 251, 256, 257
Gindely, Anton (historian), 147-148
Girondists, 388, 423
"Glorious Revolution" (1688), 122-125, 219
Gluckel of Hameln (diarist), 1-52 *passim*
Godechot, Jacques (historian), 375
Godden vs. Hales, 122
Godolphin, Earl of (English politician), 221, 222

Gorée (Dakar), 361
Goubert, Pierre (historian), 29
Gouge, Olympe de, 423
Governor, 311
Grace of Ales, 167
Grand Alliance (1702), 218, 223
Grand Duchy of Warsaw, 405, 417
"Grand Embassy," 185-186
Grand Remonstrance (1642)
Grand Trunk Canal, 308
Grantham, Battle of (1643), 105
Great Britain, history of (1600-1815), 2-4; 69-127; 211-227; 289-318; 357-362; 371-424
Great Contract (1610), 79
"Great Elector." See Frederick William, Elector of Brandenburg
"Great Fear" (1789)
Great Fire of London (1666), 45, 117
Great Northern War, 187-189
"Great revolutions," 373-374
Gribeauval, Jean-Baptiste de (military reformer), 394
"Greek Project," 354
Guberniyas, 189, 355
Gustavus Adolphus, King of Sweden (1611-1632), 151-159 *passim,* 167, 169, 175
Guy Fawkes conspiracy (1604), 81

H

Halifax, Lord (philosopher and wit), 1-52 *passim*
Haller, William (historian), 65
Hampton Court Conference (1604)
Hangö, Battle of (1714), 188
Hanover, House of, 125, 299-304 *passim*
Hapsburgs, history of, 191, 330-339 *passim,* 362-363, 371-424 *passim*
Hargreaves, Robert (inventor), 312

Hartwell, R.M. (historian), 317
Haugwitz, Ludwig (Austrian statesman), 337
Harvey, William (scientist), 242, 253-259 *passim*
Hat Act, 293
Heads of Proposals, 108
Hébert, 383
Helmont (chemist), 431
Helvetius, Claude, 270, 313-314
Henrietta Maria, Queen of England, 83-100 *passim*
Henry IV, King of France (1589-1610), 163, 165
Heraclides, 249
Hervey, Lord (English courtier and wit), 297
Hexter, J.H. (historian), 67, 126
High Commission, Court of, 91, 93
Hill, Christopher (historian), 67
Hipparchus, 249
Hobbes, Thomas (political philosopher), 63-64, 68, 265-266, 314
Hobsbawm, E.J. (historian) 7, 317, 373
Hohenlinden, Battle of (1801), 399
Hohenzollern, House of, 191, 340-349 *passim*
Holbach, Paul Thiry d', 270
"Holy Alliance" (1815), 417
Horse-racing, 429-430
Housing, changes in (1600-1815), 46
Hubertusburg, Treaty of (1763), 336, 361, 362
Huguenots, 164, 206, 211
Humble Petition and Advice (1657), 111
Hume, David (philosopher), 277
Humors, 254
"Hundred Days," 408-409
Hungary, history of. See Hapsburgs, history of
Hunter, William (anatomist), 431
Huntsman, Benjamin (ironmaster), 313

Huyghens, Christian (scientist), 209, 251
Hyde, Edward, Earl of Clarendon (English statesman), 116
Hygiene and cleanliness (1600-1815), 36-37, 205

I

Indulgence, Declaration of, 117, 118, 122
Industrial Revolution, 289-318 *passim*, 431-432
Inquiry Concerning Human Understanding, 277
Instrument of Government (1653), 110
Interregnum, the (1649-1660), 114
"Invisible hand," 315
Ireland, 95, 110, 123
Iron Act, 293
Iron and steel industry, in Industrial Revolution, 312-313
Ivan III, Tsar, 179
Ivan IV ("the Terrible"), Tsar, 179-180, 354
Ivan V, Tsar (1682-1696), 182-184
Ivan VI, Tsar (1740-1742), 350

J

Jacobins, 383, 386-391 *passim*
Jacobites, 295-296
James I, King of England (1603-1625), 3, 69-83 *passim*, 155
James II, King of England (1685-1688), 118-125 *passim*
James, Duke of York. See James II, King of England
Jansenists, 267
Jassy, Treaty of (1792), 354
Jeffreys, George (English judge), 121
Jena, Treaty of (1806), 400
Jennings, Sarah. See Marlborough, Duchess of

484 Men and Women in Revolution and War

Jesuits, 165, 267
Jews, 49-50, 338, 355
Johnson, Samuel, 277, 313
Joseph I, Holy Roman Emperor (1705-1711), 332
Joseph II, Holy Roman Emperor (1780-1790), 338-339
Junkers, 341-342
"Junto," the, 222

K

Kalmar, War of, 155
Kant, Immanuel, 278
Kardis, Treaty of (1661), 176
Karl of Södermanland. See Charles IX, King of Sweden
Karlowitz, Treaty of (1699), 332
Kaunitz, Count (Austrian statesman), 335-336
Kearney, H.F. (historian), 259
Kepler, John (astronomer and mathematician), 251, 253
Kerridge, Eric (historian), 292
"King's Friends," 302
"King in Parliament," 76-77
King William's War (1689-1697), 329
Kissinger, Henry (political scientist), 410
Klusino, Battle of (1610), 155
Knared, Peace of (1613), 155
Koch, Christopher William, 412
Koenigsberger, H.G. (historian), 148
Konigsmarck, Count, 296
Krupp Works, 429
Kuchuk Kainardji, Treaty of (1774), 354

L

Lafayette, Marquis de, 371, 378-384 *passim*
Lake Peipus, Battle of (1242)
Landesmütter, 338
La Hogue, Battle of (1692), 211
Lavoisier (chemist), 431
Le Monde, 246

La Rochelle, Siege of (1627), 161, 166
La Vallière, Louise de (mistress of Louis XIV), 203
Laud, William (Archbishop of Canterbury), 92, 94
Law of the Maximum (1793), 390; of Suspects, 389; of 22 Prairial (1794), 390
Lech River, Battle of (1632), 158
Le Chapelier Law (1791), 382
Lectures on the Industrial Revolution (1884), 291
Lefebvre, Georges (historian), 373
Legislative Assembly, in French Revolution, 382, 384
Legislative Committee, of Catherine II, 355
Leibniz, Wilhelm (mathematician and philosopher), 241, 268
Leipzig, Battle of (1813), 408
Lemontey, Pierre-Edouard (historian), 201
Leopold I, Holy Roman Emperor (1658-1705), 332
Leopold II, Holy Roman Emperor (1790-1792), 339
Leeuwenhoek (Dutch scientist), 209, 242
Lesnaya, Battle of (1708), 188
Lesynski, Stanislaus, 189
Levée en masse, 390, 394, 403
Levellers, 108, 110
Leviathan, 265
Licensing Act, 297
Ligny, Battle of (1815)
Ligurian Republic, 394, 397
Lilburne, John, Leveller leader, 108
Lincoln, Siege of (1644), 106
Livonian Knights, 179, 180
Locke, John (philosopher), 260-261, 265-266
Longman's (English publisher), 430
Long Parliament, 94-113 *passim*

Louis XIII, King of France (1610-1643), 162, 164, 200, 377
Louis XIV, King of France (1643-1714), 117, 118, 199-227 *passim*, 269, 377
Louis XV, King of France (1715-1774), 377
Louis XVI, King of France (1774-1792), 378-386
Louis the Grand Dauphin, son of Louis XIV, 203
Lowe, Thomas (surgeon), 40
Lübeck, Treaty of (1629), 157
Lunéville, Treaty of (1801), 399
Lutheranism, and Thirty Years' War, 148; in Sweden, 151-152, 173-176; effect on Peter III, 350
Lütner-am-Barenberge, Battle of (1626), 156
Lützen, Battle of (1632), 159, 167

M

Macaulay, T.B. (historian), 65, 80
Maintenon, Madame de (mistress and wife and Louis XIV), 203
Major-Generals, 111-113
Malpighi, Marcello (scientist), 242
Malplaquet, Battle of (1709), 223
Mandeville, Bernard, 314
Manchester, Earl of (Parliamentary general), 106-107
Marat, Jean-Paul, 383, 389
Marengo, Battle of (1800), 398
Mariana of Austria, Queen of Spain, 213
Maria Eleonora of Brandenberg, Queen of Sweden, 157, 169-171
Maria Theresa, Empress of Austria, 327, 330-339 *passim*
Marie Antoinette, Queen of France, 385-386

Marie Louise, Empress of France, 413
Marlborough, Duchess of, 125, 220-225 *passim*
Marlborough, Duke of, 220-225 *passim*
Marsaglia, Battle of (1693), 211
Marston Moor, Battle of (1644), 97, 106
Martinet (military reformer), 206
Mary Queen of Scots, 74, 75
Mary II, Queen of England, (1689-1694), 123-124
Marx, Karl, 67, 291, 373
Masham, Abigail (royal favorite), 125, 224
Mathematical Principles of Natural Philosophy (1687), 252
Mazarin, Cardinal and minister of France, 200, 202, 204-205
"Mazarinettes," 202
Manners; coarseness of, 21-24; improvement in 46-47
Maupeou, Rene Nicolas de (French minister), 377
May, Arthur (historian), 415
Mayer, Arno (historian), 318
Mecklenberg, 157
Medici, Marie de, Queen Mother of France, 164-167
Medicine and the medical professions, 38-43
Mendelsshon, Moses, 270
Mercantilism, 167-168, 206, 293; in Russia, 356-357
Mericourt, Theroigne de, 423
Metternich, Clemens von, 371, 410-420 *passim*
Metric system, 429
Michael (Romanov), Tsar (1613-1645), 155, 181
Midwifery, 43
Milan Decree, 401
Miloslavskys, 181-184
Militia Bill (1642), 95
Millenary Petition, 80
Modest Proposal, 277

Mohacs, Battle of (1687), 331
Mollwitz, Battle of (1741), 334
Monck, George (English general), 113
Monmouth, Duke of (illegitimate son of Charles II), 118, 121
Montcalm, General, 360-361
Montespan, Marquise de (mistress of Louis XIV), 203
Montesquieu, (political philosopher), 270, 271, 351
Moore, Sir John (British general), 403
Moryson, Fynes (diarist), 5-52 *passim*
"Mountain," the, 388-389
Mousnier, Roland (historian), 373
Music and musicians, 430-431
Muslims, 355-356
Mutiny Act (1689), 218

N

Nantes, Edict of, 211
Napier, John (mathematician), 241, 309
Napoleon Bonaparte. See Bonaparte, Napoleon
Napoleonic Code, 420, 423-434
Napoleonic Wars, 330, 391-424 *passim*
Narva, Battle of (1700), 187
Naryshkins, 181-184
Naseby, Battle of (1645), 97, 107
Nassau, Maurice Prince of (military reformer), 153
Natalia Naryshkina, 181-182
National Assembly (1789), 379-382, 386
National Covenant (1638), 94, 386
National Convention, 387-393
National Guard, 381-384 *passim*
Navigation Acts (1651-2), 110, 208, 293
Nayler, James (Quaker leader), 111
Necker, Jacques (French minister), 377-378

"Ned Lud," 432
Neerwinden, Battle of (1793), 401
Nelson, Horatio (British admiral), 396, 397
Nemtsy, 177
Newbury, Battle of (1644), 107
Newcastle, Duke of (English politician), 298, 359-360
Newcomen engine, 310
"New Model Army," 107
Newton, Isaac (mathematician and scientist), 241, 242, 247, 251-253 *passim*
Nile, Battle of (1798)
Nimwegen, Treaty of (1678), 207, 211
Nineteen Propositions (1642), 95-96
Nördlingen, Battle of (1634)
Norfolk election case (1586), 77
Novum Organum, 242
Nymphenburg, Alliance of (1741), 334-335
Nystadt, Peace of (1721), 189, 191

O

Oates, Titus, 118
Oath of the Tennis Court (1789), 379
Occasional Conformity Bill (1704), 222
Octrois, 376
Old Sarum, 305
Oliva, Treaty of (1660), 176
"Optimists," and Industrial Revolution, 317
Oprichniki, 179-180
Oprichnina, 179
Orleans, Duke of ("Philip Egalité"), 385
Orlovs, 353
Ormée, the (1652), 204
Orthodox Christianity, 179
Osborne, Thomas, Earl of Danby (English statesman), 118
Oswego, Siege of, 360
Ottoman Empire, history of (1648-1739), 331-332, 354

Oxenstierna, Axel (Chancellor of Sweden), 156, 159, 175
Oxford, Robert Harley, Earl of, 224
Oxford, Siege of (1646), 108

P

Padua, University of, 254-256 *passim*
Palmer, Robert R. (historian), 373
Parliament, history of, 61-127 *passim*, 219-225 *passim*
Paris, Treaty of (1763), 293, 306, 361-364 *passim*; (1814), 417; (1815), 417
Pascal, Blaise (mathematician), 241, 260, 266
Paul, Lewis (inventor), 312
Peerage Bill, 302
Pelerwardein, Battle of (1716), 332
Pelham, Henry (English politician), 359
Peninsular Wars, 405-408
Penruddock's Rising (1653), 111
"Pensioner Parliament." See "Cavalier Parliament"
Pepys, Samuel (diarist), 5-52 *passim*
Persian Letters, 270
"Pessimists," and Industrial Revolution, 317
Peter I ("the Great"), Tsar (1689-1725), 177-190 *passim,* 269, 350
Peter II, Tsar (1727-1730), 350
Peter III, Tsar (1762), 327, 336, 349-353 *passim*
Petition of Right (1628)
"Petitioners." See Whigs
Pettee, George S., 372
Philip II, King of Spain, 207, 213
Philip IV, King of Spain (1621-1665), 213
Philosophes, 260-262, 394
Physicians, 39-42
Pillnitz, Declaration of (1791), 383
Pitt, Thomas ("Diamond"), 304-307 *passim,* 357
Pitt, William, Earl of Chatham, 306, 327, 357-362 *passim*

Place Act (1707), 125
"Placemen," 219
Plague, in London, 32, 117
"Plain," the, 388
Plassey, Battle of (1757)
Plato, 248
"Pocket boroughs," 301
Poland, history of, 330, 336-337, 354
Polišenský, J. V. (historian), 148
Polish Partitions, 330, 336-337
"Polish-Saxon Question," 416
Political Arithmetic, 261
Politique, 161
Poltava, Battle of (1709), 188
Poniatowski, Stanislaus, King of Poland, 354
Pontiac's Rebellion (1763), 361
Pontrefact, Siege of (1648), 109
Popish Plot (1678), 118
Praetorius, Michael (composer), 430
Pragmatic Sanction, 332
Prague, Congress of, 415
Pravoslavie, 179
Prerogative, royal, 78-79, 92
Pressburg, Diet of (1687), 332; (1741), 334
Pressburg, Treaty of, 400
Preston, Battle of (1648), 94, 109
Pride's Purge (1648), 109
Priestley, Joseph (chemist), 431
Prince Rupert, Royalist commander, 105
Privileges, parliamentary, 76-83 *passim*
Proclamation Line of 1763, 361
Property Qualification Act (1710), 125
Prussia, history of, 340-349 *passim*
Prynne, William (writer), 93
Prostitution, 33; in Vienna, 338
Ptolemy, 249
Pugachev's Rebellion (1773-1775), 355
Puritanism, 65-66
Putney, army debates at, 108
Pym, John (parliamentary leader), 95
Pyramids, Battle of (1798), 396

Pyrenees, Peace of (1661), 168

Q

Quadruple Alliance. See Chaumont, Treaty of
Quakers, 108, 111
Quebec Act (1774), 362
Quebec, Battle of (1758), 360-361
Queen Anne's War (1702-1713), 329
Quesnay, 304

R

Ramillies, Battle of (1706), 223
Randall, John Herman (historian), 246
Ranters, 108
Recorde, Robert (mathematician), 241
"Reduction" of 1649, 175
Reflections on the French Revolution, 275
Reichenbach, Battle of (1762), 336; Treaty of (1813), 414
Restoration, English (1660), 113-120 *passim*
"Reversal of Alliances." See "Diplomatic Revolution"
Revolutionary Republican Women, 423
Revolutionary Tribunal, 389-391
Revolutions, nature of, 373-374
Revolutions of 1848, 420
Richelieu, Armand-Jean du Plessis de (Cardinal and French minister), 157, 160-168, *passim*, 175, 200, 206
Riksdag, 156
Riksrad, 155
Ripon, Treaty of (1640)
Rise and Fall of the Roman Empire, 297
Robespierre, Maximilien, 371, 383, 385-393 *passim*
Romanovs, 155
Rossbach, Battle of (1757), 336
Rotary motion, 311
"Rotten boroughs," 301

Root and Branch Bill (1641), 95
Rousseau, Jean-Jacques, 262, 265, 272, 275-276, 423
Royal College of Physicians, 39, 82, 257
Royal College of Surgeons, 431
"Rump" Parliament, 109
Rus, 178
Russia, history of, 177-190, 349-357; 410-420
Russo-Turkish Wars, 330
Rye House Plot, 120
Ryswick, Peace of (1697), 211

S

Saint-Simon, Duke of (French diarist), 200, 203, 205
Sans-culottes, 387-391 *passim*
Santa Cruz, Battle of (1657), 111
Sarah, Duchess of Marlborough. See Marlborough, Duchess of
Savoy, Eugene of (military leader), 223
Scheele, Carl Wilhelm (chemist), 431
Schönbrunn, Treaty of (1809), 404, 413
Schwarzenburg, Count (Austrian general), 414
Scientific Revolution, 241-278 *passim*
Seekers, 108
Sedgmoor, Battle of, 121
Self-Denying Ordinance (1645), 107
Senate, Russian, 189; French, 398
Sepoys, 359
"September Massacres" (1792), 385
Septennial Act (1716), 302
Serfdom, in Russia, 180-181, 355; in Austria, 337-338
Servetus, Michael, 256
Settlement, Act of (1652), 110; (1701), 124
Seven Bishop's Case, 121
Seven Years' War (1756-1763), 329, 358, 360
Seville, Treaty of (1729), 303

Index

Shelekhov, Gregory (Russian explorer), 354
Shelley, Mary, 276
Ship Money Case (1635), 92-93
"Short Parliament," 94
Siglo de oro, 216
Silesian Wars, 329-330, 333-338 *passim,* 348-349
"Sinking Fund," 299
"Slavophiles," 190
Slavs, 177
Smallpox, 31-32
Smerd, 180
Smith, Adam, 261, 313-316 *passim*
Sobieski, John, King of Poland, 331
Soboul, Albert (historian), 373
Social contract, 265-266
Social Contract, The, 272
Social control, 1600-1815, 11-15
Society and social life (1600-1815), 7-10
Society for the Suppression of the Slave Trade, 308
Soho Works, 310
Solemn League and Covenant (1643), 97, 106
Somerset, Earl of. See Carr, Robert
Sophia, Russian Regent (1682-1689), 182-187
Sophia Dorothea (estranged wife of George I), 296
"South Sea Bubble," 300-301
Spain, history of, 212-217 *passim*
"Spanish Match," 82, 86
Spinoza, Baruch, 209
Spirit of the Laws, 270, 271, 351
Srbik, Heinrich von (historian), 410
St. Germain-en-Laye, Treaty of, 177
St. Gotthard, Battle of (1663), 331
St. Petersburg, 188, 190
Staffarda, Battle of (1690)
Stanhope, Earl of (English politician), 299-301
Star Chamber, Court of, 91, 93
Steam engine, 310-312 *passim*

Steinberg, S.H. (historian), 149
Steinkirk, Battle of (1692), 211
Stockholm, Treaty of (1721), 189
Stolbova, Peace of (1617), 155
Streltsi, 182-183, 186-187
Stromberg, Roland (historian), 241
Succession, Act of (1701), 222
Sunderland, Earl of (English politician), 219, 221, 299-301
Surgeons, 39-40
Suvorov (Russian general), 397
Swammerdam, Jan, 209, 242
Sweden, history of, 4, 151-191

T

"Table of Ranks," 189
Tabula rasa, 265
"Tackers," 222
Taille, 200
Talavera, Battle of (1809), 404
Talleyrand, Count (French diplomat) 380, 404, 413, 416
Tartaglia, Nicolò (mathematician), 241
Tatar "yoke," 178
Tax policy; in seventeenth-century France, 200-202
Taylor, A. J. P. (historian), 411
Tea Act, 293
"Terror," the, 371, 389-391
Teschen, Treaty of (1779), 336
Test Act (1673), 118
Teutonic Knights, 179, 341
Thermidorean Reaction (1794), 391, 393
Thirty Years' War (1618-1648), 147-175 *passim,* 191
"Third Rome," 179
"Thorough," policy of, 92
Tilly (Hapsburg general), 156, 157-158
Tilsit, Treaties of (1807), 400
"Time of Troubles," 155
Toleration Act (1689), 194
Tories, 118, 219-225 *passim,* 295-296
Torres Vedras, 405
Tourbillons, 247

Toulouse, Battle of (1814), 408
Toynbee, Arnold (historians), 291
Turgot, Jacques (French minister), 377
Travel and transportation (seventeenth century), 4-6
Tsar, 179
Trevelyan, G. M. (historian), 65
Trevor-Roper, H. R. (historian), 7, 67
Tribunate, 398
Trafalgar, Battle of (1805), 401
"Tricolor Terror," 383, 386
Triple Alliance (1668), 117, 206
Triennial Act (1641), 95; (1664), 117; (1694), 218, 219
Troppau, Protocol of (1720), 420
Turin, Battle of (1706), 223
Turnham Green, Battle of (1642), 105
Turnpikes, 294, 308
Two Treatises on Government, 265

U

Ukaze of 1794, 355
Ulm, Battle of (1805), 400
Ulster, 123
Ultramontanism, 165
Uniformity, Act of (1662), 116
Utrecht, Treaty of (1713), 125, 225-227 *passim,* 293, 295, 298, 299, 358, 362-363

V

Valmy, Cannonade of (1792), 385
Valtellina Affair (1624), 166
Varangians, 177-178
Vasa, House of, 151-159 *passim*
Vasily III, Tsar, 179
Vauban (military reformer), 206
Vendée, revolt in, 387, 390
Venereal diseases, 32-33, 205
Versailles, 204-205
Vesalius, Andreas (anatomist), 255-256
Vienna, Congress of (1815), 225, 415-420 *passim;* Siege of, 331; Treaty of (1738), 332

Villiers, George, Duke of Buckingham (royal favorite), 81, 82, 86, 89-90
Vieta, Franciscus (mathematician), 241
Vimiero, Battle of (1808), 403
Vindication of the Rights of Men, 275
Vindication of the Rights of Women, 275
Vivaldi (composer), 430
Vladimir, Grand Prince of Kiev, 178
Vogt, Nicholas, 412
Voltaire, 168, 200-201, 260-270 *passim,* 331, 337, 351
Vortices, 247

W

Wagram, Battle of (1809), 404
Wallenstein (Hapsburg general), 156, 158-159
Walpole, Sir Robert (English politician), 298-304 *passim*
War of the Austrian Succession (1740-1748), 329, 333-334, 358; of Bavarian Succession (1778-1779), 330; of First Coalition (1792-1797), 383-384; of the League of Augsburg (1689-1697), 211, 329; of Polish Succession (1733-1735), 329; of the Second Coalition (1798-1802), 397-400; of Spanish Succession (1702-1714), 217-227 *passim,* 329; of the Third Coalition (1805-1808), 400-401.
Washington, George, 360, 379-380
Waterloo, Battle of (1815), 409-410
Watt, James, 309-313 *passim*
Weber, Eugen (historian), 318
Webster, Charles (historian), 256
Wedgwood, C. V. (historian), 15, 147
Wedgwood, Josiah, 306-309 *passim*
Wellesley, Arthur. See Wellington, Duke of
Wellington, Duke of, 371, 401-410 *passim*

Wentworth, Peter, 77-78
Wentworth, Thomas, Earl of Strafford, 92, 94
"Westernizers," 190
Westminster, Treaty of (1756), 336
Westphalia, Peace of (1648), 168, 174-176, 191, 209, 331, 341
Whig historians, 64-65
Whigs, 118-119, 219-225 *passim*, 295-304 *passim*
White Mountain, Battle of (1620), 156
"White Terror," 393
Whitney, Eli, 429
Wilkinson, John (ironmaster), 311, 312-313
William I ("the Silent"), Prince of Orange and Stadholder of the Netherlands, 207
William II, Prince of Orange and Stadholder of the Netherlands, 210
William III, King of England (1689-1702), 123-124, 210-212
William III, Prince of Orange and Stadholder of the Netherlands. See William III, King of England
Winchester, Siege of (1642), 105
"Winter King," the. See Frederick V, King of Bohemia
Witchcraft, 49-75; 74-75
Wolfe, General, 361
Wolfe, John B. (historian), 199, 201
Wollstonecraft, Mary, 261, 273-277 *passim*
Women; attitudes toward, 1600-1815, 24-25, 48-49; childbirth and, 28-29; diseases involving, 30-38; economic opportunities, 48; educational and religious opportunities, 47-48; Enlightment and, 271-276; French Revolution and, 422-424; Industrial Revolution and, 318; in Russia, 181; witchcraft and, 49.
Wood, William (ironmaster), 313
Woodward, E. L. (historian), 410

Y

Yachting, 429
Yorktown Campaign, 379

Z

Zagorin, Perez (historian), 67
Zemsky Sobor, 182
Zenta, Battle of (1697), 332
Zoe, Tsarina, 179
Zorndoff, Battle of (1758)